Telecourse Study Guide for

BY THE NUMBERS

Practical Applications of Business Mathematics

SOUTHERN CALIFORNIA CONSORTIUM

AUTHORS:

Michael D. Hiscox
Interwest Applied Research

Vicki L. Spandel
Northwest Regional Educational Laboratory

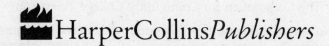

HarperCollins*Publishers*

ISBN 0-673-46351-6

2 3 4 5 6 -MAL- 95 94 93 92 91 90

INTRODUCTION

A telecourse study guide is a special kind of document. As its name implies, it must literally guide a student through a telecourse — help the student to focus his or her thinking, identify key ideas, monitor progress, and so on. In addition, it should strive to establish a context for learning so that the other course materials will be more effective. A telecourse study guide that actually accomplishes these things helps the student in much the same way as a good classroom instructor does.

Research on learning theory indicates that students tend to learn more — and feel they get more out of a course — when they see an application for what they are learning. This is especially important in a mathematics course; without this element, mathematics can become a tedious matter of plugging numbers into formulas that have no real relevance to the student. This, in turn, produces a course so boring that the content is not studied with enthusiasm. In a classroom-based course, the instructor is there to put all of the mathematics into context, to explain just why this formula or that technique is useful. But can the telecourse guide for *By the Numbers* effectively serve this role?

We think that the answer is yes. More than most other forms of mathematics, the value of what's taught in business mathematics is obvious. Simply opening the pages of any newspaper's business section will demonstrate exactly how much the business world revolves around issues of wages, interest rates, taxes, stocks and bonds, and similar topics covered in this course. But there's an even more direct relationship, since students have to deal with taxes, insurance, borrowing and saving, credit purchases, and the like in their own daily lives.

So authors of business math materials admittedly have a head start when it comes to relevance. Even so, there's still a big gap between learning the mathematics and learning how to apply it. How can a study guide demonstrate real world applications?

Several tactics can be used. One is to introduce new material in a way that helps a student establish a kind of mental framework, to make connections with his or her own current and anticipated experience and with other previous learning. Without these connections, newly introduced material may seem irrelevant or even incomprehensible. Research has shown that we all learn by integrating new information with our previous experiences. The overview within each telecourse study guide lesson is intended to establish a basis for forming this framework. It covers the same key math concepts as the text, but it does so in a way that directly relates the concepts to the students' own experiences.

Also, as stressed above, we tend to learn best when we see a purpose to that learning. Part of the function of the overview, therefore, is to demonstrate to students why they should care about pursuing the subject any further. The overviews try to give the message that "This is important material. It has implications for your future business and personal life, for the way you think. Knowing this content will help you make smart business and consumer decisions."

Because of the importance of this more personal, more experience-based approach to the content, the overviews strive to be as personal, as immediate as a classroom instructor. To this end, the overview is constructed largely of short scenarios that illustrate the concepts under discussion without a lot of mathematical complexity. Because the telecourse guide is the first material dealt with in each lesson, the focus is on making the student aware of the hows and whys of the mathematics without making the mathematics themselves a struggle. The problem sets and business applications do, in fact, sometimes challenge the students' computational skills, but in the overview, the examples are purposely simplified.

Further, the telecourse study guide—and the *By the Numbers* telecourse in general—profits from having a well-established set of objectives. The function of learning objectives, of course, is to identify the purpose of any instruction. By reviewing the objectives, students see what it is they're supposed to learn, what skills they need to attain before leaving a lesson. Indeed, mastering the objectives is an important goal for students. It is not the only goal, however; the deeper purpose of any course is—or ought to be—to prepare students to engage in the same kind of mental networking and higher thinking that provides a context for the course in the first place. In other words, we've constructed the telecourse guide to prompt the student to ask, "How can I apply these mathematical concepts when making business and personal decisions? How can I use these mathematical concepts to advantage?"

As one might suspect, each lesson of the *By the Numbers* telecourse is designed to increase opportunities for students to leave the course with more than just the haphazard memorization of a few formulas. Specifically, each chapter contains six sections, each designed to assist the student in a particular way, as follows:

☐ First, the Lesson Objectives establish a structure for learning, suggesting what elements of the course require particular attention.

☐ Second, the Lesson Overview introduces the lesson concepts and presents them in a practical context, while encouraging the students' interest in and understanding of the underlying mathematics.

☐ Third, a list of Key Terms alerts students to the important concepts covered in the lesson.

☐ Fourth, a Video Viewing Guide lays out some key questions that will be answered during the video program—and directs students to attend to those answers.

☐ Fifth, a set of Video Viewing Questions tests the students' understanding of the material presented in the video program. Any students who have difficulty with these questions are encouraged to review the overview and video program before proceeding.

☐ Sixth, the Reading Assignment and Problem Sets from the textbook and the Key Formulas emphasize the mathematical aspects of the course content; students, who are now familiar with the lesson concepts from the telecourse guide overview and the video program, are now asked to extend and apply the techniques they've learned. Also included in this section are Key Formulas that students need to know in order to master the content of the lesson.

Finally, a Solving Business Problems section asks students to apply mathematical concepts, integrate various procedures, make choices, and synthesize and evaluate options in order to decide the best actions to take to solve a realistic business problem.

Once all these steps have been completed, students should be prepared to both conduct additional activities assigned by the instructor and answer the test items from the course examination bank. Like a portion of the video questions and business problem scenarios, some examination bank items require the students to show considerable skill in analyzing and applying the math concepts of the lesson. And on many occasions, they will be required to evaluate and synthesize the relative merit of alternative actions.

In summary, we've attempted to provide a telecourse study guide that is interesting, that provokes new learning, and that allows the student some mental elbow room when applying mathematical concepts. We've also attempted to add the same relevance and life to the mathematics that a good classroom instructor would provide. If we've succeeded in achieving these goals, the guide will serve instructors and students well.

Michael D. Hiscox
Vicki L. Spandel

ACKNOWLEDGMENTS

As you might imagine, telecourses don't happen simply because they seem like a good idea to a handful of people. No matter how dedicated or convinced of the merit of their mission, one or two people cannot cause a telecourse, or even a telecourse guide, to spring to life.

The list of people who made *By the Numbers* a reality is extensive indeed. I obviously need to thank my colleagues at Interwest Applied Research, a talented group who had a lot to do with getting the idea for the course turned into a tangible product. Equally important were the staff at the Southern California Consortium, under whose auspices the course was spawned, nurtured, produced, and marketed.

Special thanks must be given to the staff at the Consortium's production office — the people who put the "tele" into the telecourse. As became obvious early on, writing about mathematics is a more practiced art form than showing mathematics on television. The problems were formidable, and we all lived in fear of producing yet another of those tedious "talking blackboard" series that characterize much of television-based mathematics. That the programs are interesting and effective is ample evidence of the special skills and dedication of the Consortium's Allison McCune Darrow, Linda Lamb, Peter Robinson, and the host of talented video professionals who worked with them.

We did not, however, have to worry about matters related to the course textbooks. Stanley Salzman, Louis Hoelze, and the late Charles Miller put together fine texts to serve as the basis for the telecourse, and Bill Poole and his staff at Scott, Foresman were supportive and helpful.

Without a doubt, though, the greatest credit for the high quality of the *By the Numbers* telecourse must be given to the project's Business and Academic Advisory Panels. As you might imagine, the gap between wanting to develop an instructionally rigorous course that reflects real-world applications and actually developing it is broad and deep — broad enough and deep enough that it could not have been bridged without the advice and counsel of these twelve knowledgeable professionals (and the hard work of Interwest's Academic and Business Liaison, Mary Lewis, in coordinating their activities).

Ensuring the instructional quality and accuracy of the course was the duty of academic reviewers Willie Felton (St. Petersburg Community Colleges, Florida), J. Roland Kelley (Tarrant County Community College, Texas), Norman Rittgers (Pasadena City College, California), Les Rosenbloom (Corning Community College, New York), John Rosich (Clark County Community College, Nevada) and John Swecz (Wayne County Community College, Michigan). Their careful reviews of the course objectives, script, and study guide drafts were key to producing an instructionally sound math course.

The course would not, however, have had such relevance to the business world had we not benefited from the knowledge and insight of our Business Advisory Panel. The helpfulness and conscientiousness of Donald J. DeMers (Boeing Company), Ron Goddard (Neiman Marcus), Jack Ludwig (The Gallup Organization), Donald Mullane (Bank of America), David Pearson (Ernst and Young) and Jan Yeomans (3M Company) made

By the Numbers special and I am deeply indebted to all of them. I should also express my thanks to their colleagues—most of them unknown to me—who verified the specifics of particular lessons as a supplement to the already rigorous reviews of the principal advisors. There's something vaguely threatening about having instructional materials reviewed by practitioners who can so readily tell the fluff from the important concepts ... and something very gratifying when those materials are judged accurate and relevant.

All in all, a team effort; dozens of people, each playing a critical role in making *By the Numbers* the best it could be. My thanks to all.

Michael D. Hiscox
Project Coordinator
Beaverton, Oregon
February 1990

CONTENTS

Mathematics in the Business World 1

Dear Dad had been laid up in the hospital for several weeks, but he was still very interested in how the family business—a small dairy farm—was getting along under the direction of his eldest son, Billy. Finally Billy found time to stop by the hospital for a visit and the talk quickly turned to the farm.

"So, Billy," Dad asked, "how are our cows doin'?"

"Not too bad, Dad," came Billy's earnest reply. "We've been getting about ten gallons a day out of them."

"Yer right," agreed Dad, "that is pretty good. Now, how much of that are ya selling as skim milk?"

"Oh, 'bout nine gallons a day," answered Billy.

"And how much is getting sold as cream?"

"Just a bit over four gallons a day, Dad."

Dad, a bit astonished at this report, reached for a pencil and scribbled a quick addition problem on a nearby notepad. He looked up from the paper with a frown on his face. "So, Billy," he demanded, "what in heaven's name are ya doin' with the rest?"

Think of all the times you encounter mathematics in your daily life. If you go to the store, you'll buy items having a wide variety of prices. If you receive a paycheck, deductions will be made. And if you look in the daily paper, you're going to find dozens of facts and figures about the world around you.

These numbers don't just happen. The prices you pay at the store are carefully calculated to produce a profit for the merchant while still being low enough to attract the purchaser. The amount of money you receive in your paycheck depends on withholdings, taxes, and other deductions that have to be calculated for each employee. And those facts and figures that you see in the paper represent a mathematical snapshot of conditions in the world around us.

Unfortunately, not all of us are as mathematically literate as we should be, which means that sometimes the mathematics goes on around us without us understanding what's really taking place. At different times, this shortcoming can be costly or embarrassing or can limit our chances for a good job and a promising career.

Throughout *By the Numbers*, you'll learn the fundamental mathematical concepts that drive the business world. We'll learn why things cost what they do, how people are paid, what it takes to get a loan, and how to track the profitability of a corporation. We'll discuss insurance, pricing, taxes, and a host of other topics with everyday application to business settings. And in this first lesson of the course, we'll give you an overview of the spectrum of content to be covered in the course. In doing so, we'll show you just how important the concepts you'll learn will be to your future life as a business person and a consumer.

LESSON ASSIGNMENTS

Each lesson in the *By the Numbers* telecourse is made up of several different assignments, each one an important step toward learning the principles, concepts, and skills covered in the lesson. Since this is the first lesson, it's appropriate that we should go through the different parts of a lesson and what each assignment does to help you master the business math content.

Incidentally, to get the most out of each lesson, we suggest that you do the tasks in the order we've laid them out. You may, for example, be tempted to watch the video program first, thinking that maybe that will save you the need of reading the telecourse guide or text assignment. That's not a good idea, however. Since all of the parts of the course were designed to be used together, you'll get more out of a lesson by going through the parts in the recommended order. The video program, for example, will be easier to understand if you've already been introduced to the content through the telecourse guide overview. Similarly, you'll find the textbook reading assignment much more meaningful after you've seen the video program.

All in all, we've tried hard to make all the components of the course work smoothly together, and we think you'll find them most interesting and instructive if you go through them in the suggested order.

**Part I:
Introducing
the Material**

Begin your study of each lesson by looking over the *Learning Objectives* in the next section. These objectives tell you exactly what you are expected to learn in the lesson.

Then read the *Lesson Overview*. This section will introduce you to the basics of the lesson, including some of the important terms you need to understand. When you've finished the Overview, go on to the *Key Terms* section and review the definitions for the terms you learned in the Overview.

**Part II:
Watching the
Video Program**

Before watching each video program, take a moment to read through the *Video Viewing Guide* included in Part II of each telecourse guide chapter. It will help you focus on the most important concepts in the video presentation. And remember, before watching the video program, be sure you're already familiar with the learning objectives for the lesson and have read through the Overview and reviewed the key terms.

Next, watch the *Video Program*. If you are watching the video program on videotape, you can stop the tape any time you'd like to review a concept in the overview. The video program counts on your having the information you read about in the telecourse guide, so you will have less trouble following the video if you read the overview carefully.

After watching the video program, be sure to complete the *Video Viewing Questions* at the end of Part II of each chapter. These questions may be used as the basis for additional discussion, or your instructor may ask that you turn your answers in for grading.

After watching the video program, you should read through the *Reading Assignment* in your textbook; the reading assignments are given in Part III of each telecourse guide chapter. You'll also want to read through the *Key Formulas* section in Part III. This section provides a handy review of the principal math concepts you encountered in the overview and the video program.

If any of the material in the Key Formulas section doesn't make complete sense to you, you'll need to go back to the textbook, the telecourse guide overview and, when possible, the video program to review the concepts you didn't master.

**Part III:
Focusing on the
Mathematics**

Next, it's time to solve some business mathematics problems. Begin this section of each lesson by working the *Problem Sets* assigned for your text in Part IV of this telecourse guide chapter or the alternate problem set assigned by your instructor. Your instructor will let you know which of the problems you solve should be turned in, if any. If you are having any trouble getting the right answers to these problems, review the appropriate sections in the text, the Key Formulas summary, and the Lesson Overview.

Finally, you may be asked to use what you've learned by applying the lesson's business math concepts to a pair of realistic *Business Applications*. At the end of most telecourse guide chapters, you'll find the descriptions of two hypothetical businesses or individuals facing a problem that can be addressed using the skills you've learned in the lesson. Your instructor may ask you to read through each of the two situations and then answer the questions that follow. Your instructor will also let you know if those answers should be turned in.

**Part IV:
Solving Business
Problems**

PART I: INTRODUCING THE MATERIAL

LEARNING OBJECTIVES

Upon completing your study of this lesson, you should be able to:

1. Provide examples of business decisions that are made based on information derived from the application of business mathematics.

2. Correctly visualize large and small quantities (e.g., billions of dollars, millions of people) and understand the relationships among such quantities.

3. Accurately describe the state of mathematics proficiency in the general population and contrast this with the needs of modern businesses for mathematical competence in their employees.

4. Perform basic operations with whole numbers, including adding, subtracting, multiplying, dividing, and estimating.

In most *By the Numbers* lessons, if you're using the hardcover textbook, *Mathematics for Business*, there are some additional objectives. In this lesson, however, the objectives are identical.

LESSON OVERVIEW

By the Numbers is a comprehensive introductory business mathematics course. But just what do we mean by comprehensive? And what do we mean by introductory?

It might be easiest to answer these questions by first deciding what business mathematics is. Unfortunately, there is no simple definition. Businesses use mathematics virtually every day and for a myriad of reasons. So is any mathematics done by a business person "business mathematics?" Probably not. Simply adding up a few numbers probably shouldn't count, but neither should solving intricate higher-level problems such as those an engineer might encounter in designing a bridge. Much of what falls between these endpoints, however, can correctly be termed business math.

Business Math: Necessary throughout Business

Business mathematics is a somewhat generic set of skills and concepts. It's not what one particular business might do in the course of daily operations; it's what almost *every* business would do. Whether you're Ted's Hot Dog Stand or Megastate Industries, there are still people to be paid, taxes to be collected, checkbooks to keep, money to invest and borrow, and so on. And, perhaps surprisingly, the mathematics that Ted uses in running his hot dog stand are conceptually quite similar to those used at the large conglomerate.

We don't mean to imply that keeping track of what goes on at the hot dog stand is of comparable complexity. It's not, and the sheer magnitude and intricacy of mathematical manipulations for a large national corporation is staggering. But we'd still claim that upwards of 90 percent of what you'll learn in *By the Numbers* applies to both types of business.

We say that the course is comprehensive because it addresses all of these widely used concepts. Unlike courses in, say, cost accounting or preparing financial statements, *By the Numbers* doesn't limit itself to just one area of business mathematics. We don't know of any math skills that are used by the majority of business people that have been left out of the course.

At the same time, the fact that there are entire courses in cost accounting tells you that *By the Numbers* gives away some depth in a given subject in order to provide this comprehensive coverage. Each of the topics we include is covered enough to give you a solid introduction to the concepts, but without going into the intricacies of the subject. That's not to say the topics are treated shallowly, though. Ideally, you'll have learned enough about each topic to both understand its importance to real-world business and apply the mathematics correctly and efficiently. You won't, however, learn the complex details that a specialist in the topic would learn.

Rather than teaching you any new math skills, this opening lesson of *By the Numbers* is designed to acquaint you with what is meant by "business mathematics" and show you how business math skills are used in the business world. Let's begin by looking at the course content to see just what kind of skills will be taught.

There's a saying that you have to learn to walk before you can run, and the equivalent principle applies to business mathematics. As you'll see, the mathematics performed throughout the course is not really too complicated; in fact, most of it is arithmetic that you learned by eighth grade. Unfortunately, if you're not adept at that arithmetic, it's going to be very hard for you to succeed at *By the Numbers*, since virtually every lesson demands considerable proficiency at adding, subtracting, multiplying, and dividing whole numbers, fractions, decimals, and percents. Therefore, *By the Numbers* starts out with two lessons that serve as a review of those basic skills.

Lesson 2 is entitled *Fractions, Decimals, and Percents* and is largely a review of those skills that you learned long ago but may not remember so well now. It's our hope that simply encountering some of these key principles will cause you to say "Sure, I know how to do that." If it doesn't, the lesson will provide you with an opportunity to re-learn and practice these important concepts.

Lesson 3 deals with *Equations and Formulas*. Business mathematics, as we've mentioned, is not a particularly complicated type of mathematics, but it does include a number of basic formulas you will have to understand and manipulate regularly throughout the course. If you're unfamiliar with how formulas work or how to apply them to solve the problem at hand, this lesson will provide the information that you need.

Lessons 2 and 3 are unusual in that most students will simply be re-learning concepts that they already mastered years earlier. What this means is that some students will have a rather easy time with Lessons 2 and 3. Don't think, though, that the rest of the course will also cover concepts that you've had before. It doesn't, and we think you'll find most of the information both new and interesting. But because having these underlying mathematical skills is so important to your success in *By the Numbers*, Lessons 2 and 3 need to be included.

Mathematical Foundations

Can you think of a business that doesn't have to deal with money? It's pretty difficult, isn't it? As they say, money is what they use to keep score in business. So knowing how money is transferred from the business to its employees, and from the business and employees to their governments, is a good starting point for applying mathematics to business.

One of the most basic characteristics of a business is that money comes in and money goes out . . . ideally more of the first than the second. This in-and-out transfer almost always takes place through a checking account. Knowing how to write checks, determine the fees associated with checking accounts, and make sure the account balances are correct is, therefore, critical for any business person. It's also important to know the alterna-

Basic Business Concepts

tives for depositing money—passbook accounts, certificates of deposit, and the like. Lesson 4, *Banking Services*, covers all these important topics.

The vast majority of adult Americans earn money at a job. That is, they earn a paycheck. Sometimes, though, how much that paycheck will be isn't completely straightforward. Complications such as overtime pay, double time pay, shift differential and split shift premiums, commissions, and piecework payments often make figuring out a worker's earnings a bit involved. Lesson 5, *Gross Earnings*, will show how different workers' earnings are calculated.

However, as you're no doubt aware, the government doesn't allow you to keep all the money you make. Certain amounts are withheld. A major deduction that affects almost every worker is a contribution required by Social Security or, as it's more precisely known, the Federal Insurance Contributions Act. The other large deduction taken from most workers' paychecks is for income tax withholding at the federal, and often state, level. Knowing how to calculate the amounts to be withheld for Social Security and income taxes is a skill business people need, and Lesson 6—*Social Security and Withholding*—will show you how to do this.

Consumers and businesses pay other kinds of taxes as well. In Lesson 7, *Sales and Property Taxes*, you'll learn how these other prevalent taxes are calculated. Whether you need this information to figure how much sales tax you might pay on a wrench from the hardware store or the property tax you'll owe on a multimillion-dollar factory, understanding these taxation concepts is important to everyone.

The amount of money withheld from your paycheck for state and federal income tax isn't necessarily the amount that you owe. Each taxpayer has to consider adjustments to income, deductions and exemptions that can affect whether more money is owed beyond the amount withheld or whether a refund is in order. Both businesses and individuals need to be able to calculate their income tax liabilities accurately—skills taught in Lesson 8, *Income Taxes*.

Lessons 9 and 10 deal with one of the most critical elements of running either a business or a household: insurance. In Lesson 9, *Business Insurance*, you'll learn the basic principles behind insurance—policies, face values, premiums—and you'll learn how an insurance company decides just how much you should pay for a given amount of protection. You'll also learn how to decide how much protection a business needs and what factors make that coverage more affordable.

While Lesson 9 uses fire insurance to demonstrate many of the concepts involved in business insurance, Lesson 10, *Personal Insurance*, addresses two other types of insurance—life insurance and motor vehicle insurance. Whether you're dealing with these kinds of insurance as an individual or on behalf of a business, you'll need to know what types of policies are available to you, what benefits you can expect, and how you'll be charged for the coverage. Lesson 10 discusses these issues.

The Mathematics of Selling

As we pointed out earlier, businesses operate to make money—almost always by selling some product or service. But how much should those products and services cost? In this group of lessons, we'll first prove to you that these decisions aren't just arbitrary, and then we'll show you the procedures business managers use to price their products.

It has no doubt occurred to you that the store where you buy groceries pays the distributor less for a bag of sugar than you pay the store when you buy it. That's because the store receives a discount, a reduction in the price of goods given to those businesses that are going to resell them. Lesson 11, *The Business Discount*, shows how these discounts are calculated, some of the factors that affect the amount of the discount, and some mathematical shortcuts that make the calculations easier. You'll also learn about invoices, the important documents that record the sale of goods and describe the terms under which the goods were purchased.

Getting goods into your store at a discount is certainly a critical part of staying in business. But it's to no avail if you can't price the goods or services at a level that attracts customers but still allows you to make a profit. In Lesson 12, *Pricing Products and Services*, you'll learn the relationship among cost, markup, overhead, gross and net profit, and the selling price. And when you're done with this lesson, you'll be able to calculate whether the selling prices of a company's products or services are enough to cover the cost of staying in business.

Not everyone has an inventory of goods to sell, but enough businesses do to make inventory control a critical business concept. Obviously, any sensible business manager would want to know what inventory was on hand and how much that inventory was worth when making business decisions. Valuing an inventory, however, is not as straightforward as you might at first think. Lesson 13, *Inventory Control*, will introduce you to the principles involved in getting an accurate report about this critical aspect of many businesses.

The Mathematics of Finance

There is so much money changing hands throughout the business world that it's almost useless to try to describe it just using numbers. Somehow, the enormity of the statement "The value of the goods and services produced in the United States in a single year is over $500 trillion" doesn't come through in written words. For the moment, suffice it to say that a lot of money passes through businesses and individuals.

What might be surprising, though, is that much of this money doesn't actually belong to the business using it. An amazing amount of money is owed by one business to another, by individuals to businesses, by businesses to individuals, and by individuals to each other. For example, each person depositing money in a bank is letting the bank turn around and loan the same money to businesses and other individuals. Similarly, every time you use a credit card, the bank that issued the credit card is loaning you a bit of money.

But what makes it worthwhile to let someone else use your money? The answer, as you probably know, is that interest is charged on the amount of the loan. In other words, the person making the loan gets back more money than was loaned out. The amount of interest paid is designed to be high enough that the person or business with the money will be willing to loan it out. Many centuries ago, businesses found out that it wasn't practical to operate on a cash-only basis, that extending credit and loaning money to individuals and other businesses was an essential part of keeping the economy going. Interest is, perhaps, the grease that keeps the economy going—and it's perhaps the single most important concept in business mathematics.

Lesson 14, *Simple Interest*, is the starting point for all of these discussions about finance. In this lesson, you'll learn the simple interest formula and how the factors it includes relate to one another. You'll use that formula to find out how much interest will be paid on any amount borrowed at a given rate, and from that, how much money will be returned at the end of the loan. You'll also be introduced to the concepts of present value and future value and shown why a dollar in hand today is almost always more valuable than a dollar coming some time in the future.

When a business borrows money, the borrowing sometimes involves a bank note and what is called a bank discount. You'll need to understand what's required in a promissory note, how they're used in business, and why promissory notes are accepted in lieu of cash in many business transactions. You'll also need to learn how a note can be discounted and how the interest on a discounted note is different from simple interest on a loan of the same amount. These topics are covered in Lesson 15, *Notes and Bank Discounts*.

But while these simple interest transactions are important, the bulk of the world's borrowing is done under compound interest. Compound interest, as you may already know, involves the payment of interest on both the amount borrowed and any interest accumulated to date. Compound interest has a considerable effect on the way payments are calculated and, particularly on loans that last many years, how big those payments will be. Lesson 16 on *Compound Interest* will cover these matters and will also discuss how compound interest affects the amount of money earned by deposits and investments made at different interest rates.

At any point in time, U.S. credit card holders owe somewhere over $100 billion in credit card debt. Billions more are owed for purchases on installment and revolving charge plans. In Lesson 17, *Credit Purchases*, you'll learn why businesses bother to extend credit to individuals and other businesses and how, once they've made this decision, they charge interest to the borrower. We'll also discuss the similarities between credit purchases and other types of borrowing and when it may or may not be wise for a business or individual to make a credit purchase.

The effect of compound interest can be truly amazing over a long period of time. A house with a cash price of, say, $100,000 could easily cost over $300,000 by the time the mortgage loan was paid off because of compound interest charges. Similarly, each dollar invested at the beginning of a working career could be worth over $30 by retirement age. Because compound interest has such an impact over long periods of time, special strategies have been developed to deal with the effects. Lesson 18 looks at the three most significant—*Annuities, Sinking Funds, and Amortization*—and shows you how to calculate the payments and interest involved in each.

Business and Financial Accounting

Whether we're taking about our hot dog stand or the giant conglomerate, there are similarities in the accounting principles used. In fact, it's probably true that there are more similarities than differences.

For example, virtually every business has to buy equipment, most of which declines in value. But since the decline in value—depreciation, it's called—can be deducted from the company's income before taxes are assessed, almost every business finds it worthwhile to formally track the depreciation of what it owns. Lesson 19—*Depreciating Business Assets*—shows how this is done. It may not be as simple as you'd like, since different depreciation methods are used for different purposes. In this lesson, we'll explain the reasons for the different approaches and examine how each is used.

Lesson 20, *Allocating Costs and Profits*, addresses another problem most businesses face—how to split up costs and profits in a way that reflects the true operation of the business. In the case of profits, for example, each business run as a partnership has to come up with a rationale for what proportion of the profits should go to each of the partners . . . and then it has to do the math to figure out what the actual amounts are. Lesson 20 shows this process. Similarly, it's often important to find out just how much of a company's money is going to produce each of its products or services. This is done by a process called cost allocation; Lesson 20 provides both the rationale and techniques for it.

If, as we said at the outset, money is what they use to keep score in business, financial statements are the scorecards. In Lesson 21 (titled, logically enough, *Financial Statements*) you'll learn about income statements and balance sheets: why each is important, what information each contains, and how to use the information to make sound business decisions. Accounting terms such as assets, liabilities, and owner's equity will be explained and we'll again show how these business math concepts apply both to the largest corporation and to the smallest proprietorship.

As you'll see in Lesson 21, there are certain things that balance sheets and income statements don't do—one of which is to present a clear picture of how money is flowing into and out of a business. Nor do the raw numbers on the financial statements clearly show whether the business is in good or bad shape. Obviously, though, every business manager needs this kind of information. In Lesson 22, *Cash Flow and Financial Ratios*, you'll learn business math techniques that use the numbers from the financial statements to create ratios that do, in fact, indicate the financial health of the business. You'll also see how a statement of cash flows supplements the income statement and balance sheet and thus helps provide a truer picture of a company's condition.

In Lesson 23, *Funding the Business with Stocks and Bonds*, you'll see how stocks and bonds provide the money that corporations need to expand, invest in equipment and new markets, or perhaps just conduct routine business operations. The similarities and differences between stocks and bonds will be examined, as will the difference between corporations, which issue stock, and proprietorships and partnerships, which don't. And, perhaps most importantly, you'll learn what makes the difference in the price of a stock or a bond and some ways that help tell when stocks or bonds are good investments.

Communicating with Numbers

By this point in the *By the Numbers* course, you will have learned a great deal about how mathematics is used throughout business. There is still, however, one skill missing—how to effectively communicate business-related numbers to business colleagues and the public.

Statistics for the Business World, Lesson 24, takes a look at how the mathematical branch called statistics helps turn piles of raw data into useful information. You'll learn about both the statistics that describe how data sets tend to cluster around an average and those that tell how they're spread out. And we'll also examine some special statistics that provide handy shortcuts to analyzing a large data set.

Even carefully crafted statistics, though, sometimes don't convey their meaning very well when there's too much data. Most business managers understandably scorn reports with hundreds of pages of attached computer printouts to sort through; they much prefer effective charts and graphs that help them see in an instant just what the data is saying. In Lesson 25, *Communicating with Graphs and Charts*, we'll examine exactly what advantages charts and graphs offer and look at the three principal graph types and their variations. You will also learn a bit about what computers have contributed to the quality and cost-effectiveness of business graphics.

The computer is a topic of more in-depth examination in Lesson 26, *The Future of Business Mathematics*. We'll discuss the different applications software for small computers that can be of great benefit to the business person, with a special emphasis on computer spreadsheets. Similarly, this lesson will talk about the kinds of business mathematics tasks that can easily be handled by a handheld business calculator. There are, however, dangers in using both calculators and computers carelessly, and we'll examine those potential pitfalls as well. The program—and the course—will close with some discussion of the major trends in computer use, with particular attention paid to innovative uses of computers, such as business forecasting and yield management.

A Note about Big Numbers

When we mentioned the $500 trillion figure for the value of goods and services produced in the United States annually, we noted how it was virtually impossible for mere numbers to convey some of the large quantities we will discuss in *By the Numbers*. It is, for example, hard to know just what to make of the fact that the United States government alone spends approximately $1 trillion each year. Now, certainly everyone admits that a trillion is a big number; in fact, it's clearly a very big number. But is it possible to visualize just *how* big it is? Perhaps not.

One problem is that we are surrounded by big numbers these days. There's a joke that goes, "a billion here, a billion there, and pretty soon you're talking big money." But many of us have started to think that way. A million dollars—a staggering sum a century ago—will seem like pocket change in some of the discussions we'll have.

It's not, of course, and most of us could make very good use of $1 million. Yet it is but *one millionth* of the federal budget. To look at it another way, the government goes through a million dollars in less than a minute. Other numbers you'll see in *By the Numbers* are in the same ballpark: the amount of consumer debt, the total value of corporate stocks, the amount of annual income tax and Social Security contributions, and dozens of others.

It would be nice if there were some way to teach an appreciation for the true magnitude of the numbers you'll encounter in this course. Unfortunately, about all we can do is encourage you to pause and think a moment about the quantities we're discussing. If you stop to ask yourself "Just what does it mean to say that consumers owe over $100 billion on their credit cards?" you may gain a valuable perspective that will improve your real-world decision-making abilities.

A Brief Word about Math Proficiency

If you read newspapers and current events magazines, you may have seen articles bemoaning the declining proficiency of U.S. citizens in mathematics. Obviously, since you are in a math class, you have some appreciation for the importance of mathematics and are dedicated to improving your proficiency. Unfortunately, you are in a minority.

The statistics are indeed worrisome. In comparisons against the scores of students from other industrialized countries, the mathematics test scores of U.S. students are consistently toward the bottom. These students also take fewer math courses than their counterparts from other countries, and they cover less in the classes that they do take.

But perhaps an even bigger problem is that U.S. employers are not able to find workers with the math skills that they need. The situation varies from employer to employer, but you'd be hard pressed to find any large company happy about the level of the math skills in prospective employees. Some employers, in fact, report upwards of *80 percent* of job applicants lack the minimal math skills they need to get hired. Arguments continue about what, if anything, can be done about this — and the situation doesn't seem likely to improve any time soon.

All this means that if you had any doubts about the potential value of a course like *By the Numbers*, you can put your mind at ease. The skills you're about to learn will be both useful to and appreciated by your current and future employers.

SOME WORDS OF ADVICE

As we stressed at the outset, the goal of *By the Numbers* is to help you master important mathematics skills in a real-world context. When you complete the course, you will have a considerable number of useful skills that can be put to work immediately on the job or in your own day-to-day life. Try to keep track of what these skills are and think about how having them might change your situation.

Unlike some math courses you may have taken, *By the Numbers* probably won't leave you wondering how you will ever apply the math that you're learning. It's likely that you will immediately see the importance of most of the concepts. In fact, we encourage you to relate each of the things you learn back to your own personal situation and interests. This will make the mathematics seem less like math and more like a handy set of useful tools that make business and consumer matters a little easier to understand in this complicated world.

If there are parts of the material you don't understand, get in touch with your instructor immediately. Each *By the Numbers* lesson assumes that you mastered the previous lesson, so it's not a good idea to leave a lesson confused about what was being taught. If you were building a brick wall, you'd stop and fix things if one of the rows weren't straight. We suggest that you take a similar approach with this course.

KEY TERMS

Each of the coming lessons has a Key Terms section that provides definitions of the mathematical and business terms used in the textbook, telecourse guide, and video program. We therefore suggest that before you read through the text assignment and watch the video program, you take a minute to look at the key terms associated with a lesson. Then when you encounter them in the text and video program, you'll already have an idea of what they mean.

PART II: WATCHING THE VIDEO PROGRAM

VIDEO VIEWING GUIDE

Before watching the video program, review the following questions. As you watch, be sure to collect the information necessary to answer them:

1. In what ways do you expect business mathematics to be similar to other mathematics courses you've taken? In what ways will it likely be different?

2. What role does basic arithmetic play in business mathematics? How about other forms of mathematics such as algebra, calculus, and statistics?

3. How closely is modern business tied to banks and other financial institutions? Is this interdependence growing or shrinking?

4. What are the major mathematical concerns of an employer trying to keep an accurate payroll? Which of these can be influenced by the employer and which are beyond the employer's control?

5. What are the basic quantities that a retail store has to deal with when selling goods—and which of them are most directly related to mathematics?

6. How often—and in what ways—do concerns about simple and compound interest affect business decision making?

7. What does the video program mean when it introduces the concept of "communicating with numbers"? Do you agree that this is an important concept?

8. What role do computers and calculators play in business mathematics? Do you think most business managers rely on them too much or too little?

VIDEO PROGRAM

This lesson's video program is Program 1—Mathematics in the Business World. Remember, if you are watching this program on videotape, take time to replay sections of the tape any time you need to review a concept.

VIDEO VIEWING QUESTIONS

Immediately after viewing the video program for Lesson 1, take time to respond to the following questions. Give your answers some careful thought; they may provide the basis for additional discussion or a longer written response.

1. In the space below, list five topics that you think will be covered in this course that you already know a lot about.

   a. _____

   b. _____

   c. _____

   d. _____

   e. _____

   Now list five topics that are completely new to you.

   a. _____

   b. _____

   c. _____

   d. _____

   e. _____

   Here is a list of the titles for the 26 *By the Numbers* lessons. Use this list to answer the next six questions.

1	Mathematics in the Business World
2	Fractions, Decimals, and Percents
3	Equations and Formulas
4	Banking Services
5	Gross Earnings
6	Social Security and Withholding
7	Sales and Property Taxes
8	Income Taxes
9	Business Insurance
10	Personal Insurance
11	The Business Discount
12	Pricing Products and Services
13	Inventory Control
14	Simple Interest
15	Notes and Bank Discounts
16	Compound Interest
17	Credit Purchases
18	Annuities, Sinking Funds, and Amortization
19	Depreciating Business Assets
20	Allocating Costs and Profits
21	Financial Statements
22	Cash Flow and Financial Ratios
23	Funding the Business with Stocks and Bonds
24	Statistics for the Business World
25	Communicating with Graphs and Charts
26	The Future of Business Mathematics

2. List the numbers of the five lessons that you think will be the *easiest* to understand.

   _____

3. List the numbers of the five lessons that you think will be the *hardest* to understand.

   _____

4. List the numbers of the five lessons that you think contain the concepts most important to a business manager responsible for *production*.

   _____

5. List the numbers of the five lessons that you think contain the concepts most important to a business manager responsible for a company's *investments*.

   _____

6. List the numbers of the five lessons that you think contain the concepts most important to the general manager of a *retail store*.

   _____

7. List the numbers of the five lessons that you think contain the concepts most important to an *individual*.

   _____

8. What single skill do you expect to learn in this course that will be of greatest value to you in your current or anticipated job?

   _____

9. What single skill do you expect to learn in this course that will be of greatest value to you as a consumer?

   _____

10. Suppose you have a friend who insists that taking mathematics courses these days is a waste of time because "all the math is done by computers anyway." Comment on the accuracy of this statement.

    _____

    _____

    _____

PART III: FOCUSING ON THE MATHEMATICS

READING ASSIGNMENT

After watching the video program, you should read one of the following Text Assignments, depending on the textbook you're using:

SOFTCOVER: Pages 1-18 from Chapter 1* of the Miller, Salzman, and Hoelzle softcover text, *Business Mathematics*.

HARDCOVER: Appendix A* of the Salzman, Miller, and Hoelzle hardcover text, *Mathematics for Business*, pages A1-A20.

As you read through the text, pay careful attention to the examples the book gives of the mathematics associated with the concepts you're learning about.

Then, after you've completed the text assignment, read through the Key Formulas below. This section provides a handy review of what you've learned. By the time you get to this point in the lesson, all of the formulas and calculations should be familiar to you. If they're not, go back and read the appropriate parts of the text and the Overview section of this lesson. You won't have much success completing the rest of your assignments if you are still confused about the information in the Key Formulas section.

KEY FORMULAS

In almost all of the lessons that follow, a Key Formulas section reviews the important formulas that you need to understand before proceeding with the math problems assigned for that lesson. You'll want to be sure that you know each one.

Since the formulas covered in the Key Formulas section are the same ones that you've encountered in the telecourse guide overview, the video program, and the text reading assignment, this section also serves as a good summary of the key mathematical points of the lesson. You may find it useful to review this section prior to taking any of the course examinations; it's likely that if you remember and know how to apply each of the formulas, you have indeed met most of the course learning objectives.

---

* Assigned at instructors' option.

PART IV: SOLVING BUSINESS PROBLEMS

PROBLEM SETS

Work the following problems in your textbook. Your instructor will tell you which problems, if any, are to be turned in. Some of the problems have answers provided in the back of the book; refer to these answers to make sure you are working the problems correctly.

SOFTCOVER: If you are using the Miller, Salzman, and Hoelzle softcover text, *Business Mathematics*, do the following problem sets:

1.1: Problems #8-16, 24-36 (even numbers only), and 42 on pages 7-8.

1.2: Problems #5-8, 19-20 (all), and 22-42 (even numbers only) on pages 13-14.

1.3: Problems #4-16 (even numbers only) on pages 17-18.

HARDCOVER: If you are using the Salzman, Miller, and Hoelzle hardcover text, *Mathematics for Business*, do the following problem sets:

Appendix A.1: Problems #20-112 (even numbers only) on pages A8-A12.

BUSINESS APPLICATIONS

In the majority of the *By the Numbers* telecourse guide chapters, we've included a pair of business scenarios that call on you to apply the skills you learned in the lesson to a real-life situation. You'll be asked to decide what you would do if you were the business person faced with the specified set of alternatives and why you'd make those decisions. The questions are never easy because in the scenarios, as in real life, there is seldom a single right answer. It is the case, however, that you can't give even plausible answers to the questions unless you are adept at the business math skills taught in the lesson.

The scenarios are designed to be used in different ways at each instructor's option. Some will ask only that you look them over and formulate your answers, while others may require a written response. Some will not include the scenarios as part of student assignments at all. In other words, look for your instructor to provide additional information on how you are to work with these scenarios.

Fractions, Decimals, and Percents 2

Hell's library

"Let no one ignorant of mathematics enter here." The Greek philosopher Plato had these words inscribed over the entrance to his famous Academy, where the students of ancient Greece came to learn. The *By the Numbers* telecourse doesn't presume to offer the comprehensiveness of Plato's Academy, but 2400 years later, his rule does have considerable relevance to business mathematics.

Virtually every subject area has its "building blocks," the knowledge and skills without which further learning cannot take place. But seldom are the building blocks so clearly critical as they are in business mathematics. To state it simply, if you are not proficient in manipulating whole numbers, fractions, decimals, and percentages, you are in for a very tough time trying to master business mathematics.

Although it's only the second of 26 *By the Numbers* lessons, this lesson is significantly different from most of the others because it addresses rather little about business. As you'll soon see, the average *By the Numbers* lesson focuses on how and why a particular math concept is important in the business world. You should finish each of these lessons understanding how the concepts you've learned are used in day-to-day business operations. In this lesson, however, the focus is on the mathematics for the simple reason that you're going to struggle during the rest of the course if you haven't mastered its contents.

PART I: INTRODUCING THE MATERIAL

LEARNING OBJECTIVES

Upon completing your study of this lesson, you should be able to:

1. Correctly define the terms fraction, proper fraction, mixed number, numerator, and denominator and identify each when encountered in a problem.

2. Determine if one number is divisible by another and use this information to determine if a fraction is written in lowest terms.

3. Find the common denominator for a group of fractions.

4. Add, subtract, multiply, and divide fractions and mixed numbers.

5. Write decimal numbers correctly in either equivalent numeric or word form when given the number in the other form.

6. Add, subtract, multiply, and divide decimal numbers.

7. Convert fractions to the equivalent decimal numbers and decimal numbers to the equivalent fractions.

8. Convert fractions to their percent equivalents and percents to the equivalent fractions.

9. Convert percents to the equivalent decimal numbers and decimal numbers to their percent equivalents.

10. List and define the three elements of a percent problem.

11. Correctly identify the base, rate, and part in business-related percent problems.

12. Know the formula for solving percent problems for part and apply it to find the part, given the base and rate.

13. Know the formula for solving percent problems for base and apply it to find the base, given the rate and part.

14. Know the formula for solving percent problems for rate and apply it to find the rate, given the base and part.

15. Correctly identify the base, rate, and part in an increase and decrease problem and apply the percent formula to solve them for the missing information.

In most *By the Numbers* lessons, if you're using the hardcover textbook, *Mathematics for Business*, there are some additional objectives for this lesson. In this lesson, however, the objectives are identical.

LESSON OVERVIEW

Perhaps when you saw our introductory admonishment about how important it is that you master the mathematics covered in this chapter, your reaction was, "No problem, I learned all this stuff by eighth grade."

The critical word here is *learned*. There's no question that you've been in classes where all these operations were discussed. And it's even likely that you had considerable proficiency at them when you were learning them. But as the saying goes, "What have you done for me lately?" What's important for *By the Numbers* is not whether you could do some particular operation a decade or more ago, but whether you mastered the skill and can do it now. And is the skill second nature? Something you can do without a lot of effort?

If you answered yes, then this lesson will be quite easy. If the answer is no, use this lesson to refresh your skills and become comfortable with the techniques. Remember, *By the Numbers* is going to be a struggle if you're not adept at working with fractions, decimals, and percents.

The Textbook

In the typical *By the Numbers* lesson, the telecourse guide chapter takes responsibility for introducing you to the important concepts of the lesson, with a focus on the role the concepts play in the business world. Neither the telecourse guide nor the video program tries to teach you all the mathematics, since you have a textbook to handle much of that instruction.

In this particular lesson, though, there's not much in the way of business concepts to introduce. We could, of course, have spent some time pointing out endless examples of how common fractions, decimals, and percents are in the business world. We suspect, however, that you already know this; besides, the telecourse guide chapter needs to be a little shorter than usual to give you time to work on the longer than average textbook reading assignments for this lesson. It's the textbook that will show you just how to master each of the lesson objectives.

Since the actual instruction will take place in the video program and textbook, we'll use this overview to alert you to some of the important concepts that are coming your way. With any luck, you can simply say, "I know how to do that" and move on to the next concept. If, on the other hand, your reaction is "Boy, I haven't heard these terms since sixth grade," we recommend some serious study.

A Note about Calculators and Computers

A common, but misguided, comment about modern-day mathematics is "There's no need to learn how to do arithmetic since everyone now has calculators and computers." Not that there isn't a huge advantage to having calculators; there is, and no one wants to go back to the days of adding long strings of numbers or dividing two large numbers by hand. Calculators and computers save vast amounts of time and modern business probably wouldn't be "modern" without them.

At the same time, what calculators and computers *don't* do is pretty significant. They don't, for example, tell you what it is that you need to solve, nor what information you'll need to get the answer. They won't tell you what operations you need to carry out, and they won't tell you if the answer you got is reasonable. And they certainly won't tell you how to set up the problem to produce the answer you need.

And while computers and calculators are good at arithmetic, they don't actually understand it. Which means that if you don't know enough to apply correctly the business math concepts you'll learn, you have no chance of getting a correct answer. So our advice to you is to use calculators and computers as tools, just as a carpenter uses a hammer and saw to build a house. But just as you'd probably think it silly if someone claimed not to need to know anything about home building because he or she owned a hammer and saw, don't claim that understanding these basic mathematical operations isn't necessary just because you have a calculator or computer.

Different Names, Same Idea

This lesson on fractions, decimals, and percents could just as well have been entitled "Parts of the Whole." That's because in spite of their different appearance and terminology, decimals, fractions, and percents are basically the same thing—numbers that represent a portion of a whole.

What this means is that any fraction can be represented as a decimal or a percent, any decimal can be represented as a fraction or a percent, and any percent can be represented as a fraction or a decimal. This is a critical concept, because business math is sort of arbitrary about when it uses one or another. An article on sale, for instance, will likely be marked "20% Off," instead of "one-fifth" or "twenty-hundredths" off. But items that are 50 percent off *are* often marked "Half Off." In either case, you'll usually have to convert the percentage or fraction to a decimal before proceeding.

If you think that life would be much easier if everything were done in decimals, for example, you're probably right. Unfortunately, centuries of mathematical tradition suggest that all three forms will continue to be used more or less interchangeably. The good news is that changing one form to another is easy and will, we hope, become second nature to you, if it isn't already.

Operations with Fractions

As we just mentioned—and aren't going to let you forget—a fraction represents a part of a whole. You probably already know that *fractions* are written as one number over another with a bar in the middle:

$$\frac{1}{2}$$

or when the typewriter or typesetter doesn't have a provision for this, two numbers separated by a slash:

$$1/2$$

You probably also remember that the number on the top is called the *numerator*; the number on the bottom is the *denominator*.

Fractions with the same denominator are said to have common denominators. This is important because having the same denominators is a requirement for adding and subtracting fractions. This, in turn, involves finding the *least common denominator* for the fractions, a technique that you can do simply by looking at the fractions but sometimes requires a little arithmetic. Either way, your goal is to end up with *like fractions*—

fractions with the same denominator. Once this is done, you can find the sum or difference of the fractions by adding or subtracting the numerators.

Adding and subtracting fractions can result in some answers that you don't often see in the business world—fractions that aren't in *lowest terms*. It's rare to see a sign advertising 9/18 off, or a 12/36 price increase. That's because people like their fractions *reduced*, which means that the fraction is written so that the denominator is as low as possible while keeping the numerator a whole number. What this means is that 9/18 isn't in lowest terms (because both 9 and 18 can be divided by 9 and still leave whole numbers), while 1/2 is. You need to be able to recognize when fractions are being reduced to lowest terms, since this is done almost automatically in business settings.

Although neither is difficult, most people find multiplying fractions easier than adding them. The difference is that the fractions don't have to have a common denominator before they can be multiplied; simply multiply the numerators, then multiply the denominators. Of course, that tends to result in some unusual fractions (like 96/128 or 144/256), so you should expect to have to reduce the result of your multiplication to lowest terms.

Dividing fractions is, as you'll remember from grade school, a matter of multiplying fractions after the second fraction has been turned upside down—*inverted*, that is. Don't get carried away and invert both fractions before multiplying; that would produce a totally incorrect response. And as with multiplication, don't be surprised to find your answer in need of being reduced to lowest terms.

Both multiplication and division of fractions can be made simpler through *cancellation*. Cancellation is somewhat similar to reducing a fraction to lowest terms, except that it's done in advance of the operation, rather than being done on the result. For example, cancelling out a pair of threes in 3/8 × 1/9 allows you to rewrite the equation as 1/8 × 1/3, which is equal to 1/24. Notice that simply multiplying the original fractions, 3/8 × 1/9, results in 3/72, which reduces to 1/24. In other words, you never *have* to cancel to get the right answer. But the idea is that since you'll have to reduce things to lowest terms eventually, why not do it at the start and multiply or divide smaller numbers? (Don't, however, make the mistake of taking the common factors out of two numerators or two denominators; that won't work. While it might be tempting to write 3/21 × 9/14 as 1/3 × 3/2, it is in no way correct. Cancellation involves one numerator and one denominator at a time.)

It may not be particularly enlightening to say that decimals are numbers written with a decimal point, but that is, in fact, what sets decimals apart from their fractional counterparts. In the overall scheme of things, though, *decimals* are nothing more than a way of writing a special kind of fraction, one with a denominator of 10, or 100, or 1,000, and so on. Decimals even sound like fractions. When spoken, there is no difference between 12/100 and 0.12; both are read "twelve hundredths."

First, we should state the obvious: You can't work with decimals if you can't work with whole numbers. But even if you are proficient with whole numbers, it's possible to make a mess of decimals if you don't keep track of a few simple rules. First, when adding decimals, line up all the decimal points in a column. Don't try to add the following:

Operations with Decimals

$$1.02$$
$$6.7741$$
$$3.1$$
$$+ \quad 6.27$$

until you've rewritten it as

$$1.0200$$
$$6.7741$$
$$3.1000$$
$$+ 6.2700$$

Notice that enough zeros have been added to make all of the numbers have four *decimal places*. Whether adding the zeros is strictly necessary depends on whether you're able to keep the numbers in the correct columns without it. Needless to say, getting the columns out of alignment is a sure way to end up with the wrong answer.

Another key to keeping errors to a minimum is to estimate the answer based on the whole number portion. In the problem above, a simple glance should tell you that the answer is certainly somewhere between sixteen and eighteen. Thus, if your answer ends up somewhere around 600, you know you've made a mistake.

This idea of estimating your answer is equally critical when you use a calculator to add decimals. Calculators are handy for adding decimals (no more rewriting numbers with the decimal points aligned, for one thing) but the answer on the calculator won't always be right. Every so often, you're going to enter a string of numbers wrong and thus get an answer way off from what's correct. You need to be able to realize "Well, that's certainly not the answer I expected, so I'd better try it again." (And don't, by the way, expect much sympathy from the business world if the wrong number gets used to make some important decision and your only defense is, "That's what my calculator said." You're expected to know when the answer isn't plausible and to correct the problem. "Garbage in, garbage out," as the computer people say, and you need to be shrewd enough to know when a result—no matter how derived—isn't right.)

Subtracting two decimals involves the same critical concept of "lining up the decimal points" that addition does. The only difference is that adding the zeros to make the numbers have the same number of decimal places is more necessary with subtraction, since you'll likely have a harder time subtracting a number from nothing than adding nothing to a number. And as with addition, estimating what the answer will be is a mandatory step.

Decimals are multiplied as if they were whole numbers, meaning that you don't have to (and probably shouldn't) bother lining up the decimal points. In fact, the decimals have nothing at all to do with the calculation until after you have the numbers multiplied. At that point, it's necessary to insert the decimal point somewhere into the answer. Just where depends on the *total* number of decimal places in the two numbers. If, for example, 0.3 is multiplied by 0.4, the answer is 0.12; the fact that each number had one decimal place means that there needs to be a total of two in the answer. But what if 0.3 is multiplied by 0.3? The answer is 0.09; an extra zero had to be attached at the left to make it possible to have two decimal places in the answer.

Division with decimals also involves moving the decimal around a bit. The trick is to convert the divisor (the number doing the dividing) to a whole number by moving the decimal point as many places to the right as it takes. This means, however, that the decimal point in the dividend (the number being divided) must also be moved the same number of places to the right. What this means is that a problem that starts out as 27.3 ÷ 0.3 ends up 273 ÷ 3, like this:

$$0.3\overline{)27.3}$$
$$91$$

In many problems, though, there will still be one or more decimal places left in the dividend. In such cases, the rule is to put the decimal in the answer at the same position as in the dividend, like this:

$$0.6\overline{)18.6\dagger6}$$
$$31.1$$

As with whole numbers, division with decimals is quite likely not to come out even. In fact, many divisions (e.g., 0.1 ÷ 3 or 2 ÷ .13) will never come out even. Obviously, at some point, you have to stop dividing and round the answer. Where to round to depends quite a bit on what the numbers you're dividing represent and what you are going to do with the answer. Let's say you've gone a seventh of the way to your friend Rob's house, which is a mile away. The *number* 1 divided into seven parts is, in fact, about 0.14285. But because of limits on how precisely the one mile was measured in the first place, it isn't sensible to say that one-seventh of the way to Rob's house is 0.14285 miles, since that answer is much more precise than it either needs or deserves to be.

Ever since grade school, you've heard people talk about "rounding off" a measurement, a figure they've read, or the answer to a math problem. Indeed, you don't have to do too many decimal divisions before the obvious necessity of rounding answers becomes clear; most of these calculations don't come out even and it would be foolish continuing the division process just hoping one more step will do it.

    Unfortunately, rounding is not always as simple as people make it out to be. First off, there's the question of whether to round or to *truncate* the number. In either case, though, you have to decide what place to round to. Is the answer to be to the nearest whole number, the nearest ten million (probably acceptable for the population of the world) or the nearest ten-millionth (necessary for the length of light waves)?

    If you decide to simply drop any digits when rounding, that's truncation. The number 48.6 truncated to the nearest whole number is 48. But, if you're going to adjust the number to the *nearest* whole number, that's simply rounding. And that means that 48.6 will "round up" to 49, while 48.4 will "round down" to 48.

    Everything is pretty straightforward until the number ends with a five in the location that has to be rounded off. For example, does 48.5 round to 48 or 49? Most math books and calculators round the number up, so 48.5 rounds to 49. This is more of a mathematical convention than the obviously right thing to do. since 48.5 is, in fact, exactly halfway between 48 and 49.

Some fractions are easy to convert to decimals. For example, 0.3, three-tenths, is pretty obviously 3/10. Similarly, 0.293 is 293/1000 and 0.41 is 41/100. This works fine, of course, for converting any decimal into a frac-

Another Note about Rounding

Converting Fractions to Decimals (and Vice Versa)

tion, but life is not quite so simple when changing fractions into decimals. That isn't to say it's difficult, however. All you need to do is divide the numerator by the denominator. Suppose you want to know the decimal equivalent of ¼. Simply divide 1 by 4, which will result in 0.25.

With any luck, though, you already know that ¼ is equal to 0.25. It would help if you also knew that ½ is 0.5, that ⅓ is about 0.333, that ⅛ is 0.125, and so on. Knowing some of these common conversions will help you considerably throughout *By the Numbers* since, as we mentioned, these conversions are made almost as second nature in carrying out business calculations.

Percents

Percents represent part of a whole. You've heard that before; the statement is also true for fractions and decimals. In fact, *percents* are very closely related to one particular kind of decimal—decimals based on hundredths; one percent is one one-hundredth of the whole. Thus, 67 percent is the same as 0.67 or ⁶⁷/₁₀₀.

But what about 32.1 percent? Even though it's harder to visualize 32.1 parts of a whole that's divided into 100 parts, that's exactly how it works. Actually, you can convert any percent to a decimal just by moving the decimal two places to the left and dropping the percent sign. Thus, 32.1% becomes 0.321, and 126% becomes 1.26.

Since converting a decimal to a percent is pretty easy, you can convert a fraction to a percent quite simply by first converting the fraction to a decimal and then converting the decimal to a percent. Thus, ⅗ becomes 0.60, which becomes 60 percent. Notice, though, that you can do the same conversion in one step by just multiplying the fraction by 100 percent. In other words, ⅗ as a percent is ⅗ × 100% = 300% ÷ 5, which is 60 percent. Of course, there really isn't any difference in these two methods; one just seems more direct than the other.

On occasion, you may encounter a fraction of a percent. If something is ¹⁄₁₀ of 1 percent, it's also 0.1 percent. Since you convert from a percent to a decimal by moving the decimal point two places to the left, 0.1 percent is the same as 0.001. Notice, by the way, that this is a pretty small amount; when someone says that something changed by, say, "two-tenths of one percent," you should immediately recognize that change as only two-thousandths of the whole amount.

**The Basic
Percent Formula**

As you'll see in the next lesson, formulas play an important part in the *By the Numbers* telecourse. Many of the concepts that you'll encounter are succinctly described in formulas, and knowing how and when to apply them is one of the most important skills you'll learn from the course. There is, however, one formula that is so basic, so central to business mathematics that it occupies a special place in our study of the subject. It's called the basic *percent formula.*

As you probably know just by observing the world around you, much of business mathematics involves problems dealing with percents. A dress is reduced 40 percent; interest rates rise by 3 percent. Many of these percent problems involve three quantities. First, there's the *base.* The base is the starting point for these problems, the number against which things are going to be compared. In the example of the dress, the base is the original cost of the dress; in the interest rate comparison, the base is the original interest rate.

The second quantity is the *rate*. The rate is easy to identify because it's the number followed by the percent sign. In our examples, the rates are forty percent for the dress and three percent for the interest rate. *Part* is what you get when you multiply the base times the rate. In many percent problems, the base and the rate are known and you'll be asked to solve for the part.

The basic percent formula is written as *Part = Base × Rate*. This is usually abbreviated to $P = B \times R$. As you can see, the formula is not very complicated, but that doesn't make it any less powerful; you'll find this formula appearing in many of the 26 *By the Numbers* lessons. In fact, it appears so often that you'll make little progress through the course if you don't understand how to apply this formula.

The simplest application of the percent formula is solving problems such as "What is 20 percent of 500?" What we are solving for is the part, and we know the base and the rate. All that is necessary to solve this problem is to multiply the base, 500, by the rate, 20 percent. In other words, Part = 20% × 500.

There's one other step, though, that you'll need to do in almost every one of these problems. That's changing the percent figure in the problem to a decimal so it can be multiplied. As you should remember, you change a percent to a decimal by dropping the percent sign and moving the decimal point two places to the left. The result is Part = .20 × 500, which means Part = 100.

With just this one technique, you can handle many of the problems in business mathematics. The key is to ask yourself whether this problem can be put in the form of "some percent of something is something else." If it can, we use the percent formula to solve the problem. Suppose we have a situation where a 10 percent discount is given on a $300 lawn mower and we want to know the dollar amount of the discount. We can restate this problem as "10 percent of $300 is the discount," where 10 percent is the rate, $300 is the base, and the discount is the part.

Finding Base and Rate

Of course, knowing the different forms of the percent formula won't do much good if you can't decide what you're trying to solve for. And because this formula is used in so many different ways in business mathematics, it's not practical to try to anticipate every variation. A better approach is to think of some general rules that you can apply in a wide variety of situations.

Identifying rate, you'll remember, is pretty simple because it is associated with the word "percent." Base and part are a little harder to tell apart, but it's not difficult if you think of base as the "starting point" and part as "a part of the base." Suppose we know that a factory produced 1,000 more machines in one year than the previous year and that that was a 20 percent increase in production. Now suppose we want to find the number of machines produced in the prior year. The rate is obviously 20 percent, but what's the part and what's the base? The 1,000 machines isn't our starting point, it's a part of our starting point. What we want to solve for—the previous year's production—is our starting point, which makes it the base. The preferable formula, therefore, is $B = P \div R$. (And if we do the arithmetic, we find that $B = 1,000 \div .20$, which means $B = 5,000$ machines.)

What if we instead knew that last year's production was 5,000 machines and that this year 1,000 more machines were produced. Now we know that 5,000 is the base and 1,000 is the part; what we don't know is the rate. Therefore, the appropriate formula is $R = P \div B$, and $R = 1{,}000 \div 5{,}000$ (which is, not surprisingly, .20, or 20 percent.)

Increase and Decrease Problems

Perhaps you can already see how useful the basic percent formula will be. There are, however, some problems that require an additional step.

When we were solving our problems about the increase in production of machines, we found that we started with 5,000 machines (the base) and, after a 20 percent increase (the rate), we found that production had increased by 1,000 machines (the part). What we didn't get from this exercise was the number of machines produced in the current year.

Not that this is hard to figure; we simply add the 5,000 machines from the base year and the 1,000 machine increase. Problems of this type are called *increase problems*, and they are very common in business mathematics. For example, if an employee gets a 10 percent raise on a $20,000 salary, the $P = B \times R$ formula tells us that the raise was $2,000. But to find the new salary, we have to add the $2,000 increase (the part) to the $20,000 base.

There are also lots of *decrease problems*, and the concept is much the same. Suppose the original price of a pair of pants is $30 and there's a 20 percent discount. The $P = B \times R$ formula tells us that the discount is $6. We don't know the new price of the pants until we subtract $6 (the part) from $30 (the base); once we do, we learn that the sale price is $24.

If you're thinking that this idea of adding or subtracting the part from the base is pretty simple, you're right. The only trick is to remember to do it. Always be careful to identify exactly what answer you're trying to get — and then don't stop until you get it.

SOME WORDS OF ADVICE

Obviously, these past few paragraphs weren't meant to replicate the several years that you spent learning about fractions, decimals, and percents in the first place. They're not even meant to replace the descriptions in your textbook, or the descriptions that will come in the video program.

What this overview can do, though, is refresh your memory for what's coming next and serve as an indicator of just how concerned you should be about the mathematical proficiency you bring to this course. Remember our warning that the course counts on you to know already how to do the arithmetic required in business mathematics. True, it's only arithmetic, but that arithmetic is critical in literally billions of dollars of business decisions made daily. If everything we've just covered is familiar to you—perhaps because you've done these manipulations regularly over the past decade or so—then you are in good shape to proceed with the course.

On the other hand, if your reaction is "Gee, I never really did understand that," we encourage you to spend some time with the explanations and problem sets in your textbook. And if things still seem muddy, see your instructor about where to go for additional help. It's unfortunate, but *By the Numbers* will be a very difficult course if you don't master the objectives associated with fractions, decimals, and percents.

One final note. In basic training in the army, they tell you, "Your rifle is your friend; get to know it." The same thing might be said about the basic percent formula. Don't leave this lesson without remembering and understanding this formula in its three basic forms. Learn to identify part, base, and rate when given a problem. (And remember that the formula alone won't give you an answer to an increase or decrease problem; an additional addition or subtraction step is necessary.)

KEY TERMS

Before you read through the text assignment and watch the video program, take a minute to look at the key terms associated with this lesson. When you encounter them in the text and video program, pay careful attention to their meaning.

Base: The starting point against which something else will be compared. Base is one of the three elements of the basic percent formula.

Decimal: A number written with a decimal point. The numbers 23.1 and 0.384 are examples.

Denominator: The number on the bottom of a fraction. In the fraction $4/7$, for example, 7 is the denominator.

Fraction: A way of representing a part of the whole by indicating how many parts the whole is divided into (the denominator) and how many parts are being considered (the numerator). If 13 parts of a whole divided into 18 parts are being considered, the fraction is $13/18$.

Improper fraction: A fraction with a numerator bigger than the denominator. Convention calls for converting improper fractions into mixed numbers.

Least common denominator: The smallest whole number that can be divided evenly by all the denominators in a set of fractions. For example, the least common denominator for the fractions $1/6$, $1/9$, and $1/2$ is 18, since 18 is the smallest number that can be divided evenly by 6, 9, and 2.

Lowest terms: A fraction whose numerator and denominator are both evenly divisible only by one. For example, while $3/5$ is in lowest terms, $3/6$ is not because both 3 and 6 are evenly divisible by three.

Mixed number: A number written as a combination of a whole number and a fraction.

Numerator: The number on the top of a fraction. In the fraction $4/7$, for example, 4 is the numerator.

Part: The result of multiplying the base times the rate. Used in the percent formula, the part is always in the same units as the base.

Percent: A way of representing a part of the whole by indicating how many of 100 parts are under consideration. For example, 41 percent indicates that 41 parts of a whole of 100 parts are being considered.

Percent formula: The formula showing that part is equal to base times rate. It is usually written as $P = B \times R$, but $B = P \div R$ and $R = P \div B$ are alternate forms.

Rate: The change in the base. Used in the percent formula, rate is given in percent.

PART II: WATCHING THE VIDEO PROGRAM

VIDEO VIEWING GUIDE

Before watching the video program, review the following questions. As you watch, be sure to collect the information necessary to answer them:

1. In what ways are fractions and decimals similar? In what ways are they different?

2. What are some of the reasons for converting fractions to other forms, such as percents and decimals? When is it more convenient to leave them as they are?

3. What, if anything, is "improper" about an improper fraction? How are improper fractions related to mixed numbers?

4. What does it mean to say that we use a "decimal" system of numbers? What are some of the reasons that a decimal number system generally works so well? When does it not work well?

5. How does the concept of "significance" relate to operations conducted with decimals?

6. To what extent does the idea of percent simply duplicate other existing ways of representing numbers? If it is largely redundant, why is it still widely used?

7. What makes the ability to quickly convert among decimals, fractions, and percents so important to a business person?

8. What is "rounding error," and is it really an error? Why or why not?

9. Why does the basic percent formula play such a big part in business mathematics? What are some examples of places it is used regularly?

10. How are increase and decrease problems different from problems that use the basic percent formula? How are they related?

VIDEO PROGRAM

This lesson's video program is Program 2—Fractions, Decimals, and Percents. Remember, if you are watching this program on videotape, take time to replay sections of the tape any time you need to review a concept.

VIDEO VIEWING QUESTIONS

Immediately after viewing the video program for Lesson 2, take time to respond to the following questions. Give your answers some careful thought; they may provide the basis for additional discussion or a longer written response.

1. Briefly, in your own words, describe what fractions, decimals, and percents all have in common.

   _____

   _____

2. For each type of number, list two common business applications where it is widely used.

   Fractions: _____

   Decimals: _____

   Percents: _____

3. Briefly explain why most fractional numbers end up represented as decimals rather than fractions when they have to be used in business.

   _____

   _____

4. Describe in words how to convert a fraction to a decimal.

   _____

   _____

   Now describe how to convert a decimal to a fraction.

   _____

   _____

5. Suppose you have a young nephew who has asked you for which fractions he should memorize the decimal equivalents. Write down the fractions (and their decimal equivalents) that you think he should memorize.

   _____

   _____

6. Comment on why discounts on store prices are generally given in percents. Why not just express them as a decimal number?

   _____

   _____

7. Write a brief rule sufficient to explain how to round any number to a specified level.

   _____

   _____

8. You have a friend who computes the answer in decimal division problems to more decimal places than you think necessary. (If your answer was 26.37, she'd get 26.37436). "Might as well be as accurate as possible," she says. Comment on the appropriateness of her approach.

   _____

   _____

9. Use the space below to identify three examples of "part" found in business, three of "base," and three of rate.

Part: _____

_____

_____

Base: _____

_____

_____

Rate: _____

_____

_____

10. Since increase and decrease problems are so common, it might help to have a rule about how to solve them. In the space below, write such a rule.

_____

_____

PART III: FOCUSING ON THE MATHEMATICS

READING ASSIGNMENT

After watching the video program, you should read one of the following Text Assignments, depending on the textbook you're using:

SOFTCOVER: Chapter 1*, pages 19-34; Chapter 2*, pages 39-68; and Chapter 4, pages 103-148, of the Miller, Salzman, and Hoelzle softcover text, *Business Mathematics*.

HARDCOVER: Chapter 1*, pages 3-29, and Chapter 3*, pages 65-98, of the Salzman, Miller, and Hoelzle hardcover text, *Mathematics for Business*.

As you read through the text, pay careful attention to the examples the book gives of the mathematics associated with the concepts you're learning about.

Then, after you've completed the text assignment, read through the Key Formulas here. This section provides a handy review of what you've learned. By the time you get to this point in the lesson, all of the formulas and calculations should be familiar to you. If they're not, go back and read

_____

* Assigned at instructors' option.

the appropriate parts of the text and the Overview section of this lesson. You won't have much success completing the rest of your assignments if you are still confused about the information in the Key Formulas section.

KEY FORMULAS

The following key formulas are important to your understanding of this lesson. Be sure that you know each one and how to use it in solving problems related to fractions, decimals, and percents.

KEY FORMULA: Decimal value = Numerator ÷ Denominator

Formula used for: Converting a fraction to a decimal.

Example:

Martin Cleaners is having a "half off" sale; the price of all cleaning services is reduced by one half. Since the fraction is ½, dividing the numerator by the denominator results in the answer 0.50. Therefore, 0.50 is the decimal value of ½.

Remember that in this formula:

1. The decimal equivalents for common fractions such as ½, ⅓, ⅔, ¼, ¾, ⅕, ⅛, and so on should be memorized.

2. The conversion of fractions to decimals is often done almost automatically, as just a routine step in working a business math problem. You should, therefore, understand how this is done so you're not perplexed about what's happening when these conversions are made.

KEY FORMULA: Percent value = Fraction × 100%

Formula used for: Converting a fraction to a percent.

Example:

Martin Cleaners, from the previous example, has decided that "half off" doesn't sound like as much of a discount as if it were given in percent. They multiply ½ × 100 percent, which gives them 50 percent. So they can, if they choose, offer "Discounts of 50%," which is the same as their original one-half off.

Remember that in this formula:

1. The percent equivalents for common fractions such as ½, ⅓, ⅔, ¼, ¾, ⅕, ⅛, and so on should be memorized.

2. The mathematics for this formula is no different from the math of converting a fraction to a decimal and then changing the decimal to a percent by moving the decimal point two places to the right. (It does, however, get the job done in only one step.)

KEY FORMULA: Part = Base × Rate ($P = B \times R$)

Formula used for: Calculating the third variable of part, base, and rate when the other two are known. This formula is called the basic percent formula.

Alternate forms: Base = Part ÷ Rate ($P = B \div R$) or
Rate = Part ÷ Base ($R = P \div B$)

Example:

Marshall Wilson paid a 4 percent sales tax on a purchase of $100. If we want to know how much sales tax was paid, we multiply $100 (the base) by .04 (the rate); the answer is $4.

Remember that in this formula:

1. The rate is usually given as a percent, but to use this figure in calculations, you'll have to change it to a decimal by moving the decimal point two places to the left and dropping the percent sign.

2. Deciding which form of the percent formula to use is mostly a matter of deciding what it is that you're trying to find. Therefore, your first step should always be to decide whether the answer you want is the part, base, or rate.

KEY FORMULA: New value = Original + Increase

Formula used for: Finding the new value from some original base when the base and rate are known.

Alternate form: New value = Original − Decrease

Example:

Wong receives an executive bonus equal to 20 percent of her $50,000 salary. The basic percent formula says that the part (the bonus) is equal to the base of $50,000 times the rate of 20 percent. This means that the bonus is $10,000. Wong is, however, more interested in what her total pay will be. To find the new value, we add the original value of $50,000 to the increase of $10,000, which gives us a new value of $60,000.

Remember that in this formula:

1. The formula works in much the same way for decrease problems, except that you subtract the decrease from the original value rather than adding the two together.

2. If a problem contains terms such as "more than" or "greater than," it's likely an increase problem. "Less than," "dropped," and "fell" indicate decrease problems.

DON'T FORGET

1. Calculators are handy for doing many operations involving decimals and percents, but be sure to estimate your answer first as a check that the numbers were entered correctly.

2. It is important that you be able to convert any fraction, decimal, or percent to any other form. At the same time, though, realize that most of the fractions and percents encountered in business are common numbers like ⅓ and 20 percent, rather than more exotic numbers like ¹²⁶/₇₁₃ or 27.121 percent. For this reason, memorizing the most common decimal/fraction conversions is helpful.

3. Convert decimals to percents by simply moving the decimal point two places to the right and adding a percent sign. Dropping the percent sign and moving the decimal point two places to the left will convert a percent to a decimal.

4. When converting between decimals and percents, it's often necessary to add zeros to the left or right side of the number as you move the decimal point. In other words, 3 percent becomes 0.03 when converted, while 0.2 becomes 20 percent.

5. The fractions resulting from various operations and conversions will not always be in lowest terms, but you should generally rewrite them that way.

6. The basic percent formula is so important that you should memorize it. But knowing the formula won't help if you can't identify part, base, and rate, so learn some of the key phrases that will alert you to which quantities are which.

PART IV: SOLVING BUSINESS PROBLEMS

PROBLEM SETS

Work the following problems in your textbook. Your instructor will tell you which problems, if any, are to be turned in. Some of the problems have answers provided in the back of the book; refer to these answers to make sure you are working the problems correctly.

SOFTCOVER: If you are using the Miller, Salzman, and Hoelzle softcover text, *Business Mathematics*, do the following problem sets:

1.4: Problems #8-16 (even numbers only), and 40-46 (all) on pages 21-22.

1.5: Problems #22-32 (even numbers only) on page 26.

1.6: Problems #6-14, 22-30 (even numbers only), and 44-46 (all) on pages 31-34.

2.1: Problems #2-44 (even numbers only) on pages 43-44.

2.2: Problems #2-24 (even numbers only) on page 49.

2.3: Problems #2-20 (even numbers only) on pages 53-54.

4.1: Problems #4-80 (every fourth problem) on pages 107-108.

4.2: Problems #2-16 (even numbers only) and 34-38 (all) on pages 113-116.

4.3: Problems #2-16 (even numbers only) and 32-36 (all) on pages 119-120.

4.4: Problems #2-20 (even numbers only) and 26-30 (all) on pages 127-128.

4.5: Problems #1-8 and 26-30 on pages 137-140.

HARDCOVER: If you are using the Salzman, Miller, and Hoelzle hardcover text, *Mathematics for Business*, do the following problem sets:

1.1: Problems #6-34 and 80-88 (even numbers only) on pages 12-14.

1.2: Problems #50-64 (even numbers only) and 77-80 (all) on pages 22-23.

3.1: Problems #51-60 (even numbers only) on pages 69-70.

3.2: Problems #20-30 (even numbers only) on page 75.

3.3: Problems #20-30 (even numbers only) on pages 79-80.

3.4: Problems #20-30 (even numbers only) on pages 85-86.

3.5: Problems #33-40 (even numbers only) on pages 95-96.

BUSINESS APPLICATIONS

Because of the longer than average reading assignment, and because the focus of this lesson is on basic mathematics rather than business concepts, there are no business application scenarios for this lesson.

Equations and Formulas **3**

"Yes, yes, I *know* that, Sidney ... *everybody* knows *that*! ... But look: Four wrongs *squared*, minus two wrongs to the fourth power, divided by this formula, do make a right."

Perhaps you know the equation $E = mc^2$. But did you ever wonder what this formula is good for? What can we do with it, and why is it written this way?

Formulas are a special kind of equation, although this admittedly isn't too helpful until you learn what an equation is. An *equation* shows the relationship between quantities in a shorthand sort of way. The equation $5x = y$, for example, tells us the same thing as, "If you have five times something called x, that's as much as if you had y." In other words, an equation says that two things are equal; the part on the left is equal to the part on the right. (In fact, sensibly enough, the two halves of the equation are called the *right side* and the *left side*.)

The equation $5x = y$ isn't really a formula, though. But $E = mc^2$ is. In this lesson, you'll learn about the difference and also learn some things about manipulating both equations and formulas. And, perhaps most importantly, you'll learn something of the important role equations and formulas play in business mathematics.

PART I: INTRODUCING THE MATERIAL

LEARNING OBJECTIVES

Upon completing your study of this lesson, you should be able to:

1. Recognize and correctly use the terms left side, right side, variable, reciprocal, and associative and distributive properties.

2. Know the addition rule and multiplication rule and use them to solve simple equations.

3. Identify which of several equations is appropriate for solving a given word problem.

4. Given a formula, describe how a change in one variable affects the other variables.

5. Use business formulas in solving word problems when the values for the variables are given.

6. Define the terms ratio and proportion, and be able to write the ratio or proportion equivalent to a word phrase.

If you're using the hardcover textbook, *Mathematics for Business*, there are some additional objectives for the lesson. Upon completing your study of the lesson, you should also be able to:

7. Given a formula and the values of all variables but one, find the value of the variable not given.

8. Given a business-related word problem, identify the variables in the problem and set up the equation necessary to solve for the missing information.

9. Define the term *coefficient* and identify examples of coefficients in business-related equations.

10. Determine whether two proportions are equivalent.

11. Solve proportions and word problems containing proportions by calculating cross products and solving the resulting equation.

LESSON OVERVIEW

Equations and formulas are sprinkled throughout *By the Numbers*. And a number of the concepts you'll study in business mathematics—interest, depreciation, markup and markdown, commissions, and so on—have formulas as their basis. It's fair to say that while *By the Numbers* isn't exactly awash in equations and formulas, if you don't have a basic idea of how to handle them, you're in for some trouble.

Let's first look at our famous equation $E = mc^2$. Perhaps the most obvious thing that this equation shows is that some quantity E is equal to some quantity m times c^2. In this case, E, m, and c are all *variables*, letters that represent numbers. It turns out that E, m, and c are also *terms* of the equation. Almost anything in an equation is a term—a single letter, a number or the product of a number, and a letter. In the equation $5E = mc$, 5 is a term, just like E, m, and c. But it is not a variable; instead, 5 is a *coefficient*. A coefficient is a number that multiplies a variable.

The important thing about an equation is that it will (at least in business math) generally have a *solution*. A solution is a number that can replace the variable and leave you with a true statement. In the simplest equations, $x = 2$ for example, the solution is already obvious. In this case, x is a variable, x and 2 are terms, and 2 is the solution, since when 2 replaces x, you get $2 = 2$, a true statement.

Most equations, however, are considerably trickier. It will take some effort to find the solution to an equation like $8 - 6p - 14 \times 3(2 + 4p) = 3$. The principle is still the same, however; there is a number that can replace the variable p to make the left side of the equation equal to the right side of the equation.

All this is pretty straightforward, but what may not be obvious to you is how an equation does anyone (besides an algebra teacher) any real good. You won't have to get very far into *By the Numbers*, however, before the answer to this question becomes very clear.

In business, you'll often encounter relationships between quantities in which one or more parts of the relationship aren't known. For example, suppose you put some money into the bank. You clearly know how much money you put into the bank and you know what the interest rate is, and you may even know how long you intend to leave it there. What you probably don't know, however, is how much money you'll receive from the bank when your principal is combined with the interest you earned.

The way to find out is by setting up an equation that relates all these variables—the money you put in, the interest rate, the amount of time the money stays in the account, and the money you take out. Notice that all four of these quantities are variables and that we know the value for three of them. What we have to do is to *solve* the equation to find the value of the variable we don't know. (This process is sometimes called *solving for the unknown.*)

As you can see, working with equations is a two-part process. No matter how well you can solve an equation, you aren't going to make any progress until the equation is set up properly. On the other hand, setting up the equation does no good if you don't have the skills needed to solve

Basic Equation Terminology

How to Use an Equation

for the unknown. Fortunately, solving equations becomes largely a matter of simple arithmetic once you understand a few basic procedures.

When Is an Equation a Formula?

To this point, we've been a little vague about the difference between an equation and a formula. Perhaps the first step toward clarification is to point out that all formulas are equations, but not all equations are formulas. That's because while equations can show any relationship (even something as obscure as $3p + 2.5z \div 6q = 37$), formulas are rules and procedures that show how one specific quantity is related to other quantities. Our example about a bank deposit would use a formula that related the interest rate, the amount of the deposit, the amount of time the deposit was earning interest, and the amount of interest earned. And as you'll see in a future lesson, once we know the formula and three of the four quantities, we can solve for the missing quantity.

Let's look at our $E = mc^2$ example. First, notice that we have an equation with a left side and a right side. Nothing special about that, though, since that's true of all equations. But in this particular equation, the variables all represent specific quantities. As every physicist knows, E stands for energy, m for mass and c for the speed of light. Therefore, $E = mc^2$ is a shorthand way of saying that when a certain mass is accelerated to the speed of light squared, a certain amount of energy will result.

Now we have to assign values to the variables. But there's a catch. We already know what the speed of light is, and it's not going to change. Which is to say the speed of light is *not* a variable; it's a *constant*. Even so, we still have two variables, so there is no solution to the equation just yet. But notice that if we choose any specific value of m, the mass, we can easily figure out the amount of energy that mass can be converted to. If we choose a different mass, we get a different energy. But regardless of what mass we choose, the relationship is always the same, and that relationship is shown by a formula.

Many of the most useful rules in business mathematics are given as formulas. Each time you use a formula, you'll know the value of most of the variables, but there will be one variable you're solving for. It might be an interest rate, or the commission on buying a share of stock, or the markup on an item offered for sale, or any number of a hundred other quantities. The key is that once you know the formula that lets you figure out the quantity in one situation, it works for any other set of values.

If you're thinking that it might be easier to forget using the formula and simply say, "You find the energy equivalent of a specific mass by multiplying the mass by the speed of light squared," most people would disagree with you. Formulas are, in general, pithy, efficient, and memorable ways of representing relationships that can get complicated. The theory is that you'll have an easier time remembering the handful of constants and variables in a formula than you would remembering, and applying, the equivalent words.

Understanding Equation-Speak

While it's handy that formulas and equations can be expressed in this sort of shorthand method, most times the business world doesn't set its problems just to match the formulas. In fact, one of the biggest criticisms business people level against mathematics courses in general is that students learn to solve problems only when the problems are already set up for them. For better or worse, though, about the only place you'll see something like $6x + 2 = 7$ is in a mathematics textbook.

For this reason, it's critical that every business person know how to get from the real-world description of a problem to its mathematical version, which can then be solved using basic math skills. This translation is made simpler by the facts that certain words and phrases keep appearing in business problems and that each of these words and phrases almost always indicates that a certain operation needs to be performed to solve the equation.

Some of these verbal expressions are very straightforward. The statement "plus a number" indicates that addition is called for, while "less than a number" is almost inevitably going to require some subtraction. Statements like "$2/3$ of a number" or "4 times as many" are likely to require multiplication. And "a total of," "the result" or "adds to" usually indicates an equality—that is, an equal sign.

Let's look first at a textbook example. Suppose someone tells you that when "three times a number is decreased by four, the result is twenty." You should already be able to quickly translate this into an equation. The "number" is the variable whose value we're attempting to find. We'll call it y, although we could pick any letter to represent this quantity. The phrase "three times the number" indicates "$3y$," while the phrase "is decreased by four" suggests that we need to subtract 4 from $3y$. The phrase "the result is twenty" suggests that 20 is going to follow the equal sign. So our equation turns out to be a rather simple $3y - 4 = 20$.

The same principle holds true for more real-life examples. If someone tells you that "Children's plane tickets cost one-half the amount of adults' plane tickets, and that the tickets for three adults and two children cost $1,600," you should be able to translate this into an equation that helps you find the cost of each ticket. Start by assigning y to the value of one child's ticket. This makes the adult tickets each worth $2y$. Since there were two children's tickets (costing $2y$ total) and three adults' tickets (costing 3 x $2y$ total), we know that the total cost of the tickets was $(3 \times 2y) + 2y$. And, since all the tickets together cost $1,600, the equation to figure out the cost of one child's ticket is $(3 \times 2y) + 2y = \$1,600$. This is the same as $6y + 2y = \$1,600$, which you can probably see is the same as $8y = \$1,600$. If we substitute $200 for y, we get a true statement ($1,600 = $1,600) which means that $200 is the cost of a child's ticket and $400 is the cost of an adult's ticket.

In real life, you'll often find that solving an equation is easier than figuring out what the equation should be in the first place. And while knowing how some common phrases translate into portions of an equation is a necessary skill, you still have to have an underlying understanding of just what it is you're trying to figure out. Regardless of the subject matter, one of the most common complaints against students who go out into the business world for the first time is that they can't clearly identify what the problem is and what information they need to solve it.

This is particularly true in mathematics, where mastering the textbook skills doesn't always translate into real-world problem-solving ability. Throughout *By the Numbers*, though, we'll do our best to show you lots of examples of how real business problems get translated into equations and then solved. As we go through this process, you should work hard to understand what's going on because this "translation" skill is every bit as important as being able to solve a mathematical equation that's already set up.

Too Much Information . . . or Too Little?

One thing that you'll consistently have to deal with is having too much or too little information to solve the problem. When writing textbook problems, the authors usually don't take up space with a lot of useless information, and this lulls students into thinking that half the battle is figuring how to use *all* the numbers they've been given. It's not like this in the business world, however. There's usually a nearly unlimited amount of information available and it's up to you to select just what's needed.

Of course, the fact that you have access to all this information may not mean that you have everything you need. Sometimes, part of the information is missing—which means you have no chance of solving the problem. As you might guess, few things are more frustrating than sitting down to get the answers you promised your boss or a client, only to find out that you don't have enough data.

The good news is that most business people develop a sense about what information they do and don't need to come up with the necessary answer. The bad news is that there aren't rules that help you decide whether some number is or isn't relevant to the problem you have at hand. Experience with a given type of problem will help. The best approach, however, is simply recognizing that when you attempt to solve a problem in the real world, all the numbers won't be just waiting for you as they are in most math course problems.

The Associative and Distributive Properties

In our earlier example with the airplane tickets, we were able to quickly see that the solution to the equation $8x = \$1,600$ was $200. As you probably know, however, relatively few equations can be solved simply by a careful glance or a lucky guess. We must have ways of modifying the equation so that all the terms containing the variable are on one side and all the numbers are on the other side. Only then can we clearly see what the value of the variable is.

We are helped in this effort by four very important rules. In fact, throughout *By the Numbers*, we will apply these four rules in order to simplify equations, and often we won't make a big deal about what we're doing. That's because these rules are so important, and used so often, that they need to become second nature to any business mathematics student.

The first of the rules is called the *associative property*. You already know this rule, even if you don't know it by its proper name. The associative property says, in so many words, that the way we group numbers doesn't matter when we are conducting operations. For instance, it's obvious that we can solve the problem $3 + 5 + 7$ by first adding 3 and 5 to get 8, and then adding 7 to get 15, *or* by adding the 5 and 7 to get 12 and then adding 3 to that, and the answer is still 15. What the associative property of addition says is that the sum will be the same regardless of how the numbers are grouped *for any numbers*. Written as an equation, we can say that the statement $(a + b) + c = a + (b + c)$ is always true.

There's also an associative property of multiplication, which says that $(a \times b) \times c$ is the same as $a \times (b \times c)$. For example, in the problem $2 \times 3 \times 4$, it doesn't matter whether we turn the problem into 6×4 (by first multiplying 2 by 3) or 2×12 (by first multiplying 3 by 4). But what there is *not* is an associative property that covers a combination of operations. In other words $(3 \times 4) + 5$ is definitely not the same thing as $3 \times (4 + 5)$. The answer to the first is 17, while the answer to the second is 27.

The second useful rule is called the *distributive property*. The distributive property says, more or less, that if you are going to add two numbers and then multiply the sum by a number, you'll get the same answer as if you first multiplied each number by that third number and then added them. As an equation, the property is written as $a \times (b + c) = (a \times b) + (a \times c)$. For example, $3 \times (4 + 5)$ is 27, regardless of whether you solved the problem as 3×9 or as $12 + 15$.

As with the associative property, don't get confused and try to apply the distributive property in the wrong situation. Don't, for instance, think that $3 + (4 + 5)$ is somehow the same as $(3 + 4) + (3 + 5)$.

The associative property will be used all the time throughout *By the Numbers*, so much so that it will scarcely be mentioned. That means that when we change $3 + y + 7$ into $10 + y$, we're not going to explain that we did this because the associative property lets us add numbers in any order. We'll just assume that you understand this and can follow what we're doing. (Which means that if you're a little shaky on this, now's the time to practice and perhaps ask your instructor for help.)

The third of our important rules is called the *addition rule*. The addition rule simply states that the same number may be added and subtracted to both sides of an equation. What the number is doesn't make any difference; the left and right sides of the equation were equal to begin with, so if we add the same number to both sides, they will stay equal. You might wonder, however, why this would be a useful thing to do. Wouldn't adding more numbers to the equation be a step backwards? Let's look at an example here.

Suppose we have the simple equation $y - 4 = 12$. At the moment, we haven't met our goal of having all of the variables on one side and all of the numbers on the other. But notice what happens if we add the number 4 to both sides. The equation now becomes $y - 4 + 4 = 12 + 4$. Of course, the reason that we choose to add 4 to both sides is because the 4 that we added to the left side cancels out the -4 that was already there. The equation can now be written $y = 12 + 4$ or $y = 16$. As you can see, adding 4 to both sides was the key step in solving this equation.

Here's an example where we'll subtract the same number from both sides. Let's start with the equation $y + 6 = 20$. The addition rule says that we're entitled to subtract 6 from both sides of the equation. Doing so results in $y + 6 - 6 = 20 - 6$, which quickly simplifies to $y = 14$. As before, the addition rule has provided a way to get only the variables on the left side of the equation and only the numbers on the right side.

The *multiplication rule* is conceptually similar. It says that the same non-zero number may be used to multiply or divide both sides of an equation. The "non-zero" condition isn't encountered all that often, but it's still important; since zero times any number is zero, zero doesn't work as a multiplier or divisor. Any other number, be it 0.274 or $37/84$ or 2,613, is fair game though.

Let's start with the simple equation $3y = 21$. As before, we can't solve the equation in this form because we haven't separated the variables and the numbers onto different sides of the equation. But since the multiplication rule allows us to divide both sides by the same number, we can choose to divide both the $3y$ and the 21 by 3. This results in

$$\frac{3y}{3} = \frac{21}{3},$$

The Addition and Multiplication Rules

which simplifies to $y = 7$. Suppose, though, that the equation had been

$$\frac{y}{3} = 21.$$

Then we would have multiplied both sides by 3, producing the equation

$$\frac{3y}{3} = 3 \times 21,$$

which simplifies to $y = 63$.

There's nothing to stop you from applying both the addition rule and the multiplication rule to the same equation; in fact, that's a very common practice. Suppose we have the equation $3y + 12 = 36$. First, apply the addition rule to subtract 12 from each side; this results in $3y + 12 - 12 = 36 - 12$, which simplifies to $3y = 24$. Then use the multiplication rule to divide each side by 3. This leaves us with

$$\frac{3y}{3} = \frac{24}{3},$$

or $y = 8$. Notice that neither one of the two rules by itself would have been sufficient to solve this problem.

Mathematically, it makes no difference in what order you apply these rules. For instance, in the equation $3y + 12 = 36$, we could have divided by 3 first, which would have given us

$$\frac{3y}{3} + \frac{12}{3} = \frac{36}{3}.$$

This simplifies to $y + 4 = 12$. Then we would apply the addition rule, this time subtracting 4 from each side, to come up with the solution $y = 8$.

Similarly, if you have an equation such as

$$\frac{2}{3}y = 12,$$

you can, of course, divide both sides by 2 and then multiply both sides by 3. But you can save a step by multiplying both sides by the *reciprocal* of the coefficient. A *reciprocal* of a fraction is simply the fraction inverted. For example,

the reciprocal of $\frac{2}{3}$ is $\frac{3}{2}$ (or 3);

the reciprocal of $\frac{45}{57}$ is $\frac{57}{45}$;

the reciprocal of   2 (or $\frac{2}{1}$) is $\frac{1}{2}$.

None of this is very complicated, but the multiplication rule does require that you be careful to get all of each side of the equation multiplied or divided by the same number. In our previous equation, $3y + 12 = 36$, it would not, for example, work to simply divide $3y$ by 3 while leaving the 12 untouched. On the other hand, be equally careful not to add a number to each side of the equation more than once. If you start with $2x - 5 = y$, don't make the mistake of adding 5 to both the $2x$ and the -5 portions of the left side of the equation; once is enough.

As you can see, the multiplication and addition rules are absolutely critical to solving business mathematics problems and to mathematics in general. Fortunately, while extremely powerful, they are simple rules to apply. The only caution is that you must do exactly the same thing to both sides of the equation if you hope to find the correct solution. The most common problem is carelessness that results in some operation being performed on only one side of the equation, which immediately makes the sides of the equation unequal — and takes away any hope of finding a correct solution.

In the last lesson, we talked about the extremely important *percent formula* and looked at the different forms the formula could have. As you should remember, the three forms are:

The Percent Formula Revisited

$$P = B \times R,$$

$$B = \frac{P}{R}, \text{ and}$$

$$R = \frac{P}{B},$$

where P is the part, B is the base, and R is the rate. Once you know whether you want to find the part, base, or rate, the choice of a formula is obvious. Until now, we suggested that you just memorize the alternate forms. But since you now know about the multiplication rule, we can give you a better understanding of the alternate forms.

Remember how the multiplication rule says we can divide both sides of the equation by the same number? In our previous examples, we used this rule to divide by a number, but we could just as well have divided by a variable that represents a number, or even by the product of a number and a variable. In other words, if we had the equation $3yz = 6y$, we can (and should) divide both sides by $3y$. The result (which simplifies to $z = 2$) is:

$$\frac{3yz}{3y} = \frac{6y}{3y},$$

We point this out because the multiplication rule is what gave us the alternate forms of the basic percent formula. Everything starts with the $P = B \times R$ form, but let's say that we want to find the base (B) instead. This is the same as saying that we want B all by itself on one side of the equation, something that's easily done if we divide both sides by R. The equation would then read:

$$\frac{P}{R} = B.$$

If we wanted to find the rate, given the part and the base, we'd want the R by itself. Starting with $P = B \times R$, we divide both sides by B, so the equation ends up as:

$$\frac{P}{B} = R.$$

Our three equations, therefore, are:

$$P = B \times R,$$

$$B = \frac{P}{R}, \text{ and}$$

$$R = \frac{P}{B},$$

just the same as the set we suggested in the last lesson that you memorize. You'll have to decide for yourself whether you simply memorize these three different forms of the basic percent formula or whether you remember only the $P = B \times R$ form and then apply the multiplication rule as necessary to solve the problem at hand. The second approach is certainly more sophisticated, and since you'll be using the multiplication rule all the time, you may find it easier than remembering the two alternate forms.

Ratios and Proportions

A *ratio* is a comparison of two quantities. When the odds of something happening are 1 in 3, those odds are a ratio comparing the odds of the event happening to the number of events being considered. And when you prepare canned clam chowder by adding one cup of condensed chowder to two cups of milk, you're forming a ratio of chowder to milk of 1 to 2.

Mathematically, what you're doing is forming a quotient of two numbers. In fact, in math, the ratio of *y* to *z* is actually written as a division:

$$\frac{y}{z}$$

In business, we more commonly write *y to z* or, sometimes, *y:z*. Either way, the concept of a ratio is very important, both in business and in everyday life.

However, ratios are even more useful when used as part of a *proportion*. A proportion says that two ratios are equal; we say that "something is proportional to something." Obviously, though, we can't just go around saying things like "one-half is proportional to one-third." That's not a true statement; one-half is *not* proportional to one-third. Even though both one-half and one-third are ratios, they aren't equal, so we don't have a proportion.

Let's look at two ratios that *are* proportional. We already learned to make clam chowder using a ratio of one cup of chowder to two cups of milk. But what if we have twice as many chowder eaters coming to dinner? Obviously, we need two cups of chowder. When we mix the first cup, we'll use two cups of milk; when we mix the second, we'll use two more cups of milk. That's a total of four cups of milk for two cans of chowder. The implication is that the ratios 1 to 2 and 2 to 4 are equal—and the chowder will taste the same whether taken from the little batch or the bigger batch.

Using Cross Products

Having a way to know whether two ratios are actually proportional would be a useful tool. Fortunately, it's easy to see by finding the *cross products*. Cross products are the products obtained when each numerator of a proportion is multiplied by the opposite denominator.

An example will make the use of cross products clearer. In the chowder example, we suspect that the result of one cup of chowder mixed with two cups of milk tastes the same as two cups of chowder mixed with four cups of milk. Written as a proportion, we think that:

$$\frac{1}{2} = \frac{2}{4}$$

is a true statement. Admittedly, it looks right, but we can prove it by finding the cross products, like this:

$$\frac{1}{2} \diagdown\mkern-19mu\diagup \frac{2}{4}$$

$$4 \qquad\qquad 4$$

Since 4 = 4 is a true statement, 1:2 = 2:4 is, indeed, a proportion.

There's a more valuable use of cross products than just checking whether two ratios we've come up with are really proportional, though. Suppose we know that our widget factory used 240 lock washers to produce 80 widgets this week and that next week we plan to produce 120 widgets. The problem of how many lock washers we need on hand can be solved using cross products. We start with the ratio we already know:

$$\frac{lock\ washers}{widgets} = \frac{240\ lock\ washers}{80\ widgets}$$

Then we substitute the anticipated 120 widgets as the denominator of the first ratio and find the cross products.

$$\frac{lock\ washers}{120\ widgets} \diagdown \frac{240}{80}$$

So 80 × lock washers = 28,800. It's then a matter of applying the multiplication rule to get the required lock washers variable all by itself on one side of the equation. Once that's done, we learn that we'll need 360 lock washers.

Incidentally, if you think about it, you may realize that using cross products has the same effect as using the multiplication rule to get the variable (the part of the proportion we don't know) on one side while putting all the numbers on the other. Our lock washer problem could, therefore, have been solved if we'd multiplied both sides of the proportion by 120, like this:

$$120 \times \frac{lock\ washers}{120} = \frac{240}{80} \times 120,$$

so lock washers = 360.

Mathematically, it doesn't matter which approach you take. In practice, you'll find problems that seem easier to handle using cross products and others that seemed laid out perfectly for applying the multiplication rule directly. Like a technician who has a lot of different screwdrivers in her toolbox so she can use whichever one is best for a particular job, a good business person will have multiple ways of solving most problems but will be able to recognize and use the easiest approach.

SOME WORDS OF ADVICE

The best advice we can give is to trust us when we tell you that understanding equations and formulas is extremely important. If all of what's been covered in this overview makes perfect sense to you, that's great. You're in good shape for the coming lessons.

But if, after you finish this lesson, there are still things that don't make sense to you, you need to invest some extra time in trying to learn the concepts, perhaps working with your instructor if things are still fuzzy. As we've stressed, you will need to deal with equations and formulas dozens of times in the *By the Numbers* course. And while none of what's covered is very complicated, things could be difficult if you don't understand the basic principles.

The addition and multiplication rules are particularly important and we encourage you to master them. We have to use these rules all the time in order to solve *By the Numbers* problems in this telecourse guide, in the video programs, and in the textbook, and we don't always pause to remind you that we are, say, applying the addition rule to get the variable alone on one side of the equation. Instead, we count on your knowing enough about how the addition rule is used to understand what we're doing.

That said, however, we need to point out that business math is not really much like an algebra course. After this lesson, the only equations that you'll see are those necessary to solve some specific business problem. But the fact that you're dealing with real-life business situations rather than mathematical equations doesn't mean that you can forget the principles in this chapter. The business math problems are mathematically much simpler than what has to be dealt with in an algebra class, but concepts such as ratios, proportions, cross products, variables, constants, coefficients, left and right sides, and so on are necessary to both.

KEY TERMS

Before you read through the text assignment and watch the video program, take a minute to look at the key terms associated with this lesson. When you encounter them in the text and video program, pay careful attention to their meaning.

Addition rule: The rule that permits adding or subtracting any number from both sides of an equation.

Associative property: The property that $(a + b) + c = a + (b + c)$. This property means that numbers can be added in any order.

Coefficient: A number that multiplies a variable. In the equation

$$\frac{1}{2}x = 3, \frac{1}{2} \text{ is a coefficient.}$$

Cross products: In a proportion, the products of each numerator with the opposite denominator. For example, in the proportion

$$\frac{3}{5} = \frac{6}{10},$$

3 times 10 (30) and 10 times 3 (also 30) are the cross products. Note that since this is a proportion, the cross products are equal.

Distributive property: The property that $a \times (b + c) = (a \times b) + (a \times c)$. This property means that the multiplication can be done after the sum is found *or* can be done separately on each term, after which the products are added.

Equation: A statement that says that two things are equal. Equations can be as simple as $y = 2$ or very complicated, but the two sides of the equation are always equal.

Formula: A special type of equation that shows the relationship between specific quantities.

Multiplication rule: The rule that permits multiplying or dividing both sides of an equation by any number.

Proportion: An equation showing two ratios to be equal. $\frac{1}{2} = \frac{2}{4}$ is an example of a proportion.

Ratio: A comparison of two numbers. Mathematically, a ratio is the quotient of two numbers (3/5, for instance), but in business, ratios are often expressed as "three to five" or "3:5."

Reciprocal: The number formed if you invert a given number. A reciprocal is often used along with the multiplication rule to eliminate a coefficient from one side of an equation.

Variable: A letter used to represent a number.

PART II: WATCHING THE VIDEO PROGRAM

VIDEO VIEWING GUIDE

Before watching the video program, review the following questions. As you watch, be sure to collect the information necessary to answer them:

1. What is an equation? How about a variable? What role might equations and variables have in business mathematics?

2. How is a formula different from an equation? How are they similar? What makes formulas more useful than equations?

3. Based on what you learned in Lesson 1 about what's covered in the *By the Numbers* course, what are some of the topics that are likely to involve formulas?

4. What are some of the reasons business problems get translated into equations? What portion of business problems could be solved without the use of equations?

5. How are the associative and distributive properties used in solving equations? Of the two, which will be used more widely in business mathematics?

6. What is a reciprocal, and how does it relate to the multiplication rule?

7. Think up some examples of ratios that might be found in common business situations. When might a business manager use a ratio to form a proportion?

8. How important is understanding cross products compared with understanding the multiplication rule? When is using cross products likely to be an effective approach?

VIDEO PROGRAM

This lesson's video program is Program 3—Equations and Formulas. Remember, if you are watching this program on videotape, take time to replay sections of the tape any time you need to review a concept.

VIDEO VIEWING QUESTIONS

Immediately after viewing the video program for Lesson 3, take time to respond to the following questions. Give your answers some careful thought; they may provide the basis for additional discussion or a longer written response.

1. Given the equation $\frac{2}{3}y + 6 = 18$, identify each of the following.

    the term(s): _____

    the variable(s): _____

    the coefficient(s): _____

    the left side: _____

    the right side: _____

2. In the space provided, write an equation to demonstrate each of the following properties.

    associative property of addition: _____

    associative property of multiplication: _____

    distributive property: _____

3. In the space provided, write an equation to demonstrate each of the following rules.

    addition rule (using addition): _____

    addition rule (using subtraction): _____

    multiplication rule (using multiplication): _____

    multiplication rule (using division): _____

4. Suppose that a friend of yours questions the need to know about formulas and equations to get along well in business. He says, "I know most of the people in my dad's office, and I don't think any of them know anything about algebra." Is he likely correct? Is the statement about knowing "algebra" an accurate way to look at the issue?

    _____

    _____

    _____

    _____

5. Ratios and proportions are often used in routine, nonbusiness activities, sometimes by people who don't even know what a ratio or proportion is. Write down three examples of proportions that might be encountered in daily home activities.

   _____

   _____

   _____

6. After having gone through Lesson 2 on fractions, decimals, and percents and this lesson on equations and formulas, decide what skills you are especially good at and which you do least well. Write two examples of each in the space below.

   Strongest: _____

   Strongest: _____

   Weakest: _____

   Weakest: _____

PART III: FOCUSING ON THE MATHEMATICS

READING ASSIGNMENT

After watching the video program, you should read one of the following Text Assignments, depending on the textbook you're using:

SOFTCOVER: Appendix A of the Miller, Salzman, and Hoelzle softcover text, *Business Mathematics*, pages A1-A16.

HARDCOVER: Chapter 2 of the Salzman, Miller, and Hoelzle hardcover text, *Mathematics for Business*, pages 36-60.

As you read through the text, pay careful attention to the examples the book gives of the mathematics associated with the concepts you're learning about.

   Then, after you've completed the text assignment, read through the Key Formulas below. This section provides a handy review of what you've learned. By the time you get to this point in the lesson, all of the formulas and calculations should be familiar to you. If they're not, go back and read the appropriate parts of the text and the Overview section of this lesson. You won't have much success completing the rest of your assignments if you are still confused about the information in the Key Formulas section.

KEY FORMULAS

Ironically, in this lesson on equations and formulas, there aren't any key formulas. There are, however, three "rules" for manipulating equations that you should review.

KEY RULE: The Addition Rule: Any number can be added to or subtracted from both sides of an equation.

Rule used for: Solving an equation by getting all the numbers to one side and the variable to the other.

Example:

Given the equation $p + 3 = 12$, the addition rule permits 3 to be subtracted from both sides. This results in $p + 3 - 3 = 12 - 3$, or $p = 9$.

Remember that with this rule:

1. Any number can be added or subtracted, but the only numbers that will do any good are ones that reduce the number of terms.

2. The addition or subtraction absolutely must be done to both sides of the equation. The two sides of the equation start out equal, so adding or subtracting any number is permissible, but only if it's done to both sides.

KEY RULE: The Multiplication Rule: Both sides of an equation can be multiplied or divided by the same number.

Rule used for: Solving an equation by getting all the numbers to one side and the variable to the other.

Example:

Given the equation $3p = 12$, the multiplication rule permits both sides to be divided by 3. This results in:

$$\frac{3p}{3} = \frac{12}{3}, \text{ or } p = 4.$$

Remember that with this rule:

1. Any number can be used for the multiplication or division, but as with the addition rule, the only numbers that will do any good are ones that reduce the number of terms.

2. The number used to multiply both sides will very often be the reciprocal of a coefficient. For example, in the equation

$$\frac{2}{3}y = 4,$$

multiplying both sides by $\frac{3}{2}$ quickly reduces the equation to

$$y = \frac{4 \ddot{o} \, 3}{2}, \text{ or } y = 6.$$

3. As with the addition rule, the multiplication or division absolutely must be done to both sides of the equation. Further, all of the terms on each side of the equation must be multiplied or divided. The wrong answer will result if only part of the terms is affected.

KEY RULE: Cross Products: Multiplying the numerators in a ratio by their opposite denominators gives equal products in a proportion.

Formula used for: Finding out whether two ratios are proportional or setting up the equation to find the missing term of a proportion.

Example:

Brown requires 7 sheets of plywood to build 20 identical children's toys. How many sheets are required for 40 toys? Here are the two ratios we're interested in, set up as a proportion. Note how their cross products result in an easy-to-solve equation:

$$\frac{7}{20} \diagdown \frac{x}{40}, \text{ so } 20x = 280, \text{ so } x = \frac{280}{20} = 14$$
$$20x \qquad 280$$

Remember that with this rule:

1. If the cross products do not turn out to be the same, the ratios are not proportional.

2. Finding cross products has much the same effect as applying the multiplication rule; it produces an equation easier to solve than what you started with. Which approach to use is largely a matter of experience and personal preference.

_____**DON'T FORGET**

1. The goal of all of your manipulations of equations should be to isolate the variable by itself on one side of the equation.

2. There are almost always several ways to solve a given equation. Some are more efficient than others, but speed is not as important as having a firm understanding of the steps being taken.

3. The addition and multiplication rules can be (and often are) used several times on the same equation. Similarly, it's often necessary to use both rules on an equation; when that happens, the order in which the rules are applied doesn't matter.

4. The addition and multiplication rules are conceptually simple, but they will lead to the wrong answer if they're not applied correctly. Remember that the same operation must be done to both sides of the equation and that all terms must be affected in the same way.

PART IV: SOLVING BUSINESS PROBLEMS

PROBLEM SETS

Work the following problems in your textbook. Your instructor will tell you which problems, if any, are to be turned in. Some of the problems have answers provided in the back of the book; refer to these answers to make sure you are working the problems correctly.

SOFTCOVER: If you are using the Miller, Salzman, and Hoelzle softcover text, *Business Mathematics*, do the following problem sets:

> **Appendix A:** Problems #2-65 (even numbers only) on pages A13-A16.

HARDCOVER: If you are using the Salzman, Miller, and Hoelzle hardcover text, *Mathematics for Business*, do the following problem sets:

> **2.1:** Problems #34-54 (even numbers only) on pages 41-42.
>
> **2.2:** Problems #17-20 and 34-44 on pages 47-48.
>
> **2.3:** Problems #1-6, 31-34, and 54-56 on pages 52-54.
>
> **2.4:** Problems #20-30, 40-50 (even numbers only), and 55-60 (all) on pages 59-60.

BUSINESS APPLICATIONS

As with the previous lesson, because the focus of this lesson is on basic mathematics rather than business concepts, there are no business application scenarios for this lesson.

Banking Services 4

"No, we don't have any dishes you can wash
to cover your little overdraft."

Not long ago, banks were regarded as safe places to store money and good places to borrow money, but not much more than that. While those time-honored operations are still the heart of our banking system, today's banks are more customer-oriented and competitive than ever before. They offer financial assistance and investment advice, issue credit cards, guard valuables, help customers finance the purchase of homes and automobiles, finance business expansions, and provide a host of other services relating to making and managing money. The term "full-service" bank isn't just a slick advertising slogan; it's an accurate description of institutions that have deliberately, if gradually, expanded their range of services to meet consumers' needs.

In this lesson, we'll discuss banking services in general, with a particular focus on checking accounts, a feature most persons and virtually all businesses find indispensable. After all, consider how impractical it would be if a large company had to pay for everything with cash. Not only would it need enormous amounts of money, but it would also face quite a challenge in keeping track of transactions, with only an odd assortment of sales slips and bills to mark the paper trail. Clearly, being able to write checks—whether for machinery, office equipment, and raw materials or groceries, rent, and car payments—represents a real convenience in both money management and recordkeeping.

Of course, neither business nor consumer checking accounts (much as we might wish otherwise) manage themselves. Handling a checking account well, as we shall see, takes some attention to detail, some math skills, and some scrupulous recordkeeping. Putting those skills together is what this lesson is all about.

PART I: INTRODUCING THE MATERIAL

LEARNING OBJECTIVES

Upon completing your study of this lesson, you should be able to:

1. Identify the component parts of a check.

2. Name and describe the two main types of checking accounts.

3. Determine the monthly service charges on an account, given the minimum balance and check fees.

4. Identify the component parts of a deposit slip, check stub, and check register.

5. Name and describe several different kinds of services provided to a business by a bank.

6. Name the transactions possible with the use of an automatic teller machine (ATM).

7. Explain the importance of reconciling a checking account.

8. Reconcile a bank statement with a checkbook record, using specified procedures.

9. Given sales, credits, and the discount charged, calculate the discount and the net deposit for a set of credit card transactions.

If you're using the hardcover textbook, *Mathematics for Business*, there are some additional objectives for the lesson. Upon completing your study of the lesson, you should also be able to:

10. List and define several different types of checking accounts.

11. Reconcile a bank statement using a T-account form.

12. Given an abbreviated check register and matching bank statement that do not reconcile, determine the reason for the discrepancy.

_____ **LESSON OVERVIEW**

Businesses today literally could not function without the capability to write checks. Having to conduct all transactions with cash would be unthinkable. Imagine a small business, Croft's Shoe Store, that wants to increase its efficiency by putting in a computer system. Croft, the owner, discovers that the new system will run about $10,000, including the software he wants. Must Croft wait until he has $10,000 cash on hand before he invests in the computer? Hardly.

For one thing, that might not happen. If Croft's is like most businesses, it's likely that cash is flowing out almost as rapidly as it comes in. The shoe store has bills to pay: rent, utilities, employees' salaries, and the cost of getting more shoes on the shelves. So, no matter how many customers are buying shoes this week, Croft's cannot simply pile up cash in the corner until there's enough to cover the computer. Too impractical and inconvenient. Instead, at the conclusion of each business day, Croft's transfers most of its cash to its account at the local bank, from which it can draw as needed to pay bills and make purchases such as the computer system.

That solves the convenience problem. But it is still critical that whoever writes checks for Croft's knows how to make them out properly and how to record each transaction so that Croft's records match those of the bank. Otherwise, the potential advantages of doing business by check quickly turn into liabilities.

Perhaps the first thing for any check writer to learn is the anatomy of a check itself (see Figure 4.1 on page 105 of the hardcover text; see page 73 in the softcover text). In this illustration, we see a typical preprinted check. Notice that the name of the bank and its address appear on the top left; the name on the account and the corresponding address appear on the bottom left. You may be interested to know that checks do not *have* to be written on preprinted forms like this in order to be negotiable. From a legal perspective, a check written on a napkin or the back of an envelope *could* be cashed, provided all the necessary information were in order. It's safe to say, though, that a preprinted check looks considerably more official and businesslike than an order to pay handwritten on a napkin. More important, the preprinted form is likely to be accepted more graciously by most tellers, since the bank's computers need to read the special number at the bottom of each check to process it correctly.

Actually, several different sets of numbers appear on this check. The bank and account numbers are recorded on the bottom left and the check number in two spots — upper right and bottom middle. The check number is very important. Suppose Croft's accountant is doing the monthly billing when the phone rings. By the time she returns to her task, she may have forgotten about the $400 check she just wrote to the janitorial service. But a quick review of the records will show her that check number 557 is not accounted for.

Notice that the check writer enters several important pieces of information: the date, name of the payee, amount (written in both figures and words), and an appropriate signature, which, in the case of a business, might be a printed stamp of the company name or an authorized check writer's name. It might occur to you that an unscrupulous payee could, under the right circumstances, alter the amount of the check. In the event

The Check

that the numbers (figures and words) representing the amount do not match, the bank will honor the check for the amount indicated in words, unless the words are not readable. In that case, the numbers will prevail.

It is a good deal easier to alter numerical figures than written words, which is why the bank cashing the check looks first to the written words in determining the correct amount. But suppose the check writer leaves sufficient space so that *both* are altered? A check for nineteen dollars might be changed to read *one hundred* and nineteen dollars. There are legal remedies available to the business (or individual) that discovers such tampering, but *discovering* it in time is the whole key to getting one's money back. Most banks will do very little about an error that goes unreported for an extended period; say, a year. And in most cases, it's safest to report errors or tamperings as soon as they're discovered, which will be within a month for the check writer who is right on the ball about balancing the checkbook.

The check writer who records each check as it is written, and who meticulously inspects each cashed check when it is returned from the bank, is almost certain to notice an inconsistency like the conversion of nineteen dollars to one hundred and nineteen. As an additional precaution, though, the bank prints the amount of the check in the lower right-hand corner. That number signifies the amount for which the check was honored, and it should match the amount entered in the check writer's original records unless (1) an error has been made in reading or recording the amount, or (2) the amount on the check has been changed.

Check Fees

Like most businesses, banks are out to make money. They make most of it through loans; that means that the more money the bank can access, the more money it can make. It is very much to the bank's advantage, therefore, to encourage each customer to deposit as much as possible, whether in a savings or checking account. Now admittedly, savings accounts (even though the customer can withdraw the money at any time) are likely to be regarded by the bank as relatively more "permanent" than checking accounts (from which most customers make withdrawals all the time). To get round this problem, and help ensure there's plenty of cash available for loans, banks often encourage customers to maintain a relatively high minimum balance even in a checking account, and many vary their fees accordingly. Further, check printing and processing, both of which cost the bank money, may be free to the customer who maintains a hefty minimum balance but may be part of the monthly service charges for the customer with the smaller account.

With a *personal checking account*, for instance, the bank supplies the customer with checks for a fee and charges a variable amount for maintaining the account, depending on how much money is in that account during any given month. The amount of the fee varies not only with the size of the account, but also with the bank itself. Such fees provide one basis on which banks compete for consumers' business. With a *flat fee checking account*, the bank may provide a wide range of services from check printing to a bank charge card for a set fee that does not vary.

Business checking accounts may entitle the holder to some special consideration. Remember Croft's Shoe Store? Let's say Croft's regularly makes purchases from Leatherworks Shoe Company. Leatherworks can arrange with its bank to have Croft's monthly check (for merchandise) routinely deposited in the Leatherworks account. In other words, in exchange for managing a business account of some size, the bank will do some of the footwork as well as the paperwork involved in checking. Such accounts do not draw interest, however. Most banks offer interest-paying checking only to individuals. But they get round this problem by offering businesses the option of an *automatic savings transfer account*. This allows the business to keep a savings account (in the same bank, of course) and to transfer funds as needed from this account to the checking account. What isn't needed to pay business expenses stays right in the savings account drawing interest.

Determining monthly fees for checking services is a relatively simple matter. Most banks provide a schedule illustrating the maintenance charges for accounts of various sizes. For example, let's say Gotham Bank, where Croft's maintains its account, charges $8 a month for accounts under $500, and $5 for accounts up to $5,000, but no maintenance fee for larger accounts. It may also charge $.20 per check, or per debit, for cashing or processing checks on accounts under $5,000, with no processing fee for larger accounts. This means that if Croft's maintains an account that never falls under $5,000, it will pay no service charges whatever. But suppose Croft's maintains an account balance of about $3,000 and writes 50 checks during an average month. In that case, Croft's will pay a $5 maintenance fee plus $.20 per check; a total of $15 (.20 × 50 = $10).

Such fees, by the way, vary considerably from bank to bank, and may be much higher than the figures we've used in our illustration. It isn't unusual these days, for example, for frequent check writers to pay total *annual* fees of $150, $200, or even more. Fees for infrequent check writers usually run from one-fourth to one-third of this amount, since a good deal of the fee is eaten up by the processing of individual checks. Banks also differ widely in what they require for a minimum balance to avoid or reduce fees. Some require only $100, while others may require $5,000 or more — far above what many customers are willing or able to keep on hand. As you might expect, fees for other services vary as well. Some banks, for example, may charge $15 or $20 for an *overdraft*, a check written on an account for which there are insufficient funds. Similar fees are levied on checks that must be returned to the writer because they are not made out properly.

To the consumer who has only a personal account, writes very few checks, and manages that account with an eagle eye, these differences from bank to bank are not so significant. It doesn't much matter what the fee on overdrafts is if you never write any. But for the company that writes hundreds of checks a month, requires frequent photocopies, may occasionally have an overdraft despite good intentions, and must often stop payments or deal with the bad checks issued by others, these fees can be critical. That company will likely want to shop around a bit in selecting a bank.

Deposit Slips and Check Registers

Customers who wish to deposit money in an account cannot simply walk up to a teller, hand over the money, smile, and leave. And a good thing it is, too. Imagine depositing $1,000 in an account on Friday only to have the teller shake his head on Monday and say, "Sorry, I just can't recall that transaction." This doesn't happen, however — or rather, it doesn't make any difference whether it happens or not — because neither banks nor their customers are allowed to rely on memory to reconstruct who deposited what amount and when. Every transaction must be accompanied by a deposit slip, a form describing that transaction, just in case of questions later.

A *deposit slip* (see Figure 4.4 on page 108 of the hardcover text; see page 76 in the softcover text) for a commercial account is somewhat more complex than that for a personal account. Note that this deposit slip requires the depositor to specify the number of hundred-dollar bills, fifties, twenties, tens, and so on deposited as cash. It also requires that each check deposited be listed separately and that it be identified by its own bank number. The total for combined currency (bills), coins, and checks deposited provides the total for the entire deposit; in this case, $3,467.29.

Businesses may use check stubs or check registers like those shown in Figures 4.7, 4.8, 4.9, and 4.10 on pages 110-112 of the hardcover text and pages 77 and 78 of the softcover text to keep track of all the checks they write. A checkbook the bank provides with a commercial account will often include such check stubs. Note that the check stub provides space for the check writer to enter the *balance forward* (the amount that was in the account after the last check was written), any *deposits* made to the account, and the amount of each *current* check (the one the check writer is making out right now). Compute the current balance by first adding the amount of any deposit to the balance forward, then subtracting from this total the amount of the current check. For example, let's suppose that Croft's Shoes has $4,445 in its business account. Following a big sale weekend, Croft's deposits $2,556.31, then writes a check to Snelling Advertising for $1,200 to cover the cost of a new radio ad. We can figure out the new balance with some simple addition and subtraction:

$4,445.00 + $2,556.31 = $7,001.31

$7,001.31 − $1,200.00 = $5,801.31 (the *current balance forward*)

As this illustration shows, figuring in individual transactions is pretty simple. It demands accuracy, of course, but there's nothing tricky about the process. What *is* a little tricky, however, is ensuring that nothing gets overlooked. If Croft's accountant forgets the late-night deposit of $500 or the last-minute $200 check mailed to the printer, the account will not balance at the end of the month.

Other Fees

Because banks derive their principal income from making loans, they are increasingly likely to charge for other services — services that, though appreciated by customers, eat up staff time and thus cut into bank profits.

One thing banks dislike doing is attempting to process checks for which there are insufficient funds — overdrafts, that is. Banks will charge a significant fee for their trouble in trying to turn a bad check into money. But to save themselves trouble and save customers time and embarrassment, many now offer *overdraft protection*; a kind of checking "insurance." If a customer's account balance is insufficient to cover a check written on that account, the bank will, for a fee, transfer sufficient funds from that customer's savings account or levy a charge against the customer's credit card account (VISA or MasterCard, for instance). Provided these other resources are in good shape, the customer with this kind of insurance will probably never write a bad check.

Other kinds of service charges are common, too. Let's say that a local amateur baseball club purchases twelve pairs of athletic shoes from our old friends at Croft's and pays with a check that bounces. If Croft's attempts to deposit this check in its business account, the bank will return the check to Croft's and assess a fee for this *returned deposit item*. Notice that not only is Croft's out some money to the bank, but getting the money from the athletic club is entirely Croft's problem, not the bank's. No wonder merchants charge customers substantial fees for returned checks.

Here's another possible scenario. Suppose Croft's purchases new carpeting for its customer service area. But the installation is sloppy, and the carpeting doesn't fit flush against the wall. Croft's can give itself some leverage against the carpet company by putting a *stop payment order* on the check, for a fee. Depending on the circumstances, the bank will then not honor the Croft's check when it is presented for payment by the carpet company, leaving Croft's and the carpet company to resolve the problem.

As we've seen, banks charge fees for most special services. So customers who need photocopies of cancelled checks or duplicate statements should expect to reimburse the bank for its effort. Sometimes, though, the banks also charge fees for doing nothing. An account that is left *dormant* (no deposits, no withdrawals) for a period of six months or more is likely to incur a monthly fee.

Remember, these various fees must be figured into the account total at the end of the month. It's easy to overlook $4 for a duplicate statement here, $20 for a returned check there, but even the smallest amounts, if not recorded, will create an imbalance in the monthly statement.

Merchants who accept credit cards in payment for purchases obviously must keep records of all such purchases and all returns. Periodically, they "deposit" their sales totals, just as if they were turning in cash, by using a *merchant deposit summary*, a record of credit card sales and refunds. The net amount, or what the merchant is actually depositing to the account, is simple to compute. It's a three-step process: First, the merchant totals the credit card sales for the month and enters that total into the appropriate space. Second, the merchant totals the refunds, or credits, and enters that total. Third, he or she determines the net deposit by subtracting the refunds from the sales total.

Credit Card Sales and Merchant Deposit Summaries

For instance, suppose that during a given day, Fiona's Party Supplies makes credit card sales in the following amounts:

$49.95
$59.95
$25.00
$21.50

Two credit card customers return purchases for the following amounts:

$100.56
$87.50

Note that these transactions put Fiona's $31.66 in the hole on its credit card sales for this day:

$188.06   (total for returns)
− 156.40   (total for sales)
−$ 31.66   (deficit)

For Fiona's sake, let's hope cash sales were more brisk, particularly considering that the company will also have to pay the bank a fee based on total sales for the period. Suppose that the credit card fee at Fiona's bank is 3 percent, based on total net sales. And let's say that Fiona's total *credit card* sales for October amount to $12,672. Returns are also heavy during this period, however, and total $4,776. This leaves Fiona's with net credit card sales of $7,896 ($12,672 − $4,776). But remember that 3 percent of this amount goes to the bank as its fee for processing the credit card sales. Thus,

$$\$7,896.00 \times .03 = \$236.88 \text{ (in fees to the bank)}$$

To find out what Fiona's *really* nets on its credit card sales for the month, we subtract the bank's fee from Fiona's former net total:

$$\$7,896.00 − \$236.88 = \$7,659.12 \text{ (payable to Fiona's account)}$$

Merchants who pay a very high fee to the bank for processing of credit card sales, or who find they have a high percentage of refunds relative to sales, may conclude that accepting credit cards isn't really worth the trouble. From the bank's perspective, however, the credit card offers an excellent money-making opportunity. Not only does the bank collect a fee from the merchant who accepts the credit cards in the first place, but it can also collect interest from customers who do not pay their accounts in full at the first billing. Small wonder that banks are generally eager to promote their credit cards.

Reconciliation of Bank Statements

Think of *reconciliation* as "matching." That's all it is. The customer must make his or her statement match that of the bank. And, it's generally wise to begin with the assumption that the bank's statement is accurate.

So, when those numbers do not match at the end of the month, it is *usually* because the customer has made a math error or forgotten something. Tracking down the problem is much simpler, much less time-consuming, if all checks, fees, and deposits are accounted for and recorded by date. If not, well, even the most energetic hunting may fail to unearth the problem. In that case, the customer is put in the uncomfortable position of, first, having to trust the bank's record totally, and second, having to do without a personal record of previous transactions.

Now, as we've hinted already, banks are near perfect when it comes to keeping accurate records, so there's some comfort in recognizing that errors on bank statements *are* indeed exceptional. At the same time, though, it's a rare business for which everything goes so smoothly that no adjustments to the financial records are ever required. For example, suppose Fred's Stereo buys $2,000 worth of supplies from Wilson Electronics. Fred's pays with a check that is, unfortunately, backed by insufficient funds. Wilson's books show a $2,000 credit representing the check from Fred's. But in fact, that credit is an illusion.

What really happens is this: The bank discovers that Fred's check is no good. Not only does it not credit Wilson's account with the $2,000, but it charges Wilson a $10 service fee for bringing the truth about Fred's check to light. All this will be reflected on Wilson's bank statement, of course. But if Wilson hasn't kept up-to-date records, the $2,010 discrepancy can come as quite a surprise, and it may take some head scratching to figure out what happened. Of course, one isolated incident won't cause huge problems with the ongoing business routine of most companies. But multiply that kind of misunderstanding by a factor of ten or twenty, and it's easy to see the value in keeping records shipshape.

The Reconciliation Process

Here, then, are some basics to keep in mind about reconciliation. First, it's important to remember that the processing of checks takes time. Let's say that Graves Publishing hires a freelance editor, McCrae, to edit a book on wildflowers. Graves gives McCrae a check (number 445) for $1,000, and promptly deducts that amount from the company's ledgers, leaving a balance of $4,350. So far so good. Keep in mind, though, that the bank as yet has no record of this transaction. If Graves' corporate bank statement arrives in the mail this afternoon, it won't include anything about check 445 to McCrae. Nor will it include this morning's $250 deposit, which brought the earlier balance (before McCrae was paid) up to $5,350. That doesn't mean, however, that Graves should not note these items and adjust the balance accordingly. Even though the bank's records can't be instantaneously up to date, those of the business itself should be.

By the way, it may occur to you that since the bank has not yet deducted the $1,000 for check 445, the money is still in the Graves Publishing corporate account. Technically that's true, but the prudent business person will consider it spent. Viewing things otherwise leads to serious trouble. For instance, suppose Graves Publishing decides that since the bank hasn't yet had time to deduct McCrae's check, and McCrae probably won't get round to cashing it for a day or so, Graves theoretically has enough in the account to cover the cost of the annual employee retreat. Based on this questionable logic, it issues a check to Crystal Mountain Resort in the amount of $4,500. Unless Graves makes a speedy deposit to make up the shortfall, whichever check is presented second will bounce. This will cost Graves an overdraft fee and probably some of its reputation as a well-managed company. In short, it's good business practice to consider the money spent from the time the check is issued; whether McCrae cashes the check the same day he receives it or two weeks later is beside the point.

The reconciliation form provided by the bank has space for entering *checks outstanding*; those, like McCrae's check number 445, that have been issued but not yet paid. These should be subtracted from the bank statement's balance to reconcile the account. The form also provides space for listing deposits not yet noted on the bank statement; these are added to the bank statement balance. These steps compensate for the account activity that the bank doesn't know about yet.

Second, remember to deduct any fees or charges that have not already been entered in the company records. Perhaps Graves issued a stop payment order during the previous period and requested photocopies of several cancelled checks for tax purposes. The account will never reconcile if these fees aren't subtracted from the company's balance.

Third, add any interest for the period. This is a new twist, relatively speaking. Not long ago, federal regulations would not allow interest on checking accounts. But in the mid 1970s, special interest-paying accounts were invented that, while technically not checking accounts, allowed the customer to write a *negotiable order of withdrawal* (NOW) that worked just like a check. NOW accounts were so well received publicly that the federal regulations were subsequently changed, and interest-bearing checking accounts are now available everywhere. On the other hand, the banks offer interest-bearing checking only to customers who meet special requirements (like a sizable minimum balance) and may not offer them to businesses at all. In other words, this step is not applicable for the majority of consumers and businesses.

Fourth, review the company records to ensure that all checks are accounted for. Prenumbered checks make this accounting simpler. If check 444 is missing, the bank statement may have an asterisk or other mark next to the reference to check 445 to show that there's a problem with the order of the checks. Of course, it's equally easy to note in the check register that check 444 wasn't recorded. When the check writer numbers the checks by hand, there's obviously more room for error. Then it's hard to know whether check 444 is missing, or whether there was no 444 because the check writer just numbered incorrectly.

Finally, it's a good idea to look over the checks themselves to ensure that the amounts and the names of the payees match what is entered in the records. Remember that unscrupulous payee in our earlier scenario who altered the $19 check to read $119? Not a common occurrence, perhaps, but far from unheard of. Nor is it out of the question for an unauthorized check to be issued and paid. This can happen quite easily in a company that doesn't keep its checkbook secure, and it's even more of a problem if the company signs checks using a rubber stamp and leaves the stamp lying around.

Such unauthorized checkwriting may be part of a scheme to defraud the company; or it may happen rather innocently. Let's say that Shields is the regular bookkeeper and check writer back at Graves Publishing. But while she's visiting relatives in Poughkeepsie, Livingston is handling the job. Livingston, who is not well acquainted with the status of Graves' various accounts, does not know that the company has refused to honor any invoices from freelance writer Thomas, whose work is far behind schedule. Thus, when she receives a $600 invoice from Thomas, Livingston promptly issues a check. The fact that the check shouldn't have been written is of no concern to the bank, however, which proceeds to deduct the $600 from the Graves account. Similarly, if Livingston later writes herself an unauthorized "bonus" check for $1,000, it, too, will be deducted by the bank. Obviously, it is up to each business to establish procedures that ensure that the company checkbook is kept secure and that opportunities for fraudulent checkwriting are kept to a minimum.

A Sample Reconciliation

To get a better sense of the steps involved in reconciliation, let's zero in on a quieter period in the life of Graves Publishing, a month when the bank statement is pretty straightforward. Of course, a large publishing company is likely to have hundreds of transactions over the course of a month, but we don't need to get that complicated for our purposes. We'll keep our scenario unrealistically simple. The balance from the bank statement reads $12,957.00. The checks outstanding are as follows:

$49.50
$200.00
$1,200.00
$525.35

Deposits not yet recorded include the following:

$500.00
$2,000.00
$200.00

And the balance in Graves' own check register reads $13,786.45. Can we reconcile these two numbers? Let's see.

First, we add together the checks outstanding, then we subtract that total from the bank statement total:

(1) $49.50 + $200.00 + $1,200.00 + $525.35 = $1,974.85

(2) $12,957.00 − $1,974.85 = $10,982.15 (the new bank statement total, after checks outstanding are subtracted)

Next, we total the deposits not yet recorded, and add this amount to (2).

(3) $500.00 + $2,000.00 + $200.00 = $2,700.00 (total deposits not yet recorded)

(4) $10,982.15 + $2,700.00 = $13,682.15 (the new bank statement total, reflecting checks outstanding and deposits)

Are we done? No, because the new bank statement total doesn't match the total in the Graves check register. According to the bank, Graves Publishing has a balance of $12,957.00. According to Graves' own records, the total should be $13,682.15, a difference of $725.15.

What's creating the discrepancy? Well, if you were the bookkeeper at Graves, several possibilities would likely spring to mind at once. First, you might think to review the cancelled checks, to make sure all were accounted for. And sure enough, there is one to Pacific Paper Supply on March 1 for $220 that wasn't recorded in the check register. There's another, as well: $442.75 to a computer repair service. Where does this leave us?

(5) $442.75 + $220.00 = $662.75 (the total for checks not yet recorded)

(6) $725.15 (the previous difference between the balances) − $662.75 = $62.40 (the amount still not accounted for)

Closer, but still not a match. Some further checking reveals that Graves put a stop payment on a check during the pay period, and the fee for this service was $20. Also, this was the month when Graves was charged $60 for a year's use of the company's safe deposit box; the bank deducts those charges from the customer's checking account. In addition, the account drew interest in the amount of $17 (which isn't likely, but remember, we're trying to give a complete example). Now, let's refigure, using the latest information.

Remember, Graves' records show a balance of $13,682.15. But the bookkeeper forgot to add the interest paid during the period. Let's do that.

(7) $13,682.75 + $17.00 = $13,699.75

Now, let's subtract the $20 stop payment fee, the $60 safe deposit box fee, and the total for the checks that were overlooked and never entered into the records.

(8) $13,699.75 − $742.75 ($662.75 for the unrecorded checks, plus $80.00 in fees) = $12,957.00

Bingo. A perfect match. Notice, however, that the agonies of reconciling the monthly statement are reduced when a company, or individual, keeps careful records of each transaction as it happens.

SOME WORDS OF ADVICE

Let's face it: These days, we really could not have business as usual without checking accounts. Businesses depend on them. So do individuals. Therefore, it's a good idea for just about anyone to become familiar with the kinds of options available in checking accounts and with the basics involved in managing such an account well.

The very first time a person writes a check, he or she is likely to proceed carefully and slowly, ensuring that each bit of information is just right and entered correctly. But after that, it all becomes so routine that it's tempting to become careless. Keep in mind, though, that accurate information is all part of a good recordkeeping system. Checks that are ambiguous or unreadable may be processed incorrectly, or may be returned along with a charge from the bank. Also, checks made out to "Cash," often written to supply a company's or individual's immediate spending needs, *can* wind up in the hands of the wrong payee. Such checks are literally like money; anyone holding such a check can cash it, often without question.

In addition, checks that are endorsed by the payee are generally payable to the holder or presenter *on demand*. In other words, if Graves Publishing endorses a check it receives from Cascade Computers, the person who presents that check at the bank may receive the cash. Graves can ensure that the money gets into its account, however, by using a *restricted endorsement*. Whoever endorses the check simply writes on the back "For deposit only." The bank then accepts the check (assuming everything is in order), but puts the money into Graves' account; it will not hand cash over to the presenter.

Checkbooks issued to companies usually come complete with either check stubs or a check register as a means of recording check information. These handy recordkeeping devices are useless, however, unless they're filled out carefully and thoroughly *as checks are written*. Waiting until things slow down a bit and then trying to fill in the blanks from memory is never a good idea.

Interest-paying checking plans are available to some consumers, but recognize that the bank is likely to have some restrictions (like a sizable minimum balance) on such accounts. It's also important to realize that the amount of interest earned in a month is unlikely to fund anything bigger than a modest dinner out unless the account balance is quite substantial. Regardless, if your checking account pays interest, it's important to record it in the check register so that reconciliation at the end of the month is simpler.

Keep in mind that banks are not in business to provide services like sending photocopies of checks or transferring funds to cover overdrafts. They do such things because if they didn't, they might lose customers to a more service-oriented bank down the road. On the other hand, virtually every service these days costs money, money that must be regularly deducted from an account in order to reflect an accurate balance. Assuming the account has a normal balance, it's fine to wait until the monthly statement arrives to deduct small fees of $.50 or even $10. But regardless of when the deductions are made, don't forget them or the checking account can't be reconciled.

Finally, it's critical to recognize that from the bank's perspective, a checking account is much more than a convenience. It represents a legal contract between bank and customer, and a serious responsibility. The bank *expects* its customers to reconcile their accounts at the end of each month, and will not be responsible for errors if customers do not hold up their end of the deal. In other words, a bank error reported the month it happens will be corrected; an error reported two years down the road is more likely to be looked on as the check writer's problem. Not such a big deal if the bank neglects to credit your account with the $4.25 worth of interest due, but a very big deal indeed if its computer puts your $2,000 deposit in someone else's account. In short, reconciling the bank statement is essential to sound business management, whether at the personal or the corporate level.

KEY TERMS

Before you watch the video program and read through the text assignment, take a minute to look at the key terms associated with this lesson. When you encounter them in the text and video program, pay careful attention to their meaning.

Adjusted bank balance: The actual current balance of a checking account after reconciliation.

Automatic teller machine (ATM): A banking machine that allows 24-hour deposits, withdrawals, and fund transfers.

Bad check: A check that is not honored because there are insufficient funds in the checking account.

Balance: The amount left in a checking account after previous checks written have been subtracted. (Also referred to as *balance forward*.)

Bank statement: A list of all charges against and deposits to a checking account; such statements are usually sent out monthly by the bank.

Business checking account: The type of checking account used by businesses. The requirements, fees, and services associated with a business account are likely to differ somewhat from those for checking accounts offered to consumers.

Check outstanding: A check that has been written but has not cleared the bank as of the statement date.

Check register: A record book provided to record checks written and deposits made to a checking account; each check or deposit is written on a different line of the register.

Check stub: A stub initially attached to the check. It remains as a record of checks written when the check is torn out.

Deposit slip: The form used for making a bank savings or checking account deposit.

Dormant account: An account that has had no activity, normally for over six months.

Flat fee checking account: A type of checking account for which the bank charges a monthly set fee.

Insufficient funds: Not enough funds in a checking account for the bank to honor the check.

Maintenance charge per month: The charge to maintain a checking account.

Merchant deposit summary: The bank form used to deposit credit card transactions.

NOW (negotiable order of withdrawal) account: A savings account that earns interest, but also allows the depositor to write *negotiable orders of withdrawal* against the account. As a result, the NOW account can be used like a checking account. These days, many types of accounts, not just NOW accounts, offer similar features.

Overdraft: Occurs when a customer writes a check for which there are insufficient funds in the account. The customer is said to be *overdrawn*.

Overdraft protection: The bank service of honoring checks written on an account that has insufficient funds.

Per-debit charge: A service charge for each check written to help defray the cost of check processing. This fee is usually the same per check regardless of the number of checks written.

Personal checking account: The type of checking account used by individuals.

Reconciliation: The process of checking a bank statement against the depositor's own personal records.

Restricted endorsement: Endorsement of a check so that only the person or company specified on the check may cash it.

Returned deposit item: The return to the bank of an item that has been deposited. This may happen due to any number of irregularities.

Stop payment order: A request that the bank not pay on a check previously written. The bank will usually charge a substantial fee to stop payment on a check.

PART II: WATCHING THE VIDEO PROGRAM

VIDEO VIEWING GUIDE

Before watching the video program, review the following questions. As you watch, be sure to collect the information necessary to answer them.

1. What different variables (for example, per-check charges and service fees) affect the cost of checking for consumers and businesses?

2. How can banks afford to provide checking account services for consumers and businesses? How do they cover the costs associated with processing checks?

3. When a check is presented for payment and there's not enough money in the account to cover it, is it the bank or the checkholder who's out the money? Who pays for the fees associated with the returned check?

4. How does a *blank endorsement* differ from a *restrictive endorsement*? What do you do to make an endorsement a restrictive endorsement? How is a *special endorsement* used?

5. What are some of the reasons that credit cards are so widely used? What advantages do they offer merchants? Are there any disadvantages to their use?

6. Why have automatic teller machines (ATMs) become as widespread as they have? What types of transactions can they handle more cost-effectively than human tellers?

VIDEO PROGRAM

This lesson's video program is Program 4—Banking Services. Remember, if you are watching this program on a videotape, take time to replay sections of the tape whenever you need to review a concept.

VIDEO VIEWING QUESTIONS

Immediately after viewing the video program for Lesson 4, take time to respond to the following questions. Give your answers some careful thought; they may provide the basis for additional discussion or a longer written response.

1. Suppose a bank hired you as a marketing consultant to advise it about new checking account features. Based on your personal opinion, which of these features would be important for a *personal* checking account? Put a 2 in front of features you consider "very important" and a 1 in front of features you consider "somewhat important." (Leave the space blank in front of "unimportant" features.)

  _____ Interest paid on the balance

  _____ No monthly service fee

  _____ No per-check charge

  _____ No minimum balance

  _____ No limit on the number of checks that can be written each month

  _____ Easy access to automatic teller machines

  _____ Automatic transfers between savings and checking accounts

  _____ Automatic covering of overdrafts

  _____ Help in reconciling checkbooks

  _____ Bonus awards for starting an account

  _____ Free safe deposit box, traveler's checks, or other services

2. Now decide which of these features would be important for a *business* checking account. As in Question 1, use a 2 to designate features you consider "very important," a 1 for "somewhat important," and leave a blank space for "unimportant" features.

  _____ Interest paid on the balance

_____ No monthly service fee

_____ No per-check charge

_____ No minimum balance

_____ No limit on the number of checks that can be written each month

_____ Easy access to automatic teller machines

_____ Automatic transfers between savings and checking accounts

_____ Automatic covering of overdrafts

_____ Help in reconciling checkbooks

_____ Bonus awards for starting an account

_____ Free safe deposit box, traveler's checks, or other services

3. Based on the video, which statement seems more accurate?

    Banks are generally offering

    _____ a wider array of banking services than two decades ago.

    _____ fewer services than two decades ago.

4. List three merchandise or customer base characteristics that would make accepting credit cards a good idea for a particular merchant.

    a. _____

    b. _____

    c. _____

5. Is there currently much banking being done electronically, or is this relatively unimportant? Is there likely to be a drop in the number of cash transactions in coming years, or will the number increase?

    _____

    _____

    _____

PART III: FOCUSING ON THE MATHEMATICS

READING ASSIGNMENT

After watching the video program, you should read one of the following Text Assignments, depending on the textbook you're using:

SOFTCOVER: Chapter 3 of the Miller, Salzman, and Hoelzle softcover text, *Business Mathematics*, pages 73-98.

HARDCOVER: Chapter 4 of the Salzman, Miller, and Hoelzle hardcover text, *Mathematics for Business*, pages 104-130.

As you read through the text, pay careful attention to the examples the book gives of the mathematics associated with the concepts you're learning about.

Then, after you've completed the text assignment, read through the Key Formulas here. This section provides a handy review of what you've learned. By the time you get to this point in the lesson, all of the formulas and calculations should be familiar to you. If they're not, go back and read the appropriate parts of the text and the Overview section of this lesson. You won't have much success completing the rest of your assignments if you are still confused about the information in the Key Formulas section.

KEY FORMULAS

The following key formulas are important to your understanding of this lesson. Be sure that you know each one and how to use it in solving problems relating to banking services.

KEY FORMULA: Adjusted Bank Balance = Statement Balance −
                     Outstanding Checks + Deposits not Recorded −
                     Fees + Credits

Formula used for: Reconciling the bank's statement of a checking
                       account balance with company or personal re-
                       cords. When the reconciliation is complete, the
                       adjusted bank balance will match the amount
                       shown in the records.

Example:

Jennings Controls shows a balance of $21,200 in its check register at the end of the month. The end-of-month account statement from its bank shows a balance of $22,350. Jennings' accountant notes that two checks (one for $500 and one for $900) have not yet cleared the bank and thus aren't recorded on the bank statement. Neither is a deposit made that day for $300. In addition, the bank statement includes a $50 charge for the rental of the company's safe deposit box. Let's see if the account balances:

Adjusted bank balance = $22,350 − ($500 + $900) + $300 − $50

Adjusted bank balance = $22,350 − $1,150 = $21,200

Since the adjusted bank balance now matches the amount shown in Jennings' check register, the account has been reconciled.

Remember that in this formula:

1. All of the checks written must be accounted for. Either they have cleared the bank and have been reflected in the bank statements, or they are outstanding and need to be subtracted from the statement balance.

2. If there's a bank fee (as for the safe deposit box rental in our example), it has to be reflected in the check register. It's not enough to simply note that acknowledging the fee helps reconcile the account; the fee

has to actually be subtracted. (Similarly, credits to the account need to be added.)

DON'T FORGET

1. Reconciling account activity is not an optional task; it is a legal requirement. Opening a checking account represents the formation of a contract between the bank and the customer, and keeping the account straight is one of the obligations the customer takes on.

2. If errors are made by the bank, they have to be pointed out promptly. If the error is allowed to persist for too long, the customer may have difficulty in getting the correction made.

3. One of the most common fees charged by the bank is a charge for each check written. If an account has this charge, be sure to take it into account when reconciling the account or the records will never balance.

PART IV: SOLVING BUSINESS PROBLEMS

PROBLEM SETS

Work the following problems in your textbook. Your instructor will tell you which problems, if any, are to be turned in. Some of the problems have answers provided in the back of the book; refer to these answers to make sure you are working the problems correctly.

SOFTCOVER: If you are using the Miller, Salzman, and Hoelzle softcover text, *Business Mathematics*, do the following problem sets:

3.1: Problems #17-23 on pages 82-83.

3.2: Problems #1-16 on pages 89-90.

3.3: Problems #4-10 on pages 95-98.

HARDCOVER: If you are using the Salzman, Miller, and Hoelzle hardcover text, *Mathematics for Business*, do the following problem sets:

4.1: Problems #1-23 on pages 112-115.

4.2: Problems #1-6 on pages 118-120.

4.3: Problems #1-15 on pages 127-130.

BUSINESS APPLICATIONS

Read each of the following scenarios and answer the questions about the decisions you would make in each situation. Give these questions some serious thought; they may be used as the basis for discussion or the development of a more complex essay. You should base your decisions on what you've learned from this lesson, applying both math skills and good business judgment to solve the problem at hand.

SCENARIO 1

Rogers is considering the relative advantages of maintaining a minimum checking account balance of $5,000. At that level, her bank levies no maintenance charges and no per-debit charges. She normally writes about twenty checks totalling $2,100 each month to cover routine expenses. If she kept just enough in the account to cover those expenses, the bank would charge her a maintenance fee of $20, plus a $.20 per-check fee for processing.

A staff member at the bank suggests that as an alternative to maintaining such a high balance in her checking account, Rogers could open a savings account with the bank and use it in conjunction with her checking account. That way, she could collect 5 percent interest on her savings, and the bank would transfer funds from savings to checking in the event of an overdraft. The bank does not charge for the transfers, but only two transfers can be made per month.

Rogers likes the idea of keeping a low minimum balance, but switching money back and forth sounds like a lot of trouble to go to. She is afraid it will be difficult to keep track of transactions with two accounts; though, of course, it's appealing to earn slightly higher interest on her money. Then again, she reasons, if it were just a matter of interest, why not put the extra money in a money market account and earn more interest yet; about 8 percent. She's pretty sure that most of the money market accounts let you write a limited number of "checks" each month.

What do you think? Which of these options should Rogers take? Is there a reason to keep the amount of money in the checking account as low as possible, or is having multiple accounts likely to be more trouble than it's worth?

- ☐ To answer these questions, you'll have to make some reasonable estimates about Rogers' checkwriting habits. What additional pieces of information do we need before we can calculate the best alternative?

- ☐ How much is it likely to cost Rogers in fees if she keeps the lowest possible balance in her account? How much interest will she earn with the interest-bearing checking option?

- ☐ How much more interest would Rogers earn if the money not needed in the checking account were put into a money market fund rather than the bank's savings account?

- ☐ About how many checks would Rogers have to write each month for it to be clearly better for her to qualify for a checking account with no per-check charge?

□   Based on the amount of money that would be earned under these different options, which seems the best alternative for Rogers?

SCENARIO 2   Currently, Elmer's Grocery, a family-owned business, accepts checks from its customers. Normally, this isn't too much of a problem. Elmer's staff know many of the customers personally and often take checks from these "regulars" without even requesting identification.

However, about 2 percent of the checks accepted per month are returned because of lack of funds. What's worse, in many cases it is impossible to track down the check writers, most of whom are occasional or out-of-town customers who rarely return to the store. In addition, Elmer's pays the bank a fee of $10 per check returned; this often amounts to several hundred dollars in service charges per month, not to mention the lost revenue on the bad checks that can't be tracked down.

A quick survey indicates that about half the customers are currently paying for their grocery purchases by check. If Elmer's stops accepting checks, it will be hard to compete with the big chain stores that always accept checks; and competing seems difficult enough as it is.

Despite Elmer's need to remain competitive, though, Assistant Manager Furley is all for a new no-check policy: "Look at the figures," he tells Manager Rigby. "We're losing about $1,000 a month in these bad checks." But Rigby isn't convinced. "I think we stand to lose a lot more if we don't take the checks," is his argument. "Yes, we're losing money, but in reality, it amounts to much less than 1 percent of our total business. Theoretically, we could lose up to 50 percent if that survey is right."

But Furley disagrees. "Lots of those people will continue coming here. Sure, we'll lose a few, but plenty of others will be willing to pay in cash once they know the new policy. In fact, if we can show them how this new policy will keep our costs low, it could even look like an advantage."

What's your opinion? Who is right here? Should Elmer's no longer accept checks, or will it lose business in the long run by instituting a policy that drives customers away?

□   Should Elmer's institute a new no-check policy? Why or why not?

□   What factors should the store consider in making this decision? What additional information, if any, is needed to provide a sound base for this kind of business decision making?

□   Rather than simply not accepting checks, are there other alternatives that should be considered as a way to reduce the amount lost to bad checks? If so, what are they?

□   Do you think that Rigby is right that a policy that Elmer's will not accept checks will probably cause it to lose many customers? Or is Furley's prediction that little business will be lost more accurate?

□   Elmer's does not currently accept credit cards. Are credit cards an alternative that Rigby and Furley should consider? Why or why not?

Gross Earnings 5

The tax consultant was helping his new client prepare the necessary tax forms. "First, I need to know your gross income," he said.

"I have no gross income," was the reply from his client.

"No gross income?"

"Right. I have only net income."

"That doesn't seem possible. How can that be?"

"I run a fishing boat."

The way in which a company handles its payroll has a lot to do, directly and indirectly, with how successful that company will be. For one thing, each company must consider what percentage of its total resources it can afford to spend on hiring and training staff. If that percentage is too high, profits suffer; if it's too low, the company may not have the staff necessary to expand its market.

In addition, though, company managers must learn to look at things from the employees' perspective. Ours is a society in which workers tend to specialize. Few people are equally skilled in farming, teaching, medicine, and sales. They usually have one or two areas of expertise and seek a position that not only makes use of their specialized knowledge but rewards it with an appropriate wage. The more skilled and experienced the worker, the more in demand he or she is likely to be. This means that only those companies that are in a position to offer competitive wages and benefits can attract the most qualified employees—employees whose work increases company productivity.

Of course, a company's capacity to attract and keep good employees depends on a wide range of factors, some of which have nothing whatever to do with wages and income. Yet there's no question that effective payroll management is important to most workers. They want to be paid fairly and on time. In this lesson, we'll consider some of the key features of good payroll management and will compare several different methods for calculating wages.

PART I: INTRODUCING THE MATERIAL

LEARNING OBJECTIVES

Upon completing your study of this lesson, you should be able to:

1. Calculate gross earnings, given salary or wage rate, and hours worked.

2. Calculate the overtime wage, overtime earnings, and total pay, given base wage and using a time-and-a-half rate.

3. Define the terms double time, shift differential, and split-shift premium.

4. Calculate gross earnings for employees who work on commission.

5. Explain the purpose of a sliding scale or variable commission plan as a method of pay.

6. Define draw and quota.

7. Calculate gross earnings based on piecework or differential piecework basis.

8. Calculate gross earnings based on piecework with a guaranteed hourly wage basis.

9. Calculate gross earnings based on piecework basis when overtime earnings are involved.

If you're using the hardcover textbook, *Mathematics for Business*, there are some additional objectives for the lesson. Upon completing your study of the lesson, you should also be able to:

10. Explain how account sales and account purchases work.

11. Calculate gross earnings for employees who work under premium payment plans.

12. Apply the concepts of draw and quota in calculating gross earnings based on commission.

13. Calculate gross earnings based on piecework rates when chargebacks and dockings are involved.

LESSON OVERVIEW

Workers can offer a host of reasons for accepting a particular job: They like the challenge, they like the people they work with, or they just enjoy the work itself. These are all valid reasons for holding any job, but in the final analysis, very few people work simply for the joy of it. They expect to be paid for what they do. From the workers' perspective, getting paychecks at the end of each pay period may seem very routine. But from the employer's side, it is anything but. Managing the payroll in a company with more than a handful of employees is a major responsibility.

To begin with, payroll management demands some careful record-keeping and a thorough knowledge of the industry. Business managers need to know what other companies are paying for comparable work and how the wages for a given job are generally computed. Companies that pay an hourly wage must also know, usually to the nearest quarter or tenth hour, how much time each employee has worked and how much of that time, if any, will be paid at an overtime or premium rate. Such record-keeping may be partially the employee's own responsibility, but in the end, the payroll office must be certain that the information it uses to calculate wages is accurate and up to date. This means having some sort of system for keeping track of each employee's hours, rate of pay, overtime, and other pertinent information that may affect that employee's paycheck.

Many companies use timecards, which may be either filled in by hand or run through a time clock that automatically fills in the day, date, and time in or out. The information from each employee's time card is then transferred to a payroll ledger or to a computerized payroll program that will handle all the calculations.

Payroll Management

It is particularly important that these records be kept up to date, and this is one reason many companies have chosen to computerize their payroll. It's much faster than hand calculating data for, say, fifty or a hundred employees. And for a company with several hundred or several thousand employees, computerization is virtually a must. Most computerized payroll programs will automatically keep track of hours worked, overtime, premium pay, and any appropriate deductions and will even print out the checks.

Within limits, a company can choose how long each *pay period*, the time between paychecks, will be. Some companies pay weekly, some biweekly (every two weeks) and some monthly. Virtually all employees are paid at least once a month, though it's sometimes legal to go as long as about thirty-five days between pay periods. Most workers have financial obligations (rent, mortgage, utilities, insurance) that come due on a monthly cycle, so it would be highly inconvenient for most people to be paid, say, every six months. In addition, it wouldn't be fair for a company that is not financially solvent to employ people for three or four months, then tell them, "Sorry, we don't have enough resources to cover your paychecks." This scenario is not so farfetched as it sounds. In a single year, thousands of companies go bankrupt in the United States alone, many of them without enough money left to meet their final payroll.

Of course, when an employee does not get paid on time, it does not always mean that the money isn't there. Sometimes it's just a matter of bad management. Perhaps the information has not yet been transferred from timecards, or perhaps the monthly wages have not yet been computed because of a equipment failure. A late paycheck caused by some emergency is not a big deal to most people. However, a company that is routinely behind in its payroll is likely to incur some ill will from employees, some of whom may be sufficiently annoyed to seek work elsewhere. Any company that misses a pay period completely—simply does not issue any checks for the month—will likely be subject to legal sanctions if employees report their problem to the appropriate state agency (usually the Department of Labor) or to the federal government.

Also, in many states, employees who are fired without notice must be issued paychecks on the same day to cover any work already performed. And even when notice is given, the employer may be required to issue a paycheck to a terminated employee within a very short period, perhaps 48 hours. Clearly, a company that does not have current payroll records could end up with some serious legal problems to go with its administrative difficulties.

Computing Gross Earnings

Not all employees work for an hourly wage, but for the moment, let's focus on those who do. Computing total gross earnings for such employees is a matter of straightforward multiplication, according to this formula:

Gross earnings = Number of hours worked × Rate per hour

For instance, suppose Nevins works at Mo's Bake Shop, a family-owned business that caters to tourists. Nevins's hours are not fixed. Because of the nature of the business, she puts in a long day when there are lots of people buying baked goods and goes home early on days when sales are slow. Let's say that during a given week she works 38 hours altogether and her hourly rate is $6.50. In that case, her gross earnings can be computed as follows:

Gross earnings = 38 × $6.50 = $247.00

Maybe Mo's will issue Nevins a check for $247.00, less her deductions, at the end of the week. If the bakery pays employees biweekly or monthly, it will just keep a record of her earnings on file for the time being.

Now let's complicate our scenario a little. Suppose it is the height of the vacation season, with lots of tourists stopping by for a morning croissant and tea or a late-night muffin and cocoa. This means Nevins is working very long hours, particularly on weekends. Let's say her timecard for the week shows these totals:

Mo's Bake Shop
Timecard for: Eloise Nevins
Position: Bakery Manager
Rate: $6.50/hour

Sunday	–	0
Monday	–	8
Tuesday	–	10
Wednesday	–	12
Thursday	–	8
Friday	–	14
Saturday	–	14

As this timecard indicates, Nevins has put in a very full week. Under the *Fair Labor Standards Act* (FLSA), which covers most full-time workers, a workweek is defined as 40 hours; those 40 hours are considered *straight time* hours. Anything over that is considered *overtime* and is generally compensated at a *time-and-a-half* rate, or 1½ times the employee's usual rate of pay. Her time card indicates that during this particular week, Nevins has put in a total of 66 hours, or a full 40-hour normal workweek plus 26 hours of overtime. We compute her wages for this week using the following formula:

Gross earnings = Earnings at regular rate
 + Earnings at time-and-a-half rate

Thus,

Gross earnings = (40 × $6.50) + (26 × $6.50 × 1.5), or

$260.00 + $253.50 = $513.50 (for the week)

Notice that during this particular week, Nevins's hours well exceeded the 40 hours covered by the regular workweek. Sometimes, however, an employee works overtime some days but not others, and the total hours for the week may not exceed 40. When this happens, company policy (or a union contract) determines whether that employee receives overtime compensation. For instance, suppose Nevins's timecard for the week looks like this:

Mo's Bake Shop
Timecard for: Eloise Nevins
Position: Bakery Manager
Rate: $6.50/hour

Sunday   –   0
Monday   –   4
Tuesday   –   2
Wednesday   –   2
Thursday   –   4
Friday   –   16
Saturday   –   10

Nevins has worked a double shift on Friday and overtime Saturday. Yet because her hours are so short on the other days, her total for the week is only 38 hours, not enough to qualify her for the overtime rate unless Mo's pays on a *daily overtime* schedule. In that case, Nevins would have 8 hours of overtime for Friday and 2 for Saturday.

Premium Pay

Americans love convenience. A lot of us would rather eat out on holidays than spend our time off cooking and cleaning. We want to do our banking or shopping after work, or maybe even after dinner or during the early morning hours. People who need a quart of milk, a tank of gas, or a last-minute birthday gift in the middle of the night like the idea that there's someplace they can get it. Merchants have tried hard to be responsive to consumers' growing demand for convenience, but face it: Somebody has to pump the gas at 3:00 a.m. or run the cash register at the convenience store. But the number of people who prefer to work these unusual hours is fairly small. To make such jobs more appealing, companies have come up with a number of *premium rates*, including *double time*, *shift differential*, *split-shift premium*, and *compensatory time*. Let's consider each of these briefly.

Some companies pay *double time* (double the employee's regular rate, that is) for hours worked on holidays. Were that the case at Mo's, Nevins would receive $130.00 for the 10 hours she put in last Saturday if that were Christmas Day (10 hours × $13.00, which is double her regular rate of $6.50). Double time for special days is not dependent on the total hours an employee works for the week. In other words, when Nevins works at the bake shop on Christmas, she receives double time wages, even if that is the only day she works that week.

Many companies have extremely busy times during the business day followed by slow periods during which not much is happening. A restaurant, for instance, may have a busy lunch hour, followed by a quiet afternoon with few customers, followed by a dinner hour rush. Of course, the restaurant could simply close up for a few hours each afternoon, but closing up is a big job in itself; plus, the restaurant would lose out on the small amount of business it might gain during that time. On the other hand, the restaurant doesn't want to pay employees just to stand about waiting for customers to come through the doors.

Take Charlie's Chili House, which solves the problem by hiring most employees to work a *split shift*, 11:00 a.m. to 2:00 p.m. and 5:00 to 8:00 p.m. Charlie's pays the employees who are on this divided schedule a split-shift premium, an extra $2.50 per hour, to compensate for the inconvenience it causes them. Notice that Charlie's could solve the problem another way, by hiring people to work the afternoon shift and hiring a different crew to work evenings. But then the restaurant would face the problem of finding well-qualified staff willing to work only three hours per day, and that could prove difficult.

Let's say Charlie's then discovers that it can do a lot of business by staying open until midnight and catering to late-night workers, shoppers, and after-theater snackers. A great idea for boosting profits, but where will they find people to serve chili and wash dishes at 11:00 p.m.? They'll have an easier time finding them, probably, if they offer a *shift differential*, a premium payment given to employees willing to work a shift from 4:00 p.m. to midnight.

It is often to a company's benefit to maintain a smaller crew during slow periods. And for some companies, the higher pay for overtime can mean a serious drain on resources. Put these two factors together, and it may be to the company's benefit to offer *compensatory time*, or *comp time*, to employees who work overtime hours. Comp time, where legal (it is not a legally acceptable replacement for overtime pay in some states) is usually offered at $1\frac{1}{2}$ times the overtime hours worked. In other words, an employee who has worked 20 hours of overtime will receive 30 hours of comp time. The employee receives no wages for comp time, just time off during the regular work schedule. Some employees value this time off and consider it as good as receiving extra wages. Not all share this perspective, however, and employees can object if an employer *insists* on reimbursing them for routine overtime with comp time rather than extra wages.

Salaries

As the proportion of workers in service industries grows compared to those in manufacturing jobs, the number of people paid a salary rather than an hourly wage is increasing. A salary is usually expressed as an annual salary, though some people prefer to think in terms of earnings per month or earnings per week. For instance, let's say that Bleeker, an assistant manager in a small print shop, receives a monthly salary of $1,550. Bleeker's annual salary (12 × $1,550) is then $18,600. If Bleeker is paid monthly, his gross pay on each paycheck will be $1,550. But he might be paid weekly (52 times per year), biweekly (26 times per year), or semi-monthly (24 times per year). Regardless, we can always find the amount of Bleeker's gross pay per pay period by dividing the annual salary by the number of pay periods.

We can also, of course, determine Bleeker's equivalent hourly wage, even though he is not paid on this basis. For this purpose, we ignore vacations and assume a 40-hour workweek, and since there are 52 weeks in a year, Bleeker works 52 × 40 hours per year, or a total of 2,080 hours. Since we know his annual salary, we can determine his hourly wage by dividing the total amount of Bleeker's annual compensation by the number of hours worked:

$18,600 ÷ 2,080 = $8.94 (rounded down to the nearest penny)

This information could be of considerable interest to Bleeker, who, if he is offered a $10 per hour position at the library will need to be able to calculate whether that's more or less than his current $18,600 per year job.

But one thing that complicates the calculation is that many persons on salary do not work 40-hour weeks. Salaried employees are usually paid for the completion of specific tasks set forth in their job description and are expected to put forth whatever effort is required to complete those tasks. Bleeker might be lucky. He might have a relatively easy job, an understanding employer, and time to go golfing on Wednesdays without any decrease in his pay. Or he might find himself with a job that cannot be completed in fewer than 60 hours per week, no matter how hard and fast he works.

The FLSA recognizes the unfairness of routinely providing additional compensation to nonsalaried employees while expecting salaried employees to good-naturedly put in whatever hours are required. Thus, employees in certain salaried positions (teachers, for instance) are compensated for overtime *in certain circumstances*. A teacher who is required to attend an after-hours professional development seminar or chaperone the Saturday night basketball game, for example, will usually be compensated for that time, though the hours spent correcting student papers at home or reading professional literature will usually not be compensated. Often, the circumstances under which professionals receive overtime compensation are decided in contract negotiations between employers and unions representing the professionals.

Incentive Rates: Piecework

So far we've talked about compensating employees on the basis of the time they spend on the job. Often, this is the fairest way to approach things. For example, say that Schmidt provides childcare for Wolfe. Schmidt is not being paid to complete any particular task (other than generally supervising the children) during her childcare hours. In other words, no "product" results from her efforts.

Nor does it make any sense to say that on good days she might finish the job in half the time. No, her time and attention are mostly what Schmidt is being compensated for, together with the fact that Wolfe considers her qualified to fill this position. In short, it makes perfect sense to compensate Schmidt by the hour. But sometimes the nature of the job suggests that some other method of compensation might be more appropriate for both employer and employee.

For instance, suppose Bean sews custom leather boots for a living. His employer would understandably be reluctant to pay him by the hour. If he hurried through the job, the employer might come out very well (provided Bean didn't hurry so much that the work suffered), but Bean might justifiably feel rushed for no good reason. But if Bean dawdled along, taking his time about things, Bean's extra wages would reduce profits or, alternately, force his employer to raise prices.

In circumstances like these, it makes sense to pay according to the number of items produced—by a *piecework* rate, that is. Paying by the piece, rather than by time spent on the job, is considered one form of *incentive rate*. The idea is that Bean, or anyone paid in this manner, will be motivated to work harder and faster if the pay depends on completion of the task.

Earnings calculated on a piecework rate are found by this formula:

Gross earnings = Pay per item × Number of items

Suppose that Big Country Western Boots pays Bean $5.00 for each pair of boots he sews. During a given day, Bean makes 15 pairs of boots. Thus,

Gross earnings = $5.00 × 15 = $75.00

The company might also offer a *differential piece rate* plan, under which a worker is compensated at one level up to a certain production total and at a higher level if more items are produced. The differential piece rate approach doesn't always apply well. We might suppose, for instance, that there would be some maximum number of boots that Bean could fashion during the month and still turn out fine work. He is already a highly skilled craftsman, not a novice in the process of learning his trade. Trying to motivate him with the lure of higher wages would probably do little to speed his efforts.

On the other hand, let's consider Murphy, who packs stereo speakers and who is paid for each box he packs. If Murphy is fairly new to this job, he may be working well below his eventual capacity. In other words, it makes sense to encourage him to work faster. He'll earn more money, and the company won't need to hire additional packers. With that in mind, Murphy might be paid according to a schedule like this one:

1-100 boxes	= $.50 per box
101-200 boxes	= $.55 per box
201 boxes or more	= $.60 per box

Let's say that during his first day on the job, Murphy packs 110 boxes. The rate for the first 100 boxes will be $.50 per box. The rate on the remaining 10 will be $.55 per box. Thus, Murphy's wages for the day will be

($.50 × 100) + ($.55 × 10) = $50.00 + $5.50 = $55.50

As it turns out, Murphy has a talent for this job. By the end of the year, he is packing 220 boxes per day. Then his wages will be

($.50 × 100) + ($.55 × 100) + ($.60 × 20) =

$50.00 + $55.00 + $12.00 = $117.00

Notice that if Murphy had been paid for the same job on a *time rate*, he would have realized little or no increase in pay by the end of the year, despite his increased efficiency. And that's the whole point: Why should Murphy struggle for ever-greater efficiency if he's just being paid for the time he spends in the shipping department? But because he was paid by the piece, his time became more productive by the end of the year, both for him and for his employer. Notice, too, what a difference the differential pay rate makes in his total wage. If he had been paid for the 220 crates on a straight piece rate of $.50 per box, his total for the week would have been $110.00, about 7 percent less than what he actually earned. A graduated scale provides significant motivation, *assuming* that an increase in worker productivity is realistically achievable.

The worker who is very new to a job or who is learning a technically difficult task may find a piece rate extremely frustrating. Suppose, for instance, that a worker is paid to do hand stitching on custom lampshades. The work is exacting, precise, and often frustrating. If it goes very slowly during the period that the worker is just learning, then a piece rate method of compensation won't produce enough income to meet minimum wage requirements. To avoid this sort of situation, the company may adopt an either/or approach, in which the employee is compensated at the piece rate or at an hourly rate, whichever is higher.

Of course, the company is not likely to continue this approach indefinitely. Unless the expectations are inherently unreasonable and no one is meeting the quotas, there will come a point at which the company will expect the employee to gain enough speed so that the piece rate regularly exceeds the hourly wage compensation. And if the employee never improves, the employer is likely to start looking for a replacement who performs the work faster.

Also, even piece rate workers usually have to be paid at or above the federal guaranteed minimum wage, so that is the least they can earn. Such a guaranteed rate is particularly important for agricultural workers, whose productivity frequently depends on conditions beyond their control. If a poor growing year has resulted in fruit that's few and far between, workers might not be able to pick enough at piecework rates to earn a minimum wage, no matter how hard they work. But they can take some comfort from the fact that they'll make at least the federal minimum wage, regardless of what they would have earned at the piece rate.

Even so, there's no denying the fact that not everyone feels perfectly comfortable with this payment approach. Consumers are likely to raise the issue of quality: When workers are encouraged to work as rapidly as possible, aren't they likely to become sloppy or careless, to let things go that they might otherwise take time to fix, in order to make as much money as they can? Perhaps. But then, there are no guarantees of high quality with time rates of payment, either.

Further, there are some built-in safeguards with the piece rate approach. For one thing, no law requires an employer to accept work that is clearly of inferior quality. Remember Murphy and the speaker boxes? If Murphy's work is sloppy, or if the speakers he packs become damaged because he's working too fast to be careful, his employer is likely to refuse to pay for such useless efforts. The work that isn't completed correctly, called *dockings*, will not be included or may even be subtracted from Murphy's total, thus encouraging him to take a little more time in the future. And, of course, if Murphy's slapdash technique persists, he is likely to be out of a job altogether.

Commissions

A second form of incentive pay involves *commissions*, or payment based on a fixed percentage of sales or a fixed amount per item sold. This form of payment is very common for salespeople in a wide range of industries, from shoes to insurance.

With *straight commission*, the sales representative receives a fixed percentage of all sales, called the rate of commission. Salespersons on straight commission receive no base salary. Let's say, for instance, that Guthrie sells real estate and has a 5 percent commission. If she sells a house for $100,000, her pay is computed as follows:

Gross earnings = Commission rate × Sales

Gross earnings = .05 × $100,000 = $5,000

This may look like a pretty fair return on a single sale. But remember: We have no idea how many hours of research, public relations, and paperwork went into that sale. Guthrie's hourly wage may be considerably less impressive than her commission would lead us to believe. Further, we must also consider that with commission, there is no guarantee of income. If Guthrie sells a house every month, she's making a decent living. If this is her only sale for six months, things look much less prosperous.

With some jobs, calculating commission sale by sale would be just too tedious and time consuming. For instance, suppose that Robbins works in a clothing store, where she is paid a 6 percent commission. She will not calculate her earnings every time she sells a scarf or pair of socks but will wait till the end of the pay period and calculate her earnings based on total sales. Further, before she can figure out what she is owed, she will need to deduct any *returns* (merchandise customers have brought back to the store) and any *allowances* (merchandise sold at discount). (Normally, a business is less willing to pay a commission on discounted merchandise, which is already yielding little or no profit to the company.)

Let's suppose then that Robbins' sales for the month of April amount to $12,762, and that she has returns and allowances of $1,443. Her commission is 6 percent. What are her earnings for April?

Gross earnings = Commission rate × Sales

Gross earnings = .06 × ($12,762 − $1,443) = $679.14

That's not a very big monthly check, and unless Robbins has some other source of income, she is likely to have difficulty running a household on such small pay. It may be that she's in a job with no future; maybe this store isn't very popular and sells very little merchandise. Or maybe Robbins really doesn't have a knack for making sales.

But let's suppose neither of these situations is true. Let's suppose instead that Robbins has exceptional potential but just needs a little experience. And let's further suppose that the average salesperson in this clothing store has sales exceeding $35,000 per month after returns. Robbins' employer believes that she will eventually surpass this amount and does not want to lose her. Chances are, though, that Robbins can only survive just so long on less than $700 per month. An employer who is sufficiently serious about wanting to keep Robbins around can "invest" in her or, more accurately, in her eventual value to the company, by paying her a combination *salary plus commission*.

This might be a permanent arrangement, or the money might be a kind of interest-free loan against future commissions, called a *draw*, which Robbins would repay sometime in the future. A commission with a salary base provides a way for an inexperienced salesperson to build sales skills, get to know the merchandise, and establish a good client base, and still have some guaranteed income to pay the bills while "learning the ropes." It's money well spent for the company that ends up with a crackerjack salesperson who might otherwise have gone with another company or gone into another field altogether.

Many companies also want to reward their top-producing salespeople. They can do this with a *sliding scale*, also known as a *variable commission scale*. Robbins at the clothing store might make 6 percent on her first $10,000 worth of sales, 7 percent on the next $10,000, and 8 percent on all sales over $20,000. Suppose that Robbins eventually makes $32,000 worth of sales in a given month, and at about the same time is offered a sales job with another company. The second job includes a base of $500 per month, plus commissions of 7 percent. Should Robbins take it? Let's see. For now, let's suppose that her present job involves no draw. Thus, we compute her wages as follows:

Gross wages from commissions = Commission rate × Sales, or

(.06 × $10,000) + (.07 × $10,000) + (.08 × $12,000) =

$600 + $700 + $960 = $2,260

In order to have a proper base of comparison, let's assume for now that Robbins's total sales at the other job would also come to $32,000 for the month. Thus, we use the following formula:

Gross earnings = Base salary + Gross wages from commissions, or

$500 (the fixed amount) + (.07 × $32,000) =

$500 + $2,240 = $2,740

Notice that without the base, the jobs would be roughly comparable. As it is, though, the second job appears to be the better choice. But sometimes the information the math calculations alone give us can be misleading. Robbins will have to consider, for instance, whether she is really likely to sell $32,000 worth of merchandise at her second job. Perhaps the new job is with a store that has very few customers or sells only inexpensive goods. The second job is better *only* if she can equal or better her current sales volume.

SOME WORDS OF ADVICE

The company that keeps accurate, thorough, up-to-date payroll records has two management plusses on its side. First, that company is in a better position to know how its resources are being spent, and whether it's committing too high a percentage of revenue to workers or not enough. Second, when a company pays its workers a fair wage based on industry standards and meets its payroll obligations in a timely fashion, it stands a better chance of keeping workers happy and hanging onto those it most wants to keep.

Payroll management is not a small task. In today's companies, workers do not all arrive at 9:00 a.m. and punch out at 5:00 p.m. Many work irregular hours or split shifts. Their pay rates and benefits are different. Keeping track of this information is a formidable task that, for all but the smallest companies, usually demands some computerized support. Any company trying to keep manual records on more than a few employees might do well to consider the benefits of computerizing its payroll.

As we have seen, there are great advantages to knowing what others in the industry are paying for comparable work. A startup company may, of course, be forced into simply paying what it can afford until it has more resources to draw upon. But the more competitive a company can be in offering fair wages, the more options it has in selecting from qualified candidates to fill key positions. On the other hand, a company that overpays employees simply undermines its own profits. And in the end, it doesn't always do the employees a service, since they can earn those higher wages only as long as the company is able to prosper.

Finally, the wise manager must ensure that wages are computed in a manner that is appropriate given the nature of the work performed. It's not very feasible to pay a security guard by the number of crimes prevented, but it makes perfect sense to pay a hat maker for the number of hats produced instead of by the hours he or she spends making them. And it usually makes better sense to pay a professional—say a teacher, plant manager, or bank president—a salary than to pay by the hour or by the task performed. The trick is to ensure that the method of calculating compensation will be fair to the employee while also encouraging the best possible performance and the highest standards of quality.

KEY TERMS

Before you watch the video program and read through the text assignment, take a minute to look at the key terms associated with this lesson. When you encounter them in the text and video program, pay careful attention to their meaning.

Commission: A fee paid to an employee for transacting a piece of business or performing a service. Commissions are most often paid for the sale of goods and services.

Compensatory time: Time off given an employee to compensate for overtime previously worked; it is generally given in lieu of overtime pay.

Differential piece rate: A piece rate scale that pays a higher rate for each unit of production as the number of units produced is increased.

Double time: Wages paid at twice the regular hourly rate. Double time is most often paid for working holidays.

Draw: An amount paid by an employer to salespeople, often at regular intervals. A draw is perhaps best viewed as a loan that is to be repaid within a certain period out of the income that the salesperson will earn through commissions.

Fair Labor Standards Act: A federal law that addresses certain wage and hour work conditions; it is the FLSA that establishes the length of the workweek, the federal minimum wage and requirements for overtime pay.

Gross earnings: The total amount of money earned by an employee before any deductions are taken.

Incentive rate: Any of several payment systems (e.g., commission, piecework) based on the amount of work completed.

Overtime: The hours worked by employees in excess of their agreed work schedule. For most workers, this is set by the FLSA as work in excess of 40 hours per week or 8 hours per day, but it may be some other standard established by a union contract or employment agreement.

Pay period: The time period for which an employee is paid; how often employees receive paychecks. Weekly, biweekly, semimonthly, and monthly are the most common pay periods.

Piecework rate: A method of pay by which an employee receives a set amount of money per item completed.

Premium rate: A higher than normal amount of pay, usually given for additional hours worked or additional units produced.

Quota: An expected level of production. A premium may be paid to employees who exceed their quotas.

Salary: A fixed amount of money paid to the employee each pay period; it is not based on the number of hours worked or the amount produced in the pay period.

Salary plus commission: A pay arrangement wherein an employee receives a commission in addition to a base salary.

Shift differential: The premium paid for working a less desirable shift, such as evenings or nights.

Sliding-scale commission: A rate of commission that depends on the total amount of the sales, with the rate increasing as sales increase. Also called a *variable rate commission*.

Split-shift premium: A premium paid for working a split shift; for example, an employee who is on four hours, off four hours, and then on four hours would receive this premium in addition to eight hours of pay.

Straight commission: A pay system where earnings come entirely from commissions; no base salary or draw is provided.

Time-and-a half rate: $1\frac{1}{2}$ the normal rate of pay for any hours worked in excess of an agreed-upon amount (usually 40 hours per week or 8 hours per day); time-and-a-half is the normal rate paid for overtime work.

Time rate: A pay system in which earnings are based on hours worked, not on the work accomplished. Hourly employees are paid a time rate; employees on commission, piecework, or salary systems are not.

PART II: WATCHING THE VIDEO PROGRAM

VIDEO VIEWING GUIDE

Before watching the video program, review the following questions. As you watch, be sure to collect the information necessary to answer them.

1. What are the critical points to consider in deciding whether to pay someone a wage, a salary, a commission, or some other type of pay?

2. How can a person compare the pay for two jobs, one of which pays a salary and one an hourly wage?

3. When is overtime pay necessary and how is it calculated from the employee's base hourly wage?

4. What is the most important reason that companies pay double time, shift differentials and split-shift differentials?

5. Is selling on commission likely to be more or less profitable for the employee than performing the same sales job on a salary? How about for the employer?

6. What are the important factors in determining whether a job should be paid on a piecework basis?

7. The composition of the workforce is changing. What are some of the changes, what are the implications for employers, and what effects do these changes have on the way people are paid for their work?

VIDEO PROGRAM

This lesson's video program is Program 5 — Gross Earnings. Remember, if you are watching this program on videotape, take time to replay sections of the tape whenever you need to review a concept.

VIDEO VIEWING QUESTIONS

Immediately after viewing the video program for Lesson 5, take time to respond to the following questions. Give your answers some careful thought; they may provide the basis for additional discussion or a longer written response.

1. Suppose you were given a job selling new cars at a dealership with a good history and a lot of traffic coming through the door. Which of these five methods of pay would you prefer to work under? Rank them from 1 (best) to 5 (worst) by placing a number in the blank in front of the method.

   _____ Straight commission

   _____ Commission plus base salary

   _____ Commission plus draw

   _____ Straight salary

   _____ Hourly wage

2. Suppose you were given a job planting seedlings in a logging area that was being replanted. Which of these five methods of pay would you prefer to work under? Rank them from 1 (best) to 5 (worst) by placing a number in the blank in front of the method.

   _____ Straight salary

   _____ Hourly wage

_____ Piecework basis

_____ Differential piecework basis

_____ Salary plus piecework basis

3. Based on the video, which seems more accurate? Premium payment systems (such as shift and split-shift differentials) are largely paid by employers in order to:

_____ compensate employees for the inconvenience of working unusual hours.

_____ attract and retain employees who otherwise wouldn't work for them.

4. Based on the video, which seems more accurate? Compared to payment on the basis of salary and wages, piecework pay is

_____ generally more fair.

_____ generally less fair.

_____ Neither – it depends on the particular job at hand.

5. Different systems of pay have come about largely because the type of work being done is simply better suited to one system or another. Look at each of the tasks that follow and decide whether it is better suited to a wage or salary, piecework pay, or a commission arrangement. You needn't select the pay method currently used for the task, but you should be able to defend your choice if you propose a different system. (Check only one column for each task.)

Wage/ Salary	Piece- work	Commis- sion	
_____	_____	_____	Selling stocks and bonds
_____	_____	_____	Providing financial consulting to clients
_____	_____	_____	Selling automobiles
_____	_____	_____	Performing mechanical repairs on automobiles
_____	_____	_____	Washing and waxing automobiles
_____	_____	_____	Taking tolls at a toll booth
_____	_____	_____	Writing tickets for parking violations
_____	_____	_____	Towing cars that violate parking laws
_____	_____	_____	Working as a bank teller
_____	_____	_____	Writing chapters of a technical manual for a computer
_____	_____	_____	Writing poetry for a literary magazine
_____	_____	_____	Putting up wallboard in newly constructed houses
_____	_____	_____	Soliciting funds for a symphony orchestra

_____ _____ _____ Playing professional baseball

_____ _____ _____ Training thoroughbred racehorses

6. Suppose that you were named president of a large department store chain and that you had the flexibility to design whatever way of paying your employees you thought was fair. Given that you have to account for a wide range of employees, all the way from yourself to the part-time gift wrappers, which of the following do you think you'd need to include in your system? (Check as many as apply.)

_____ Time-and-a-half overtime pay

_____ Double time pay

_____ Salaries

_____ Straight commissions

_____ Commissions plus base salary

_____ Sliding-scale commissions

_____ Sales quotas

_____ Draws

_____ Shift differentials

_____ Split-shift differentials

_____ Piecework pay

_____ Differential piecework pay

_____ Guaranteed minimum wage

PART III: FOCUSING ON THE MATHEMATICS

READING ASSIGNMENT

After watching the video program, you should read one of the following Text Assignments, depending on the textbook you're using:

SOFTCOVER: Pages 155-172 from Chapter 5 of the Miller, Salzman, and Hoelzle softcover text, *Business Mathematics*.

HARDCOVER: Pages 137-164 from Chapter 5 of the Salzman, Miller, and Hoelzle hardcover text, *Mathematics for Business*.

As you read through the text, pay careful attention to the examples the book gives of the mathematics associated with the concepts you're learning about.

Then, after you've completed the text assignment, read through the Key Formulas here. This section provides a handy review of what you've learned. By the time you get to this point in the lesson, all of the formulas and calculations should be familiar to you. If they're not, go back and read

the appropriate parts of the text and the Overview section of this lesson. You won't have much success completing the rest of your assignments if you are still confused about the information in the Key Formulas section.

KEY FORMULAS

The following key formulas are important to your understanding of this lesson. Be sure that you know each one and how to use it in solving problems related to calculating gross earnings.

KEY FORMULA: Gross earnings = Number of hours worked × Rate per hour

Formula used for: Determining gross earnings for workers paid an hourly rate.

Example:

Markland earns $7.00 an hour at her assembly line job. In a week where she works exactly 40 hours, her gross earnings would be 40 × $7.00, or $280.00.

Remember that in this formula:

1. The wage rate is always given in dollars per hour and the time worked in hours. This is because wage earners are paid by the hour, rather than the day, week, or month; people paid in those units are usually being paid a salary.

2. This is how the gross earnings are calculated. Markland does not take home $280, since taxes and other deductions have to be subtracted.

KEY FORMULA: Overtime earnings = Wage rate × Overtime factor × Overtime worked

Formula used for: Finding the gross pay for overtime work performed by hourly employees.

Example:

In one exceptionally busy week, Markland worked 60 hours. For all the hours of overtime, she received time-and-a-half pay. By multiplying her wage rate of $7.00 an hour by the overtime factor (1.5) for the hours of overtime worked (60 − 40 = 20), we find that she made $210 in overtime.

Remember that in this formula:

1. Overtime is usually paid for all hours over 40 worked in a week. The amount might have to be adjusted, though, if any part of the overtime is made up by compensatory time.

2. The "overtime factor" is usually 1.5 (for regular overtime paid at time-and-a-half) or 2.0 (for overtime paid at double time); time-and-a-half pay is much more common.

3. This formula combines two steps into one. It works equally well to figure out the overtime wage rate first and then multiply that by over-

time worked. We could, for example, multiply the $7.00 per hour straight time rate by 1.5 to find her overtime rate (in this case, $10.50 an hour). When this is multiplied by the same 20 hours of overtime, we find, not surprisingly, that Markland still made $210 in overtime.

4. Don't get confused and multiply the total hours worked by the overtime rate. In our example, Markland worked 60 hours, but only 20 of those were overtime hours. To figure out how much Markland made that week, you'd have to calculate the straight time earnings ($280) and the overtime earnings ($210) and add them together. In our example, Markland made $490 for working 60 hours in one week.

KEY FORMULA: Commission earnings =
Commission rate × Value of units sold

Formula used for: Determining the earnings of a person paid on commission based on the value of the total sales.

Alternate Form: Commission Earnings = Commission rate × Number of units sold.

(Use this form when the commission rate is based on the number, as opposed to the value, of the units sold.)

Example:

Gregory receives a 3 percent commission for the sale of each used car, based on the value of the car. The commission from selling a $2,000 car would, therefore, be .03 × $2,000 = $60, while the commission for a $6,000 car would be $180.

Remember that in this formula:

1. The commission is usually given in percentage form, but that has to be converted to a decimal before multiplying. In our example, Gregory's 3 percent commission meant that we multiplied by .03.

2. Adjustments for variable commission rates have to be handled separately. If Gregory receives 3 percent on the first $50,000 he sells and 4 percent on the rest, you have to do two multiplications and add the results to get his commission on $70,000 of sales. This would mean that Gregory earned .03 × $50,000 *plus* .04 × $20,000 (the amount paid at the higher rate), which is $1,500 + $800, or $2,300 total.

DON'T FORGET

1. The calculations discussed in this lesson are used to figure out gross earnings. This is not the employee's take-home pay; that amount is substantially smaller because of withholdings for taxes and deductions for insurance, retirement plans, and the like.

2. Many of these calculations require more than one step. To figure total gross earnings for wages, for example, calculate the overtime earnings and the straight time earnings separately and then add them together. The same process is used for commissions paid on a sliding scale or

piecework paid on a differential piecework basis. In each case, figure out how much work was done at each rate, find the dollar value of that work, and then add the dollar values together.

PART IV: SOLVING BUSINESS PROBLEMS

PROBLEM SETS

Work the following problems in your textbook. Your instructor will tell you which problems, if any, are to be turned in. Some of the problems have answers provided in the back of the book; refer to these answers to make sure you are working the problems correctly.

SOFTCOVER: If you are using the Miller, Salzman, and Hoelzle softcover text, *Business Mathematics*, do the following problem sets:

5.1: Problems #3-39 (odd numbers only) on pages 163-165.

5.2: Problems #5-27 (odd numbers only) on pages 171-172.

HARDCOVER: If you are using the Salzman, Miller, and Hoelzle hardcover text, *Mathematics for Business*, do the following problem sets:

5.1: Problems #4-6, 16-18, 22-24, 28-30, 48-50, 55-58 on pages 146-149.

5.2: Problems #17-32 on pages 156-158.

5.3: Problems #6-10, 28-30, and 36-42 on pages 162-164.

BUSINESS APPLICATIONS

Read each of the following scenarios and answer the questions about the decisions you would make in each situation. Give these questions some serious thought; they may be used as the basis for discussion or the development of a more complex essay. You should base your decisions on what you've learned from this lesson, applying both math skills and good business judgment to solve the problem at hand.

SCENARIO 1

Holt is an experienced computer salesperson with a good reputation in the business and a loyal following of customers. He works for Valley Data Systems, which sells mostly moderately priced microcomputer network systems and pays Holt a straight commission of 6 percent. He usually sells from one to three systems per month, sometimes doing slightly better in the winter. The average price for a system is about $16,000. Holt's wife has worked part-time as a receptionist for a number of years, making an average yearly income of about $12,000. They have no children. When Holt's wife becomes seriously ill and is unable to continue working, they need to re-evaluate their financial situation. Suddenly they are without her income and also have some medical expenses not covered by insurance.

Holt decides he should look for a new, better paying position to offset the additional family expenses. There are two options. Mission Computer has offered him a sales position that pays straight commission at 8 percent. Mission sells more expensive computer systems, averaging $35,000 or more. Sales have not been brisk lately, but Mission assures Holt that such slumps are common and only temporary. The company is eager to have him on board.

The second option involves a position at a Midwest Sporting Goods. Holt knows very little about sports equipment, but the manager tells him that his experience in sales is the critical factor; he will pick up the rest quickly. The position includes a base salary of $500 per month for the first two years and a 6.5 percent commission on all sales. The $500 base is repayable to the company without interest at a rate of $250 per month, beginning with the third year of employment. Sales have been moderate to good for Midwest, and it is considering opening a new store. The top salesperson, who has been with the company for almost ten years, averages $24,000 to $25,000 in sales per month. Holt is less than confident about his ability to sell tents and ski equipment but supposes that his general knack for representing products well could see him through. He will lose his contacts in business, though, since those people know him primarily as a computer salesperson. What do you think? Which position should Holt take? Or should he simply remain where he is at Valley Data Systems?

☐ Which of the three positions seems to offer the highest *potential* gross earnings? What assumptions did you need to make to figure that out?

☐ Which of the three positions seems to offer the highest *guaranteed* gross earnings? Why did you come to that conclusion?

☐ What are the risks involved with each of the three positions? Is there one Holt should rule out because the earnings might simply be too low?

☐ Should Holt accept one of the new positions he has been offered? If so, which one and why?

SCENARIO 2

Woodbright Cabinets has a reputation for quality which it is eager to maintain. It has eight cabinet makers on staff, including one senior craftsman, three fabricators, and four apprentice carpenters who primarily do measuring and installation. All eight have been paid at an hourly rate up to now, with daily overtime and double rate for Saturdays, Sundays, and holidays. The regular rates are $12.50 per hour for the apprentice carpenters, $14.00 per hour for the three fabricators, and $16.50 per hour for the craftsman, who primarily does design work and finishing. Average overtime is about 10 hours a week each, except for the finishing craftsman, who generally puts in at least 20 hours of overtime weekly and often more.

For the moment, the company has more work than it can handle, and it's considering adding additional staff. Qualified workers are readily available, though the plant manager, Barnes, is apprehensive about making the total payroll any bigger since the future sales of the cabinets are still somewhat uncertain. Further, as the crew's overtime increases steadily, payroll is getting tougher and tougher to meet, and Barnes isn't sure they can afford to take on anyone new. "We've got to be careful," he tells his assistant manager, McGrew. "We don't want to get ourselves into a position where we're asking people to do work we can't pay them for."

McGrew agrees but feels that something has to be done. A review of the company budget suggests that Woodbright is spending far more on payroll than others in the industry. "Maybe the answer is to manage things differently," McGrew remarks. "If we're going to stay competitive, I suggest we stop paying by the hour and begin paying by the finished product — you know, by the finished cabinet. We can work out a price list, so that each type of job has its own payment rate."

Barnes is intrigued by the idea but has some misgivings. "I don't know of anyone else in our kind of work who is paying that way," he tells McGrew. "If that approach made sense, you'd think someone else would have thought of it."

But McGrew persists. "We can't keep eating all this overtime," he tells Barnes. "It's killing us. The overtime increases our production cost by about 30 percent, and that means we'll have to price ourselves right out of business just to stay alive. Trust me — piece rate is the only way to go here." What do you think? Is McGrew's analysis of the situation correct? Or are there things he is overlooking?

- ☐ Should Woodbright Cabinets shift to a piece rate schedule of payment for its employees? Why or why not?

- ☐ What reaction are the employees at Woodbright likely to have to a major change in the way they are paid?

- ☐ What are some of the most important factors for any company to consider in determining how it will compensate its employees for the work they do? Have Barnes and McGrew considered these factors carefully enough to make a decision?

- ☐ Barnes and McGrew can't figure out why they are having such difficulty making ends meet when business is basically good. What do you see as the most likely explanation?

Social Security and Withholding 6

President Herbert Hoover gave his salary back to the government. Now Congress wants everybody to do it.

When we hear that a school district's teachers are paid an average of $28,000 per year or that apprentice electricians in the Midwest are earning $13.00 per hour, we are hearing about *gross wages*. Those figures do not represent the money these workers get to take home at the end of each pay period. In fact, calculating gross pay—whether it's based on hourly wage or on salary—is just the first step in putting together a payroll.

To determine *net pay*, what is commonly called take-home pay, we must subtract *deductions* from gross income. The primary deductions for most workers are Social Security tax and federal and state income tax. But most workers have other deductions as well; union dues, for instance, or corporate pension contributions. These sorts of deductions vary from company to company and are not required under federal or state law. They are simply part of an employee's private contractual arrangement with the employer. They do, however, affect net pay.

In this lesson, we'll focus primarily on the legally required deductions: Social Security tax and income taxes. We'll see how net pay is calculated when gross pay and tax rate are known and examine a few of the factors that influence tax rates for various workers.

PART I: INTRODUCING THE MATERIAL

LEARNING OBJECTIVES

Upon completing your study of this lesson, you should be able to:

1. Explain the history and purpose of the Social Security tax.

2. Calculate FICA tax given the earnings and the FICA rate.

3. Use a FICA tax table to determine Social Security taxes.

4. Given information on employee earnings and the FICA rate, calculate the employer's FICA contribution for a pay period.

5. Calculate FICA tax when total earnings exceed the FICA maximum.

6. Explain the difference between Social Security tax rates for the self-employed and those employed by others.

7. Be able to complete a W-4 form and understand its purpose.

8. Use a tax table to determine federal withholding tax, given an employee's earnings in a pay period.

9. Given the gross wages, taxes, and other deductions for an employee, calculate net pay.

10. Give examples of the problems that can result when payroll records are not accurately maintained.

11. Given FICA and federal taxes withheld, calculate the quarterly amount payable by an employer to the IRS.

If you're using the hardcover textbook, *Mathematics for Business*, there are some additional objectives for this lesson. Upon completing your study of the lesson, you should also be able to:

12. Calculate the Social Security tax due for a self-employed person making a given amount during a quarter.

13. Understand the relationship between number of withholding allowances and the federal tax withheld, and estimate the appropriate number of deductions for an employee in specified circumstances.

14. Calculate an employer's Federal Unemployment Tax Act insurance payments for a small set of employees, given their earnings during a pay period.

LESSON OVERVIEW

Most employees would probably say that they'd prefer to take home their gross wages and just keep the money that is currently deducted for taxes. But after a little thought, they might well change their mind. If the services that depend heavily on taxes (highway and park maintenance, public education, research and development, for example) were suddenly to be paid for with voluntary contributions, these services might rapidly cease to exist. To put it simply, the tax deductions from wages provide the income needed to run the country. And individual workers benefit from these deductions in both direct and indirect ways.

The History of Social Security

Social Security is a form of tax used by the federal government to fund people's retirement, to pay survivors' and disability benefits to workers and their families, and to help fund the Medicare health insurance program. Social Security did not exist prior to 1935, when the Federal Insurance Contributions Act (*FICA*) was passed by Congress. Before that time, it was up to workers to plan for and fund their own retirement. For many, this proved extremely difficult. Unless an employee earned a high enough wage to permit substantial savings, it was all but impossible to set aside enough money to keep a family above the poverty level through the retirement years, even if family members remained in relatively good health. Medical problems of any kind often proved financially disastrous.

Social Security was designed to reduce these problems through a structured savings program in which workers would set aside a portion of their income each month in the form of a Social Security tax. The money collected by the government in this manner would either be paid out to other, eligible workers in the form of benefits or invested to earn additional income until it was needed. Because the number of workers who participate in the system has increased substantially, and because Social Security premiums have risen regularly over the past several decades, the amount of money within the fund has grown enormously and is now in the hundreds of billions of dollars.

Social Security is not welfare. It is an earned benefit. Therefore, the size of a worker's Social Security check depends on how long he or she has worked and the total amount of income earned. Time on the job translates into work credit; thus, a person who never works or who quits before accumulating a minimum amount of credit will not qualify for Social Security benefits. On the other hand, it is not necessary to work 40 or 50 years or earn very high salaries to get sizable Social Security benefit; most people who work about ten years at an average wage level receive benefits at or near the maximum.

Social Security Contributions

Social Security is most often thought of as retirement income, and that is usually what it turns out to be. If the worker should die or become severely disabled, however, benefits may go to the worker's dependents. And as mentioned above, Social Security contributions help fund the Medicare national medical care program.

Unlike most pension funds, Social Security benefits are subject to automatic cost of living adjustments. This means that the value of the benefits is not seriously affected by inflation. It also means, of course, that each year the government will probably have to pay out more money in the form of benefits. For this reason, some people have worried whether contributions would be sufficient to cover increases in benefits and, indeed, whether the system could remain financially sound over time.

In 1983, a number of amendments designed to ensure the solvency of the Social Security system over the next 75 years were enacted by Congress. The amendments included various tax increases and benefits reductions. Perhaps the most significant change was a new law requiring retired persons with substantial income from other sources to pay taxes on a portion of their Social Security benefits. However, it was estimated that fewer than 10 percent of recipients will be affected by this new regulation, at least for the immediate future.

Amendments to the Social Security system also extended the normal retirement age from 65 to 66 for persons born from 1943 through 1959, and to 67 for persons born in 1960 or thereafter. In part, this change reflects the fact that Americans are living longer and working longer than ever before in history. In addition, though, it effectively delays for a year or two the time at which Social Security recipients can collect full benefits and keeps workers contributing to Social Security longer. The combined effect of these changes is to produce less of a burden on the national Social Security fund. In addition, the 1983 amendments required federal workers hired after 1983 to participate in the system; prior to that time, federal government employees had been exempt from Social Security tax. With more workers making contributions, obviously, the fund has a better chance of remaining sound.

There is a ceiling on the amount of income subject to Social Security tax. Workers who earn more than this amount need not pay any additional Social Security for that year. The ceiling amount is determined by Congress, and is subject to change in future years as the average income level changes. The ceiling amount, which was only $4,800 prior to 1966, rose from $25,900 to almost $50,000 during the 1980s. The proper amount of Social Security tax is withheld from each worker's paycheck by the employer, who then turns it over to the government. This is not an optional sort of arrangement; the employer has a legal obligation to collect the money and faces sizable fines if the appropriate deductions aren't made.

Social Security is a little different from most forms of taxation in that benefits eventually accrue directly to the workers who pay the tax. In other words, people who pay money into the fund eventually take money back out, almost as if they'd put it in a savings account. Of course, the money doesn't just sit idle in the meantime, waiting for workers to collect their benefits. The government uses and invests the money for its own purposes, but it always ensures that enough remains within the fund to cover what is currently owed.

Income Tax Concepts

Income tax is the single largest source of revenue for the federal government. Money collected through taxes is used to finance a wide range of things, including highway and national park maintenance, higher education, research projects, national defense, and space exploration, just to name a few. Workers who pay income tax never see the money again, but they do receive indirect benefits from the services and facilities funded through their tax dollars.

Virtually all workers who earn more than a minimum income level are required to pay federal income tax. Unfortunately, determining what is owed is, for some workers, a complex task, and the correct answers are sometimes difficult to sort out. For one thing, certain expenditures or exemptions may reduce the amount of taxable income. Families with many dependents are not required to pay as much tax for a given amount of income. Further, taxpayers may deduct certain items: interest on mortgage payments or certain medical expenses, for instance.

Businesses pay income taxes as well. (In fact, the income earned by businesses that aren't corporations is taxed as personal income for the businesses' owners.) Corporations pay taxes at different rates from individuals, but even so, the ideas of deductions and exemptions still apply. A business may deduct, over time, the cost of a new computer or an air pollution control system, or may have certain income taxed differently because of the way it was earned. For both personal and corporate taxes, what items qualify for exemptions and deductions are determined by law. Like all elements of tax law, these are changing all the time.

In 1986, in fact, personal income tax laws underwent the most sweeping changes in the history of federal income tax. The full ramifications of these reforms are likely to be debated for some time to come. Among other things, the 1986 reforms created just two personal tax brackets: a 15 percent bracket and a 28 percent bracket, based on level of annual income. Prior to that time, there had been fifteen different brackets, ranging from 11 to 50 percent. The change was designed to simplify the federal tax system. However, because of numerous other changes, some observers would argue that the system as a whole remained as complex as ever.

Employers are required by law to deduct federal income tax from employees' paychecks, just as they have to take out Social Security contributions. This is true even for temporary employees. It is not true, however, of businesses and independent consultants who may be hired by a company to perform a specific service, such as giving legal advice or painting an office. Such contractors are responsible for managing their own taxes. (The business hiring a contractor must, however, file a 1099 form with the Internal Revenue Service to document what the contractor was paid.)

Income tax is based on gross earnings and is thus calculated prior to any other deductions (such as Social Security, for instance). Determining the amount of taxable income is a joint responsibility of employer and employee. The employee, usually at the time of employment, fills out a W-4 form on which he or she notes the number of withholding allowances that are being claimed. This is not an arbitrary number; in other words, a worker cannot claim ten withholding allowances just because she wants to. Definite guidelines, relating primarily to the number of dependents a worker has, are established by the government.

Once an employer has the information contained on the employee's W-4 form, the employer can refer to a tax table printed by the federal government to determine the amount of tax owed by that employee. Most larger companies use payroll software that has the tax tables built in, so the computer automatically figures the tax owed and deducts it from the gross pay. And while it's certainly possible for a small company to compute the deductions by hand, many hire a "payroll service" to do all of the math and keep track of the deductions.

Remember that self-employed persons have no deductions taken from their gross pay. They are responsible for calculating and mailing to the government their own Social Security and income tax payments.   Most self-employed persons pay taxes at least quarterly, and since they may not be on a fixed income, they need to estimate the amount of tax owed. This can be tricky. For instance, a legal consultant may do a booming business one quarter with income of about $20,000, but have very little work the next quarter, when her income falls to about $6,000. Since estimated tax is based on *annual* income, a worker whose income is this changeable will have to combine some good math skills with business intuition to arrive at a plausible estimate. (And since there are significant penalties for underpaying income tax throughout the year, keeping the tax payments in line with tax obligations is more than just an interesting exercise.) The corporate employee with a regular weekly income and an employer to handle a good share of the calculating does not usually have these worries.

If employers had to send the government information about income tax withholding and Social Security payments each pay period, the paperwork, for both the government and the employer, might become overwhelming. To simplify matters, the government asks that most employers account for the tax withholding every three months by filing a quarterly federal tax return. Of course, in order for this form to be totally accurate (and it is the employer's responsibility to ensure that it is) the company must maintain thorough, precise records of each employee's gross pay and deductions.

Don't get the idea, though, that a company can go for three months without giving any of the money deducted from employees to the government. Large employers usually have only three days after the end of the pay period to deposit the withheld money to special tax deposit accounts established at local banks. Employers with smaller tax liabilities get longer to pay, but only very small payrolls get to go the full three months between deposits.

Social Security Withholding

As mentioned, corporations have separate corporate income tax to deal with, but with respect to personal income tax, the employer sends in only what is deducted from employees' paychecks. In other words, if the Munchie Muffin Company deducts $15,000 for federal income tax during a pay period, that is the amount the company will put in the tax deposit account. Social Security, though, is another matter.

An employer is required by law to match the Social Security premiums of each employee. This is the reason that Social Security premiums are lower for employees than for self-employed persons. The total contribution is the same for persons of comparable income, but the self-employed person pays the full contribution, while the corporate employee pays only half of the full amount owed, the other half being paid by the employer. Thus, if Munchie Muffin collects $7,000 in Social Security payments from its employees during a pay period, Munchie must match that amount and deposit $14,000 in FICA payments for that pay period.

Other Withholdings

As mentioned earlier, most workers have several other deductions made from their paychecks each pay period. Some, like parking, may be a fixed amount for all workers. Others, like health insurance, may vary from worker to worker but still aren't related to pay.

But most workers end up paying a least some additional taxes that are based on earnings. State and local income taxes are common, as are unemployment insurance and state disability or workers' compensation insurance. Fortunately, all of these deductions are calculated the same way: by multiplying the tax rate times the applicable earnings.

Let's say that Willig earns exactly $1,000 in a pay period and that his state collects three percent of the employee's pay for state income tax. This means that in addition to Social Security contributions, federal income tax, and any other deductions, Willig will have $30 ($1,000 × .03) taken out for state income tax.

SOME WORDS OF ADVICE

It's a good idea for any employee to know precisely how taxes are calculated and how payroll deductions are determined. For example, filling out a W-4 form is not a task to be taken lightly, since it has substantial bearing on take-home pay. Further, the information on that form should be revised periodically. Circumstances change. Workers marry and divorce, gain and lose dependents. These new circumstances may well warrant a new W-4 form. Moreover, some change is probably called for if a worker is consistently having more or less income tax withheld in a year than is owed. And it's important to recognize that while the government will sometimes accept overwithholding without too much question, under-withholding of taxes is risky and can result in a substantial penalty.

Most workers know approximately how much they're paying each month (or year) in Social Security taxes, but many do not know just how much they'll receive in benefits upon retirement. The Social Security Administration is happy to provide this information, and asking for it is a good idea, for more than one reason. First, knowing one's retirement income is clearly important to good financial planning. But in addition, should there be an error in the computation, and it does happen, a worker normally has a grace period of only three years in which to correct the error. After that, it is often too late. Remember, this information is not automatically provided to workers; it must be specifically requested from the Social Security Administration.

Even a small company will end up withholding tens of thousands of dollars from employees' paychecks during a year, and the federal and state governments expect, not unreasonably, that a company's payroll records will be accurate and up-to-date. Close is never good enough in payroll matters, so even small companies have to master the intricacies of using withholding tables, completing quarterly tax reports, and making tax deposits. A company that's not confident that it is handling withholdings correctly should seek help from its accountant, or perhaps hire a payroll service to attend to the details on its behalf.

KEY TERMS

Before you read through the text assignment and watch the video program, take a minute to look at the key terms associated with this lesson. When you encounter them in the text and video program, pay careful attention to their meaning.

FICA: Federal Insurance Contributions Act. A federal act (law) requiring that a specified amount of money be collected from the paycheck of almost all employees and used to pay pensions, survivors' benefits, disability, and Medicare.

Gross earnings: The total amount of money earned by an employee before any deductions are taken.

Income tax withholding: Federal income tax withheld from gross earnings by the employer.

Net pay: The amount of money actually received by an employee after deductions are taken out of gross pay.

Personal income tax: A tax, based on income earned, that is charged to individuals by states and by the federal government.

Social Security: See FICA.

Withholding allowances: Allowances for employees and their spouses and dependents, that determine the amount of withholding tax taken from gross earnings.

PART II: WATCHING THE VIDEO PROGRAM

VIDEO VIEWING GUIDE

Before watching the video program, review the following questions. As you watch, be sure to collect the information necessary to answer them:

1. How has the amount of Social Security contributions changed for most taxpayers in recent years?

2. How is the amount of the Social Security contribution for each taxpayer determined?

3. In what ways does tax liability differ for corporate employees and self-employed persons?

4. How important is it for an individual taxpayer to correctly estimate the appropriate number of withholding allowances entered on a W-4 form? What are the implications of an inappropriate estimate?

5. When might it be important for a business manager or individual taxpayer to have professional consultation in determining tax liability?

6. What are the employer's primary responsibilities with respect to Social Security contributions and employees' income tax payments?

7. What are the employee's responsibilities with respect to Social Security tax and income tax?

8. How, if at all, does Social Security tax differ from other forms of tax withheld from employees' paychecks?

VIDEO PROGRAM

The lesson's video program is Program 6 — Social Security and Withholding. Remember, if you are watching this program on videotape, take time to replay sections of the tape any time you need to review a concept.

VIDEO VIEWING QUESTIONS

Immediately after viewing the video program for Lesson 6, take time to respond to the following questions. Give your answers some careful thought; they may provide the basis for additional discussion or a longer written response.

1. According to the video, which of the following factors would likely have some direct effect on the amount of an employee's take-home pay? (Check as many as apply.)

_____ The employee's age

_____ The amount of gross pay

_____ The amount of the Social Security deduction

_____ The number of withholding allowances claimed

_____ Contributions to a company pension plan

_____ Union dues

_____ A company monthly parking fee

_____ The quality of the worker's performance

_____ Length of time in the position

2. On this scale of 1 to 10, where would you rank the importance of an employee's knowing how to calculate his or her _own_ Social Security or income tax deductions?

Not   **Extremely**
important   **important**

1- - - - -2- - - - -3- - - - -4- - - - -5- - - - -6- - - - -7- - - - -8- - - - -9- - - - -10

3. On this scale of 1 to 10, where would you rank the importance of Social Security benefits as a source of income for retired persons?

Not   **Extremely**
important   **important**

1- - - - -2- - - - -3- - - - -4- - - - -5- - - - -6- - - - -7- - - - -8- - - - -9- - - - -10

4. According to the video, ensuring the accuracy of Social Security contributions and income tax deductions is a responsibility shared by the employer and employee. Briefly, name two steps in this process that are definitely the _employer's_ responsibility:

a. _____

b. _____

Now name two steps that are definitely the _employee's_ responsibility:

a. _____

b. _____

5. Name two specific ways in which the calculation of Social Security contributions or federal income tax is different for employees and self-employed persons:

a. _____

b. _____

6. According to the video, which of the following factors would most likely suggest a need to evaluate and perhaps modify the number of withholding allowances claimed on an employee's W-4 form? (Check as many as apply.)

_____ A rise in the inflation rate

_____ A very large tax refund at the end of the year

_____ The birth of a new child in the family

_____ A job change

_____ A raise in pay

_____ A new tax law forbidding deductions of interest on credit card debt

_____ A penalty for underpaying federal income tax

_____ A cost of living adjustment in Social Security benefits

PART III: FOCUSING ON THE MATHEMATICS

READING ASSIGNMENT

After watching the video program, you should read one of the following Text Assignments, depending on the textbook you're using:

SOFTCOVER: Pages 173-192 from Chapter 5 of the Miller, Salzman, and Hoelzle softcover text, *Business Mathematics*.

HARDCOVER: Pages 164-190 from Chapter 5 of the Salzman, Miller, and Hoelzle hardcover text, *Mathematics for Business*.

As you read through the text, pay careful attention to the examples the book gives of the mathematics associated with the concepts you're learning about.

Then, after you've completed the text assignment, read through the Key Formulas below. This section provides a handy review of what you've learned. By the time you get to this point in the lesson, all of the formulas and calculations should be familiar to you. If they're not, go back and read the appropriate parts of the text and the Overview section of this lesson. You won't have much success completing the rest of your assignments if you are still confused about the information in the Key Formulas section.

KEY FORMULAS

The following key formulas are important to your understanding of this lesson. Be sure that you know each one and how to use it in solving problems related to withholding.

KEY FORMULA: Social Security tax = Gross income × FICA tax rate

Formula used for: Determining the amount of Social Security tax an individual must pay.

Example:

Simply multiply the gross income times the rate of tax. For instance, if a worker's gross annual income is $40,000 and the Social Security tax rate is 7.51 percent, the amount of tax owed will be $40,000 × .0751 = $3,004.

Notice that in converting 7.25 percent to the correct decimal, we must move the decimal point two places *to the left* before multiplying. Otherwise, we would wind up with a total of $290,000 ($40,000 × 7.25), approximately seven times this worker's income!

Remember that in this formula:

1. Social Security tax is paid only up to a maximum income level; for instance, in a given year, there might be no Social Security tax on income over $50,000. This ceiling changes from time to time, as does the rate of the tax.

2. Social Security taxes have tended to go up steadily, both because the tax rate is higher and because the ceiling goes up.

3. Self-employed persons pay a higher Social Security tax. This is because the Social Security contribution of corporate employees is matched by the employer.

4. Social Security tax can easily be computed by hand but is usually determined by a table just to save a little calculating time.

KEY FORMULA: Net pay = Gross earnings − FICA tax − Federal withholding − State withholding − Other deductions

Formula used for: Calculating the take-home pay of a worker, given the gross pay.

Example:

Say that a given employee earns a total of $450 during the pay period but has the following deductions: FICA, $32; federal income tax withholding, $43; state income tax withholding, $25; health insurance, $18. The net income for this employee during this pay period will be $450 − ($32 + $43 + $25 + $18) = $332.

Remember that in this formula:

1. Net pay is what the employee can take home to spend; gross pay is the total amount earned during the period.

2. The amount of federal tax varies not only with income, but also with the number of withholding allowances the worker claims.

3. The number of withholding allowances a worker may legitimately claim varies *mainly* with the number of dependents. The number of withholding allowances claimed is determined by the employee (not the employer) under guidelines set by the federal government.

4. The amount of income tax is comparable for self-employed persons and corporate employees at the same income levels (in other words, self-employed workers do not pay *more* income tax). Remember, though, self-employed persons do have higher FICA deductions, since they don't have an employer paying half the total contribution.

5. While federal income tax rates and Social Security tax rates are consistent across the country, the nature and amount of other deductions varies from company to company and from state to state. In particular, workers pay higher state income taxes in some states than others.

KEY FORMULA: SDI deduction = Gross income × Rate

Formula used for: Many states require workers to pay a state disability insurance (SDI) premium that is a percentage of their earnings.

Example:

Calculate this by multiplying the amount of gross income times the rate of the premium. Thus, if a worker earns $400 during a pay period, and the SDI rate is .9 percent, the total deduction will be $400 × .009 = $3.60.

Remember that in this formula:

1. State disability insurance is only one deduction calculated according to this formula; others include state and federal unemployment taxes, some local taxes, and occasionally even taxes to support mass transit or special economic improvements. In each case, the tax rate is multiplied by the amount of gross income below the ceiling income, if any.

2. Most states require an SDI premium on only a portion of income, with no premium on additional income over that level.

3. For any of the deductions calculated this way, the rate varies from state to state. Even more important, not all states have the same deductions. For example, workers in some states don't pay any state income tax at all, while their counterparts in neighboring states might pay as much as 10 percent.

DON'T FORGET

1. To determine Social Security contributions or income tax liability, multiply *gross pay* times the appropriate tax rate.

2. Tax tables provided by federal and state governments save considerable calculation time—but be sure they're current!

3. Remember that while the rate at which Social Security contributions are determined does not vary with income level, there is a cutoff point beyond which no Social Security contributions are deducted from income earned.

4. Income tax rate, on the other hand, does vary with income level, but there is no cutoff point; beyond a certain minimum level, workers pay federal income tax on all income earned.

5. Social Security contributions and federal income tax rates are established by federal law and are subject to change over time.

6. Federal tax liability is affected by withholding allowances, but no such allowances apply to Social Security tax.

7. Employers must match their employees' Social Security contributions dollar for dollar; self-employed persons receive no such matching benefits and thus must pay both halves of the contribution.

PART IV: SOLVING BUSINESS PROBLEMS

PROBLEM SETS

Work the following problems in your textbook. Your instructor will tell you which problems, if any, are to be turned in. Some of the problems have answers provided in the back of the book; refer to these answers to make sure you are working the problems correctly.

SOFTCOVER: If you are using the Miller, Salzman, and Hoelzle softcover text, *Business Mathematics*, do the following problem sets:

> **5.3:** Problems #5-29 (odd numbers only) on pages 179-180.

> **5.4:** Problems #1-39 (odd numbers only) on pages 189-191.

HARDCOVER: If you are using the Salzman, Miller, and Hoelzle hardcover text, *Mathematics for Business*, do the following problem sets:

> **5.4:** Problems #12-40 (even numbers only) on pages 171-172.

> **5.5:** Problems #8-32 (even numbers only) and 33-36 on pages 180-182.

> **5.6:** Numbers #4-24 on pages 189-190.

BUSINESS APPLICATIONS

Read each of the following scenarios and answer the questions about the decisions you would make in each situation. Give these questions some serious thought; they may be used as the basis for discussion or the development of a more complex essay. You should base your decisions on what you've learned from this lesson, applying both math skills and good business judgment to solve the problem at hand.

SCENARIO 1

Grant is a self-employed artist who sells hand-finished furniture she makes herself. Her monthly income is highly variable, but her annual income has been remarkably consistent, averaging about $30,000 per year and increasing a few percent each year over the last several years. Her Social Security rate (given that she's a self-employed worker) is about 15 percent on the first $50,000 of income.

Grant has received a job offer at the Selected Artists Gallery, where she would continue her painting but also teach classes. The gallery would market and sell her work but would pay her no commission. Instead, she would receive a salary of $35,000 per year to cover her painting and teaching responsibilities. All required materials and supplies would be provided by the company, and all work produced by Grant would be the property of Selected Artists. The job includes an annual cost of living raise, which is variable but has averaged 4 percent per year over the last several years. In addition, Grant would have other mandatory deductions of $50 per month and must make a monthly pension contribution of 4 percent of her income, which is matched by her employer. She would also receive some significant health and medical insurance benefits.

What do you think? Should Grant accept the position with Selected Artists, or would she be better off to remain self-employed? What are some of the financial considerations involved? What nonfinancial considerations might influence Grant's decision? Which job offers the better rate of pay right now? Which is likely to offer the better rate of pay down the road?

☐ Should Grant accept the position with Selected Artists Gallery? Why or why not?

☐ The arrangement with Selected would substantially change how Grant is compensated for her paintings. What are the advantages and disadvantages of each approach?

☐ What specific steps are involved in setting up a fair comparison between these two positions (or any two jobs, for that matter)?

☐ How much money will Grant save by having an employer contribute part of her Social Security contribution? Does this seem an important reason to take the Selected position?

SCENARIO 2   Klein is a divorced mother of three school-age children. She works as a surgical nurse and receives an annual gross income of $42,000. She claims two withholding allowances on her W-4 form and usually receives a federal income tax refund of $1,000 or more, which she and the children spend on a vacation together. They look forward to this experience each year, viewing it as sort of a gift from the Internal Revenue Service.

Klein's tax consultant suggests, however, that this is an unsophisticated way of looking at the matter. He encourages Klein to increase the number of withholding allowances she is claiming from two to four. If she increases the withholding allowances, she will likely have little, if any, refund at the end of the year and could even wind up owing a small amount (probably less than $50) in federal taxes. But this change would effectively increase her monthly net income by just over $90 — an amount, the consultant points out, that she would then be free to invest as she saw fit. Klein isn't sure this would be such a good idea, however. She isn't sure she wants the responsibility of managing "investments." Everything seems very simple as it is, and she likes being able to count on that big tax refund each year; her children look forward to the vacation, too, and she doesn't want to disappoint them. Why complicate life?

The tax consultant tells her that managing the investments is no big deal; if she wants, she can just put the $90 into a money market account each month and let it sit there. Or she could buy a certificate of deposit every now and then. Either way, she should make close to $100 a year in interest. Of course, she'll have to pay some taxes on that interest, but even so, she'll certainly come out ahead. Besides, the government wants you to complete your W-4 accurately, and while he personally doesn't know of anyone who got in trouble for overwithholding, it's technically not right.

What do you think? Should Klein follow the consultant's advice and increase her withholding allowances to four? What are the implications of doing this? What benefits is she likely to gain? What problems is she likely to encounter?

☐ Should Klein follow her tax consultant's advice in this case? Why or why not?

☐ About how much money is Klein currently giving up, given that she'll have to pay taxes on any interest she earns on the extra money?

☐ Klein's tax consultant is assuming the extra $90 per month will be invested to earn interest. But maybe Klein will spend the money instead, leaving her with no money at the end of the year. Do you think there is any merit in using overwithholding as sort of a forced savings plan? Why or why not?

☐ In general, under what circumstances should an individual taxpayer consider revising the number of withholding allowances on a W-4 form?

Sales and Property Taxes 7

Taxation without representation is tyranny.

James Otis

Taxation with representation ain't so hot either.

Gerald F. Lieberman

Because paying taxes is inevitable and usually unavoidable, it's easy to overlook the fact that in paying taxes, citizens are really purchasing services like road repair, education, or police protection, in much the same way that consumers purchase other kinds of services from private businesses. Of course, there are important differences. When consumers purchase services from a private agency, they can sometimes refuse to pay if those services do not meet their expectations. As taxpayers, we have the right to protest if we do not like the way the government spends our money and we can sometimes vote on how it's spent. But when it comes to deciding how tax dollars will be allocated, it's the decision of the community as a whole, not the decision of the individual taxpayer, that counts most. An individual taxpayer may not like the idea that a certain percentage of property tax goes to school funding, for instance; but once that kind of decision has been made, individual taxpayers cannot request that their contributions be spent differently.

Ultimately, no matter how much they complain, most citizens do acknowledge that tax dollars provide benefits. After all, government provides services of the size and scope most private agencies would be hard pressed to take on; highway construction, for instance, or maintenance of state parks. Such services would be very difficult for citizens to provide individually, or even collectively, without government help. A few taxpayers could educate their children at home, a few others might propose that the parks be closed. But how many would also want to recruit their own police protection, build their own roads, install water and sewer pipes, build hydroelectric dams, or hire their own firefighters? Because tax dollars are used to serve these general public needs, individuals in our society usually do not have to worry about doing these things for themselves.

In this lesson, we'll consider two important types of tax that help fund government services: sales tax and property tax. The large majority of people who own property in this country are taxed on that property. Property tax rates are highly variable from one area to another, however, and a handful of states don't have property taxes. Similarly, sales tax affects *most* people who purchase goods and services, but not all. A couple of states have no statewide sales tax and many areas don't have local sales tax. Further, the kinds of purchases that are taxed differ from one region to another. This lesson takes a closer look at each kind of tax, the way in which tax revenues are calculated, and a few of the ways in which tax revenues are used.

PART I: INTRODUCING THE MATERIAL

LEARNING OBJECTIVES

Upon completing your study of this lesson, you should be able to:

1. Give examples of the ways merchants calculate sales tax due, as well as some of the concerns a merchant has in collecting and recording the tax.

2. Calculate the tax due and total amount due, given a sales tax rate and the amount of a sale.

3. Define fair market value and assessed valuation.

4. Express a given property tax rate in percent, dollars per $100, dollars per $1,000, and mils.

5. Use the fair market value to find assessed valuation, given the ratio between the two.

6. Determine the property tax, given the assessed valuation and tax rate.

If you're using the hardcover textbook, *Mathematics for Business*, there are some additional objectives for this lesson. Upon completing your study of the lesson, you should also be able to:

7. Find the amount of a sale when the sales tax rate and the total price including tax are given.

8. Define excise tax and give examples of products and services on which an excise tax is paid.

9. Calculate the excise tax due, given the tax rate and the amount of the product or the total of the sale, as appropriate.

10. Calculate the property tax rate, given the assessed valuation, and the amount of the tax payment or the assessed valuation, given the tax rate and tax payment.

11. Determine the total tax payment due, given the assessed valuation and the tax rates of the individual taxing authorities.

The largest single source of revenue for federal and state governments is income tax, a tax based on workers' salaries or wages. Federal income tax funds the national defense, space exploration, housing and welfare programs, some education and environmental programs, and the administration of government itself. State income tax funds similar kinds of programs at the state level. Often, states do not get all the resources they need from income tax alone. Both state and local governments, however, can draw from two other sources: sales tax and property tax. These two types of tax are the focus of this lesson.

Sales Tax Concepts

Almost all states now have a statewide sales tax. And within those states, some counties and cities have their own sales tax as well. So, if a consumer buys a couch from a store that charges a 6 percent state sales tax and a 1 percent city sales tax, the consumer will pay a total of 7 percent in sales tax (6% + 1%) on that item. And if there's an additional county tax of 1 percent, the total sales tax will be 8 percent (6% + 1% + 1%).

Notice how much difference this apparently small amount of tax can make in the final cost of an item. A $500 couch, for instance, will cost the consumer $540 if there is an 8 percent sales tax. By the way, that $540 is not the figure that will be reflected on the price tag. That's because from the merchant's point of view, the couch really *does* sell for $500. None of the sales tax revenue goes into the merchant's pocket. The merchant merely collects the money and then turns it over to the government.

Every tax must have some way of determining how much each taxpayer will pay. With income tax, for instance, the basis is what the taxpayer earns. Workers who earn more, overall, tend to pay more tax. With sales tax, the basis is what the customer purchases. Though in some states certain items are exempt from sales tax, it's generally fair to say that consumers who spend the most money will usually pay the highest amount of sales tax.

What purchases get taxed is a matter determined by the state legislature when it passes the tax bills. Prescription drugs may be exempted, for instance, and in some states, tax isn't charged on food items. Interestingly, however, while a consumer may purchase a steak at the local supermarket and pay no sales tax on it, if she buys that same steak at the restaurant down the street, there will be a sales tax. Of course, in that case, what she's being taxed on is not just the food itself, but the "luxury" of eating it in a restaurant where someone else does all the work.

Whether consumers pay sales tax on mail order items depends on where they live. Let's say that Washington resident Armstrong orders a pair of $75 hiking boots from a company in Seattle. She'll have to add Washington state sales tax to the order. But if she orders the same hiking boots from a company in Montana that has no facilities or employees in Washington, will she have to pay sales tax? While the laws could be changed at any time, at the moment she doesn't pay a penny in sales tax.

Some lawmakers, and some consumers, look on sales tax as one of the more fair forms of taxation, noting that persons who can afford to spend the most will pay the largest share of tax. This sounds logical enough in theory, though it's hard to say whether those who can afford to spend the most are the same people who in fact do spend the most. Proponents of sales taxes often suggest that having a sizable sales tax allows governments to lower other taxes (income tax or property tax) because the sales tax will produce much of the necessary revenue. Taxpayers generally tend to be skeptical about such arguments, however; perhaps justifiably so, since the majority of citizens paying sales taxes also pay income and property taxes.

Computing Sales Tax

Calculating sales tax is a one-step arithmetic problem, nothing more. And since only a simple multiplication is required, the process isn't difficult. (Still, consumers who don't carry pocket calculators with them everywhere will do well to know how to estimate these taxes by hand.) Remember, though, to convert the percentage of tax to a decimal before multiplying. Thus, a tax of 5 percent becomes .05 and a tax of 3 percent becomes .03. Simply multiply this decimal by the purchase price to determine the amount of tax owed.

A quick way to mentally calculate sales tax on larger purchases is to think of a 5 percent rate, for instance, as meaning $5 of tax for each $100 owed. This kind of approximation isn't very useful, of course, on small purchases, but then a customer buying a candy bar isn't likely to be too concerned about sales tax. To the customer contemplating buying a new automobile, though, the sales tax could be well over $1,000.

Perhaps surprisingly, sales personnel usually do not have to worry about computing sales tax—either by hand or with the aid of a calculator. Most cash register systems these days are computerized, and the computer can be programmed to figure the sales tax on various items automatically. In a grocery store, for instance, each item is coded with a bar code, a series of vertical lines that mean little to the consumer but are quite readable to the computer. When the clerk passes a product over the bar code scanner, the computer identifies the item and automatically registers any state, local, or excise (luxury) tax that applies to that item. Obviously, though, not every store is this computerized, so merchants also work with tax tables, looking up the amount owed on taxable items. This isn't quite as efficient or fast as computerized calculations, but it does reduce human error in computing sales tax compared to manual calculations.

Excise Taxes

The federal, state, or local government sometimes charges special taxes on certain items that, for one reason or another, it decides to tax differently. These are still sales taxes in the sense that they are charged at the time of the sale, but they apply only to a single item. Originally, the idea was to put a *luxury tax* on some nonessential items; the government would get extra income without causing much hardship to anyone. Of course, one person's "luxury" may be another's "essential," and one could quibble about things like diesel fuel being taxed as luxury items. In truth, these days luxury taxes are better viewed as *excise taxes*, taxes that are charged on specific items. The list of items that are taxed in this way is broad and varied; the federal government taxes tires, airplane tickets, even coal, while local governments commonly put taxes on such things as hotel rooms, theater tickets, and rental cars.

Sometimes, the rationale for applying an excise tax is a little difficult to unearth. For example, telephone service and gasoline are both subject to excise taxes. But is a telephone a luxury? Is gasoline? To the traveling salesperson who depends on both to make a living, this might seem a very strange way of looking at things. But the government has a slightly different perspective. Basically, any item or service is a candidate for being taxed if enough of the lawmakers at the local (or state or national) level want the revenue produced by the tax. Besides, much of the excise tax charged on gasoline and diesel fuel is used to help pay for repairs on roads; local taxes on hotel rooms might support a new convention center. In other words, an excise tax is often simply a sort of users' fee.

Unlike most sales taxes, excise tax is often included in the purchase price of an item, and it's sometimes based on a flat fee rather than a percentage of the total price. For instance, the customer who fills his gas tank often pays in the neighborhood of $.20 a gallon in federal and state excise taxes, but that amount remains the same regardless of whether the gas sells for $1 or $2 per gallon. And because of the way excise taxes work, consumers are often unaware that they are even paying such a tax. Or they may know it but not know how much of the purchase price goes for taxes.

Property Tax

The basis of property tax is ownership of real property or personal property. *Real property* is defined as land or anything attached to the land, including buildings, roadways, wells, and so forth. *Personal property* includes any possessions that are movable: cars, trucks and automobiles, mobile homes, paintings, antiques, furniture, even clothing. Virtually all areas of the country have property tax in some form.

Each item of property taxed must first be *assessed* to determine its *fair market value*. The fair market value is the amount the property could reasonably be expected to sell for on the open market. This value is not determined by the property owner, but rather by a professional assessor who looks at hundreds or thousands of comparable properties and who is well acquainted with what buyers are currently paying (which is another way of saying that the assessor knows the current market). He or she will likely know, for instance, whether nearby freeway access adds much to the value of a commercial property, or whether a residential property is enhanced by having a fenced yard. These and hundreds of similar factors will be considered in determining the fair market value. This is not the figure on which the property tax is based, however.

Instead, property tax is based on the *assessed valuation*. In some areas, this is 100 percent of the fair market value; in other words, it's the same figure. But in other areas, the assessed valuation is some smaller percentage of the fair market value, perhaps 50 or 75 percent. Let's say Newman lives in an area where the property tax is 6 percent. His house has a fair market value of $100,000 but an assessed valuation of 50 percent of that figure, or $50,000. Newman will thus pay a property tax of $50,000 × .06, or $3,000. That's only half what he would pay if the assessed valuation equalled the fair market value of his home.

Determining Assessed Valuations

Many things influence property values for both commercial and residential property. But the bottom line is: What could the property sell for, given current market conditions? Location may have as much to do with property value as any other factor, but even the value of a location is not constant. Surroundings change with time. Consider a home on a quiet lane in the country, a property with an average fair market value. Over time, however, say that this quiet lane is transformed into a six-lane arterial highway, bringing its share of noise and pollution into the area. As scenic hills and woodlands are cleared to make way for shopping centers, parking lots, new roads, and office buildings, residential property values in the area may change dramatically.

Notice that while the house hasn't actually moved an inch, its location has changed just as much as if it had. The impact of this change will need to be assessed carefully. The assessed value may go down if most prospective buyers feel the home no longer offers the peace and tranquility of country living; or it may increase, given that it is now more convenient to shopping, offices, and the other conveniences afforded by city life. Obviously, assessing property values is not a simple task.

Keep in mind that while the property assessment determines the taxable value of property, it does not determine what the *property tax rate* will be. That depends on how much tax money is to be collected by a given tax; that is, on the amount of the tax levy. Who decides what the tax levy will be depends on the situation. The U.S. Congress determines federal taxes, state legislators usually determine state taxes, and local officials determine local taxes. In every case, those decision makers are ultimately responsible to the people who elected them. But sometimes, particularly on local tax matters, the voters themselves decide whether to pass a tax levy. When this happens, the voters are directly deciding whether to charge themselves a certain amount of money in order to buy some service.

Calculating Tax Rates

The tax base is another factor that's involved in calculating the tax rate. The tax base is the assessed valuation of everything that will be taxed under the particular levy. A metropolitan area with lots of complex roads to maintain, lots of city parks and sidewalks, large school systems, county-financed health centers, a big library, and so forth will have a lot to spend tax dollars on, but will likely have a large tax base to match. A rural area with a small school, gravel roads, no sidewalks, no parks, and no local health facilities is going to need less tax revenue. On the other hand, though, the rural area also has relatively less of value to tax to raise the needed funds.

The tax rate is simply the tax levy divided by the tax base. If a levy for $1 million to fund a library is passed in an area with a tax base of $500 million, the tax rate is $1 for each $500 dollars of assessed valuation. If the library needed twice as much from the same taxpayers, the tax rate would be $2 for each $500. But suppose that the tax base also became twice as big. Then it would be necessary to collect the $2 million on $1 billion of assessed valuation. This means the rate is back down to $2 per $1,000, which is the same as $1 for each $500 of assessed valuation.

So the rate depends on two things: how much money is needed (the tax levy) and the value of the property that can be taxed (the tax base). Let's say that a local community is planning to build a new high school using money from an education budget funded by property taxes. In this case, the amount of tax money needed increases by whatever amount it costs to fund the new school. If the total assessed value of taxable property in the area is *not* increasing, individual taxpayers will have to pay a higher tax rate.

Compare that situation with a similar circumstance in which a community builds a new school because it anticipates 500 families moving into the area. Again, the amount of tax money needed will go up because of the school construction. However, there will probably be a lot of new construction in the area (homes, stores, offices) to accommodate the new residents. That means that the tax base will go up, which means that more money can be collected without changing the tax rate.

Taxes vary from area to area across the country, even for highly comparable properties. Let's say that Wade owns a three-bedroom ranch house on a one-acre piece of property in rural North Dakota. The house is assessed at $70,000. A very similar house, built the same year, with the same number of square feet, on the same size piece of land just outside San Francisco might be assessed at ten times that amount. What makes the difference? Proximity to a major city, for one thing. And availability of land, for another. In San Francisco, large numbers of buyers are competing for a small amount of available property, and a one-acre parcel close to the city would be considered a rare find. But in rural North Dakota land is more abundant, while the potential buyers are more rare. This difference has an enormous impact on land values.

Changes in
Assessed
Valuation

Because property is constantly increasing or decreasing in value, it must be reassessed periodically. Any major change (constructing a new building, remodeling an existing building, or improving the property with a new road or utilities) is likely to invite a new assessment of that property, and with it an increase in the property tax owed. Even if the property goes unchanged, assessment is likely to be conducted on a regular cycle (often every three to five years) because inflation alone will tend to increase property values. And sometimes owners themselves request an assessment; for example, when they think that a general increase in assessments applied to their neighborhood shouldn't apply to their property.

Property owners sometimes have an almost irrational fear of assessment because they link it with a sure increase in taxes. But that increase is not automatic. For one thing, property values do not necessarily increase appreciably with each new assessment. For another, the tax rate is often lowered when the assessed valuation is increased. The thing that makes taxes go up is the need to raise more money; if the amount of money to be raised remained constant, an increase in assessed valuation would be matched by a drop in the tax rate.

SOME WORDS OF ADVICE

Most states charge a state sales tax, but the rate does vary from state to state. If you travel, it's a good idea to keep track of the rate for each state, so you have no surprises when it comes to paying for items. Certain things are likely to be exempt; local citizens and merchants can tell you which items these are. Keep in mind that in an area with state or local sales tax, the price marked on the item is not the total cost; it does not include the sales tax.

New sales and property taxes are being proposed constantly, and voters sometimes have a say in whether to accept these new taxes or do without the services they would fund. Knowing how to compute these taxes can help you, as a voter, make a responsible decision. You need to know, first, exactly how the money will be used and, second, how many dollars it will cost you individually to support the new tax. If you know the proposed tax rate and the assessed valuation of your property, you can easily determine what any new tax will cost you.

Keep in mind that two factors determine how much property tax you will pay: one is the assessed valuation of all the taxable property in your area, and the other is the amount of money needed to fund proposed services. If these increase or decrease together, the tax rate tends to remain pretty stable. If funding needs increase faster than the assessed valuation, the tax rate goes up. When the reverse is true, the tax rate goes down.

Finally, remember that there is a direct link between taxes and community services. Very few citizens are good sports all the time when it comes to paying taxes. And some complaints are legitimate, if rates are unfairly high or if services are lacking. But the real question is not whether taxes in general are a good idea, but whether the community is receiving its fair share of quality services for the tax dollars it is spending. Only by gaining a thorough and accurate picture of how your tax money is spent can you really answer this question.

KEY TERMS

Before you read through the text assignment and watch the video program, take a minute to look at the key terms associated with this lesson. When you encounter them in the text and video program, pay careful attention to their meaning.

Assessed valuation: The value assigned by the assessor to a piece of property for property tax purposes. This value may or may not match the fair market value of the property. It cannot be higher than the fair market value, but it may be a smaller percentage of that value.

Assessment: The procedure by which a local official called the assessor inspects a property and makes an estimate of its fair market value.

Excise tax: A tax charged on specific items selected for taxation by state or local government agencies. Also called a *luxury tax*, excise tax was originally applied to items considered nonessential (such as fishing rods, firearms, alcoholic beverages, cigarettes, and pet food). These days, however, there are also excise taxes on such essentials as tires and gasoline.

Mil: One tenth of a cent or one thousandth of a dollar. In decimal figures, one mil is .001 of a dollar; ten mils equal one cent. (Sometimes spelled mill.)

Personal property: Property that is movable and not attached to land. This might include furnishings, automobiles, boats, mobile homes, or money. Personal property is distinguished from real property (land and buildings), which is considered unmovable. Real property is often taxed by state and local governments; personal property is also taxed, but by fewer governments.

Property tax rate: For property, find the tax rate by dividing the total amount of tax revenue needed by the total assessed valuation of taxable property.

Real property: Land, buildings, and other improvements (such as a well) attached to the land.

Sales tax: A tax consumers pay on items they purchase. Almost every state charges a sales tax; in some areas, the consumer will also pay a county or city tax (and sometimes both).

PART II: WATCHING THE VIDEO PROGRAM

VIDEO VIEWING GUIDE

Before watching the video program, review the following questions. As you watch, be sure to collect the information necessary to answer them:

1. What is the basis for sales tax? In other words, how does the government decide who pays and how much they pay?

2. What is the basis for property tax? Why not just have a bigger sales tax and forget about property taxes, or vice versa?

3. How are sales and excise (or luxury) taxes similar? What are some of the ways that they're different?

4. Why is property reassessed periodically? Is it to get more money for the government, or is it principally to make sure that taxes are assessed equitably?

5. What factors are most likely to affect property values for commercial property? For residential property?

6. Under what circumstances would the amount of property tax paid by a property owner increase? Under what circumstances would the rate of property tax paid by a property owner increase?

7. How might life in your community be different if there were no sales or property tax?

VIDEO PROGRAM

The lesson's video program is Program 7 — Sales and Property Taxes. Remember, if you are watching this program on videotape, take time to replay sections of the tape any time you need to review a concept.

VIDEO VIEWING QUESTIONS

Immediately after viewing the video program for Lesson 7, take time to respond to the following questions. Give your answers some careful thought; they may provide the basis for additional discussion or a longer written response.

1. Name two important conceptual differences between sales tax and property tax.

   a. _____

   b. _____

2. Sales and property taxes are automatically computed for the consumer. Given that, is it worthwhile for taxpayers to be able to calculate sales and property taxes for themselves? Why or why not?

_____

_____

3. Put a check next to the five factors you think would have the greatest long-term impact on *residential* property values.

_____ Current property tax rate

_____ Initial cost of property

_____ Quality of the environment (air and water)

_____ Quality of schools

_____ Size of the metropolitan area

_____ Whether the community's population is growing

_____ Proximity to major highways

_____ Proximity to railroads

_____ Proximity to major cities

_____ Cost of electricity and other utilities

_____ Property value of similar properties across the country

_____ Whether residents like living in the community

_____ Occupations of people in the community

_____ Education level of people in the community

_____ Average age of residents in the community

_____ Whether land is suitable for farming

_____ Climate

4. Now put a check next to the five factors you think would have the greatest impact on *business* property values.

_____ Current property tax rate

_____ Initial cost of property

_____ Quality of the environment (air and water)

_____ Quality of schools

_____ Size of the metropolitan area

_____ Whether the community's population is growing

_____ Proximity to major highways

_____ Proximity to railroads

_____ Proximity to major cities

_____ Cost of electricity and other utilities

_____ Property value of similar properties across the country

_____ Whether residents like living in the community

_____ Occupations of people in the community

_____ Education level of people in the community

_____ Average age of residents in the community

_____ Whether land is suitable for farming

_____ Climate

5. Using the list from Question 4, list three factors that would have a greater impact on the value of property used for manufacturing than for office or retail purposes.

a. _____

b. _____

c. _____

6. If both sales and property tax were discontinued in a given community, which of the following do you think might result? (Check as many as apply.)

_____ More people would want to move to the community

_____ Income tax for residents would also go down

_____ Some schools would close

_____ Commercial property values would go up

_____ Selling homes would become easier, and homes would sell for more

_____ The community would attract lots of new businesses

_____ Parks would no longer be well maintained

_____ Spending would increase, especially on expensive items

_____ People would drive their cars more

_____ Employment would increase

7. Imagine a small town with a population of about 3,000 people. The town has almost no industry; it is basically an agricultural community with lots of ranches and farms. The downtown commercial section of the community is limited in size, with only a few shops. Suddenly oil is discovered, and almost overnight the community changes. A major oil company buys leases on much of the nearby land, and the community is projected to triple in size during the next two years. New schools will need to be built, a couple of new trailer parks will open, and there will be substantial new housing construction for the first time in ten years. In three or four sentences, describe how you think these changes will affect property values and property taxes in this community.

_____

_____

_____

_____

PART III: FOCUSING ON THE MATHEMATICS

READING ASSIGNMENT

After watching the video program, you should read one of the following Text Assignments, depending on the textbook you're using:

SOFTCOVER: Pages 447-452 from Chapter 11 of the Miller, Salzman, and Hoelzle softcover text, *Business Mathematics.*

HARDCOVER: Pages 199-212 from Chapter 6 of the Salzman, Miller, and Hoelzle hardcover text, *Mathematics for Business.*

As you read through the text, pay careful attention to the examples the book gives of the mathematics associated with the concepts you're learning about.

Then, after you've completed the text assignment, read through the Key Formulas below. This section provides a handy review of what you've learned. By the time you get to this point in the lesson, all of the formulas and calculations should be familiar to you. If they're not, go back and read the appropriate parts of the text and the Overview section of this lesson. You won't have much success completing the rest of your assignments if you are still confused about the information in the Key Formulas section.

KEY FORMULAS

The following key formulas are important to your understanding of this lesson. Be sure that you know each one and how to use it in solving problems related to sales and property taxes.

KEY FORMULA:	Tax rate = Amount to be collected ÷ Total assessed value
Formula used for:	Determining the rate of property tax, given the total assessed value and the amount of money to be raised by the tax.
Alternate form:	Total amount levied = Total assessed value × Tax rate

Example:

If the community authorizes a levy of $1 million to pay for a new recreation center and the total assessed valuation of the community is $1 billion, the tax rate will be $1,000,000 ÷ $1,000,000,000. This is the same as 1 ÷ 1,000, which is .001. In this case, then, the tax rate is $1 for every $1,000 of assessed valuation.

Remember that in this formula:

1. The tax rate in this formula will come out as a decimal number, like .001 or .02. This decimal can then be converted into any other means of expressing tax rate, such as dollars per hundred or dollars per thousand.

2. The amount to be collected is the amount levied by any one tax. In our example, we were given the levy for the new recreational center and we found the tax rate for that project. The rate for this tax is completely different from the rate for the school district, the water district, or the state government. Each property owner pays taxes equal to the sum of the money due from all these individual taxes.

3. The total assessed value refers to the sum total of *all* taxable property within the area covered by the levy. Often property owners will be part of several different tax bases. For instance, two property owners might be taxed for the same city government but for different school districts. The tax base for the city government will, therefore, be different from the tax base for either of the two school districts.

KEY FORMULA:	Tax = Tax rate × Assessed valuation
Formula used for:	Determining the tax to be paid on a specific property or group of properties.
Alternate form:	Tax rate = Tax ÷ Assessed valuation

Example:

If the annual tax for the local school district is $5.33 per $1,000 of assessed valuation, a taxpayer with a home assessed at $150,000 would pay ($5.33 ÷ 1,000) × $150,000, which is very close to $800.

Remember that in this formula:

1. You will be solving for a dollar figure, the *amount* of tax to be paid by an individual property owner. (Remember, though, that the total property tax bill will be the sum of all the individual taxes.)

2. The tax rate may be expressed as a percentage (for example, 1 percent), as mils per dollar (10 mils per $1), as dollars per hundred ($1 per $100) or as dollars per thousand ($10 per $1,000).

3. If the tax rate is expressed in mils, remember to move the decimal point *three* places to the left to convert mils to a decimal figure. For example, 15 mils becomes .015 and 500 mils becomes .500.

4. The way in which the tax rate is expressed (whether it's 6 percent or $6 per $100 or $60 per $1,000) does not affect the amount of tax owed. In other words, the effective rate for a given piece of property in a given area remains the same no matter how that rate is expressed.

5. Remember, the *assessed valuation* may or may not be the same figure as the fair market value of a property. The fair market value is the price the property could reasonably be expected to sell for on the open market. The assessed valuation is a percentage of the fair market value. For instance, say a house has a fair market value of $160,000, meaning that we would expect it to sell for about that amount. The assessed valuation might be 100 percent of that figure, in which case it would be the same: $160,000. Or it might be 50 percent of the fair

market value, or $80,000. Or it might be 25 percent of the fair market value, or $40,000. These percentages vary from area to area and are set by local government officials in charge of assessment. In other words, knowing the fair market value of a property will not allow you to predict the taxes for that property until you *also* know the percentage of fair market value at which the assessed valuation is set.

KEY FORMULA:	Sales tax = Selling price × Tax rate
Formula used for:	Determining the amount of sales tax charged on an item (or items) having a certain selling price.
Alternate form:	*This formula is a special case of the familiar P = B × R formula; see the comments below.*

Example:

If a desk sells for $700 and there is a sales tax of 5 percent, find the amount of the tax by multiplying $700 × .05. This tells us the sales tax is $35.

Up to this point, we've found the amount of the tax, but *not* the total cost of the item to the customer. To find that, we must add the original selling price to the amount of the tax. Thus, the total cost is $700 + $35, or $735.

This is the total amount (selling price + sales tax) the customer pays for the desk. But remember, the price written on the sales tag will be $700. The $35 sales tax is added on when the customer pays for the purchase.

Remember that in this formula:

1. This formula is based on the familiar P = B × R formula used in many business math calculations. In this example:

   P = part, which in this case is $35, the amount of sales tax;

   B = base, which in this case is $700, the price of the desk; and

   R = rate, which in this case is 5 percent (.05), the percentage of the selling price assessed as sales tax.

2. If both the state and the county (or city) charge sales tax, these figures must be added together to determine the total sales tax levied. For instance, a state sales tax of 6 percent plus a local tax of 2 percent results in a total sales tax of 8 percent.

3. This formula may or may not work for calculating an excise tax. That's because excise (or luxury) taxes may be a percentage of the total sale like sales tax, or they may be assessed as a flat fee based on the amount sold. For instance, an excise tax on imported sweaters might be 4 percent of the wholesale selling price, while excise tax on gasoline might be $.10 per gallon.

DON'T FORGET

1. Fair market value and assessed valuation are not the same thing. Fair market value is the price a professional assessor estimates a property could sell for on the open market. The assessed valuation is some percentage of that fair market value assigned to the property for the

purpose of determining property tax. Sometimes the assessed valuation is equal to 100 percent of the fair market value, but not always. It may be only half or three-fourths (or some other fraction) of the fair market value. Remember that property tax is always computed on the assessed valuation, not on the fair market value of the property.

2. Property values change with time and new assessed valuations are assigned periodically, when property is improved or when a specified length of time has passed. Property tax rates also change, but not necessarily at the same time. If either the rate or the assessed valuation changes, the amount of property tax will change.

3. Property taxes can be expressed in a number of ways: as a percentage of assessed valuation, as dollars per hundred, as dollars per thousand, or as mils per dollar of assessed valuation. These variations do not affect the total amount of tax owed by a given property owner. They are just different ways of calculating the amount of the tax, which remains constant no matter how it is expressed.

PART IV: SOLVING BUSINESS PROBLEMS

PROBLEM SETS

Work the following problems in your textbook. Your instructor will tell you which problems, if any, are to be turned in. Some of the problems have answers provided in the back of the book; refer to these answers to make sure you are working the problems correctly.

SOFTCOVER: If you are using the Miller, Salzman, and Hoelzle softcover text, *Business Mathematics*, do the following problem sets:

    4.2: Problems #27 and 33 on pages 114-115.

    11.1: Problems #1-26 on pages 451-452.

HARDCOVER: If you are using the Salzman, Miller, and Hoelzle hardcover text, *Mathematics for Business*, do the following problem sets:

    6.1: Problems #2-38 (even numbers only) and 39-42 on pages 204-206.

    6.2: Problems #2-34 (even numbers only) and 35-42 on pages 210-211.

BUSINESS APPLICATIONS

Read each of the following scenarios and answer the questions about the decisions you would make in each situation. Give these questions some serious thought; they may be used as the basis for discussion or the development of a more complex essay. You should base your decisions on what you've learned from this lesson, applying both math skills and good business judgment to solve the problem at hand.

SCENARIO 1   Andreas has a dream. He wants to own and operate his own ice cream parlor. He has a large amount of his own money to invest in this venture and thinks he can secure a loan at the bank for another $25,000 or so. Given that, he has two options, both of which seem fairly appealing.

Option A involves a small, very busy ice cream store in a downtown area that's currently undergoing a lot of renovation. The store is located about three blocks outside the heart of the downtown shopping district in an area of older shops and apartments, many of which are now being torn down or remodeled. A new parking area is being constructed nearby; Andreas is unsure what other changes or improvements are planned. There are a number of offices within walking distance of the area, so there is a lot of foot traffic. Andreas thinks business will probably continue to be good. Currently, the property has an assessed valuation of $75,000 and the property taxes are $2.20 per $100 for the current year.

Option B involves a somewhat larger ice cream store on the outskirts of a rapidly expanding suburban area with substantial growth projected over the next five to ten years. Right now, the shop is in a very small shopping complex with only two other stores (a small grocery and a dry cleaning establishment), but the area is zoned for commercial development and Andreas has heard rumors that the area will soon have a major mall serving thousands of patrons. It's a little hard to imagine, though, since right now there are only bare fields for as far as the eye can see. Still, some new housing developments are springing up within a mile or two. There will be little or no foot traffic for now, though; customers must drive to this store. The property has an assessed valuation of $120,000 and property taxes are $19.25 per $1,000.

Andreas likes the location of Property B better. He likes the idea of living in the country himself. Also, he'd like to live close to the store and knows that housing is less expensive in the suburbs. On the other hand, business is at least 30 percent better at Store A, which makes it look more desirable. But who can say whether that will hold true for the future?

What do you think? Should Andreas buy Property A in the heart of the downtown district? Or should he take a chance on B, which is now pretty much out in the country? Which will be the better business move in the long run? And which factors should Andreas consider in making his decision?

☐   Would you advise Andreas to buy Property A or Property B? What reasons would you give?

☐   What is likely to happen to the assessed valuation of each of the two properties?

☐   Should Andreas be trying to get the property with the higher assessed valuation or the lower, or doesn't it make much difference?

☐   Which of the two properties costs more? Is there any way to tell which is the better deal from their assessed valuations?

☐   What additional information could Andreas get that would make his decision easier? How would he go about getting that information?

McDuff is trying to decide whether to remodel her house. It's among the smaller homes in the neighborhood, and with two children living at home, it's beginning to feel crowded. McDuff does a lot of entertaining and could use more space. Plans include a new kitchen/family room combination with a greenhouse and expansive deck.

SCENARIO 2

The current assessed valuation of the house is $82,500. After the addition, that assessed valuation is projected to increase to $110,000. However, the assessor says he cannot give a final figure until he sees the actual addition; it might be a little higher or a little lower than the estimate, which he's basing on his review of the building blueprints.

The property tax rate in McDuff's area is now **4** percent. She lives in a rapidly growing suburb with lots of new families moving into the area, new housing going up all around, and new stores and shopping centers opening regularly.

McDuff would really like to build the new addition, even though it means borrowing some money. However, she is worried about the taxes on a property with a higher assessed valuation. At her current level of income she can afford to repay the loan with little trouble, but if her monthly payments increase too much because of higher taxes, she'd have difficulty making ends meet. She wonders if she should just forget the whole remodeling idea.

What do you think? What potential advantages or disadvantages exist for homeowners who build onto their homes, or for any property owners who make improvements? Are there factors McDuff is overlooking that would help her in making her decision?

☐ Should McDuff go ahead and build the addition? Why or why not?

☐ What specific math computations should McDuff perform to help her analyze her situation?

☐ Is McDuff overly concerned about the effect that increased property taxes will have? Just how much more in taxes is she likely to pay each year if she proceeds with the remodeling?

☐ To what extent, if any, is the increase in taxes likely to be offset by the increased value of her house?

☐ From a tax standpoint, would McDuff be better off to sell this house and buy another that already has the features she wants? Would this make her taxes higher or lower, or would it depend on the specifics of the new house? If the latter, what specifics would be particularly relevant?

Income Taxes 8

Almost every American who works and earns income over a certain minimum level must pay federal income tax. Indeed, for many workers, income tax competes with housing costs as the single largest expense during the year. And not surprisingly, it is also the single largest source of income for the federal government.

As we shall see, a wide range of factors determines how much federal income tax each taxpayer pays. The calculation starts with the amount of income the worker earns (the worker's gross earnings) but that's just the beginning. Consider this common example: Two workers earn the same salary doing the same job, but each pays different amounts of income tax. Why? Different lifestyles: one is single, lives alone in an apartment, and has numerous money-making investments; the other is married, has four children, owns a home with a substantial mortgage, and has only a modest passbook savings account. Since marital status, dependents, investment income, and mortgage costs all affect the amount of tax owed, their tax returns look very different indeed.

In this lesson, we'll examine how federal income tax is calculated and consider the variables that affect bottom line figures. We'll also touch briefly on state income taxes; where they exist, they can take another substantial bite out of a worker's paycheck. And we'll explore how income tax laws have changed since the Tax Reform Act of 1986 and delve into some ways the federal government spends its tax revenues.

PART I: INTRODUCING THE MATERIAL

LEARNING OBJECTIVES

Upon completing your study of this lesson, you should be able to:

1. List the steps involved in determining income tax liability.

2. List the factors that affect adjusted gross income.

3. Given gross income and adjustments to that income, calculate adjusted gross income.

4. Given adjusted gross income, number of exemptions, and the amount of tax withheld, use a tax table to determine the balance due or refund from the Internal Revenue Service when deductions are not itemized.

5. List possible deductions and explain how or why deductions vary among taxpayers.

6. Define excess deductions and standard deductions and calculate excess deductions, given total deductions and standard deduction amount.

7. Determine taxable income, given adjusted gross income, excess deductions, and value of exemptions.

If you're using the hardcover textbook, *Mathematics for Business*, there are some additional objectives for the lesson. Upon completing your study of the lesson, you should also be able to:

8. Discuss the relationship between itemized deductions and the standard deduction and, given the necessary information, determine whether it is advantageous to itemize deductions.

9. Calculate the income tax due, given income, itemized deductions, and the number of exemptions.

LESSON OVERVIEW

Anyone who has ever received a paycheck knows that what you earn and what you take home are two very different things. Employees who work for a company have money subtracted from their paychecks to cover everything from state and federal income tax to Social Security contributions, union dues, pension contributions, and medical insurance, not to mention a host of incidental expenses. Self-employed workers don't have these contributions deducted from their earnings, but they must pay income tax and make Social Security contributions all the same. Regardless of the way the income is earned, the federal government wants part of it in taxes.

Many state governments also want part of the income. A handful of states have no statewide income tax, so a few workers do not pay this tax at all. But in some states, state income tax rates are over half of federal tax rates. Similarly, not all companies have pension plans or medical insurance programs or unions. In other words, paycheck deductions are not uniform. But almost every worker pays federal income tax. The only exceptions are those with income so low that it does not exceed allowable deductions and exemptions; they literally have nothing left over to tax.

Instructions and rules governing how and when to pay federal income tax are established by Congress and summarized in written form by the Internal Revenue Service (IRS), the U.S. government's tax collecting agency. The IRS is responsible for managing all the paperwork associated with processing tax returns—and it is substantial indeed. While the taxes of millions of people are straightforward, the complete set of laws governing income tax and the instructions explaining how to apply those laws are notoriously complicated. After all, tax laws and instructions are written, necessarily, to take into account every possible sort of situation among the tens of millions of taxpayers currently affected. No wonder some people make a lucrative living just explaining the laws and instructions and helping people fill out their tax returns.

Help with Understanding Tax Laws

Tax consultants have their work cut out for them, since changes in tax laws are frequent and sometimes dramatic—as with the tax reforms of the 1980s. And each change is likely to affect people differently. These days, two workers can earn about the same, but rarely do they have identical mortgage payments, investments, childcare expenses, and so on. Tax consultants are sometimes better prepared than individual taxpayers to cope with special circumstances and apply current tax laws in a flexible way that fits the individual taxpayer's circumstances.

However, even tax consultants are not all alike. They vary not only in terms of experience and skill, but also in the degree to which they are willing to assume responsibility for errors. Most accept responsibility for errors in mathematical calculations; if the taxpayer supplies all the right figures but the consultant adds or subtracts incorrectly, the consulting agency will take responsibility for the error. They will even pay any interest or fines incurred as a result. Consultants cannot, however, take responsibility for the information entered on the form. Only the taxpayer Smith can say whether she did indeed take a business trip to Miami on August 24, and only the taxpayer can verify the purpose of that trip and the amount of the expenses. Smith must provide the copy of the relevant contract, hotel receipts, restaurant receipts, mileage records, and so forth. The consultant's job is to say how much of that business expense, if any, is legally deductible, then to advise the client whether to subtract these business expenses from her adjusted gross income.

Of course, businesses themselves have to pay tax on the money they earn. The earnings from proprietorships and partnerships go directly to the owners, so the business earnings are taxed as part of the personal income of those owners. In other words, the business itself doesn't file a tax return. But a corporation, which has stockholders rather than direct owners, must file a corporation tax return. In any business, though, the complexity caused by the different sources of income, depreciation of equipment, deduction of expenses, and so on makes calculating the tax on business income a fairly formidable job, usually left to specialists.

Incidentally, the IRS itself also provides assistance and consultation in the completion of tax returns. But (perhaps surprisingly) if the IRS answers a question incorrectly, you, as the individual taxpayer, are still responsible for the correct completion of your return. (And the fact that the IRS itself sometimes gives the wrong answers to tax questions is a good illustration of just how complicated certain portions of the tax law can be.)

The Changing Nature
of Tax Laws

Tax laws have changed frequently since the federal income tax was first made law in 1913. That's not hard to understand; the income tax pays for the services provided by the federal government, so as the type and scope of those services change, so does the amount of money required to pay for them. Also, the country's views on what income should be taxed and what deductions should be allowed changes over time. All in all, there will probably never be a time when the tax code becomes "final."

Even so, the reforms in income tax laws made during the mid-1980s were exceptionally broad and revolutionary. Those reforms are far too complex to summarize here. In fact, even professional tax consultants (including IRS representatives) are continuing to work out the details of how and when new laws should be applied. However, we can review the key changes:

☐ The number of tax brackets was reduced from fifteen to two. As a result, workers with income under a certain level are taxed at the lower rate, and those with income over that level are taxed at the higher rate. These percentages are built into tax tables to simplify the calculation.

☐ Many deductions previously allowed were either restricted or phased out altogether. For instance, interest on credit card accounts, formerly deductible from taxable income, was gradually phased out as a deduction, as was interest on auto loans. This makes it less advantageous to pay for merchandise over time, making consumers somewhat less likely to run up a big credit card bill or borrow a large sum to buy a new car. (This is an example of how tax laws can have far-reaching effects on the way consumers use their money.)

☐ Long-term *capital gains* (profits from the sale of investments held for a certain minimum period) are now taxed at the same rate as other income. Prior to the 1986 tax reforms, such investments served as a kind of tax shelter; capital gains were taxed at a lower rate than other income. But to give you an idea of how frequently tax laws are changed, note that by 1989 the U.S. Congress was again considering changing the way capital gains are to be taxed.

Historically, the issue of tax reform has always generated controversy. Some people feel we should pay higher income taxes; otherwise, they argue, funding for needed social services and programs will suffer. Accordingly, we must either provide the government with more money or face cutbacks in education, research, transportation, medical services, and other critical areas. Others argue that current tax revenues are more than sufficient to support needed programs. To them, what's really needed is better money management. Of course, the debate doesn't stop there.

No matter what deductions are allowed or disallowed, protest follows. Some taxpayers may feel that restrictions on certain deductions cost them money, while "loopholes" permit others to claim more deductions than they ought to be entitled to. For example, not everyone was happy about phasing out interest deductions on auto loans and credit card accounts. These critics charge that borrowing and spending promote economic expansion, which should be encouraged. Others feel that the new restrictions don't go far enough. Many oppose the still-allowable deduction on home mortgage interest. They claim it is biased against renters and that it, like other interest-based deductions, should be abolished. Public support for home mortgage deductions has been extremely strong, however, making many politicians afraid to tamper with it too much.

If it has to do with income, you can be certain the IRS has a form for recording it. While not every taxpayer needs every form (thankfully) there are at least three — the W-2 form, the W-4, and the 1099 — that every working person needs to know about.

The W-2 form. Employers provide the W-2 form to each of their employees at the end of the year. The W-2 form records total wages or salary that the employee has earned from the company during the year and the total amount of income tax that the employer has withheld. An employer is required to provide a W-2 form for each employee who receives earnings of any kind, no matter how short the term of employment. Say Walker hires Davis at 9:00 a.m. on Monday and fires him at 9:00 a.m. Tuesday. Assuming she pays him for his brief association with the company, she must report his earnings and withholdings on a W-2 form.

The information on this form is entered by the employer, but employer and employee share mutual responsibility for ensuring that the information is accurate. Employees must verify that the total earnings figure is correct. Likewise, it's up to the employer to ensure that the correct amount of tax, based on those earnings, is withheld.

Withholding tax is deducted from employee earnings every pay period by the employer; the employee has no say in this and couldn't, for example, say "I've got some extra expenses this month; how about we don't withhold as much from this check." But employers can't just keep the money and send it in in one lump sum. Rather, the government requires that it be deposited into special "tax deposit accounts." This means, in effect, that employees are paying income taxes to the federal government each pay period, not just once a year when tax returns are filed.

Actually, the yearly tax return serves as a kind of summary, a final accounting as it were. This is the time for determining whether more tax is owed or a refund is forthcoming. For example, if the W-2 form indicates that Bill Baxter paid $10,000 in federal income tax for the year but he owes just $8,000, he can expect a $2,000 refund.

Although personal tax returns are traditionally filed on April 15 of each year, workers are taxed on income earned from January 1 through December 31 of the preceding year. The April 15 deadline (which can be extended) is designed to allow employers enough time to prepare W-2s, taxpayers enough time to complete their returns, and the IRS more flexibility in processing incoming returns. As chaotic as tax time is now, imagine the scrambling that would occur if *all* returns had to be mailed in January 1, just one day after workers finished earning the money on which they were being taxed.

The W-4 form. Another important form is the W-4, which indicates the number of *personal exemptions* a worker can claim. As discussed in earlier lessons, the higher the number of exemptions, the smaller the amount of tax withheld from that worker's pay. But individuals cannot simply claim any number of exemptions they like; a general rule is one exemption for the taxpayer and one for each of his or her dependents. A dependent can be a child, spouse, or parent who is supported entirely or in large part by the taxpayer's income.

W-4 forms must be filled out carefully or the wrong amount of tax will be withheld. Persons who claim too few exemptions pay more tax than they need to during the year and thus are extending the government a kind of interest-free loan. On the other hand, those who claim more exemptions than they're entitled are likely to owe more money at the end of the year, and run the risk of a paying a penalty for underpaying.

The 1099 form. On the 1099 form is recorded income that does not come from regular wages or salary. It is used by companies to record fees paid during the year to independent consultants, not regular employees. The company does not withhold taxes from an independent consultant's check, since that person is responsible for making his or her own tax payments and Social Security contributions. (And, of course, such consultants are not entitled to company benefits, so no deductions are necessary for that reason.) To illustrate, if consultant Hemmingway earns $25,000 from the Bressler Electric Company, he receives the full $25,000. Then it's up to Hemmingway to pay his taxes, cover his Social Security contributions, and fund his own medical or other benefits out of that money. The 1099 form simply shows that Hemmingway earned $25,000 during the year, and that amount is added to Hemmingway's adjusted gross income.

Self-employed workers like Hemmingway must file quarterly returns and send in estimated tax payments that are roughly comparable to withholding. These quarterly returns are based on the income tax expected to be owed during the year. For instance, Hemmingway might estimate his income at $48,000 and make estimated tax payments accordingly. At the end of the year, he would file an annual return to which he would attach all his 1099s, perhaps showing his total income for the year was only $45,000, not $48,000. If that's the case, he'd likely have a refund coming.

We usually think of income in terms of hourly wages or salary, or perhaps consultant fees. In other words, compensation for work performed. But, as far as the government is concerned, interest on investments is also defined as income and is taxable at the same rate. So if Wiley earns $500 in interest on her savings and other investments during the year, she must add that $500 to her income. The bank, or whoever manages her investments, will provide her (and the IRS) with a 1099 form on which interest is reported.

Adjusted Gross Income and Taxable Income

The terms *adjusted gross income* and *taxable income* may sound interchangeable, but they're not. *Adjusted gross income* is figured first; it includes wages and salary plus consultant fees, tips, honorariums (e.g., for making a speech), bonuses, interest payments, or anything else the government defines as income. But not everything that would seem to be income is counted to figure adjusted gross income; some sources of income are exempted.

Sometimes it's difficult to know what is exempt. For instance, most persons do not pay any federal income tax on Social Security benefits. Now, however, with the Tax Reform Act, people at higher income levels — those who have significant income from sources other than Social Security — are taxed on a portion of their benefits. Similarly, a person who received an award in honor of his or her contribution to a company might very well be taxed on that award if it were presented in the form of cash. But the proverbial gold watch (or a similar token of appreciation) might or might not be taxed, depending on how current laws are interpreted.

Some adjustments are allowed to reflect special circumstances, such as a move necessitated by taking a new job. A deduction like this must be carefully documented, however, and it's important to make sure that the adjustment is legitimate. For instance, suppose Bailey takes a new job in the office building across the street from her current place of employment.

She also decides to move into a new condominium downtown so that she won't have the inconvenience of commuting in rush-hour traffic. According to the federal government, her relocation is a personal convenience; consequently, she cannot deduct expenses associated with this move from her adjusted gross income.

But let's say Bailey is offered a job in another city 1,000 miles to the north, a job she cannot reasonably accept without moving. In that case, she can deduct moving expenses including hiring a moving van to transport her furniture, motel and food expenses during the time she is moving, and the gas needed to get to her new home. Such expenses might even include traveling to the new site to look for a place to live. But the exact circumstances under which various adjustments can be made are complicated, so it's often necessary to consult the IRS or a professional tax consultant for advice.

Once we've added together *all* income totals for the year and subtracted any allowable adjustments, we know the adjusted gross income. But remember, federal income tax is not based on adjusted gross income. In order to determine the *taxable income*, we must now subtract both exemptions and deductions.

As noted earlier, a taxpayer is allowed one exemption for him- or herself and one for each dependent. Each exemption allows the taxpayer to subtract a given amount (determined by the tax laws in effect at the time) from the adjusted gross income. For instance, if the amount of the exemption in a given year was $1,100, a taxpayer entitled to two exemptions could subtract $2 \times \$1,100$ ($2,200) from the taxable income.

Deductions are also subtracted when taxable income is calculated from adjusted gross income. The tax laws say that if you spend your money on certain things, you shouldn't be charged any tax on the income that paid for these things. (Some examples are the interest paid on home mortgages, donations to charity, large medical expenses, and business expenses that aren't paid by an employer.) As a result, the taxpayer's adjusted gross income is reduced by the amount spent on these deductible items in order to find the taxable income.

Calculating Taxable Income

The government assumes that virtually all taxpayers will have some deductions in the form of donations to charity, childcare, interest on mortgage payments, and so forth. To simplify matters for itself and for the taxpayers filling out returns, the government allows every taxpayer a kind of allpurpose deduction known as the *the standard deduction*. This amount is different for married persons filing jointly, married persons filing separately, single persons, or heads of household. But it is the same for all taxpayers who fit into one of those categories.

Each taxpayer has to decide whether or not use the standard deduction when calculating taxable income. Obviously, persons with total yearly deductions less than the standard deduction amount are better off taking the standard deduction. For instance, suppose that Martin Melrose has an adjusted gross income of $20,000. He is allowed two exemptions at $1,000 each ($2 \times \$1,000 = \$2,000$). That brings his taxable income down to $20,000 − $2,000 (for the two exemptions), or $18,000. Now let's say that the standard deduction is $3,000. Since Melrose has deductions of only $2,000 he doesn't need to (and shouldn't) itemize deductions.

The Standard Deduction

On the other hand, what if Martin has deductions of $5,000, well over the $3,000 standard deduction? In that case, he'll save himself money by claiming the deduction for the full $5,000.

Even a person with no legitimate deductions receives the standard deduction amount as a kind of minimum possible deduction. But if higher deductions are claimed, they must be itemized before they can be subtracted from taxable income. That is, they must be listed separately on a tax return and properly documented. What does the government accept as proper documentation? Again, a tax consultant can usually advise a taxpayer on what's required. Note that itemized tax returns for people with numerous deductions, such as extensive business deductions, often require several supplemental forms and schedules, resulting in a tax return that is several pages long.

Using Tax Tables

Tax tables may look complicated, but they're really not. The secret to using them lies in reading the fine print. The first thing to look up is the *general* level of taxable income. A worker's actual taxable income is rarely a nice, even number. Rudolph's taxable income probably isn't $25,000; a more likely figure would be something like $25,213.27. That looks tougher to work with, but the tables make it simple. Rudolph's taxable income is *about* $25,000, so we find that figure in boldface numbers on the chart and zero in.

If line 37 (taxable income) is —		And you are —			
At least	But less than	Single	Married filing jointly	Married filing separately	Head of a household
			Your tax is —		
25,000					
25,000	25,050	4,596	3,754	4,995	3,777
25,050	25,100	4,610	3,761	5,009	3,791
25,100	25,150	4,624	3,769	5,023	3,805
25,150	25,200	4,638	3,776	5,037	3,819
25,200	25,250	4,652	3,784	5,051	3,833
25,250	25,300	4,666	3,791	5,065	3,847

Looking down the lefthand column, we find the number $25,200 — getting closer. Rudolph's income is in fact *at least* $25,200 but *less than* $25,250, so that's the row in which the correct tax will be listed. (Incidentally, in this example, Rudolph could have had another $36.72 in taxable income and not paid any more tax because he would still have made less than $25,250.)

Notice, however, that the amount of tax varies according to whether Rudolph is married and filing jointly, married and filing separately, single, or single and the head of a household. In other words, there are four tax amounts at this income level, and the correct one depends on Rudolph's status. Until we know that, we cannot determine his tax. Let's say Rudolph is single. In that case, his tax for this year, according to the table in the text, would be $4,652. Notice that if he were married and filing jointly, his tax would be $3,784, almost $1,000 less.

Records of income are critical for every taxpayer. All W-2 forms must be included with the income tax return prepared at the end of the tax year. In addition, taxpayers who itemize must keep thorough records on all expenses when they are incurred. Don't expect to think up all of the deductions the night before the tax return is due; the IRS demands precise and timely documentation and is likely to disallow deductions supported only by after-the-fact guesses. Notebooks designed for recordkeeping are available at stationery and office supply stores. Taxpayers who make use of such books are likely to have most of the documentation they need at the end of the year.

Keeping Good Records

Make no mistake, good documentation takes time. A business executive with lots of deductible expenses may have something to add to the record book — a lunch receipt, a mileage record, a purchase of supplies, an airline ticket receipt — every day. When the April 15 deadline is months away, it's tempting to dump everything into a big envelope and sort it out later, or worse, to tuck receipts and other documents all over the place. But the taxpayer who keeps records in this fashion is likely to face a tough choice: Risk taking a deduction with no way of proving it's legitimate (possibly incurring penalties for underpayment of taxes) or give up a deduction to which he or she is rightfully entitled.

Every year, a million or so taxpayers who file federal income tax returns are *audited*. An audit is a review of the return conducted by the IRS for the purpose of verifying the correct amount of tax owed. These audits reveal that a substantial number of taxpayers owe the government more money than they indicated on their returns — sometimes through honest mistakes, sometimes not. Not surprisingly, like any company trying to collect on an unpaid bill, the federal government is eager to get its hands on this money. Understandably, the IRS is reluctant to disclose exactly what set of circumstances triggers an audit. Most people correctly assume that they *could* be audited at some point, and the government does nothing to change this impression. However, the chances of any individual taxpayer being audited are fairly small.

Being Audited

There are, however, certain types of returns that are much more likely to be audited. Many audits are triggered by something unusual in the tax return (claiming an unusually high refund, for instance) or by certain types of deductions. Deductions for home offices and business use of personal computers, for example, are often incorrectly claimed, so a return that claims such deductions is more likely to be audited than an equivalent return without them. Audits, or at least an inquiry from the IRS, are also more likely for people who fail to report income. Remember, everyone who pays you income reports that fact (using 1099 or W-2 forms) to the IRS. If the income you claim differs from the IRS computer's record of what you've been paid, questions are almost certainly going to be raised.

Taxpayers tend to fear and loathe audits, but they're really nothing more than a routine check to determine the correct amount of tax owed. It is the IRS's way of saying, "We're not convinced by the information included with your return that the amount of tax you say you owe is accurate." Of course, the taxpayer has an opportunity to present the needed information, provided he or she can come up with it. And, in fact, many taxpayers who are audited end up owing exactly the amount of tax they claimed they did, and some even end up owing less. Nevertheless, audits uncover billions of dollars of underpaid taxes. In other words, while a taxpayer who reports all income and has only legitimate, supportable deductions has nothing to worry about, the audit process consistently produces additional tax payments, penalty and interest charges, and occasional fines and prison terms for tax evasion.

SOME WORDS OF ADVICE

All taxpayers need to be familiar with current tax laws, at least on a general level. You don't have to be an expert. But you should have a sense of when and how to file a return, what deductions are allowed, and the documentation necessary for those deductions. You must also know how the government defines your "income."

Taxpayers whose returns are complex, meaning those who have unusual sources of income or extensive deductions, are often well-advised to seek the assistance of a qualified tax consultant. For one thing, such consultation may well save the taxpayer money. Consultants often know of legitimate deductions that may not occur to the taxpayer. For another, consultants can save a taxpayer interest payments and penalties that result from underpaying taxes. At the very least, the consultant is likely to save the taxpayer some time and frustration. The completion of routine tax forms is fairly simple, but unusual circumstances often make the fee charged by a professional tax consultant (which, by the way, is tax deductible) a good investment.

The importance of keeping scrupulous records of all income and all deductible expenses cannot be overemphasized. True, it takes time and effort. But the effort will be financially rewarding if legitimate and well-documented deductions exceed the standard deduction and save the taxpayer money.

If you are audited, don't panic. Having a dental checkup doesn't mean your teeth have cavities. Similarly, being audited won't cost you money you don't already owe. But don't expect much understanding from the IRS if you've no support for your deductions.

Finally, remember that the responsibility for providing truthful, accurate, and complete information still rests with you, the taxpayer, even if your tax preparer is a professional. If there is an error, you will be responsible for paying any additional tax owed, even if the error was not your fault. And if the error did result from false or incomplete information provided to the consultant, you may also wind up paying a penalty for underpayment. The moral? Whether you are concerned with the taxes of a business, a family, or an individual, take responsibility for knowing your own tax situation and the requirements of reporting it.

KEY TERMS

Before you read through the text assignment and watch the video program, take a minute to look at the key terms associated with this lesson. When you encounter them in the text and video program, pay careful attention to their meaning.

Adjusted gross income: The total of all income received from wages, salaries, interest, dividends, and investments, less any adjustments to income, such as moving expenses.

Excess deductions: The difference between the total of the itemized tax deductions and the standard deduction amount.

Personal exemptions: Automatic deductions allowed by the government for each taxpayer and his or her dependents.

Standard deduction: A figure representing the automatic deductions allowed by the federal government for persons in a given category (e.g., married persons filing jointly). Itemized deductions over this amount may be subtracted from adjusted gross income, but every taxpayer, even one with no deductions, is entitled to the standard deduction.

Taxable income: The actual amount of income on which the taxpayer pays income tax. It is the adjusted gross income minus exemptions minus allowable excess deductions.

1099 form: A form for reporting income other than wages and salaries. A 1099 is used to report consultant fees, interest, stock dividends, royalties, and other earnings that are not part of an employee's wages or salary.

W-2 form: A wage and tax statement given each year to an employee by his or her employer. The W-2 form reports the total wages earned by that employee during the year, as well as the total amount of income tax withheld by the employer.

W-4 form: A from that sets forth the number of personal exemptions an employee is claiming.

PART II: WATCHING THE VIDEO PROGRAM

_____ VIDEO VIEWING GUIDE

Before watching the video program, review the following questions. As you watch, be sure to collect the information necessary to answer them:

1. Summarize some key changes from the 1986 Tax Reform Act. How have these changes affected individual taxpayers? How about taxpayers who are also business owners?

2. How important is it for individual taxpayers to know the most recent tax law changes? What are some sources of this information?

3. Who should seek the help of a professional in preparing a tax return?

4. Following the tax reforms of the mid-1980s, are individual taxpayers likely to be paying more or less income tax than before tax reform? How might business owners be affected?

5. Give some examples of currently accepted deductions. What deductions have recently been restricted or eliminated?

6. What are the steps in determining adjusted gross income? After adjusted gross income is determined, what needs to be done to determine taxable income?

VIDEO PROGRAM _____

The lesson's video program is Program 8—Income Taxes. Remember, if you are watching this program on videotape, take time to replay sections of the tape any time you need to review a concept.

VIDEO VIEWING QUESTIONS_____

Immediately after viewing the video program for Lesson 8, take time to respond to the following questions. Give your answers some careful thought; they may provide the basis for additional discussion or a longer written response.

1. Name the two principal differences between adjusted gross income and taxable income.

   a. _____

   b. _____

2. On this scale of 1 to 10, rate how important you think it is for a taxpayer to personally have comprehensive knowledge of current tax laws.

   Not Important   **Extremely Important**

   1- - - - -2- - - - -3- - - - -4- - - - -5- - - - -6- - - - -7- - - - -8- - - - -9- - - - -10

3. Which of the following would likely affect the final amount of personal federal income tax a taxpayer owes? (Check as many as apply.)

   _____ The number of deductions claimed by the taxpayer

   _____ The kinds of deductions claimed by the taxpayer

   _____ The taxpayer's place of residence

   _____ The taxpayer's age

   _____ Whether the taxpayer is married or single

   _____ The taxpayer's length of employment

   _____ The taxpayer's job title

   _____ Current government spending

   _____ State of the U.S. economy

   _____ Current interest rates (e.g., interest banks are paying)

   _____ Current conditions on the stock market

   _____ Current conditions in the real estate market

   _____ The total number of taxpayers in the U.S.

4. Which of the factors in Question 3 would clearly have an immediate, direct effect on the amount of federal income tax owed? Which would clearly have only indirect, long-term effects?

   Direct effects: _____

   _____

   Indirect effects: _____

   _____

5. Put a plus (+) by each of the following items that would need to be reported as *income* on a federal income tax return. Put a minus (−) by each item that could be reported as a *deduction* from taxable income on a federal income tax return. If an item qualifies as *neither* income nor a deduction, leave it blank.

   _____ Interest on savings

   _____ Interest paid on a home mortgage

   _____ Money made through gambling

   _____ Tips

   _____ Salary

   _____ Lottery winnings

   _____ Cost of dental checkups

   _____ Cost of new clothing

   _____ Moving expenses

   _____ Cost of a business lunch

   _____ Money made in the stock market

6. Name two types of expenses that were allowed prior to the major mid-1980s tax reforms but disallowed afterwards.

   a. _____

   b. _____

7. Briefly describe the relationship between a personal income tax return and the tax returns for a business owned by that taxpayer.

   _____

   _____

8. Name any two characteristics that would increase the probability of a taxpayer's personal tax return being audited.

   a. _____

   b. _____

9. Briefly discuss the individual taxpayer's responsibility for ensuring that information on a federal tax return is accurate.

   _____

   _____

PART III: FOCUSING ON THE MATHEMATICS

READING ASSIGNMENT

After watching the video program, you should read one of the following Text Assignments, depending on the textbook you're using:

SOFTCOVER: Pages 453-462 from Chapter 11 of the Miller, Salzman, and Hoelzle softcover text, *Business Mathematics.*

HARDCOVER: Pages 212-222 from Chapter 6 of the Salzman, Miller, and Hoelzle hardcover text, *Mathematics for Business.*

As you read through the text, pay careful attention to the examples the book gives of the mathematics associated with the concepts you're learning about.

Then, after you've completed the text assignment, read through the Key Formulas below. This section provides a handy review of what you've learned. By the time you get to this point in the lesson, all of the formulas and calculations should be familiar to you. If they're not, go back and read the appropriate parts of the text and the Overview section of this lesson. You won't have much success completing the rest of your assignments if you are still confused about the information in the Key Formulas section.

KEY FORMULAS

The following key formulas are important to your understanding of this lesson. Be sure that you know each one and how to use it in solving problems related to income tax calculations.

KEY FORMULA: Excess deductions =
Total deductions − Standard deduction

Formula used for: Calculating whether a taxpayer should use the standard deduction or itemize deductions.

Example:

Let's say that the standard deduction amount for a given year is $3,000 for married persons filing jointly. Tim Elrich, who fits this category, has deductions of $4,500. His excess deductions are $4,500 − $3,000, or $1,500. Since this number is greater than zero, he is better off itemizing deductions.

Remember that in this formula:

1. Excess deductions are those over and above the standard deduction.

2. The standard deduction amount is set by the government and may change from year to year; this makes it important to know the right amount for a particular year.

3. The standard deduction is different for married people filing jointly, married filing separately, single people, and for single heads of household. Be sure to select the right figure to determine taxable income.

KEY FORMULA: Taxable Income = Adjusted gross income − Deductions − Exemptions

Formula used for: Calculating the amount of income on which tax will be paid once adjusted gross income and the value of exemptions and deductions are known.

Example:

Suppose Kate Wilkinson has an adjusted gross income of $32,000. She has deductions of $4,000 and four $1,000 exemptions (4 × $1,000 = $4,000). Kate's taxable income is $32,000 − $4,000 − $4,000, or $24,000.

Remember that in this formula:

1. Taxable income and adjusted gross income are not the same thing.

2. Taxable income is the figure to use when looking up the amount of tax owed in the tax tables.

3. Adjusted gross income includes *all* income earned during the year — not just wages and salary, but also tips, interest on and earnings from investments, and any other miscellaneous income. For instance, if Larry Randall receives an end-of-year bonus of $1,000 for his outstanding contributions to the company, he must include that $1,000 in his adjusted gross income. If Larry earns another $2,000 in royalties on his romance novel, he must report that money as income, too.

4. Any adjustments to income, such as deductible moving expenses, are subtracted from adjustable gross income. Allowable adjustments vary from year to year and situation to situation, though, so it is wise to seek the advice of a reputable tax consultant in determining what is currently allowable.

5. One personal exemption is allowed for the taxpayer and for each of his or her dependents. For example, a married couple with two children might claim four exemptions if filing jointly. If the two married persons in this example were filing separately, however, they could not *each* claim four exemptions. A person cannot be claimed as a dependent on more than one tax return, nor can a person claim a personal exemption as head of household on one return and then be claimed as a dependent on another return.

DON'T FORGET

1. The amount of the personal exemption is set by the government and is changed from time to time. So are the tax rates, the standard deduction amount, and what deductions are allowable. You will be given various figures to use in solving the problems in this course, but in filling out an actual tax return, it would be essential to look up the correct figures for the year in question.

2. Deductions differ for each taxpayer and must be itemized and calculated on a case by case basis. For this reason, no two taxpayers who itemize are likely to have *identical* returns.

3. Marital status is very important in using tax tables to determine the amount of federal income tax owed; tax rates are different for single persons, married persons filing jointly, married persons filing separately, and single heads of household.

4. Tax tables are used to find the total amount of tax owed for the year, but this figure must be compared to the tax already paid, either through quarterly tax returns or withholding from paychecks. Employees can compare the tax table figure to the amount of tax reported on a W-2 form (or forms). This comparison shows whether the taxpayer still owes money or has a refund coming.

PART IV: SOLVING BUSINESS PROBLEMS

PROBLEM SETS

Work the following problems in your textbook. Your instructor will tell you which problems, if any, are to be turned in. Some of the problems have answers provided in the back of the book; refer to these answers to make sure you are working the problems correctly.

SOFTCOVER: If you are using the Miller, Salzman, and Hoelzle softcover text, *Business Mathematics*, do the following problem sets:

11.2: Problems #3-32 on pages 459-462.

HARDCOVER: If you are using the Salzman, Miller, and Hoelzle hardcover text, *Mathematics for Business*, do the following problem sets:

6.3: Problems #3-32 on pages 220-222.

BUSINESS APPLICATIONS

Read each of the following scenarios and answer the questions about the decisions you would make in each situation. Give these questions some serious thought; they may be used as the basis for discussion or the development of a more complex essay. You should base your decisions on what you've learned from this lesson, applying both math skills and good business judgment to solve the problem at hand.

SCENARIO 1   Joe Flanders took a new job this year that requires him to travel extensively. Accepting the position meant moving; his relocation involved two trips to look at new homes, select one, and close the deal. Altogether, he spent over $4,500 on moving expenses, including the cost of a moving van.

His new job involves selling and marketing new products across the country. Flanders's last job involved selling to local downtown clients. But now he deals with dozens of national accounts and is always booking another airline flight. While he receives a generous commission for his efforts, the company provides no travel allowance. This means he finances his own travel, lodging, meals, and so on

While he likes the travel (one of the reasons he took the position), he isn't used to documenting his expenses. In his old job he sat behind a desk all day and took orders over the phone. If he had a luncheon or occasional trip, he filled out an expense form and got reimbursed. However, his new company requires only that he submit monthly reports on sales progress by region, something he spends quite a bit of time on each month.

As the year ends, he has a pretty good record of his travel expenses on a calendar. He's scribbled in where he went and on what dates. And he's saved some receipts, all stuffed in a large manila envelope in his desk file.

About this time, he talks with his tax consultant, who advises him to itemize his year's expenses. This makes Flanders very nervous; what about that documentation? He thinks quickly. If he takes his moving expenses as an adjustment to income but does not claim his on-the-job travel expenses, he'll save about $1,500 on his income tax. However, if he claims his business expenses, he could save another couple of thousand dollars (based on estimates of what he's spent during his ten months on the job). If he does both, the government will owe him a substantial refund. If he does neither, he'll owe the government a substantial amount of money, which he'll be forced to borrow to cover his tax liability.

Flanders isn't sure what to do. He'd just as soon let his tax consultant figure it all out. But the consultant won't have anything to do with it until Flanders gets the records in some order. Unfortunately, Flanders hates detail work and now isn't sure he can organize the receipts. The thought of pulling out that bulky, crinkled manila envelope scares him. But do the receipts really have to be organized and added up? He was, after all, smart enough to save his receipts; he just didn't organize them too well. Why not estimate the deductions? The receipts are there if someone wants to sort through them. He'll even take a little less of a deduction than he thinks he's entitled to, just to be sure he's not paying less than he truly owes.

What do you think? How should Flanders handle his adjustments and deductions?

☐ Should Flanders deduct his moving expenses as an adjustment to his gross income? Why or why not?

☐ Should Flanders itemize his federal tax return and claim deductions for his business expenses? Why or why not?

☐ If Flanders is audited, is the documentation he has likely to be sufficient to support the business expense deduction? If not, what else does he need to do?

☐ Flanders figures that he will make an estimate of his business expenses that's lower than what he thinks it actually is. Is this a sensible approach? Why or why not?

☐ What, if anything, would happen to Flanders if the IRS disallows deductions or adjustments he makes?

☐ What responsibility, if any, does Flanders's tax consultant have in this matter? If you were Flanders, what responsibility would you expect your tax consultant to assume?

SCENARIO 2   Bill and Helen Carpenter have been married five years and have filed a joint tax return every year during that time. Both work at professional-level jobs, and they aren't having any trouble making ends meet. Currently, they live in an apartment where they pay rent of $1,000 per month. They're considering buying a home but can't decide if it's a good investment for them or not. Their combined income is close to $80,000, and they expect it to increase slowly but steadily during the next few years.

Both intend to keep working for the foreseeable future. They like their jobs; they like to travel. They do not plan to have any children. Right now they put about $1,000 a month into various short- and long-term investments and are hoping to increase that amount as their income goes up. Both have excellent insurance coverage through their jobs.

While Bill and Helen do not quite have sufficient savings for a $35,000 down payment on the kind of home they want, they have over $30,000 in long-term investments. They also have annuities that they don't plan to touch before retirement and they have $4,000 in a passbook savings account. They estimate it might take them a couple of years to save enough money for the down payment, or they could borrow the additional $20,000 they need right now, using the long-term investments as collateral. Repaying that debt, together with covering mortgage payments that they estimate would run about $1,500 per month, will stretch their budget to the limits.

Scraping by is something the Carpenters aren't used to and they don't find it a very appealing possibility; they think they might be happier renting forever. But their advisor has pointed out that there could be some real tax advantages to owning a home. Virtually all of that $1,500 monthly mortgage payment would be interest that could be deducted from their income tax, which means that the government would, in effect, be paying for part of the house. Besides, with inflation and interest rates uncertain, it doesn't always pay to wait to buy. And what will they do with the money if they don't buy a house? They'll invest it and then end up paying tax on the income that the investments make. All in all, a house might be as financially sound an investment as they could make.

What do you think? Would the Carpenters be making a mistake to buy a house they don't really care about owning and that might cause a financial burden? Or are they losing financial advantages by waiting?

☐ Should the Carpenters borrow the money they need for the down payment and buy the house? Why or why not?

☐ What are some of the primary advantages they will realize if they buy the house now? The primary disadvantages?

☐ From a financial perspective, what would likely happen over the next five to ten years if the Carpenters follow your advice?

☐ Obviously, their investment advisor thinks that the mortgage interest deduction is something the Carpenters should pick up on. Is he overrating the value of this deduction?

☐ What *specific* mathematical calculations should the Carpenters perform in getting together the information they need to make a good decision?

☐ What *specific* factors (mathematical or nonmathematical) should anyone in the Carpenters' position be sure to consider in making a decision like this one?

Business Insurance 9

A man bought a box of expensive cigars and immediately insured them against loss by fire. When he had smoked them, he put in a claim to the insurance company, saying they had indeed been destroyed by fire.

Not surprisingly, the company refused to pay, and the matter was brought to trial. The judge, after carefully examining the policy, pointed out that the cigars had, in fact, been destroyed by fire, so the policy applied.

The claimant was quite pleased until the judge pointed out that the insurer was not actually required to pay anything.

"Why not?" demanded the indignant cigar smoker.

"The policy," explained the judge, "clearly states it does not cover losses caused by arson."

Each year, thousands of businesses suffer some kind of damage from fire. Unfortunately, many have no insurance to protect them against fire loss. Some cannot (or feel they cannot) afford this type of insurance; others rationalize that the risk of fire is not sufficiently high to justify the cost.

On the surface, statistics might support this kind of thinking. While they vary dramatically by location and type of business, the odds that any given business will suffer fire damage in a given year are pretty low, perhaps less than one chance in a hundred for some. But for that unlucky one in a hundred, the consequences can be financially fatal.

Moreover, averages do not tell the whole story. Far from it. For a variety of reasons, some businesses are more at risk than others. Not surprisingly, it is the businesses that most need insurance that also tend to pay the highest premiums. Those businesses that take steps to lower the risk of fire or other types of damage usually lower their insurance costs in the bargain.

It's important to keep in mind that merely having insurance in no way reduces the likelihood that disaster will strike. It may give the business owner peace of mind, but the reality is that an insured business is no less likely to catch fire or have a customer trip on the doorsill than one that is uninsured. What insurance can do, however, is give the insured business a means of carrying on with as little expense, wasted effort, and inconvenience as possible.

In this lesson, we'll discuss how the costs of insurance are determined and how the nature of a policy affects payment on a claim. We'll also look briefly at a few of the things a business can do to minimize the risk of damage and claims and at the same time reduce the cost of insurance.

PART I: INTRODUCING THE MATERIAL

LEARNING OBJECTIVES

Upon completing your study of this lesson, you should be able to:

1. Define the terms policy, face value, and premium.

2. List important factors that determine the rate and total amount of a premium.

3. Using a table of rates per hundred dollars of insurance, calculate the annual premium for fire insurance, given building rating, area rate and property value.

4. Define coinsurance, discuss the reasons for coinsuring, and calculate the liability of insurer and insured, given the percentage of coinsurance and the amount of the loss.

5. Discuss the rationale for insuring a property with multiple carriers.

6. Identify the categories of potential loss and liability a prudent business person should consider in determining comprehensive business insurance coverage.

If you're using the hardcover textbook, *Mathematics for Business*, there are some additional objectives for this lesson. Upon completing your study of the lesson, you should also be able to:

7. Describe the effect of short-term and cancellation rates and use a short-term rate schedule to calculate the refund due for a cancelled insurance policy.

8. Calculate the amount paid by each of multiple carriers, given the amount of their coverage and the amount of the loss.

9. Find the liability of multiple carriers when a coinsurance requirement is not met.

10. Explain the advantages of group insurance to a business and its employees and calculate the financial advantages to each, given the individual and the group rates.

LESSON OVERVIEW

Buying insurance is a form of gambling on the future. The purchaser makes a prediction about the likelihood that something will go wrong, then weighs this potential risk against the amount of loss the business can afford to withstand on its own. By balancing the likelihood of having a loss against the impact of loss, a business can determine how much it ought to invest to protect itself. If the prediction is accurate, the business buys just the insurance it needs. Spending more is wasteful; spending less could endanger the company unnecessarily if something does go awry.

The way in which insurance works is not unlike a lottery; its purpose is much different, of course, but it's based on the same principle of creating extensive funding through multiple contributions. In the lottery, many persons pay in but only a few win. The combined contributions of all players are pooled to pay off the holders of the winning tickets.

The Principle of Spreading Risk

Similarly, the idea behind insurance is that many contributors each pay a little in order to finance the cost of a few contributors' losses. For instance, let's imagine a small insurance company has 2,000 customers, each of whom pays $1,000 to purchase a fire insurance policy offered by the firm. The company providing the insurance now has $2 million (2,000 × $1,000) to spend. It cannot spend all that money paying off claims, of course. It has to buy or rent facilities, purchase equipment, pay staff, pay taxes, and still net some profit. But let's say the company can cover all its expenses, make a substantial profit, and still have $1.5 million left over. That amount is available to cover claims.

If it's a good year, perhaps the claims amount to only $50,000. That means extra profits for the company and leftover money to invest for the future. If that sort of trend continues in the years to come, the company (or, more likely, state government insurance regulators) may decide it's charging more than it needs to for this type of insurance. So in the future, policy holders might need to pay only $500 per year for the same coverage.

Now let's change our scenario and suppose that things do not go so well one year. Claims exceed the $1.5 million that the company budgeted for them. That means the company will have to cut costs, reduce profits, dip into its investments and, if the trend continues, perhaps go into debt. It can't survive long without bringing the claims and premiums back into balance, of course. A bad year is one thing. But if the excess claims continue, where will the company get the extra money in the long term? Most likely, it will have to ask state insurance regulators for permission to raise policies.

Our example here is greatly simplified, of course. But it should help you understand the concept of insurance from the point of view of the company providing the protection. When the insurance industry got its start many centuries ago, it's a good bet that the first "agents" based their charges on whatever the traffic would bear. They had to make an educated guess about the likelihood that something would go wrong and they would have to pay on the policies they had sold. But over the years, experience has taught insurance companies when, how, and why trouble is likely to strike. These days, insurance is no longer a matter of guesswork.

Insurance Ratings

Modern insurance companies have volumes of data illustrating the history of many different kinds of businesses. When restaurant owner Rossini wants a fire insurance policy on his restaurant, the price of the policy will be based on computerized analyses of how many claims have been filed by restaurants like his and how much those claims cost the company.

The information in Rossini's insurance company's "history of restaurants" file provides a critical beginning for negotiations, but as you might guess, it's hardly sufficient. After all, restaurants are not all alike. Let's say Rossini's restaurant is brand new and designed by an architect who specializes in fire-resistant construction. It's constructed primarily of brick, stone, plaster, steel, and tile; not a flammable substance in the lot. The kitchen is equipped with safety features, and the most technologically advanced sprinkler system on the market is woven into the ceiling construction. The restaurant is all on ground level, and there are several wide, well-lighted, easily accessible exits, making it unlikely that anyone would be trapped inside if a fire broke out. Clearly, Rossini has given a lot of thought to making his business safe. Why should he pay the same rates for insurance as Bigler across town?

Bigler also runs a restaurant. It's old, dilapidated, and built primarily of wood. The carpeting is flammable, the walls papered and badly grease-stained. The kitchen appliances are outdated, the wiring faulty, the ventilation poor. Worse yet, the restaurant is crowded into the second floor of the building, which means that the thirty or so people the restaurant seats would have a hard time getting out in a hurry if there were a fire. In short, the risk of fire is much greater at Bigler's. And if there were a fire, it would probably do more damage than at Rossini's, where it might more easily be controlled.

Given these differences, Rossini is likely to pay considerably less for a given amount of insurance coverage than Bigler pays. (In fact, in the real world, Bigler might be refused insurance coverage altogether till he cleaned up his act a bit.) Insurance companies look at a range of factors, like the construction and design of a building, to decide the likelihood that the building will suffer fire damage. This results in an *insurance rating*. Many factors may go into this rating, and they're likely to vary a little from one insurance company to another. But any company will look at the overall design of the building, the materials used in construction (whether they're sound and fire resistant), the manner in which the building is used, whether it's open to the public, the size of the building, and its location.

Bigler's restaurant, for instance, seems the perfect target for fire damage. But its risk profile improves a little when we learn it's situated right across the street from the fire station. Rossini's restaurant, by comparison, is ten miles out of town, accessible only by a narrow, unlighted two-lane road. It's still a good risk (given the way it's constructed), but its out-of-the-way location is likely to boost the insurance rates over what they'd be if the restaurant were easy for fire trucks to reach.

The insurance company will ordinarily assign two ratings to a building. One, the building classification, is based on the design and construction of the building itself. The other, the territorial rating, is based on the location of the building and the quality of fire protection available within that location. As we indicated in the preceding example, proximity to a fire station is an important factor in rating location. But it isn't the only factor. A building in the city limits, with ready access to a good water supply, would generally be judged safer than one far outside the city limits where there are no hydrants for extinguishing a fire. Similarly, a business in an open area with plenty of room for firefighters to move around might have a different rating from one buried in a basement off the main street, accessible only by a narrow alleyway. And, of course, there's the question of how likely a fire is to spread to adjacent buildings.

These two ratings—the building classification and territorial rating—are built into tables (like those shown in your text) that indicate insurance costs *per $100* of coverage. Keep in mind that some people want and need a lot more coverage than others. Rossini, with his big new modern restaurant, may need several hundred thousand dollars worth of coverage. Bigler's restaurant, much smaller and not so flashy, has a much lower market value. He needs less coverage, and may even pay less altogether for his insurance, but the cost per $100 will still be higher for Bigler than for Rossini.

For instance, say Rossini has a building classification of A (high safety) and a territorial rating of 3 (moderate). According to this information, his insurance would then cost him perhaps $.37 per $100 of coverage. If he insures his restaurant for $300,000, he'll pay $.37 × 3,000, or $1,110 in annual premiums. Let's say Bigler has a building classification of C (low safety) and a territorial rating of 2 (he's tough to get to, but he is close to that fire station). His insurance will cost him $.54 per $100 of coverage. He'd be paying a lot more than Rossini if his restaurant had the same market value, but it doesn't. He needs only $70,000 worth of coverage, so he'll pay $.54 × 700, or $378, in annual premiums.

But remember, at this point neither Rossini nor Bigler is likely to have all the coverage he needs. A restaurant, like most businesses, is more than just a building. The contents of a building may be insured by the same policy as the building, but this portion of the premium is figured separately. That's because, as common sense would suggest, the building contents for one sort of business are likely to be very different from those for another. Sam's Rental is jammed with cameras, video equipment, tools, small appliances, and miscellaneous equipment of every description. Grimley's Feed Store houses bins of grain, racks of harness, and bits of hardware. Spitting Image Photo has a glass case full of film in the front and expensive film developing equipment in the back. It wouldn't make sense to try to come up with some sort of "typical" contents or "average" amount of insurance coverage. Every business is different from every other business. What does make sense, though, is to consider the building contents in rating the building. And that's just what insurance companies do.

Don't Forget the Contents

The contents of any building must be appraised or assessed in some manner before they can be insured. In the case of routine inventory, like film or hardware, the business can simply provide the insurance company with a record of what it pays for items in its inventory and what it has on hand at any one time. Equipment is a little different, though, because it isn't resold on a regular basis. Many business assets—an X-ray machine in a medical office, for instance, or a dentist's chair—*depreciate* (decline in value over time). So the business must keep a record of when such purchases were made, what they cost, and what their current market value is.

For some items, such as medical equipment or computer systems, market values are pretty much a matter of record. But suppose a business deals in original artwork or Oriental rugs or one-of-a-kind pets. Not everyone knows the value of a Picasso print or a rare albino lizard. Items this specialized must be *appraised* by someone with knowledge of the field.

And this appraisal must be made available to the insurance company before insurance costs can be determined.

Except for artwork and similar "collectibles," almost everything from computers to carpeting wears out over time. But that doesn't mean its market value eventually drops to nothing, or that there comes a time when it's no longer worth insuring. Both the business owner and the insurance agency must recognize that insurance costs have to be based in part on what it would cost to replace the contents in question. For instance, let's say the computer that sits on the reception desk at Uptown Dentistry is ten years old. It's worth only a fraction of its original market value, but if it's damaged in a fire the business will still have to replace it, and it's likely to spend much more than it could have sold the original computer for. How to solve this problem? Some insurance companies will, for an increased premium, cover the replacement costs on specific items like Uptown's computer. What this means, of course, is that Uptown is, in essence, paying the insurance on an expensive computer it doesn't own rather than the cheap one it has. That may or may not be a shrewd idea.

The premiums for the insurance on the structure and the insurance on the content will be added together to determine a total premium. Remember Rossini's restaurant? We already determined that he would pay an annual premium of $1,110 on just the building. Insuring the contents of a building with that rating (A-3) will cost Rossini perhaps $.46 per $100 of coverage. So, if the contents are valued at $200,000, the cost will be $2,000 \times .46 = \$920$. That makes Rossini's *total* premium $1,110 plus $920, or $2,030 per year.

Notice, by the way, that the rate for insuring $100 worth of contents is just a little higher than the rate for insuring $100 worth of the building itself. That's not unusual. For one thing, many fires start somewhere inside the business and burn outward. When that sort of thing happens, it's the contents, not the walls of the building, that burn first. In addition, depending on the nature of the business, it can be more difficult to get to and protect the building contents than to put out a fire that starts on the roof or by one of the outside walls. And finally, a fire that does only minor damage (say to one of the exterior walls) may result in total destruction of a building's contents because of smoke or water damage. After firefighters get through hosing down Wanda's Wallpaper Shop, the building may be standing, but there may not be much left that anyone would want to use to paper walls.

Limited Insurance

So far we've talked as if business owners always insure their property for its full market value. That is far from the case, however. Insurance costs have risen dramatically in recent years, and business owners are always looking for ways to save money. If a business owner feels that the risk of fire at his or her business is remote, then it may seem prudent to spend less on protection. Of course, only time will tell whether such a decision was truly a wise one.

Insurance companies themselves recognize that total destruction of a business through fire is fairly rare. In fact, in most fires, total damage is considerably less the assessed market value of the property. For this reason, insurance companies may include a *coinsurance clause* with the policy. With coinsurance, part of the risk of fire may be assumed by the holder of the policy (who is normally the property owner). An 80 percent coinsurance clause, for instance, says in effect, "Look — it's highly unlikely that fire damage to this property would be more than 80 percent of the market value, so for all practical purposes, we can look on that 80 percent coverage as *full coverage*." The remaining 20 percent of market value represents the policy holder's risk. In other words, if the property *were* totally destroyed by fire, the policy holder would have to bear 20 percent of the replacement costs. Meantime, though, he or she saves money by insuring the property for a little less than full value.

Take our friend Rossini, whose restaurant is valued at $300,000 with contents valued at another $200,000. That's a total of $500,000, or half a million dollars. With an 80 percent coinsurance clause, Rossini could insure his building for $240,000 and its contents for $160,000. Using the same rates we applied earlier ($.37 per $100 for the building and $.46 per $100 for the contents), Rossini's total premium for both building and contents would be $1,624 per year, almost $400 less than it would cost him to insure it for the full market value.

Of course, there's nothing to stop the business owner from insuring for 60 percent, or 50 percent, or just 25 percent of the market value. The question is: How much price cutting is too much? When is the business owner inviting more risk than is prudent? Rossini, for instance, may personally believe that the chances of his restaurant catching on fire are negligible. The data files at the insurance company indicate he's wrong, but he's entitled to his opinion. Suppose that instead of insuring his building for the recommended $240,000 (80 percent of its market value), he insures it for just $40,000, one-sixth the recommended amount. That fraction is the key to what Rossini can claim in the event of a fire: Because he insured the property for *one-sixth* the recommended amount, the insurance company will only pay *one-sixth* of the total damage, up to but not exceeding $40,000, the face value of the policy.

Short-Term Policies

The premiums quoted by insurance companies usually reflect an annual rate, or coverage for a period of one year. For a business that plans to stay in the same location and retain the same basic equipment and inventory, an annual premium makes perfectly good sense. But sometimes business needs change.

For instance, suppose a business is planning to sell a portion of its inventory or to sell the building in which it's currently housed. If these plans are fairly definite, the owners may not wish to pay for a full year's worth of insurance on property they will own for only a few months. In that case, some insurance companies will provide a *short-term policy* for a period of one to eleven months, depending on the needs of the buyer.

Now, it might occur to you that while this is a very good deal for the buyer, it's not such a good deal for the insurance provider, which is losing a portion of the premium by cutting the policy short. To make up for a little of the lost profit, the company prorates the cost of the premium. This works much the same as if they charged a fee to the client for the privilege of having a short-term policy. In other words, let's say the business wants the policy to run for six months, not the full twelve. Will the insurance company just cut the cost in half, since the policy runs half a year? No. It wants a little something extra for its trouble, so the insured is more likely to pay 70 percent or so of the full-term cost. That may seem a little steep, but it's really no different in principle from a shoe store that offers a bargain price to the customer who buys three pairs of running shoes instead of just one. The greater the volume of the purchase, whether the product is shoes or insurance, the better the rates are likely to be.

Multiple Carriers

Some businesses carry fire insurance with more than one company. There are several ways this could come about. Perhaps the business is so large, and its market value so high, that no single company wants to bear all the risk of handling the insurance. In looking at a multimillion-dollar shopping mall or luxury apartment complex, for instance, an insurance company may say, "Well, if this place is destroyed we couldn't cover the cost, no matter how much we charged you in premiums. So we'll insure what we can afford to replace (about one-fourth) but the other three-fourths will have to be covered by someone else." The owner, therefore, may need three or four separate carriers in order to get sufficient coverage.

But even modest-sized businesses sometimes have *multiple carriers*. This often comes about when a business changes hands or expands over the years so that its needs change or someone new is making the business decisions. For instance, consider a family-owned furniture business that originally had very simple needs and just one insurance provider. When the business passes from one generation to the next, the new manager may feel the business needs more coverage but that it can be better served by a different company. Instead of getting rid of the old policy, though, the manager decides to hang onto it. Sometime down the road (say, when the business opens its new 50,000-square-foot showroom) there could be a need for even more coverage. Then a third insurance company, offering very competitive rates, sends one of its most persuasive representatives to have a look at the remodeled downtown store and winds up with yet another share of the furniture store's insurance business. This approach is not necessarily good business, since it's possible that the first company could have handled all of the furniture store's insurance needs at a lower cost than the sum of the three premiums. Still, it happens.

Fire Insurance: Only the Beginning

No doubt it's occurred to you by now that no matter how complete a business's fire insurance protection, it's only a fraction of the total insurance coverage the business needs. If a customer slips and falls on the waxed floor at the furniture store, or if an armed robber stops by Rossini's Restaurant late one Friday night and takes all the cash in the register, no amount of fire insurance will help pay the damages.

Fire insurance receives as much attention as it does for two reasons. First, it's a basic type of insurance that makes sense for virtually every business. Second, it's an excellent example of critical insurance concepts such as rates, risk profiles, and the balance between claims and premiums. Virtually every type of insurance involves premiums that are based on the probability of something happening to the insured, and that probability is based on the claims that have been paid to similar policy holders in the past. Fire insurance is a good way to illustrate these points, but it would be a mistake to think that fire insurance is the only (or, for some businesses, even the most important) insurance concern.

For example, most businesses also carry liability insurance. This protects the business in the event that someone other than an employee is injured on the property and sues the business for damages. Product liability insurance is a special type of liability insurance that protects manufacturers, distributors, and sellers against claims resulting from injuries and damages caused by their products. And doctors, lawyers, and some other professionals must have *malpractice* insurance to protect themselves against claims resulting from mistakes made in their work.

Employers are usually required by law to provide *workers' compensation* to protect employees who are injured on the job. This is especially critical in businesses where the work itself or the location is dangerous. For example, roofers, bridge builders, welders, and coal miners are far more likely to suffer serious injury on the job than, say, grocery clerks or receptionists, all other things being equal. Still, every job has its occupational hazards, and even a technical writer or a musician will generally have to be covered by workers' compensation insurance. As you might guess, though, the rate charged to cover the technical writer will be much less than the rate to cover a miner.

In addition, most businesses with more than a handful of employees provide *group* medical or dental *insurance* as a company benefit. Group rates usually make such insurance more affordable to employees than it would be if they purchased it as individuals. Often a portion of the premium is covered by the company as part of its employee benefits package, making the insurance a considerable bargain for the insured.

SOME WORDS OF ADVICE

As a consumer considering the purchase of fire insurance, take time to shop around. The insurance business is highly competitive, and one company may offer better rates than another. Don't make a decision on the basis of rates alone, though. Equally important is the knowledge and expertise of the agent with whom you'll be dealing. As a business owner, you want someone who has some familiarity with your industry and who can therefore assess your needs thoroughly and fairly.

Be realistic about those needs. Don't hesitate to ask the insurance agent the basis for determining your needed coverage or premium; you should know these details. But in addition, do an independent evaluation of your own property, considering just how safe it really is. Avoid being underinsured unless you are certain the business has enough resources to survive any possible loss. Even then, keep in mind that fire insurance may be far more economical in the long run than selling investments or closing down the East Coast office if you're put in the position of paying for your own loss.

Take some steps to reduce your company's risk. Insurance is fine protection after the fact, but after all, it's almost always cheaper and certainly less inconvenient to prevent claims in the first place. Do some comparative pricing: What would it cost to have a sprinkler system installed? How does that cost compare to the higher premiums you'll pay without it? Your insurance company can usually offer some practical advice on these matters; it's as eager as you are to reduce your risk.

Finally, remember that an insurance policy is a legal contract. In signing it, therefore, it's important for you to know what your legal obligations are, and what those of the insurance provider are. As a policy holder, for instance, you are obligated to pay your premiums in full and on time. Failure to do so will normally disqualify you for coverage.

The insurance provider is also required to live up to the terms of the contract, but be sure you know what those are. For instance, some policies do not cover fires resulting from arson. Better to know that before signing than when it's time to file a claim. In addition, remember that the provider will never pay more than the total damage or the face value of the policy, and may not pay even that much. If you, the purchaser, insure your property for less than the recommended rate, your insurance coverage is reduced accordingly. The *face value* on the policy indicates the maximum reimbursement you could expect to receive under any conditions; it is not a guarantee of payment.

As a property owner, you're entitled to evaluate your own risk and to buy as much or as little insurance as you think is appropriate. Realize, though, that insurance company recommendations are based not on hunches but on years of carefully and systematically analyzing the needs of businesses like yours and predicting how likely it is you will one day use the insurance coverage you pay for.

KEY TERMS

Before you read through the text assignment and watch the video program, take a minute to look at the key terms associated with this lesson. When you encounter them in the text and video program, pay careful attention to their meaning.

Business owner's package policy: A business insurance policy insuring many additional perils beyond fire.

Coinsurance clause: A fire insurance clause that places part of the risk of loss upon the insured.

Face value: The amount of an insurance policy. This is the maximum amount the policy holder can collect under any circumstances.

Group insurance: An insurance policy that covers a group of people employed by the same company or belonging to the same organization.

Insured: See *policy holder*.

Insurer: The insurance company. Also called the *insurance provider*.

Multiple carriers: Two or more insurance companies sharing in an insurable risk.

Policy: A contract between the insured and an insurance company.

Policy holder: A person or business that has purchased insurance. Also known as *the insured*.

Premium: The amount of money charged for an insurance policy.

Short-term/cancellation rate: A rate used when charging for short-term policies and the refunds given when policies are cancelled by the policy holder.

Underwriter: An insurance company employee who determines the risk factors involved in the occurrence of various insurable losses. The underwriter's work helps determine the insurance premium.

Workers' compensation insurance: Insurance that provides payments to an employee who is unable to work due to a job-related injury or illness.

PART II: WATCHING THE VIDEO PROGRAM

VIDEO VIEWING GUIDE

Before watching the video program, review the following questions. As you watch, be sure to collect the information necessary to answer them:

1. How are fire insurance premiums determined for a given business?

2. What are some of the factors that cause fire insurance rates to go up or down for a given business? To what extent does a business have control over what it will pay for fire insurance?

3. What is the basic idea behind a coinsurance clause? In other words, what is the thinking that prompts an insurance company to include such a clause?

4. Under what conditions would a short-term policy make good business sense?

5. Under what conditions would a company need multiple carriers?

6. How, when, or why do a company's fire insurance needs change with time?

7. What are some of the other insurance needs of a business beyond basic fire insurance? Which of them pertain to the majority of businesses and which to only a few?

VIDEO PROGRAM

This lesson's video program is Program 9 — Business Insurance. Remember, if you are watching this program on videotape, take time to replay sections of the tape any time you need to review a concept.

VIDEO VIEWING QUESTIONS

Immediately after viewing the video program for Lesson 9, take time to respond to the following questions. Give your answers some careful thought; they may provide the basis for additional discussion or a longer written response.

1. Make a simple list of all of the types of insurance discussed in the video lesson.

_____

_____

_____

_____

2. Imagine that you are the owner of a company that has a number of different branches, each dealing with a different product or service. In the space below, list four factors that you would use to decide how much fire insurance coverage you would purchase for each branch.

   a. _____

   b. _____

   c. _____

   d. _____

3. Give two reasons why you, as a business owner, might consider insuring your property for less than its full market value.

   a. _____

   b. _____

4. Based on information presented in the video, which of the following factors do you think would be likely to affect fire insurance rates? (Check all that apply.)

   _____ Location of the business

   _____ Age and health of the policy holder (the business owner)

   _____ Age of the building in which the business is housed

   _____ Contents of the building in which the business is housed

   _____ Architectural design of the building

   _____ Type of heating system used in the building

   _____ Number of windows and doors

   _____ Kinds of businesses that surround the insured business

   _____ Whether the business is open to the public

   _____ Number of employees

   _____ Whether the business offers its employees health insurance

   _____ Nature of the business (e.g., law firm, pet shop, shoe store)

5. Name three things a business could do to keep fire insurance rates as low as possible.

   a. _____

   b. _____

   c. _____

6. Based on the video, for which of the following businesses do you think fire insurance rates might tend to be higher than average for businesses of similar size and market value? (Check all that apply; be prepared to give a reason for your answer.)

   _____ Restaurant

   _____ Shoe store

   _____ Medical clinic

_____ Furniture store

_____ Clothing warehouse

_____ Self-service storage company

_____ Telephone company

_____ Plumbing company

_____ Automobile manufacturing plant

_____ Pet store

_____ Greenhouse

_____ Stationery store

_____ Accounting firm

_____ Farm

7. In a sentence or two, summarize how insurance rates are determined by insurance companies.

_____

_____

_____

_____

_____

PART III: FOCUSING ON THE MATHEMATICS

_____ **READING ASSIGNMENT**

After watching the video program, you should read one of the following Text Assignments, depending on the textbook you're using:

SOFTCOVER: Pages 463-470 from Chapter 11 of the Miller, Salzman, and Hoelzle softcover text, _Business Mathematics_.

HARDCOVER: Pages 228-240 from Chapter 7 of the Salzman, Miller, and Hoelzle hardcover text, _Mathematics for Business_.

As you read through the text, pay careful attention to the examples the book gives of the mathematics associated with the concepts you're learning about.

Then, after you've completed the text assignment, read through the Key Formulas below. This section provides a handy review of what you've learned. By the time you get to this point in the lesson, all of the formulas and calculations should be familiar to you. If they're not, go back and read the appropriate parts of the text and the Overview section of this lesson. You won't have much success completing the rest of your assignments if you are still confused about the information in the Key Formulas section.

KEY FORMULAS

The following key formula is important to your understanding of this lesson. Be sure you know how to use it in solving problems related to insurance coverage.

KEY FORMULA: Amount insurance company will pay (assuming 80 percent coinsurance) = Amount of loss × Amount of policy ÷ 80% of market value

Formula used for: Determining the total amount the insurance company will pay on a claim when the business in question is insured for less than 80 percent of its market value, assuming an 80 percent coinsurance clause.

Example:

Suppose Klein owns a business with a market value of $100,000. With an 80 percent coinsurance clause, "full coverage" requires a policy with a face value equal to 80 percent of the market value ($100,000 × .80 = $80,000). But let's say that Klein doesn't think the risk of fire is very great at his tire warehouse. He wants to cut his insurance costs way down and has a policy with a face value of only $20,000, or one-fourth the amount required for full coverage. To Klein's surprise and dismay, fire breaks out in the warehouse, resulting in damage of $40,000. How much of this $40,000 will the insurance company pay? At first glance, it might seem it would pay $20,000, or the face value of the policy. That is not the case, however. Klein has chosen to insure his property for only a fraction of the market value; thus, the insurance company will cover only a fraction of the damage. Let's use the key formula to see how much that will be.

Total amount insurance company will pay =

$40,000 × ($20,000 ÷ $80,000), or

$40,000 × 1/4 (because $20,000 is 1/4 of $80,000), or

$10,000 (1/4 of $40,000)

It is up to Klein to come up with the other $30,000. What if he had insured the warehouse for the full $80,000? Then how much would the insurance company have paid? Let's see:

Total amount insurance company will pay =

$40,000 × $80,000 ÷ $80,000, or

$40,000 × 1 = $40,000

Had Klein insured his business for the recommended amount, he would have had full coverage *up to* $80,000. In this case, with a loss of only $40,000, the entire amount would have been paid by insurance and none of the loss would have fallen on him personally. Of course, we can also presume that Klein would have paid a good bit more for this full coverage; but after his $40,000 loss, he's likely to feel it would have been worth it.

Remember that in this formula:

1. The amount the insurance company will pay never exceeds the face value of the policy or the amount of the damage. In other words, if Klein is insured up to $80,000 but suffers a loss of $100,000, the company will still pay only $80,000. Similarly, if Klein is insured up to $80,000 but the loss is only $40,000, the company will pay only the $40,000.

2. The *amount of the policy* is the same as the *face value* of the policy; it's the maximum amount of coverage available.

3. The insurance company is not bound to pay the full face value of the policy if the insurance coverage is less than the recommended amount. In other words, with an 80 percent coinsurance clause, the recommended amount of coverage would be 80 percent of the market value. If coverage were only 40 percent of the market value, that would be just one-half of the recommended amount, and the insurance company would cover only one-half of the loss.

4. The coinsurance concept is based on historical evidence that few fires in businesses of the type owned by the policy holder are likely to cause damage equalling the full market value of the property. A coinsurance clause does not prevent the policy holder from purchasing more insurance. The policy holder may, for instance, insure the property for the full market value in order to place all the risk on the insurance company if he or she wishes to pay the higher premium.

_____**DON'T FORGET**

1. The face value of the policy is the maximum amount the insurance company will pay on a claim under any circumstances. This is not necessarily the amount the company *will* pay in any given situation, however.

2. When using a fire insurance rate table, be sure to consider both the building classification for the business in question and the territorial rating. Both are important in determining the annual premium.

3. Remember that the premiums for a building and its contents are calculated separately. The rate is usually a little higher for the contents.

4. The figures in an annual rate table usually represent the cost *per $100 of insurance purchased*. Multiply this figure by one-one hundredth (.01) of the face value of the policy to determine the premium.

5. When there are multiple carriers, each provides coverage for a portion of the risk. That portion is equal to the ratio of the face value on a given policy to the total amount of coverage. If the face value on one carrier's policy is $50,000 and the total coverage is $200,000, that carrier will pay only one-fourth the amount paid on any claim.

PART IV: SOLVING BUSINESS PROBLEMS

PROBLEM SETS

Work the following problems in your textbook. Your instructor will tell you which problems, if any, are to be turned in. Some of the problems have answers provided in the back of the book; refer to these answers to make sure you are working the problems correctly.

SOFTCOVER: If you are using the Miller, Salzman, and Hoelzle softcover text, *Business Mathematics*, do the following problem sets:

> **11.3:** Problems #1-26 on pages 467-470.

HARDCOVER: If you are using the Salzman, Miller, and Hoelzle hardcover text, *Mathematics for Business*, do the following problem sets:

> **7.1:** Problems #2-44 (even numbers only) and 45-68 on pages 236-238.

BUSINESS APPLICATIONS

Read each of the following scenarios and answer the questions about the decisions you would make in each situation. Give these questions some serious thought; they may be used as the basis for discussion or the development of a more complex essay. You should base your decisions on what you've learned from this lesson, applying both math skills and good business judgment to solve the problem at hand.

SCENARIO 1   Peterson runs a small TV and stereo repair shop. She's had fire insurance with the same company for the past 30 years and has had no complaints on her service, nor on the rates, for that matter. During that time, she's had two small claims for minor fires, both the result of faulty wiring in the building. Neither fire did any serious damage to the building or its contents, and Peterson has since repaired the wiring. The insurance company responded to both claims in a timely and businesslike fashion, covering the cost of the damages in full, and with no subsequent increase in premiums. The same agent, Frost, has handled Peterson's account for the entire ten years Frost has been with the company. Frost is a friendly and knowledgeable sort, easy to deal with and good about answering questions.

This year, Peterson is considering remodeling and expanding the shop. The business owns a good-sized piece of adjacent property, and Peterson would like to add onto the building and perhaps put in a small warehouse as well. Business is booming, and she doesn't like the idea of having all the repair work right out there in the front room where it's the first thing customers see. She'd like to spruce the place up—put in a real reception area, a counter, some comfortable chairs, maybe a good stereo system playing music for customers while they're waiting.

A new insurance company in town recently sent one of its representatives to talk with Peterson about her insurance needs. The new rep, Conklin, hinted strongly that Peterson's old policy was outdated, especially now with the remodeling plans. Furthermore, Conklin claimed that his company could beat Frost's rate per $100 of coverage, though the overall premium would be higher simply because Peterson was "grossly underinsured, based on current needs." Conklin shared some statistics on current costs to repair fire-damaged property, and they were worrisome, all right. He also suggested to Peterson that several features of her business contributed to a higher risk of fire.

Peterson is unsure about what to do. She really likes the company she's been with, and Frost has provided excellent service. Besides, she's only six months into her new policy, and the premium is paid for the full year. If she cancels now, won't she lose a lot of money? On the other hand, the idea of being underinsured is scary. Just because she hasn't had a fire in the last ten years doesn't mean she couldn't have one next week. Maybe, as Conklin told her, she's "just been very, very lucky." Anyhow, she doesn't have to stay with an insurance company out of loyalty, does she? Isn't this strictly a business decision?

What do you think? Is Peterson better off to stay with a company she's been with for a long time? Is she foolishly putting her business at risk by not taking out more insurance? How much faith should she put in Conklin's evaluation, and how could she go about making a more informed decision?

☐ Should Peterson stay with her old company or take out a new policy with Conklin's company? What are some of the potential advantages in each choice?

☐ What specific mathematical calculations should Peterson complete and what information should she gather before making her final decision? Do you think Frost could be of help in making this decision?

☐ Are there any factors Peterson is overlooking that you would caution her to think about?

☐ The obvious question is "Why not just ask Frost what he thinks of Conklin's analysis?" Is this a good strategy, or is there some drawback to this approach? Should Peterson just add some insurance from Conklin's company to the coverage she already has from Frost?

☐ What are the most important factors (mathematical or non-mathematical) for any business person to consider in selecting an insurance provider or in changing from one provider to another?

SCENARIO 2

Asante has run a chemical company for fifteen years. During that time, he's carried a fire insurance policy with an 80 percent coinsurance clause and has always insured the company for "full protection" under that clause, though it's been expensive to do so. He has never had a claim, though his agent tells him that's unusual for a company of his type. With many flammable chemicals stored in the building and many employees handling them, the odds of having some sort of fire sooner or later are fairly high, based on the insurance company's records of similar firms. Asante maintains, however, that the company is not typical and that its risks are greatly reduced by the fire-resistant construction of the building, the excellent sprinkler system, and a thorough training program provided to all staff. In fact, Asante isn't convinced that his insurance provider pays enough attention to these things when setting the premiums.

Right now, Asante pays over $20,000 per year for insurance on the building and contents, and his agent tells him to expect an increase of at least 10 percent based on their most recent evaluation of repair and replacement costs. Asante thinks it's time to consider a policy with a lower face value. If he cannot get credit for the steps he's taking to reduce fire hazards, then perhaps the best way to save money is to buy a new policy with reduced coverage. There are plenty of places to put the other money; the business has short-term loans to pay off, and he'd like to add at least one new employee. A quick calculation suggests he could save about $8,000 per year by reducing his coverage; that seems like a good deal, especially considering that he has yet to get one dime of his insurance investment back in claims. Besides, with his great record over the past fifteen years, it really seems as if the company is overinsured.

What do you think? Is Asante paying too much for coverage he doesn't need? Or is his current insurance coverage a prudent investment he's likely to be glad he made? Are there other options he ought to consider?

☐ Should Asante keep the insurance coverage he has now, or should he reduce it?

☐ If you think he should reduce it, what percentage of the market value would be a good figure? Why did you choose this?

☐ What specific steps should Asante follow and what mathematical calculations should he make to ensure that his decision is the best one possible?

☐ Are there factors Asante is overlooking that you would caution him to think about?

☐ Asante is currently most concerned about his fire insurance premiums, but there are undoubtedly other types of coverage he either has or should have. What are some examples?

Personal Insurance 10

The insurance company president was furious with his new agent. "Why in the world would you write a million-dollar life insurance policy on a man 104 years old! That's the stupidest move I've seen in all my years."

"But I was just doing what you taught me to do," protested the agent.

"What I taught you to do?!," exploded the president.

"You're the one who told me that we should base our policies on the likelihood of the applicant dying during the policy period," explained the agent.

"Yes, that's right. So what?"

"Well, I carefully looked up the information like you told me, and I found out that in the entire country, almost nobody that age dies in a given year."

These days, it's possible to insure just about anything from condominiums to pet piranhas, from walnut orchards to fishing vessels. Most people insure things that are of value to them personally or things important to their ability to make a living. Sometimes, these are one and the same. A dancer may insure her legs. A singer may insure his voice, a piano player or surgeon, her hands.

Most insurance consumers, however, have somewhat more conventional needs. While insurance policies on pet piranhas and distinctive noses are fairly rare, two types of personal insurance—life insurance and motor vehicle insurance—are very common in our society today. In fact, virtually all adult Americans will, at some point, have at least one of these types of insurance, and the majority can expect to have both.

In this lesson, we'll look at some options relating to these important types of insurance, discuss how premiums are determined and the factors that can cause those premiums to go up or down, and consider the various benefits involved in insurance coverage. As we'll see, motor vehicle insurance is a necessity for anyone who drives a car, or other vehicle, on today's busy streets and highways. Such insurance is valued primarily as an investment in peace of mind, a hedge against the potentially astronomical costs associated with motor vehicle accidents.

Life insurance, on the other hand, is a little different. As we shall see, this is the one form of insurance that can pay off even if nothing goes wrong, and that gives it status as a financial investment as well.

PART I: INTRODUCING THE MATERIAL

LEARNING OBJECTIVES

Upon completing your study of this lesson, you should be able to:

1. Describe how motor vehicle insurance rates are established and identify factors that affect the cost of insurance for a given vehicle owner.

2. Describe the circumstances covered by liability, property damage, comprehensive, and collision insurance.

3. Calculate premiums for different types of vehicle coverage, given the rate and amount of coverage, and use these to determine the total premium due for all coverage.

4. Define a deductible and calculate how the amount of the deductible affects the premium and the amount of coverage in the event of a loss.

5. Describe no-fault insurance and explain the advantages and disadvantages of this insurance as applied in different states.

6. Explain the purpose and importance of uninsured motorist insurance and calculate the amount of the premium.

7. Describe youthful operator factors in auto insurance premiums and calculate the annual premium for a youthful operator, given the annual premium for an adult operator.

8. List reasons for purchasing life insurance.

9. Define term, ordinary life, limited payment, and endowment life insurance and, given a description of a life insurance policy, correctly categorize it.

10. Accurately describe how universal life and variable life insurance policies combine insurance coverage and investment potential.

11. For different policy types and values, calculate annual life insurance premiums for men and women of various ages, given a table showing the premium per $1,000.

12. Given the annual premium and the appropriate premium factors, calculate the payment due for monthly, quarterly, and semiannual payments.

If you're using the hardcover textbook, *Mathematics for Business*, there are some additional objectives for this lesson. Upon completing your study of the lesson, you should also be able to:

13. Given the annual premium and the appropriate premium factors, calculate the additional cost of a policy when payments are made monthly, quarterly, and semiannually.

14. Explain nonforfeiture options and describe the common options available upon cancellation of a policy.

15. Given a table of nonforfeiture values, calculate the cash value, paid-up insurance, and extended insurance available for a cancelled policy of specified value and years in force.

16. Compare the common settlement options for receiving life insurance benefits on the basis of when and what payments are made to the beneficiary.

17. Given a table of monthly payments per $1,000 of face value, calculate, as appropriate, the monthly payments or total benefits from a policy with a specified face value under a particular settlement option.

LESSON OVERVIEW

Most adult Americans would find it difficult to get along without a car. Aside from the fact that many find driving pleasurable, especially those lucky enough to find an open stretch of road to enjoy, most find that a car makes life a whole lot more convenient. Most employed Americans drive their cars to work, and even in cities that boast good public transportation networks, most people still rely on automobiles to get them where they want to go.

Let's face it, though: Driving is hazardous, especially for those who live in the more populated metropolitan areas, where heavy traffic clogs the highways at all times of the day and night. It wasn't always that way. In the early 1900s, before Henry Ford's first cars rolled off the assembly line, an automobile was a genuine rarity. Now there are well over 100 million vehicles on America's highways. And anyone who's ever commuted through a major city during rush hour is likely to feel that most of those 100 million vehicles are headed to the same destination.

Those who drive a car (or any vehicle, for that matter) need some form of motor vehicle insurance. There are a number of options to choose from, partly because there are different sorts of problems against which drivers need to protect themselves and partly because the needs of drivers are diverse. Let's briefly consider the types of insurance first, then look at a couple of hypothetical drivers for whom insurance agents would probably assemble very different sorts of coverage.

Liability insurance protects the driver in the event that he or she injures someone or something with a car. For instance, a driver might run into a pedestrian or bicycle rider. Or, if there were a collision with another vehicle, the other driver or passengers of that vehicle might be injured. A person who suffers such injuries is very likely to sue the responsible driver to recover medical costs, costs that can be extremely high. Because such risk is impossible to escape totally, liability coverage is required by law in most states before a car can be driven.

Liability insurance is often combined with personal *medical coverage* in the event that the driver and his or her own passengers are also injured.

Liability Insurance

The amount of coverage tends to be smaller than the regular liability coverage because claims are usually smaller, but it can, of course, be increased if the insured is willing to pay a higher premium.

Many experts suggest $1 million or more of liability insurance, in part because beyond a certain basic premium level the cost of increasing the coverage is often nominal. For instance, it might cost a driver about $1,000 a year to carry 100/300 liability coverage, meaning that in the event of an accident, the insurance company would pay up to $100,000 to cover injuries to one person or up to $300,000 to cover injuries to more than one person. But for an additional $100 a year, just 10 percent of the original premium, the driver might be able to more than double his or her protection—to 250/500. But, you may be wondering, would a motorist realistically need so much liability coverage? Quite possibly. Complicated bodily injuries resulting from an auto accident may take years to treat and may require the attention of medical specialists. What's more, determining responsibility for the accident and the extent of the damages may mean legal representation on both sides, the filing of a lawsuit, and the awarding of damages by a court. Together, medical and legal costs can easily run into the hundreds of thousands of dollars; for this reason many drivers, though by no means all, feel it's prudent to carry as much liability insurance as they can afford.

Property damage insurance covers damage to the property of others — property other than vehicles, that is (which we'll get to in a moment). For example, say Baxter comes home on a very foggy night, misses the turn to his driveway, and takes a section out of neighbor Clausen's fence. Or Wilson forgets to set his parking brake, and while he's visiting his mother-in-law his car coasts unaided down the hill and into the living room of the surprised Longman family. Property damage insurance would cover the cost of repairing Clausen's fence or putting the Longmans' house back together.

Both liability insurance and property damage insurance tend to be more expensive in some areas than others. In the heart of a big city where there are more people, there are also more people to injure and property to run into. Any time risk increases, insurance rates go up right along with it.

Comprehensive Insurance

Comprehensive insurance covers theft and damage caused by vandalism, hail, falling trees, and other such events, events unassociated with driving a car. With this type of insurance, the appropriate amount of coverage depends on both the vehicle and how much minor damage the owner is willing to pay for personally. Everyone, of course, must worry about theft to some degree. But there's no question that certain makes and models of cars are more likely to be stolen than others. Thieves do not always take the whole car, of course. They may just take a hood ornament, stereo, or set of wheels. These items are also covered by comprehensive insurance.

Or, say Barker takes her car to the Rocky Mountains. While she's parked at a roadside lookout getting some great photos to show the folks back home, her roof is dented by a falling rock. If she has comprehensive insurance, her company will pay for the repairs. Most drivers, even those who don't consider themselves fussy, will want to repair a roof that's been caved in by a runaway boulder. But comprehensive insurance can also cover the little annoyances that only some drivers care about. For instance, while Barker is heading through Yellowstone Park, a curious grizzly peers into her window and scratches the paint a bit in the process. If Barker's the carefree, nonchalant type, she may not even notice the small imperfection. But if she's particular, she can take comfort in the fact that the comprehensive coverage in her policy will cover the damage. (As we'll see, though, the *deductible* on her policy means that she will be paying some, if not most, of the bill for these minor repairs.)

Collision insurance, as its name suggests, pays for repairs to a vehicle involved in an accident. Most collisions occur between two vehicles, but there are other possibilities. Remember Wilson, who forgot to set his parking brake? Well, after his car rolls through the front wall of the Longmans' house, his collision insurance will come in handy to fix the car.

Collision Insurance

Most collision and comprehensive insurance policies have a deductible, or a portion of any claim that is paid by the insured. A deductible amount could be as low as $50, or as high as $1,000. Not surprisingly, the higher the deductible, the lower the premium for coverage. Deciding on a deductible is a little like betting on the amount of damage you expect. Suppose that fixing the bear-claw scratches in Barker's car costs $250. If she has a $50 deductible, she'll pay $50 and her insurance company will pay the other $200. But if her deductible is $250, she'll pay the entire bill by herself. But she can take some comfort from the fact that the premiums she's been paying for the policy with the higher deductible have been considerably less than she would have been charged for a policy with a $50 deductible.

Insurance premiums on both comprehensive and collision insurance are influenced not only by the *territory* in which the owner lives, but also by the make, model, and age of the insured automobile. This is simply because it costs more, generally speaking, to replace or repair newer, more expensive cars than it does older, less costly models (something to think about when purchasing an automobile in the first place). While car buyers are busy touring showrooms, thinking about sunroofs, air conditioning, sound systems, and turbo power, they may not feel like doing much comparison shopping on insurance rates. But perhaps they should. Motor vehicle insurance can be one of the major costs involved in owning and maintaining any automobile, and there are huge differences in the premiums charged for various cars.

Uninsured or *underinsured motorist insurance* protects a vehicle owner in the event of a collision with a driver who is not insured or who doesn't have enough insurance to cover the damages. Insurance companies are often obligated to pay only in the event of an accident for which the insured bears responsibility. If it's "the other guy's fault," the assumption is that the other insurance company will pay. But what if there is no other insurance company? Or the coverage is too small to take care of the damage?

Uninsured Motorist Insurance

In that case, uninsured or underinsured motorist insurance provides the needed coverage. Even when state laws mandate that drivers have liability insurance, the required limits are often too low to cover serious accidents. What's more, despite state laws, many cars are driven without any insurance. For this reason, experts consider uninsured motorist insurance a "must have" coverage, especially in light of its rather low cost (generally less than $100 per year).

Notice that with most liability or collision insurance policies, before anyone pays for anything, it must be established who's at fault. Sometimes, this is fairly obvious. If an intoxicated driver speeds through a red light

No-Fault Insurance

into a parked car in front of half a dozen witnesses, then determining responsibility may be just a matter of filing an accident report. But if two cars collide in an unmarked intersection with no one else around, sorting out the details can be extremely complex. It may take a combination of police reports, legal depositions (sworn statements), photographs, diagrams, discussion, and negotiation by attorneys on both sides, or even a court hearing. All this is both time consuming and expensive.

Given the legal complexities of fixing blame for an accident, several states have adopted *no-fault insurance* laws, under which the policy holder's own company reimburses the insured for damages and all medical costs associated with an accident, regardless of who caused it. This eliminates the need to determine responsibility and ensures that even a driver who has no uninsured motorist coverage will be protected. Supporters say that under no-fault laws, everyone gets a prompt and just settlement, without tying up the courts and having a lot of money go to attorneys' fees. The implication is that premiums can then be lower.

There are, however, those who strongly oppose no-fault. Opponents argue that no-fault insurance, despite its built-in efficiencies, has failed to reduce insurance costs to the extent promised. Moreover, they argue, because this type of coverage sometimes precludes pain and suffering damages except in the case of permanent injury or death, some victims are not compensated for damages caused by others. And above all, they say, the entire legal system is based on the right to collect damages from the party causing the damage, so why should auto accidents be an exception?

On the other hand, many people say that the no-fault laws in most states don't go far enough. Often, there are exceptions to the no-fault concept (damages over a certain amount, for example) that critics say dilute the whole concept. Only a handful of states have adopted what might be considered full no-fault insurance laws, and even in these places, reviews have been mixed.

The Generic Policy: Why It Doesn't Work

You may be thinking that things would be a lot simpler if there were just some sort of generic coverage called "auto insurance" that took care of everything at once. Well, perhaps that sounds simple, but the needs of drivers are different, and while some are almost paranoid about insuring against every conceivable eventuality, others want only bare-bones, no-frills protection and resist paying for anything more. Under certain circumstances, their logic is hard to fault.

Consider Andy Fraley, a farmer in a rural area who drives the back roads and rarely meets another car. Fraley drives a 20-year-old pickup with good tires and a well-tuned engine, but there its commendable qualities end. Fraley's pickup, which has seen two decades of rough roads and rougher weather, has virtually no finish left. There are just a few tired threads where the upholstery used to be. Fraley isn't concerned about scratches and dents and wouldn't dream of having such things repaired. Odds of theft? Remote. In short, Fraley considers comprehensive insurance a waste of money. Similarly, on the off chance he should swerve off the road and knock down a neighbor's mailbox, he'd prefer to pay for it himself than go through the hassle of filing an insurance claim, so he doesn't carry property insurance either. He *does* carry collision and liability insurance, but his rates are low because of the age of his truck and the area in which he lives. Also, he carries the minimum recommended amount. He's never had an accident, and since he puts fewer than 5,000 miles a year on his truck, his good luck may well continue.

Harvey Welmore, on the other hand, commutes more than 50 miles a day through heavy city traffic. He drives a brand-new European sedan and surveys it bumper to bumper morning and night, searching for "battle scars." Welmore has a good driving record, but that's partly a matter of luck. He speeds routinely and does most of his driving on eight-lane freeways where careful driving and survival are synonymous. Welmore carries every type of motor vehicle insurance his company offers, and if they come out with a new type of coverage tomorrow, he'll be waiting in line, check in hand.

Notice that both Welmore and Fraley are familiar with their own needs and with some of the factors that influence both their coverage and what they pay for it. Insurance companies like that kind of awareness. It makes it easier to ensure that drivers get the right kinds of coverage at a price that's, if not low, at least fair.

Whoever said "What goes up must come down" certainly wasn't referring to insurance premiums, which in recent years have tended to go up and then go up some more. Knowing some of the factors that influence cost can help drivers anticipate their needs, spend their insurance dollars wisely, and (where possible) take steps that hold premiums down to the minimum. We've already noted a number of these factors, including the territory or area in which the driver lives and works, the driver's driving record, and the make, model, and year of the car itself.

The Cost of Premiums

In addition, the age and sex of the driver are significant. Statistically, young male drivers have more than their share of accidents, so they also must pay more for their insurance. This is simply the insurance company's way of saying, "Look, we'll insure you, but we know from experience that you belong to a group that has lots of accidents. You're asking us to take a bigger risk, so you'll have to pay us more to do it." An 18-year-old male driver with a good record may be tempted to take offense at this seemingly biased thinking, but that would be pointless.

There's nothing personal in the insurance companies' position. They base their rates on the compiled statistics from hundreds of thousands of policies and the resulting patterns of recorded accidents and claims. They then combine the information on age and driving record with information on make of car, territory, level of coverage needed, and other relevant factors, and they mathematically compute a premium which they feel is fair to both sides. The math is complex but the underlying concept is simple: Insurance companies need to charge enough so they're sure to take in more on premiums than they'll pay out on claims. Otherwise, they can't make a profit and probably can't even stay in business.

As we noted earlier, motor vehicle insurance cannot be considered a financial investment in the traditional sense—though anyone who's been involved in a serious accident can tell you it's almost always cheaper to pay premiums, however high, than to pick up the tab on automobile repairs and related medical expenses. Primarily, though, auto insurance premiums buy protection. Let's look now at another form of personal insurance that often goes a step further by offfering some investment potential.

At its most basic level, life insurance is like auto insurance in that premiums are paid to the insurer so that money will be given back in case something bad happens. Auto insurance protects against damage to vehicles;

Life Insurance

life insurance is intended to provide a family or a business with income in the event that a major income or service provider dies.

In determining how important life insurance is, the question to ask is this: How difficult would it be for the family, or business, to carry on as usual in the event something happened to the person in question? There's no simple answer to that question, of course, since every situation is different. Take a family in which one spouse works outside the home while the other has major housekeeping and childcare responsibilities. If the employed spouse dies, the major income for the family is suddenly gone; life insurance provides important protection against such an occurrence. But if the other spouse dies, his or her responsibilities have to be assumed by someone else, someone who may charge a lot of money to clean house, cook, and care for children. In other words, it may be wise to insure that person's life, too, at least until the children are grown or until the other spouse's income is high enough to take care of any added housekeeping or child-rearing costs.

Similarly, a business may invest in something called *key person* insurance, which protects the business in the event that its owner or manager dies. In the case of a small business, particularly, the loss of a key person can be devastating, for the business may well depend on that person's specialized knowledge, expertise, and reputation for its very survival. Key person insurance provides income that either allows a partner to buy out the insured's portion of the business or buys the business some recovery time, time in which to train new staff, bring in a consultant, purchase equipment, change location, or do whatever else may be needed to remain competitive.

Like motor vehicle insurance, life insurance can take many forms. But while drivers tend to combine many different types of insurance within one policy, buyers of life insurance tend to opt for one kind or another. Let's consider a few of the primary choices.

Types of Life Insurance

Term insurance is the most basic form of life insurance. Money is paid in premiums and given back only if the insured dies. As its name suggests, such insurance is provided for a specific term, say 10 or 20 years, and then expires (even if the insured is still living); it then must be renewed to continue the coverage. It is the cheapest possible coverage for the life insurance dollar, but it provides a *death benefit* and nothing more. In other words, the only way anyone can collect money on a term insurance policy is if the insured dies. That suits some people just fine, because a death benefit is what they buy life insurance for.

Term insurance is not, however, an investment. The premiums paid during any policy period are completely dependent on what the company feels the odds are of the insured dying. For this reason, a year's worth of term insurance costs a 20-year-old only a fraction of what it would cost a 70-year-old, if the 70-year-old could be insured at all. Remember, though, the money paid for term insurance is money gone forever unless the insured dies during the coverage period.

An *ordinary* or *whole life* policy combines a death benefit with an investment component. The insured pays a consistent premium until death or retirement, whichever occurs sooner. Then, at retirement, the accumulated premium dollars turn into a kind of retirement income, from which the insured can draw monthly payments for life.

A *universal life* policy works much the same way except that the insured can vary the amount of the premium to reflect current income. For most workers, income goes up over time. So, as they can afford it, these workers can pay an increasingly higher premium; but because the basic cost of maintaining the death benefit stays fairly stable, the extra money from the higher premium goes into retirement benefits as an investment. Usually, it earns about the interest one would expect on a money market account at the bank, and sometimes there's a guaranteed rate of interest that the insured can count on no matter what happens to the money market rates.

With a *variable life insurance* policy, the insured can invest tax-deferred (no income tax until retirement) income in the form of premiums, just as with universal life. The big difference is that a variable life policy gives the insured some choice in determining how the money will be invested — in stocks, bonds, or other assets. Moreover, the insured may have a chance to switch the investments up to twice a year. Apparently, many people like this feeling of control over their insurance savings, for this rather recent type of policy now makes up a major part of the industry's total life insurance business.

As with motor vehicle insurance, life insurance premiums tend to vary from one consumer to another. And as you might expect, the most important factors in determining premiums are age and general state of health. As we mentioned, a person 20 years old can expect to pay a lower premium than someone who's 70, because the death rate among persons age 70 is much higher than for those age 20. However, as the 20-year-old gets older, term insurance premiums go up to reflect the increasing odds that the company will have to pay a death benefit.

Factors Affecting Premiums

Keep in mind that life insurance is different from some other types of insurance in one important respect. Not everyone has auto accidents, or is struck by lightning, or loses business assets in a fire. But sooner or later, everyone dies. From the insurance company's perspective, the challenge is to ensure that it takes in enough money to make up for the inevitable "loss" and still net a profit. For this reason, life insurance companies are scrupulous about evaluating their own risk.

Once people are beyond a certain age, an insurance company is likely to request that they take a physical examination to determine whether they are overweight, have high blood pressure, or suffer from heart disease, diabetes, or some other significant health problem. Females tend to live a little longer than males (roughly three years, on average) so their premiums are a little lower. Persons who smoke tend not to live quite so long, on average, as those who do not, so their premiums are higher.

Occupation may be a factor, too. If Helen deVries discovers after taking the two-mile walking tour of New York City that her new shoes are a size and a half too tight, she may feel like strangling the salesperson who assured her they would "loosen up just fine." But insurance company records will undoubtedly indicate that Helen's salesperson is probably safe. On the whole, the statistics suggest, it is much safer to sell shoes than it is to rescue boats at sea, fly helicopters, or tame circus lions. So for now, pilots and lion tamers must expect to pay higher premiums for life insurance than shoe clerks.

Many life insurance policies also have clauses to cover special situations. Some will not cover suicide, for instance — or at any rate, not for the first few years of the policy. Similarly, the insurance may not cover deaths from a *pre-existing condition*. In other words, if Keating, who knows she has a life-threatening blood disease, takes out a life insurance policy worth a few million dollars and then dies soon afterward from that blood disease, the death benefit probably won't be paid. In practice, insurers sometimes require physical examinations and almost always require application forms on which the prospective policy holder must list all known medical problems. In Keating's case, she probably could have gotten the insurance only by knowingly misstating her health on the application, which would probably release the insurance company from its obligations if it was determined that the pre-existing condition caused her death.

Cash Values

Policies that combine a death benefit with a savings plan build *cash values* over time, and this money can be used in several ways. For instance, the policy holder can borrow against it, usually at a highly competitive rate of interest. Of course, the money borrowed must be repaid; otherwise, the death benefit is decreased proportionately.

Similarly, the money can be used to purchase *paid-up insurance*. Say Velma Morgan has a $100,000 policy with a cash value of $15,000. She can spend the cash value — all of it — to buy herself, say, $30,000 worth of paid-up insurance. Now, if she dies, her *beneficiary* (the person she designates to receive the benefits) receives $30,000, not the original $100,000. On the other hand, the policy remains in effect for as long as Velma lives, and she'll never have to pay another premium.

But let's say that Velma doesn't want to decrease the death benefit. Unfortunately, she can't afford the premiums just now, either. So, what to do? Well, she can spend her $15,000 cash value, until it's gone, to cover the premiums. Even if the premiums run $1,000 a year, she's set for a good long while; and whatever she doesn't need to spend in a given year will continue to earn interest until she does spend it. However, if she's still alive after the $15,000 is used up, she must then come up with another way of paying the premiums or lose her insurance policy.

Policy holders and their beneficiaries sometimes get the idea that they can have both the full death benefit and the full cash value on a policy. Not true. The cash value can be used like any other savings to keep the policy in force. Or it can be taken out and spent — to buy a car or take a trip. But if it is spent in this way and not replaced, the amount of the death benefit is lowered. In other words, it is an either/or sort of arrangement.

Benefit Options

Life insurance beneficiaries have several options for receiving their benefits. They can, of course, take the total death benefit in a lump sum, which many choose to do. If they need the money to pay off a large debt or have some creative investment ideas in mind, this approach may make the most sense. But if the lump sum is sizable, there are tax and investment implications that should be considered.

There are other ways. A *fixed-period annuity*, for instance, provides monthly income for a set period of time, say ten years. The amount of the monthly check depends on the size of the death benefit. Obviously, $10,000 must be spread much thinner to span ten years than, say, $60,000.

A *fixed-amount annuity* works much the same way except it's the monthly *income* that's predetermined, with payments continuing till the money is gone. For instance, if Ida Radnor receives her husband's death benefit of $5,000 and wants to receive it in monthly increments of $1,000, she can do so; she just can't do so for very long. But if the benefit was $500,000, Ida Radnor could receive $1,000 monthly payments (much more, actually) for the rest of her life.

Many persons like the option of *payments for life with a guaranteed number of years*. With this sort of option the life insurance company checks its tables to see how long the beneficiary would normally be expected to live and sets the amount of payments accordingly. Take Ida Radnor, who's now 76. The tables indicate people her age live an average of close to eight years—92 months, to be precise. On her $5,000 settlement, they offer her $55 a month guaranteed for 92 months. If she dies before the 92 months are up, the $55 per month will go to her heirs for the remaining months.

SOME WORDS OF ADVICE

Not everyone has the same insurance needs, but the majority of adults in our society need life insurance, motor vehicle insurance, or both. With life insurance, there's often an advantage to buying while one is young, while premiums are low. With motor vehicle insurance, by contrast, youth produces higher premiums. But no matter what sort of insurance you buy or when, it pays to shop around and to ask questions. For one thing, deciding just how much insurance to buy is difficult; you'll need to balance carefully the amount of premiums against the benefits in light of your own personal situation.

Keep in mind that insurance rates vary not only from company to company but also from one sort of policy to another. And as we've seen, there are lots of options. In buying motor vehicle insurance, take time to evaluate your needs realistically. Some drivers need much more coverage, and different types of coverage, than others. On the other hand, beware of being underinsured. The risk of an accident may seem low, but if it does occur, the consequences can be very expensive.

In choosing a life insurance policy, ask yourself whether it makes more sense for your needs to buy a straightforward term policy to simply get a death benefit or whether there might be more advantage in choosing a policy with a savings component. Some financial advisors will tell you to buy a term policy (the cheapest form of life insurance) and invest what you'll save on premiums in something that pays a higher return. If you're a disciplined investor, that advice may make good sense. The problem is, some people are not; if you tend to spend just what you earn, there may be some advantage in having the insurance company sock those funds away for you.

With any kind of insurance policy, there is almost always a way to lower premiums. You may not want to move from the city to the country just to lower your motor vehicle insurance rates. But you can and should give some serious thought to the type of automobile you purchase and what it would cost to repair it; those costs will be reflected in your insurance premiums. And, though it seems obvious to say it, you can keep your rates down simply by driving safely. A poor driving record will inevitably raise your premiums and may even make you uninsurable in time.

Finally, if you have a life insurance policy that accumulates cash values, recognize that while that cash is a useful resource, it is not a bonus over and above the death benefit. If you spend it and do not replace it, you not only use up the cash value, but you may lower the death benefit as well. Therefore, be certain you understand the implications of paid-up insurance or extended term insurance before selecting one of these options. Remember, too, that if you borrow on your life insurance policy and do not pay the money back, your death benefit goes down in proportion to the amount you borrow — a fact that has surprised many a beneficiary who didn't take time to sort out the relationship between death benefits and cash values.

KEY TERMS

Before you read through the text assignment and watch the video program, take a minute to look at the key terms associated with this lesson. When you encounter them in the text and video program, pay careful attention to their meaning.

Adult operator: A driver over a certain age, usually 25.

Annuity: Periodic payments of a fixed amount of money.

Beneficiary: A person designated by the insured to receive insurance benefits.

Cash settlement option: Life insurance benefits paid in cash in one lump sum.

Cash value: The value in cash remaining after a policy holder has cancelled or borrowed against a life insurance policy.

Collision insurance: A form of automobile insurance that pays for repairs to the insured's car in case of an accident.

Comprehensive insurance: A form of automobile insurance that covers theft or damage from fire, vandalism, falling trees, or similar events.

Decreasing term insurance: A form of life insurance in which the insured pays a fixed premium for a certain period of time, during which the amount of insurance coverage decreases periodically.

Deductible: A certain portion of insured costs that is paid by the insured, with the balance of the loss being paid by the insurance company.

Face value of the policy: The amount of an insurance policy.

Fixed-amount annuity: A settlement option that pays a fixed amount per month to life insurance beneficiaries.

Fixed-period annuity: A settlement option that pays monthly benefits for a fixed period to life insurance beneficiaries. The amount of the monthly payment depends on the total amount of the death benefit.

Liability or bodily injury insurance: Coverage that provides protection from suit by an injured party.

Medical insurance: Insurance providing medical protection in the event of accident or injury.

Mortality table: A table showing statistics on life expectancy, survival, and death rates. Also known as an actuarial table.

No-fault insurance: Motor vehicle insurance that pays directly to the insured no matter who causes the accident.

Ordinary life insurance: A form of life insurance in which the insured pays a constant premium until death or retirement, whichever occurs sooner. Upon retirement, monthly payments are made to the insured until his or her death. Also known as *whole* life (because the insured pays during his or her whole working life).

Paid-up insurance: An option in which the insured uses the cash value from a cancelled policy to purchase paid-up insurance for a given amount.

Payments for life: A life insurance settlement option that pays an annuity for life.

Payments for life with a guaranteed number of years: A life insurance settlement option that pays a certain amount per month for the life of the insured or beyond; if the insured dies before the time has expired, the monthly benefits will be paid to the insured's beneficiaries.

Policy: A contract between the insured and the insurance company.

Premium: The amount of money charged for an insurance policy.

Property damage insurance: A type of automobile insurance that pays for damages caused to the property of others.

Term insurance: A form of life insurance providing protection for a fixed length of time.

Uninsured/underinsured motorist insurance: Insurance coverage that protects the insured in the event of an accident with a driver who is uninsured or underinsured.

Universal life insurance: A policy providing life insurance protection together with the promise of cash values higher than those provided through traditional insurance.

Variable life insurance: A policy providing life insurance protection and savings with the option of allowing the insured to determine how the balance of the premium (over and above what's needed to cover the death benefit) will be invested.

Youthful operator: A driver under a certain age, usually 25.

PART II: WATCHING THE VIDEO PROGRAM

VIDEO VIEWING GUIDE

Before watching the video program, review the following questions. As you watch, be sure to collect the information necessary to answer them:

  1. Why are there so many different types of motor vehicle coverage?

2. What are the major factors that determine the rates on motor vehicle insurance? Why do rates tend to be higher for younger drivers? Is it fair that they pay a higher rate? Why or why not?

3. What are some advantages and disadvantages of no-fault insurance?

4. How risky would it be for a driver to simply forgo insurance?

5. What are some reasons for purchasing life insurance? Are there some people who have no need for life insurance? Why?

6. Would you consider an ordinary life, universal life, or variable life policy a good way of investing money for retirement? Why or why not?

7. Why are there so many different options for receiving benefits? How does the beneficiary determine which option is best?

8. Where do life insurance companies get the figures in their actuarial tables? How do you know these figures are accurate?

9. What is the relationship between the cash value of a policy and the death benefit of that policy?

VIDEO PROGRAM

This lesson's video program is Program 10—Personal Insurance. Remember, if you are watching this program on videotape, take time to replay sections of the tape any time you need to review a concept.

VIDEO VIEWING QUESTIONS

Immediately after viewing the video program for Lesson 10, take time to respond to the following questions. Give your answers some careful thought; they may provide the basis for additional discussion or a longer written response.

1. On a scale of 1 to 10, rate how important it would be for you to have each of these four kinds of insurance on a motor vehicle you drove.

Liability Coverage:

Not Important		Extremely Important

1- - - - -2- - - - -3- - - - -4- - - - -5- - - - -6- - - - -7- - - - -8- - - - -9- - - - -10

Collision Coverage:

Not Important		Extremely Important

1- - - - -2- - - - -3- - - - -4- - - - -5- - - - -6- - - - -7- - - - -8- - - - -9- - - - -10

Comprehensive Coverage:

Not Important		Extremely Important

1- - - - -2- - - - -3- - - - -4- - - - -5- - - - -6- - - - -7- - - - -8- - - - -9- - - - -10

Uninsured/Underinsured Motorist Coverage:

| Not
Important | | | | | | | | | Extremely
Important |

1- - - - -2- - - - -3- - - - -4- - - - -5- - - - -6- - - - -7- - - - -8- - - - -9- - - - -10

2. Imagine that you are the owner/manager of a small company on the outskirts of a mid-sized city. You have just purchased a company car that you and your employees will use for a variety of business purposes. How much motor vehicle insurance coverage do you think you should buy for the car? (Put a value, such as $50,000, in the space in front of each option.)

   _____ Liability

   _____ Collision

   _____ Comprehensive

   _____ Property damage

   _____ Uninsured motorist

   _____ Medical

3. Name one potential advantage and one potential disadvantage of no-fault insurance:

   Advantage: _____

   _____

   Disadvantage: _____

   _____

4. Insurance costs for motor vehicle and life insurance have tended to increase steadily in recent years. Name two factors that you believe have contributed to this increase:

   a. _____

   b. _____

5. Which of the following factors would be likely to affect the cost of premiums for motor vehicle insurance? (Check as many as apply.)

   _____ Age of the driver

   _____ Driving record of the driver

   _____ Driver's sex

   _____ Driver's occupation

   _____ Where the driver lives or works

   _____ Whether the driver carries life insurance

   _____ Whether the driver is married

   _____ Whether the driver often carries passengers

   _____ Age of the vehicle

   _____ General operating condition of the vehicle

   _____ Road conditions in the area·

_____ Extent of traffic in the area

_____ Average speed limit in the area

_____ Make and model of the vehicle

_____ Whether the driver has had driver's education training

6. There are a few companies whose motor vehicle insurance premiums are lower for drivers who do not smoke. Give one reason you think this might be so:

_____

_____

_____

7. On a scale of 1 to 10, rate how important you think it would be for the following individuals to carry some form of life insurance. (Be prepared to support your answers.)

A young, married father of three children:

Not   Extremely
Important   Important

1- - - - -2- - - - -3- - - - -4- - - - -5- - - - -6- - - - -7- - - - -8- - - - -9- - - - -10

An unmarried, retired woman with no children and no dependents:

Not   Extremely
Important   Important

1- - - - -2- - - - -3- - - - -4- - - - -5- - - - -6- - - - -7- - - - -8- - - - -9- - - - -10

A middle-aged, unmarried head of a small company:

Not   Extremely
Important   Important

1- - - - -2- - - - -3- - - - -4- - - - -5- - - - -6- - - - -7- - - - -8- - - - -9- - - - -10

8. Which of the following factors could have a major influence on the cost of life insurance premiums? (Check as many as apply.)

_____ Age

_____ General health

_____ Smoking/drinking habits

_____ Weight

_____ Height

_____ Occupation

_____ Place of residence

_____ Number of children

_____ Sex

_____ Marital status

_____ Hobbies

9. Name two advantages to having a life insurance policy with a large cash value:

a. _____

_____

b. _____

_____

PART III: FOCUSING ON THE MATHEMATICS

_____ **READING ASSIGNMENT**

After watching the video program, you should read one of the following Text Assignments, depending on the textbook you're using:

SOFTCOVER: Pages 471-484 from Chapter 11 of the Miller, Salzman, and Hoelzle softcover text, *Business Mathematics*.

HARDCOVER: Pages 240-260 from Chapter 7 of the Salzman, Miller, and Hoelzle hardcover text, *Mathematics for Business*.

As you read through the text, pay careful attention to the examples the book gives of the mathematics associated with the concepts you're learning about.

Then, after you've completed the text assignment, read through the Key Formulas below. This section provides a handy review of what you've learned. By the time you get to this point in the lesson, all of the formulas and calculations should be familiar to you. If they're not, go back and read the appropriate parts of the text and the Overview section of this lesson. You won't have much success completing the rest of your assignments if you are still confused about the information in the Key Formulas section.

_____ **KEY FORMULAS**

The following key formulas are important to your understanding of this lesson. Be sure you know how to use it in solving problems related to personal insurance.

KEY FORMULA: Premium = Number of thousands ×
                      Rate per thousand

Formula used for: Figuring the premium for a life insurance policy, using a table that lists rates per $1,000 of insurance purchased.

Example:

To find the rate, you need to use a table such as the one in your text. Let's say that Ben Ross wants to buy $30,000 of ordinary life insurance. Ross is now 30 years old. To find the rate, we look down the Age column to 30, then across to find the column for Ordinary Life. Where the two intersect, we find the rate 14.97. This means Ross must pay $14.97 for *each $1,000* of insurance he purchases. How many thousands does he want? Thirty, since 30 × 1,000 = $30,000. Thus, the cost will be 30 × $14.97 = $449.10. Note that this is Ross's *annual* premium.

Remember that in this formula:

1. The *premium* is the amount the insured owes annually.

2. The *number of thousands* is found by dividing the total amount of insurance purchased by 1,000. Since Ross wanted $30,000 worth of insurance, the number of thousands = 30,000 ÷ 1,000 = 30.

3. The *rate per thousand* can be determined only from the appropriate insurance table. In order to use the table properly, you must know the insured's age and the type of insurance desired. Rates will vary according to both these factors.

KEY FORMULA:	Total auto insurance premium = Liability premium + Comprehensive premium + Collision premium + Uninsured motorist premium + Other premiums
Formula used for:	Determining the total auto insurance premium charged.

Example:

Davidson decides to cover his car with 250/500 liability insurance, collision and comprehensive insurance with $200 deductibles, personal injury insurance, uninsured motorist insurance, and rental car and towing coverage. The total amount she pays her insurance company is the *sum* of all of the individual charges.

Remember that in this formula:

1. The premiums may not be quoted as annual premiums. If, for example, they are semiannual premiums, you'll need to multiply the total by two to find your annual cost.

2. The premiums for some types of insurance (liability and personal injury, for example) depend on the amount of coverage. Others (collision and comprehensive) depend on the deductibles. A few (rental and towing) are fixed costs.

DON'T FORGET_____

1. Many different types of motor vehicle insurance are included together within one policy. These individual premiums must be added together to determine the total premium for the policy.

2. Most insurance premiums are calculated with the use of one or more tables. Generally, the tables for liability and property damage (motor vehicle insurance) include classification by *territory*.

3. The tables for comprehensive and collision (motor vehicle) insurance include classification by *age group* and by *class* of vehicle (also called the *rating* or *symbol*). Age group refers to the age of the vehicle, not the age of the driver. The class refers to the relative cost of insuring the vehicle; this depends on a combination of the cost of the vehicle, the cost to repair it, and the likelihood of something happening to it.

4. Premiums for young drivers (usually under age 25) must be multiplied by a youthful operator factor to determine final cost. This factor is found in a table.

5. Premium rates in life insurance tables (see the example in the text) are often given *per $1,000* of coverage. Where that is the case, remember that the figure listed is not the total premium, but must be multiplied by the number of thousands of coverage to determine the total premium.

PART IV: SOLVING BUSINESS PROBLEMS

PROBLEM SETS

Work the following problems in your textbook. Your instructor will tell you which problems, if any, are to be turned in. Some of the problems have answers provided in the back of the book; refer to these answers to make sure you are working the problems correctly.

SOFTCOVER: If you are using the Miller, Salzman, and Hoelzle softcover text, *Business Mathematics*, do the following problem sets:

11.4: Problems #6-20 on pages 475-478.

11.5: Problems #10-24 on pages 483-484.

HARDCOVER: If you are using the Salzman, Miller, and Hoelzle hardcover text, *Mathematics for Business*, do the following problem sets:

7.2: Problems #1-22 on pages 246-247.

7.3: Problems #2-30 and 38-44 (even numbers only) on pages 258-260.

BUSINESS APPLICATIONS

Read each of the following scenarios and answer the questions about the decisions you would make in each situation. Give these questions some serious thought; they may be used as the basis for discussion or the development of a more complex essay. You should base your decisions on what you've learned from this lesson, applying both math skills and good business judgment to solve the problem at hand.

SCENARIO 1   John and Irma Clark have contributed to the purchase of a $7,500 used car for their teenage son Ted. The Clarks paid $5,000 of the cost; Ted paid the remaining third from his own savings. The car is five years old and has 45,000 miles on it. Ted will use it to drive to work at his part-time job (he works 6:00 to 10:00 p.m. at a local grocery) and to drive to school. He is also eager to use the car for weekend trips, though his parents are trying to discourage that.

Irma Clark, who admits she's a worrier by nature, wants to insure the car as heavily as their budget will allow. She feels that every type of motor vehicle insurance exists for a reason: "If there weren't a problem, the insurance company wouldn't sell that kind of coverage."

John Clark, however, favors a more conservative view. He points out that the car is far from new, that Ted is a careful driver, and that most of his driving will be done close to home on well-lighted roads with low speed limits. He suggests keeping the liability coverage down to 50/100 (rather than the 250/500 recommended by the insurance company representative) and forgetting about collision, comprehensive, and uninsured motorist coverage. "Those are just frills tacked on to boost insurance profits," he tells Irma. "This car isn't about to be stolen and an occasional dent and ding won't matter. If Ted *does* get in an accident, the other people's insurance will pay for anything that's their fault. And if Ted caused the accident, we'll just pay to get the car fixed."

Irma is only half convinced. She agrees that the insurance premiums are high and they've already spent a fair amount on the car. They need to save for Ted's college tuition; they can't be spending money on everything. John is probably right; for this first car, a more conservative insurance package makes the most sense.

What do you think? Are the Clarks budgeting their money wisely by avoiding insurance "frills" most drivers don't really need? Or are they overlooking risks they should be thinking about and inviting bigger expenses in the long run?

- ☐ Should the Clarks go with the insurance package John Clark has outlined? Or should they be adding some of the components he wants to take out? Why?

- ☐ What specific insurance coverage would *you* recommend? Why?

- ☐ What errors, if any, has John made in analyzing the insurance situation for Ted's car?

- ☐ Perhaps you don't feel you have enough information about the Clarks to decide the best approach. What additional information would help you decide what coverage to get?

SCENARIO 2   Harry Bates, age 45, recently married for the first time. His wife, who's been married before, has two children in their early teens, both of whom Harry and his new wife want to send to college. The tuition is no problem on Harry's current salary, but their savings are fairly small (they tend to spend quite a lot on recreation and entertainment) and Harry worries that if something should happen to him, the money would not be there. His wife is a surgical nurse, but she could not afford household expenses *and* college tuition on a nurse's pay.

Harry has never had life insurance, but he thinks now might be the time. He isn't sure how to proceed, though. An agent has recommended a variable life insurance plan to run for 20 years, till Harry retires. The agent tells Harry that this plan will give him the protection he's looking for, plus some retirement income. This sounds like double-talk to Harry. Since when does insurance provide income? The straightforward term policy seems like the better deal. The premiums are only about half what he'd be paying with the variable policy, and if something should happen to him, his wife and her children would receive over $100,000, more than enough to meet the tuition needs.

One thing bothers Harry, though. The company requires him to take a physical for either policy. Harry knows he's at least 20 pounds over-weight. He smokes, too (though less than a pack a day, and he's trying to cut down). The insurance agent admits that these factors could cost Harry a little money on premiums, but adds that the premiums could go down in the future if Harry loses weight and quits smoking.

There's one other option, too. Recently, Harry got an offer in the mail for life insurance at a guaranteed rate of just $90 per year. The ad claimed that Harry could not be turned down, that he would not need a physical, and that his premium (just $7.50 a month) would never increase. They didn't even say anything about smoking. Maybe that's the best deal of the three. It's surely the least expensive, so it seems to offer the most for the money.

What do you think? Would it be a shrewd move for Harry to go with the offer he's received in the mail if he can save some money doing it? Or should he stick with one of the policies from a well-established, reputable company? If so, is the variable policy or the term insurance better suited to Harry's needs?

☐ Which policy should Harry select? Why?

☐ No matter how you answered Question 1, do you think vari-able life or term life is better suited to Harry's needs? Or is there another option better than either of those two? Why or why not?

☐ It would seem that Harry needs to make some calculations to determine just what each policy really costs compared to its benefits. What calculations would you recommend?

☐ Are there any other alternatives Harry should consider? What about taking the money that would go for premiums and in-vesting it in something else? Would that be a good idea? Why or why not?

The Business Discount 11

The ambitious and successful wholesale sales rep ran into one of his customers at a restaurant. The customer looked depressed, so the wholesaler asked what the problem was.

"I promised my wife I'd get her a Pomeranian, but the best price I can find is $200, and that's just too much money," the customer replied.

"Well, I'd be depressed, too," agreed the sales rep. "Why, that's absurd — $200 for a Pomeranian! Listen, it so happens we have a special customer discount this month on Pomeranians and I can get you one for . . ." he punched a few keys on his calculator, "only $140."

"Hey, that's great," said his customer, now very happy. "When can I take delivery?"

"Let me just make a phone call to check," said the sales rep, who then rushed to the restaurant telephone. Calling his office, he got his partner on the phone.

"Hey, George, how's business?" asked his partner.

"Not bad, not bad at all. In fact, just made another sale. Only one thing, though . . . . What's a Pomeranian?"

Everybody loves a bargain, and retail merchants are no different from consumers in this respect. They too like to save money, especially if they can save it on merchandise they want and need anyway.

Manufacturers and wholesale distributors also like discounts, for a variety of reasons. In much the same way that a sale in a department store attracts consumers, business discounts attract retail merchants. That means more immediate cash in the hands of the manufacturers and wholesalers, cash they can use to purchase equipment and supplies or to produce and market new products. Because of these indirect benefits, the producer or distributor often winds up making far more in the long run than the business gave up by discounting the product and selling it a little cheaper. In other words, discounts aren't just good for public relations and advertising; in the long run, they're good for the business pocketbook, too.

In this lesson, we'll consider some widely used types of business discounts: the *trade discount*, which is routinely offered to wholesalers and retail merchants alike; the *series*, or *chain*, *discount*, which is offered on certain products or to certain merchants; and the *cash discount*, offered as an incentive for prompt payment of bills. We'll also briefly discuss some important considerations to keep in mind when reading an invoice.

PART I: INTRODUCING THE MATERIAL

LEARNING OBJECTIVES

Upon completing your study of this lesson, you should be able to:

1. Given a sample invoice, correctly read the information in the different parts and correctly explain their meaning.

2. Provide the correct meaning for each of the abbreviations commonly used on invoices.

3. Given an invoice showing the quantities of several items and their unit prices, calculate the extension totals and the invoice total.

4. Given the list price and trade discount for an item, calculate its net cost.

5. Define and calculate series (chain) discounts and discuss several circumstances under which these might be offered.

6. Given a series discount and the list price of an item, calculate the net cost by taking the discounts separately.

7. Given a series discount and the list price of an item, calculate the net cost by multiplying the complements of the single discounts.

8. Use a table to find the net cost equivalent of a series discount and use that figure to calculate the net cost of an item having a specified list price and series discount.

9. Express a given series discount as an equivalent single discount.

10. Calculate the list price of an item, given its net cost and its single or series discount.

11. Distinguish among ordinary dating, postdating, end-of-month dating, and receipt-of-goods dating and, given the terms and effective date, determine the net payment date and the last date for taking the cash discount under a specified invoice dating method.

12. Given an invoice total, trade discount, and cash discount terms, determine the total due for any specified payment date.

13. Calculate the discount available for partial payment of an invoice, given the terms and the amounts of the invoice and payment.

If you're using the hardcover textbook, *Mathematics for Business*, there are some additional objectives for the lesson. Upon completing your study of the lesson, you should also be able to:

14. Given the list price and available trade discounts for the same item, determine which of two suppliers offers the more advantageous net price.

15. Given the net price from each of two suppliers offering different cash discounts, determine which supplier is more advantageous for goods paid for on any specified payment date.

LESSON OVERVIEW

To understand how business discounts work, we need to be somewhat open-minded in our thinking about buyers and sellers. We usually think of consumers as buyers and retail merchants as sellers. That's fine, except that this is only one of many buyer-seller relationships. In fact, retail merchants are also buyers themselves, who purchase the goods they sell either from the producer or manufacturer or from a "middleman" like a *wholesale* distributor. Sometimes there are several wholesalers between the original manufacturer and the retailer, sometimes just one, and sometimes none. But keep in mind throughout this discussion that whereas consumers are virtually always the buyers in any situation, the retail merchant shifts hats regularly and is sometimes the buyer, sometimes the seller.

The Invoice

Every business transaction is recorded through some sort of written record. A sale is recorded through an *invoice*, which documents the nature of the merchandise (often including a written description), the amount of merchandise sold, the unit price, the *extension total* for a given type of merchandise, discount terms as appropriate, and a final total with an acceptable date of payment. In short, all the particulars governing how the sale will be handled, and what will change hands at what price, are included on the invoice. The invoice not only clarifies the terms of the sale, but also provides any business a useful written record of its income or expenses, depending on whether the business is in the role of buyer or seller.

It is critical that a business person be able to read an invoice accurately; not knowing how to read an invoice or not taking the time to decode it properly can literally cost the business money. For instance, suppose Henley's Fishing Supplies orders $1,000 worth of merchandise from World Manufacturing Company. When the merchandise arrives, Henley's staffers promptly inspect and inventory it, mark it for sale and put it on the shelves. They file the invoice for payment 30 days later.

Had they bothered to look more closely, though, they would have noticed that World billed them for two items they never received—$200 worth of fishing reels and $150 worth of wading boots. They would also have noticed that the invoice total was $1,250, not $1,000 as they'd expected. And that the bill was due in full 20 days following receipt of the goods, not the 30 days Henley's assumed. What's more, a *5/10, n20* notation on the invoice, if properly interpreted, would have informed Henley's that they were entitled to a 5 percent *cash discount—if* they paid within ten days—an offer Henley's might well have wanted to take advantage of.

Obviously, there was a lot on that invoice that warranted the attention of Henley's staff.

As it stands, not only has Henley's lost out on a cash discount savings of $50 or more but, unless someone quickly discovers the discrepancy between the shipment and the hastily filed invoice, it's likely to wind up paying for merchandise it never received and therefore certainly cannot sell. Further, its records are now inaccurate. A year from now, when staffers try to put together a summary of purchases and sales, it may be tough to figure out why there's nothing in the inventory or the sales receipts relating to the mysterious fishing reels and wading boots. By then, it may be too late for anyone to put the pieces back together and figure out what happened.

Business invoices, especially those for large companies with hefty orders, are likely to be crammed with data and to look pretty formidable. So perhaps we can sympathize with Henley's staff, who were so eager to get the goods on the shelf that they paid little attention to the invoice. But regardless of the excuse, their response is certainly unwise. What if World Manufacturing says that it *did* ship the fishing reels and waders and that Henley is just trying to get out of paying for them? Henley's legal position depends on the exact circumstances of the shipment and the paperwork, but Henley's could have a hard time getting out of paying for the shipment. Besides, an argument between World and Henley's over this $250 worth of goods might affect their entire business relationship. In any event, it should be clear that negligence and delays in checking invoices often cause problems that take more time to solve than would have been needed to deal with the invoice properly in the first place.

Henley's failure to deal with this invoice was probably just because the employees were in a hurry. But if they were reluctant to deal with the data because they felt they couldn't understand it, they were overestimating the difficulty of the task. True enough, reading an invoice takes time and some basic knowledge. That's because a typical invoice packs a lot of information into a small space, much of it written in a kind of code that looks a little like a foreign language to someone seeing it for the first time.

The code isn't intended to confuse buyers, though. On the contrary. It's intended to ensure consistency in the way different people read and interpret the invoice. For instance, all merchandise is sold in *units* of one sort or another: barrels, boxes, crates, quarts, dozens, pounds, or maybe just "each." These terms are not written out on most invoices; they're abbreviated. And the abbreviations have to be standardized. Otherwise, when Black in Seattle writes "C" on the invoice, Bates in San Francisco might take it to mean "crate," while Forster in St. Louis thinks it means "carton," and Wooster in Atlanta reads it as "100." To avoid this sort of confusion, the same abbreviations are used all the time and are never varied. It pays for the business person to memorize these abbreviations or at least know enough to look up abbreviations that aren't clear so there's no misunderstanding in interpreting someone else's notations.

Shipping Terms

Shipping terms like *FOB, COD,* and *FAS* commonly appear on invoices, too. They clarify the conditions under which goods are shipped from seller to buyer, particularly who pays for the shipping and who is responsible in the event that goods are lost or damaged in transit. It is important that both buyer and seller understand the terms of this arrangement *before* the goods leave the seller's hands. If something does happen to the merchandise en route, misunderstandings about who pays can be tough to straighten out and can jeopardize future business relations. In fact, a set of laws called the Uniform Commercial Code often applies to buying, selling, and shipping goods, and in order to avoid potential problems, the UCC has precise definitions of what these terms mean.

For instance, if merchandise is marked "FOB shipping point," the buyer is responsible for paying all shipping costs and actually owns the merchandise from the time it leaves the seller's hands. That means that the seller is *not* responsible for paying insurance that would cover the items in the event the shipment is lost, nor for fixing or replacing it if it is damaged in transit. Unfortunately, if the buyer did not understand the terms of shipment, the need to replace damaged goods may come as a nasty surprise. If the buyer protests, however, the seller is likely to say, "Check the invoice," which is usually mailed in advance of the shipment. A buyer who simply protests that he or she didn't know what the shipping terms meant is only showing ignorance and is unlikely to get much sympathy from an experienced seller (and none at all from the legal system).

By the way, shipping and insurance costs, whether assumed by the buyer or the seller, are not likely to be reflected on the invoice. That's because trade and cash discounts are never applied to these extra costs, so to avoid confusion, the seller customarily includes on the invoice only those costs that relate directly to the merchandise itself. The cost of shipping and insurance must be added later.

Many invoices these days are generated by computer, so the chances of math errors are small. Yet as our earlier illustration with Henley's Fishing Supply illustrates, computers have no sense of whether what's in the shipment matches what's printed on the invoice. Besides, there's always the chance that the wrong data has been entered into the computer or the *per-unit price* on an item does not reflect the discounts that the buyer and seller agreed to. Obviously, it does no good to accept a discount and then lose it to a data entry error. A buyer who's been offered, say, a 20/10/10 discount must check to see whether the extension total for that item reflects the anticipated discount. If it doesn't, perhaps there was an oversight on the part of the seller or a misunderstanding about the buy-sell agreement.

To take advantage of a cash discount, it is often necessary to calculate the due date for the payments. This would be simple enough if the terms offered were always consistent, but they're not. For instance, an invoice may specify that payment is due within 30 days. Fine. But 30 days calculated from when? If there is no other notation, the buyer can assume that the 30 days is figured from the date of the invoice. Let's say that's November 7. There are 30 days in November, so $30 - 7 = 23$ days remaining this month, plus another seven days in December to make the full 30, so the money is due December 7.

But the due date might be written *as of* November 10, in which case the buyer would have 30 days after November 10 to pay. Notice, too, that the calculations would be a little different if the invoice were dated December 7 or January 7; those months have 31 days. Thirty days from December 7 is January 6, not January 7. That one day could mean the difference between qualifying or not qualifying for a discount. It might even put the buyer in the position of owing late charges on an overdue bill.

As the written summary of their sales transaction, the invoice is important to both buyer and seller, and it is imperative that both take time to read it thoroughly and to ensure that what it says reflects their under-

**Taking Advantage
of Discounts**

standing of the sales agreement. Let's look now at some specifics that affect the nature of that agreement itself.

The Trade Discount

All discounts, including the standard *trade discount*, are based on *list price*, or the proposed price at which an item is offered for sale to the public. Clearly, not all goods are sold to consumers at their list price. In fact, it's generally illegal for manufacturers and distributors to try to force retailers to sell their products at only at list price. Very often, the merchant will sell them for less as part of a sale or special promotion. Sometimes, as in the case of an automobile that is in great demand, the merchant can sell the product at *more* than the suggested list price. But even though the selling price is often different, every product has a list price, and it's from this list price that discounts are given.

Obviously, the retail merchant could not afford to buy goods at the list price. For instance, a clothier who bought raincoats for $80, then turned around and sold them for $80, would be doing nothing more than performing a public service by making shopping a little more convenient for consumers. He wouldn't even break even on the deal since he'd have to use a portion of his $80 to pay rent, taxes, utilities, and other expenses, which the merchant incurs whether he makes a profit or not. Soon the raincoat merchant and all others like him would go out of business and consumers would have to buy their goods directly from the manufacturer. Of course, happily for consumers, that isn't the way it works. We say happily because if it *did* work like that, the consumer would need to go to one manufacturer to buy a raincoat, another for shoes, another for ballpoint pens, and so on. Shopping could easily turn into a full-time enterprise.

But luckily, the business world recognizes the need for each person in the merchandising network to make *some* profit in order to stay in business. The way this comes about is for the manufacturer and each successive wholesaler to offer the next buyer in line a *trade discount*, a price that allows the buyer to purchase goods at some percentage off the list price. The buyer who purchases an item at discount can afford to mark it up for sale to the public, and out of the difference, he or she can pay business expenses and still make a profit.

The amount of the trade discount varies from item to item, depending partly on the cost of production and somewhat upon the volume of business the buyer offers the seller. For instance, if Big City Department Store can afford to buy 200 raincoats at a time, Stitchright Manufacturing may offer it a slightly higher discount than it offers to the Corner Clothier, which only orders six coats at a time. After all, some of the costs of selling raincoats (like making the initial sales call, printing the invoice, or arranging for shipment) aren't that much less for small orders than large ones.

In pricing their merchandise, manufacturers and wholesalers have the same sorts of concerns that the retailer will later have in selling to the public. They need to keep costs down and profits up. That usually means more willingness to negotiate price on bigger sales, or on sales of merchandise that is less popular. Maybe raincoats are hot sellers this year. Not only is the weather cold and rainy across the country, but every fashion magazine is promoting the trenchcoat look. But perhaps another item, say wool socks, is all but unsalable. If only a few consumers want wool socks this year, those retailers who are good sports about taking already manufactured socks off the hands of producers are likely to be rewarded with a substantial trade discount. This, in turn, permits them to lower prices to consumers. And since the lower prices may make consumers buy more socks, everybody wins: The manufacturer can sell socks that weren't going to sell, the retailer can sell socks at a lower price but still make a profit, and the consumer can buy socks at a lower price.

You may be wondering how sellers go about offering different discount rates on different items, or to different buyers. Well, let's begin by saying that they do *not* set discount rates whimsically or on impulse. Rather, they use a mathematical approach designed to make any sale even more appealing for the buyer: the series discount.

Series Discounts

A *series discount* is also called a *chain discount*. As its name implies, a chain discount is like a succession of "sales," one right on top of the other. An item is discounted once based on list price, then discounted again based on the remaining balance (list price minus the first discount), and sometimes even discounted a third or fourth time.

For instance, suppose Corner Clothier is given a 40/10 discount on battery-operated, glow-in-the-dark umbrellas; very trendy this year, according to the marketing representative who first introduced them to CC's purchasing agent. And let's say that the list price on these unusual accessories is $100. The first discount (of 40 percent) knocks the $100 cost down to $60, since $100 \times .40 = 40$ and $100 - 40 = 60$. But on this balance of $60, Corner Clothier is entitled to *another* 10 percent off; so the final cost will be $54, since $60 \times .10 = 6$ and $60 - 6 = 54$.

At this point, the manufacturer (sensing opportunity) may tell Corner Clothier that if it is willing to order 100 of the umbrellas instead of the 30 it originally asked for, it can qualify for another 20 percent off. This would bring the per-unit price down to $43.20 ($54 \times .20 = 10.80$ and $54 - 10.80 = 43.20$). Now, a hundred glow-in-the-dark umbrellas is a lot. But remember, the list price on this item is $100, so if Corner Clothier is paying just under $45 per unit, the potential for profit is great. Perhaps it can afford to offer the item "on sale," say for $79.95, and still come out well ahead. Will battery-operated umbrellas capture the public imagination? Who can say? The point is, a chain discount can tempt a buyer to consider a product that wouldn't seem so appealing at a higher price, or to buy more than he or she might otherwise be willing to purchase.

There are all sorts of reasons that chain discounts might be offered. One, as we've seen, is to encourage merchants to buy more. Another might be to open a new market, say in a different geographic area. For instance, consider Buddy Pet Supplies, which up until now has only sold to markets in the Midwest. Buddy would like to branch out, to take on some new accounts in the Northeast and on the West Coast. But the trouble is, those pet stores already have suppliers they're working with. And they have no complaints about products or service. What's more, if these retailers buy from Buddy, they'll have to pay substantial shipping costs to get the merchandise to their stores. There's also an additional delay involved because of the distance, and then there's the hassle of long-distance negotiations. All this adds up to the kind of sales resistance that Buddy could do without. The store can break down some of that sales resistance, though, by offering a series discount on some or all of its merchandise.

Let's say Buddy's regular trade discount is 35 percent. It can't compete on the West Coast with that rate, though, because retailers there are already getting 35 percent off from their other suppliers. So, Buddy might begin by offering West Coast buyers a 35/10 series discount on selected items or on all the merchandise they order. Those retailers that agree to buy in greater volumes, and that would include the bigger stores and those with multiple outlets, might qualify for an even better 35/10/5 series discount.

Some products are seasonal, or may be seasonal to some buyers. Take water skis. Manufacturing water skis costs pretty much the same in January as in June, but water skis would be a tough sell in most of the country in January. Rather than shut down the factory, though, the water ski manufacturer may find it better to offer additional discounts during the winter months to keep retailers buying. So the retailer who normally qualifies for a 40 percent trade discount on water skis may be offered a 40/15 series discount in January, an additional 15 percent off for buying off-season.

Calculating a Series Discount

Keep in mind that the figures in a series discount are never added together, nor are they averaged. In other words, a 40/10 discount is not the same thing as a 50 percent discount. The totals on a single item might be fairly close, but "close" usually isn't good enough in the business world. For instance, as we've seen, a 40/10 discount on a $100 item amounts to a cost of $54; that's four dollars more than the buyer would pay with a regular trade discount of 50 percent.

Well, you might say, that's approximately the same thing. True. But approximations can lead to big differences in volume buying. Unlike individual consumers, retailers rarely buy one of anything. They tend to order dozens or hundreds or thousands, or even tens of thousands, of a given item. On an order of 10,000, a $4 per unit difference adds up to $40,000 — hardly insignificant, even for the most casual business manager. Still, you might be saying to yourself, it would simplify things for the business manager to be able to think in terms of a *single* discount equivalent instead of a whole string of numbers. Most managers would agree with you, and as it happens, the *single discount equivalent* is simple to calculate.

Calculating the net cost equivalent. Each number in the discount series has a decimal equivalent. In the 20/10 series, the decimal equivalents are .20 and .10, or 20 percent and 10 percent. These numbers, in turn, have *complements*. The complement is simply the difference between the decimal and the whole number *one*. So, the complement of .40 is .60 (1 − .40 = .60). And the complement of .10 is .90 (1 − .10 = .90). When two complements are multiplied together, the result is the *net cost equivalent*. In this case, the net cost equivalent is .60 × .90 = .54. If we multiply the list price by the net cost equivalent, we can find the price. Not surprisingly, multiplying the $100 list price of our umbrellas by .54 gives $54.

We now know how much we have to pay, but we don't quite know the discount. We're very close, however; to find the single discount equivalent, all we do is subtract the net cost equivalent from 1. In our example, we subtract .54 from 1 and get .46. In other words (as we suspected from our earlier calculations) a 40/10 discount is pretty close to 50 percent. But remember, in the world of business, pretty close doesn't count. We need to know *precisely* what the amount of the discount is.

Using tables. In calculating the single discount equivalent, most business people use tables. They're not necessary, really, since the calculations (just simple multiplication) are not that complex. But the tables do save time. They also help ensure accuracy. The number in the table is the *net cost equivalent*, the product of all the discount complements in the series. In other words, the only step left, when using a table, is to multiply this net cost equivalent times the original list price to find the cost of the item at a given discount.

Notice, however, that this figure is *not* the amount of the discount; it's the amount the buyer must *pay*. The trouble with shortcuts is that when someone else does part of the calculating for you, as with a net cost equivalent table, it's easy to lose track of where you are in the whole math process. Just remember if you use a net cost equivalent table that the figure you come up with will be the amount the buyer pays the seller.

Since a 40/10 series discount is mathematically the same as a straight discount of 46 percent, you may be wondering what all the fuss is about. Why not just set the discount at 46 percent and be done with it? The answer is simple: This wouldn't give the seller any flexibility. Remember, earlier we noted that sellers often vary the discount from product to product or buyer to buyer. So, some buyers may qualify for only the first discount in the series, or 40 percent. Others, those who buy more or buy a wider range of products, for instance, may qualify for an additional 10 percent off, so the 40/10 series applies to them. And on some products or during certain times of the year, the seller may extend the series again, to 40/10/5 perhaps, for qualified buyers. In short, the series discount gives the seller some leverage in catering to those buyers who purchase certain products, or buy more, or in some way increase the seller's profits.

Cash Discounts

Retailers obviously tend to favor consumers who pay their bills on time. Wholesalers and manufacturers feel exactly the same way, and with good reason.

A strong cash flow gives a business buying power: money for new inventory, money to put on new staff, money to expand. When cash flow is slow, the business may need to borrow to cover its needs. Borrowing costs money and can drain cash reserves even more, especially for the business that is already weighted down with other debts. Ready cash minimizes the need for borrowing and allows the business to use its own money to meet expenses, almost always the cheaper way to go.

Ideally, from the seller's point of view, the buyer would pay each bill the moment he or she received the invoice. But let's be realistic. The buyer needs cash reserves, too, and so is likely to wait until the last possible minute to pay; unless, of course, there's some motivation to do otherwise. The *cash discount* can provide that kind of motivation. It's the seller's way of saying to the buyer, "Look, you're going to pay this money eventually anyway. Pay me early, and I'll make it worth your while by charging you a little less. That's how important it is to me to get the money as soon as possible."

Of course, the difference between the company that pays promptly and the one that really drags its financial heels may be only 30 days or so. Is that enough to really make such a big difference? Well, it could be. Think of it this way. Suppose you took a new job and your employer said, "We'll pay you $2,000 a month. You can have the first $2,000 now, or at the end of the month." Which would you choose? For most people, this would be a simple choice because $2,000, or any amount of money, is worth more now than in the future. Why? Well, for one thing, inflation makes the cost of living go up steadily, meaning that virtually anything we buy as consumers costs a little less now than it will cost later, other things being equal. If income goes up too, that's another matter. But in this case, you don't make anything by waiting; you get the same $2,000 whether you take it now or 30 days from now. But in addition, let's say your monthly expenses are only $1,000. In that case, you could take the extra $1,000 and invest it, thereby increasing its value. You couldn't do that, though, unless you could get your hands on the money.

The business person must think the same way. From his or her standpoint, today's money is worth a little more than tomorrow's. In fact, because of increased buying power and investment return, the business person expects to make more in the long run than he or she loses by allowing the cash discount. Were this not so, businesses would discontinue the practice. But let's consider an example to clarify how it works.

Suppose Miller's Feed Store buys a load of grain from Golden Field Supply and receives a $1,000 invoice with a *2/10, n/30* notation. This means that Miller's has 30 days in which to pay the full $1,000, the net amount owed. But if Miller's pays Golden Field within 10 days of the invoice date, it will qualify for a 2 percent discount on the grain. In this case, that amounts to $20. Now, in the business world, $20 is clearly not a fortune. But it isn't insignificant, either. After all, this is just one of many bills that Miller's owes. Over the course of a year, it could easily save thousands of dollars simply by taking advantage of cash discounts. In addition, remember that the actual profit stores make may be only a few percentage points. That 2 percent cash discount results in a direct increase in profit; for the store otherwise showing an 8 percent gross profit, the effect of a 2 percent cash discount is to raise gross profits a whopping 25 percent.

If Miller's takes advantage of the cash discount, as well it might, Golden Field loses $20. It doesn't mind, though. As it happens, it doesn't need to spend that $1,000 (or $980, to be precise) just now. That's because lots of other buyers have also taken Golden Field up on the cash discount offer, so the company is flush right now. Instead of using Miller's money to pay bills, it can invest it long-term at 12 percent compound interest and earn back much of the $20 discount within the first month. Besides, when other buyers learn of the cash discount offered by Golden Field, they may wish to purchase grain from this supplier, too. That means a growing market and expanding profits.

Dating Methods for Invoices and Cash Payments

Some cash discounts are offered on an *end-of-month*, or *proximo*, basis. The notation on the invoice looks like this: *2/10 EOM* or *2/10 prox.* This means that the buyer has until the tenth of the *following month* to take advantage of the 2 percent cash discount. And if the invoice is received on or after the 26th of the month, it is customary to extend the discount period not just to the next month, but to the month after that. In other words, an invoice received on January 28th with a *2/10 EOM* notation would not be due until *March* 10. The extension is intended to give the buyer a little additional time, a sort of grace period, in which to come up with the money.

In some cases—with a *COD* (cash on delivery) shipment, for instance—the invoice may arrive with the merchandise. Very often, though, the invoice is sent on ahead, as soon as the sale is negotiated, and the merchandise arrives some time later. If it's arriving from out of state, or from out of the country for that matter, it may take days or weeks to reach its destination. Say Ruskin in Los Angeles orders lampshades from a company in New York. She receives the invoice on May 5, just two days after placing her order. The lampshades aren't in L.A. yet, though. They had to be packed in New York and put aboard a truck. Right now they're somewhere east of Chicago, still four days short of arrival.

Meanwhile, what does Ruskin do? Pay the bill? That's not necessary. The lampshade company marked her invoice *3/15 ROG*, meaning that she has 15 days *from receipt of goods* to qualify for a cash discount. It doesn't matter when the invoice is dated; the discount days don't start elapsing until the shipment is in the buyer's hands. So, if the truck breaks down in Chicago and doesn't reach L.A. till May 20, Ruskin has 15 full days from that date, or until June 4, to qualify for the discount.

Since most sellers who offer cash discounts are happy to see any portion of the money come in early, they still offer cash discounts on *partial payments*. So, for instance, if Miller's Feed Store pays half its $2,000 bill ($1,000) in time for the cash discount, it will receive the 2 percent discount on that amount. In other words, it is to the buyer's advantage to pay any portion of the bill quickly if a cash discount is available.

Keep in mind, incidentally, that the net cost to a buyer is the list price minus *both* the trade discount and any cash discount. Taking one kind of discount does not disqualify the buyer from taking the other. In general, however, the cash discount is calculated on the amount due according to the invoice (less any freight and insurance that might have been added), not on the list price. In other words, don't make the mistake of calculating the cash discount on the list price, as you would the trade discount.

SOME WORDS OF ADVICE

Whether you are in the position of buyer or seller, take time to become familiar with the codes and format of an invoice. You must be able to read this document accurately, or you will have no way of knowing whether the terms of the sale are those to which you agreed and whether the merchandise ordered has all been properly billed at the agreed-upon price. Further, if you are a buyer, you may lose opportunities to qualify for cash discounts if you don't read the fine print. Some sellers will spell it out for you; they want their money, so they put the terms of the discount in bold letters where they hope you can't miss it. You may miss it anyway, though, if you don't attend to the invoice and simply hope everything is in order.

As a seller, consider the value of series or cash discounts to attract more buyers or to promote sales of less popular or lesser-known products. Almost everyone loves a bargain, and some buyers will go so far as to borrow the money they need to take advantage of cash discounts. Cutting prices is, however, a good deal only when the increased sales more than offset the loss in profit on each individual item. Discounts obviously should be offered only after considerable thought about their impact on sales and profits.

As a buyer, check to see whether you qualify for cash or series discounts. If the seller doesn't offer them outright, ask; such discounts may be negotiable, especially if you can show that it would be to the seller's advantage to do business with you. Maybe your business is growing; maybe you have plans to open a new store in a region nobody else has touched. Your potential to increase sales or open new markets could literally mean money in your pocket (or at least less money out).

Cash discounts are likely to benefit you no matter which side of the buy-sell agreement you're negotiating from. As a seller, you benefit from the improved cash flow and flexibility that up-front cash payments provide. As a buyer, you can save money by paying early. Obviously, though, it's important to verify that you have no better use for the money. You don't have to take cash discounts, and you shouldn't if your own cash flow is likely to become a problem if you pay all invoices immediately.

Another word of caution to buyers: Don't let the lure of a discount tempt you into buying things you neither want nor need. No merchandise, however attractively priced, is really a good buy if you can't resell it. If it just sits on your shelves collecting dust, then *anything* you've paid for represents a loss to the company. Worse, if you make such purchasing mistakes too often, you may wind up with a reputation for being out of touch with consumers' needs. If you're offered a too-good-to-pass-up sort of bargain, try to figure out the reason behind it. Sometimes it's quite legitimate. An off-season special on an album of Christmas songs, for instance, could be a real money-saver if you normally handle holiday music and have lots of empty warehouse space.

But how about that gigantic series discount on inflatable palm trees? Before you get carried away with the bargain price, stop and think: The first number that has to make sense is the selling price. Perhaps you can't sell inflatable palm trees to consumers at $20 or $10 or even $1, and your business will be in trouble if you load up on them. No discount is sufficient to offset the absence of a good market for the product.

KEY TERMS

Before you read through the text assignment and watch the video program, take a minute to look at the key terms associated with this lesson. When you encounter them in the text and video program, pay careful attention to their meaning.

As of: See *Postdating*.

Cash discount: A discount offered by the seller allowing the buyer to take a discount on the amount due if payment is made within a specified period of time.

Chain discount: A discount involving two or more separate discounts. Also known as a series discount.

COD: A shipping term meaning "cash on delivery."

Complement: When related to discounts, the number that must be added to a given discount to get 1 (or 100 percent).

Consumer: The ultimate user of a product or service; the last buyer in the chain.

Destination: The city or town where goods are being shipped.

Discount: An amount subtracted from the list price of a product or service.

End-of-month dating: In cash discounts, the time period beginning at the end of the month the invoice is dated. Also known as dating *proximo* (meaning "the following").

Extension total: On an invoice, the product of the number of items times the unit price.

FAS: Free alongside ship (or simply *free alongside*). This term is used to indicate that the price quoted by the seller includes all costs of transporting the goods and, further, that the shipper is responsible for the goods in transit.

FOB: Free on board. When goods are shipped "FOB shipping point," the buyer pays shipping and insurance costs and is responsible for the goods from the time they leave the seller's hands. When goods are shipped "FOB destination," the seller pays shipping and insurance costs and is responsible for the goods until they reach the destination specified on the shipping invoice.

Invoice: A written record of a sales transaction that helps both buyer and seller keep track of sales and purchases.

Invoice total: The total amount owed on an invoice; this is the sum of all extension totals. Note that this total does not include shipping or insurance costs.

List price: The manufacturer's suggested retail price, or the final price to the consumer. All discounts are based on this price.

Net cost: The cost after all allowable deductions have been taken.

Net cost equivalent: The product of the complements of trade discounts in a series. This number is the *percentage paid*; when multiplied by the list price, it equals the net cost.

Ordinary dating method: A method for calculating the discount date and the net payment date. Days are counted from the date of the invoice but do not include the date of the invoice.

Partial payment: A payment that is less than the total owed on an invoice; a cash discount can still be earned on the partial payment.

Postdating: Dating in the future, or "as of" dating on an invoice.

Proximo dating: In cash discounts, the time period beginning at the end of the month the invoice is dated. Also called *end-of-month* or *EOM* dating.

Receipt of goods (ROG) dating: ROG dating is used in cash discounts; time is counted from the date that goods are received.

Retailer: A business selling directly to the consumer.

Series discount: See *chain discount*.

Shipping point: The location from which merchandise is shipped by the seller to the buyer.

Single discount: A discount expressed as a single percentage, not as a series.

Single discount equivalent to a series discount: A series or chain discount expressed as a single number or percentage.

Trade discount: A discount offered to businesses. A trade discount may be expressed as a single number (e.g., 25 percent) or as a series (e.g., 20/10/5). Either way, it is based on the list price.

Wholesaler: The middleman; someone who buys from the manufacturer or another wholesaler and sells either to the retailer or to another wholesaler.

PART II: WATCHING THE VIDEO PROGRAM

VIDEO VIEWING GUIDE

Before watching the video program, review the following questions. As you watch, be sure to collect the information necessary to answer them:

1. How do the roles of buyer and seller interrelate with the roles of manufacturer, wholesaler, retailer, and consumer?

2. What are some reasons why it is important for both buyers and sellers to know how to read an invoice properly?

3. What is the purpose of an invoice? Identify as many as possible. (There are several.)

4. What are some reasons sellers offer series discounts?

5. Can you identify a general rule for when is it wise for a buyer to take advantage of special discounts offered by the manufacturer or wholesaler?

6. Are some products more likely to be subject to series discounts than others? If so, which ones and why?

7. Some buyers are more likely to qualify for series discounts than others. What kinds of buyers? Why?

8. What is the primary reason why sellers offer a cash discount? When should a seller not offer a cash discount?

9. There are circumstances under which a discount is not a good deal. What are some of these circumstances?

VIDEO PROGRAM

The lesson's video program is Program 11 – The Business Discount. Remember, if you are watching this program on videotape, take time to replay sections of the tape any time you need to review a concept.

VIDEO VIEWING QUESTIONS

Immediately after viewing the video program for Lesson 11, take time to respond to the following questions. Give your answers some careful thought; they may provide the basis for additional discussion or a longer written response.

1. Give three examples of misunderstandings, confusion, or even legal problems that can result from not accurately reading an invoice

   . . . if you are a buyer.

   _____

   _____

   _____

   . . . if you are a seller.

   _____

   _____

   _____

2. Name any two reasons a series discount might be offered on a product:

   a. _____

   b. _____

3. Imagine that you are a seller who deals in all of the following products. On which of these products do you think you would be *very likely* to offer a series discount as opposed to a single trade discount? (Check as many as apply. Be prepared to give reasons for your response.)

   _____ Windshield wipers

   _____ Nails

   _____ Swimsuits

   _____ Pocket calculators

   _____ Original oil paintings

   _____ Automobile tires

   _____ Fertilizer

   _____ Watermelons grown in Texas

4. A seller is often willing to extend a buyer additional time in which to qualify for a cash discount. Name one reason you think this might be so:

   _____

   _____

5. Which of the following factors do you think might influence a merchant's ability to qualify for a series discount? (Check as many as apply. Be prepared to give a reason for your response.)

   _____ Nature of the business

   _____ Size of the business

   _____ Number of employees

_____ Number of different outlets (retail stores) operated by the business

_____ Geographic location of the business

_____ Future goals of the business

_____ Financial health of the business

_____ Past performance in paying bills

_____ Whether the business is a wholesaler or retailer

_____ Current advertising strategies used by the business

6. Imagine that you are a wholesale distributor of automotive parts. One of your retail accounts has been notoriously slow in paying its bills. On a scale of 1 to 10, how likely would you, as a seller, be to offer this retailer a cash discount? (Be prepared to give a reason for your response.)

Not   **Very**
Likely   **Likely**

1- - - - -2- - - - -3- - - - -4- - - - -5- - - - -6- - - - -7- - - - -8- - - - -9- - - - -10

7. In your own words, sum up in a sentence or two how a buyer can know whether a discount is really a good value:

_____

_____

_____

_____

PART III: FOCUSING ON THE MATHEMATICS

READING ASSIGNMENT _____

After watching the video program, you should read one of the following Text Assignments, depending on the textbook you're using:

SOFTCOVER: Chapter 6 of the Miller, Salzman, and Hoelzle softcover text, _Business Mathematics_, pages 197-228.

HARDCOVER: Chapter 8 of the Salzman, Miller, and Hoelzle hardcover text, _Mathematics for Business_, pages 272-301.

As you read through the text, pay careful attention to the examples the book gives of the mathematics associated with the concepts you're learning about.

Then, after you've completed the text assignment, read through the Key Formulas below. This section provides a handy review of what you've learned. By the time you get to this point in the lesson, all of the formulas and calculations should be familiar to you. If they're not, go back and read

the appropriate parts of the text and the Overview section of this lesson. You won't have much success completing the rest of your assignments if you are still confused about the information in the Key Formulas section.

KEY FORMULAS

The following key formulas are important to your understanding of this lesson. Be sure that you know each one and how to use it in solving problems related to business discounts.

KEY FORMULA: Net cost = List price − Trade discount

Formula used for: Determining the net cost of an item when the list price and discount are known.

Example:

The list price on an oak rocker is $200 and the trade discount is 25 percent, or $50, since 200 × .25 = 50. Thus, the net cost is $200 − $50 = $150.

Remember that in this formula:

1. The net cost is the cost to the wholesaler or retailer; this formula is not used to find the net cost to the individual consumer, who does not qualify for a trade discount.

2. The list price is the manufacturer's suggested retail price, or the cost of the item to the consumer.

3. The trade discount may be a single figure, as in our example with the rocker, or it might be a series discount. In the event it's the latter, a single discount equivalent must be calculated before the net cost can be determined. See the next formula for an example.

KEY FORMULA: Percentage paid × List price = Net cost

Formula used for: Determining the net cost on an item when the list price and the percentage paid (also called the net cost equivalent) are known.

Example:

The list price of a radial tire is $100. The series discount is 10/20. Using the complements on these two figures, we can determine the net cost equivalent, or the percentage paid. Thus, .90 × .8 = .72. This means that the buyer will pay .72, or 72 percent of the list price. So the net cost is .72 × $100 = $72.

Remember that in this formula:

1. The *percentage paid* is the same as the *net cost equivalent*.

2. If a straight trade discount is used, the percentage paid is the same as *100 percent − the amount of the trade discount*. Let's say the trade discount is 25 percent. Then the amount paid is 100 percent − 25 percent = 75 percent.

3. If a series discount is used, as in the example, calculate the percentage paid by multiplying the complements of each number in the series. The complement is simply *1 − the decimal equivalent of the number*. The decimal equivalent of 10 is .10. Thus, the complement is .90, or 1 − .10.

4. If you are using a net cost equivalent table, you need only multiply the correct number from the table times the list price to find the net cost.

5. When using the net cost equivalent table, keep in mind that the order of the numbers in a discount series makes no difference at all to the final net cost. A 10/30/20 discount is *mathematically* the same as a 10/20/30 or a 30/20/10. Just be sure all the numbers are accounted for, regardless of order, before doing the final calculation.

KEY FORMULA: Net cost = List price − trade discount − cash discount

Formula used for: Determining the net cost when both a trade discount and a cash discount are taken.

Example:

The list price on an above-ground swimming pool is $500. The trade discount is 20/10, and the cash discount is 2 percent (assuming payment within 10 days). Let's calculate the trade discount first, using the complements method discussed above. The amount paid will be .80 × .90, or .72. Thus, the discount is 1 − .72, or .28. So the trade discount is $500 × .28 = $140. The cash discount is 2 percent of the amount due, which is $500 − $140 = $360 × .02 = $7.20. Now we can use the formula to determine net cost. Net cost = ($500 − $140) − $7.20 = $352.80.

Remember that in this formula:

1. You need to determine the *amount* of the trade discount and the amount of the cash discount, not just the percentages.

2. The amount of the cash discount is based on the amount due to the seller, not the list price (as is the case for a trade discount).

DON'T FORGET

1. All trade discount calculations are based on *list price*, or the price at which merchandise is offered to the public.

2. When you calculate the net cost equivalent for a series discount, the order of the discounts in the series makes *absolutely no difference*. Thus, a 20/10 discount and a 10/20 discount are no different in terms of the final net cost. (They may be very different, though, when it comes to the practical business negotiations between buyer and seller; see the discussion in the Overview.)

3. *Never* add the numbers in a series discount together. A 20/10 series discount is not the same as a trade discount of 30 percent.

4. Be careful about rounding the net discount equivalent; for example, a net discount equivalent of .509 should not be rounded to, say, .5. If

you round this number, the amount of the discount is going to be slightly inaccurate, which could cause a substantial over- or under-payment if the amount of the order is large.

5. When using the table of net cost equivalents, simply multiply the correct number times list price to find net cost. (Incidentally, there are times when tables of numbers are used in business math because the related math is either difficult or extremely tedious. This isn't one of these cases; net cost equivalents are easy to figure out. But since a seller or buyer might have to calculate many prices, it's worth having a table to save a little effort each time.)

6. In a cash discount notation, such as *2/10, n/30*, the first number is the amount of the discount. It is followed by the number of days allowed to get the discount. In this case the buyer has 10 days within which to qualify for a 2 percent discount and 30 days within which to pay the net owed. Incidentally, the days shown for a discount never includes the date of the invoice; net 30, for example, means that payment is due on the thirtieth day starting from the day after the invoice date.

7. A buyer who makes a partial payment within the cash discount period qualifies for a discount on the amount paid.

PART IV: SOLVING BUSINESS PROBLEMS

PROBLEM SETS

Work the following problems in your textbook. Your instructor will tell you which problems, if any, are to be turned in. Some of the problems have answers provided in the back of the book; refer to these answers to make sure you are working the problems correctly.

SOFTCOVER: If you are using the Miller, Salzman, and Hoelzle softcover text, *Business Mathematics*, do the following problem sets:

6.1: Problems #14-20 on page 202.

6.2: Problems #18-20, 30-32, and 36-39 on pages 207-208.

6.3: Problems #12-14 and 23-25 on pages 211-213.

6.4: Problems #4-6 and 17-19 on pages 219-220.

6.5: Problems #6-9 and 20-24 on pages 225-228.

HARDCOVER: If you are using the Salzman, Miller, and Hoelzle hardcover text, *Mathematics for Business*, do the following problem sets:

8.1: Problems #22-34, 50-54, and 62-68 (even numbers only) on pages 281-283.

8.2: Problems #16-42 (even numbers only) on pages 287-288.

8.3: Problems #28-36 on pages 294-295.

8.4: Problems #8-13, 24-36, and 38-43 on pages 299-301.

BUSINESS APPLICATIONS

Read each of the following scenarios and answer the questions about the decisions you would make in each situation. Give these questions some serious thought; they may be used as the basis for discussion or the development of a more complex essay. You should base your decisions on what you've learned from this lesson, applying both math skills and good business judgment to solve the problem at hand.

SCENARIO 1   Elmira's Gift Shop is a little low on inventory. Owner Elmira Finch is fearful of losing sales when buyers eye the empty shelves and sparse window displays. She would like to add new merchandise to make the business look a little more prosperous, but it's hard to do just now with the cash flow so low and sales down.

A new company, Rainbow Visions, offers Elmira an excellent buy on its specialty line of stained glass fixtures, including lamps, windows, terrariums, and other decorative items. The craftsmanship on the stained glassware is excellent, and it would certainly make an attractive addition to the front window. Better yet, Elmira can get the items at a 40/10 series discount if she is the first retailer in the area to take Rainbow up on its offer—with an additional 10 percent discount if her order is $1,500 or more. Rainbow also offers a cash discount of 5 percent on payments made within 10 days following receipt of the goods.

Elmira doesn't have the cash on hand to take advantage of this offer, but she could cover the cost by taking out a short-term loan from the bank at 16 percent simple interest. If business is good, she should be able to repay the loan within a month or two. But what if it isn't? Besides, maybe it would be wiser to spend that $1,500 on enlarging the store's current inventory of gift items, rather than taking on something new. After all, who knows how well the Rainbow Visions products might sell? Other gift shops don't seem to carry much in the way of stained glass, and Elmira feels a little suspicious about the amount of the discount. "There must be something wrong," she tells one of her staff, "or they would never discount a new product that much." At the same time, she recognizes that the stained glass products would distinguish Elmira's from her competitors.

What do you think? Should Elmira borrow the money to put in a new product line, or would that just be foolishly risking the future of the business on a product with no track record? Use the methods you've learned in this lesson to answer the following questions:

☐   Is Elmira right to be so suspicious of this seemingly good deal? Or is there likely to be a perfectly legitimate reason for this discount?

☐   Suppose Elmira bought $1,500 worth of goods from Rainbow Visions, paid for it immediately with cash, and sold it all at list price. About how much money would she take in?

□ The scenario doesn't tell us much about the discounts Elmira is receiving on the products she currently sells. Is this important information? If so, why?

□ Should Elmira take advantage of the cash discount offered by Rainbow Visions? Why or why not? Or does it depend on the specific circumstances?

□ What are the most important factors (mathematical and non-mathematical) for Elmira, or any business person, to consider in making a decision of this type?

SCENARIO 2

Oso Toy Company is having difficulty pushing its new product line of battery-operated robots. Oso's marketing director, Halsey Fitzgibbon, believes this toy has the potential to top all others in sales, *if* Oso can ever get reluctant retailers to put it on the shelves. Response so far has been dismal, despite ad campaigns in the trade press and extensive trade show involvement.

The regular trade discount on the robot is 30 percent, with a list price of $120 on the smaller XR1 model and a list price of $160 on the deluxe XR7, which responds to voice commands. Fitzgibbon suggests promoting the robots with a 30/15 discount to retailers who have larger volume sales and even an additional 10 percent to those on the East Coast, where Oso hasn't had much of a market yet.

But company president Delores deLucci doesn't think much of the idea. She thinks the proposed discount is too big, for one thing; it will make retailers think poorly of the product. She feels Oso's reputation as a designer and seller of quality toys depends on "not overselling—as if we were desperate." Besides, she tells Fitzgibbon, it wouldn't be good for business overall to reduce profits even more on a product that has basically done so poorly. Might as well stick with their current best-sellers, like their top video games. Why take a chance, especially this time of year with the holiday buying season coming?

Fitzgibbon's view remains different; he's unpersuaded by what he calls deLucci's "overly cautious attitude." He looks on the series discount pricing as an opportunity for Oso to make up for some of its losses on the early marketing efforts. Besides, he points out to deLucci, it's unfair to judge the marketability of any product till it's been before the public, which the robots haven't—thanks to the reluctant retailers. Oso's preliminary marketing studies suggest that the list prices are right in line with what consumers will pay, so he's certain that the problem is getting retailers to buy the robots in the first place.

What do you think? Is series discounting a good business strategy in this case, or will it just cause profits to drop even further? Use the methods you've learned in this lesson to answer these questions:

□ Should Oso Toys offer a series discount on the robots? Why or why not?

□ If they do offer a series discount, do you think Fitzgibbon's proposed figures are good ones, or would you suggest a bigger or smaller discount? Why?

□ Are there specific mathematical calculations that Fitzgibbon and deLucci need to make that will help them make a decision that's less guesswork?

☐ The scenario doesn't tell us much about why the retailers aren't buying the robot, so it's possible that Fitzgibbon is cutting prices when he doesn't need to. If you were in deLucci's shoes, what questions would you want answered before you made a final decision about whether to approve the discount?

Pricing Products and Services 12

The people in my apartment are kinda weird. The lady next door tried to hold up a department store with a pricing gun . . . . "Hand over all your money or I'll mark down everything in the store."

Steven Wright, Comedian

As consumers, we often think more about whether we can pay for goods and services than about how the price was established in the first place. But those prices don't just come out of thin air. In a successful business, they're almost always the result of careful decision making.

In the world of business, a merchant cannot simply say to himself, "Gee, I think I'll mark these tennis racquets up about 50 percent. They look as if they're worth it, and that amount should bring in a healthy profit." He might get lucky, of course, and make just the right guess. But suppose he doesn't. If the price is too high, no one will buy the tennis racquets, and he'll be left with too much inventory. If the price is too low, sales won't cover his costs and operating expenses. Too many bad pricing decisions like that, and the company will go out of business. In other words, guesswork can be risky; a price that seems profitable may not actually be profitable at all, given a closer mathematical look.

In this lesson, we'll consider the related concepts of cost, price, markup, and markdown. We'll also demonstrate the mathematics that lets merchants calculate the missing information when they have just some pieces of the pricing puzzle. And, most importantly, we'll focus on the challenge the merchant faces in pricing merchandise in a way that attracts customers and still nets a good profit for the business.

PART I: INTRODUCING THE MATERIAL

LEARNING OBJECTIVES

Upon completing your study of this lesson, you should be able to:

1. Define and use correctly the key terms associated with this lesson (see the Key Terms section).

2. Explain, in general terms, the interrelationships among cost, price, markup, and markdown, and describe the impact of these interrelationships on the business person's daily life.

3. Calculate markup based on cost or on selling price.

4. Explain the difference between markup based on sales and markup based on cost, show how each is calculated, and discuss the significance of these different approaches from the business person's perspective.

If you're using the hardcover textbook, *Mathematics for Business*, there are some additional objectives for the lesson. Upon completing your study of the lesson, you should also be able to:

5. Give several reasons for selling goods at markdown prices, and show how markdown is calculated.

6. Given the percentage of markup, calculate the selling price multiplier and explain how this number is used.

7. Explain what is meant by *perishable goods*.

8. Explain how and why the calculation of markup on perishable goods versus nonperishable goods may differ slightly.

9. Use a profit wheel or profit chart to find selling price, cost, or percentage of markup.

10. Solve markup problems when a certain percentage of the items are unsalable.

LESSON OVERVIEW

It's no secret that businesses operate to make a profit. And in these days of rapidly shifting consumer demand and rising costs, profits are not always easily attained. One of the secrets is good pricing techniques. Consumers won't shop where they feel they can't get a bargain; but the business that prices its products *too* low, in an effort to appeal to consumers, may wind up unable to cover its own expenses.

The Basic Pricing Formula: $C + M = S$

All pricing decisions begin with one key formula: $C + M = S$, in which $C = cost$, $M = markup$, and $S = selling price$. Let's take a closer look at these three factors, one at a time.

Cost, the *C* in the formula, is whatever it costs the merchant to get the goods onto the shelf, ready to sell to the public. The bulk of this cost is eaten up by the wholesale price that the merchant pays to the manufacturer, wholesaler, or distributor from whom the merchant buys the goods. But cost might also include some insurance, as well as shipping or handling. For instance, say that Rugby Imports buys a load of rattan chairs from its wholesale distributor, South Seas, Inc. The wholesale cost of the chairs is $900, but to this cost South Seas adds $50 to cover insurance, plus another $50 to cover their shipping costs. Thus, the full cost to Rugby will be $900 + $50 + $50 = $1,000. Notice that this is *not* the cost of the rattan chairs to the public; this is the cost to Rugby, the merchant. The general public rarely has an opportunity to buy goods at wholesale cost.

Selling price, the *S* in the formula, is what the consumer pays to buy the product from the merchant. Let's suppose that there are ten chairs in the shipment to Rugby. So Rugby's cost per chair is $1,000 ÷ 10 = $100. Rugby isn't going to sell the chairs for this price, however; that wouldn't make any sense. Rugby, like any merchant, is in business to make a profit. So Rugby will *mark up* the chairs by some amount, let's say by $50 each. In that case, the price tag on each chair will be $100 + $50 = $150. That's how much it will cost a customer to go home with a new rattan chair from Rugby.

The difference between the selling price and the cost is *markup*, the *M* part of the formula. In our example with Rugby, M = $150 − $100 = $50. This markup is also known as *margin* or *gross profit*; the three terms can be used interchangeably. Be careful, though, in interpreting the term "gross profit." It can be a little misleading, since the business can have millions of dollars of gross profit and still not be making any money. The *net profit* is what the merchant makes after paying all the expenses associated with running the business. The gross profit, by contrast, includes not only the net profit, but also the operating expenses for the business, which may be considerable.

Overhead: The Cost of Doing Business

Consider our friend Rugby. He might make a very healthy profit on his rattan chairs if he could just open a sidewalk stand right where the chairs were unloaded from the delivery truck and sell them all on the spot. But, of course, that isn't how most real-life businesses work. Rugby can't leave his merchandise sitting on the sidewalk; he's got to have a store where he can display it. That means he's going to pay rent, or a mortgage, and property taxes (on the land and building if he owns them, and certainly on the inventory). He'll probably have to heat and maybe air condition the store. He'll certainly need lights and running water and telephones.

And if the store needs a little fixing up, he might find himself painting, rewiring, putting in carpeting, and installing some furniture and equipment—a desk where he can do his work and a computer to manage the inventory. Unless business is rather poor, he'll also need to hire some staff, and that means more costs for salaries and benefits. Finally, he'll probably need to do some advertising; if he doesn't, almost no one will know about his goods regardless of their price.

All of these items taken together constitute *overhead*, also called *operating expenses*. You may already be thinking that a lot goes into a business's overhead. Very true. In fact, our quick sketch of Rugby's needs is minimal; he'll be adding dozens of items to this bare-bones list before he's through. And every one of them means an expense to the business and a cut in profits.

Keep in mind that the merchant has only limited control over cost — what he or she pays the wholesaler to buy the merchandise in the first place. Merchants can sometimes buy at discount — if they purchase large quantities or buy products off season, for instance. And of course, like any good consumer, the merchant will shop around for the best price. But when the wholesale cost is higher than the merchant would like, the merchant has little choice but to pay it anyway, or just do without the merchandise.

By contrast, overhead costs can vary substantially. Even when two stores are selling the identical product, for which they paid the same price, the overhead costs can be very different. How fancy is the store? Does the business do a lot of advertising? How much is spent for heat and lights? True, a business cannot run without electricity, but through good management, it can control the amount of electricity it requires. Similarly, it cannot operate without hiring employees and paying them a fair wage; but it can take steps to ensure it isn't overstaffed or staffed with the wrong kind of employees for the work that needs to be done.

There's Markup, and then There's Markup

The variable over which the business person has the most control is selling price, which is regulated through markup. Markup is generally expressed as a percentage of some basic amount. Let's look at a simple example.

Imagine an individual consumer, Iris Meechum, trying to get some sense of the relative cost of certain items within her budget. This would be simpler if Meechum had a benchmark of some kind, a base cost. She might decide to use her salary. Let's say it's $2,000 per month. By relating every budgetary expense to this base, Meechum could get some sense of how these various expenses compared to one another. For instance, if her rent was $500, she could look on that as $\frac{1}{4}$ or 25 percent of her salary ($500 ÷ $2,000 = .25). If she spent $100 per month on entertainment, she could look on that as 5 percent ($100 ÷ $2,000 = .05) of her salary.

Notice that this information tells Meechum that she is spending five times as much on rent as on entertainment. And next month, if she takes a $1,000 trip to Mexico, she'll know she's spending ten times her usual amount on entertainment. There's nothing magical, of course, about expressing her expenses as a percentage of her monthly salary. She could, for example, have expressed them as a percentage of her monthly rent. Then her salary would be 400 percent ($2,000 ÷ $500 = 4) of her monthly rent. This, admittedly, doesn't make quite as much sense, but it's a perfectly valid way of having some consistent way of looking at costs.

Whether to express markup based on cost or selling price depends mostly on the perspective of the merchant. Most manufacturers, for example, base their markup on the cost of the finished goods, which is also the basis for figuring the value of their inventories. But most retail stores think it more sensible to look at markup based on selling price. This is simply because most other business-related costs (including sales tax, sales commission, and advertising) are also related to selling price, and basing everything on selling price adds consistency. Wholesalers may relate markup to cost or to selling price, depending on how they usually value their inventory.

Any kind of business *could* calculate either kind of markup. But, traditionally, markup has a certain meaning within each industry. So when two merchants in similar businesses discuss "markup," they don't usually have to add "based on cost" or "based on selling price."

It's important to understand, by the way, that whether markup is based on cost or selling price has nothing to do with the *amount* of the markup; it's just a different way of looking at the same number. To see why this is so, let's return for a moment to Rugby and the rattan chairs. Recall that the cost on a chair was $100, the markup was $50, thus, the selling price was $150. If we divide the amount of the markup by the cost, the result is $50 ÷ $100 = .50, or 50 percent. In other words, the markup based on *cost* is 50 percent. Or think of it this way: Rugby marks the chairs up by 50 percent of what it costs him to get them into the store in the first place.

Suppose, though, that we divide the markup by the selling price. Now the result is $50 ÷ $150 = .333, or 33.3 percent. This is another way of saying that the markup based on *selling price* is about 33 percent, or that 33 percent of the selling price is markup and 67 percent (100% − 33% = 67%) is the cost of the goods. Notice, as we indicated earlier, that the *amount* of the markup ($50) doesn't change. But the *percentage* of markup changes depending on whether we're comparing it to cost or selling price.

Incidentally, it's simple to convert markup on cost to markup on selling price or vice versa. One formula will do the trick:

Markup on cost = % of markup on selling price
÷ (100% − % of markup on selling price).

As mentioned, most times one or the other type of markup will be standard throughout a certain type of business. But it's not too difficult to switch from one kind to the other with just this formula and a little multiplication.

Pricing and Profit

Knowing how to price merchandise is, to a large degree, a matter of sound business judgment. This good judgment takes experience, knowledge of consumer needs, some sense of what the market will bear, and an accurate perception of what others in the same industry are doing. But it also takes a good understanding of the mathematics involved. The business person must know, in real dollars-and-cents terms, where the breakeven point for the business is, the point at which all costs are covered (more on this later). Even more importantly, he or she must have a precise answer to this critical question: What is the maximum amount I can charge for this article of merchandise or service, and still sell it?

Sometimes it's very tempting for the merchant to reduce prices in order to undercut competitors. Perhaps this is a good idea, perhaps not. To some extent, it depends on the nature of the merchandise, whether it's in generally high demand anyway, and whether it's likely to be something consumers will comparison shop for. Most consumers will look a long time before buying an automobile or a piano, for instance; few will shop around for kitchen matches, thumbtacks, or shoe laces. So competitive pricing on these small items may be a waste of the merchant's time and profit.

Then, too, there's something to be said about the psychology of dropping prices *too* low. Customers may think they're getting a real bargain—or they may suspect there's something wrong with the merchandise and may not want it at any price. Cheaper doesn't always mean more salable.

Remember, too, that even though an item generally sells for more than cost, that's no guarantee of a profit. Suppose Danforth runs a small variety store and competes against big chain stores that buy in volume for less money. The chain stores sell waffle irons for $25 and make a profit. Can Danforth do the same? Let's say the cost to Danforth for each waffle iron is $15 and her overhead is $10.

Here's how these figures work in the basic formula. Recall that overhead is one portion of markup; the other part is the net profit. Since cost plus markup equals selling price, we also know that cost plus overhead plus profit equals selling price. In this case, $15 + $10 + profit = $25. Or, $25 + Profit = $25, which unfortunately means that profit = 0. If she wants to make any profit at all, Danforth will either have to reduce overhead, buy the waffle irons for less, or sell them for more than the chain stores are getting. If none of these options seems practical, she may have to forget about waffle irons altogether.

Incidentally, it's this net profit, or what is left of the gross profit once all the overhead has been paid, that is the real key to business success. When net profit is sufficiently high, the business can afford to expand, open new sites, hire more employees, take on more inventory, market a new product line, launch a new advertising campaign, or embark on a hundred other business ventures. When net profit is low, the business person's options are severely limited.

Time for a Sale?   Few merchants expect to sell all of their merchandise at regular price. In the American marketplace, discounts have become a way of life, and merchants are often forced to discount some items in order to compete effectively.

The amount of the discount is referred to as the *markdown*, while the selling price after the markdown may be termed the *reduced price*, *sale price*, or *actual selling price*. The reduced price is simply the difference between the original selling price and the markdown. Recall, for instance, that the selling price on Rugby's rattan chairs was $150. Let's suppose, though, that for whatever reason, rattan chairs just aren't moving this season. Perhaps consumer tastes have shifted in a way that Rugby Imports didn't anticipate, so that Rugby's advertising and creative displays don't seem to be helping. Perhaps the only thing left to do is mark the chairs down. Rugby decides to begin with a fairly conservative markdown: $20. That means the reduced price will be $150 − $20, or $130.

The percentage of markdown is always based on the original selling price, which in this case is $150. Thus, the percentage of markdown is $20 ÷ $150 = .133, about 13 percent. If Rugby thinks that a 13 percent markdown doesn't sound too exciting, then he might avoid mentioning the percent figure and simply advertise the chairs as "$20 off the original price" or "Marked down from $150." And sometimes the price tag doesn't note the original price at all; it just includes the sale price and the percentage of the markdown. If the buyer is curious, though, figuring out the original price isn't difficult.

For instance, let's say that Hilda's Boutique has a sale on feather hats. One hat has a sale price of $60, and it is marked "50% off the original price." What was that original price? Well, if 50 percent has been discounted, then the $60 represents the remaining 50 percent of the original price. Thus, the selling price is $60 ÷ .50 = $120. In other words, the hat originally sold for $120. The amount of the discount, the markdown, is $120 − $60 or, as you'd suspect, $60.

Breaking Even   You may be wondering how retailers come up with the right discount price. After all, putting goods on sale is not an indication that the merchant no longer cares about making a profit. The merchant will try very hard to set a price that lets the store come out a little ahead, even if the profit isn't very big. This isn't always possible, however. It depends on how high the overhead costs are, how much the merchant paid for the goods, and how hard those goods are to sell, even at discount.

A good place for the merchant to begin discount calculations, usually, is by figuring out the *breakeven point*, the point at which the store brings in just enough money to cover the cost of the goods plus the operating expenses associated with maintaining or storing those goods. Let's return for a moment to Rugby Imports and those tough-to-sell rattan chairs. We'll suppose for the time being that Rugby's operating expenses are 25 percent, based on cost. That means that if it costs Rugby $100 to buy a rattan chair, the overhead will be .25 × $100 = $25. So the breakeven point on the rattan chair is cost plus overhead, or $100 + $25.00, or $125.

What does this information tell Rugby? Two things. First, in order to make any net profit whatever, he will have to sell the chairs for more than $125 apiece. Anything below $125 represents an *operating loss* for the business. Second, in order even to recover the cost on a chair, he'll have to sell it for $100 or more. Anything below $100 represents an absolute loss to the business, since the merchant isn't even getting back what it cost him to buy the chair from the wholesaler. For instance, if Rugby is forced to mark the chairs clear down to $50 in order to sell them, then the business has an absolute loss of $50 per chair: $100 (the cost of the chair) − $50 (the discounted selling price).

In our discounting example, Rugby planned to sell the chairs for $130, a $20 markdown from the original $150 price. If the breakeven point is $125, then the markdown price means a potential net profit of $5 per chair ($130 − $125). Not very big, but better than a loss!

To this point, we've treated overhead, the operating expenses, as a single figure that seemed easy to come by. Unfortunately, things aren't quite so straightforward in the real world.

It's relatively simple, of course, just to figure the total value of all the inventory in the store at cost, and the total operating expenses for the business, and then divide to come up with the overall overhead factor. For instance, suppose that one month Rugby's sales total $100,000 while his operating expenses are $25,000. He divides $25,000 by $100,000 and learns that his operating expenses are 25 percent of his sales. Unfortunately, though, this approach would be accurate only if the overhead were the same for every dollar's worth of goods he sells.

In reality, though, actual overhead is much higher on some items than on others. For instance, in a pet shop, it costs more to keep $500 worth of puppies healthy and salable than to keep $500 worth of dog food ready to go. A grocery store spends more maintaining fresh meat and dairy products than it spends maintaining potato chips and dry beans. For that matter, $500 worth of rattan chairs (though they don't rot and don't require care and feeding) take up more floor space than, say, $500 worth of jewelry. Assuming the rent he pays for the store is significant, Rugby may feel it's not quite fair to figure the overhead on a rattan chair quite the same way he figures overhead on a pair of jade earrings worth the same amount. In short, a retailer really needs to differentiate among items when determining overhead costs, though this certainly complicates the math when it comes time to determine the breakeven point and the appropriate markdown for a given item.

Two other factors are important in determining overhead rates, too. One is that overhead costs, even for the same retailer, can vary dramatically

Overhead: The Cost of Doing Business

from month to month for many reasons. For instance, it costs more to air condition a Phoenix department store in August than in December; it costs more to heat a Minneapolis motel in January than in May. What's more, few retailers maintain truly consistent inventory from month to month; as the inventory changes (some products are discontinued, others added on) the cost of maintaining them may also shift. Expansion and remodeling also bring about changes in overhead costs, as do additions or reductions in staff. Tax increases also add to overhead. In other words, a retailer cannot just come up with one overhead figure for all time; overhead costs must be refigured routinely, sometimes as often as every month.

In addition, it's helpful for any retailer to know what others in the same industry are spending on overhead. Take our importer Rugby. Suppose he discovers that most other import store owners are spending from 30 to 40 percent on overhead; that makes his 25 percent look pretty good. Conversely, if the industry average were 20 percent, it might be time for Rugby to consider looking for less costly facilities, cutting back on advertising, paying less in overtime, or otherwise finding some ways to economize.

The Selling Price Multiplier: A Pricing Shortcut

It may have occurred to you that if the amount of markup were different for every single item in a store, pricing would be a full-time job in itself. Retailers would literally be so busy pricing items they wouldn't have time to sell anything. That's one reason, in fact, that retailers attempt to keep the calculation of overhead simple, even though that simplification distorts the truth a little. Thus, a grocer, as an example, may have one overhead rate for canned goods, another for frozen goods, another for produce, and another for refrigerated goods. But the grocer is not likely to have one overhead rate for canned peas, another for canned corn, and another for canned beans. There's a point beyond which precision pays no dividends because it requires too much of the retailer's time.

Similarly, when it comes to pricing, it's helpful if certain groups of goods all have the same percent of markup. It saves time. For instance, let's say that Viola MacAdoo runs a sporting goods store where she stocks approximately 3,000 different items. If MacAdoo had to calculate 3,000 different markup rates, she would never finish pricing her inventory. But if she had, say, *ten* different rates, and every one of the 3,000 items fit into one of these ten categories, her task would be relatively simple.

What's more, she could make pricing simpler yet with use of a fraction known as the *selling price multiplier*. In order to use this fraction, MacAdoo has to know her markup based on cost and she has to know how to convert a decimal to a fraction. With these two things in mind, let's see how the selling price multiplier works.

Let's say that MacAdoo sells bicycles and that her markup on this item is 40 percent, based on cost. That percent is the same as .40, which in turn is the same as $4/10$ or $2/5$. To figure out the selling price multiplier, we simply add this fraction, which represents markup based on cost, to one: $1 + 2/5 = 5/5 + 2/5 = 7/5$. The selling price multiplier for the bicycles is $7/5$. This means that the selling price on any bike will be $7/5$ of the cost. Suppose, for instance, that the wholesale cost on a child's bike is $60. That bike will sell for $7/5 \times \$60 = \$84$. Notice, by the way, that if MacAdoo is fairly skilled in math, as many retailers are, she can do a lot of this calculating in her head. Most retailers know the selling price multiplier on many of the items they buy wholesale. So when MacAdoo is negotiating for the purchase of this bike, she already has a good idea what she'll be charging for it. And if she's a shrewd merchant, who knows what bikes are selling for these days, she may also have a good sense of whether $84 is a price at which the bikes will sell.

She can use the selling price multiplier another way, too. Let's say that the selling price multiplier on golf clubs is 4/3 (because markup is 1/3, based on cost). MacAdoo knows from experience that she can sell a certain set of golf clubs for $600, but no more than that. Given that, how much can she afford to pay the wholesaler? Well, the $600 represents 4/3 of the wholesale cost. So, 4/3 times the wholesale cost equals $600. If we divide both sides of this equation by 4/3, we see that the wholesale cost is $600 ÷ 4/3 = $450. In other words, MacAdoo can pay up to $450 for a set of golf clubs and still make her desired profit margin without pricing herself out of the market. Of course, if she can get the clubs for less (say, $400) her potential profit goes up.

As you can see, this is very helpful information for her to have when negotiating with the wholesaler. And there's no question that this simple shortcut saves merchants time. Remember, however, that the selling price multiplier cannot be used when markup is based on selling price. It works only when markup is based on cost.

So why, besides tradition, would anyone bother to calculate the markup based on sales at all? Because the sales volume determines, to a large extent, the health of a company. Most companies do not depend on huge profits on any one item to make a profit; they depend instead on selling many items at moderate profit. Thus, a prudent business person may feel it is wise to spend no more than a certain percentage of sales revenue on advertising, rent, or other overhead expenditures. Knowing what percentage of sales is converted into profits makes it easier for the business manager to decide when to hire a new employee, order new supplies, and so forth.

Pricing Perishables

Most products can't sit endlessly on merchants' shelves, awaiting sale. They reach a peak of marketability, after which their capacity to pull in a profit declines dramatically. In discussing such *perishables*, we may think immediately of fresh food, an obvious example. But in reality, almost every product is perishable in some sense. Sports equipment goes out of season; furniture, clothing, and automobiles go out of fashion; computer hardware and software become outdated; landscaping materials wilt and fade.

Virtually every product is susceptible in some way to the effects of time; some within a very short period, others over several years. The question, therefore, is not so much "Is this product perishable?" but "For how long, or during what period, will this product or service retain its maximum marketability?" And if that time period is shorter than the time normally required to sell the inventory, then pricing decisions have to be made differently. The merchant's overriding goal in pricing perishables is to set the selling price high enough so that products that do sell will make up for those that do not, or for those that must be sold at discount.

The whole process rests on these four simple steps:

1. Determine the cost of the total purchase.

2. Determine the selling price for the total purchase.

3. Estimate the percentage of merchandise that is likely to be sold.

4. Divide the total sales (#2) by the amount of merchandise (#3) to obtain the selling price per item or per pound.

Let's look at an example to see how this works. Florence Azuki, who runs a small pet store, has an unusual purchasing opportunity. She can buy a lot of 100 parakeets at $5 per bird from an overseas supplier who has excess stock. On the one hand, she feels that this price is too good to pass up, yet her experience tells her that within the first month about 20 percent of the parakeets will die or become diseased. She also knows that under normal circumstances, given the care and maintenance required, she must have a markup of 50 percent on the parakeets, based on cost.

The key point here is that Azuki doesn't expect that all of the merchandise (the parakeets) will be marketable. As an experienced retailer who's been in this situation before, she'll use the four steps we've just outlined to come up with a price that will protect her business from a loss in the event that her predictions come true and she does lose a portion of her inventory.

First, she starts with the total cost of her purchase: 100 parakeets at $5 each makes $500. Now, knowing the total cost and knowing that her desired markup on the parakeets is 50 percent of cost, she can determine their selling price by using the basic formula: $C + M = S$. Thus, $C + .50C = S$, or $1.5C = S$. Since the cost is $500, $1.5 \times \$500 = S$, and S, the selling price, equals $750.

In short, Azuki must take in $750 for this lot of parakeets. Remember, though, she cannot count on selling all 100 birds. According to her estimates (Step 3), she expects to sell only 80. So, she has to make the whole $750 on 80 parakeets. To find out the cost of each bird, then, she simply divides the total selling price ($750) by the number of birds (80), and the result is about $9.40. In other words, given that some of the birds won't be sold, Azuki will price the birds that do sell somewhat higher; $9.40 instead of the $7.50 price she'd use if she thought all the birds would sell. Keep in mind though, if Azuki gets lucky and any of the 20 other birds are sold, everything she makes on the sale of those parakeets will be profit because the sale of the first 80 birds, which she is counting on, will cover all expenses.

Saving Some Time

You may be wondering at this point whether merchants run about with formulas and figures and selling price multipliers in their heads all the time. Well, yes. Many do just that! At the same time, though, there are a number of shortcuts they can use. They rely on calculators and computers, of course. In addition, many use profit wheels or profit charts to help determine the amount of markup on any item.

A *profit chart* lists wholesale costs down one side and various percentages of markup across the top. The retailer simply finds the correct numbers on the chart and, presto, there's the selling price. The one disadvantage with a profit chart is that it is, of necessity, limited. It isn't practical to create a chart so big it lists every conceivable cost or percentage markup a merchant might want to use. An alternative is the *profit wheel* (see illustration), a device that also does some of the calculating for the merchant but allows more flexibility in selecting numbers.

Of course, no profit wheel, profit chart, calculator, or computer will be of much help to the merchant who doesn't know his or her own industry or who doesn't have up-to-date information on costs or overhead. You have to begin somewhere. Formulas are very useful to the person who knows what information to plug into those formulas. But in the end, there can be no doubt that business know-how, experience, and a good intuitive sense of consumer needs all contribute to good pricing practices.

Profit wheel. Courtesy of Leland Company.

Pricing Services
Instead of Products

Business math courses usually discuss pricing concepts in terms of merchandise: a quart of milk, a pair of pants, a bicycle, and so on. That makes good sense; such examples are clear-cut and do a good job of illustrating the mathematics involved. But a growing percentage of American businesses don't sell products. Instead, they provide services: they repair computers, complete tax returns, provide day care, things like that.

Don't get the idea that the mathematics of pricing doesn't apply to service businesses; it most certainly does. There's a certain cost of providing the service, a markup that needs to cover overhead and net profit, and a selling price. An accounting firm, for example, may pay staff $50 in wages for completing a certain type of tax return. Perhaps the cost of the office space, advertising, telephones, and all the other overhead adds another $20. And, of course, there's the profit for the firm; let's say $10. How much does the accountant charge for each tax return? Even for services, cost plus the markup (the overhead plus net profit, that is) equals selling price. Since $50 + $20 + $10 = $80, our accounting firm should be charging $80.

Admittedly, though, a lot of small service businesses get by without consciously setting a selling price for their services based on cost and markup. This is especially true for businesses like many kinds of consulting, for example, where no two jobs seem quite the same. Still, the C + M = S formula works just as well for services as for merchandise, and you can guarantee that any business where the selling price isn't high enough to cover the costs and overhead is in trouble.

Similarly, it may seem a little strange to talk about using a simple formula like C + M = S to decide the selling price of a new multimillion-dollar jetliner or office building. But the idea still works just fine. It costs a certain amount to get the goods ready to be sold, then you add the overhead of selling the product and the desired net profit. Even when the C, M, and S figures are in the millions, the formula is still perfectly correct.

SOME WORDS OF ADVICE

Most of us are so accustomed to thinking like consumers that it's hard to put ourselves in the position of the merchant, but it's important to do this in order to really appreciate how pricing works. In attempting to make a profit, a business must balance what it spends on merchandise against what it can sell that merchandise for. It is important to recognize, for instance, that the business that only recovers its cost (what it takes to buy the merchandise from the wholesaler or distributor) will not break even. Just to keep from losing money, the business must be able to sell merchandise for a high enough price to cover both the cost and the operating expenses: the overhead.

The problems you're asked to do in this lesson generally present you with a markup based on some percentage of either selling price or cost. In many ways that means that the hard work has already been done, because one of the toughest challenges the retailer faces is determining what that percentage of markup should be. And while math skills are a great help, the merchant must also know the market for his or her product and have a general sense of how other competitive merchants are doing in the same field. Whether we're talking of parakeets, rattan chairs, golf clubs, or corn flakes, there's no one "right" price that the merchant will magically come upon by plugging the right numbers into the right formulas. Each retailer's situation is different. Effective pricing calls for the ability to juggle a whole range of factors, mathematical and nonmathematical, and to know not only what formulas to use but what numbers to put into those formulas.

Keep in mind, too, that while we usually think of businesses as making a profit, that is not always the case. There is nothing to guarantee that there will always be a profit (and you should not make that assumption in your calculations as you're working the problems for this lesson). Even when the sales price is much higher than wholesale cost, there is no profit for the merchant unless overhead is also covered. No business person is likely to intentionally set a selling price lower than what it cost to buy the goods, but many will set a selling price that doesn't cover both cost of goods and the overhead.

This brings up another important point. It may seem to us, as consumers, that merchants occasionally charge high, even outrageous, prices for their merchandise. No doubt some do. At the same time, though, there's no way to make a fair judgment about that without knowing first what it cost the merchant to buy the goods in the first place, and second what it costs the merchant to sell those goods. It's only reasonable that the merchant have an opportunity to recover those costs. Remember, no matter how much consumers love a bargain, merchants have to make a profit to stay in business. The business that consistently gives consumers too good a bargain won't be around long.

Consumers may feel they have little or nothing to say about what merchants spend on overhead, but this is not quite true. Indirectly, consumers may have a lot of influence. For instance, a consumer shopping for a business suit may shun the little corner discount store where a hundred suits are crowded onto a tiny rack and everything is self-service. She may prefer to go to the large, spacious store that's air-conditioned, where merchandise is well-displayed, where there's soft classical music in the background and free coffee for customers, where the dressing rooms have upholstered chairs and plush carpeting, and where one salesperson can afford to spend an hour or two with a single customer.

It all sounds very pleasant, but remember that it costs money. The merchant has to pay for the coffee, the carpeting, the air conditioning, and the extra room. Covering that kind of overhead requires raising the price of the suit. As a consumer, you might not worry too much about overhead; besides, it may be worth it to you to pay a little more if you can shop in comfort. That's fine, so long as you realize that when patronizing this sort of merchant, you are helping pay the business's higher overhead costs.

What about the merchant who seems to be offering everything at discount all the time? Is that reasonable? Common sense and the formulas applied in this lesson suggest that it isn't; not if the discounts are significant and are widespread throughout the merchandise of the store. When merchants seem to be discounting everything, it's likely that the "original selling price" is not really the price that came out of the C + M = S formula; it's an inflated price designed to make what would normally be the selling price look like a sale price. Philosophically, you might not approve of this approach, but it's certainly not illegal or even, to most people, unethical.

There are guidelines for what truly constitutes a "sale." The National Retail Merchants Association considers a sale to be when merchandise is in stock at a regular price and then the price is reduced for a limited time, not to exceed two weeks. Obviously, many advertised "sales" don't meet this definition. But such suspect advertising shouldn't bother a smart consumer, for whom the key question is "How does this retailer's actual selling price compares to what the product sells for from others?" If it's higher, the discounted price is no bargain; if it's lower, you may want to ignore the questionable promotion and buy the product anyway.

Above all, whether you're acting as a consumer or a business buyer, don't be afraid to shop around. That's what the merchant does when he or she buys the goods in the first place. Through the simple act of buying items that are fairly priced and refusing those that aren't, the consumer encourages sound pricing practices for the future.

_____**KEY TERMS**

Before you watch the video program and read through the text assignment, take a minute to look at the key terms associated with this lesson. When you encounter them in the text and video program, pay careful attention to their meaning.

Cost: The price paid to the manufacturer or supplier after trade and cash discounts have been taken. It includes transportation and insurance charges. This is not the cost to the buyer; that amount is the selling price.

Irregulars: Items that are flawed or blemished and must be sold at a reduced price.

Markup: The difference between cost and selling price. Also known as _margin_ or _gross profit_.

Markup on cost: Markup calculated relative to the cost of the goods or services.

Markup on selling price: Markup calculated relative to the selling price of the goods or services.

Markup with spoilage: Markup calculated to include deductions for spoiled or unsalable merchandise.

Net profit: The difference between gross margin (or gross profit) and overhead (or operating expenses). After the cost of goods and the operating expenses are subtracted from total sales, the remainder is net profit.

Overhead: The expenses involved in operating a business. Wages, salaries, rent, utilities, and advertising are examples of overhead. Also known as *operating expenses*.

Perishables: Goods that have a limited time during which they are salable at their normal price. Because it spoils, fresh food is a particularly important example of a perishable. However, goods such as fashionable clothing or new automobiles can become worth less over time and are thus also perishable in a sense.

Profit chart: A chart or table used by business people to calculate markup and selling price.

Profit wheel: A tool used by business people to calculate markup and selling price.

Selling price: The sum of the wholesale cost of an item plus the markup on that item, as in the formula $C + M = S$.

Selling price multiplier: A fraction that is multiplied by the cost of an item to get the selling price.

Spoilage: A decline in the quality of merchandise that makes it unsalable. Usually considered to calculate markup on perishable items such as fresh food.

Unsalable items: Merchandise that cannot be sold due to spoilage, damage, or manufacturing defects. Usually considered when calculating markup.

PART II: WATCHING THE VIDEO PROGRAM

VIDEO VIEWING GUIDE

Before watching the video program, review the following questions. As you watch, be sure to collect the information necessary to answer them.

1. Do business managers seem to worry more over net profit or gross profit? How do you know?

2. How important is the basic $C + M = S$ formula in the day-to-day pricing decisions made by merchants?

3. What are some of the principal factors involved in determining the "right" price for an item?

4. To what extent do good pricing decisions depend on math skills? To what extent is good pricing a matter of sound business judgment?

5. Is markdown inevitable for most businesses? Why or why not? What is the relationship between markdown and profit?

6. What happens when a merchant has an operating loss on one or more products? What can the merchant do to either avoid or make up for that loss?

7. What are some similarities and differences in pricing approaches between product-oriented and service-oriented industries? In which type of industry is pricing more difficult? Why?

VIDEO PROGRAM

This lesson's video program is Program 12 — Pricing Products and Services. Remember, if you are watching this program on videotape, take time to replay sections of the tape whenever you need to review a concept.

VIDEO VIEWING QUESTIONS

Immediately after viewing the video program for Lesson 12, take time to respond to the following questions. Give your answers some careful thought; they may provide the basis for additional discussion or a longer written response.

1. Suppose you were called on to consult for some people who wanted to start a small retail shoe store. On a scale of 1 to 10, how important would you tell them good math skills will be in running the business?

   Not   Extremely
   Important   Important

   1- - - - -2- - - - -3- - - - -4- - - - -5- - - - -6- - - - -7- - - - -8- - - - -9- - - - -10

2. On a scale of 1 to 10, how important would you tell them business knowledge and experience will be in running the business?

   Not   Extremely
   Important   Important

   1- - - - -2- - - - -3- - - - -4- - - - -5- - - - -6- - - - -7- - - - -8- - - - -9- - - - -10

3. Based on the video, which seems more accurate? Product-based industries and service-based industries are

   _____ more alike than different with respect to pricing concerns.

   _____ more different than alike with respect to pricing concerns.

4. Based on the video, which seems more accurate? All things considered, pricing decisions seem more difficult

   _____ in a service-based industry.

   _____ in a product-based industry.

   _____ Neither — there doesn't seem to be any difference.

5. Sometimes business managers need to make estimates based on their knowledge and experience. Other times it seems wiser to rely on hard data. Suppose you were a business manager. Which of the following do you think would demand precise data as opposed to an experience-based guess? (Check the appropriate column for each type of information.)

Guess   Data

_____ _____ Current property tax rate for the business site

_____ _____ Selling price multiplier

_____ _____ Amount of a given product that would sell during the next month

_____ _____ Number of customers the business can expect over the next month

_____ _____ Percentage of overhead spent on advertising

_____ _____ Percentage of overhead that should be spent on advertising

_____ _____ Ratio of overhead to cost

_____ _____ Ratio of overhead to selling price

_____ _____ Overhead for other similar businesses in the area

_____ _____ Projected increase in overhead costs for the coming year

_____ _____ Increase in overhead costs for the past year

_____ _____ Amount of operating loss in dollars

_____ _____ Amount of absolute loss in dollars

_____ _____ Net profit

_____ _____ Gross profit

6. Suppose that you managed a sporting goods store and you were trying to come up with the right price on a pair of skis. Which of the following factors do you think should influence your final price? (Check as many as apply.)

_____ Wholesale cost of the skis

_____ Markup on other items in the store

_____ Retail price of skis at other stores in the area

_____ Projected overhead costs

_____ Retail prices on other merchandise in the store

_____ Overall profit margin for the business

_____ A sudden hike in property taxes for the business

_____ Current business volume (numbers of sales)

_____ Amount of money spent on advertising

_____ Amount of money spent on staff salaries

_____ Cost of business facilities

_____ Time of year

_____ Effectiveness of advertising

_____ Quality of the merchandise

_____ Desire for higher profit

_____ Pressure from consumers to lower prices

PART III: FOCUSING ON THE MATHEMATICS

READING ASSIGNMENT

After watching the video program, you should read one of the following Text Assignments, depending on the textbook you're using:

SOFTCOVER: Pages 233-254 from Chapter 7 of the Miller, Salzman, and Hoelzle softcover text, *Business Mathematics*.

HARDCOVER: Chapter 9, pages 309-335, and pages 340-347 from Chapter 10 of the Salzman, Miller, and Hoelzle hardcover text, *Mathematics for Business*.

As you read through the text, pay careful attention to the examples the book gives of the mathematics associated with the concepts you're learning about.

Then, after you've completed the text assignment, read through the Key Formulas here. This section provides a handy review of what you've learned. By the time you get to this point in the lesson, all of the formulas and calculations should be familiar to you. If they're not, go back and read the appropriate parts of the text and the Overview section of this lesson. You won't have much success completing the rest of your assignments if you are still confused about the information in the Key Formulas section.

KEY FORMULAS

The following key formulas are important to your understanding of this lesson. Be sure that you know each one and how to use it in solving problems relating to retail merchandise pricing.

KEY FORMULA: $C + M = S$

Formula used for: Determining selling price, cost, or markup when the other two factors are known.

Alternate forms: $C = S - M$ or $M = S - C$

Example:

Memory Lane Photo pays $50 for a case of film. The markup is $30. Therefore, the selling price will be $50 + $30 = $80.

Remember that in this formula:

1. C = cost, or what the merchant pays for the merchandise. This is not the same as the cost to the general public.

2. M = markup (also known as margin or gross profit). Markup includes both overhead and net profit. That means that if markup and overhead are equal, there is no profit; the merchant just breaks even. If markup is a little less than overhead, the retailer has an operating loss.

3. S = selling price of the item, or the price the buyer pays to purchase the item from the merchant. When the selling price isn't even high enough to cover the cost, the business has an absolute loss.

KEY FORMULA: Base × Rate = Part

Formula used for: Finding the percentage of markup based on cost or on selling price.

Alternate forms: Rate = Part ÷ Base or Base = Part ÷ Rate

Example:

An umbrella that costs the merchant $20 sells for $30. What is the percentage of markup based on cost? What is the markup based on selling price? First, note that the formula C + M = S shows that $20 plus the markup equals $30. Thus, the amount of the markup, in this case, is $10. When we're figuring out the percentage of markup based on cost, the base in the formula is the cost. The part is the amount of the markup. The percentage of markup equals the rate. Since we're solving for rate, we use the second form of this basic formula: Rate = Part ÷ Base. Thus, percentage of markup based on cost is $10 ÷ $20 = .5, or 50 percent.

We can use the same formula to solve for markup based on selling price. This time, since we're figuring the percentage of markup based on selling price, the selling price is the base in the formula. The amount of markup is still the part. Thus, Rate = $10 ÷ $30 = .3333, or 33.3 percent. Markup based on selling price is therefore about 33 percent.

Remember that in this formula:

1. The rate is equal to the percentage of the markup. The solution to the problem yields either a fraction (1/3, 1/4, etc.) or a decimal (.333, .25, etc.), which must then be converted to a percentage. Remember that "percent" means hundredth. Thus, 25/100 is equal to .25, or 25 percent. To convert a decimal to a percentage, move the decimal point two places to the left. Thus, .05 becomes 5 percent, .25 becomes 25 percent, .001 becomes .1 percent, and so on.

2. When you are solving for markup based on cost, cost is equal to the base in the formula. When you are solving for markup based on selling price, selling price is the base in the formula.

3. Whether you are solving for markup based on cost or on selling price, the amount of the markup is equal to the part in the formula.

KEY FORMULA:	Markup on selling price = Markup on cost ÷ (100% + Markup on cost)
Formula used for:	Converting one form of markup to the other for the purpose of making comparisons between the two.
Alternate form:	Markup on cost = Markup on selling price ÷ (100% − Markup on selling price)

Example:

A computer has a markup of 25 percent based on cost. What is the markup on selling price? If a tent has a markup of 50 percent based on selling price, what is the markup based on cost?

Let's begin with the computer. Since the markup based on cost is 25 percent, the markup based on selling price is 25% ÷ (100% + 25%), or .25 ÷ 1.25 = .20, or 20 percent. In other words, a markup of 25 percent based on cost is the same as a markup of 20 percent based on selling price.

Now let's look at the tent. Here the markup based on selling price is 50 percent. Thus, the markup based on cost is 50% ÷ (100% − 50%), or .50 ÷ (1 − .5), or .5 ÷ .5, or 1. In other words, the markup based on cost is 100 percent. Since 50 percent of the selling price was markup, we know that the retailer simply doubled the cost of the tent in pricing it.

Remember that in these two formulas:

1. It is not necessary to know dollar amounts. You need only know the percentage of markup.

2. The denominators in the fractions of the two formulas look alike at first glance, but they're not. When solving for markup on selling price, add 100 percent to the markup on cost in the denominator of the formula. When solving for markup on cost, subtract markup on selling price from 100 percent in the denominator of the formula.

KEY FORMULA:	Reduced price = Original price − Markdown
Formula used for:	Determining the reduced or sale price of an item when the original selling price and the amount of markdown are known.

Example:

A coat that originally sold for $100 has been marked down 20 percent. What is the reduced price? Since markdown is always based on selling price, the amount of the markdown is 20% of $100, or $100 × .20 = $20. That means that the reduced price is $100 − $20 = $80.

Remember that in this formula:

1. The reduced price is the sale price, or the price following markdown.

2. It is necessary to know either the reduced price or the amount of the markdown to solve the problem.

3. Since markdown is always based on selling price, it is possible to determine the amount of markdown by knowing the selling price and the percentage of markdown, as in the example.

4. The original price is the same as S, selling price, in the basic C + M = S formula.

KEY FORMULA: Selling price multiplier = Markup on cost + 1

Formula used for: Finding the selling price when markup on cost is known.

Example:

The wholesale cost of a radio is $100. Markup is 25 percent based on cost. What is the selling price of the radio? First, we convert 25 percent to a fraction: $25\% = .25 = 25/100 = 1/4$. The selling price multiplier, then, is this fraction plus one, or $1/4 + 1$, or $1/4 + 4/4 = 5/4$. That means that the selling price on the radio will be $5/4 \times \$100$, or $125.

Remember that in this formula:

1. It is essential to know the markup based on cost. Markup based on selling price is of no help in finding the selling price multiplier.

2. The selling price multiplier is always expressed as a fraction. Therefore, you need to convert a decimal or percentage to a fraction in order to use the formula. There are some tables in the texts to help you with this. But if you don't have a table handy, remember that "percent" means hundredth. You can convert a percentage to a decimal by moving the decimal point two places to the left: thus, 25 percent becomes .25. This is read twenty-five hundredths. That means it's the same as the fraction $25/100$, which can be reduced to $1/4$. If you find this kind of conversion difficult, you should work on it enough that using the selling price factor becomes simple for you. (You might want to go back to Lesson 2 of this course to review this type of computation.)

DON'T FORGET_____

1. Cost is what the merchant pays for goods. Don't confuse it with selling price, or what the consumer pays.

2. In the basic C + M = S formula, M, or markup, equals the sum of overhead and net profit. In order for the merchant to have any net profit, S, the selling price, must be higher than C plus the overhead portion of M.

3. Markdown is always based on selling price. Thus, a markdown of 25 percent means that 25 percent has been taken off the original selling price.

4. When using the Rate = Part ÷ Base formula to solve for markup based on cost, let cost = the base. when solving for markup based on selling price, let selling price = the base. in either situation, the part is the markup, and the rate is the percentage of markup.

5. The selling price multiplier is simply a shortcut for finding selling price when markup on cost is known. This number is always expressed as a fraction. First, find the fractional equivalent of the markup on cost, then add it to 1 and convert the whole to a fraction. Thus, a markup of $.40 = 4/10$ or $2/5$; $2/5 + 1 = 2/5 + 5/5 = 7/5$.

PART IV: SOLVING BUSINESS PROBLEMS

PROBLEM SETS

Work the following problems in your textbook. Your instructor will tell you which problems, if any, are to be turned in. Some of the problems have answers provided in the back of the book; refer to these answers to make sure you are working the problems correctly.

SOFTCOVER: If you are using the Miller, Salzman, and Hoelzle softcover text, *Business Mathematics*, do the following problem sets:

> **7.1:** Problems #6-26 (even numbers only) on pages 239-240.
>
> **7.2:** Problems #4-24 (even numbers only) on pages 247-248.
>
> **7.3:** Problems #6-20 (even numbers only) on pages 253-254.

HARDCOVER: If you are using the Salzman, Miller, and Hoelzle hardcover text, *Mathematics for Business*, do the following problem sets:

> **9.1:** Problems #8-30 (even numbers only) on pages 315-316.
>
> **9.2:** Problems #11, 12, and 20-28 on pages 319-320.
>
> **9.3:** Problems #18-50 (even numbers only) on pages 328-330.
>
> **9.4:** Problems #12-30 (even numbers only) on pages 333-334.
>
> **10.1:** Problems #2-12 (even numbers only) on pages 345-346.

BUSINESS APPLICATIONS

Read each of the following scenarios and answer the questions about the decisions you would make in each situation. Give these questions some serious thought; they may be used as the basis for discussion or the development of a more complex essay. You should base your decisions on what you've learned from this lesson, applying both math skills and good business judgment to solve the problem at hand.

SCENARIO 1

Halsey sells leather jackets in an exclusive shop in a suburban shopping mall. The usual selling price for a fashionable line of men's fall jackets is $200 apiece, but they're moving more slowly than Halsey expected. Next year the jackets may be out of style, though Halsey feels confident he could still sell some at discount.

Meanwhile, Fitch, a competitor across the way, is selling jackets of inferior quality for $100 apiece and sales are brisk. Nearly every morning, Halsey is dismayed to see another customer leaving Fitch's with a large package he assumes is a $100 jacket.

Halsey figures his overhead is 50 percent, based on cost. He paid $100 apiece for the twenty jackets he now has in stock. He is considering discounting them but wonders whether he can make enough to cover expenses and still realize a profit. Sales on other merchandise are also running a little slow, so he could use some cash.

What do you think? Is discounting the jackets a good idea? Or is Halsey just acting out of impulse in a desperate attempt to compete effectively with Fitch? Are there other, more competitive strategies he might try?

- Should Halsey discount the $200 jackets? Why or why not?

- If he does discount them, what should he charge? Why?

- Does Halsey have all the information he needs to make a good business decision? If not, what other information is needed?

- What specific mathematical calculations should Halsey make before deciding what to do?

- What are the most important factors for Halsey, or any merchant, to consider in making a decision about whether to discount merchandise?

SCENARIO 2   Miller Furniture likes to advertise "daily discounts" as a way of attracting business. The company feels good about its city-wide reputation for selling quality furniture at near-cost levels.

Currently, Miller's markup is 25 percent based on cost, with overhead approximately 20 percent of cost. In order to keep their reputation as the city's best bargain, they'd like to reduce their standard markup to closer to 10 percent of cost. This is a little different from other merchants in town, whose markup generally runs 30 to 40 percent of cost.

Miller has an opportunity to buy a shipment of furniture with a regular wholesale list price of $50,000. Because of the size of the lot, however, the wholesaler is willing to discount the furniture by 20 percent, provided Miller will take all of it. The shipment is roughly twice what the store really needs to add to inventory at this time, and Miller has some concerns about selling it all. In addition, the inventory includes some pieces that Miller doesn't usually carry. On the other hand, there's nothing wrong with a little variety, and it does seem like a good buy. Sales have been down a bit lately, and Miller could use a bargain that would allow it to boost profits. Maybe this is just the opportunity Miller's been looking for.

What do you think? Should Miller buy the furniture? Is it really a bargain, given the store's current rates for overhead and markup, or will it have trouble making a profit? Is the plan to cut markup realistic; or should Miller rethink its pricing strategy?

- Should Miller buy the furniture? Why?

- If it does buy it, what should the markup be in order to guarantee Miller a reasonable profit? How do you know?

- Does Miller Furniture have all the information it needs to make a good business decision in this situation? What specific mathematical calculations should it make and what steps should it take to ensure that its decision is the best one possible?

- What are the steps Miller must take to be able to cut the markup rate? Do you think it can and/or should cut the markup?

- What are the most important factors, mathematical and non-mathematical, for Miller Furniture or any merchant to consider in determining the correct markup on merchandise?

Inventory Control 13

The length of time between when a business receives merchandise and when it is sold is one of the major indicators of a business's success. And, for a number of reasons, some stores seem more adept at moving merchandise quickly than others. But the store whose shelves are constantly empty isn't going to make much money either; shoppers aren't going to patronize a store where they can't count on finding the products they want. All in all, understanding inventory control and accounting matters is a critical requirement for any business selling or using products and materials.

In this lesson, we'll look at a few of the methods businesses use in valuing their inventory. We'll compare those methods and briefly discuss why some work better under certain conditions or for certain types of inventory than others. As we shall see, the approach a business takes to inventory control is highly dependent on the nature of that business: on what it sells, how fast it needs to turn its inventory around, and how precise its measure of inventory needs to be. There is one thing virtually all retail businesses have in common, though, and that is the need for good, thorough inventory management in some form. For as we'll discover, the key to business success lies not in having the biggest inventory on the block, but in managing a company's inventory well.

PART I: INTRODUCING THE MATERIAL

LEARNING OBJECTIVES

Upon completing your study of this lesson, you should be able to:

1. Discuss inventory (stock) turnover and its relationship to the efficiency of the business as a whole.

2. Given the necessary inventory values, determine average inventory, and use this information to calculate turnover at retail or turnover at cost.

3. Distinguish between perpetual inventory and periodic inventory and describe the role that computers and uniform product codes play in inventory control.

4. Contrast the specific identification method of inventory valuation with the average cost method and calculate the average cost valuation, given the relevant purchase information and quantity in inventory.

5. Distinguish between the FIFO and LIFO methods of valuing inventory and describe the relationship between the change in purchase price over time and the value of inventory under each system.

6. Given the quantity and cost of several purchases of an item and the quantity in inventory, calculate the inventory value using both FIFO and LIFO methods.

If you're using the hardcover textbook, *Mathematics for Business*, there are some additional objectives for the lesson. Upon completing your study of the lesson, you should also be able to:

7. Calculate the value of the inventory at the end of a period using the gross profit method, given starting inventory value, purchases, net sales, and markup on selling price during the period.

8. Calculate the value of the inventory at the end of a period using the retail method, given starting inventory value at cost and retail, purchases at cost and retail, and net sales during the period.

LESSON OVERVIEW

Consider two stores, both of which sell watches. The first, Goodwin's Jewelers, seems to sell out everything it gets in stock. It can scarcely get merchandise displayed in the case before it's out the door and Goodwin's has to reorder. At the second store, Reston, Ltd., many of the watches on display have been in stock for more than a year. Orders for new merchandise tend to be small and infrequent. So, all things being equal, Goodwin's seems to be the more thriving business. But of course, things are rarely equal from one business to another. There are perhaps dozens of variables, unaccounted for in our scenario, which could be contributing to the differences in "busy-ness" at these two stores.

For one thing, prices could be higher at Reston, Ltd. In fact, maybe the prices are so much higher that Reston needs to sell only one watch to pull in the same profit that Goodwin's makes on five or six. Then there's that reordering business. It seems that Goodwin's is always having to bring in new merchandise. But maybe one reason is that it orders in small quantities, like a cook who buys butter by the quarter pound and is forever running to the store for just "one stick more." Perhaps Reston deliberately orders more generously because its purchasing manager knows the market so well that she is able to anticipate sales for six months to come. Sometimes, high-volume orders save a business money by enabling the purchaser to qualify for business discounts, so perhaps Reston's manager also has an eye on the company pocketbook when she places these large orders.

In short, there is no simple way to account for apparent differences among retail businesses. Even if we pulled up a chair by each front door and watched customers come and go, it wouldn't help us very much. The business that looks busy and thriving is not always the one bringing in the highest profits. What we really need here is some hard data to support our hypothesis that Goodwin's is in fact doing better than its competitor. And, as we'll see in this chapter, one of the best places to begin that data collection is with a closeup look at the *inventory*, the sum total of all the merchandise a business has for sale.

Valuing the Inventory

Inventory valuation usually begins with a *count*, some sort of assessment of what the business has on hand. It's also important, of course, to determine the value of that merchandise; volume isn't everything. Take our hypothetical watch dealers. Perhaps Goodwin's has over 1,000 watches in inventory at any given moment, but their value is only about half that of the 100 or so very expensive watches in stock at Reston, Ltd. Then, too, it's critical to measure the flow of inventory in and out of the business. After all, retailers can't hope to make much money if they're simply warehouses for products they can't sell. So taking inventory isn't a one-time task; it's an ongoing requirement for all businesses that want to know how much they're selling and how fast they're selling it.

But before the inventory can be valued, it's necessary to understand just what goes into making up an "inventory." Inventory is the sum total of all the goods a business has available for purchase at any given time. Not everything the business owns is classified as inventory, however.

Take Harvey's Roadside Restaurant, for instance. Harvey's, not surprisingly, deals primarily in food; and food is its primary inventory. It may also have a few miscellaneous items for sale, such as coffee mugs, souvenir keychains, road maps, and the ever-popular "I Ate at Harvey's and Survived" T-shirts. But most of Harvey's inventory is items like bread, milk, cooking oil, hamburger buns, coffee, and so forth. Of course, Harvey's *owns* a great many other things, too: stoves and dishwashers, furniture, a cash register, dishes, linens, and so forth. These items, essential to running a restaurant, are part of the business's assets but not part of its inventory.

Here's the difference. Items in his inventory are those that Harvey will turn around and sell to the public. Noninventory assets are still valuable and still could be sold to get Harvey some money were he to close the business. But they are more permanent; they're not intended to be sold. This difference is important because the value of such items is measured differently from the value of business assets, though both would have to be calculated with some accuracy should Harvey want to establish an accurate value of his business.

Inventory Turnover

Turnover is a measure of the speed with which goods are sold. In calculating turnover, a business manager is asking, "From the time these products come in the door, how long does it take until they are sold and I need to reorder?"

Turnover is often indicated by a ratio, which is expressed as a decimal. A turnover ratio of 3.5, for instance, means that within a given period of time, say one month, a given product or set of products will sell out three and a half times. Say, for instance, that Harvey orders his cocoa in five-pound packages. If his turnover on cocoa is 3.5 for a given month, that means he'll go through three and a half five-pound packages during that period of time. Of course, every item has a separate turnover rate, and it's wrong to compare two different items, even if they seem similar. For example, if Harvey begins to order cocoa in twenty-pound packages, his turnover ratio will be different. Actually, individual turnover ratios aren't all that valuable; turnover ratios are primarily useful in comparisons, and then only when we know a little of the behind-the-scenes information on which those turnover figures are based. Let's see why that is.

Suppose, for the sake of simplicity, that the average turnover at Harvey's—not just on cocoa, but on food items in general—is about 3.5, measured monthly. Is that good? We can't say, at least not until we have some basis for comparing turnover at Harvey's to that at other comparable restaurants. Let's say that turnover at Alfie's Diner down the street, a restaurant of comparable size, is 5.5 monthly. Is Alfie's doing a better business? We still don't know, because we don't know what quantities Alfie orders. Clearly, if Alfie orders items in quantities half the size of Harvey's, he's selling less in spite of having the higher turnover ratio.

In real life, though, Alfie's probably orders food from the same suppliers in much the same quantities as Harvey's. If that is indeed the case, then the turnover ratios indicate that Alfie's is serving more people, or at least using up food faster. But while this one-to-one comparison is likely to offer Harvey some limited information, he needs a broader base of comparison to really evaluate how well his business is doing. He may find it in a trade journal, which is likely to publish average turnover ratios for restaurants of various types and sizes. Let's imagine that Harvey subscribes to such a journal and discovers from his reading that roadside diners the size of Alfie's and Harvey's have an average turnover of 5.5 to 7.2 monthly. This information (based on the industry as a whole, not just on one or two cases) gives us some perspective. Now we can see that Alfie, by industry standards, is just on the low edge, and Harvey is managing his inventory in a way that, if not wrong, is at least very different from the way others in the same business do it.

Tracking Turnover Over Time

Remember how we stressed that simply knowing that Harvey had a 3.5 turnover for his cocoa wasn't of much use? That's true, but it would be very valuable for Harvey to know how that number changes over time; month-to-month comparisons, for instance. It could be that Harvey's current 3.5 turnover ratio just represents a brief slow period. Maybe severe winter weather is keeping business down a little. If Harvey has kept good data on his turnover rate over the past year, then he'll already know about the "January slump." That way, he won't overorder in December and get stuck with a lot of food that no one will come in to eat.

Over time, Harvey can learn what's typical for different seasons, months, even days of the week. He can get as precise with his inventory management as he's willing to take the trouble to get. He may find out that his turnover ratio peaks in July and August, at about 5.8, when his regular trade is supplemented with some tourist business. Then next August, if his turnover reaches 6.3, Harvey can feel pretty confident that things are going exceptionally well. But if his ratio drops to 4.6, he can begin figuring out what's going wrong.

Harvey will also want to pay some attention to how one item is doing in comparison to another. For instance, if the turnover on chicken increases faster than the average for other food items, perhaps Harvey should consider adding more chicken dishes. If turnover on eggs drops significantly, Harvey would be smart to analyze why his customers aren't buying egg dishes. If he doesn't pay attention to turnover ratios or even bother calculating them in the first place, he won't have any of these clues about shifts in the preferences of his customers.

If he doesn't adapt to match customers' wishes, turnover will slow even more. At that point, Harvey is likely to discover that slow turnover can trigger a whole collection of problems: Customers complaining that the food isn't fresh or that they can't get what they want. Limited storage space for new products and too much money spent storing merchandise that doesn't sell well. And perhaps a growing reputation as the kind of business that doesn't care about its customers.

Of course, this is not to suggest that simply keeping an eye on turnover will solve all business problems. However, comparing the turnover of one business to that of another comparable business, or comparing turnover month to month or item to item, *can* give an alert business manager valuable clues about how the business is progressing.

Rapid Turnover: What Most Managers Want

Most business managers strive for rapid turnover. It's one sign of a healthy business. When products are steadily disappearing from the shelves, that's a good indication that the business is stocking what customers want. Rapid turnover has several advantages to both retailers and consumers.

Among the primary advantages is the business's capacity to offer fresh, new merchandise. No one wants to eat stale food or buy wilted flowers. When turnover is slow, perishable items suffer, and that turns customers away. It makes merchants unhappy, too, because whatever can't be sold at the regular price must either be sold at markdown prices or, in some cases, just tossed out. That means at the very least reduced profits, and at worst a total loss for the business. Rapid turnover on products customers are happy to pay for means a steady cash flow for the business.

Unfortunately, while calculating inventory turnover is a critical part of managing the business, it doesn't always save the business manager from making some difficult business decisions. Consider Ed's Discount Tire Center, for instance. Let's say that Ed has a chance to take advantage of a volume discount on a big order of 1,000 tires. It looks like a good deal, and perhaps it is. The only problem is, Ed doesn't have space at the store to stack that many new tires, so he has to rent storage space. That's expensive, and not very handy, either, since he now has to move his inventory around as customers make purchases.

There's another problem too, though. Once Ed decides to take advantage of the discount, he'll have a lot of money tied up in those 1,000 new tires. Of course, if he can sell them at a good price and bring in lots of money, he'll soon recover what he has spent and the high-volume trade discount will have proven itself to be a good investment. But if business should drop off, for whatever reason, Ed could be in trouble. Until he recovers the money he's spent on the inventory, his financial options are limited. He may have difficulty paying taxes, meeting payroll, or advertising his new service department. In short, the business manager has to take care that purchasing does not get too far ahead of what can be sold at the current rate of turnover. If it does, the business will have no cash to spend.

On the other hand, a turnover ratio that's too fast can spell problems, too. When shelves are constantly being emptied out before they can be restocked, a store may acquire a reputation as a place with no selection, a place that never seems to have what customers are looking for. Too many "Sorry—Out of Stock" signs encourage consumers to look somewhere else next time.

It may have occurred to you that the desirable speed with which inventory flows in and out must vary from one business to another. At Harvey's Roadside Restaurant, for instance, a week one way or the other makes a big difference on the salability of inventory. Food doesn't keep forever (even under the best of conditions) and most customers don't want three-week-old chicken. But at Ed's Tires, it's a different story. A few extra weeks in storage will make absolutely no difference in the salability of a rubber tire. Ed might feel quite successful if he can turn his whole inventory over once every few months, whereas that sort of turnover ratio would spell disaster to someone in the restaurant business.

Of course, as we've hinted already, there's a limit to how much inventory Harvey or Ed, or anyone, can or should keep on hand at one time. Storage costs money, and if a business is going to pay just to keep things in stock, it had better be sure that what it's storing can eventually be sold at a good price. If all the special off-road tires Ed ordered in January are still part of October's inventory, it's time to ask whether they're overpriced, whether ordering them in the first place was a mistake, and whether it makes sense to pay to store them any longer.

Inventory Shrinkage

Virtually all inventory is subject to a phenomenon known as *inventory shrinkage*, a reduction in inventory *after* it has been purchased by the store. Inventory shrinkage has several causes. It may result from some unforeseen internal problem that causes products to become unsalable. For instance, if the refrigeration goes out at Harvey's Restaurant, the spoilage that results will cause a shrinkage in inventory.

Inventory shrinkage also results from breakage or other kinds of damage. A customer at the Crystal Bright gift shop may hold up a $500 vase to see how it looks with the sun shining through it—and drop it on a glass shelf of ceramic figurines. Or perhaps a customer at Toy World will take a wind-up clown out of the box to see how it works, wind it a little too tight, break the springs, and then return it to the box without saying anything.

But the biggest cause of shrinkage in many retail stores is theft, sometimes by employees, sometimes by customers. In spite of merchants' dedicated efforts, billions of dollars worth of goods are stolen each year. When customers at Music City Stereo slip cassette tapes into their coat pockets and stroll out the door without paying, the store's inventory is affected. In many businesses, the price of goods has to be raised significantly to cover the shrinkage loss resulting from shoplifting and larger thefts.

Some inventory shrinkage must probably be accepted as part of the cost of doing business. The cooks at Harvey's, no matter how careful, are likely to drop an occasional egg or burn some bacon. Sooner or later, the refrigeration may go out, or the stove may go berserk and scorch six apple pies. Short of cautioning the cooks and inspecting the equipment regularly, there isn't much Harvey's can do to prevent this sort of problem altogether.

Most retail businesses, however, take precautions to protect themselves against shrinkage that results from customer carelessness, vandalism, employee theft, or shoplifting. For instance, customers who drop or break merchandise may be required to pay for it, especially if the incident occurs at a relatively small business that cannot afford this sort of loss. Thus, the unlucky customer who drops the $500 vase at the tiny Crystal Bright gift shop has probably purchased it. Had the same thing happened in the glassware section of a large department store, she might have been forgiven. But that's not because people are so much nicer at the department store; it's simply that the vase is a much smaller part of their total inventory, so its loss, though regrettable, is not devastating.

Crystal Bright probably has a sign warning customers about the unhappy consequences of breaking something. It may even have a sign asking customers not to handle merchandise or not to look at some things without assistance. A store like Toy World is likely to ask its customers not to open boxes. And as a consumer, you may have noticed that many boxes are getting tougher to open! They're likely to be well-glued or stapled, or sealed in tough plastic. That helps protect what's inside from prying hands and careless inspections. So while a package may be difficult to get into once you've bought it, take some consolation in the fact that the price may be a little lower than it would be if money had to be added to the cost to cover breakage.

Shoplifting is a lot harder to get by with these days, too. Many stores post signs warning that shoplifters, if caught, will be prosecuted. Hidden cameras are common. And merchandise often has special tags that, if not removed within the store by an employee, will trigger a signal from a scanning device when the customer tries to leave. This sort of equipment is not inexpensive, and the fact that stores are willing to pay for it is testimony to how potentially costly shoplifting can be.

There's probably never been a time when inventory management did not represent something of a challenge, even to the smaller businesses. But let's face it; a hundred years ago things were much less complicated for the typical business person. Because transportation was a whole lot slower in those days, people tended to shop within a mile or two of home, so each retailer had only a limited clientele to serve. Total mass production was still in the future; many items were still made by hand. And regardless of how the products were made, there wasn't nearly so much selection. These factors combined meant that stores tended to carry much less inventory: fewer products and smaller numbers of each item.

Perpetual Inventory

Things are different now. It's the day of "one-stop shopping," with numerous stores that try to offer everything to everyone all the time. It's an ambitious idea and one that has taken inventory management to new heights of complexity. These days, there are literally hundreds of thousands of products. Rather than simply noting that he has "72 pairs of men's socks," today's retailer might be forced to track the inventory for 72 different *kinds* of men's socks.

Bigger stores these days usually computerize their inventory, an innovation that permits *perpetual*, or ongoing, inventory management. With this sort of system, each item purchased is entered into the inventory as soon as it is unpacked and put on the shelves. The quantity, size, and cost are all noted. Later, when the item is purchased, it is automatically deducted from the inventory when the the sales clerk enters it into the computer. As a result, the inventory is always correct, and computer printouts can tell the manager precisely what's in stock at any given time — and what the store is about to run out of. This simplifies reordering tremendously.

Computerized Inventory and Pricing

The whole procedure is made easier by something called the *uniform product code*, or UPC. This familiar code is made up of a series of bars that are imprinted on the packaging of an item or on a tag the manufacturer attaches to the item. Each item has its own code, and while the codes may look like gobbledygook to humans, they're perfectly readable to a computer scanner. The whole process goes something like this.

Say that Big City Grocery orders 20 cases of mayonnaise. These items could be written into Big City's inventory listing by hand, but there's no need for that. A UPC is printed right on the label of each jar by the manufacturer. A Big City employee, using a hand scanner, enters the product code and the number of jars into the inventory as she stocks the shelves. Later, as consumers buy the mayonnaise, the checkout clerk passes each jar over a built-in scanner on the checkout counter. The scanner tells the cash register what to charge for the mayonnaise; it also tells the store's main computer to deduct that item from the inventory. When computer printouts show that Big City is running low on mayonnaise, the manager can reorder this item. In fact, these days the computer's software will likely print out the order for more mayonnaise automatically just as soon as the inventory falls below some minimum level set by the store manager.

Notice, by the way, that with this system pricing of products is automatic; there's no need for the individual tag on each item telling the sales clerk what to charge. That doesn't mean that Big City is locked into one price on the mayonnaise, though. It can discount it or raise the price just by reprogramming the computer to interpret the bar code differently. Say the computer now reads this code as $1.79; it can be reprogrammed to read the same code as $1.69 or $1.89 or any other number. The computer can even be programmed to charge a special sale price for, say, two weeks and then change back to the regular price.

As you might guess, though, in order for this system to work properly, it's essential that every item have its own code. If mayonnaise and cheese and bleach all shared the same code, they'll all have to share the same price as well. What's more, the store manager would never know whether to reorder bleach or cheese. If you think of all the products found in a large grocery or department store, you can see that getting all the codes, prices, and reorder levels right is a big job.

But think how difficult it would be to keep track of all of this information by hand, and you'll understand why installing computerized inventory systems turns out to be cost effective for many businesses, even when the systems cost hundreds of thousands of dollars. The UPC pricing and inventory system offers far more up-to-date inventory information than could ever be obtained otherwise. Take Big City Grocery, for instance. The manager here can get current information on the turnover rate and current inventory for any item in the store, in just the time it takes to print the information out of the computer. That kind of data management enables the store to be far more responsive to shoppers' needs and preferences. If oriental mushroom soup isn't selling well, the store can order less or drop that item altogether and make room for something else that customers seem to want more.

While customers may not recognize the improvements in inventory control, they do realize that clerks do not have to punch prices into the cash register by hand, so checkout goes much faster. Customers also get itemized receipts of their purchases, something most appreciate. Further, because the inventory management is less time consuming, it's easier for the store to hold prices down. In a large store, the sheer volume of merchandise on hand at any one time makes inventory management a full-time job in itself, and then some. When much of the work is done by computer, it's not only faster but more cost effective as well. And that means the store won't need to raise prices in order to cover the cost of its own inventory control.

Of course, no system is perfect. Don't get the idea, for instance, that a manager whose inventory is computerized can just sit back and let the computer take over all the work. While computers do their specialized tasks with impressive speed and efficiency, there are a lot of things they cannot do at all—like moving products from the storage room out into the store, for instance. And what if those cases of mayonnaise never get entered into the inventory in the first place? Even if they're obviously sitting on the shelf, they don't exist as far as the inventory is concerned. Similarly, if Mrs. McFeeney wheels her cart round the corner too fast and knocks 30 jars of mayo off the assistant manager's prize display, the computer will not make note of this event; someone will need to enter the proper data to show what happened. In other words, while the computer system manages the inventory, someone must manage the computer.

Physical Inventory

As mentioned, inventory at the bigger department, variety, and grocery stores just keeps growing all the time. The typical grocery store today stocks over 10,000 different items and may have several dozen of any one item on hand at any given time. So counting these items one by one, which is what *physical inventory* is all about, is an overwhelming task. Nevertheless, it's a necessary one for any business that wants to have a truly accurate picture of its total inventory.

Wait a minute, you may say: If a store has computerized inventory, isn't that accurate enough without putting someone through the torture of painstakingly counting out everything from anchovies to zucchini? Well, most of the time, for most purposes, yes. But some inventory may still be unaccounted for. Remember Mrs. McFeeney and the 30 jars of mayo? A large store will likely suffer accidental losses like this every day. Then there's that case of pickles forgotten behind a shelf in the back room, the extra dog food that was returned but not taken out of inventory, and the thousands of items "picked up" by shoppers who never paid for them. In short, there's a great deal the computer can't account for. At a store the size of Big City Grocery, in fact, these miscellaneous items will add up to many thousands of dollars' worth of merchandise over the course of a year. There's only one way for the store to find out precisely what it has, and that's by taking a physical inventory—actually counting up the items.

Because physical inventory is so time consuming, a store the size of Big City Grocery may only do it once a year. And even then, such stores are likely to hire outside help. If they put their own employees on the task, they'd either have to hire new staff anyway to take care of customers or shut the store down altogether for "inventory week," not a desirable alternative. A much smaller business, however, may take inventory every few months, or even every month, especially if it's not computerized. Physical inventory taken at regular intervals is called *periodic inventory*, and it's common practice at smaller operations where inventory is neither too extensive nor too diverse.

You may be thinking that once a year isn't very often to get a clear picture of where you stand. Don't forget, though, that in these large stores there is the computerized record—which, despite its shortcomings, is likely to be reasonably accurate. This information will be verified, though, with records of purchases, or invoices, which the company keeps on file, and with records of sales. So even though those forgotten pickles in the back room weren't noted in the inventory, they're sure to be noted when it's time to pay the pickle company's invoice. Cross-checking among several databases helps a business like Big City Grocery ensure that its records are as accurate as possible. This, in turn, increases the likelihood that whoever does the ordering will stock plenty of popular, top-selling items and discontinue those no one seems to want.

The Ever-Changing Inventory

It has no doubt occurred to you by now that inventory management would be much simpler if nothing ever changed: that is, if stores always ordered the same products in the same quantities at the same prices. But for most businesses, inventory changes continuously, in one way or another. Unpopular products are eliminated; new and more popular products are added or their volume increased. Retailers buy more when products are "in season," or the business expands, or a growing market warrants it; they buy less when business is slow or the purchase of seasonal items falls off. And, of course, the prices of most items (even at wholesale cost) tend to rise steadily due to inflation, so selling prices have to change as well.

All this change complicates inventory management. What's particularly tricky is valuing the inventory. Remember, inventory management is more than just counting total numbers of items; it requires determining what those items are worth. When prices have shifted over time, that can be really difficult.

Consider, for instance, Southwest Furniture, which now has ten dining room tables of a certain style in stock. The tables are all the same size, all made of cherry; they all come with four chairs. The difference is that Southwest Furniture bought the first four for $200 apiece. It paid $250 for the next four and $300 for the last two. So, how much is this inventory worth? Well, that depends on how you choose to look at it. Let's consider some alternatives.

The weighted average method. One way to value inventory is the *weighted average method*. This involves first determining the total amount the business has spent on the inventory in question and then dividing that amount by the number of items. In this case, Southwest has spent ($200 × 4) + ($250 × 4) + ($300 × 2) = $2,400. There are ten tables, so the weighted average cost per table is $2,400 ÷ 10 = $240. Notice, by the way, that this figure can be used to find the value of remaining inventory when some of the tables have been sold. Let's say, for instance, that Southwest sells four dining tables next week, so six remain in stock. Their value will be $1,440 ($240 × 6), according to this method of inventory valuation. But there are other methods, and if we use one of them, the value of the six tables will look different.

The FIFO Method. The *FIFO*, or *first in, first out, method* of inventory valuation assumes that the first products a business purchases will be the first ones sold. This is the normal flow of merchandise, and it's sometimes an accurate assumption, assuming that turnover is reasonably rapid and that products do not change in style or quality. For instance, the nails sold by a hardware store may not change from week to week, nor year to year, for that matter. So we wouldn't normally expect a customer to come in demanding the "new, improved" nails. The store simply orders more nails for the warehouse as it puts the last of the old stock out for sale, so it sells them more or less in the same order in which they arrive.

Let's assume for now that it's like that with the cherry tables. In that case, we can assume that the six tables still in inventory are the ones most recently purchased. Last time the store bought tables, at $300 each, it bought two. If there are six in inventory, we need four more to make up the difference $(6 - 2 = 4)$. And, in fact, the previous shipment included four tables at $250 each. So the value of the six tables, using the FIFO method, is $(2 \times \$300) + (4 \times \$250) = \$1,600$. Notice that this is $160 more than the value of the same inventory using the weighted average method.

The LIFO Method. The *LIFO*, or *last in, first out, method* of inventory valuation assumes that the last products ordered will be the first to sell. Now let's imagine for a moment that it's like that with our dining tables, too. In that case, the six tables still in inventory are assumed to be the first six ordered. That means they'll include all four of the $200 tables plus two of the $250 tables, for a total inventory valuation of $(4 \times \$200) + (2 \times \$250) = \$1,300$. That's $140 less than the weighted average valuation and $300 less than the FIFO valuation.

Which is the most accurate valuation in this case? We can't say. The FIFO method is probably most reflective of how the inventory is actually sold, and it is the method that most merchants use. Even so, the value of the inventory can still be calculated by any of these three common methods, and a business can, to some extent, choose how it will value its inventory, regardless of how that inventory moves. In other words, a store can use the LIFO method of accounting without actually handling inventory in the last in, first out manner.

As our examples with Southwest Furniture show, the LIFO method tends to result in a lower inventory valuation. This decreases the total value of the business. So if Southwest Furniture were thinking of selling out to another, larger store, this method would put it at a disadvantage. It would make the business seem to be worth less, since the value of a furniture store's inventory is a major component in the value of the business as a whole. On the other hand, suppose Southwest has no thoughts of selling. But it is a little concerned about taxes. The lower the value of the inventory, the lower property taxes will be. And because the books will show it has been selling the later, generally more expensive inventory, the cost of goods is higher. This means that the store's profit will be lower and it will owe less income tax.

Determining the right approach to inventory valuation is not a simple task. Deciding which method to use has a lot to do with the tax laws and industry practices that affect a given business, and making the right decision about valuing inventory will likely require the help of a qualified accountant, preferably one who has dealt with similar kinds of businesses in the past.

SOME WORDS OF ADVICE

Many business consultants look on inventory management as a key to business success. After all, the value of any retail business is, to a large extent, reflected in the value of its inventory. Moreover, the manager who is thoroughly familiar with the ebb and flow of inventory is in a much better position to order products that will sell and to price them effectively. Managers who do not know how fast their products are selling or which products are selling better than others cannot hope to compete with those who take the time and trouble to put themselves in touch with consumers' needs.

It's hard to deny, though, that taking inventory is a large, complex, time-consuming task. Tedious, too, some would add. So it's no doubt tempting to just forget the whole thing, or to do it in a sort of slapdash, general impression kind of way without getting too hung up on details. But the advice on that sort of approach is simple: Forget it. When it comes to good inventory management, shortcuts do not work. Besides, they aren't really shortcuts in the long run. As we've seen in our various scenarios, the business that engages in haphazard inventory management often finds itself spending too much money on inventory it cannot hope to sell or tossing out goods that are no longer salable. Careful inventory management costs money, but it saves the business much more over time by giving the manager precisely the information needed for sound purchasing decisions.

Larger businesses or those with complex, diverse inventory often find it cost effective to computerize their inventory system. A computerized system combines pricing and inventory management and provides more current information on inventory than any sort of manual system can possibly hope to do. Keep in mind, however, that as we noted earlier, there are limits to what even the best computerized system can accomplish. Computerized inventory management does not, for instance, eliminate the need to take physical inventory and cross-check inventory data with records of purchases and sales.

Virtually every major industry has trade journals that summarize general data on inventory turnover for businesses of a given type and size. Managers are well-advised to compare their own business performance with that of others. Certainly every business is unique, so slight deviations from these averages one way or the other are not cause for alarm nor for rejoicing. The question to ask is: What's causing those deviations? Significant differences in performance suggest a need to look a little deeper into how a business is being run.

Finally, in determining how best to value an inventory, the prudent business manager will seek the advice of a qualified business consultant or accountant. Needs differ according to the type of business and the nature of its inventory. Keep in mind, though, that this is not a whimsical sort of decision that can be altered arbitrarily. The government likes to see some sort of consistency, for tax purposes, in the way a business determines its worth. So, no fair using the LIFO method for taxes and then switching to the FIFO method just when it's time to sell the business. As a business manager, you have to determine in advance how you'll look at your inventory, and then—except in very special circumstances—stick with that perspective.

KEY TERMS

Before you watch the video program and read through the text assignment, take a minute to look at the key terms associated with this lesson. When you encounter them in the text and video program, pay careful attention to their meaning.

Average inventory: A total inventory valuation determined by dividing the sum of all inventories taken by the number of times the inventory was taken.

FIFO (first in, first out) method: An inventory valuation method that assumes that the first goods purchased by the business will also be the first goods sold.

Inventory turnover: The number of times during each year (or other period of time) that the average inventory is sold.

Inventory valuation: The process of determining the value of merchandise in stock. Four common methods of inventory valuation are FIFO, LIFO, weighted average cost, and specific identification.

LIFO (last in, first out) method: An inventory valuation method that assumes that the last goods purchased by the business will be the first goods sold.

Operating loss: A loss resulting when the selling price of merchandise is lower than the retailer's cost of buying that merchandise.

Periodic inventory: A physical inventory taken at regular intervals.

Perpetual inventory: A continuous inventory system that normally utilizes a computer.

Physical inventory: An actual physical count of each item in stock at a given time.

Specific identification method: An inventory valuation method that keeps track of each item individually and values the item at its actual cost.

Stock turnover: See *inventory turnover*.

Uniform product code (UPC): A bar code that is issued on each product and product size. This coding provides the basis for a computerized perpetual inventory system.

Weighted average method: An inventory valuation method in which the cost of all purchases during a given time is divided by the number of units purchased.

PART II: WATCHING THE VIDEO PROGRAM

VIDEO VIEWING GUIDE

Before watching the video program, review the following questions. As you watch, be sure to collect the information necessary to answer them.

1. How important is it to a business to maintain good inventory control?

2. Does the importance of sound inventory management vary from business to business?

3. What are some of the advantages in perpetual inventory management using UPCs and computerized inventory control from the business manager's perspective? From the consumer's perspective?

4. What are some of the advantages associated with rapid inventory turnover? Are there potential disadvantages to rapid inventory turnover?

5. What is the main difference between the LIFO and FIFO methods of calculating inventory? Under what circumstances might a business choose to use one method rather than the other?

6. What are some factors that make inventory management more challenging to some businesses than to others?

7. What are some things a business could do to make its inventory control simpler and more efficient?

VIDEO PROGRAM

This lesson's video program is Program 13 — Inventory Control. Remember, if you are watching this program on videotape, take time to replay sections of the tape whenever you need to review a concept.

VIDEO VIEWING QUESTIONS

Immediately after viewing the video program for Lesson 13, take time to respond to the following questions. Give your answers some careful thought; they may provide the basis for additional discussion or a longer written response.

1. Suppose you were called on to consult for some people who wanted to start a small retail shoe store. On a scale of 1 to 10, how important would you tell them *good inventory control* will be in running their business?

Not   Extremely
Important   Important

1- - - - -2- - - - -3- - - - -4- - - - -5- - - - -6- - - - -7- - - - -8- - - - -9- - - - -10

2. Which of the following businesses would you expect to have particularly rapid inventory turnover? (Check as many as apply.)

_____ Hardware store

_____ Restaurant

_____ Live bait shop

_____ Flower shop

_____ Grocery

_____ Furniture store

_____ Bookstore

_____ Auto dealership

_____ Pet store

_____ Stationery store

_____ Record store

3. Name one potential advantage, and one potential disadvantage, to rapid inventory turnover.

Advantage: _____

_____

Disadvantage: _____

_____

4. Which of the following factors do you think would likely contribute to inventory shrinkage? (Check as many as apply.)

_____ Inflation

_____ Poor packaging

_____ Slow turnover

_____ Breakage

_____ Careless handling during shipment

_____ Growing costs of storage space

_____ Poor store security

_____ Lack of shoplifting control devices

_____ Shifts in consumers' buying habits

_____ Poor lighting in the store

_____ Poor inventory control

5. Name one reason a business might use the LIFO method of inventory valuation.

_____

_____

6. Name one reason a business might use the FIFO method of inventory valuation.

_____

_____

7. On a scale of 1 to 10, how important do you think it is for a business to take physical inventory at least once per year?

Not   Extremely
Important   Important

1- - - - -2- - - - -3- - - - -4- - - - -5- - - - -6- - - - -7- - - - -8- - - - -9- - - - -10

8. Which of the following factors do you think affect *total* inventory value? (Check as many as apply.)

_____ Inflation

_____ Property tax rates for the business

_____ Method of inventory valuation

_____ Size of the business

_____ Turnover ratio

_____ Date on which inventory is taken

_____ Types of products inventoried

_____ Inventory shrinkage

PART III: FOCUSING ON THE MATHEMATICS

READING ASSIGNMENT

After watching the video program, you should read one of the following Text Assignments, depending on the textbook you're using:

SOFTCOVER: Pages 255-264 from Chapter 7 of the Miller, Salzman, and Hoelzle softcover text, *Business Mathematics.*

HARDCOVER: Pages 347-361 from Chapter 10 of the Salzman, Miller, and Hoelzle hardcover text, *Mathematics for Business.*

As you read through the text, pay careful attention to the examples the book gives of the mathematics associated with the concepts you're learning about.

Then, after you've completed the text assignment, read through the Key Formulas below. This section provides a handy review of what you've learned. By the time you get to this point in the lesson, all of the formulas and calculations should be familiar to you. If they're not, go back and read the appropriate parts of the text and the Overview section of this lesson. You won't have much success completing the rest of your assignments if you are still confused about the information in the Key Formulas section.

KEY FORMULAS

The following key formulas are important to your understanding of this lesson. Be sure that you know each one and how to use it in solving problems relating to inventory management.

KEY FORMULA: Turnover at retail = Sales ÷
                      Average inventory at retail

Formula used for: Finding the turnover ratio when both sales totals
                       and the value of inventory at retail are known.

Example:

Griffith Enterprises has sales of $32,155.50 during the month of May. The average value of its inventory *at retail* during this period is $9,894. Its turnover ratio is therefore $32,155.50 ÷ $9,894 = 3.25. In other words, Griffith turned over its entire inventory three and one-fourth times during the month of May.

Remember that in this formula:

1. The *turnover ratio* indicates the number of times, on average, that the entire inventory has been sold out and replaced during the period in question. The turnover ratio for any individual items within this inventory total may be slightly higher or slightly lower. For instance, the turnover ratio on a popular item at Griffith might be 6.5 for the month while the turnover ratio on another, much less popular item is only 0.3. But on average, the ratio indicates that items had to be replaced just over three times.

2. The sales total is equal to the amount sold, or the gross sales figure, during the period. In other words, if Griffith added up all the figures on all the sales receipts for May, the total would be $32,155.50. This total does not include deductions for expenses or profits.

3. The average value of the inventory at retail is just that; an average. For instance, suppose that the total value of the inventory at retail were $9,729 on May 1 and $10,059 on May 31. Then the average for the month would be ($9,729 + $10,059) ÷ 2 = $19,788 ÷ 2 = $9,894. This doesn't mean that it's wrong to give a "May 1" or "May 31" value; that's OK. But neither one is the "average May inventory." For that, you need to calculate an average.

KEY FORMULA: Turnover at cost = Cost of goods sold ÷
                      Average inventory at cost

Formula used for: Finding the turnover ratio at cost when the cost
                       of goods to the buyer (retailer) and the average
                       inventory at cost (usually the wholesale price) are
                       known.

Example:

Griffith Enterprises (from the preceding example) paid $19,441.71 for the merchandise it sold during May; in other words, that figure represents the cost (to Griffith) of the goods sold. Suppose the markup is 40 percent based on selling price. We can use this figure to calculate the average inventory at cost, based on what we know from the preceding example. Recall that Griffith's average inventory at retail was $9,894. If markup is 40 percent of retail, then the value of the inventory at cost must be 60 percent of this figure (100% − 40% = 60%). Thus, the value of the inventory at cost − .6 × $9,894 = $5,936.40. Now we can put these figures into the formula to determine turnover at cost: $19,441.71 ÷ $5,936.40 = 3.275.

Remember that in this formula:

1. Even though you are working with cost figures rather than retail figures, you are still looking for the same information: the number of times, on average, that the entire stock at Griffith was sold out and had to be replaced. The slight difference between the two turnover figures (3.275 vs. 3.25) is due to the impact of inventory shrinkage—the fact that some items, though already paid for by the store, did not produce any income.

2. The *cost of the goods sold* refers to the cost to Griffith Enterprises (to the retailer, that is). Be careful not to confuse cost with selling price. In the preceding formula, you were working with retail figures. In this formula, you are working with wholesale (cost to the merchant) figures.

3. The value of the inventory at cost may already be known to the merchant, depending on the method he or she uses to value the inventory. When it is not known, however, it can be calculated based on the value at retail if the amount of markup is known. In this case, for instance, we knew that since the markup represented 40 percent of the selling price, the cost had to represent the remaining 60 percent.

DON'T FORGET

1. Calculate average inventory by dividing the total inventory valuation for a period by the number of times that inventory was taken. For instance, if the inventory valuation on June 1 was $4,000 and the value on June 30 was $6,000, then the average for the period would be $4,000 + $6,000 ÷ 2 = $5,000.

2. It is important not to mix retail and wholesale figures when calculating average inventory or inventory turnover. Use one set of figures or the other.

3. Inventory turnover and *stock turnover* are the same thing. Both are a measure of how many times the inventory had to be replaced as a result of sales.

4. Inventory turnover is a ratio of sales to value at retail or cost of goods sold to average inventory at cost. In isolation this figure has little meaning. It takes on meaning only as a basis for comparing the turnover at one business to that at another or for comparing the turnover within a given business from month to month or item to item.

5. The weighted average method values inventory items at the average cost of purchasing them. To determine the average value of an item by this method, determine total values for all items in the inventory

(based on actual cost to the business), then divide by the number of items in the inventory. For example, if a shoe store buys 10 pairs of boots at $50 each and another 10 pairs at $60 each, then the average value is $(10 \times \$50) + (10 \times \$60) \div 20 = \$500 + \$600 \div 20 = \$1,100 \div 20 = \$55$.

6. The FIFO method of valuing inventory assumes a natural flow of goods, in which the first items purchased by a business will also be the first items sold. The last items purchased, then, are presumed to be those remaining in the inventory, and the total inventory value is based on the cost of these items.

7. The LIFO method of valuing inventory assumes a reverse situation, in which the goods most recently purchased by the business are the first to be sold. In this case, the first items purchased are assumed to be those remaining within the inventory, and the total inventory value is based on the cost of these items.

PART IV: SOLVING BUSINESS PROBLEMS

PROBLEM SETS

Work the following problems in your textbook. Your instructor will tell you which problems, if any, are to be turned in. Some of the problems have answers provided in the back of the book; refer to these answers to make sure you are working the problems correctly.

SOFTCOVER: If you are using the Miller, Salzman, and Hoelzle softcover text, *Business Mathematics*, do the following problem sets:

    7.4: Problems #1-24 on pages 261-264.

HARDCOVER: If you are using the Salzman, Miller, and Hoelzle hardcover text, *Mathematics for Business*, do the following problem sets:

    10.2: Problems #1-24 on pages 350-351.

    10.3: Problems #1-20 on pages 358-361.

BUSINESS APPLICATIONS

Read each of the following scenarios and answer the questions about the decisions you would make in each situation. Give these questions some serious thought; they may be used as the basis for discussion or the development of a more complex essay. You should base your decisions on what you've learned from this lesson, applying both math skills and good business judgment to solve the problem at hand.

SCENARIO 1 Ed Frank owns a sporting equipment store called The Good Sport. It started as an outlet for Ed's own interest in fly fishing and was originally a very small, one-person operation with fewer than 200 items in its inventory. Now the business has expanded; it has seven employees (besides Ed) and an inventory of nearly 1,500 items, including mountain bikes, tennis and ski equipment, and camping gear. Ed is seriously considering a new line of golf equipment as well, and he plans to build on next year. The shelves are overflowing and a lot of the merchandise is stored in a small rental facility over five miles from the store.

Ed hasn't taken physical inventory in over eight months, even though he's added a number of new items during that period. There just never seems to be time to do it; other, day-to-day activities have to take precedence. Ed's accountant suggests that the store go to a computer-based perpetual inventory system so he can know just where he stands at all times. The accountant points out that much of Ed's merchandise comes precoded with UPCs from the manufacturer, so Ed and his staff would save time by not having to put their own price tags on. Furthermore, they'd have more current information to use in their ordering and could probably cut down on the amount of merchandise they have to mark down to sell.

The accountant's arguments are compelling, but Ed isn't fully convinced. He thinks the new system will be too expensive, and besides, he doesn't want to "waste a lot of time training people to do something new when they can hardly keep up with their current responsibilities." Moreover, he tells her, it just isn't practical for such a small business. And what if it breaks down?

Right now, sales are averaging around $50,000 per month, with fluctuations of 10 percent either way, but the overall trend is up. Ed uses his sales receipts to value his inventory and to get a general idea of turnover, which he thinks is around once per month. "I'd say that's pretty good," he tells his accountant, "and no matter what people say, you can get better information looking at the shelves and listening to what customers tell you than you can get from looking at some computerized inventory data."

Ed's accountant acknowledges that, on the whole, Ed is a good manager, with a strong sense of what the customer wants. The business is doing well, she tells him, but it could be doing better. Right now, for instance, there are some inconsistencies between information on the invoices (purchase records) for the business and what the sales receipts show is going out the door. Some merchandise is unaccounted for. Further, she points out, sooner or later the government is likely to complain that Ed's inventory data isn't precise enough for tax purposes. For that reason alone, the computerized system could be a good investment.

What do you think? Is computerizing a good idea for Ed's business, or would he just be rushing into a new set of problems he isn't prepared for? What are some of the benefits he might be overlooking? Are there disadvantages the accountant is not alerting Ed to? Would the system solve the kinds of problems The Good Sport faces?

☐ Should Ed computerize his inventory? Why or why not?

☐ Do you think Ed has the information he needs to make a good business decision right now? If not, what additional information should he collect?

☐ Ed is worried about the cost effectiveness of installing a computerized system. How would he go about conducting a mathematical analysis of whether the system will save him money? What factors does he need to consider?

☐ Ed mentioned the possibility of the computer breaking down. Do you personally think this is something that should keep him from considering a computerized system?

☐ What are the most important factors (mathematical or non-mathematical) for Ed, or any business manager, to consider in deciding whether to install a computerized perpetual inventory system?

SCENARIO 2

Helen Flores runs a gardening supply business that specializes in landscaping equipment for residential yard maintenance. Helen lives in a warm climate where sales are pretty consistent year round. Hers is a modest-sized business with a well-established clientele, and it has done well in recent years, though growth has been only moderate. Helen doesn't foresee moving out of the small shop she leases from a large local nursery for at least several more years.

When Helen started the business, she made a lot of decisions that she didn't really think through too carefully. One of those was how she values her inventory. Now she's wondering if she should take some different approach to valuing her inventory. While profits are not going up, her property taxes are; without any strong signs pointing to business expansion, it's getting to be a serious worry.

Helen has always used the weighted average method to value her inventory. And given the differences in what she pays for her merchandise across time, she still thinks it may make the most sense. In her business, she is often able to take advantage of seasonal discounts on items like lawnmowers and hedge trimmers, so sometimes her own costs go down a little even though she holds her prices pretty steady. It's these business discounts that have kept Helen going, really, despite the increases in taxes. Unfortunately, such discounts apply only to a few items in Helen's total inventory.

A business associate suggests that Helen consider the LIFO or FIFO method of valuing her inventory. Helen isn't sure which, if either, would work for her. A review of the company books suggests that although the numbers of various items Helen has purchased have remained remarkably consistent during the past few years, her costs have risen 10 to 20 percent on many items. For example, Helen bought ten tree trimmers in January and paid $50 apiece. In March she bought ten more, but this time she paid $56 apiece; in June, she bought five more and paid $60 apiece. Since the trimmers were all identical, the increase in price was totally due to inflation. Since she has only eight left, it will soon be time to reorder, and no doubt the price will be up again. What's more, this is just one of several dozen examples.

With costs going up that rapidly, Helen isn't sure whether the weighted average method reflects the true value of her inventory. Maybe some other method would be better, but which one? And in what ways would this change the value of her inventory or her tax situation? Maybe she should check further into this LIFO and FIFO business, or maybe the differences aren't significant enough to warrant changing to a whole new system.

What do you think? Is Helen's current method of valuing her inventory probably as good as any? Or is there another method that would fit her situation better? If so, what would you recommend, and why?

☐ Should Helen stick with the weighted average method of valuing her inventory, or would another system work better in her situation? If you think she should change, what method would you recommend? Why?

☐ Does Helen have enough information right now to make a good business decision? What specific mathematical calculations should she make, and what other steps should she follow, to ensure that her decision is the best one possible?

☐ Helen hasn't mentioned anything about consulting an accountant. Is this something she needs to do, or does the fact that Helen understands her own business better than anyone make consulting an accountant a poor investment?

☐ Helen's business is not all that unique; she knows several other companies that operate in much the same way as hers. Should she be influenced by the inventory valuation methods these other companies use? Why or why not?

☐ Wouldn't it be simpler if there were only one kind of inventory valuation method? Wouldn't most companies do just as well with any method? If not, why not?

Simple Interest 14

"Each hour."

HERMAN® COPYRIGHT © 1989 UNIVERSAL PRESS SYNDICATE.
Reprinted with permission. All rights reserved.

No matter how carefully businesses or individuals plan, sooner or later their needs and wants may outrun their cash on hand. That means they'll need to borrow money. Fortunately, there are many people who are more than willing to let others use their money. But not for free; they want something in return. And why not? If we look at things from the lenders' side, it's potentially costly for businesses or individuals to do without their own money even for a little while. After all, the convenience and opportunity that the borrower gains by using someone else's money are precisely the advantages the lender gives up. So paying for the use of money is the most common way of making that lost opportunity and the inconvenience worthwhile.

The notion of charging *interest* on borrowed money is hardly new; in fact, it's probably been around as long as money itself. One of the earliest pieces of writing ever found (from about 2500 B.C.) details the interest to be charged on a loan. What's different in the modern world, though, is the fact that borrowing is a lot more systematized these days. If borrowing had been an isolated, rare occurrence, it's highly unlikely the banking system we know today would ever have evolved. But modern banking evolved because, as we hinted a moment ago, borrowing is a very common practice for both businesses and individuals. And that's why certain businesses, like banks, are able to make a profit "buying" and "selling" money. They pay interest on deposits and earn interest on the money they lend. When a bank is successful, it has plenty of money on hand to lend. And as anyone who reads advertisements knows, banks with the resources encourage borrowing—with interest, of course.

By and large, this is a world of *compound interest*, meaning that interest is charged (or earned) not only on the amount borrowed, but on any interest owed as well. Because compound interest has more long-term money-making potential, most loans extended by banks and other formal lending institutions are based on compound interest. Similarly, credit card accounts are based on compound interest. However, simple interest loans (loans where the interest is charged only on the principal) are often available on a short-term basis from banks and credit unions. And it's probably safe to say that most personal loans between friends or relatives involve simple interest, though there are certainly exceptions.

In this lesson, we'll see how simple interest is calculated and consider ways that businesses and individuals can use formulas relating to simple interest in making important borrowing decisions.

PART I: INTRODUCING THE MATERIAL

LEARNING OBJECTIVES

Upon completing your study of this lesson, you should be able to:

1. Define the term *interest* and explain how simple interest differs from compound interest.

2. Know the basic simple interest formula and use it to calculate the amount of interest, given the principal, rate, and time.

3. Know or derive alternate forms of the simple interest formula and use them to calculate principal, interest, rate, or time, given the other three.

4. Given any two dates, determine the number of days between them, both by calculation and by using a table.

5. Distinguish between exact interest and ordinary interest and calculate the difference in interest between the two, given principal, rate, and time.

6. Define the term *maturity value* and calculate the maturity value of any loan, given the principal, rate, and time.

7. Define the terms *present value* and *future value* and suggest some business situations in which calculating present value would be useful.

8. Accurately describe the capabilities of handheld business calculators in calculating the present and future value of money.

If you're using the hardcover textbook, *Mathematics for Business*, there are some additional objectives for the lesson. Upon completing your study of the lesson, you should also be able to:

9. Know or derive the formula for present value and use the formula to calculate present value, given future value, rate, and time.

10. Understand the significance of the time value of money and calculate time value, given principal, rate, and time until the loan is due.

11. Calculate the present value of a loan having a given maturity value.

12. Given the time value of money, derive the present value of a loan by calculating its maturity value.

13. Calculate the present value of a loan at a specified date after the loan has been made, both with and without a change in interest rate.

LESSON OVERVIEW

Whenever interest is involved, borrowing costs money. So it's only logical to ask why anyone would think about borrowing. For businesses, as for individual borrowers, the answers are varied and complex, yet they boil down to two broad, general reasons. First, there may be an immediate, important need for cash that the borrower cannot meet. For the individual, it might be a medical emergency, for instance. For the business, it might be lack of funds to make rent or tax payments or to cover some other ongoing business expense.

The second general reason for borrowing is that there may be an opportunity that will be lost unless the borrower can quickly come up with the resources to take advantage of it. For instance, the individual borrower may want money to take advantage of a sale on tires for the car, or to buy a refrigerator that the store has on sale for a limited time. Similarly, a business may want to expand, open new markets, take advantage of a trade discount to expand its inventory, or provide its staff with new training. Such improvements are designed to increase a business's money-making potential. Thus, the company that borrows to expand inventory, buy new equipment, advertise more broadly, or help employees fine tune their skills often winds up recapturing much more than its original investment. In short, borrowing money, if it's done thoughtfully and with the right kind of planning, often makes good financial sense.

Simple versus Compound Interest

As we'll keep stressing, simple interest is charged only on the *principal*, the amount originally borrowed. Compound interest, on the other hand, is charged not only on the principal but on any accumulated interest. Here's a simplified example to help illustrate the difference. Let's say that Clemens borrows $1,000 for one year at 10 percent simple interest. At the end of the year, Clemens owes the $1,000 principal, plus 10 percent of that amount (or $100) in interest, for a total of $1,100. Even if Clemens makes no effort to pay off the loan before the end of the borrowing period, the amount he owes doesn't increase.

Let's suppose that at the same moment, Goldberg also borrows $1,000 for one year at 10 percent interest compounded quarterly. That means that every three months, the lender figures up the interest Goldberg owes. Assuming that he hasn't paid anything on the debt yet, for the following quarter interest accumulates not only on the unpaid principal, but also on the interest Goldberg *owes so far*. This means that by the end of the year, if he hasn't paid off anything on the loan, Goldberg will owe $1,103.81, or $3.81 more than Clemens. Well, you might say, that doesn't seem like a very large difference over a full year. And you're quite right. It isn't very big—not on a loan of this size and not at this rate of interest. But what if the two loans had been for $100,000 and the interest rate had been higher, Clemens's at 18 percent simple interest, Goldberg's at 18 percent compounded monthly? Then the total amount owed would have been much bigger: $115,000 versus $119,562, or a difference of over $4,500.

Why Banks Might Charge Simple Interest

In our example with Clemens and Goldberg, the rates and borrowing periods are consistent. If they were not, the comparison between their debts would get more complex. For instance, it's cheaper to borrow $1,000 at 10 percent compound interest for a year than it is to borrow the same $1,000 at 12 percent simple interest. Obviously, the interest rate isn't the only consideration. But assuming that the rates are equal, charging compound interest nets the lender a higher return in the form of interest. Why then would banks, which set their own interest rates within limits imposed by the federal government, ever consider charging anything else?

Well, if you think back to the Clemens-Goldberg comparison, you'll recall that the difference on interest with a one-year, $1,000 loan was negligible, less than $4. But from the borrower's perspective, the psychological difference may be very great. Borrowers like the idea that they can get a simple interest loan; it "feels" cheaper. It's also appealing because the interest on a simple interest loan is a little simpler to compute and explain. And, finally, banks or other lending institutions that offer simple interest loans may be able to convince customers that they are offering a better deal, even when the difference to the borrower is negligible.

Take our friend Clemens. If he thinks the Golden Valley Bank won't give him a simple interest loan, he may just borrow the money from his wealthy Aunt Pearl, who not only has the money to lend but might offer it at 9 percent simple interest. On the other hand, Clemens might prefer not to go to Aunt Pearl if he doesn't have to. In short, Clemens and many others like him like the professional feeling of borrowing from a bank, and will do so *if* they can get the money about as cheaply as they could get it from friends, relatives, or business associates. On a single simple interest loan, the bank loses the few dollars it might have gained by charging compound interest, but it earns much more by attracting customers who would go elsewhere for the money if this sort of loan were not available.

There is a catch, though: Simple interest loans from banks or other lending institutions tend to be short-term, usually less than a year. The effects of compound interest become much more significant as the time period stretches out, so when the term of the loan is short, the lender isn't making all that much of a concession by charging simple interest. But borrowers who want money for extended periods generally have no choice but to pay compound interest.

Whether or not a simple interest loan is available from a bank depends on a lot of factors that the borrower can't control. Face it, if none of the banks in town wants to offer a simple interest loan, there's not a lot of sense in insisting on one. Besides, as we've stressed, a short-term simple interest loan can easily cost more than a compound interest loan if the rate is just a little bit higher.

But if Aunt Pearl is going to loan the money, she's pretty likely to charge simple interest. For one thing, Aunt Pearl probably doesn't know how to calculate the amount of compound interest due. (In fact, she may not even know what compound interest is.) She is likely to feel like she deserves some interest for loaning out her money, but she's unlikely to try to squeezing the last dollar in interest out of her nieces and nephews. And since she's not competing for customers against a number of other lenders, the interest rate she charges will probably be a bit arbitrary.

The amount of interest owed on a simple interest loan is a function of three factors: principal, rate, and time. This relationship is expressed in a very important formula: $I = PRT$. The bigger any of these factors (P, R, or T) the greater the amount of interest owed. For instance, the borrower will be charged more interest on a loan of $3,000 than on a loan of $2,000, given the same rate and borrowing period. Similarly, the interest on $1,000 for six months will be higher at 12 percent than at 8 percent. This all seems pretty obvious, right?

What's sometimes less obvious to borrowers, though, is the fact that the third factor, *time*, is variable. It's also the factor over which the borrower (usually) has the most control. For instance, a borrower might take out a one-year loan but repay the money in only three months. In that case (assuming no prepayment penalties), she would owe only a quarter the amount of interest she would have owed had she kept the money for the full year. Let's use some real figures to see how this works.

Say, for instance, that Davidson borrows $2,000 at 12 percent per year for one year. We can use the basic simple interest formula $I = PRT$ to determine how much interest she'll owe at the end of the year. $P = \$2,000$, $R = 12$ percent per year, and $T = 1$, so $I = \$2,000 \times .12 \times 1$, which is $240. But if she pays off the loan after three months, notice how the formula changes: $I = \$2,000 \times .12 \times \frac{3}{12}$ (because three months is $\frac{3}{12}$ of a year). In that case, Davidson owes just $60 in interest, a fairly substantial savings. Of course, she may not have the money to pay off the loan. After all, she probably borrowed the money for a year because that's how long she needs it. But if she does have the funds, she can save herself some money by reducing the time she keeps the bank's money.

Interest rates make the front page of newspapers' business sections just about every day, a testimony both to the popularity of borrowing in today's business world and to the variability of the rates themselves. The interest rates charged by banks are a function of many factors, not the least of which is the general state of the economy at a particular time. However, just what makes a healthy economy is a matter of dispute, as is almost any assessment of how the economy is acting or going to act. Nevertheless, there are some basic economic theories about how interest rates are affected by the economy, and we'll mention them here. Keep in mind that these days there seem to be pretty constant exceptions to all the rules, and you shouldn't count on this rather simplified description to explain things all the time. (Economics isn't called "the dismal science" for nothing.)

Simple Interest for Nonbank Loans

Time: The Variable Factor

How the Economy Affects Interest Rates (Maybe)

Historically, when times were good, people saved more money. That meant more and bigger bank deposits and more money generally available for borrowing. For better or worse, however, Americans today don't usually save most of their extra money; instead, they spend it, often as the down payment for things that they buy with loans. So good economic conditions in the U.S. often mean that more people start borrowing money for things other than emergencies. A family or a business with a good income and a bright future feels more comfortable borrowing for things beyond bare necessities: new housing or office space, travel, furniture, equipment, and automobiles. So while the rate of borrowing is up, the supply of money isn't all that much higher. That means that money is in shorter supply and people who have money to lend can charge more for it. As you'd expect, the price of money, the interest rate, goes up.

By contrast, borrowing decreases in hard times. People tend to avoid borrowing for nonemergency purposes because they fear they will be unable to repay the money. They may not even have money for a down payment, so there's no thought of borrowing money. That means banks have money available but fewer customers to take advantage of it. So interest rates drop. Just as prices often drop at the shoe store if no one is buying shoes, banks lower their interest rates if no one is "buying" money.

What to Charge Customers for Money

Don't get the idea that there is one overall "interest rate." Not so; there are several. The *prime rate* is the rate at which banks lend money to their preferred customers, those with the highest presumed likelihood of repaying the money. Preferred customers are generally well-known to the bank, are usually large companies, have an excellent credit rating, and have usually borrowed many times in the past and always paid the money back on time. The prime rate is, at least theoretically, the lowest rate at which the bank will lend money.

Obviously, not every customer qualifies for a loan at this rate. Say McDuff wants to borrow money to begin a new business. He's a whitewater rafting expert and plans to give guided tours on the Defiance River, just as soon as he can afford to buy the boats. Golden Valley Bank may be attracted by the interest it would earn from loaning McDuff $50,000. But the risk is high. McDuff has just moved from another state and has no local credit references and no history of doing business with Golden Valley. It may also occur to the loan officer that the whitewater boats that McDuff is going to buy don't make great security for the loan. The point is, if it lends him the money at all (which is doubtful), it's certain his interest will be well over the prime rate.

The *federal funds rate* is the rate at which banks borrow from each other to increase their own reserves. Say that Golden Valley wants to give McDuff his $50,000 loan (at an interest rate several percentage points over prime) and also wants to increase its loans to the community in general. Perhaps the community is growing, and the bank could make good money by making loans for new construction and business expansion. The trouble is, Golden Valley is currently a small rural community with a limited number of depositors. So the bank doesn't have enough money on hand to cover a greatly increased amount of lending. It could send McDuff and others to another bank, of course, but then it would be sending away business. More likely, Golden Valley Bank would try to borrow money from another bank. A bank that has more cash available than it can loan out to its own customers might like to loan part of it to Golden Valley since, like any other customer, Golden Valley must repay this loan with interest.

Banks also borrow at times from the Federal Reserve Bank, in which case they pay interest at the *Federal Reserve discount rate*. As you might expect, the rates at which banks borrow also determine, to some extent, the rates that they turn around and charge their customers. In this, they're no different from any other merchant. When Superfit Shoes pays more to the shoe manufacturer to get shoes on its shelves, customers must also pay more to take those shoes back off the shelves again. Similarly, the more banks must pay to get money to loan, the more their customers must pay to borrow it. What this means is that the various interest rates tend to go up and down together, even though there are rarely times when everything changes in precisely the same way.

Like any other business, the banking business is competitive. So to some extent, interest rates are also determined by what other banks in the area are charging. Let's say the community of Golden Valley has three banks within a ten-mile radius. If the Golden Valley Bank's two competitors are offering short-term loans at 15 percent simple interest, it will hardly behoove Golden Valley to be charging 16 percent. The little extra they make on one or two loyal customers will be more than offset by the dollars they lose on potential customers who go elsewhere.

Sooner or later, it occurs to anyone calculating either simple or compound interest that the calculations would be somewhat simpler if all borrowing periods were rounded to the nearest month. That would mean that on a short-term loan, borrowers could keep the money for as little as one month ($\frac{1}{12}$ of a year) or as long as a full year ($\frac{12}{12}$). When a loan is first set up, of course, the borrower (and the lender, too, for that matter) generally have something like this in mind.

Ordinary versus Exact Interest

For instance, suppose VanCleef borrows $1,000 to install a new ventilation system at his furniture refinishing shop. The loan is for six months, or $\frac{6}{12}$ of a year. VanCleef doesn't need to repay the money until the whole six months is up, but he can save some interest if he does. So, if things are going well in the furniture business, VanCleef might repay the loan in, say, 71 days. That's all well and good, but now we're stuck with this uneven number to complicate the calculations.

There are a couple of ways the bank might handle this. They might say, "Well, 71 days is more than two months, so let's just round it up to three months for the sake of simplicity and figure the interest accordingly." That simplifies calculations, all right, but VanCleef might not think it was very fair, especially if he discovered that the bank down the street was willing to calculate the interest right to the day. That's the second option, and the one that's likely to appeal a lot more to VanCleef. Fortunately for borrowers, that's the option banks now choose, too.

Notice that when interest is calculated by the month, the fraction that represents the borrowing period is always expressed in twelfths because there are twelve months in a year. This fraction may, of course, be reduced to its lowest terms. Thus, six months, may be expressed as $\frac{6}{12}$ or as $\frac{1}{2}$. Three months may be expressed as $\frac{3}{12}$ or as $\frac{1}{4}$. And so on. When interest is calculated by the day, however, the denominator (the bottom number of the fraction that represents the borrowing period) is either 365 or 360.

Why two numbers? Because there are two different approaches to figuring daily interest. The *ordinary interest* approach assumes 360 days per year, and this is the approach used by most banks. The *exact interest* approach, as its name implies, assumes the full 365 days per year — in other words, the actual number of days that exist in all but leap years (which have 366). The exact interest approach is used by a number of credit unions, and—if they know about such things—is preferred by consumers because it results in a slightly lower amount of interest owed. Remember VanCleef, the furniture refinisher? Recall that he borrowed his $1,000 for 71 days. Let's suppose that the interest rate is 10 percent. Using the ordinary interest method, VanCleef would owe $1,000 × .10 × $71/_{360}$ = $19.72. Using the exact interest approach, VanCleef would owe $1,000 × .10 × $71/_{365}$ = $19.45. The difference isn't very big; 365 days is, after all, only about 1.5 percent more than 360. But the larger the loan and the higher the interest rate, the more difference that 1.5 percent makes.

What's more, given thousands of customers, those pennies can add up to higher profits for banks—which, not surprisingly, favor the ordinary interest method. It might occur to you that one reason lenders would favor this method is that 360, as a nice even number, is a lot easier to work with than 365. That's true if you're doing the calculations by hand, and seven or eight decades ago, it might have been a factor in encouraging lenders to use the ordinary dating method. In this day of calculators and computers, though, simplicity of calculation is no longer a factor. Banks favor the ordinary interest method chiefly because it produces more revenue for them (even though, admittedly, it does so pennies at a time).

Credit: A Form of Borrowing

If you want to borrow money, one way is to march into a bank and request a loan. But that's only one way. For some people, it's simpler to "borrow" by charging purchases on a credit card. No doubt there are a lot of consumers who do not even think of this as borrowing; but that is, in fact, what it is.

Consider our furniture refinisher, VanCleef, for instance. He happens to hold a major credit card with a credit limit of $3,000. When VanCleef needs $500 worth of supplies for his store, he could take out a short-term loan with the bank to cover the purchase. But that would take time. He'd have to drive to the bank, apply for the loan, wait for the application to go through, and so forth. In this case, it's a lot simpler and faster to drive to the store, pick out what he needs, hand over his card, and say, "Charge it." Simpler, maybe, but not necessarily cheaper.

The thing is, interest is charged on credit accounts just as on loans. This interest is the charge that the merchant or bank, depending on who extends the credit, levies for managing the account and waiting a period of time for the buyer's money. The bigger the charge, and the longer the merchant or bank has to wait, the higher the interest.

All credit accounts are based on compound interest. There are a number of reasons for this, but one important reason is that there is no telling how long the consumer will take to repay the money. By charging compound interest, the creditor feels more comfortable about a longer loan period. As long as the consumer regularly pays some minimal amount on the balance owed, and as long as the accumulating interest does not push that balance over the customer's credit limit, the customer can continue to owe the money almost indefinitely.

How Present Value Grows Into Future Value

This lesson is all about interest. But so far we've talked mainly about interest charged on loans. Interest owed, that is. Keep in mind that a bank, or any lender, looks at that interest from a very different perspective. Remember that $50,000 loan to McDuff, the white water rafter? From McDuff's perspective, that's a $50,000 debt. But to the bank, it's a $50,000 *investment*, one that will increase in value over time because of the interest

McDuff pays. Any loan, in fact, is a kind of investment from the lender's point of view. And in granting the loan, the lender must weigh the potential return on investment against future needs.

Sometimes, individuals or companies know they're going to need a specific amount of money by some given time in the future. They may be able to come up with that money out of regular earnings. But an alternative is to invest a smaller amount now and let it grow by accumulating interest. The amount of that current investment is the *present value* of some specific future amount (a *future value*), given a known interest rate and period of investment.

For instance, let's say that Ellis is a veterinarian. She expects to need a new $1,000 microscope for her laboratory in about three years. She doesn't have the money now, but she does have an opportunity to invest some money with a guaranteed return of 10 percent for the three years. So she can earn the $1,000 if she has enough to invest. The question is, what is the present value of $1,000, given a three-year investment period at a simple interest rate of 10 percent? The formula for solving this problem is $P = MV \div (1 + RT)$, in which P = present value, MV = the *maturity value*, or future value, of the money (in this case, $1,000), R = rate (10%), and T = time (3 years). Thus, $P = \$1,000 \div (1 + (.10 \times 3)) = \$769.23$. In other words, Ellis needs only about $770 now in order to have the full $1,000 in three years, given a simple interest rate of 10 percent.

The concept of present value is useful in another context, too. We usually take it for granted that people who lend money want it back as quickly as possible, but this isn't necessarily true. As we've mentioned, a quick payoff deprives the lender of interest, and it was to earn the interest that the money was lent in the first place. Say that Melrose lends Gilbert $2,000 for six months at 20 percent annual simple interest. If Gilbert doesn't pay the debt until the end of the six months, he'll owe Melrose $2,200. And Melrose is looking forward to that money; in her mind, that $2,200 represents the future value of the loan. So if Gilbert offers to pay off the debt after just three months, Melrose will not necessarily be pleased.

That may be because Melrose doesn't have anyone else waiting to pay her 20 percent interest to borrow the money for the remaining three months. In fact, let's suppose that the best thing she can find to do with the money Gilbert pays back is to put it in a money market account paying 8 percent. Given this situation, we say that the *time value of money* has fallen from 20 to 8 percent. In other words, as long as Gilbert has Melrose's money, she is earning an investment return of 20 percent. But if he pays it off early, she can only reinvest it at an average return of 8 percent. And that means a loss to her.

So, when Gilbert offers to pay $2,100 (the $2,000 of principal plus three months' worth of interest) Melrose says no, she will not accept that amount. What she wants is enough money to get her the full $2,200 when invested at the currently available rate of 8 percent. Only now, since she is getting an 8 percent return instead of a 20 percent return and since she has only three months (one-fourth of a year) left in which to do it, Gilbert will have to give her more to invest.

How much more? Remember, the formula for solving this problem is $P = MV \div (1 + RT)$, in which P = present value, MV = the maturity value, or future value, of the money (in this case, $2,200), R = rate (8%), and T = time (now only three months, or .25 year). Thus, $P = \$2,200 \div (1 + (.08 \times .25)) = \$2,156.86$, or about $57 more than Gilbert was planning to pay. It's just Gilbert's bad luck, by the way, that the time value of money happened to go down. If Melrose had suddenly found someone willing to pay a higher rate to borrow the money just as soon as it was paid back, then she would probably have eagerly settled for the normal interest rather than trying to charge Gilbert more.

Keep in mind that the time value of money is always changing, while the interest rate on a given loan is usually fixed for a certain period. That was the case with Melrose and Gilbert. Gilbert might have saved himself some money, incidentally, by establishing an agreement with Melrose at the outset that there would be no penalty (no additional charge, that is) for early payment of the debt. In fact, various laws limit the amount and conditions under which lenders can charge borrowers penalties for pre-paying loans.

The Business Calculator: A Shortcut

Being able to calculate present and future values is handy for virtually any investor or borrower. Fortunately, modern business calculators make the process extraordinarily simple. You need only know the present, or future, value desired, the time allowed for investment, and the rate of interest. Enter these values into the calculator beginning with the amount, followed by the time and rate. Many calculators even have a special key marked *PV* for present value. Punch this button and the result is calculated for you in an instant.

But remember, while the calculator is doing the math, you need to be sure you enter the data correctly and in the right order. And, as with any calculation you perform on a calculator, you have to know whether the result is reasonable. If your calculator tells you that the future value for a $3,000 loan is $12.54, something's not right — and you have to be smart enough to know that. Math errors in calculating things like interest and present value can cost companies a considerable sum of money. Our advice is to always make sure the answer the calculator gives you is roughly the same as what your mental calculations tell you to expect.

SOME WORDS OF ADVICE

As a borrower, take time to check out simple interest alternatives. As we've noted, ours is an economy that runs by and large on compound interest. But for short-term loans of modest amounts, there are often simple interest options available. And whenever the simple interest rates are equal to compound rates, the borrower will certainly save money with simple interest, even though the savings may be quite modest.

That brings up an important point, however. A one-year simple interest loan at 10 percent is cheaper than a compound interest loan at 10 percent, but it's not cheaper than a one-year compound interest loan at 8 percent. The point here is that it's a good idea to know in advance just how long the borrowing period will be and to determine the precise amount of interest owed, or charged, for that period. Only then is it possible to make a true comparison of one loan to another.

If you buy on credit, it's only prudent to equate that kind of purchasing with the borrowing of money. That's what it is, really. Creditors charge interest on credit accounts just as bankers charge interest on loans. Keep in mind, though, that if you pay the full balance on a credit card account within the first month, you can usually avoid paying interest. But if you pay only a portion of the balance, the money you pay will be credited only to the principal. That means that with the next payment, you'll pay on the remaining principal plus the accumulated interest. If you're contemplating a major credit card purchase and you plan to take many months to pay it off, you might want to consider taking out a short-term, simple interest loan instead. Odds are good that the rate will be lower; if you can afford to pay the full balance within a year, this is often a good alternative.

Remember, too, that despite our previous scenario with Gilbert and the uncooperative but financially astute Melrose, most short-term loans do not involve any penalty for early payment. Banks are usual happy to get their money back quickly (they're figuring interest on a daily basis anyway) and they can usually lend it out to someone else. So, as a borrower, keep in mind that you can save money—sometimes lots of it—by paying early. In general, there's little reason to keep the money longer—unless, of course, you plan to invest it at a substantially higher rate of return than the interest rate you're paying.

Finally, whether you're a borrower or lender, be sure all terms of any agreement are in writing. If you do business with a bank or other professional lending agency, of course, you won't have any choice about this. In fact, you're likely to be surprised by the amount of detail even the simplest of simple interest loans can generate. But as bankers know from centuries of experience, when it comes to loans, borrower and lender may remember the terms of the agreement differently. A written agreement helps ensure that the basics of the loan (the principal, rate, and time) look just the same no matter which side of the loan you're standing on.

KEY TERMS

Before you read through the text assignment and watch the video program, take a minute to look at the key terms associated with this lesson. When you encounter them in the text and video program, pay careful attention to their meaning.

Banker's interest: See *ordinary interest*.

Compound interest: Interest charged or received on both principal and interest.

Exact interest: Simple interest calculated using 365 days in a year.

Interest: A fee paid for borrowing money or received for lending money.

Interest, rate of: The percentage of the principal charged as interest. Interest rates are most often quoted as annual (percent per year) rates.

Maturity date: The date a loan is due.

Maturity value: The total amount—principal and interest—that must be repaid when a loan is paid off. Also known as *future value*.

Ordinary interest: Simple interest calculated using 360 days in a year. Also known as *banker's interest*.

Present value: An amount that can be invested today at a given rate to produce a given amount in the future.

Principal: The amount of money borrowed, loaned, or deposited.

Simple interest: Interest charged or received only on the principal.

Time: The length for which a loan is assessed interest. Most commonly, this is the number of years or fraction of a year for which the loan is made.

Time value of money: The average interest rate at which money can be loaned (or otherwise invested) at a given time. Also called simply the *value of money*.

PART II: WATCHING THE VIDEO PROGRAM

VIDEO VIEWING GUIDE

Before watching the video program, review the following questions. As you watch, be sure to collect the information necessary to answer them:

1. On the whole, which is more common: simple interest or compound interest? Why do you think this is so?

2. Why do individuals or institutions charge interest at all? How important is the interest on loans to a bank's profitability?

3. What factors affect the current rate of interest charged by a bank or other lending institution? Under what circumstances might that interest rate go up or down?

4. How important is the length of time the loan is outstanding in determining the total amount of interest a borrower pays on a loan?

5. Is simple interest generally a "better deal" than compound interest? Why or why not?

6. When a credit card customer charges a purchase, will he or she be charged simple or compound interest? Why is this likely the case?

7. How does a business (or individual) determine when and if borrowing at simple interest makes good financial sense?

VIDEO PROGRAM

The lesson's video program is Program 14 — Simple Interest. Remember, if you are watching this program on videotape, take time to replay sections of the tape any time you need to review a concept.

VIDEO VIEWING QUESTIONS

Immediately after viewing the video program for Lesson 14, take time to respond to the following questions. Give your answers some careful thought; they may provide the basis for additional discussion or a longer written response.

1. Which of the following factors do you think would affect the current rate of simple interest charged by a bank? (Check as many as apply.)

   _____ Simple interest rates at other banks

   _____ Current volume of customer borrowing

   _____ Current compound interest rates

   _____ Current state of the national economy

   _____ Current state of the local economy

   _____ Current rate of inflation

   _____ Time of year

   _____ Customers' reasons for borrowing

2. On a scale of 1 to 10, how important do you consider the general state of the economy in a bank's determination of the interest to charge on short-term loans?

   Not   **Extremely**
   Important   **Important**

   1- - - - -2- - - - -3- - - - -4- - - - -5- - - - -6- - - - -7- - - - -8- - - - -9- - - - -10

   How about on long-term loans?

   Not   **Extremely**
   Important   **Important**

   1- - - - -2- - - - -3- - - - -4- - - - -5- - - - -6- - - - -7- - - - -8- - - - -9- - - - -10

3. If simple interest were no longer available from banks or other lending institutions, which of the following do you think would be likely to happen? (Check as many as apply.)

   _____ Interest rates would go down.

   _____ More money would be available for borrowing.

   _____ Economic expansion would slow down.

   _____ The number of long-term loans would increase.

   _____ Borrowing money would become more difficult.

   _____ The number and variety of products offered to consumers by retail merchants would drop.

   _____ Unemployment would rise.

   _____ Some banks would close.

4. How likely do you think it is that simple interest rates will go down substantially in the next five years? (Give a reason for your answer.)

   _____

   _____

5. Using your own words, define the term *interest* in a sentence.

   _____

   _____

6. Imagine that you are the owner and manager of a small, very successful business and that you have been asked to loan $10,000 to a reliable business associate. You have the money and can easily afford to do this. Based on current real-life economic conditions nationally and in your own geographic area, what rate of simple interest will you charge? *Be specific*. Now list the two major factors that you considered in determining this rate.

Proposed Rate: _____

Factor 1:

_____

_____

_____

Factor 2:

_____

_____

_____

7. Now imagine that as the owner and manager of a small, thriving business, you need $10,000 to make a business purchase. List the three factors that would (or should) influence your decision about whether to borrow the money:

a. _____

b. _____

c. _____

PART III: FOCUSING ON THE MATHEMATICS

READING ASSIGNMENT

After watching the video program, you should read one of the following Text Assignments, depending on the textbook you're using:

SOFTCOVER: Pages 273-296 from Chapter 8 of the Miller, Salzman, and Hoelzle softcover text, *Business Mathematics*.

HARDCOVER: Chapter 11 of the Salzman, Miller, and Hoelzle hardcover text, *Mathematics for Business*, pages 368-399.

As you read through the text, pay careful attention to the examples the book gives of the mathematics associated with the concepts you're learning about.

Then, after you've completed the text assignment, read through the Key Formulas below. This section provides a handy review of what you've learned. By the time you get to this point in the lesson, all of the formulas and calculations should be familiar to you. If they're not, go back and read the appropriate parts of the text and the Overview section of this lesson. You won't have much success completing the rest of your assignments if you are still confused about the information in the Key Formulas section.

_____ **KEY FORMULAS**

The following key formulas are important to your understanding of this lesson. Be sure that you know each one and how to use it in solving problems related to simple interest.

KEY FORMULA: $I = PRT$

Formula used for: Finding the amount of simple interest that is owed when the principal, the rate, and the time (the period of the loan) are all known.

Alternate forms: $P = I \div RT$ or $R = I \div PT$ or $T = I \div PR$

Example:

Zither borrows $500 at 10 percent for six months, which is one-half year. How much interest will she owe? $I = PRT$, so $I = \$500 \times .10 \times \frac{1}{2} = \$25$, which means the total interest for the period will be $25. Or suppose Casey receives $100 in interest on a $2,000 investment for six months. What is the interest rate? $R = I \div PT$, so $R = 100 \div (2,000 \times \frac{1}{2}) = .10$, or 10%.

Remember that in this formula:

1. I = the amount of interest owed, not the rate; R is the rate.

2. P = the principal, which is the amount borrowed or invested.

3. T, or time, is always expressed in years or as a fraction of a year. For instance, if Zither (in the first example) had borrowed the money for one full year, then the formula to find the amount of interest would be $I = 500 \times .10 \times 1$. If she had borrowed the money for seven months, the formula would be $I = 500 \times .10 \times \frac{7}{12}$, because there are twelve months in a year. And if she had borrowed it for 53 days, the formula would be $I = 500 \times .10 \times \frac{53}{360}$ (using the number of days assumed for ordinary interest).

4. When you are solving for T, the result will often be a decimal or fraction that represents some fraction of a year. For instance, .5 or $\frac{1}{2}$ (which are the same) represents half a year. This is the same as six months. The ordinary interest system assumes 360 days in a year, so six months is also equal to 180 days ($\frac{6}{12} \times 360 = 180$).

KEY FORMULA: Time in days = $(I \div PR) \times 360$

Formula used for: Finding the number of days for which money was deposited or borrowed, assuming ordinary (360 days per year) interest.

Example:

Suppose that Oswald earned $60 on a $1,200 deposit at 10 percent. To find the number of days, we use the basic time formula and multiply by 360: $T = (I \div PR) \times 360$. Thus, $T = (60 \div (1,200 \times .10)) \times 360 = .5 \times 000 = 100$ days.

Remember that in this formula:

1. *Time in days* is no different from the T or time in any of the other formulas except that it is expressed in days rather than in years.

2. The number 360 is based on the ordinary interest method of calculating interest, which assumes 360 days in a full year (rather than the 365 assumed by the exact interest method).

KEY FORMULA: $MV = P + I$

Formula used for: Finding the maturity value (also referred to as future value) on a loan or deposit when the amount of the principal and the rate of interest are known.

Example:

Wallaby deposits $1,000 for six months and earns $50 in interest. What is the maturity value on this deposit? $MV = \$1,000 + \$50 = \$1,050$.

Remember that in this formula:

1. MV, or the maturity value, is the total amount that the depositor or creditor receives at the end of the borrowing period. It is the same as the *future value* of a given amount at a given interest rate for a given period.

2. Knowing the interest rate is not enough. You need to know both the amount of interest and the amount of the principal. In our example with Wallaby, we provided these numbers. But suppose we'd presented the example this way: Wallaby deposits $1,000 for six months at 10 percent annual interest. What is the maturity value? In that case, you would need first to solve for the amount of interest: $I = PRT$; thus, $I = \$1,000 \times .10 \times \frac{1}{2} = \$50$. Then add the amount of interest ($50) to the principal ($1,000) to determine the maturity value.

3. It's important not to confuse maturity value and principal. The principal is the original amount of the deposit or loan. The maturity value is the amount that deposit or loan grows into as interest accumulates.

KEY FORMULA: $MV = P(1 + RT)$

Formula used for: Finding the maturity value on a loan or deposit when the principal, rate, and time are known but the amount of interest is not known.

Example:

Let's use the previous example with Wallaby to see how this formula works. Recall that Wallaby deposited $1,000 for six months at 10 percent annual interest. Thus, $MV = \$1,000 (1 + .10 \times \frac{1}{2})$, or $MV = \$1,000 \times 1.05 = \$1,050$.

Remember that in this formula:

1. The parentheses tell you that you must multiply R by T and then add 1 before you multiply by P. In other words, P, the amount of the principal, is multiplied by the sum of 1 + RT.

2. It is important to remember that the number inside the parentheses is the number *1*, not the letter *I*. The 1 represents the full amount of the principal itself. The *RT* part of the formula (when multiplied by the principal) gives us the interest. These two elements together (principal plus interest) give us the maturity value.

3. It is not necessary to know the amount of the interest in advance. You can use this formula any time you know the principal, rate, and time (which are known at the time the loan or deposit is made).

KEY FORMULA: $P = MV \div (1 + RT)$

Formula used for: Finding the present value when the maturity value, rate, and time are known.

Example:

Rawlings needs $5,250 in six months. If he deposits the money at 10 percent interest, how much must he deposit now to reach his goal? Based on the formula, $P = \$5,250 \div (1 + .10 \times \frac{1}{2}) = \$5250 \div 1.05 = \$5,000$. In other words, the present value of $5,250 at 10 percent for six months is exactly $5,000.

Remember that in this formula:

1. P = present value, which conceptually is the same thing as the principal. It is the amount of money that, if deposited today at a given interest rate and for a given period, would grow to some future value or maturity value.

2. MV = the maturity value of a given amount. This formula is useful only when the maturity value, or future value, is known.

3. It is necessary to find $1 + (R \times T)$ first, then to divide MV by the result.

4. The denominator of the fraction on the righthand side of the formula is 1 (one) + RT, not I (interest) + RT. It is not necessary to know the amount of interest to use this formula.

_____DON'T FORGET

1. R, the rate of interest, is always expressed as a decimal when you solve simple interest problems. In the presentation of the problem, though, it is likely to be expressed as a percentage. To convert a percentage to a decimal, move the decimal point two places to the left. Thus, 10% becomes .10, 5% becomes .05, and 12.5% becomes .125.

2. Time is always expressed in years or fractions of a year. When the time in months is known, use 12 (for 12 months) as the denominator. Thus, 6 months = $\frac{6}{12}$, or $\frac{1}{2}$. Three months = $\frac{3}{12}$, or $\frac{1}{4}$. And so on. When time in days is known, use 360 or 365 as the denominator,

depending on whether you are solving for ordinary or exact interest. Nearly all the problems we assign ask you to solve for ordinary interest, so assume 360 days in a year unless the problem specifies that you should do otherwise. Thus, 17 days becomes 17/360, 253 days becomes 253/360, and so on.

3. To easily recall the formulas for P, R, and T (derived from the basic I = PRT formula), always use I as the numerator and the two "leftover" elements as the denominator. For instance, when you solve for P, the correct formula becomes P = I ÷ RT.

4. Present value and principal are essentially the same thing mathematically, so even though P in the formulas sometimes represents principal and sometimes present value, it's not critical to keep them separate. Similarly, maturity value (the principal plus amount of interest) and future value are mathematically the same thing.

5. Some of the formulas in this lesson incorporate the letter *I*, which represents the amount of interest; some involve the number *1*. These look very similar. Be careful not to confuse them or you'll wind up with some very strange "solutions."

PART IV: SOLVING BUSINESS PROBLEMS

PROBLEM SETS

Work the following problems in your textbook. Your instructor will tell you which problems, if any, are to be turned in. Some of the problems have answers provided in the back of the book; refer to these answers to make sure you are working the problems correctly.

SOFTCOVER: If you are using the Miller, Salzman, and Hoelzle softcover text, *Business Mathematics*, do the following problem sets:

8.1: Problems #9, 10, 15, 16, and 43-50 on pages 281-286.

8.2: Problems #35-44 on page 296.

8.3: Problems #17-26 on page 302.

HARDCOVER: If you are using the Salzman, Miller, and Hoelzle hardcover text, *Mathematics for Business*, do the following problem sets:

11.1: Problems #14-16, 18-21, and 36-40 on pages 372-373.

11.2: Problems #6-8, 14-16, 28-30, 40-42 (all), and 44-54 (even numbers only) on pages 379-380.

11.3: Problems #39-42, 47, and 48 on pages 385-387.

11.4: Problems #31-39 (odd numbers only) on pages 392-393.

11.5: Problems #6-30 (even numbers only) on pages 398-399.

BUSINESS APPLICATIONS

Read each of the following scenarios and answer the questions about the decisions you would make in each situation. Give these questions some serious thought; they may be used as the basis for discussion or the development of a more complex essay. You should base your decisions on what you've learned from this lesson, applying both math skills and good business judgment to solve the problem at hand.

Wally and Alma Brewster would like to buy a new motor home, but they can do it only if they borrow $5,000 toward the down payment. Central Valley Bank will loan the Brewsters the money for up to three years at 15.5 percent simple annual interest. But the loan officer cautions them that this is a special adjustable rate, and it could fluctuate somewhat (up or down) every six months during the borrowing period. He also tells them that while the currently advertised fixed rate for similar loans is 14.5 percent for preferred customers, they cannot yet qualify for this lower rate because they have only had an account with the bank for a very short period and they have no history of borrowing and repaying previous loans.

SCENARIO 1

The bank rate seems a little high, but there is an alternative. The Brewsters could also borrow the money from Wally's Uncle Bill, who says yes, he'll give them the money; but he'd like to make $500 on his investment, "no matter when they repay the loan." But that's not too big a concession because Uncle Bill then tells them that he is planning a vacation in the Bahamas in about a year and wants all the money, the $5,000 in principal plus the $500 interest, paid back before he goes.

Wally and Alma are hopeful about being able to repay the money within six months, no matter where they borrow it from. Wally has been promised a bonus within three months; if he doesn't get it, repayment could be more difficult, and Alma might have to look for work herself. She is not employed currently but feels pretty confident she could get a part-time job if she needed to. After all, the economy is booming and even more economic growth is predicted for the future.

What do you think? Should the Brewsters borrow the money from the bank, or should they take Uncle Bill up on his offer? What are some of the advantages or disadvantages either way? Use the methods you've learned in this lesson to answer these questions:

☐ Should the Brewsters borrow the money from Central Valley Bank or from Uncle Bill? Why? When should they plan to repay the money? Why?

☐ Do you think the Brewsters have enough information to make a good decision? What specific mathematical calculations should they make, and what other steps should they follow to ensure that their decision is the best one possible?

☐ Suppose the Brewsters borrow from Uncle Bill, then find they can repay the loan within three months. Should they do so? What alternatives might make better financial sense? Why?

☐ What are the most important factors (mathematical or non-mathematical) for the Brewsters, or any borrower, to consider in making a decision of this type?

SCENARIO 2   Doug Kelly runs a bakery. It's a small, family-owned business and it's doing well, but it needs to expand. Kelly plans to do some remodeling of the kitchen and needs $10,000 to do it. The problem is, he doesn't have the money he needs—not all of it anyway. He has about $6,000 right now. There are a few options for coming up with the balance. For instance, he could invest the $6,000 in a money market account, which is paying 0.5 percent effective annual interest now and is expected to go higher over the next six months or so. He'd be able to add more money to the account every month, so it wouldn't be too long before he'd have the $10,000.

As an alternative, he could borrow the additional $4,000 he needs. Milltown Bank will give him a rate of 15 percent simple annual interest on a $4,000 loan for up to one full year. That would give him a little time to repay the money after the new kitchen goes in. And Kelly is sure this improvement will quickly yield higher profits for the business. The bank loan would also allow him to do the remodeling now, before inflation increases costs.

There's one other option, too. A business associate, McVee, would like to borrow Kelly's $6,000 for six months "at any simple interest rate that's reasonable." Given that the bank wants him to pay 15 percent, Kelly figures that McVee wouldn't balk at paying, say, 13 or 14 percent, more money than Kelly could get investing the money himself. This seems like an appealing option; his original $6,000 would be earning great interest and he could concentrate on saving up the remaining $4,000. But Kelly isn't sure how risky such an investment would be. What if McVee didn't repay the money? There are so many factors to consider, Kelly feels fairly confused. Meanwhile, McVee is putting on plenty of pressure. He is more than willing to draw up a written agreement, and he's not quibbling over interest rates. That certainly makes the offer more tempting.

What do you think? Should Kelly invest his money in the relatively safe money market account for 8.5 percent? Or borrow the last $4,000 he needs and remodel the kitchen now? Or should he lend McVee the money for six months and work to save the last $4,000 himself? Use the methods you've learned in this lesson to answer these questions:

☐ Which of the three options will put Kelly in the best business position? Why?

☐ Do you think Kelly has enough information right now to make a good business decision? What specific mathematical calculations should he make and what other steps should he follow to make sure his decision is the best one possible?

☐ If Kelly lends the money to McVee, how much interest should he charge? What factors should go into determining this rate? Why might it differ from the bank's rate?

☐ The interest rate on money market accounts is expected to rise, according to the scenario. What, if anything, does that indicate about the economy in general? How much attention should Kelly pay to this information (or to other economic indicators) in making his decision?

☐ According to the scenario, the interest rate for Kelly's potential money market fund is "expected to go higher over the next six months." Should Kelly count on this? Why or why not? What conditions would lead to someone's even making such a prediction?

Notes and Bank Discounts 15

Bankers Williams and Jackson were fishing in the middle of the lake when their boat hit a log and sank. Williams, a good swimmer, called to his struggling associate. "Don't try to swim," he hollered. "Just stretch out; you won't sink."

Jackson calmed down, so Williams decided he'd better swim to shore for assistance. "Jackson," he yelled. "I need to get help. Can you float alone?"

Jackson wailed back. "I'm a banker, you idiot. Of course I can float a loan. But don't you think this discussion should wait until Monday?"

Many everyday items that consumers and businesses buy—groceries, gasoline, paper clips and the like—are often paid for with cash right on the spot. Few business or individuals, however, have enough cash on hand to pay for all the things they want or need. Sometimes a consumer or business needs to borrow money, but only for a relatively short time; say, less than a year. In such cases, the bank may be willing to provide a short-term simple interest loan.

Banks recognize that the interest from short-term loans can provide a good source of income while helping borrowers buy needed goods and services. In this lesson, we'll explore two of the primary means of borrowing for the short term: simple interest notes and discount notes. We'll look at how to compute the interest and rate of interest for each and thereby make a sound comparison between the two.

PART I: INTRODUCING THE MATERIAL

LEARNING OBJECTIVES

Upon completing your study of this lesson, you should be able to:

1. Define the term *promissory note* and explain how such a document is used in business and personal borrowing.

2. Given a promissory note, be able to identify the maker (payer), the payee, the term or due date, the face value, and the interest rate.

3. Find the due date of the loan, given the date of the note and the term.

4. Find the time of a note, given the date of the note and either the due date or the term.

5. Explain how a simple discount note differs from a simple interest note and define the terms *bank discount* and *proceeds*.

6. Know the formula for bank discount and use it to calculate the discount on a discount note, given the face value, discount rate, and time.

7. Calculate the proceeds from a discount note, given the face value and the bank discount.

8. Given the proceeds desired from a discount note (along with the time and rate), calculate the necessary face value of the note.

9. Explain why the discount rate of a discount note is not the same as the interest rate and calculate the effective rate of interest for a discount note, given the discount, proceeds, and time.

10. Given the discount, term, and face value of a U.S. Treasury bill, find the purchase price and the effective rate of interest.

If you're using the hardcover textbook *Mathematics for Business*, there are some additional objectives for the lesson. Upon completing your study of the lesson, you should also be able to do the following:

11. Describe the rationale for businesses (a) accepting promissory notes for payments due and (b) discounting these notes to a bank.

12. Explain the difference between notes discounted with and without recourse and the effect this difference has on the fees charged by the bank.

13. Given the date, term, face value, and rate of a note and the discount date and rate, calculate the proceeds to the payee when a note is discounted to a bank.

14. Define rediscounting and factoring, explain how they are used in business transactions and, given the necessary information, calculate the proceeds to the original discounter.

15. Given the details of a hypothetical business purchase, calculate whether the opportunity to make a special purchase of goods warrants (a) borrowing money with a simple discount note or (b) factoring receivables.

LESSON OVERVIEW

It's a rare person indeed who hasn't at some point borrowed money for some purpose. Most people have borrowed fifty cents for a parking meter or vending machine or borrowed money for lunch or for some other modest purchase. Such borrowing is fairly routine, of course, and is not documented; people do not, as a rule, deal with paperwork for fifty-cent loans. It isn't worth the bother because the potential loss is too small. Nor do "lenders" usually charge interest for such small amounts of cash. But as soon as the amount of money involved is bigger than the lender is willing to risk losing, things change, even between friends or family members.

Two friends or relatives who want to formalize a borrowing agreement can do so with a *promissory note*. This is a written promise made by the borrower to repay a given amount of money at a stated interest rate by some agreed-upon time. Signing the note makes it official and, generally, legally binding (although this is not the place to get into the finer points of contract law).

Promissory Notes

It may occur to you to wonder whether a friend or relative shouldn't just trust the borrower to repay the money. In many cases, that's probably how it works. But the introduction of a promissory note does not necessarily imply lack of trust. It simply makes the arrangement more businesslike. Remember, the note summarizes all the basic terms of the agreement: the amount borrowed, the date on which the money is issued, the date on which the loan must be repaid, and the amount and rate of the interest. In short, the promissory note helps clarify all the details of the arrangement so that the borrower and lender will not have to depend on memory later. And if there is a disagreement, well, all the information needed to clear up the argument is right there on the note. Further, a lender, even if he or she is a relative or close friend, may well feel that the signing of a promissory note shows good faith, a real pledge to repay the loan in a timely fashion.

Banks also issue promissory notes. Their versions tend to look considerably more formal than a promissory note between two friends, which can be as simple as a handwritten statement bearing the borrower's signature. In addition to basic information concerning the amount of the loan, the period of repayment, and the interest rate, the bank's preprinted form usually contains a great deal of information describing the bank's rights in the event that the loan is not repaid on time or is never repaid. And, of course, certain factors are determined by current bank policy: interest rate, for one thing. But when Edwards borrows $500 from his Uncle Burt, the amount of interest can be anything the two can agree upon. If Edwards is Uncle Burt's cherished nephew, the interest rate might even be zero.

Collateral is anything of value that may be offered to the lender as a way of securing a loan. If the borrower cannot repay the money, the collateral becomes the property of the lender. Usually, it is then sold to help pay off the debt. Requiring collateral is common practice at banks, particularly with customers who are not well known or who do not have an established account at the bank. This is the bank's way of protecting itself, of reducing the loss if the borrower doesn't repay the loan.

Collateral and Credit Risk

Almost anything of value has potential as collateral, but banks tend to be choosy in deciding what to accept. They are primarily interested in liquid assets, those that can easily be turned into cash. An original painting, for instance, though it might have a very high assessed value, would be less appealing to the bank than a savings account of equivalent size. That's because if the borrower defaulted on the loan, the bank could get the cash from the savings account immediately. The painting would need to be sold at auction, and the bank would take a chance on finding a buyer willing to pay enough for the painting to cover the cost of the loan.

Furthermore, banks are not in business to sell merchandise. Retrieving the collateral and then selling it takes time. Someone must handle these transactions, and that someone must be paid by the bank. Further, keep in mind that by law the bank cannot make a profit on the collateral it collects and then resells. Anything over and above the amount owed on the loan and the expenses of repossessing and selling the collateral must be returned to the borrower. This means that the bank will never come out ahead when the borrower doesn't repay the loan. So, when determining what to accept as collateral, banks tend to look more favorably on such items as certificates of deposit, Treasury bills, stocks or bonds, and so forth. They will also accept property such as cars and houses, since their value is usually easily established and selling them is relatively easy. But most banks would be reluctant to accept a pet boa constrictor or a collection of baseball cards, no matter what their value in the eyes of the owner.

Of course, as we've indicated already, collateral simply provides added security. It gives the bank a fallback position, as it were. What banks try to do in the first place is to ensure that each borrower is a good risk, a person or business with a high likelihood of repaying the loan. In order to check this out, the bank will ask the applicant to provide a credit history, which usually includes current and previous salary levels, credit accounts held, current money owed (including, for individuals, credit card debt, mortgage or rent payments, car payments, and so forth), previous loans, and any other pertinent financial information. Businesses are usually required to submit financial reports: income statements and balance sheets. References are usually required, too; the bank will want to know whether the borrower made timely payments to the creditors it already has.

In addition, the bank may request a report from a *credit bureau*, a business that specializes in preparing such reports. Credit reports contain information on previous jobs held and debts paid or unpaid. They may also include information on major loans and unpaid taxes. If the applicant has ever filed for bankruptcy, it will be reflected in the report. Or, if the applicant has ever been turned down for a credit card or has had a credit card account cancelled, such information is likely to be included.

A good history with the bank lending the money is particularly helpful. Banks will often be eager to loan money to customers who previously borrowed from them and repaid the loan on time. They also like to loan money to people whose accounts in the bank are greater than the amount of the loan. A customer with a $10,000 savings account at the First Federal Bank is likely to have an easy time getting a $1,000 loan. Often, in fact, the bank will go out of its way to make sure such customers know how easy it is to qualify for short-term loans. After all, banks want to loan money when the risk of losing it is low. Loans mean profits. So they encourage borrowing, but only by customers who can demonstrate an ability to repay.

Co-Signers   Asking borrowers to put up collateral is one way banks have of protecting their interests. Another is to ask the borrower to have a *co-signer*, someone who will assume joint responsibility for repaying the loan. It is common practice for young borrowers, whose credit rating is not yet well-established, to have a parent or other adult co-sign on a loan. But in fact, any borrower whose ability to repay is in some doubt may have difficulty obtaining a loan without a co-signer.

The co-signer's position is not an enviable one. He or she gets none of the benefits (the loaned money goes to the borrower) but *all* of the liability of the loan. That is, if the borrower fails to repay the loan, for whatever reason, the obligation to pay falls to the co-signer. From the bank's perspective, the co-signer is no different from the borrower in terms of liability. In other words, the co-signer isn't just responsible for a portion of the loan or half the loan, but for all of it. Any portion that the borrower does not repay the co-signer must repay. Depending on the terms of the loan, that may mean that the bank has the right to seize the collateral put up by the co-signer, take money from the co-signer's bank account, or even take it directly out of the co-signer's wages. In summary, co-signing is not an obligation to be undertaken lightly.

Reasons for borrowing money are, of course, as varied and numerous as the businesses and individuals who borrow, and we certainly cannot explore all of them here. But let's briefly consider the wisdom of borrowing, first from the bank's point of view and then from the borrower's.

Borrowing: A Sound Idea?

First, though it comes as a surprise to many customers, banks don't usually care too much about the reasons behind a loan. They do like some general idea of how the money will be used. After all, banks do not want to become involved in loaning money for illegal purposes, such as the purchase of stolen goods. Also, with many kinds of loans (most car loans, for example) the thing the borrower is buying is the collateral for the loan, so the bank wants to know the details. And all other things being equal, banks like to see their loans going for what they term "productive" purposes. But in general, the bank is far more interested in the borrower's ability to repay than in the purpose of the loan itself.

Let's say Carlson wants to borrow $20,000. Will he be more likely to get the loan if he tells the bank he is putting new playground equipment in at the daycare center than if he says he's going to buy himself a new sports car? Not usually. His probability of getting the loan depends much more on whether the bank believes it will get its money back on time. Whether Carlson uses the money to better the community or just to put some fun into his own life is largely his business. It is important for consumers to understand this point of view because, in the event that a loan application is turned down, the reason almost certainly lies in the applicant's apparent ability to repay, *not* in the reason for the loan.

Now let's consider the issue from the borrower's perspective. Borrowing money means debt. No question of that. But, ironic as it seems, going into debt temporarily sometimes makes good financial sense. For instance, suppose Simmons, a cattle rancher, can get winter feed for his livestock at a substantial discount if he pays for it in May. The problem is, Simmons doesn't have the cash in May. But if he doesn't buy now, he'll lose out on the discount. If he borrows the money, he goes into debt for the period of the loan, but he saves a lot of money on something he's going to have to purchase eventually anyway.

Of course, it might occur to you that by the time Simmons pays interest on the loan, his savings on the feed will no longer be as great. True. The question is, will the savings be greater than the interest? That's simple enough to determine. Simmons has only to figure out what he'll repay on the loan (principal and interest), then compare that to what he'd pay for the feed at the regular price. Because trade and seasonal discounts are often substantial, borrowing often turns out to be the less expensive course of action in the long run. And don't forget that borrowing also gives Simmons the power to take action now while the price of the feed is known. By delaying a decision, the business person often loses a certain measure of control over a situation. For instance, supply and demand can influence prices dramatically any time a decision to buy is delayed for any substantial period. By next fall, the price of feed may go up far more than Simmons or anyone else could have anticipated, thereby widening the gap between what the loan would have cost and what the feed costs at the higher price.

In other words, borrowing often gives businesses more opportunities, more choices. Money that finances expansion, whether through inventory, facilities, or new personnel, often increases a business's money-making power substantially. Companies with outdated equipment and too few employees to carry the workload will usually have a tough time competing with those that are modernized and well staffed.

Of course, this isn't an argument for indiscriminate borrowing. A prudent business manager must decide when to borrow, how much, and for what purpose. Putting new carpeting in the reception area might reap benefits if it gives the business a more successful and professional image and therefore attracts customers. But if nobody notices, or worse, if clients think the company is charging them too much so it can afford fancy carpet, then the company would have been better off not to have borrowed in the first place.

Simple Interest Notes versus Discount Notes

Whether or not to borrow in the first place is the first big decision a business or individual consumer faces. The next question is *how* to borrow. With short-term loans there are two main options: simple interest notes and discount notes. Both are based on simple interest, but they work a little differently.

With a *simple interest note*, the borrower receives the face value of the note and pays interest over and above that face value by the end of the borrowing period. For instance, say Sam's Auto Repair Shop borrows $2,000 to put in a new engine analyzer. If Samantha pays simple interest at 10 percent and keeps the money for one year, she'll have to repay $2,200: the principal of $2,000 plus $200 in simple interest. The full sum, $2,200, is repayable at the end of the borrowing period.

But let's say that the only sort of short-term simple interest loan this particular bank offers is a *discount note*. A $2,000 discount note will not give Sam $2,000 to spend. The discount will be subtracted from this amount beforehand. Let's say, for purposes of comparison, that the annual discount rate is also 10 percent. The discount is figured on the face value of the note, which is $2,000, so the amount of the discount, based on a one-year borrowing period, is $200. This means that the bank actually gives Sam's Auto Repair $1,800 ($2,000 − $200) to spend on its engine analyzer. That's fine, provided the $1,800 is enough to cover the cost of the system. But it might not be. What if Sam really needs $2,000? In that case, she'll need a discount note of about $2,200 in order to have roughly $2,000 to take home from the bank.

What about the interest rate? We know the amount of the interest. That's $200, the amount of the discount. The discount *is* the interest on a discount note. At the end of the borrowing period, Sam must pay the bank $2,000: the $1,800 plus the discount fee of $200. But notice that Sam isn't paying interest on $2,000; she didn't receive that much. She's paying $200 in interest on only $1,800. To determine the rate of interest, divide the amount of interest ($200) by the amount of the principal ($1,800), and the result is just over 11 percent. This is higher than the 10 percent charged on the simple interest note, even though Sam would pay $200 in interest either way. Or, to look at it another way, a 10 percent *discount rate* on a loan doesn't mean that the interest rate is 10 percent; it's not.

By the way, discount notes are sometimes called *interest-in-advance notes* because the amount of interest is discounted right up front, at the time of borrowing. The term interest-in-advance is a little misleading, though. The borrower does not really pay the interest in advance; the amount of interest is subtracted from the face value of the note before the borrower ever gets the loan money. The borrower repays the principal (the amount of the loan after discount) *plus* the interest at the end of the borrowing period. Take Sam in the preceding example. She goes home with $1,800 but must repay the full $2,000 at the end of the borrowing period; that's when the interest is actually paid.

You may be wondering whether a borrower is generally better off with a simple interest note or a discount note. There is no ready answer to this question. The bottom line, as you might expect, is the rate of interest. Because the discount is subtracted from the face value of the note, the consumer who needs $2,000 in cash will have to borrow more with a discount note than with a simple interest note in order to have a comparable amount of money to spend. As you might guess, it can get a little complicated trying to figure out just what interest rate and how much interest is being charged. Fortunately, the federal Truth in Lending Act requires that banks tell consumers precisely what the *effective rate of interest* will be on any type of loan, including discount notes, and how much interest will be charged.

Discounting Notes and Factoring

A business can look financially sound on paper yet be very low on cash reserves. This is because one of the primary assets of many businesses is the money that is owed by others, money that the business will presumably have sometime in the future but cannot get its hands on right now. But what if it could? There is a way.

In fact, banks (and some businesses, too) buy notes or accounts receivable held by other businesses. The process of receiving cash for a note is known as *discounting a note* (not to be confused with a discount note, which is not the same thing at all). The process of receiving cash for accounts receivable is known as *factoring*, and the businesses that buy the accounts are *factors*.

Of course, banks and businesses do not buy notes or accounts at face value. That would make little sense because then, when they collected on the notes or accounts, they would only be recovering what they had already spent and not making a cent for their trouble. But, in fact, these businesses charge a substantial fee, enough to make it worthwhile for them to provide this service.

Perhaps it seems odd that a business would sell its accounts receivable at a discount when it could just wait and collect the money itself and not have to give up a portion of its profits. But keep in mind that sometimes businesses with poor cash flow need immediate funds, either for expansion or to cover ongoing expenses they're unable to meet. Imagine, for instance, a business with $50,000 owed to it by customers. A tidy sum, but not of much value to the business if it can't collect the money until some time in the future. Perhaps some of the accounts are slow to repay. Perhaps others are not due for 30 or 60 days. Meanwhile, the business is becoming desperate for cash, perhaps to cover quarterly taxes or meet other bills of its own. If the bank will give this business $45,000 for the accounts now, it loses a little money, yes, but the cash problem is solved for the time being. And that transaction may help keep the company going.

The bank, of course, must have some assurance that it will be able to collect. So, most probably, it will buy notes or accounts receivable only with *recourse*. That means that if the bank cannot collect from those who owe the money, it has recourse; it can go back to the business and demand that the business itself repay the debt. Remember those slow-to-pay accounts we just mentioned? Well, suppose some of those accounts belong to companies that are having financial difficulties of their own. A bank that buys the notes or accounts with recourse knows that if the business owing the money goes bankrupt, the business from which the bank took over the account must come up with the money.

SOME WORDS OF ADVICE

Whether borrowing money makes good financial sense is a decision only the individual consumer or business person can make. After all, a sensible decision can only be made in light of current needs and a thorough comparison of the potential advantages and disadvantages that will result from borrowing. If a business stands to lose its competitive edge by not expanding or by not taking advantage of economical buying opportunities, then not borrowing money could be the wrong decision. On the other hand, going into debt is costly. Using someone else's money is clearly more expensive than using your own, so it is a bad idea to borrow money without a good reason.

If you are in the position of lending money to a relative or friend, think about the advantages of having the terms of the loan in writing in the form of a promissory note. In the event that the borrower does not repay, a written note provides some evidence regarding the terms of the agreement and increases the likelihood that you would have some success in a legal action to collect the money.

As a borrower, you are also well advised to have the terms of the agreement in writing, even if you're just borrowing from a friend or relative. A written agreement minimizes the chances of disagreement later about how much was borrowed and how much interest is owed. If you're borrowing from a bank or other lending institution, the terms of the agreement will certainly be in writing, in the form of a note. But there are other important factors to think about.

A bank is likely to require collateral to secure the loan. Keep in mind that banks will not accept just anything as collateral, so your choices may be limited. But it's wise to give serious thought to this decision. Whatever you pledge as collateral will belong to the bank in the event that you are unable to repay the loan. Of course, you probably have every intention of repaying at the time of borrowing. But good intentions are not always enough. Borrowers sometimes have bad sales periods or lose their jobs, or incur new, unforeseen debts (medical expenses or equipment repairs, for instance) that make repayment difficult. These aren't the sorts of circumstances under which a borrower can afford to also lose office equipment or a house that has been pledged as collateral.

If someone asks you to be a co-signer on a loan, you should take the request with the same seriousness you'd take a request to loan the money to him or her personally. This means that you'll want some assurance that the person for whom you are co-signing can repay the loan. In the eyes of the bank, borrower and co-signer are equal partners. Thus, if the borrower cannot pay, the debt (all of it, not just half) will fall on the co-signer. Remember that the act of co-signing says that you are responsible fully and completely for any portion of the loan that goes unpaid. As a co-signer, you may also be asked to put up collateral of your own.

The federal Truth in Lending Act requires that banks and other lending institutions disclose the true or effective rate of interest charged on a loan. Nevertheless, laws cannot guarantee that loan officers will be clear and concise in their presentation of information about interest rates. You, as a responsible consumer or business borrower, must protect your own rights by asking enough questions to ensure that you understand how much interest you owe and what the rate of interest on your loan will be before you sign the paperwork. Borrowing money, whether for a business or a personal need, is a serious matter. Answer those questions to your own satisfaction before you place yourself in the role of debtor.

KEY TERMS

Before you read through the text assignment and watch the video program, take a minute to look at the key terms associated with this lesson. When you encounter them in the text and video program, pay careful attention to their meaning.

Collateral: Goods pledged as security for a loan. In the event a loan is not paid, the collateral can be seized by the lender and sold to pay the debt.

Discount or bank discount: The amount of interest charged on a note.

Discount note: See *simple discount note*.

Discount period: The borrowing period on a discount note.

Discount rate: The percentage by which the face value of a discount note is reduced before the proceeds are given to the borrower.

Discounting a note: The process by which the holder of a note sells the note to a bank before its maturity date, thereby obtaining cash earlier than would otherwise be possible.

Effective rate of interest: The true rate of interest on a discount note, which is different from the discount rate.

Face value: The amount printed on the face of a note.

Factor: A person who buys the accounts receivable of a business (that is, the money owed to the firm).

Interest-in-advance note: Another term for a discount note. The term comes from the fact that the discount, or interest, is deducted from the face value of the note at the time of borrowing.

Maker: The person borrowing the money on a note. The term comes from the fact that the person borrowing "makes" the bargain and signs the note agreeing to repay the money with interest.

Maturity value: The amount that must be repaid by the maker of the note when the note is due. For a simple interest note, the maturity value equals face value plus interest.

Payee: The person who loans money and to whom a loan will be repaid.

Payer: Another term for the maker, the person who pays back a loan.

Proceeds: The amount of money a borrower receives after subtracting the discount from the face value of a note.

Promissory note: A document in which one person agrees to pay money to another person at a certain time in the future and at a certain rate of interest.

Recourse: The right of a business that purchases a note from another to collect from the seller of the note if the maker of the note does not pay.

Rediscounting: The process in which one financial institution discounts a note at a second institution.

Simple discount note: A note whose interest is deducted or discounted in advance, with only the balance, or proceeds, going to the borrower.

Simple interest note: A short-term (less than a year) note, in which interest is figured only on the principal, not on any unpaid interest.

Term of the note: The period of time until a note is due. A six-month note has a term of six months.

Truth in Lending Act: An act passed by the U.S. Congress in 1969 that requires all interest rates to be given as comparable percentages so U.S. consumers have a better chance of understanding exactly how much interest they will owe on a given loan.

Treasury bills: Also known as T-bills. A form of simple discount note in which the maker, or borrower, is the government and the payee is the consumer.

PART II: WATCHING THE VIDEO PROGRAM

VIDEO VIEWING GUIDE

Before watching the video program, review the following questions. As you watch, be sure to collect the information necessary to answer them:

1. What are the major differences between simple interest and discount notes? Under what circumstances might each be preferable?

2. In deciding whether to borrow money, what are some factors for a business to consider?

3. When is borrowing likely to be a wise business decision?

4. In many ways, our economy is based on a system of borrowing. What are some of the economic advantages and disadvantages to such a situation?

5. If you borrow money from the bank, it will calculate the interest and send you a statement showing the amount owed. Knowing this, how important do you think it is for an individual to be able to calculate for him- or herself interest on money borrowed?

6. If you were in the position of a banker or loan officer, what sorts of things do you think you would accept as collateral on a loan? Why? Are there things you definitely would not accept?

VIDEO PROGRAM

This lesson's video program is Program 15—Notes and Bank Discounts. Remember, if you are watching this program on videotape, take time to replay sections of the tape any time you need to review a concept.

VIDEO VIEWING QUESTIONS

Immediately after viewing the video program for Lesson 15, take time to respond to the following questions. Give your answers some careful thought; they may provide the basis for additional discussion or a longer written response.

1. Name any three factors that distinguish a simple interest note from a discount note:

   a. _____

   b. _____

   c. _____

2. Which of the following factors, according to the video, affects the total *amount* of interest paid on a short-term note? (Check as many as apply.)

   _____ The term of the note

   _____ The annual rate of interest

   _____ The face value of the note

   _____ The value of the collateral, if any

   _____ Whether it's a simple interest or a discount note

   _____ The purpose of the loan

   _____ The length of time it takes the borrower to repay the loan

3. A bank would be likely to issue a promissory note for which of the following types of loans? (Check as many as apply.)

_____ A 6-month loan to finance a European vacation

_____ A 1-year loan to build an addition on a home

_____ A 30-year home mortgage

_____ A 5-year loan on an automobile

_____ A 9-month loan to repay a college tuition debt

4. Imagine that you are a banker trying to decide whether to grant a loan to an applicant. Based on the information presented in the video, on a scale of 1 to 10, how important would you consider the loan applicant's *credit rating* in making this decision?

Not   **Extremely**
Important   **Important**

1- - - - -2- - - - -3- - - - -4- - - - -5- - - - -6- - - - -7- - - - -8- - - - -9- - - - -10

On a scale of 1 to 10, how important would the purpose of the loan be to you, as a banker, in making this decision?

Not   **Extremely**
Important   **Important**

1- - - - -2- - - - -3- - - - -4- - - - -5- - - - -6- - - - -7- - - - -8- - - - -9- - - - -10

5. Suppose that banks made a decision to stop granting short-term loans for any purpose. Based on information presented in the video, which of the following results do you think would be most likely? (Check as many as apply.)

_____ The economy would begin to grow much more rapidly.

_____ Businesses would begin offering a wider selection of merchandise.

_____ The kinds of services and products offered by businesses would be limited.

_____ Fewer businesses would extend credit to consumers.

_____ More businesses would demand cash for their merchandise or services.

_____ Business persons would be tempted to take more risks in expanding.

_____ Banks would grow richer.

_____ A lot more people would start their own businesses.

PART III: FOCUSING ON THE MATHEMATICS

READING ASSIGNMENT

After watching the video program, you should read one of the following Text Assignments, depending on the textbook you're using:

SOFTCOVER: Pages 297-324 from Chapter 8 of the Miller, Salzman, and Hoelzle softcover text, *Business Mathematics*.

HARDCOVER: Chapter 12 of the Salzman, Miller, and Hoelzle hardcover text, *Mathematics for Business*, pages 409-435.

As you read through the text, pay careful attention to the examples the book gives of the mathematics associated with the concepts you're learning about.

Then, after you've completed the text assignment, read through the Key Formulas here. This section provides a handy review of what you've learned. By the time you get to this point in the lesson, all of the formulas and calculations should be familiar to you. If they're not, go back and read the appropriate parts of the text and the Overview section of this lesson. You won't have much success completing the rest of your assignments if you are still confused about the information in the Key Formulas section.

KEY FORMULAS

The following key formulas are important to your understanding of this lesson. Be sure that you know each one and how to use it in solving problems related to simple interest notes and discount notes.

KEY FORMULA: $I = PRT$

Formula used for: Figuring out the amount of simple interest paid when a certain amount of money (the principal) is borrowed for a certain length of time at a certain interest rate.

Alternate forms: $P = I \div RT$ or $R = I \div PT$ or $T = I \div PR$

Example:

Omnitech Systems borrows $10,000 at 12 percent annual interest for one year. It will pay $10,000 $\times$ 12% per year $\times$ 1 year, which is $10,000 $\times$ .12 $\times$ 1, or $1,200.

Remember that in this formula:

1. I = simple interest, P = principal (the amount borrowed), R = rate (the rate of interest, that is), and T = time, or the period for which the money is borrowed.

2. T, or time, is expressed as a fraction of a year, assuming that the interest rate is given in percent per year, as it almost always is. For instance, if the borrowing period is three months, then time would be expressed as the fraction $3/12$ (three months over twelve months), which is equal to $1/4$. If the borrowing period is 60 days, then the time would be expressed as the fraction $60/360$, which is equal to $1/6$. (Note that for purposes of solving simple interest problems, a year is considered to have 360 days; this figure simplifies the math calculations.)

3. R, or the rate of interest, is put into the formula as a decimal. Interest rates are given in percentages, but we need to put the rate in the formula as a decimal. This means that an interest rate of 10 percent would be expressed as a decimal figure of .10. Notice that the decimal point is moved two places to the left. An interest rate of 20 percent would be expressed as .20, a rate of 15.5 percent as .155, and so forth.

KEY FORMULA:	Maturity value = Face value + Interest
Formula used for:	Calculating how much money (principal and interest) will have been paid when the loan is completely paid off.
Alternate forms:	Face value = Maturity value − Interest or Interest = Maturity value − Face value

Example:

A local restaurant obtains a simple interest note for $10,000; the note is payable in one year. The lender charges 14 percent interest for the loan. Using the I = PRT formula, we learn that the bank will receive $1,400 in interest. This makes the maturity value for the note $11,400, or the face value of $10,000 plus the interest of $1,400.

Remember that in this formula:

1. The face value on a simple interest note is simply the amount borrowed. This amount is written right on the front of the note; that is why it is referred to as face value. The face value on a discount note is not the amount given to the borrower. It's the amount repaid at the end of the borrowing period. This amount is also written on the front of the note.

2. The maturity value on a simple interest note is equal to the face value (what was borrowed) plus any interest that the borrower must pay. This is another way of saying that the maturity value is the amount that must be repaid to the lender by the end of the borrowing period.

KEY FORMULA:	B = MDT
Formula used for:	Calculating the amount that the lender subtracts from the amount of a loan for interest on a discount note. (This formula doesn't apply to simple interest notes.)
Alternate forms:	M = DT + B or D = MT + B or T = MD + B

Example:

Nelson's Book Store arranges for a discount note of $10,000. The discount rate is 10 percent and the note matures in one year. When the note is signed, $1,000 (the face value times the 10 percent per year discount rate times one year, or $10,000 × .10 × 1) is withheld by the lender.

Remember that in this formula:

1. B = the bank discount, the amount the bank (or other lending institution) subtracts from the principal at the time of borrowing. This bank discount is equal to the interest that the borrower pays on the loan, but it may also be thought of as a fee charged by the lender.

2. M = the face value or maturity value of the loan. Keep in mind that with a discount note, the face value and maturity value are the same. In other words, the amount written on the front of the note is the amount that the borrower must repay at the end of the borrowing period. If the face value of a discount note is $5,000, that is what the borrower repays. That does not mean the borrower goes home with $5,000, however; the bank will subtract its discount from that amount, sending the borrower out the door with perhaps $4,500, depending on the amount of the discount. Notice that with a discount note, the face value is not equal to the amount that the borrower actually receives. It is, however, equal to the amount that must be repaid.

3. D = the discount rate, which is changed from a percentage to a decimal when used in this formula. For instance, if the discount rate on a $1,000 note is 10 percent per year, that is .10 per year. In other words, the amount of the discount for the full year would be 1,000 × .10, which is $100. Of course, not all borrowers take exactly a year to repay a loan, which brings us to the final part of the formula.

4. T = time, which (as with simple interest notes) is expressed as a fraction of a year. Six months, for instance, is half a year, and would be expressed as 6/12 or ½. Five months would be expressed as 5/12, one month as 1/12, and so forth. Thus, if the discount rate on a $1,000 note is 10 percent per year, and the borrower repays the money after six months, the amount of the bank discount = $1,000 × .10 × ½, which is $50. In other words, as we might expect, a borrower who uses money for six months pays only half the discount of a borrower who uses the same amount at the same rate for a full year.

KEY FORMULA:	Proceeds = Face value − Bank discount
Formula used for:	Determining the amount that the borrower actually gets from a discount note after the bank discount is taken out. (This formula doesn't apply to simple interest notes.)
Alternate forms:	Face value = Proceeds + Bank discount or Bank discount = Face value − Proceeds

Example:

In the previous example, we determined that the bank discount on Nelson's $10,000 note was $1,000. Subtracting this $1,000 from the face value of $10,000, we find that the proceeds from this note are $9,000.

Remember that in this formula:

1. The *proceeds* are the amount that goes out the door with the borrower. As we mentioned above, if a borrower takes out a six-month discount note for $1,000 at an annual discount rate of 10 percent, the discount equals $1,000 × .10 × ½, or $50. Then the proceeds equal the face value of the note minus the amount of the discount, or $1,000 − $50, or $950. In other words, the borrower goes home with $950. Remember, though, the borrower must repay the full $1,000 at the end of the six-month borrowing period.

2. The face value is equal to the maturity value, what must be repaid. On a discount note, the face value is *not* the same as the principal. This is one way in which simple interest notes and discount notes differ. The principal on a discount note is equal to the amount that the borrower actually receives. In the preceding example, for instance, the principal is $950 (not $1,000, as it would be if this were a simple interest note).

KEY FORMULA: $M = P \div 1 - DT$

Formula used for: Determining the maturity value of a discount note, given the proceeds. This is the total amount of money that the borrower repays to the lender when the note is due.

Example:

Reynolds's lender offers her a one-year discount note at 10 percent per year. If Reynolds needs to receive $5,000 as the proceeds from a discount note, how large a note will she need? According to the formula, M = $5,000 ÷ 1 − (.10 × 1), which is $5,000 ÷ .90, or about $5,556. In other words, the amount of the discount note must be about $5,556 if Reynolds is to have the full $5,000 to spend. At the end of the borrowing period, Reynolds will repay $5,556.

Remember that in this formula:

1. M = the maturity value or face value of the discount note. (The two are the same.)

2. P = the proceeds, *not* the principal as in some other formulas. Remember that the proceeds equal the amount the borrower actually receives. You can also think of P as the amount that the borrower needs, since you will use this formula to determine how large a discount note a borrower must request in order to go home with a given amount.

3. D = the discount rate.

4. T = the time, or period of borrowing.

DON'T FORGET

1. T, or time, is always expressed as a fraction of a year when the interest rate is given as an annual rate. The denominator of the fraction is either 12 (for 12 months) or 360 (for 360 days per year).

2. With a discount note, the *amount* of the discount and the *amount* of interest are the same, but the rates are different and the interest rate is always higher. The interest rate is based on the principal, or what goes home with the borrower; the discount rate is based on the face value of the note, or what is repaid at the end of the borrowing period.

3. The interest rate quoted by a bank or other lender is usually expressed as an annual rate. Thus, 8 percent interest means 8 percent *annual* interest. In simple interest terms, this means that a borrower who needs a loan for only six months pays 4 percent interest (half of 8) and a borrower who needs the money for only three months pays 2 percent (one-fourth of 8).

4. With a discount note, the face value and maturity value are equal. With a simple interest note, the maturity value is always higher because interest is added to the principal at the end of the borrowing period.

PART IV: SOLVING BUSINESS PROBLEMS

PROBLEM SETS

Work the following problems in your textbook. Your instructor will tell you which problems, if any, are to be turned in. Some of the problems have answers provided in the back of the book; refer to these answers to make sure you are working the problems correctly.

SOFTCOVER: If you are using the Miller, Salzman, and Hoelzle softcover text, *Business Mathematics*, do the following problem sets:

8.3: Problems #1-8 on page 301.

8.4: Problems #6-26 (even numbers only) on pages 309-312.

8.5: Problems #29-32 on pages 319-320.

Supplementary Exercises: Problems #2-16 (even numbers only) on pages 321-324.

HARDCOVER: If you are using the Salzman, Miller, and Hoelzle hardcover text, *Mathematics for Business*, do the following problem sets:

12.1: Problems #1-8 and 35-39 on pages 415-417.

12.2: Problems #6-38 (even numbers only) on pages 423-425.

12.3: Problems #6-36 (even numbers only) on pages 430-432.

12.4: Problems #2-20 (even numbers only) on page 435.

BUSINESS APPLICATIONS

Read each of the following scenarios and answer the questions about the decisions you would make in each situation. Give these questions some serious thought; they may be used as the basis for discussion or the development of a more complex essay. You should base your decisions on what you've learned from this lesson, applying both math skills and good business judgment to solve the problem at hand.

SCENARIO 1

Business Is Blooming Flowers, a good-sized shop in a large shopping complex, has an opportunity to purchase a large volume of merchandise just before the winter holidays. A trade discount allows Blooming 25 percent off all potted plants and trees purchased by the last day of November. But in order to take advantage of the discount, Blooming must pay cash. The minimum order is $3,000 worth of plants, after discount.

Unfortunately, the business has little cash on hand and cannot afford to spend more than a few hundred dollars on new inventory. However, the accounts receivable show $5,000 owed to the business by reputable vendors. Blooming could raise the money by selling all or a portion of these accounts receivable to the bank at a 15 percent discount rate.

Business has been only moderate lately. There is one other flower shop nearby and it is advertising "great prices on holiday flowers and plants." If Blooming doesn't do the same, it may lose customers. On the other hand, the manager, Fred Bloom, is concerned about stripping the business of its resources. If the accounts receivable are sold for immediate cash, where will the business get its routine income over the next few months? Bloom wants to hire an assistant in order to extend the store's hours into the evening and take advantage of the 6:00 to 9:00 p.m. business, a period during which the other florist's shop is closed. If he sells his accounts receivable, his planned-for 30 percent profit will be only half what it would be if he collected the money himself. Then how can he afford to hire new staff?

What do you think? Is selling the accounts a good idea? What are some potential advantages to the business? What are the relative risks? Are there factors Bloom is overlooking?

- ☐ Should Bloom sell the accounts receivable to the bank? Why or why not?

- ☐ Are there calculations that Bloom needs to perform before he can determine whether to sell his receivables? If so, what are they?

- ☐ What are the most important factors (mathematical or non-mathematical) for Bloom to consider in making this decision?

- ☐ Bloom could, of course, sell the receivables but keep the money in reserve rather than using it for the special purchase of new stock. Is there any merit in this approach? Why or why not?

Joe's Juicy Burgers is a very small restaurant that specializes in orders to go. It has no seating area at all, much to the dismay of customers, who now stand in long lines to buy what they consider "the best burgers in town." There is no shortage of business; in fact, more than once Joe's has run out of food before closing time.

For $30,000, Joe's could put an extra grill in the kitchen and build a small eating area that would seat 18 to 20 patrons. The addition would also expand the waiting and serving area so that more customers could come inside to wait for their orders. The counter would be bigger and more attractive.

It all sounds very appealing, except for one thing: Owners Flora and Joe Grimsky have nothing to put up for collateral except the business itself. That seems a little risky to Joe, but Flora is all for the expansion. "We can't go on like this," she tells Joe. "Customers can't get in the door. They're standing in the rain. We can't expect them to stay loyal forever if we don't do something about this situation. Some of them will settle for a not-so-great lunch, even at a higher price, if they can go inside somewhere and sit down to eat it. We'll wind up losing business."

Joe agrees but points out some things Flora hasn't considered. "If we put in tables and add more equipment to the kitchen," he tells her, "we're going to have to add more staff. I'm serving people as fast as possible now. New tables are great, but they don't solve the problem completely. The only way to make the line move faster is to hire help. And suppose business drops off and we can't cover the loan. We'll lose our restaurant."

Joe and Flora decide to go so far as to explore the options for borrowing. Two banks in town are more than willing to grant the $30,000 loan with the restaurant as collateral. One bank offers a one-year simple interest note with an annual rate of 12 percent. A second bank offers a one-year discount note with a discount rate of 10 percent. Joe and Flora think the second offer sounds like the better deal, but they aren't sure. They're a little confused about what "discount rate" really means. Besides, the first decision is whether to borrow at all.

What do you think? Should the Grimskys expand? Or should they try to get by the way things are for now? If they do borrow the money, which bank's offer should they consider? Why?

□ Should Joe and Flora take out the $30,000 loan?

□ If they do decide to borrow the money, which bank should they do business with? Why?

□ What specific mathematical calculations should Joe and Flora perform to determine which of the two loans offered gives them a better deal financially?

□ What are the most important factors (both mathematical and nonmathematical) Joe and Flora should consider in deciding whether to borrow money in the first place?

□ What general advice would you offer businesses in making borrowing decisions like those Joe and Flora face?

Compound Interest 16

Several prominent historians were invited to a special meeting to determine the greatest inventor of all time. The discussions were heated — one historian proposed Edison, another supported Henry Ford, a third claimed that Orville Wright deserved the honor.

Everyone argued long and hard for their choice, except one quiet little man who had been sitting in the corner listening but saying nothing. Finally, close to exasperation, one of the panelists turned to him and said, "See here, Collins, let's have your opinion on this matter."

"Well," came the quiet reply, "you've got to admit that the person who decided to charge compound interest was certainly nobody's fool."

American statesman, philosopher, and inventor Benjamin Franklin reportedly said, "Money makes money, and the money that money makes makes more money."

Franklin certainly knew what he was talking about. In his lifetime he made enough money to retire at 42 and devote himself to public life. When he died in 1790, at age 84, he left $5,000 to the residents of Boston with but one stipulation: that the money be left alone to earn interest for 100 years. By 1891, the original sum had grown to the tidy sum of $322,000, enough to finance a school and have $92,000 left over to set aside for a second hundred years. In 1960, almost 70 years later, the second investment reached nearly $1.5 million. It is still growing, thanks to compound interest.

Today, the vast majority of investments pay compound interest: interest paid not just on the principal, but also on the accumulated interest. That's good news for investors, since as we shall see in this lesson, the difference in real dollars between compound interest and simple interest (which is paid on principal alone) is potentially enormous. For example, had Franklin's $5,000 investment paid only simple interest, his money would have grown to about $50,000 rather than the nearly $2 million it provided with interest compounding.

But fortunately for Bostonians, Franklin was determined to prove his belief that "money makes money" by testing his theory out for a century after his death. Of course, one need not wait a century to see an investment grow significantly; many current investments can, thanks to interest compounding, double in as little as seven or eight years. In this lesson, we'll explore how compound interest works and examine some of the everyday applications of compound interest, chief among them the use of compounding in passbook savings accounts.

PART I: INTRODUCING THE MATERIAL

LEARNING OBJECTIVES

Upon completing your study of this lesson, you should be able to:

1. Calculate compound interest by summing the interest earned for each period of the investment or loan.

2. Explain the effect that shorter compounding periods have on total interest and calculate the difference in interest, given an identical principal, rate, and term but different compounding periods.

3. Using a compound interest table, calculate the interest on a loan or investment, given the principal, rate, compounding period, and term.

4. From a business perspective, contrast the advantages and disadvantages of passbook accounts and time deposits for company funds.

5. Using appropriate interest tables, determine the interest earned on passbook and time deposit accounts having a specified principal, rate, and term.

6. Using a table giving the present value of a dollar, calculate the present value of any future value, given the principal, rate, and term.

If you're using the hardcover textbook, *Mathematics for Business*, there are some additional objectives for the lesson. Upon completing your study of the lesson, you should also be able to:

7. Using the compound interest formula, directly calculate the interest on a loan or investment having up to four compounding periods, given the principal, rate, compounding period, and term.

8. Distinguish between the effective rate and the nominal, or stated, rate and calculate the effective rate for any nominal rate by using a compound interest table.

9. Given the principal, rate, and penalties for early withdrawal of a time deposit, calculate the amount received if the deposit were withdrawn at a specified point prior to maturity.

10. Describe the effect that changes in interest rates or compounding periods have on the interest on an investment or loan and evaluate the

merit of investments offering different earnings with different liquidities for a given business situation.

11. Use the compound interest formula in conjunction with a compound interest table to approximate the time required for an investment to grow to a specified compound amount at a specified rate.

12. Use the compound interest formula in conjunction with a compound interest table to approximate the rate at which an investment will grow to a specified compound amount over a specified term.

13. Know the present value formula and use it in conjunction with a compound interest table to determine the amount that must be deposited at a given rate for a given period to produce a specified future value.

LESSON OVERVIEW

Principal is the basis for all interest charges. Simple interest is, well, simple; it's calculated on the principal only. For instance, if Meyer borrows $1,000 from Lynch for one year at a simple interest rate of 10 percent per year, Meyer must repay $1,100 ($1,000 × 1.10): the $1,000 principal plus $100 in interest.

Compound interest, on the other hand, is calculated on principal *plus* interest. By and large, this is a world of compound interest, and some common sense suggests why. Take our example with Meyer and Lynch.

Since Meyer is repaying the loan within a year, Lynch may be happy to make just $100 on the deal. But suppose Meyer wanted the money for *10* years. During those years, inflation will have substantially reduced the buying power of the $1,000 in principal and the $100 in yearly interest. In addition, had Lynch not loaned the money to Meyer, he might have invested it in some money-making proposition that would be earning him an ongoing profit. All in all, Lynch may feel he's entitled to quite a bit more consideration for giving Meyer the extended use of his money. He might like the option of having new interest accumulate on a regular basis so that the total interest he receives actually represents a good return on his money.

If Meyer wants to pay off the loan sooner, that's fine, and he may be charged only for the interest accumulated to date. In fact, the chance to avoid interest charges is likely to give Meyer some incentive for paying off the loan a little faster. But the major reason for compounding the interest is to ensure Lynch an appropriate profit for lending his money. After all, if all transactions were simple interest, the value of the money lenders got back from borrowers would often be *less* than when they loaned the money. Obviously, under such circumstances, no one would be foolish enough to loan anyone any money; that, in turn, would have a disastrous effect on businesses, consumers, and the economy in general.

Now let's look at things from the perspective of a bank depositor opening a passbook savings account. Suppose your local bank offered *simple* interest of 8 percent on passbook savings. The rate sounds incredibly good, perhaps, in comparison to what other banks are offering. But remember, interest is earned only on your initial investment, the principal. A deposit of, say, $500, would entitle you to $40 in interest at a simple interest rate

Compound Interest for Passbook Accounts

of 8 percent. Every year, you'd get $40 more. After 10 years, you would have earned $400 in interest, so the account would now have $900 in it. But in the eleventh year, you'd still earn only the same $40 calculated from the $500 original principal. If you wanted to earn more than $40 interest per year, you would have to deposit more money.

On the other hand, the bank that offered compound interest would pay interest not only on the $500 deposit, but also on any future interest that money earned, so long as the money was left on deposit. If previous interest payments meant there was, say, $700 in the account, the year's interest would be earned on $700, not the original $500. In fact, in our example, before 10 years were up, the compound interest account would be earning twice as much interest per year as the simple interest account. And were the money to stay in the account for, say, 50 years, the compound interest account would be paying over *10 times* the yearly interest. It isn't difficult to see which bank would be more likely to get the deposits of smart investors.

These days, while many personal business transactions are based on simple interest, most commercial business dealings are based on compound interest. It's commercially more lucrative for banks and other businesses. But in addition, it's more realistic. When people or businesses borrow large sums of money, they generally need an extended period of time in which to repay that money. Compound interest, unlike simple interest, gives the lender ongoing reimbursement for making that money available to the borrower. Long-term loans, mortgage payments, other types of credit payments, and most short- and long-term investments are all based on some system of compound interest.

How Fast Will the Money Grow?

Several factors affect the rate at which money accumulates with compounded interest. These include the rate of interest, the time involved, and the period of compounding.

Obviously, an 8 percent interest rate will build an investment faster than a 5 percent interest rate. But in the real world, the interest rates offered by various banks rarely differ by such large amounts. Perhaps one bank will offer 5.25 percent interest on passbook savings, while another will offer 5.5 percent. The second would still seem to be the more desirable rate, and all things being equal, it would be. In the world of banking, though, things are often not equal. Before choosing a bank, it's wise to find out, for instance, if there are any penalties or service charges that could effectively reduce the yield. Some banks impose a service charge for an account that falls below a certain minimum balance, for instance; others impose a penalty for frequent withdrawals. Some charge a fee for accounts that are closed within the first year, so that the depositor may wind up paying all the interest, and then some, in a service fee.

In addition, some banks pay interest only on the lowest balance maintained in the account during a given period. For instance, suppose Holt has $5,000 in an account at Great State Bank, an institution that has a low balance rule. And let's say that Holt withdraws $4,000 to pay a debt. Even if she quickly replaces the $4,000 by selling her car, her interest for the period will be based on a deposit of $1,000, not the $5,000 she started with.

But that's not always as serious a shortcoming as it first sounds. Many banks, but not all, pay interest *from the day of deposit to the day of withdrawal*. Under such an approach, interest is calculated daily and is based on the exact amount in the account each day, without consideration of when money is deposited or withdrawn. With such an approach, Holt, in our preceding example, would have lost interest on the $4,000 only during those days she had it out of the account. That $4,000 would have started earning interest again on the very day she redeposited the amount.

At first it might seem that a given rate of interest would produce about the same amount of interest whether it was compounded annually, quarterly, weekly, or daily. In fact, however, the *period of compounding* makes a substantial difference over time. To illustrate, imagine an investment of just $1 per week over a year's time at 10 percent compound interest. At the end of the first year, that $52 would grow to $54.65 if the interest were compounded annually. The same investment would produce $54.78 if interest were compounded daily. Well, you might think to yourself, that's not much of a difference: $0.13. Big deal.

But remember, we're talking about a very small investment. Had the investment been $100 per week, the difference during the first year would be $13. Still not impressed? Then consider this: the difference in interest on that same $100 per week investment would be more than $3,000 after 10 years and more than $124,000 at the end of 30 years. In short, the period of compounding does affect the rate of growth, even when the base interest rate remains constant. It just takes a little time to see the effect.

There's a limit to the effective rate at which growth can accelerate, however, even when the compounding period is shortened. As we've just seen, it makes a big difference, over time, whether interest is compounded annually or daily. But that's a big jump. It makes much less difference whether interest is compounded monthly versus weekly. And the difference between daily compounding and *continuous compounding*, in which the interest is compounded virtually every instant, is minimal.

For example, suppose that an investor deposits $1,000 at 12 percent interest for 10 years. At simple interest, that $1,000 would grow to only $1,200, not much of an increase at all. At 12 percent interest compounded annually, the investment would grow to a more impressive $2,105.85. If the interest were compounded quarterly, the investment would grow to $2,262.04. Monthly compounding would produce $2,300.39. (Notice that the increases grow proportionately smaller as we reduce the period of compounding.) Daily compounding would produce $2,320.09, only about a $2 per year gain over monthly compounding. And continuous compounding would produce a compound amount of $2,320.11, only $0.02 more than daily compounding over the 10 years.

In fact, continuous compounding has little application in the banking industry. It's generally applied to concepts like inflation or the general growth in consumer prices and the cost of living. It's a very useful concept for discussing inflation because it suggests that prices are rising continuously—all the time—not just in weekly or monthly spurts. And that, of course, is much closer to the way it really works. Inflation rates are based on the analysis of hundreds of price increases; they certainly do not all happen at once, nor do they occur at regular, predictable intervals. At any given moment, though, it's safe to say that the price of something, somewhere, is going up; and the accumulated effect of those continual price increases is what we call inflation.

There's no problem, though, with the idea of making interest payments to an account at periodic points in time. And the more frequent those interest payments are, the more compound interest the account will eventually bear. At the same time, the additional advantages of very short compounding periods are quite small.

Passbook Savings versus Time Deposit Accounts

The right kind of investment depends on what you plan to do with the money. A passbook savings account is ideal for the short-term investor who wants a *liquid* investment — in other words, one that can be converted to cash in a hurry when the depositor wants to go on vacation or make a down payment on a new refrigerator. A *passbook account* generally pays lower interest than other forms of investment, but it usually allows for immediate withdrawal of money without notice and without penalty (though, as we've noted, there are exceptions). As a general rule, the bank isn't going to pay as much for using money that a depositor can take back at any time as it will for money it can count on keeping for a fixed period of time.

A big advantage of passbook savings accounts and similar bank deposits is safety. Federal insurance on banks is provided by the Federal Deposit Insurance Corporation (FDIC); insurance on credit unions is provided by the National Credit Union Share Insurance Fund. Both agencies provide insurance on individual accounts of up to $100,000. A family can, and usually should, increase its protection further by opening separate accounts under different names (each account is insured separately) or having accounts in more than one bank. Since the insurance protection is backed by the U.S. government itself, such an account is considered to have almost no risk. On the other hand, higher risk tends to produce higher potential return, and serious investors often feel that passbook accounts simply do not produce enough yield. They are excellent places to put "rainy day" money, money to cover emergencies or impulse purchases, but long-term savings often call for another approach.

Time deposits (TDs) — which often take the form of certificates of deposit (CDs) — are another form of savings account offered by financial institutions like banks. The actual time of deposit for such an investment may range from a single week to a number of years, and the amount of deposit may vary from as little as $100 to $100,000 or more. A time deposit is a kind of contractual agreement between the depositor and the financial institution, and as with most contracts, each side receives a certain kind of benefit.

The depositor receives a higher rate of interest than would usually be available with a regular passbook savings account. In exchange for this higher interest, he or she agrees to leave the money on deposit for a definite period, say, six months. In fact, six-month certificates have been consistently the most popular with American investors. Most people, it seems, feel pretty comfortable about letting go of their money for half a year but much less comfortable about having it tied up longer than that, even given the reward of higher interest.

Bank and credit union time deposits are insured like passbook accounts, so there's not too much difference in the safety of the money. But there is an important conceptual difference between CDs and passbook accounts. The interest rate on *certificates of deposit* is fixed for the life of the certificate. With a passbook savings account, it's a little different. If Elm City Bank suddenly increases its passbook interest rate from 5 to 6 percent, every account on deposit benefits automatically. But the purchaser of a CD can benefit from an interest rate increase only by purchasing another certificate; those purchased previously are locked in to whatever interest rate was offered at the time.

That's both an advantage and a disadvantage to CDs. If interest rates go up substantially, you'll regret having money in a CD that's paying far less than is currently available. Conversely, you can look like a financial wizard if you lock in a CD rate and then interest rates in general drop several percentage points. (And if you get a long-term CD—one with a term of, say, five years—whether general interest rates go up or down compared to the CD's fixed rate is what determines whether the CD was a good or a bad investment.) In any event, rates on certificates of deposit vary widely and change constantly, so shopping around is a good idea. And since convenient access to the deposit is not an issue for CDs, some investors will even go out of town to get better rates.

CDs sometimes permit early withdrawal but usually only with a penalty, which may be substantial. For example, let's say Wilson purchases a six-month CD for $1,000, but finds after three months that he'd really like to have that money for the down payment on a new car. Depending on the rules of the institution with which he's doing business, he can probably get his $1,000 back early. But odds are he'll lose any interest his investment has accumulated to date. Sometimes, if the date of withdrawal is sufficiently close to the date of maturity, the bank will pay interest at the passbook rate for part of the investment period. That's better than nothing, but it still nets Wilson less interest than the same investment would have earned in a regular passbook account and nowhere near the interest he'd have earned if he'd left the money alone until the CD matured.

Present Value

Despite the advice of financial advisors, individual investors do not always take the time or trouble to plan future purchases or investments. Experts point out, for example, that the ideal time to decide to buy a new car is three or four years before the old one breaks down so that the money needed to buy it can be saved up. But in real life, most consumers are considerably more whimsical than that and often wind up depending on whatever resources the family happens to have at hand when the urge to buy strikes.

Businesses, however, must generally operate a little differently if they are to be successful. A business manager must anticipate future needs as well as monitor what's going on today. For instance, farmers cannot wait until machinery has fallen apart before they think of replacing it. In order to budget resources effectively, they must know when and how they'll be spending money.

Let's say a farmer determines that a pickup truck currently in use will do for another three years but will then have to be replaced. That may mean an investment in three years of, say, $20,000, taking into account inflation and annual increases in the price of pickups. The next question is, how much money will the farmer need to put aside *now* in order to ensure that the $20,000 will be available when he needs it?

That is simply another way of asking what is the *present value* of $20,000 invested at a given rate of interest for three years? Let's say that the farmer can get interest of 5 percent compounded semiannually. At that rate, in order to reach his $20,000 goal, he'll need to invest $17,246 today. (Incidentally, there are ways to calculate that amount by hand, but it's a lot easier to use a special calculator or table that finds present values.) In actuality, of course, the farmer probably won't put the whole $17,246 in the bank in one lump sum. He may not have that much right now, so he may need to deposit the money in six-month increments. That's fine. Each time he does so, he can project the compound interest on his current investment and match that against the present value of the $20,000 he ultimately needs.

If he's a shrewd business person, he may have another thought, too: the price of pickups may be increasing at a rate higher than the rate of interest on his investment. In our admittedly conservative example, he's getting only 5 percent compounded semiannually. Maybe the price of pickups is increasing at a rate of 10 percent per year. At this rate, his money won't grow fast enough to match anticipated price increases. If he does have the necessary $17,000 in cash, he might be money ahead to buy that pickup now.

SOME WORDS OF ADVICE

In considering any kind of investment, whether for personal or business purposes, it's a good idea to analyze current and projected financial needs carefully. A passbook savings account, for instance, is a handy and sensible place to put money needed for everyday financial matters. It's safe. It offers *some* interest, though any service charges or penalties should be subtracted from this amount to get a true picture of the yield. And it's convenient, since the money can usually be withdrawn without penalty if it's needed suddenly. On the other hand, for the family or business with more money than it needs for anticipated expenses, putting large sums of money into passbook savings rarely makes good business sense. The return isn't particularly high, so if the money isn't going to be needed for a period of time, there are more profitable investments.

Time deposits are a good alternative for the individual or business investor who can get along without a given amount of money for a definite period. It's rarely a good idea to invest limited resources in this manner, however, since the money is not readily accessible in the event of an emergency. It may be unavailable altogether or, more likely, be available only after a penalty for early withdrawal reduces the interest, perhaps to nothing. The terms of the agreement should be reviewed fully prior to any such investment, of course, so that there are no surprises. Investors should also keep in mind that many banks reserve the right to "roll over" any matured certificates; that is, at the end of the investment period, they will automatically take the accumulated funds and interest from one CD and invest them in another (perhaps lower-paying) CD, unless the customer specifically requests otherwise.

Whether one is opening a passbook savings account or investing in a time deposit certificate, it often pays to shop around a bit. In the final analysis, the interest rate on a passbook savings account may be less critical than the period of compounding, though neither will make a great difference if the investment is small and left on deposit for only a short period. Some holders of passbook savings accounts put aside a given amount, say $2,000, to cover emergencies, and then add little or nothing to the account (other than the interest that accumulates). But that isn't always a good plan. Some banks demand activity and may even close an account down—or at the least, impose a penalty stiff enough to wipe out any interest—if there are no deposits or withdrawals for an extended period. So while passbook accounts are simple and straightforward, they still require periodic attention.

Finally, it's very good practice to make certain any money put on deposit in any form is insured by an agency of the federal government. This also applies to any long-distance banking investments. Remember, a higher yield is of little comfort if the money is not insured and the institution later goes broke; without that insurance, the entire investment may be lost. Remember, too, that there are limits on the amount of coverage provided to any one account, so it's often a good idea to split deposits over $100,000 among different banks.

KEY TERMS

Before you read through the text assignment and watch the video program, take a minute to look at the key terms associated with this lesson. When you encounter them in the text and video program, pay careful attention to their meaning.

Certificate of deposit (CD): A type of time deposit account; the depositor receives a certificate specifying that an amount has been deposited and will be repaid with interest on a specific date.

Compound amount: Final amount calculated on both principal and past interest. Applies to money deposited in an account with compound interest rates.

Compound interest: Interest charged or received on both principal and interest.

Continuous compounding: An account offering interest compounded every instant. (It's easier to think of continuous compounding as a mathematical concept than to try to visualize how it works in real life. The effect of continuous compounding differs little from that of daily compounding.)

Daily compounding: Interest paid for every day that money is on deposit in a savings account.

Insured money market accounts (IMMAs): Accounts insured up to a certain maximum by the federal government. Such accounts generally offer a higher rate than passbook accounts in exchange for a penalty for early withdrawal.

Passbook account: A common form of savings account used for day-in and day-out deposit of money. Such accounts generally offer a relatively low rate of interest but allow the money to be withdrawn at any time.

Period of compounding: The amount of time between additions of interest to a deposit or loan. For example, if a bank offers 8 percent interest compounded quarterly, the period of compounding is three months.

Present value: The amount that can be deposited today at a given rate of interest to yield a certain sum in the future.

Stated rate: Rate of interest quoted by a bank. The so-called effective rate may be slightly higher because of the frequency of compounding.

Time deposit account: Savings account in which the depositor agrees to leave money for a certain period of time.

PART II: WATCHING THE VIDEO PROGRAM

VIDEO VIEWING GUIDE

Before watching the video program, review the following questions. As you watch, be sure to collect the information necessary to answer them:

1. From a business person's perspective, what are the practical differences between simple and compound interest?

2. A *liquid* investment is more easily transformed into spendable cash than an *illiquid* investment. Provide an example of each type and discuss the advantages and drawbacks of each.

3. Are businesses better off to borrow money at compound or simple interest? Actually, how much choice do they have in the matter?

4. What is the relationship between the compound amount and the period of compounding?

5. What is the relationship between the period of compounding and the frequency with which interest is compounded?

6. How does the state of the economy affect the interest rates offered to depositors and charged to borrowers? (Note: This question isn't directly answered in the program, but you should be able to figure it out from the information that is provided.)

7. As a consumer, how would you go about determining whether to buy now or save your money and make a major purchase at some later date? Provide an example and show the mathematics you used to make your decision.

8. Suppose you were in charge of a business with $50,000 that wasn't needed for immediate expenses. What questions would you have to have answered before you could decide what to do with the money?

VIDEO PROGRAM

The lesson's video program is Program 16 — Compound Interest. Remember, if you are watching this program on videotape, take time to replay sections of the tape any time you need to review a concept.

VIDEO VIEWING QUESTIONS

Immediately after viewing the video program for Lesson 16, take time to respond to the following questions. Give your answers some careful thought; they may provide the basis for additional discussion or a longer written response.

1. On a scale of 1 to 10, how high would you rate the importance of understanding compound interest in making a good business decision?

Not   **Extremely**
Important   **Important**

1- - - - -2- - - -3- - - - -4- - - -5- - - - -6- - - - -7- - - - -8- - - - -9- - - -10

2. After viewing the video, how would you personally rank the following factors in making a wise investment? Number them 1 to 6 (with 1 the most important, 6 the least.) To answer the question, you'll need to imagine yourself running a hypothetical business that has certain current and future needs, so be ready to defend your ranking in terms of the needs of your imaginary business.

_____ Liquidity (ability to reconvert the investment to cash)

_____ Compound interest rate

_____ Length of the compounding period (quarterly, annually, daily, etc.)

_____ Current rate of inflation

_____ Safety

_____ Current tax bracket at the time of the investment

3. Name at least two factors not listed in Question 2 that influence you in considering a personal or business decision about investing money:

a. _____

b. _____

4. Briefly, how would you define the relationship between risk and return on investment, based on information in the video?

_____

_____

5. Which of the following investments is most liquid? Mark it with a plus sign. Which is least liquid? Mark it with a minus sign. Now put a check by each one you feel is a fairly liquid investment.

_____ An insured money market certificate

_____ A passbook savings account

_____ A new home

_____ Undeveloped land

_____ An expensive automobile

_____ Commercial real estate, such as a store or hotel

_____ Gold

_____ A certificate of deposit

_____ A painting or other work of art

_____ A race horse

6. Given the same investments, which has the lowest risk? Mark it with a plus sign. Which has the highest risk? Mark it with a minus sign. Now put a check by each one you feel is a fairly low-risk investment.

_____   An insured money market certificate

_____   A passbook savings account

_____   A new home

_____   Undeveloped land

_____   An expensive automobile

_____   Commercial real estate, such as a store or hotel

_____   Gold

_____   A certificate of deposit

_____   A painting or other work of art

_____   A race horse

7. Name two ways investment decisions made by individual consumers are likely to differ a little from investment decisions made by large corporations.

a. _____

b. _____

PART III: FOCUSING ON THE MATHEMATICS

READING ASSIGNMENT _____

After watching the video program, you should read one of the following Text Assignments, depending on the textbook you're using:

SOFTCOVER: Pages 331-350 from Chapter 9 of the Miller, Salzman, and Hoelzle softcover text, *Business Mathematics.*

HARDCOVER: Chapter 13 of the Salzman, Miller, and Hoelzle hardcover text, *Mathematics for Business*, pages 443-471.

As you read through the text, pay careful attention to the examples the book gives of the mathematics associated with the concepts you're learning about.

Then, after you've completed the text assignment, read through the Key Formulas below. This section provides a handy review of what you've learned. By the time you get to this point in the lesson, all of the formulas and calculations should be familiar to you. If they're not, go back and read the appropriate parts of the text and the Overview section of this lesson. You won't have much success completing the rest of your assignments if you are still confused about the information in the Key Formulas section.

KEY FORMULAS

The following key formulas are important to your understanding of this lesson. Be sure that you know each one and how to use it in solving problems related to compound interest.

KEY FORMULA:	Interest = Compound amount − Original principal
Formula used for:	Determining the net cost of an item when the list price and discount are known.
Alternate forms:	Compound amount = Original principal + Interest or Original principal = Compound Amount − Interest

Example:

If the compound amount is $1,500 and the original principal is $1,200, then the interest earned on the investment was $1,500 − $1,200, or $300.

Remember that in this formula:

1. The interest is the money earned on the principal over time.

2. The compound amount includes both principal and past interest. It equals the total value of all the money credited to a given account.

KEY FORMULA:	$A = P (1 + i)n$
Formula used for:	Determining the compound amount, given the principal, the interest rate, and the number of compounding periods.

Example:

Suppose we need to find the compound amount A for a deposit of $500 at 8 percent compounded quarterly for two years. First, we have to remember that because the compounding occurs four times a year, the 8 percent must be divided by 4; thus, $i = 8/4 = 2\%$ interest per compounding period. Over two years, there are eight compounding periods (four periods per year times two years). Thus, $n = 8$. The equation is now $A = \$500 \times (1 + .02)8$. Since 1.02 to the eighth power is 1.17166, we multiply this figure times the principal of $500 to find the compound amount. This means that $A = \$500 \times 1.17166$, which is $585.83. In other words, at the end of two years, the initial $500 principal will have grown to $585.83.

Remember that in this formula:

1. A = compound amount, or the final amount of the deposit after all interest is calculated.

2. P = number of dollars deposited.

3. i = rate of interest per period . If the annual interest rate is 8 percent, and the interest is compounded quarterly, or four times per year, the interest rate per period will be $8/4$, or 2 percent.

4. n = the number of times the money is compounded during the time of calculation; that is, the number of compounding periods. If the money is compounded semiannually over a period of three years, then n = 2 + 2 + 2 = 6. In other words, the interest will be compounded six times over the course of the three years.

5. Because calculating, for instance, 1.028 is a bit tedious, there are tables and calculators that will do much of the math for you. Your text, for example, has a table that lets you look down the lefthand column to find n and across the top of the table to find the correct rate of interest; at the place where the row and column meet there's a decimal, like 1.17166, that is equal to (1 + i)n. Once you know that number, you just multiply it times the principal to get the compound amount. In fact, when you have the appropriate table available, you can simply think of the formula this way: Compound amount = Principal × Decimal number from table.

KEY FORMULA: P = A ÷ (1 + i)n

Formula used for: Determining the present value of an investment. Present value, remember, is the amount of money that must be invested at a specified interest rate for a specified time in order to achieve a specified amount at the end of that time.

Example:

Suppose Jan Robbins needs $8,000 in three years. How much must she deposit at 6 percent compounded semiannually to meet this goal? First, notice how similar this formula is to the one for finding compound amount; i and n are handled the same way. So if the interest is compounded at 6 percent semiannually (or twice per year), the interest rate *per period* (i) will be 6/2, or 3 percent. Across the total time of deposit, three years, there will be six compounding periods: 3 (years) × 2 (compounding periods per year) = 6 compounding periods. The equation becomes P = $8,000 ÷ (1.03)6. Thus, P = $8,000 ÷ 1.1597, which means P is a little over $6,898. That's how much Jan Robbins must deposit in order to have the $8,000 she needs in three years.

Remember that in this formula:

1. P represents *present value*, or the amount that a person would need to deposit at a given interest rate to accumulate a given future amount. Present value can also be viewed as the principal that's going to grow to the compound amount, so it's not wrong to think of P as principal in this formula.

2. Just as for the previous formula, there are tables to simplify the mathematics. But there's one difference: the table you use isn't a table of (1 + i)n; it's a table of 1 ÷ (1 + i)n. In other words, the division has already been taken care of, so you actually solve the problem as a multiplication problem; you do *not* divide by the number from the table. Therefore, think of this formula as reading this way: Present value = Compound amount × Decimal number from table.

3. To use Table 9-4 correctly, you need to know the number of compounding periods for the total time of deposit and the percentage rate at which the money is compounded per period. These figures are de-

termined the same way for present value as for the compound interest formula.

4. Determining present value is a lot like figuring compound interest because it's really the same problem looked at from another angle. We go into the problem with a different piece of information; instead of knowing the amount of the original deposit, we know how much money we need by some future date. We use this information to figure out how big the original deposit must be to accumulate enough interest to reach that goal.

DON'T FORGET

1. Compound interest differs from simple interest. It's calculated on the basis of both principal and accumulated past interest.

2. The period of compounding may have as much impact on the compound amount (or final total deposit) as small variations in the interest rate itself. This is particularly true for larger investments.

3. Calculate the compound rate *for the period* by dividing the annual compound interest rate by the number of compounding periods in the year. When interest is compounded quarterly, there are four compounding periods in a year. Thus, if the annual compound rate is 10 percent, the quarterly compound rate is 2½ percent ($10/4$). Be sure to determine the compound rate for each period before attempting to determine the compound amount.

4. Most calculations of compound interest or present value make use of tables. When you use compound interest or present value tables, much of the calculation has already been done. In the formula for determining compound amount, $A = P(1 + i)n$, the value of $(1 + i)n$ is often available from a table. In the formula for determining present value, $P = A \div (1 + i)n$, the value of $1 \div (1 + i)n$ is also available from a table. In either case, simply multiplying the number from the table by the principal or compound amount (as appropriate) gives the answer. Using these tables simplifies the math calculations. However, be sure to work with the interest rate *per period* and the *total* number of compounding periods, or you'll get the wrong answer.

PART IV: SOLVING BUSINESS PROBLEMS

PROBLEM SETS

Work the following problems in your textbook. Your instructor will tell you which problems, if any, are to be turned in. Some of the problems have answers provided in the back of the book; refer to these answers to make sure you are working the problems correctly.

SOFTCOVER: If you are using the Miller, Salzman, and Hoelzle softcover text, *Business Mathematics*, do the following problem sets:

> **9.1:** Problems #3-27 (odd numbers only) on pages 337-338.
>
> **9.2:** Problems #2-16 (even numbers only) on pages 343-344.
>
> **9.3:** Problems #2-18 (even numbers only) on pages 349-350.

HARDCOVER: If you are using the Salzman, Miller, and Hoelzle hardcover text, *Mathematics for Business*, do the following problem sets:

> **13.1:** Problems #12-42 (even numbers only) on pages 449-451.
>
> **13.2:** Problems #8-42 (even numbers only) on pages 459-462.
>
> **13.3:** Problems #6-32 (even numbers only) on pages 465-466.
>
> **13.4:** Problems #14-24 (even numbers only) on pages 470-471.

BUSINESS APPLICATIONS

Read each of the following scenarios and answer the questions about the decisions you would make in each situation. Give these questions some serious thought; they may be used as the basis for discussion or the development of a more complex essay. You should base your decisions on what you've learned from this lesson, applying both math skills and good business judgment to solve the problem at hand.

SCENARIO 1

Frank and Sylvia Rath have just started a small family business, a take-out restaurant featuring Hungarian food. They have borrowed $20,000 at 8 percent interest, compounded semiannually, to get their enterprise under way and are repaying this investment at the rate of about $400 per month. The restaurant has been open for just over six months, and so far things are going well. Business has not been booming, but it's increasing steadily at the rate of about 5 percent per month, with no signs of dropping off. If business continues to increase, the Raths hope to pay the loan off a little early, and there is no penalty for doing so. On the other hand, if business should take a serious downturn, they would have difficulty making the $400 payment. Even with the modest increases in the rate of business, it seems there is little extra money left over at the end of the month.

Recently, Frank Rath has learned that he is the beneficiary of a $5,000 insurance policy belonging to his late aunt. The money certainly comes at a welcome time; the question is what to do with it. There seem to be three options. Frank could apply the $5,000 directly to the $20,000 loan, thereby substantially reducing the principal and with it the number of payments remaining. Or he could put the money into a passbook savings account for himself and his wife. They currently have no personal savings, having put all of their resources into the restaurant, and Sylvia likes the idea of regaining a little financial cushion. The passbook account at their local bank pays a little over 5 percent interest compounded daily.

A third option would be to invest in a certificate of deposit. The local bank is currently paying 9 percent on six-month CDs and 9.5 percent on CDs running one year or more. The high interest rate is very appealing to

Frank, but Sylvia is apprehensive about tying up their money for so long. "It's scary not having anything we can spend if we need to," she tells him. "Let's just keep it where we can get at it. We're making the payments on the loan without any difficulty; I don't see that we need to put the money there. I like the idea of having something in case of an emergency." Frank sympathizes but feels that a passbook account isn't a very prudent business investment. "We can do better," he tells Sylvia, "without much more risk. Either of the other options makes better business sense."

What do you think? Should the Raths use the money to help pay off the loan? Buy a CD? Or should they follow Sylvia's suggestion and just put it into a regular passbook account?

☐ Which of the three options do you think the Raths should take? Explain why.

☐ Sylvia is concerned about sudden emergencies. Which of the three options is most prudent, given Sylvia's concerns?

☐ Frank says "We can do better without much more risk." Is he right? If so, which of the options offers the best balance between risk and return?

☐ Frank knows that the CD pays more than the passbook account, but he hasn't said much about the advantages of paying off the loan early. How would he go about calculating whether paying off the loan would be better than putting the money in a CD?

☐ Suppose Frank and Sylvia can't agree and finally decide to divide the money and put it into two or three of the options? What might be the advantage of such an approach, and what are the drawbacks?

SCENARIO 2

Gilbert owns a small shoe repair business that he started from scratch, first working out of his basement. The business now operates out of a cramped but functional corner store in a moderate-sized shopping center. The value of the business is estimated at about $75,000 and Gilbert's business advisor tells him that this value will probably increase at the rate of 10 percent, compounded annually, for the next five years. After that, though, the growth rate will decline considerably; business might even drop off some.

Gilbert has been offered $60,000 for his business and is trying to decide whether to accept it. Since he would not need the money to live on (he plans on getting a full-time job if he sells the business), he could invest the entire $60,000 in CDs paying 8 percent compounded quarterly or in a passbook account paying 6 percent compounded daily. Gilbert feels ready for a change, but it seems like a big decision. Also, he isn't altogether happy with the offer; it strikes him as a little low. Still, he doesn't have any other prospective buyers; the number of people eager to get into the shoe repair business seems to be decidedly limited.

What do you think? Should Gilbert sell the business and invest the money? Or should he hold out for a better price down the road? If he does sell, should he try to bargain for more money? If so, how much more?

☐ Gilbert's business is apparently worth $75,000, but he has a buyer willing to pay $60,000 cash now. Assuming his consultant's estimates are accurate, how much difference does it make financially whether he accepts the $60,000 now or sells in five years?

□ If Gilbert sells now, he expects to put the money into CDs or a passbook account. Are there other options that he should be considering? If so, what are they?

□ Gilbert's business consultant advises him that inflation is likely to remain fairly low (less than 5 percent) during each of the next five years. Assuming that's an accurate prediction, should that information make Gilbert more or less willing to sell?

□ Gilbert did have another potential buyer, but that buyer offered to pay only $20,000 in cash and then pay $1,000 per month for the next five years. Was Gilbert smart to reject that offer, or was it a better deal than his current offer?

Credit Purchases 17

Reprinted by Permission: Tribune Media Services.

Everyone has known people who take pride in "paying as they go" rather than relying on credit. That's perhaps an admirable idea in theory, but the simple truth is that it's practically impossible to put into practice anymore. Turn on the shower and you're using water—on credit—from the water company. Flick on an electric light, switch on the stereo, pop some bread in the toaster—and there's more credit from the electric company. Not to mention air conditioners, water heaters, refrigerators, office lights, and central heating, all things we generally take for granted.

So when people say they don't like the idea of credit, it could be they haven't given sufficient thought to the alternative. Think what a nuisance it is when you don't have change for the parking meter or the public telephone. What if *everything* were like that? What if you couldn't toast a bagel unless you had a nickel or turn on the television unless you slipped a dime in the slot? Clearly, paying as you go, however appealing philosophically, has some real drawbacks in practice. Today's merchants sell trillions of dollars' worth of merchandise on credit every year, and it's a rare U.S. family that doesn't do at least a few thousand dollars of business on credit each year. In fact, credit buying now accounts for a major portion of many retailers' sales.

In this lesson, we'll explore some advantages and disadvantages of buying on credit, look at some different ways merchants offer credit, and carefully examine some important formulas consumers can use to determine how much they're paying in finance charges when they buy on credit.

PART I: INTRODUCING THE MATERIAL

LEARNING OBJECTIVES

Upon completing your study of this lesson, you should be able to:

1. Explain the importance of credit purchasing in modern business and consumer transactions, including some estimates of the magnitude of credit use.

2. Provide examples of open-ended credit accounts and describe the differences between open-ended account finance charges calculated on the unpaid balance and the average daily balance methods.

3. Given a simplified history of credit purchases, returns, and payments, calculate the finance charges and balance due at the end of the period using the unpaid balance method.

4. Given a simplified history of credit purchases, returns, and payments, calculate the finance charges and balance due at the end of the period using the average daily balance method.

5. Calculate the total installment cost, finance charges, and amount financed for a purchase, given the cash price, down payment, and payments.

6. Know the formula for approximate annual percentage rate and use it to estimate the APR for a purchase, given the cash price, down payment, and payments.

7. Use a table of finance charges for given APRs to calculate the finance charges for a specified amount financed.

8. Describe and contrast the elements of the United States Rule and the Rule of 78.

If you're using the hardcover textbook, *Mathematics for Business*, there are some additional objectives for this lesson. Upon completing your study of the lesson, you should also be able to:

9. Following the United States Rule, find the amount due on the maturity date of a loan on which one or more prepayments have been made.

10. Following the Rule of 78, calculate the amount of unearned interest and finance charges due when a monthly installment contract is paid in advance.

LESSON OVERVIEW

It's no secret that buying on credit has become a way of life in the U.S. Almost all adult consumers have at least one major credit card; some have half a dozen or more. Consumers buy everything from clothing and small appliances to big-ticket items like automobiles, boats, motor homes, and South Pacific cruises on credit. Some consumers are very credit wise, planning their spending carefully. Others, however, may not be aware of the total amount they're spending when they pay for an item or service over time.

As we shall see in this lesson, credit is not free. It is a service that retailers extend for a fee. Thus, consumers who buy on credit pay not only the initial cash price of the item but interest as well, interest the creditor normally assesses in the form of a *finance charge*. How much they pay depends on the credit terms: the percentage charged and the time allowed to repay the loan.

To understand better how this works, think of credit buying as borrowing money. In essence, that's what it is. Consider Leaman, who buys a $1,000 refrigerator on time. Let's say he pays $200 down and finances the remaining $800. For all practical purposes, this is the same as if Leaman borrowed $800 and repaid it with interest. By the time Leaman sends in the last monthly payment, he will have paid *more* than $1,000 for the refrigerator. If he takes only a few months to pay, the interest on the loan might be small; say, $40 or $50, depending on the terms. But if he takes two *years* to pay, it might be much more than that—several hundred dollars, perhaps.

The Rationale for Offering Credit

You may be wondering, by the way, whether it's fair for the seller of the refrigerator to make all this money over and above the selling price. There's no simple answer to that question, and it's no different, really, from asking whether $1,000 is a "fair" price for a refrigerator in the first place. What's fair in any situation is whatever the buyer and seller can agree to.

But just for a moment, look at things from the seller's perspective. He'd like to sell the refrigerator to Leaman today, only Leaman doesn't have the money. So if the seller insists on cash, he'll lose a sale. He could say, "Well, too bad for Leaman; there are plenty of other buyers." Absolutely right. The trouble is, maybe they don't have $1,000 in cash either. So in order to sell more refrigerators, the seller comes up with a compromise. He'll do without some of his money for a while, but he'll have to charge something for this inconvenience. After all, if the seller had the money, he could be buying more refrigerators or modernizing the accounting system or, at the very least, earning interest by putting the money in the bank. Since the seller is giving up the opportunity to use his own money to make more money, it's reasonable to expect the buyer to pay something extra for credit.

Remember, the seller had to pay a wholesaler to get that refrigerator into the store in the first place. Chances are, he's got a certain amount of cash tied up in it already, so when Leaman takes it out the door without fully paying for it, he puts the seller (the retailer, that is) in a difficult position. If Leaman fails to pay the rest of the money, the retailer suffers a loss. Most of the time, fortunately, consumers do pay their bills on time, so the risk is fairly small—but it's there, all a part of doing business. The interest the seller charges Leaman helps offset that risk, as well as the cost of doing without his money for a time.

It's entirely possible that the store owner may sell 20 refrigerators this month instead of the five he would have sold on strictly cash terms. That gives the retailer more money to spend on new inventory. And the wholesaler, delighted at what a good customer the appliance store owner has become, may extend credit terms and a substantial discount on the next order of refrigerators. Now the retailer is buying for less, perhaps needs less cash than before, and finds it easier than before to turn around and offer credit to his customers. In other words, credit buying tends to become a kind of self-perpetuating cycle.

In fact, it's no exaggeration to say that if credit buying were suddenly discontinued, and everyone had to pay cash or do without, the economy would slow perceptibly. Leaman wouldn't be buying his refrigerator, for instance. (And while he was saving up for it, he might not be buying much of anything else, either.) The appliance store would lose that sale and probably a number of others as well. The store, in turn, wouldn't be ordering much from the wholesaler, and the company that manufactured the refrigerators wouldn't have much need to increase production.

Then it might postpone orders for new equipment, scrap plans for expansion, and even let some workers go as a result of the slowdown in refrigerator orders. Chances are that those workers would have a tough time finding new work if this cash-only policy existed in other parts of the business community, too. For then manufacturing in all fields might be slow and methodical. Why rush if there's no market? And by the time Leaman did finally save up the money for the refrigerator, he might have to special order it, since the retailer would no longer find it profitable to keep refrigerators in inventory if they sold at the rate of only one every few months.

The saga of Leaman and his refrigerator is pure fiction, of course. But we can predict with great certainty that in the absence of credit, some major decline in economic growth would be almost inevitable. There is no point manufacturing goods of any kind if there is no one to buy them. And there can be no doubt that the number of available buyers goes up dramatically when retailers offer credit.

As we stressed, though, there's a cost associated with all of this credit buying: the finance charge. Let's take a closer look now at how those finance charges are calculated.

The United States Rule

The *United States Rule* derives its name from the fact that it applies in the U.S., but not necessarily in other parts of the world where retailers offer credit. The premise of the rule is simple: Any payment made by a buyer will be applied first to interest owed on a debt and then to the principal.

Suppose, for instance, that Romano takes out a one-year simple interest note for $2,000 at 10 percent annual interest. After three months, she pays $500. At first, we might assume this would reduce her debt to $1,500, but it's not quite that simple. Remember, the note is accumulating interest every day that it goes unpaid. So in order to find out how much Romano still owes, we first need to calculate the interest after three months. We use the simple interest formula $I = PRT$. So in this case, $I = 2{,}000 \times .10 \times 3/12 = \$50$.

Remember, the United States Rule says that Romano's $500 payment must *first* be applied to the interest owed. So $50 out of the $500 goes to interest. That leaves $500 − $50 = $450 to apply to the principal: $2,000 − $450 = $1,550 remaining of the principal after Romano pays the $500. Interest from this point on will be calculated on the $1,550, not on the original $2,000.

Installment Buying

The United States Rule doesn't always apply, though. With *installment buying* the question of paying off the interest first is considerably less relevant. Say that our friend Romano bought a piano on time. Let's say the price was $2,000; she paid $500 down and financed the rest with monthly payments of $70 for two years. Each of those $70 payments would go toward paying both a portion of the principal and a portion of the interest owed on the $1,500. Notice that with this installment plan, the schedule of payments and the amount of each payment are determined in advance, and those payments include interest.

But when Romano takes out the one-year note, she may not be required to repay *any portion* of the money until the year is up. The United States Rule simply says that if she *does* pay any portion of the debt prior to the maturity date, her payment will apply to interest first.

There are two primary ways in which retailers typically offer credit to buyers. One is through installment buying, the approach used by Romano to purchase the piano in the previous example. Installment buying typically, though not always, involves a down payment that covers a portion of the purchase price, with the balance paid in periodic payments (usually monthly) of a predetermined size. Those payments, added together, usually come to considerably more than the balance owed on the cash price for the purchase. The difference equals the finance charges, or what the seller charges the buyer for extending credit through this kind of loan.

Take Romano, for instance. Recall that she paid $500 down on her $2,000 piano. That leaves a balance of $1,500. But she is paying $70 per month for two years, or 24 months. That's a total of 24 × 70, or $1,680. In other words, her total cost is $500 (the down payment) plus $1,680, or $2,180, which is $180 more than the cash price of the piano. That $180 is the finance charge.

Installment buying is well-suited to the purchase of large items like pianos—or refrigerators, computers, boats, automobiles, or anything else that most consumers simply would not have enough cash on hand to purchase. It's also normally reserved for items that consumers do not buy very often. Most people who buy pianos do not buy them on a monthly basis, for instance; many buy just one in a lifetime. Similarly, most consumers buy a refrigerator or a new couch or an automobile only occasionally. Normally, then, even with extended payment schedules, one item is completely paid for before the consumer buys another like it.

Open-End Credit

Other sorts of purchases are different. People do not usually buy one shirt, for instance, wear it for 10 or 15 years, and then buy another. Moreover, this type of purchase is far less expensive than those we've been talking about. So it wouldn't make much sense for the buyer *or* the seller if inexpensive items like shirts, jeans, shoes, books, or cosmetics were paid for on the installment plan. What's more, given the number of such purchases a consumer might make in a month, buyers and sellers wouldn't have time to do anything but fill out and approve credit application forms.

Let's take a hypothetical shopper, George Bean, who likes to do business at the Carry-All Variety Store, the sort of store that stocks everything. Bean has a charge account here, so shopping is simple. At the end of the month, they just send him a statement summing up what he owes. During May, Bean buys toothpaste, deodorant, shampoo, socks, a baseball mitt, wine, some compact discs, ribbons for his typewriter, a garden hose, lightbulbs, flowers, thumbtacks, and a power lawn mower. Imagine paying for all this merchandise on the installment plan! Who could keep it straight? Let's see ... 20¢ a month on the toothpaste, 25¢ on the socks ... no, that would be ridiculous.

Unfortunately, you couldn't lump all the purchases together and break the total down into installment payments either. For one thing, Bean probably didn't buy them all on the same day, so any approach like that would end up with Bean's paying too much or too little in finance charges. What's more, he'll no doubt buy a whole raft of new items next month. All in all, Carry-All's installment purchase plan wouldn't work for these purchases. What the store can do, however, is offer Bean *open-end credit*.

Under this system, Bean is billed monthly for all purchases made during the previous billing period. He pays whatever he chooses, and his current *unpaid balance* swells or shrinks, depending on his spending habits for the period. That doesn't mean he can pay just 5¢ or 10¢, of course. He'll owe some reasonable minimum, based on the total balance at any given time. Let's say that Bean's purchases for May total about $300. The store might require that he pay a minimum of 10 percent of that amount, or $30.

It's important to understand that with open-end credit, if Bean pays off the total balance the *very first time* the store sends him the $300 bill, he probably won't owe any interest at all. That's because many stores look on payment within a short period — say, 30 days — the same way they look on cash. Retail stores, like consumers, need some time to pay their bills, too. On the other hand, if Bean decides to pay just the $30 minimum, that will be subtracted from the $300 he owes, and the store will begin to charge him interest on the $270 balance.

During the next month, June, Bean might buy a $100 hammock at Carry-All. The store will not charge him interest on that $100 purchase, though. Not yet. The June interest will be figured only on the unpaid $270 from the preceding month. Let's say that the store's monthly finance charge is 2 percent. That means that George's June statement will include the $270 plus .02 × $270 (in finance charges) plus the new $100 purchase, for a total of $270 + $5.40 + $100 = $375.40 and a new minimum payment of $38.

Bean undoubtedly has some *credit limit* associated with his account, a maximum outstanding balance that he can have. He might be allowed to charge up to, say, $1,000, at which point Carry-All will say, "That's it — no more purchases until a portion of this is paid off." Essentially, though, as long as Bean keeps paying *something* each month, he never has to pay the account off entirely. The store extends him credit — well, forever. Hence the term *open-end* credit.

George Bean's account in this scenario is an example of a *revolving charge account*, one in which the charges from one month are simply carried over into the next month. Notice how different this is from installment buying, in which a customer pays for a specific item in a very systematic fashion. With open-end credit, Bean can decide whether to send in the $30 minimum, or $40, or $50. Or the full amount, for that matter. And if he does send in $50, the store doesn't worry about whether Bean views it as going for the garden hose or the hammock. It doesn't matter.

Country Club Billing versus Itemized Billing

Shoppers like George Bean, who buy lots of different items during a given month, may have difficulty remembering just what they've bought and when. In fact, when the credit card bill comes in the mail, it's likely to contain a few charges that will cause Bean to scratch his head and say "I wonder what that was for?"

Not long ago, consumers like Bean, who had difficulty keeping track of their purchases, could count on *country club* billing to jog their memories. Country club billing includes more than just a list of purchases; it also includes an individual carbon-copy record of each purchase made during the billing period. Handy for the consumer, but expensive and time-consuming for the retailers — which is precisely the reason that most retailers these days use itemized billing.

As its name suggests, *itemized billing* involves a detailed listing of all purchases but no individual records. For instance, if George Bean buys five pairs of socks on May 5, his itemized bill will show that he bought $14.99 worth of merchandise from the men's clothing department on that date. But the Carry-All billing department isn't likely to get more specific than that. So it will behoove George to save his sales receipts and check them against his itemized bills at the end of the month.

Well, you might say, that sounds like a lot of work. Sure it is. But, consumer credit counselors say, that's the price you pay for the buying power that goes with credit. Of course, George (or any consumer) can just take the retailer's word for the fact that he currently owes $375.40. The retailer is probably right. Mistakes are not unheard of, though. Suppose that $25 garden hose George bought on May 10 had a leak in it, so he returned it on May 11, only the store failed to enter that return into its computerized billing system. If George saved all his receipts, including the one for the returned hose, he can straighten this little matter out; otherwise, he could wind up paying the $25, hose or no hose.

Creditors use two basic methods for calculating finance charges: the *unpaid balance method* and the *average daily balance* method. In order to compare the two, let's leave George Bean to his shopping for a moment and look in on another credit card user, Karen Nolte. Let's say that Nolte has two credit accounts, one with Citywide Department Store and another with Fairprice Department Store. Citywide calculates finance charges using the unpaid balance method. It works like this.

At the beginning of a given billing period, Nolte has an unpaid balance of $100. Let's say that Citywide's monthly finance charge is 2 percent. During the billing period, Citywide will calculate interest at this rate on the $100 Nolte currently owes. During this billing period, Nolte makes another $50 purchase, and pays the store $25. What's her balance at the end of the period? Let's see.

First, let's figure out her interest on the unpaid balance. That's $100 × .02 = $2. This amount is added to her bill. Notice that for this month, she owes no interest on the $50 purchase. (That will be calculated during the next billing period.) Thus, the total amount she owes is $100 + $2 + $50, or $152. But she pays $25, so we deduct this from the total owed: $152 − $25 = $127. This is the amount on which Citywide will calculate interest for the *next* billing period.

Now let's see how Fairprice does business. We'll begin again with a balance of $100 on June 1. And to keep things simple, we'll say that the billing period begins with the first of the month (though usually, it begins around the fifth or a little later). Suppose that Nolte makes another $100 purchase on June 10, but she returns that purchase June 20. And she makes another $50 purchase June 25. What's her bill for the period?

To figure this out, we must first calculate the interest or finance charges, which Fairprice bases on the average daily balance, or the average amount Nolte owed on any given day during this period. We figure this out by adding together what she owed each day, then dividing by the total number of days in the period. Her balance was $100 on June 1, and that

**Calculating
Finance Charges**

remained her balance for 10 days: thus, $100 × 10 = $1,000. She then spent another $100, bringing the balance up to $200 for another 10 days: thus, $200 × 10 = $2,000. She returned the $100 purchase on June 20, dropping the balance back to $100 for another five days: $100 × 5 = $500. Then she spent $50 more, raising the balance to $150 for the last five days: $150 × 5 = $750.

The average daily balance is the sum of all these daily balances divided by the number of days in the period: $1,000 + $2,000 + $500 + $750 ÷ 30 = $141.67. Notice that this figure is *not* what Nolte owes. This is simply the figure used by the merchant to determine the finance charges. Let's say those charges are 2 percent monthly. For this month, Nolte owes $147.67 × .02 = $2.95 *in interest*. For *principal* she owes $100 + $100 − $100 + $50 = $150. Thus, the store will bill her for $150 + $2.95 = $152.95.

Notice, by the way, that although Nolte doesn't have to pay for that $100 purchase she returned, the fact that she kept the merchandise for 10 days did affect her finance charge because it increased her average daily balance. In this case, it cost her only a few cents, but she was paying the store interest on the higher balance for those 10 days. And there's some fairness to this, if you think about it; since the item wasn't available for sale during that period, the store couldn't sell it to recover the money it had spent on it.

Monthly versus Annual Finance Charges

Monthly finance charges have a way of looking rather small. They usually range from 1 to 2 percent or so, and that doesn't seem like much, does it? Remember, though, that the monthly finance charge is only $1/12$ of the total annual finance charge (because there are twelve months in a year). So, 2 percent *monthly* translates into an annual interest rate of 2 × 12 = 24 percent. And that might be substantial interest indeed on a good-sized debt.

Say that Alice Porter buys a $500 painting. The monthly finance charge at 2 percent would be just $500 × .02 = $10. But the annual rate is $500 × .24 = $120, almost one-fourth the cost of the item itself. Of course, interest charges aren't automatic. Alice can avoid them by paying off the debt early. But the point is, it's important for Alice to understand the *potential* cost of a credit purchase in the first place, so that she has an accurate idea of what she's paying for the privilege of deferring payment.

Because it is so easy for consumers to misunderstand how interest is calculated, in 1969 Congress passed the Truth-in-Lending Act which requires creditors to report all finance charges honestly and openly to buyers and to share with them the *annual percentage rate* (*APR*) of interest charged. Thus, the seller of the $500 painting would be obliged to point out to Alice that although she would only owe $10 in interest if she paid the bill off after the first month, the annual interest rate was actually *24* percent, not 2 percent, and she would owe 2 percent of *each month's* unpaid balance until the entire bill was paid, no matter how long that took. Further, since that 2 percent monthly charge would be levied not only on the unpaid principal but also on any accumulated interest, the effective annual rate is even higher than 24 percent.

This legislation is not intended to make things hard for sellers. Rather, it's intended to enable buyers to make responsible purchasing decisions. It isn't in anyone's best interest for consumers to become overextended, buying items they lack the ability to pay for. Knowing the true cost in advance puts a consumer in a much better position to gauge his or her ability to pay.

On the face of it, it might seem that most creditors would prefer that customers pay in cash. They'd get their money a lot quicker, and they wouldn't have all the bookkeeping hassle that goes with extending credit. Remember, though, the creditor makes some money by waiting. Each month that the buyer doesn't pay the full balance on a debt, the creditor earns interest on any portion of the debt that remains. That's not to say that most stores look on credit as a money-making proposition; for most, it's more a service necessary to remain competitive. Even so, if you look at it from the lender's side, credit is a sort of investment.

Of course, in order for it to be a good investment, the creditor has to make more than he or she could make investing the money some other way. For instance, it wouldn't make much sense to charge 10 percent annual interest if the creditor could earn 15 percent putting the money earned on cash sales in the bank. In fact, one reason finance charges are as high as they are is that creditors want a rate of return at least as high as they would have to pay to borrow the "missing money" from a bank.

Notice that we referred to the creditor as "earning" interest. That's what he or she does by "selling" credit as a service. *Unearned interest*, then, is interest that might have gone to the creditor but does not because the buyer pays the debt off early. Say, for instance, that the total interest on a 12-month loan is $300. But the borrower pays the loan off three months early and saves about $25. It is sometimes referred to as a "refund" to the borrower, though this terminology is a little confusing because the borrower doesn't actually receive anything; he or she simply doesn't have to pay quite as much to the lender.

Not surprisingly, lenders and creditors are somewhat reluctant to give up their interest. For this reason, they sometimes impose a penalty for early payment of a loan or debt. The penalty will rarely be equal to the full amount of unearned interest, but it might equal a good portion of it—enough so that the borrower will want to weigh carefully the advisability of early payment. While it almost always saves money to pay off a debt early, don't forget that the money could be invested instead. Since the spread between the interest charged on a debt and that paid on an investment may be just a few percentage points, penalties could make paying off a loan early less attractive than one would first think.

Unearned Interest and Penalties for Early Payment

SOME WORDS OF ADVICE

For a consumer, it's obviously important to learn to use credit responsibly. It's a convenience, undoubtedly, and it's very useful for buying needed goods and services, either as an individual consumer or on behalf of a business. Buying on credit can be costly, though, with finance charges adding substantially to the cost of an item.

Think of credit buying as borrowing money; after all, that's essentially what it is. If you wouldn't borrow money to make a large purchase, you certainly shouldn't think it's somehow OK to use a credit card. In fact, the annual percentage rate you'll pay on a credit card debt will be well over what the bank would charge you on a short-term loan of comparable size.

Before making any major purchase, be sure to note the APR and the total finance charges. They can surprise you. Remember that the monthly finance charge is *not* the annual interest rate. Creditors like to quote monthly charges precisely because they have a way of sounding nice and manageable. How much less intimidating 1.5 percent monthly sounds than 18 percent annually; yet they're exactly the same. Realize too that 12 times the monthly interest is not quite equal to the effective APR. That's because interest on credit balances is almost always compounded. That 18 percent annual rate, for instance, may actually be closer to 19 percent, given the effects of compounding. But since the potential creditor is obligated by law to provide the borrower with the true effective annual rate, tell you how it is determined, and specify in dollars the amount you'll pay in finance charges, there's no reason for not knowing the precise numbers.

Even so, it's a good idea to know how the finance charges are calculated. For instance, you might owe nothing in interest if you pay off the bill at the end of the first billing period. In effect, you get a 30-day (or so) grace period in which buying on credit works just like buying with cash. But methods of calculating finance charges vary from creditor to creditor, so it pays to take a close look at how your charges are determined.

Chances are, most if not all the creditors with whom you do business will use itemized billing. That means that it's up to you as a buyer to keep track of what you buy and when and to make sure that your monthly bills are accurate. If you don't save receipts, think about starting. Billing systems are incredibly accurate, but no system is flawless. If you use a charge card to buy 20 or 30 items a month, odds are that your memory is not going to do the trick when it comes time to verify the accuracy of the bill.

KEY TERMS

Before you read through the text assignment and watch the video program, take a minute to look at the key terms associated with this lesson. When you encounter them in the text and video program, pay careful attention to their meaning.

Amount financed: The difference between the cash price of an item and the down payment.

Annual percentage rate (APR): The true or effective rate of interest. It is *slightly* higher than 12 times the monthly finance charge (the reason being that credit financing is based on compound, not simple, interest).

Average daily balance method: A method of calculating the balance owed on a revolving charge account. The balance is found on the account at the end of each day, these daily totals are summed, and the result is divided by the number of days in the billing period (usually 30 or 31).

Country club billing: A type of billing received on revolving charge plans in which actual carbon copies of charges are returned.

Deferred payment price: See *total installment cost.*

Down payment: An initial amount paid on the principal at the time an item is bought.

Installment loan: A loan paid off in a series of equal payments made at equal intervals. A car loan is one example of an installment loan.

Itemized billing: A method of credit card billing in which purchases are listed but no actual receipts returned to the user.

Open-end credit: An account that is not paid off in a fixed period of time; MasterCard and VISA accounts are examples of open-end credit.

Revolving charge account: An account based on open-end credit.

Rule of 78: A method of calculating interest charges that need not be paid (unearned interest) because the loan was paid off earlier than planned. According to the Rule of 78, installment payments are disproportionately weighted to ensure that the bulk of all interest owed is paid off early in the payment period, with increasingly greater portions of each payment going toward the principal.

Total installment cost: The down payment, plus the total amount paid on installment. This amount is equal to the deferred payment price, though the two are calculated differently.

Truth-in-Lending Act (Regulation Z): A federal law passed in 1969 that provides for uniform methods of disclosing information on finance charges and interest rates.

Unearned interest: The interest that a lender would normally have received but does not receive because the loan is paid off early.

United States Rule: A method of handling partial loan payoffs; any payment is first applied to the interest owed on a loan, with any remaining balance applied to the principal.

Unpaid balance: The balance outstanding on a revolving charge account at the end of a billing period.

Unpaid balance method: A method of calculating the finance charge on a revolving charge account using the previous month's ending balance.

PART II: WATCHING THE VIDEO PROGRAM

_____ **VIDEO VIEWING GUIDE**

Before watching the video program, review the following questions. As you watch, be sure to collect the information necessary to answer them:

1. In what ways is the availability of credit important to the business community in our society?

2. In what ways is credit important to the individual consumer?
   To Buy now or Pay later

3. What are some advantages and disadvantages of buying on credit? Of selling on credit? *Buying - Paying more - getting now - Increase sales / more time to collect*

4. What is the primary difference between installment buying and open-end credit? *Monthly Payment decided in advance / Revolving Payments vary.*

5. What impact would discontinuing credit buying have on our economy? What specific positive or negative effects would you anticipate?

6. What is the major difference between itemized billing and country club billing? Which is preferable from the consumer's point of view? How about from the merchant's point of view?

7. What is the importance of the Truth-in-Lending Act of 1969 to the consumer? How can consumers take advantage of this legislation?

8. Why are some merchants more willing to extend credit than others?

VIDEO PROGRAM

The lesson's video program is Program 17—Credit Purchases. Remember, if you are watching this program on videotape, take time to replay sections of the tape any time you need to review a concept.

VIDEO VIEWING QUESTIONS

Immediately after viewing the video program for Lesson 17, take time to respond to the following questions. Give your answers some careful thought; they may provide the basis for additional discussion or a longer written response.

1. On a scale of 1 to 10, how important would you consider credit buying to be to you and your friends and family?

Not
Important   Extremely
                                                              Important

1- - - - -2- - - - -3- - - - -4- - - - -5- - - - -6- - - - -7- - - - -8- - - - -9- - - - -10

2. As a consumer, name two advantages of buying on credit.

   a. _____

   b. _____

3. As a business person, name two advantages of buying on credit.

   a. _____

   b. _____

4. Which of the following do you think might happen if credit card buying were suddenly discontinued in the U.S.? (Check as many as apply.)

   _____   Consumer spending would decline.

   _____   Profits for most merchants would go up.

   _____   Economic growth would slow down.

   _____   Savings and investments would increase.

   _____   Fewer consumer goods and services would be readily available.

   _____   Banks would grant more loans and make more money.

   _____   Interest rates on bank loans would rise.

   _____   More consumers would sell their old possessions.

5. Name one important difference between installment buying and open-end credit.

Same Monthly Payment

6. Which of the following would a consumer be most likely to purchase on installment? (Check as many as apply.)

_____ A television set ✓

_____ A camera

_____ Shoes

_____ Clothing

_____ Food

_____ An automobile ✓

_____ Furniture ✓

_____ Farm machinery ✓

_____ A computer ✓

7. Name one reason a retailer might refuse to accept credit cards.

_____

_____

8. Which of the following businesses do you think might *not* extend credit to customers? (Check as many as apply, and be prepared to explain your answers.)

_____ A grocery store

_____ A hot-dog stand ✓

_____ A bowling alley ✓

_____ A shoe store

_____ A pet shop ✓

_____ A live bait shop ✓

_____ An amusement park ✓

_____ A movie theater ✓

_____ A department store

_____ A furniture store

_____ A watch repair store ✓

_____ A computer store

_____ A beauty parlor ✓

_____ A roller-skating rink ✓

_____ A zoo ✓

_____ An airline

_____ A restaurant

PART III: FOCUSING ON THE MATHEMATICS

READING ASSIGNMENT

After watching the video program, you should read one of the following Text Assignments, depending on the textbook you're using:

SOFTCOVER: Pages 383-406 from Chapter 10 of the Miller, Salzman, and Hoelzle softcover text, *Business Mathematics*.

HARDCOVER: Chapter 14 of the Salzman, Miller, and Hoelzle hardcover text, *Mathematics for Business*, pages 478-504.

As you read through the text, pay careful attention to the examples the book gives of the mathematics associated with the concepts you're learning about.

Then, after you've completed the text assignment, read through the Key Formulas below. This section provides a handy review of what you've learned. By the time you get to this point in the lesson, all of the formulas and calculations should be familiar to you. If they're not, go back and read the appropriate parts of the text and the Overview section of this lesson. You won't have much success completing the rest of your assignments if you are still confused about the information in the Key Formulas section.

KEY FORMULAS

The following key formulas are important to your understanding of this lesson. Be sure that you know each one and how to use it in solving problems related to credit purchases.

KEY FORMULA: Approximate APR = Monthly finance charge × 12

Formula used for: Finding the *approximate* annual percentage rate (APR) when the monthly finance charge, or percentage rate, is known.

Example:

A department store has a monthly finance charge of 1.8 percent. Its annual percentage rate, therefore, is about 1.8 × 12 = 21.6 percent.

Remember that in this formula:

1. APR stands for annual percentage rate, or the annual amount of interest assessed on a loan or credit loan.

2. The APR calculated through this formula is only an approximate rate, though it is close enough to the *effective annual percentage rate* for most consumers to make sound purchasing decisions. The effective annual rate is slightly higher because interest on a credit loan is compounded; that is, it is charged not only on the remaining principal, but

also on any unpaid interest. For example, the effective annual rate in the example will likely be over 22 percent.

KEY FORMULA:	Amount financed = Cash price − Down payment
Formula used for:	Determining that portion of a credit loan on which the borrower will pay interest.
Alternate forms:	Cash price = Amount financed + Down payment or Down payment = Cash price − Amount financed

Example:

Suppose Duncan buys a camper for $6,000 and pays $2,000 down. The amount financed will then be $6,000 − $2,000 = $4,000.

Remember that in this formula:

1. The *cash price* is the amount on the price tag. It is what the buyer would pay for the item if he or she paid cash.

2. The down payment is whatever the buyer pays to the seller at the time of purchase. The lowest acceptable down payment is usually some minimum portion of the selling price, such as 10 percent, but the buyer *may* pay much more than this. The down payment is subtracted directly from the principal, or cash price, so that the buyer pays no interest or finance charges on the down payment. For this reason, it is often to the buyer's advantage financially to pay as much down as possible.

3. The amount financed is the same as the amount on which the buyer will pay interest.

KEY FORMULA:	Deferred payment price = Cash price + Finance charge
Formula used for:	Determining how much an item will cost altogether when some portion of the total cost is financed.
Alternate forms:	Cash price = Deferred payment price − Finance charge or Finance charge = Deferred payment price − Cash price

Example:

Suppose that Duncan pays the balance on his camper with 24 monthly payments of $200 each. That's a total of 24 × $200 = $4,800. Since the balance on the camper was $4,000, the finance charge is $4,800 − $4,000 = $800. This is the amount Duncan pays over and above what the camper actually costs. Thus, the deferred payment price is $6,000 + $800 = $6,800. This is another way of saying that it cost Duncan $800 to pay for the camper on time instead of paying cash.

Remember that in this formula:

1. The deferred payment price is equal to the total amount the buyer pays to purchase an item on time.

2. It is critical to know the amount of the finance charge. Knowing the cash price and the down payment would not be enough.

3. The finance charge can be determined if the cash price, monthly payments, and down payment are all known. The finance charge is the difference between the total installment cost and the cash price.

KEY FORMULA: Total installment cost = Down payment + (Amount of each payment × Number of payments)

Formula used for: Finding the total amount that the buyer pays to purchase an item on time.

Alternate form: Down payment = Total installment cost − (Amount of each payment × Number of payments)

Example:

Recall that Duncan paid $2,000 down on his camper and then made 24 monthly payments of $200 to cover the balance. Thus, the total installment cost on Duncan's camper is $2,000 + ($200 × 24) = $2,000 + $4,800 = $6,800.

Remember that in this formula:

1. The total installment cost is equal to the deferred payment price. They are just calculated a little differently.

2. It is important to know the amount of each monthly payment and the total number of monthly payments. Therefore, the formula is useful only for problems involving installment purchases; it is not useful with problems involving open-end credit.

KEY FORMULA: Approximate APR = 24 × Finance charge ÷ Amount financed × (1 + Total number of payments)

Formula used for: Finding the approximate annual percentage rate on a credit loan when the monthly finance charge is not known.

Example:

Recall that the finance charge on Duncan's loan to buy the camper was $800, and the amount financed was $4,000. He paid for the camper with 24 equal monthly payments. Thus, the approximate APR on this loan is 24 × $800 ÷ $4,000 × (1 + 24) = 4,800 ÷ 100,000 = .192, or 19.2 percent.

Remember that in this formula:

1. It is not necessary to know the monthly finance charge. In fact, this formula is most useful when that piece of information is missing.

Otherwise, it would be simpler to compute the APR simply by multiplying the monthly charge by 12.

2. The finance charge is equal to the total amount the buyer pays over and above the cash price.

3. The amount financed is equal to the difference between the cash price and the down payment.

4. There must be a consistent monthly payment. Thus, this formula is useful for problems involving installment buying but not for problems involving open-end credit.

KEY FORMULA: Finance charge per \$100 = Finance charge ÷ Amount financed × \$100

Formula used for: Determining the total finance charge per \$100.

Example:

The finance charge for Duncan was \$800, and the amount financed was \$4,000. Thus, the finance charge per \$100 is \$800 ÷ \$4,000 × 100 = .20 × 100 = \$20. This is another way of saying that for each \$100 financed, Duncan paid \$20 in interest.

Remember that in this formula:

1. The finance charge is equal to the total amount the buyer pays over and above the cash price.

2. The amount financed is equal to the difference between the cash price and the down payment.

3. The result indicates the amount per \$100 that goes into covering finance charges. In other words, for every \$100 of the \$4,000 he financed under this payment plan, Duncan paid \$20 in finance charges.

KEY FORMULA: Unearned interest = Finance charge × Number of payments remaining ÷ Total number of payments × (1 + Number of payments remaining) ÷ (1 + Total number of payments)

Formula used for:

Determining how much a buyer can save in interest by paying off a loan early, according to the Rule of 78. Under this rule, finance charges are distributed disproportionately throughout the period of payment, so that the greater portion of the total finance charge is covered early in the period. If the loan is for 12 months, then 12/78 of the finance charges are covered in the first month, 11/78 in the second month, and so on. Paying off a loan in the second or third month would save a buyer a large portion of the total finance charge; paying off a loan in the eleventh month would save the buyer only 1/78 of the total charge.

Example:

A loan payable in 12 monthly installments has a finance charge of \$600. How much interest could the buyer save by paying off the loan six months early? At this point, there are six payments remaining. Thus, the unearned interest is $600 \times {}^{6}\!/_{12} \times (1 + 6) \div (1 + 12) = 25,200 \div 156 =$ $161.54 (approximately).

Remember that in this formula:

1. Unearned interest derives its name from the fact that this interest would be earned by the creditor, or lender, if the loan went unpaid until the maturity date. But since the loan is paid off early, the lender has no opportunity to earn this interest, and it is "refunded" to the borrower. This doesn't mean that the lender hands the borrower cash; it simply means that the lender does not charge the borrower interest that he or she would otherwise have owed.

2. The portion of unearned interest declines markedly as you go further into the borrowing period. Thus, the borrower can realize a substantial savings by paying off the loan before he or she is halfway into the borrowing period; the savings are much smaller after that time.

3. It is important to know the total number of payments in the borrowing period, as well as the number of payments remaining at the time the loan is paid off.

4. The name Rule of 78 comes from the fact that the buyer or borrower making twelve monthly payments pays off $^{12}\!/_{78}$ths of the interest with the first monthly payment, $^{11}\!/_{78}$ths of the interest with the second payment, on down to $^{1}\!/_{78}$th for the last monthly payment. As you'd expect, adding up $^{12}\!/_{78}$ths plus $^{11}\!/_{78}$ths plus $^{10}\!/_{78}$ths and so on equals $^{78}\!/_{78}$th, or all the interest.

DON'T FORGET

1. Under the United States Rule, the money paid on a loan is applied first to the interest, then to the principal.

2. Finance charges include *all* charges above and beyond the cash price of an item.

3. You can convert monthly finance charges to approximate APRs by multiplying the monthly charge by 12. For example, a monthly rate of 1 percent translates to an APR of 12 percent. But remember that this is an approximation. Because of compounding, the effective annual interest rate is slightly higher.

4. The total installment cost is equal to the *total cost* of buying on credit. It includes the down payment and all subsequent monthly payments.

5. As always, to convert an interest charge expressed as a percent to a decimal, move the decimal point *two* places to the left. Thus, 10 percent becomes .10, 5 percent becomes .05, and so on.

6. Approximate APR may be calculated by one of two formulas (see Key Formulas section). But the results of this calculation are *not* sufficient to satisfy federal requirements under the Truth-in-Lending Act. The precision required of lenders by law involves very complex mathematics and the use of government tables. These approximate figures are, however, usually accurate enough to enable consumers to make responsible purchasing decisions.

PART IV: SOLVING BUSINESS PROBLEMS

_____**PROBLEM SETS**

Work the following problems in your textbook. Your instructor will tell you which problems, if any, are to be turned in. Some of the problems have answers provided in the back of the book; refer to these answers to make sure you are working the problems correctly.

SOFTCOVER: If you are using the Miller, Salzman, and Hoelzle softcover text, *Business Mathematics*, do the following problem sets:

> **10.1:** Problems #12-20 (even numbers only) on pages 390-392.

> **10.2:** Problems #2-24 (even numbers only) on pages 397-398.

> **10.3:** Problems #2-20 (even numbers only) on pages 403-406.

HARDCOVER: If you are using the Salzman, Miller, and Hoelzle hard-cover text, *Mathematics for Business*, do the following problem sets:

> **14.1:** Problems #2-12 (even numbers only) on page 482.

> **14.2:** Problems #5-24 on pages 488-491.

> **14.3:** Problems #2-28 (even numbers only) on pages 499-500.

> **14.4:** Problems #1-14 on pages 503-504.

_____**BUSINESS APPLICATIONS**

Read each of the following scenarios and answer the questions about the decisions you would make in each situation. Give these questions some serious thought; they may be used as the basis for discussion or the development of a more complex essay. You should base your decisions on what you've learned from this lesson, applying both math skills and good business judgment to solve the problem at hand.

SCENARIO 1

Chadwick and Delgetti run a small accounting firm. They rent an office over the local bakery. The space is tiny, but right now it's all they can afford. The business is successful and well able to pay its bills, but the cash flow is slow. They have made a practice of buying nothing on time, of paying for everything with cash; that's how Chadwick prefers it, and since he owns the controlling interest in the business, Delgetti is forced to go along with this plan. He feels it might be time for a change, though.

They're talking of buying a new computer system for $5,000. At the current cash flow rate, they'll need to save up for about 10 months before they can afford the computer. Delgetti doesn't think they should wait. They have enough right now—$500—for an acceptable down payment. And they can pay off the balance in 12 payments of $450 each, which is just about the extra money the business can afford per month. "We'll be so much more efficient," Delgetti tells Chadwick. "The computer will make money for us, and we'll wind up saving money in the long run."

Chadwick is unconvinced, though. "Buying on credit is a bad habit," he tells Delgetti. "It's irresponsible—for a person or a business. We'll wind up paying more than we should for the computer. All that does is make some salesperson rich. I don't want our firm doing business that way. We expect our clients to pay their bills within 30 days, so I don't see how in all good conscience we can expect less of ourselves. When our cash flow increases, we'll be able to afford more. Till then, we'll just have to get by."

Delgetti, still very much in favor of the credit approach, points out that the cash flow isn't likely to *get* stronger until they have a way of generating more business; the computer could provide that by increasing their speed and efficiency in processing accounts. The firm is currently handling 30 accounts, and Delgetti estimates that they might be able to handle up to 40 percent more if they were computerized. "And I think that estimate is conservative," he tells Chadwick confidently.

What do you think? Would it be a good idea for Chadwick and Delgetti to buy the computer on the installment plan? Or should they wait 10 months till they can afford to pay cash? What are some of the advantages to waiting? What are the potential advantages to buying now? Do you think Chadwick's attitude is part of a sound business philosophy, or is he being unreasonably old-fashioned in his thinking?

- ☐ Should Chadwick and Delgetti buy the computer on installment right now or wait till they can pay cash? Why?

- ☐ Do you think they have enough information to make a good business decision? Why or why not? What mathematical calculations should they make and what steps should they follow to ensure that their decision is the best one possible?

- ☐ Delgetti estimates that the business might be up to 40 percent more efficient with the computer. How could Delgetti use this figure to determine whether the computer is a good investment for the business?

- ☐ What are the most important factors (mathematical and non-mathematical) for Chadwick and Delgetti to consider in making this decision?

SCENARIO 2   Maria Marquez is an artisan who makes jewelry, hand-sculpted out of gold, silver, and precious stones. She has her own business, Marquez Creations, and rents space in a small complex where other people sell hand-crafted items. Her only real competition is from a commercial jeweler up the street. His inventory is quite different, but Marquez knows he's taking some business away from her because he offers credit, which she does not. Customers may open an account at the competitor's store, Discount Jewelry, and may also use bank cards. Marquez offers neither option. Her business has been strictly cash only; in fact, she often requests payment in advance.

She is thinking, though, about allowing a few established customers to open accounts and pay for their purchases on time. It might make a difference. Her own costs have gone up markedly in the past year, so prices have risen almost 10 percent. It is getting harder for customers to pay cash. Still, the idea of waiting for her money is not appealing.

Marquez does some checking and learns that Discount Jewelry charges a monthly finance rate of 1.5 percent. Marquez's assistant, Calder, suggests going them one better and dropping the rate at Marquez Creations to 1 percent monthly. He thinks that rate will lure customers, but Marquez disagrees. "Any monthly rate will sound low," she tells Calder. "If we're going to do this, let's make it worth our while and charge 2 percent monthly. That way, it won't be so painful to wait for the money." Together they do some figuring and estimate that in the early months, they'll bring in another $500 to $1,000 worth of business per month by offering credit. Still, Marquez is not convinced it's the right decision. There's something appealing about getting your money right on the spot. Perhaps they should consider accepting bank cards but not offering their own credit account; that might be a wise compromise.

Calder strongly disagrees with that option. He is totally persuaded that the store should have its own credit system, but he insists that the 2 percent rate is too high. "If people think we're scalping them, we'll lose more business than we'll gain by offering credit," he tells her.

What do you think? Is it a good idea for Marquez Creations to offer credit to customers? Should they maintain their own accounts, or let the bank do it and just accept customers' bank cards? If they do offer their own credit system, what monthly finance rate do you think they should charge? Is Calder right in thinking that customers will notice the increase from 1.5 to 2 percent, or is he overreacting to a minor difference in rates?

☐ Should Marquez Creations offer its own credit accounts? Or should it just accept bank cards from customers? Or both? Or neither? Why?

☐ If they do establish their own credit system, what do you think the monthly finance charge should be? Why? What factors should they consider in determining this charge?

☐ Do you think Marquez and Calder have enough information right now to make a good business decision? What mathematical calculations should they make and what specific steps should they follow to ensure that their decision is the best one possible?

☐ Suppose that Marquez decides to offer credit and charges 2 percent, only to have competitors follow suit. At that point, would Marquez be wise to raise her rate? Explain.

Annuities, Sinking Funds, and Amortization 18

"I advise you to go on living solely to enrage those who are paying your annuities. It is the only pleasure I have left."

The French philosopher Voltaire wrote these words in a letter to one Madame Du Deffand toward the end of the eighteenth century. In an age when most people had to work all their lives, Voltaire became rich enough to retire by the time he was 40. But while he was a successful writer, the income he earned was nowhere near enough to account for his affluent retirement.

The secret? Voltaire made it known that he would loan money to young noblemen who had not yet received their inheritance but who were eager to have some money to spend. Voltaire charged a straightforward 10 percent annual interest rate; 10 percent per year for the rest of his life, that is. The young men were so eager to get their hands on some cash that they didn't worry about the years ahead. And besides, Voltaire consistently looked so sickly and pale that the noblemen expected him to die any minute, thus freeing them of the need to make any more payments.

Voltaire lived to be 82 ... and needless to say, he died a very rich man.

Because individuals and businesses alike seldom have enough cash to cover all their necessary purchases, they must either borrow to buy what they need or invest money to increase their assets. We usually talk about borrowing or investing in terms of lump sums: Reynolds borrows $50,000 for a new tractor; Plum City Electronics invests $200,000 in a new branch office. In real life, though, whether we're talking about individuals or businesses, lump sum payments are not as common as periodic payments. When money is borrowed, it is usually repaid a little bit at a time. Similarly, individuals and companies usually build toward future investments through a series of periodic deposits. Later, they may withdraw the money the same way, a portion at a time.

Individuals and business managers with an eye on the future often have a pretty good idea how much money they're going to need both for specific future purchases and to cover ongoing expenses. This kind of planning makes money management infinitely more efficient. The reason is simple: Using the kind of math we're going to talk about in this lesson, the money manager who plans ahead can determine just how much must be saved or invested in order to meet future needs.

Of course, all this math would be trivial were it not for two factors: inflation and interest. Both influence the value of money continuously. A dollar does not have the same value today that it had a year ago, nor the value it will have one year from now. Most money that's saved (unless it's tucked away in a cookie jar somewhere) is earning interest. And *all* money, whether it's hiding out in the cookie jar or tied up in stocks on Wall Street, is subject to some erosion from inflation. Ideally, the interest rate on investments will stay ahead of the inflation rate, so that the value of money increases significantly faster than it can decrease.

There are no guarantees about this, of course, and no one's crystal ball is infallible. As we shall see in this lesson, however, money managers can use some very handy formulas to make an educated—and often very realistic—approximation of future needs, then use that information to guide their investing and borrowing.

PART I: INTRODUCING THE MATERIAL

LEARNING OBJECTIVES

Upon completing your study of this lesson, you should be able to:

1. Explain what an annuity is and give several business examples.

2. Know the formula for finding the amount of an annuity and, using a table of annuity values, calculate the amount of an annuity resulting from a specified series of deposits at a fixed interest rate.

3. Define the present value of an annuity and use a table to calculate the present value of an annuity that would result from a specified series of deposits at a fixed interest rate.

4. Given a specified payment plan at a fixed interest rate, calculate the equivalent cash price of the payments.

5. Contrast a sinking fund with an annuity and give business-related examples of the use of sinking funds.

6. Given the interest rate and payment frequency, use a sinking funds table to determine the periodic payment required to produce a specified amount at a point in the future.

7. Establish a sinking funds table for a sinking fund established to produce a specified value from a specified series of payments.

8. Define the concept of amortization and cite business- and consumer-related examples of amortized loans.

9. Given the interest rate and payment frequency, use an amortization table to determine the periodic payment required to pay off the loan at the end of its term.

10. Establish an amortization schedule for a loan with a specified payment schedule and interest rate.

11. Determine the monthly payments necessary to amortize a fixed-rate home mortgage of specified term and interest rate.

12. Determine the total cost and total interest on the purchase of a property, given a mortgage loan of specified term and interest rate.

If you're using the hardcover textbook, *Mathematics for Business*, there are some additional objectives for this lesson. Upon completing your study of the lesson, you should also be able to:

13. Given two proposals with different down payments, interest rates, and periodic payments, use a table of present values to determine which proposal is most advantageous.

14. Determine the payments to a sinking fund required to produce a specified future value that covers both principal and interest (or appreciation or inflation) accumulated over the life of the fund.

LESSON OVERVIEW

The majority of financial transactions in our society are simple, mainly because the amount of money involved is relatively small. For instance, let's say that Ives goes to Northland Bakery and buys a dozen cinnamon rolls for $4. He pays cash. It's an impulse purchase; Ives was only planning to go out for the morning paper, but he smelled the rolls baking and couldn't resist. Well, no matter; a $4 purchase won't make a big dent in Ives's budget. As he's emerging from the bakery, though, he spots the new car he's been wanting across the street. Wouldn't it be nice, he thinks to himself, if he could just stop in at the dealership and buy it, as he did the cinnamon rolls?

Of course, if Ives were as impulsive about automobiles as he is about cinnamon rolls, his budget would soon be in chaos. On the other hand, though, if he had known five years ago that he was going to want that car, he might be in a perfect position to buy it today. Unfortunately, people don't usually plan ahead *that* far—or do they?

When Impulse Spending Won't Work

Like Ives, most people make spur-of-the-moment purchases sometimes; certainly, few of us would want to account for every dollar we spend. At the same time, though, businesses—and most individuals, for that matter—cannot afford to make too many purchases on impulse. They need to plan how much they'll spend and when, and how they'll get the income to cover those expenses. Otherwise, they may wind up spending more money than the business has power to earn.

Take Brightwood Research and Development, for example, where our friend Ives is employed. Let's suppose that Brightwood is a relatively new company, about 10 years old. They feel like they should have a retirement plan; most of their competitors have one and the employees seem enthusiastic. On paper, the concept looks sound enough; employees who have been with the company 10 years or longer will retire on a fixed monthly income based on a total percentage of their earnings.

Ives has done a little multiplication to figure out how much this would be, and in his case it comes to roughly $600 per month. Not a fortune, but combined with other sources of income, he's confident it should make him reasonably comfortable.

Unfortunately, Brightwood hasn't yet been as diligent about its math homework as Ives. The retirement plan looks very sensible on paper, but there's no accompanying investment program to finance it. They've done no projections of how many employees were going to be retiring and when, nor have they yet considered what the monthly expenditure on retirement income would be or how they would finance that expenditure. The result? The retirement plan never gets off the ground.

True enough, our scenario is fictional. But for all too many companies, a mismatch between long-term financial commitments and funding sources is a constant problem. What might Brightwood have done differently? To begin with, it obviously needed to take the time to figure out just what the retirement program would cost before deciding it would be a workable benefit. That information would, in turn, let the company take advantage of a long-term investment tool, such as an annuity account or sinking fund, that can assure a solvent retirement program. Let's take a closer look at the benefits and procedures associated with these two investment approaches, beginning with annuities.

Annuities: More Than Insurance Plans

When many people hear the term *annuity*, they think at once of a series of payments made by a life insurance company when a person retires. This is one form of annuity, but it's not the only one. In the broader sense, an annuity is *any series of equal, periodic payments.* Those payments might be part of a retirement program or investment program or the repayment of a loan. Home mortgage payments are a kind of annuity. So are car loan payments or Social Security benefits. Within the context of this lesson, we'll *generally* be talking about an annuity as a series of equal periodic *deposits* designed to create an account from which the investor can later make equal periodic withdrawals. Keep in mind, though, that if *either* the payments into or withdrawals from the account are equal and periodic, the account is an annuity.

The time between payments to the account is known as the *payment period.* For instance, let's say that Alice Kent is saving to return to college and has set up a fund into which she makes quarterly deposits of $1,000. (Alice could, of course, invest her money more often if she wished, or vary the amount. But then she would not have an annuity.) The time from the beginning of the first payment period to the end of the last payment period is known as the *term of the annuity.*

Let's say that Kent must continue her quarterly deposits of $1,000 for a period of five years in order to have enough to finance her schooling. In that case, the term of the annuity is five years. Keep in mind, by the way, that Alice, like many persons with an annuity, will not take out all the money in one lump sum when she enrolls at the university. She'll take out as much as she needs to finance her first term's tuition and leave the rest intact to continue earning interest until she needs to make another withdrawal. This gradual withdrawal of funds increases the value of the annuity in the long run.

The *amount of the annuity* is the final sum on deposit. Alice has what is known as a *simple annuity*, one in which the deposit dates match the compounding period. As we've pointed out, this is not necessary, but it does simplify calculations. The formula for determining the amount of the annuity looks complex but isn't; that's because the complicated part has already been done for us and listed in a table. Let's see how it works, using Alice's example.

Calculating
Annuity Values

We'll suppose that her money is deposited at a rate of 12 percent, compounded quarterly. We need to use a special formula: $S = R \times s_{\overline{n}|i}$. In this formula, think of S as the sum total of the annuity's value. R stands for the amount of each deposit; in this case, $1,000. The amount of the deposit is multiplied by the value of $s_{\overline{n}|i}$ pronounced *s angle n at i*. This value, given in the form of a decimal number, comes from a special table; you'll find an appropriate table in your textbook. You can tell if you've got the right table because you'll see the $s_{\overline{n}|i}$.

Use the table this way: Remember that n equals the number of periods in the term of the annuity. In this case, since Alice is making quarterly deposits for five years, that number will be 4×5, or 20. The i stands for the interest rate, which in this case is 12 percent annually, or 3 percent per quarter: $12/4 = 3$. Thus, we look up the figure for $s_{\overline{20}|3}$, and that figure is 26.87037449. We simply multiply this figure by $1,000, the amount of each quarterly deposit, to find the total value of the annuity at the end of the term: $26,870.37. What we've learned from this calculation is that by making $1,000 deposits every three months for five years, Kent ends up with almost $27,000 dollars.

In our example, Kent has what is known as an *ordinary annuity*, which means that she makes her deposits at the end of the compounding period. Most annuities work this way. But suppose Alice deposited her money at the *beginning* of the current period, on October 1. In that case, she would have what is known as an *annuity due*, for which the full amount is calculated a little differently. We use the same formula and the same table, but *add one period* to account for the interest earned by the early deposit of the first $1,000, making the total number of periods 21. This changes the $s_{\overline{n}|i}$ figure to 28.67648572, making the total $1,000 $\times$ 28.67648572 = $28,676.49. But remember, though Alice earned interest for 21 periods, she didn't make 21 *deposits*; she made only 20. So, to find the final, true total for an annuity due, we must subtract $1,000 from this preliminary total: $28,676.49 − $1,000 = $27,676.49. As you can see, the difference between an ordinary annuity and an annuity due is not very great—about 1 percent in our example.

We should also point out that Alice is the holder of an *annuity certain*, one that makes definite payments to the investor (or a beneficiary) over a specified period of time. This makes perfect sense for her situation since she is investing with a specific goal in mind (her college tuition) and has a definite date when she'll stop making deposits. A retirement plan that pays benefits for 10 years is another example of an annuity certain, as are the 60 payments needed to pay off a car loan.

Not all annuities are set up this way, though. A *contingent annuity* has variable beginning or ending dates. As its name implies, those dates are contingent upon the occurrence of some other event. Perhaps the most common example is an insurance policy that pays a fixed sum per month beginning at a certain age but ending with the insured's death. Since the number of payments to be made can't be known in advance, such a payment plan is said to be a contingent annuity.

**Gambling on
Contingent
Annuities**

Any contingent annuity based on a person's projected lifespan is a kind of gamble. People who live longer than the average get a better deal than they paid for, largely because people who die sooner than average collect less. Let's say, for instance, that Frank Miller invests in an annuity that pays him or his surviving spouse, Elly Miller, a fixed sum of $1,000 per month from age 65 until the death of the surviving spouse. This may sound like a good deal on the face of it, but is it really? The answer depends entirely on how long Frank and Elly live.

The mathematics involved in calculating contingent annuities involve a knowledge of probability theory that goes well beyond what we're prepared to present here, but we can oversimplify a bit to make a point. Let's say that Frank and Elly initiated their annuity fund at age 25, so they've been contributing to it for 40 years, investing a total of $60,000 during that time. Of course, the fund is worth considerably more than that; remember, those contributions have been earning compound interest from the beginning. Now let's say that the mortality tables predict that Frank will live to be 75, Elly 80. If they live exactly that long, the amount they collect in payments will be exactly what they "deserve," taking into account the interest they earn and the administrative fees charged by the insurance company.

Suppose, though, that Elly lives to be 90. If so, the insurance company will have to pay 10 extra years of benefits. But Frank and Elly didn't pay anything additional to cover these 10 extra years. The money for the payments came from someone who died sooner than the tables expected and who therefore collected fewer benefits than average. The decision to invest in such an annuity is, therefore, largely a gamble based on how longevity matches against the mortality tables.

It might occur to you that insurance companies need to be very precise in estimating the amount of money they will need to cover annuity payments to people like the Millers. Quite right. They review the mortality tables carefully, check out the current health of their clients, and use sophisticated probability statistics to make the most precise predictions possible about the amount of money they'll spend and when. This information determines what rates of interest the company will pay on an annuity investment and how large individual annuity payments will be.

**Present Value:
How Much
Is It Worth Now?**

Most of us, when thinking of investing money, try to imagine how much a given sum will grow to in the future, given a specified interest rate and schedule for investing. That's a common way of thinking about investments, and it works fine for the sort of open-ended savings plan in which the investor has no prespecified financial goal, perhaps because he or she is investing everything that present budgetary constraints will allow.

Sometimes, though, when future needs are known, it is helpful to turn things around and to think of how much some future sum would be worth today; in other words, if an investor needed $50,000 at the end of 10 years, how much would she need to invest at, say, 10 percent compounded annually to meet that goal?

When we're discussing annuities, there are two ways to think about the concept of *present value*:

1. The present value is the lump sum that, if deposited all at once *right now*, would eventually grow into the same total as the periodic deposits by which investors normally contribute to an annuity, *or*

2. The present value is a lump sum that, if deposited today, would permit the depositor to make withdrawals of some prespecified amount sometime in the future.

Remember Alice Kent, our prospective college student? Let's use her situation to look at present value in each of these two ways. Remember that Alice was making $1,000 deposits quarterly, a sensible way of building an annuity fund. Now granted, most people do not save for their college education by making one gigantic deposit in the bank. But when we're considering present value, the question is *what if* the investor did that? In other words, if Alice were to set up her annuity fund with just one big deposit, how much would she need to put in in order to have as much as she'd acquire through quarterly deposits of $1,000?

The formula for determining present value is very similar to that for determining the total value of an annuity at the end of the term. The big difference is that we'll be using a different table to look up the information needed to solve the problem. We begin with $A = R \times a_{\overline{n}|i}$ in which A equals the amount of the lump sum deposit, R equals the amount of the regular quarterly payments, and $a_{\overline{n}|i}$ is the figure from the table used to determine the present value of an annuity.

Recall that Alice is saving for five years, at 12 percent compounded quarterly. Thus, there are 20 investment periods and the interest per quarter is 3 percent. Given these figures, the table for present value of an annuity tells us that $a_{\overline{n}|i}$ is 14.87747486, so we must multiply the $1,000 by 14.87747486, and the result is $14,877.47. In other words, Alice would need to deposit just under $15,000 in *one lump sum* in order to have in her account, at the end of five years, the same $27,000 she'd earn by investing *$1,000* per quarter. And, of course, if Alice had the $15,000 to invest this way, she could do so, knowing that her future educational needs were thus taken care of.

Buyers do comparison shopping all the time. But sellers can do that, too. In fact, the concept of present value makes it essential. For example, let's say that Ed Neeley is going to sell his classic 1930s Cadillac and he has two prospective buyers, who make very different offers. Neeley isn't sure which offer is the better deal for him, and since they're so different, it's hard to know how to begin comparing them. Our formula for present value can help because it puts the two offers into comparable terms. Let's see how this works.

Freeman offers $70,000 cash. Olson offers $25,000 down and $5,000 twice a year for five years. Now, if we just totaled the money that Olson is offering, $25,000 plus $50,000 ($5,000 × 2 × 5), we'd come up with $75,000, which makes that offer a little better. But is it? Remember our early point about the constantly changing value of money. In order to compare the two offers fairly, we need to determine the *present* value of Olson's proposed $5,000 semiannual annuity.

Let's say that Neeley knows that money can be invested at 10 percent compounded twice yearly. In that case, there will be 10 compounding periods (twice per year for five years), and the compound rate per period will be 5 percent (10% ÷ 2). The R in the formula for present value of an annuity is $5,000; that's how much Olson will contribute with each pay-

**Analyzing the
Value of Payments
over Time**

ment. Using the table for present value of an annuity, we find the value of $a_{\overline{n}|i}$ to be 7.72173493. Thus,

$$A = R\, a_{\overline{n}|i}$$
$$A = \$5,000 \times 7.72173493$$
$$A = \$38,608.67$$

In other words, Olson's annuity would be worth a little less than $37,000. But we must add to this the amount of the down payment: $25,000 + $37,608.67 = $62,608.67. Notice that while Olson would *eventually* pay more than Freeman, the present value of Olson's offer is much less. But we couldn't be sure of that until we put them into equal terms. That $62,608.67 figure, by the way, is known as the *equivalent cash price*. In other words, Olson's offer, as it stands, has the same value as if he were paying just over $62,000 in cash for the classic car. Which is to say that Neeley should prefer Freeman's $70,000 cash offer.

Sinking Funds for Business Investments

As we indicated earlier in this chapter, the most successful businesses tend to be those that anticipate their needs and plan to meet them. You might recall, for instance, our initial example with Ives and the Brightwood retirement fund. Ideally, a company with a retirement program determines what it needs to finance such a program, then invests accordingly to ensure that its commitment can be met.

Similarly, a company might put aside money to cover a very specific purchase: new equipment, for instance, the remodeling of an office, or the construction of a new store or warehouse. Some companies issue bonds in order to raise money needed to get the company started or to promote expansion, then design investments to cover the payment and interest on those bonds as they mature. Whatever the nature of the purchase or expenditure, the basic idea is not much different from that of a family making regular savings deposits that will go toward a vacation or a new house. The fund set up to receive these deposits is known as a *sinking fund*, and the deposits are one form of *annuity* payment.

With an ordinary annuity, the amount to be invested is known; what's unsure is how much the accumulated investments will be worth at some point in the future. With a sinking fund, the question is turned around. The amount that's needed in the future is known; the question is, how much must the investor set aside at a given rate of interest in order to ensure that the money will be there?

Let's suppose, for instance, that Oxidation Chemicals is planning to install new pollution control equipment in five years. The cost will be $200,000. The company wants to set up a sinking fund to cover this cost and can invest the money at 8 percent compounded quarterly. The question is, how much must Oxidation set aside each quarter?

To find out, we use the formula for the value of each payment into a sinking fund, $R = S \times (1 \div s_{\overline{n}|i})$. Like the other formulas in this lesson, this one looks considerably more formidable than it is, since (as with the others) most of the math has been done for us and incorporated into a handy table. In this formula, R represents the amount of the monthly payment, in this case unknown, while S represents the total needed at the end of the term. Values for $(1 \div s_{\overline{n}|i})$ are given in a sinking fund table. As usual, to use the table, we must determine both n, or the total number of compounding periods, and i, the interest rate. In this case, there will be 20 compounding periods (4 times per year × 5 years). The annual 8 percent rate translates to 2 percent per quarter. And S, the amount needed, is $200,000. So the formula becomes

R = \$200,000 \times 0.04115672 (from the table)

R = \$8,231.34

In other words, Oxidation Chemicals must contribute a bit over $8,000 quarterly to its sinking fund for five years in order to finance the purchase of the pollution control equipment.

Notice that there are several ways the company could use this information. For instance, suppose they cannot afford this kind of contribution. Better to know that now while there is still time to plan. They may be able to establish a fund that pays a better rate of investment, in which case their quarterly contributions can be lower. Or they may need to sell stock, issue bonds, borrow a portion of the money, or find some other way of raising the needed capital.

If they do have the money for the sinking fund, they can buy their $200,000 of pollution control equipment with about $164,000. But if they have to borrow the money, Oxidation will pay well over $200,000 due to the interest that must be paid on the borrowed amount. In fact, they'll pay more in interest on the loan than they're able to earn on their investments. This is a common situation. Banks and other lending institutions must charge more interest on money lent out than they pay on money taken in through deposits. After all, banks, like any business, must earn a profit on what they sell; banks "sell" the use of money. If the interest rates on money going out were the same as on money invested, then it would be very difficult for banks to come out ahead. So this *interest rate spread*, or the difference between rates on loans and rates paid on deposits, is essential to keep the lending institution in operation.

Amortization: Buy Now and Pay for Quite a While

Annuities and sinking funds provide two creative ways of taking care of tomorrow's spending needs. But what about today? Some purchases are too expensive to afford right now, yet they won't wait.

Let's say that a progressive little company, Cliff's Catering, has set up an annuity to take care of the retirement needs of the company's six employees. They have a sinking fund to cover the cost of that new refrigeration unit they anticipate needing in about four years. A model of planning and investing, right? Unfortunately, they need a bigger delivery truck *right now*. This purchase cannot be put off; they're losing business because they can't serve bigger clients. This is a purchase that makes sense, but they don't have the money to cover it. They'll have to borrow the money.

Repayment schedules on loans may be set up in all sorts of ways, but perhaps the most common is to *amortize* the loan. Amortization implies that the principal and total interest will be paid off through a series of equal periodic payments. It is commonplace for loans on homes or other real estate (including land) to be amortized. Similarly, loans on trucks and automobiles, farm machinery, office equipment, or virtually any major purchase may be amortized. The key is that the payments on an amortized loan are equal in size and each covers a portion of the interest owed as well as a portion of the principal.

The formula for determining the amount of each payment on an amortized loan is much like those we've used previously. Again, it's essential to know the rate of interest and the compounding period. This information allows the user to extract the right figure from an amortization table. For instance, let's say Marie Haas buys land for $50,000. She pays $20,000 down and amortizes the remaining $30,000 at 10 percent compounded quarterly for 10 years. To find out what her quarterly payments will be, we use the formula $R = A \times (1 \div a_{\overline{n}|i})$, in which A represents the amount of the amortized loan and R is the amount of each payment. Since the interest rate is 10 percent per year, that translates into 2.5 percent per quarter for 40 payment periods. Thus, the amount of each payment will be $30,000 × .03983623 (from the table for amortization), or about $1,195.

While amortized loan payments are all equal, the amount of each payment that goes toward principal or interest is *not* equal across the term of the loan. After all, when the loan is first made, the principal is large and so is the resultant interest. But at the end of the loan, there's relatively little principal on which to charge interest. If the loan weren't amortized, payments toward the beginning of the loan would be huge, while payments at the end would be tiny. With amortization, borrowers spend proportionately more paying off interest early in the repayment period and apply proportionately less toward principal. The payments are all equal, but the split between the amount going to interest and the amount going to principal changes dramatically. With a 30-year mortgage, for instance (one form of amortized loan), a buyer may be paying only a few dollars a month toward principal during the first year or two of the loan. The remainder is eaten up by interest. But in the last year of the loan, almost all of the payment is used to reduce the principal.

We can check to see, for instance, how much interest Marie Haas pays on her first $1,195 payment and how much goes to principal. She owes $30,000. We can determine the interest on this amount for the first period using the simple interest formula $I = PRT$. Remember that the first period is one-fourth of a year and the annual interest rate is 10 percent. Thus, the interest owed for the first quarter is $30,000 × .10 × ¼, or $750. Marie's first payment is $1,195. Of that, $750 goes toward interest. This means that $1,195 − $750, or only $445, is applied toward the principal. Following her first payment, Marie still owes $30,000 − $445, or $29,555, on her land. The second quarter, Marie will owe $29,555 × .10 × ¼ = $738.86 in interest. Notice that it's gone down just a little, which means that the amount going to pay off the loan is increasing. Gradually, over time, the proportions reverse themselves, so that toward the end of the borrowing period, the buyer with an amortized loan is spending a larger portion of each payment on principal and a much smaller portion on interest. But this takes time, and it's sometimes astonishing to buyers to find out how slowly those big house payments are actually buying the house.

Amortize — or Set Up a Sinking Fund?

You may be wondering why, when amortization is so convenient, anyone would go to the trouble of setting up a sinking fund. There are several reasons. First, keep in mind that an amortized loan puts the buyer in the position of a borrower, who must then repay that loan at the lender's rate of interest. With a sinking fund, on the other hand, the buyer is still spending money, but it is money that, temporarily at least, is *earning interest* for the buyer rather than costing the buyer interest. This means that in the long run, the buyer who uses a sinking fund to increase assets can make the same purchase at a lower total cost than the buyer who amortizes a loan to cover the purchase.

The difference can be dramatic. Imagine Kelso, one of the world's most patient prospective homeowners. Instead of taking out a 30-year mortgage on the house of her dreams, Kelso sets up a 30-year sinking fund to save the money necessary to pay cash for the house. You might be surprised that the total Kelso would have to put away to buy the house will likely be less than *10 percent* of what it would cost the more normal buyer who amortizes the loan.

Of course, sinking funds require advance planning, and almost no one would approach home buying as Kelso did. A young couple wanting a house, for instance, may not be willing to wait a decade or two for a sinking fund to mature. (And even if they were, the price of their dream house is likely rising yearly, perhaps rising faster in some years than the value of their sinking fund.) All in all, amortization provides a useful way of satisfying immediate needs when there isn't time to plan or the will to wait.

SOME WORDS OF ADVICE

The need to plan for the future is implicit in every part of this lesson. Impulse buying may be fine for small purchases, but it is not a wise investment strategy for large sums of money. Annuities and sinking funds, by nature, are tools for creating future financial security. But to use either well, it is important for the individual or business to have clear-cut financial goals, to have some sort of timelines for saving and spending in mind, and to know what return is afforded by the intended investment. As we've seen, the value of money changes over time. But the process is not magical; it's simply a reflection of the sometimes amazing effect of compound interest.

Knowing what kind of investment approach to use in a given situation is important. Keep in mind that a sinking fund creates a large sum of money that's usually targeted to a specific purchase. A business may use a sinking fund, for instance, to cover the purchase of new equipment. An annuity, on the other hand, is usually used to provide funding for an extended period. An annuity might be set up to fund an individual's retirement or education, for instance.

When it comes to setting up a program of either sort, it pays to compare options. Interest rates may be considerably higher with some programs than others, and in the case of an annuity, this difference will translate into higher monthly or quarterly payments to the investor somewhere down the road. (That half-point difference that made almost no difference when you select a 90-day certificate of deposit looms a lot bigger for a 30-year annuity.) Further, some programs offer more options for making withdrawals than others. While this isn't important to every investor, some like knowing they'll have the option to take their investment return in the form of one lump sum *or* relatively higher payments for a limited, guaranteed time *or* relatively lower payments for life.

If you find yourself offered a payment plan instead of a lump sum payment, the concept of present value can help you select the better deal. Keep in mind that money in the hand today is generally worth more than money in the future *if* the amounts are equal. But they may not be. Trying to compare a cash payment to a series of payments can seem like comparing apples to oranges; sometimes the amount that looks smaller is really larger in the long run. Present value makes the two approaches comparable, so it's simple to determine which offer is more attractive.

Amortization is such a convenient way of paying for a large purchase that it's become very commonplace in our business world. It's fair to say that most consumers amortize a loan at some point in their business or personal lives, so it makes sense to keep a few precautions in mind. First, though this seems very basic, it's well to ensure that the payments are manageable.

It's also worth doing a simple multiplication to find out how much those payments are going to add up to. Sometimes, the result can be a bit surprising. Keep in mind that when a loan is amortized, the total purchase price (down payment plus the sum of all monthly payments) will exceed the original asking price — usually by a substantial amount. The difference depends on the size of the down payment (which is subtracted directly from the asking price and is therefore applied only to principal, not interest) and on the interest charged on the loan. Suffice to say, though, that there's a certain irony in watching a $10,000 car that really costs $15,000 depreciate down to $2,000. (There's not much to be done about this situation, but it's at least nice to understand what's happening.)

Monthly payments on an amortized loan are equal, but the proportion of each payment that goes toward interest is far higher early in the term of the loan than it is later on, when a larger portion goes toward the principal. This means, in practical terms, that the buyer doesn't make much headway early on toward reducing the size of the loan. Don't make the mistake of thinking that just because you've made $50,000 in payments on your $150,000 mortgage, it would take about $100,000 to pay off the loan. In reality, most of that money went to pay interest and you've likely reduced the principal by only a few thousand dollars.

KEY TERMS

Before you read through the text assignment and watch the video program, take a minute to look at the key terms associated with this lesson. When you encounter them in the text and video program, pay careful attention to their meaning.

Amortization schedule: A table showing the equal payment necessary to pay off a loan for a specific amount of money, including interest, for a specific amount of time.

Amortized loan: A loan on which principal and interest are paid off through a sequence of equal (but disproportionately allocated) payments.

Amount of an annuity: The sum of the compound amounts of all the periodic payments into an annuity, compounded to the end of the term; in other words, the total value of an annuity at the end of the term.

Annuity: A series of equal periodic payments.

Annuity certain: An annuity with fixed beginning and ending dates.

Annuity due: An annuity whose payments are made at the beginning of each payment period (and therefore draw interest throughout the period).

Contingent annuity: An annuity with variable beginning or ending date.

Equivalent cash price: A single amount today equal to the present value of an annuity; in other words, the equivalent amount a buyer would need to pay if he or she were paying cash rather than making periodic payments.

Interest rate spread: The difference between the interest rate charged on loans and that paid (by the same institution) on deposits.

Ordinary annuity: An annuity whose payment is made at the end of a given period of time.

Payment period: The time between payments into an annuity.

Present value of an annuity: (1) A lump sum that, if deposited today, would eventually grow into an amount equivalent to the final total produced through periodic payments into an annuity; or (2) a lump sum that, if deposited today, would permit periodic withdrawals of a specified amount for a specified period in the future.

Simple annuity: An annuity in which payment or contribution dates match the compounding period (e.g., annuity payments are made quarterly and interest is compounded quarterly).

Sinking fund: A fund set up to receive equal periodic payments in order to pay off an obligation at some fixed time in the future.

Term of an annuity: The time from the beginning of the first payment period until the end of the final payment period.

PART II: WATCHING THE VIDEO PROGRAM

VIDEO VIEWING GUIDE

Before watching the video program, review the following questions. As you watch, be sure to collect the information necessary to answer them:

1. In your own words, how would you define the concept of an annuity? Give three different examples of annuities.

2. For what purposes would an individual or business set up an annuity? A sinking fund? Would those purposes differ and, if so, why?

3. Give one example of an *annuity certain* and one example of a *contingent annuity*.

4. Explain why a *sinking fund* could be considered one form of annuity, and then explain how a sinking fund is different from an annuity.

5. Describe the influence of inflation on the value of a sinking fund or an annuity.

6. Define the concept of *present value* as it relates to an annuity and explain how a business investor, seller, or lender might use this information.

7. Why are loans amortized? What are some advantages and disadvantages of amortized loans?

8. Under what circumstances might a small business set up a sinking fund to cover a business expense? Under what circumstances might it choose to amortize a loan to cover the same expense? What are some similarities and differences in these two financing approaches?

VIDEO PROGRAM

This lesson's video program is Program 17—Annuities, Sinking Funds, and Amortization. Remember, if you are watching this program on videotape, take time to replay sections of the tape any time you need to review a concept.

VIDEO VIEWING QUESTIONS

Immediately after viewing the video program for Lesson 17, take time to respond to the following questions. Give your answers some careful thought; they may provide the basis for additional discussion or a longer written response.

1. Suppose that you are 25 years old and want to retire at age 60 on an income of $3,000 per month. You could just put extra income in the bank and save for your retirement, or you could set up an annuity. Name two advantages that the annuity would offer over simply setting up a savings account.

   a. _____

   b. _____

2. Name two purposes for which a small business might set up an annuity.

   a. _____

   b. _____

3. Suppose that a friend who manages a small business wishes to establish a fund to finance retirement benefits for 10 employees. The oldest employee will retire in five years. Would you recommend an annuity or a sinking fund? Explain your reasons.

   _____

   _____

4. In your own words, describe the difference between an annuity certain and a contingent annuity, and provide one example of each.

   _____

   _____

5. For which of the following decisions would knowledge of present value be critical? (Check as many as apply.)

_____ Deciding between two offers on a piece of real estate

_____ Choosing between two annuity programs offered by different companies

_____ Deciding whether to set up a sinking fund or amortize a loan to pay for a purchase

_____ Determining the amount of each periodic payment into a sinking fund

_____ Determining the amount of an annuity at the end of the term

_____ Deciding between a contingent annuity and an annuity certain

6. In your own words, state the major purpose for amortizing a loan, from the consumer's (buyer's) perspective.

_____

_____

7. Name the primary advantage to an amortized loan, from the seller's perspective.

_____

_____

8. Name one circumstance under which an amortized loan could work to the *seller's* disadvantage.

_____

_____

9. Which of the following would most likely be influenced by inflation? (Check as many as apply.)

_____ The amount of an annuity

_____ The present value of an annuity

_____ The interest rate paid on an annuity

_____ The interest rate paid on a sinking fund

_____ The cost-effectiveness of amortizing a loan

_____ The availability of amortized loans

_____ The cost-effectiveness of setting up a sinking fund

PART III: FOCUSING ON THE MATHEMATICS

READING ASSIGNMENT

After watching the video program, you should read one of the following Text Assignments, depending on the textbook you're using:

SOFTCOVER: Chapter 9, pages 351-370, and Chapter 10, pages 407-422, of the Miller, Salzman, and Hoelzle softcover text, *Business Mathematics*.

HARDCOVER: Chapter 15 of the Salzman, Miller, and Hoelzle hardcover text, *Mathematics for Business*, pages 511-544.

As you read through the text, pay careful attention to the examples the book gives of the mathematics associated with the concepts you're learning about.

Then, after you've completed the text assignment, read through the Key Formulas below. This section provides a handy review of what you've learned. By the time you get to this point in the lesson, all of the formulas and calculations should be familiar to you. If they're not, go back and read the appropriate parts of the text and the Overview section of this lesson. You won't have much success completing the rest of your assignments if you are still confused about the information in the Key Formulas section.

KEY FORMULAS

The following key formulas are important to your understanding of this lesson. Be sure that you know each one and how to use it in solving problems related to annuities, sinking funds, and amortization.

KEY FORMULA: $S = R \times s_{\overline{n}|i}$

Formula used for: Determining the amount (final total sum on deposit) of a simple annuity.

Example:

Teller Enterprises invests $1,000 quarterly for five years in an account paying 12 percent compounded quarterly. What is the value of the annuity at the end of this five-year term? In this formula, R represents the amount of the quarterly investment. We look up the figure for $s_{\overline{n}|i}$, keeping in mind that the quarterly interest rate is 3 percent (12% ÷ 4), and the number of compounding periods is 20 (5 years × 4 periods per year). For this problem, the value of $s_{\overline{n}|i}$ is 26.87037449. Thus, the value of the annuity at the end of the term will be $1,000 × 26.89037449, or $26,890.37 (rounded).

Remember that in this formula:

1. S represents the value of the annuity, or the total amount on deposit, at the end of the term.

2. R represents the amount of the periodic deposit, in this case $1,000.

2. R represents the amount of the periodic deposit, in this case $1,000.

3. The value for $s_{\overline{n}|i}$ has already been calculated for you, and can be determined from the appropriate table for *amount of annuity*. Be careful to use the correct table (or the correct column within a larger table) in looking up this amount.

4. Be sure, in using the table, to calculate the interest rate for the *compounding period*, which in most cases is only a portion of the annual interest rate. In this case, the compounding period is one quarter and the rate is *3 percent*.

5. This formula is designed only for simple annuities, or those in which the payment period matches the compounding period.

6. The formula assumes that the annuity is an *ordinary annuity*, or one in which payments are made at the end of the payment period. To determine the value of an annuity due, or one in which payments are made at the beginning of the payment period, increase the value of *n* by one. Then deduct the amount of one payment (or deposit) from the final total. In this instance, that would change the final total to $1,000 × 28.67648572 = $28,676.49 − $1,000 = $27,676.49.

KEY FORMULA: $A = R \times a_{\overline{n}|i}$

Formula used for: Finding the present value of an annuity in which *R* dollars are deposited for *n* periods at an interest of *i*.

Example:

Gloria Deets has set up a 10-year annuity with quarterly contributions of $500 at 8 percent compounded quarterly. As an alternative, what if Gloria were to invest her money in one lump sum now? How much would she need to invest in order to wind up with the same total that her $500 quarterly contributions will produce at the end of 10 years? To answer this question, we first determine *n* and *i*, then use the proper table to find the value of $a_{\overline{n}|i}$. In this case, *n* is equal to 40 (4 periods per year for 10 years), and *i* is equal to 2 percent (8% ÷ 4). Using the table for *present value of annuity* we find that $a_{\overline{n}|i}$ is equal to 27.35547924. Thus, the present value is $500 × 27.35547924 = $13,677,74. This is the amount Gloria would need to deposit today if she wanted to create an annuity of comparable value with a single deposit.

Remember that in this formula:

1. A equals the present value of the annuity.

2. R equals the amount of the periodic deposit, in this case $500.

3. The value of $a_{\overline{n}|i}$ is taken from a table and need not be calculated separately. But it is important to use the correct table: *present value of annuity*.

4. This formula is useful only when the values for *n* and *i* are known. Keep in mind that *i* represents the periodic interest rate (versus the annual interest rate), and *n* represents the total number of compounding periods (not just the number per year).

KEY FORMULA: $R = S \times (1 \div s_{\overline{n}|i})$

Formula used for: Determining the amount of each payment that must be made into a sinking fund in order to produce a final value of S, given n periods and an interest rate of i.

Example:

Preston Heating Co. wants to create a sinking fund to pay off $100,000 worth of bonds that will come due in five years. The interest rate available is 8 percent compounded annually; Preston will make annual contributions. How much must they contribute each year? In this case, $n = 5$, since contributions are made annually and interest is compounded annually; $i = 8$ percent. And $S = \$100,000$, the total amount needed at the end of the eight years. The figure for $(1 \div s_{\overline{n}|i})$ is taken from the table for *sinking fund* values. Thus, $R = \$100,000 \times .09401476 = \$9,401.47$. In other words, Preston will need to contribute just over $9,000 annually in order to reach its goal and pay off the bonds.

Remember that in this formula:

1. R equals the amount of each periodic payment.

2. S equals the total amount desired in the sinking fund.

3. The value of $(1 \div s_{\overline{n}|i})$ has already been calculated and can be taken from the *sinking fund* values table. *Be sure to use the correct table.*

4. As always, the values of n and i must be determined before the table can be used. Keep in mind that n equals the total number of periodic payments, while i equals the effective rate of interest for the compounding period.

Key Formula: $R = A (1 \div a_{\overline{n}|i})$

Formula used for: Determining the periodic payment, R, needed to amortize a loan of A dollars for n periods at an interest rate of i.

Example:

Pete Sills buys a piece of land for $15,000. He pays $5,000 down and amortizes the rest over a period of three years with quarterly payments at a rate of 20 percent compounded quarterly. What will Pete's quarterly payments be? In this case $n = 12$ (4 payments per year $\times$ 3 years) and $i = 5$ percent (20% $\div$ 4). The amount amortized is $10,000 ($15,000 minus the $5,000 down payment). And the value of $(1 \div a_{\overline{n}|i})$ is taken from the table for *amortization* rates. Thus, $R = \$10,000 \times .11282541 = \$1,128.25$. In other words, Pete will pay about $1,100 four times a year for three years in order to pay off the balance on the land.

Remember that in this formula:

1. R equals the amount of each periodic payment.

2. A equals the total amount amortized. This is often less than the asking price if the buyer, like Pete, makes a down payment. Remember to subtract the amount of the down payment from the total cost before inserting figures into the formula.

3. The value of $(1 \div a_{\overline{n}|i})$ has already been calculated and can be taken from the table on *amortization* values. Be sure to use the correct table.

4. The total cost of a purchase with an amortized loan is always higher than the cash price because of interest. In this case, the total amount that Pete Sills pays for the land is $5,000 (the down payment) + $1,128.25 (the amount of each payment) × 12 (the number of payments), or $18,539. Thus, he pays more than $3,000 over the cash price.

_____**DON'T FORGET**

1. With annuities, sinking funds, and amortization, much of the math has already been done for you, so that you need only take the appropriate values from a table (or perhaps your business calculator) and insert them into the right formula. But it is critical to use both the right formula *and* the right table. So the first question to ask is, what is the value you are trying to find?

2. Present value can be interpreted two ways. It can mean either (1) the lump sum amount that, if deposited today, would eventually have a value equal to periodic deposits made over the same period of time at the same interest rate; or (2) a lump sum that, if deposited today, would permit periodic withdrawals of a given amount for a given period beginning at a specified date in the future. Regardless of how it is defined, the same formula is used to solve for the value.

3. A sinking fund is a type of annuity, a series of periodic payments. The primary difference is that when you solve for a regular annuity, the amount of the periodic payments is known and the value of the final amount on deposit is unknown. With a sinking fund, the value of the final amount on deposit is predetermined; what is unknown is the amount of each periodic payment necessary to produce that value.

4. In solving for the amount of each payment on an amortized loan, remember to deduct the amount of the down payment first. Only the loan balance is amortized; don't make the mistake of using the purchase price in your calculations.

_____

PART IV: SOLVING BUSINESS PROBLEMS
_____

_____**PROBLEM SETS**

Work the following problems in your textbook. Your instructor will tell you which problems, if any, are to be turned in. Some of the problems have answers provided in the back of the book; refer to these answers to make sure you are working the problems correctly.

SOFTCOVER: If you are using the Miller, Salzman, and Hoelzle softcover text, *Business Mathematics*, do the following problem sets:

9.4: Problems #8, 9, 14-16, and 21-25 on pages 355-356.

9.5: Problems #10-14 (all) and 16-24 (even numbers only) on pages 361-362.

9.6: Problems #14-22 (even numbers only) on pages 368-370.

10.4: Problems #17-20 on page 412.

HARDCOVER: If you are using the Salzman, Miller, and Hoelzle hardcover text, *Mathematics for Business*, do the following problem sets:

15.1: Problems #10-12, 19-20, 23-27 (all), and 32-48 (even numbers only) on pages 517-519.

15.2: Problems #22-36 (even numbers only) on pages 525-526.

15.3: Problems #2-24 (even numbers only) on pages 530-532.

15.4: Problems #16-36 (even numbers only) on pages 542-543.

BUSINESS APPLICATIONS

Read each of the following scenarios and answer the questions about the decisions you would make in each situation. Give these questions some serious thought; they may be used as the basis for discussion or the development of a more complex essay. You should base your decisions on what you've learned from this lesson, applying both math skills and good business judgment to solve the problem at hand.

SCENARIO 1

Bill Conklin runs a garbage service on a lake with no road access. Business has grown in the past three years, and Bill is run ragged trying to keep up, given that he has only one small boat with a 25 horsepower motor. He feels he can get by for two more years—possibly three—but at the end of that time, he will need a larger pontoon boat and a 75 horsepower motor to keep up with the demand for his services. The boat he's considering costs $25,000 now, and prices are expected to rise at about 10 percent compounded quarterly.

The dealer who sells the boats is urging Bill to buy now, "before prices go up." The dealer is willing to take Bill's current boat on trade and values it at about $5,000; that amount can be deducted from the price of the new boat. The dealer is willing to finance the balance at a rate of 16 percent compounded quarterly for a period of three years. During that time, Bill would make quarterly payments on the pontoon. Bill hasn't quite figured how all this breaks out. He thinks he could afford to spend roughly $400 per month right now, and his income is rising steadily but slowly.

He hates the idea of going into debt, though, and the local banker has suggested setting up a sinking fund. He offers a rate of 12 percent, compounded quarterly. The appealing part of this option, from Bill's perspective, is that it would let him accumulate the cash he needs to cover the cost of the pontoon without having to borrow money from anyone. He could still trade in his present boat for a down payment, though of course the value of his old boat and motor are likely to decline over the next few years while the price of the new boat is going up. All in all, which would be the more financially sound decision? Bill isn't sure.

What do you think? Should Bill set up the sinking fund for the pontoon? Or would it make better business sense to buy the boat now, since he obviously needs it, and simply amortize the loan? Which approach is more affordable for Bill in his present situation? Is his current income sufficient to make either option realistic?

- ☐ Should Bill buy the boat now and amortize the loan? Or would he be better off to set up a sinking fund? Explain your answer.

- ☐ What are the comparative *total costs* to Bill, given these two options?

- ☐ Name at least one advantage that each option offers from Bill's current perspective.

- ☐ What are the most important factors (mathematical and non-mathematical) for Bill to consider in making this decision?

- ☐ Suppose Bill had the money to pay cash for the pontoon boat. Would this be a wiser course than either of the other options? Why or why not? Under what circumstances would the payment of cash definitely *not* be a wise business decision for Bill?

SCENARIO 2

Helen Honeywell is selling her vacation property and has had two offers. She is not sure which, if either, to accept. Helen bought the property 10 years ago for $40,000. Since that time, property values have risen an estimated 10 percent per year, compounded quarterly.

One buyer, Zinford, has offered $70,000 in cash, but in return for this cash deal, Zinford wants Helen to throw in the living and dining room furniture, valued at $1,500. The second buyer, Withers, offers $20,000 down and the balance in quarterly payments of $3,600 for a period of five years; the money can be invested at 12 percent compounded quarterly. Withers couldn't care less about Helen's furniture.

Helen is not sure which of these offers, if either, she should accept. Her brother George tells her that cash in hand is "always better than payments over time." But Helen isn't sure. It's true, there are things she'd like to buy with that $70,000. The cash offer is tempting and, as George points out, the cash could probably be invested at maybe 8 or 10 percent interest. But is it really the more financially sound decision? Withers is willing to pay over $20,000 more than Zinford; certainly this must be the better offer, even if she does have to wait a while for all the money.

What do you think? Is either offer one that Helen should accept, given the estimated current value of her property? Which offer will put Helen in a better financial position, or are they comparable? Which offer, if either, would you advise her to take?

- ☐ Should Helen accept the offer from Zinford or Withers? Or neither? Explain.

- ☐ What is the actual difference in dollars between the offers?

- ☐ Under what circumstances is a cash offer on property (or any purchase) likely to be appealing to the seller? Under what circumstances is it likely to be less appealing?

☐ What factors (mathematical or nonmathematical) should Helen consider in making her final decision?

☐ Suppose that Helen's property were currently appraised at $80,000 and she did not want to come down below this price, but she did want to sell soon. What counter-offer could she make to Zinford? What counter-offer could she make to Withers?

Depreciating Business Assets 19

A business asset that has seen a lot of wear and tear will inevitably be worth less than one that's fresh and new. Take the case of Maxim's, the famous Parisian restaurant renowned for its food and service. One night, Maxim's was host to the French writer Georges Feydeau, who ordered one of the specialties, fresh lobster. But when the dish was served, the writer noticed that the lobster was missing a claw. A waiter was summoned.

The waiter pointed out that lobsters are combative animals and that because of the close quarters in the lobster tank, fights producing such damage are not uncommon.

"No matter," Feydeau told the waiter. "I want you to take this one back and bring me the victor."

Virtually everything a business buys — vehicles, equipment, furniture, buildings themselves — depreciates over time. That is to say, its newness wears off, it must be repaired (or, eventually, replaced), and its resale value goes down. That's the bad news. The good news is that businesses can deduct *depreciation* from taxable income, with the result that less of the business's gross income goes to pay taxes.

Businesses that invest in their own future tend to prosper in the long run, even when the advantages don't *immediately* translate into dollars. New equipment costs money, so, like most individual consumers, business owners must think carefully before spending. Take the Handy Print Shop, a small operation serving offices in the downtown district of a growing town. Handy Print could use a new color photocopy machine, but the cost is prohibitive. But what if Handy could recover some of that cost through tax deductions spread over the life of the machine, say, for the next five years? Now it has an incentive to make the purchase. The tax deductions make it more affordable.

What's more, Handy Print isn't the only business to come out ahead in this situation. The seller of the photocopy machine makes more sales if businesses like Handy Print can afford to buy new equipment. Without the tax incentive, Handy Print might have tried to limp by for another few years with its old color copier, and that wouldn't do much for profits at the copy machine company. Not to mention the fact that Handy Print customers are delighted by the new purchase; their favorite print shop is suddenly offering better service.

Of course, our illustration with Handy Print is a simple one. As we'll see in this lesson, not everything a business buys can be depreciated. Nor are all assets depreciated at the same rate. Further, while there are rigorous government regulations to guide tax-related aspects of depreciation, business managers often have to decide which of several approaches is best suited to the financial needs of the business. In this lesson, we'll talk about some different approaches to depreciation and contrast their effects.

PART I: INTRODUCING THE MATERIAL

LEARNING OBJECTIVES

Upon completing your study of this lesson, you should be able to:

1. Define and correctly use key terms associated with depreciation, including tangible and intangible assets, cost, useful life, salvage value, and book value.

2. Use the straight-line method of depreciation to determine the annual depreciation of a business asset, given its cost, salvage value, and useful life.

3. Explain accelerated depreciation, the declining-balance method, and the sum-of-the-years'-digits method and give examples of declining balance methods.

4. Given its cost, salvage value, and useful life, calculate the annual and accumulated depreciation and the book value of a business asset at any point in time using the double-declining-balance method of depreciation.

5. Given its cost, salvage value, and useful life, calculate the annual and accumulated depreciation and the book value of a business asset at any point in time using the sum-of-the-years'-digits method of depreciation.

6. Given its cost, salvage value, and useful life, calculate the annual and accumulated depreciation and the book value of a business asset after any number of units using the units-of-production method of depreciation.

7. For any specified method of depreciation, construct a depreciation schedule for a business asset, given cost, salvage value, and useful life.

8. Describe the key features of the modified accelerated cost recovery system (MACRS) of depreciation and be able to categorize assets into the appropriate recovery periods.

9. Using a table of MACRS depreciation rates, find the amount of depreciation in a specified recovery year for a business asset, given its description and purchase price.

If you're using the hardcover textbook, *Mathematics for Business*, there are some additional objectives for this lesson. Upon completing your study of the lesson, you should also be able to:

10. Given the cost, salvage value, and useful life of a business asset, construct the depreciation schedules necessary to determine which method provides the largest depreciation in a given year.

11. Contrast the amount of depreciation available at different points of an asset's useful life when using straight-line, declining-balance, and sum-of-the-years'-digits methods.

12. For a given set of projected business cash flow requirements, select which method of depreciating a costly business asset is likely to be most compatible with those requirements.

13. Given a specified method of depreciating a business asset, calculate the depreciation of the asset when it is held for a partial year.

LESSON OVERVIEW

The basic idea of *depreciation* is simple enough: A business makes a purchase, records how that purchase depreciates over time, and each year deducts the depreciable amount from taxable income. So far, so good. But why not take the *entire* deduction right away, at the time of the purchase? Remember our friends at Handy Print? Think how it might help their business to deduct the full $50,000 they paid for the color photocopier in the same year they made the investment. True, it would help—for that year.

But an expensive piece of equipment like this doesn't just make the company money for a year. Instead, the business continues to benefit from the investment over a long period. An asset normally loses its original value gradually, over a period of many years, not all at once. Depreciation, then, is designed to spread the value of the asset across the years of its useful life, thereby providing a truer approximation of the financial gains and losses that asset represents to the business.

There are two basic types of assets in which businesses invest. The most common are *tangible*, or physical, assets: equipment, machinery, furniture, buildings, tools, and so forth. *Intangible* assets include such things as client or customer lists, patents and copyrights, or franchise. Any asset, whether tangible or intangible, can be depreciated, provided it has a *useful life* of one year or more and provided the length of its useful life can be estimated with some accuracy.

What Can Be Depreciated

Land is a tangible asset that cannot be depreciated for the simple reason that its useful life is indefinite. Though its usefulness for certain purposes (e.g., forestry, agriculture) may vary with time, land may retain its basic value for countless years. And more often than not, barring erosion or other damage, land tends to *appreciate* in value over time. The concept of depreciation simply doesn't apply to an asset that *gains* value rather than losing value as the years go by.

Similarly, though there is no rigid dollar limit on depreciation, smaller purchases like staples, pencils, and copier paper are not depreciated. Sometimes this is because the tax laws allow items of less than a $200 or so to be expensed. But in the case of supplies, it's more because they're consumable. It doesn't make any sense to talk about the value of a box of staples a year from now; most of them will have been used up by then. But it makes perfect sense to talk about the value of the printing press itself, an asset that will still be useful to the company a year from now.

Some Other Important Terms

A few other terms are also useful in discussing depreciation. One is *cost*, or the total amount paid for the asset. Recall that with Handy Print's photocopier, the total cost was $50,000. This figure is important because it provides the basis for all calculations of depreciation, regardless of the approach used.

Equally important is the projected *useful life* of the asset. We'll suppose in our scenario that the useful life of the photocopier is set at five years. As you'll soon see, though, the concept of "useful life" is not quite what it seems in the world of depreciation. When you think of useful life, don't think of how long a piece of equipment will last. Instead, think simply of the period over which the depreciation will be taken. This will help you get around the considerable problem of trying to understand why someone could think that each and every photocopier, regardless of make, model, design, or amount of use, could suddenly fall apart after exactly five years. They don't, and you shouldn't think that this is what's implied by useful life.

The *salvage value* of an asset (also called the scrap value) is theoretically its value when it's retired, traded in, disposed of, or simply worn out. In other words, it's what's left after all the depreciation is taken. Sometimes, an asset has no significant salvage value. Suppose Finley's Ice Cream Cones has a very impressive $15,000 sign made for the corporate headquarters. Unfortunately, the sign isn't worth much to anyone except Finley, so the scrap value is exactly that — what the sign is worth as scrap. But a five-year old delivery van may have a substantial trade-in value. As a result, its owners will not depreciate the entire cost of the van, but will depreciate only the difference between the cost and the salvage value.

Notice that the salvage value of an asset is essentially its resale value on the open market, and that this value needs to be estimated when the asset is placed in service. At the end of the "useful life," though, the salvage value may not exactly match the truck's value on the open market. Nevertheless, all the depreciation has been taken, and the salvage value isn't readjusted.

Accumulated depreciation is the total amount of depreciation taken to a particular point in the useful life of an asset. Let's say Winthrop's business has a $16,000 pickup truck, which he depreciates at $3,000 in the first year and another $3,000 in the second. The accumulated depreciation at the end of the second year is $3,000 + $3,000, or $6,000. The *book value* of the truck at this point is the original cost ($16,000) minus the accumulated depreciation ($6,000), or $10,000. Keep in mind the rule that book value can never be lower than salvage value.

When Is Depreciation Not Depreciation?

It may trouble you to learn that simply viewing depreciation as a periodic deduction of a portion of an asset's cost over its useful life is bound to cause problems. For better or worse, this "traditional" view of depreciation isn't used any more for federal tax purposes. (And since the principal idea behind depreciation is to recover the cost of an asset by deducting it from taxable income, the regulations that the Internal Revenue Service adopts for depreciation are pretty important.)

The Economic Recovery Tax Act of 1981 was the culprit in changing both the concept and techniques of depreciation. Under the previous, so-called *traditional methods*, the amount of depreciation charged in a given year had some relationship to the actual decline in the value of the asset. As we pointed out with the photocopier, not every asset declined in value exactly as it was being depreciated, but the intention was there. The asset got "used up," so its value dropped; and as it dropped, the owners got to deduct the drop in value from taxable income. And it simply wasn't fair to take more depreciation than the drop in the asset's value, which is to say that the accumulated depreciation was never more than the cost minus a reasonable salvage value.

Under the new law, traditional depreciation was replaced as a concept by *cost recovery*. An asset was put into a specific category and the percentage of the cost that could be deducted each year of the *recovery period* was specified. Salvage value had no relevance; a business eventually recovered the entire cost of the asset through these deductions from taxable income. And, perhaps surprisingly, it didn't even matter whether the asset was new or used. So, as you can see, the traditional view of depreciation doesn't help much when considering cost recovery.

Unfortunately, it's not easy simply to do without traditional depreciation. Suppose that the value of Kelly's business consists primarily of depreciable assets. Odds are that Kelly would not want to go without a reasonable estimate of the value of those assets at any point in time, regardless of what the IRS is willing to let her deduct. And perhaps Kelly's state government isn't willing to go along with the U.S. government's idea of what makes a sensible depreciation system and thus makes her use a traditional method for state taxes. All in all, the Economic Recovery Act of 1981 added "cost recovery" as a concept without eliminating the need to understand—and often calculate—traditional depreciation.

The Reasons Behind Cost Recovery

If you're the curious sort, you might well wonder why the U.S. Congress would suddenly decide to change the way in which depreciation is handled for tax purposes. The answer has to do with the true cost of buying new assets, which, as we've seen, isn't the figure on the price tag. Depreciation makes assets cheaper for businesses, and the faster the cost is deducted from taxes, the better businesses like it. The cost recovery method was Congress's way of stimulating widespread buying and therefore widespread production of goods. Once businesses started buying all those assets, the economy would prosper—enough, perhaps, that the tax money the government lost by giving these generous deductions would be more than made up by the fact that companies were making more money and therefore paying more taxes.

Perhaps because depreciation had been such a standard business concept for so long, the new cost recovery system continued to be referred to as "depreciation." But it's critical to understand that cost recovery depreciation applies for tax accounting, not depreciation in the traditional sense. Don't worry much about the decline in the actual value of an asset when dealing with cost recovery; you'll only get confused. Remember, though, that many businesses still use a traditional depreciation method for their own internal accounting. Let's look at a few of those methods before returning to cost recovery methods.

The Straight-Line Method

The *straight-line method* of depreciation is the simplest approach mathematically and the easiest to understand. It's based on the idea that an asset loses an equal amount of its value during each year of its useful life. The depreciable amount is based on the difference between the original cost of the asset and its salvage value.

The straight-line method requires that both a useful life and a salvage value be established when the asset is put in place. If the asset's useful life is, say, seven years, one-seventh of the depreciable amount will be taken each year. (Remember, in traditional depreciation, the useful life is supposed to be a realistic reflection of when the asset is likely to stop being productive for the company.)

Let's suppose that a dentist, Dr. DeBerry, buys new furniture for his waiting room. The original cost of the furniture (a couch, coffee table, and two chairs) is $2,500. The expected life is, say, seven years, and the salvage value at the end of that time is $400. To find the annual depreciation, we first figure out the depreciable amount: $2,500 (the cost) − $400 (the salvage value) = $2,100. Remember that this amount will be depreciated over a period of seven years, so the annual depreciation amount will be $2,100 ÷ 7 = $300. Which is to say that (in the days before cost recovery) $300 could be deducted from Dr. DeBerry's taxable income each year to reflect the declining value of this furniture.

This $300 is also the amount subtracted each year to determine the current book value of the furniture. Thus, at the end of the first year, the book value is $2,500 − $300 = $2,200. At the end of the second year, the book value is $2,200 − $300 = $1,900, and so on. After seven years, Dr. DeBerry cannot depreciate the furniture further; he's already taken $2,100 in depreciation, all that's allowed. Now perhaps DeBerry never keeps patients waiting and, since scarcely anyone has had a chance to sit on it, the furniture doesn't really need to be replaced. That's all well and good, but it has no impact on depreciation; all the allowable depreciation has been claimed and there's no more to be had.

Company accountants sometimes work out a *depreciation schedule* to keep closer track of business assets and their changing value from year to year. Such a schedule shows the amount of depreciation for that year, the accumulated depreciation (or total to date), and the current book value of the asset. Here, for instance, is what such a schedule might look like for Dr. DeBerry's furniture.

DEPRECIATION SCHEDULE: OFFICE FURNITURE

Year	Amount of Depreciation	Accumulated Depreciation	Book Value
0	None	None	$2,500
1	$300	$300	$2,200
2	$300	$600	$1,900
3	$300	$900	$1,600
4	$300	$1,200	$1,300
5	$300	$1,500	$1,000
6	$300	$1,800	$700
7	$300	$2,100	$400

Notice that the accumulated depreciation total at the end of seven years is equal to the *total* depreciable amount; that means that at the end of seven years, the furniture is no longer a depreciable asset for the company. Notice, too, that the book value at the end of seven years is equal to the salvage value DeBerry assigned the furniture when it was placed in service.

As anyone who's bought a new car can testify, many assets lose value faster in their first few years than in their later life. As a result, the straight-line method may not be as realistic a reflection of the true value of an asset as a method that has more of the depreciation taking place earlier in the useful life. Methods of *accelerated depreciation*, of which the declining-balance method is one, allow the asset owner to take a higher rate of depreciation early on, with decreasing depreciation later.

Depreciation with a *declining-balance method* is based on the straight-line rate, but it's applied a little differently. Three rates are possible: 200 percent of (or twice) the straight-line rate; 150 percent of (or one and a half times) the straight-line rate; and 125 percent of (or one and a quarter times) the straight-line rate. As you might guess, since the 200 percent depreciation rate provided by the *double-declining-balance* method allows owners to recovery their money sooner, it's most widely used.

Declining-balance methods are also known as "constant percent" methods, and they're perhaps easier to understand when you think of a constant percentage of the asset's *book value* being depreciated each year. In other words, while straight-line depreciation is based on a constant *amount* of annual depreciation (so that it represents an increasing percentage of the book value), declining-balance methods take a constant *percentage* of the book value, which results in a decreasing amount.

Let's say that the Hasty Tasty Pizza Company buys a new delivery truck for $20,000. The truck has an estimated useful life of five years and a salvage value of $2,000. That means that the depreciable amount will be $20,000 − $2,000 = $18,000. Hasty knows it will take a big loss on the truck early in its life (and, besides, the company wants every possible tax advantage to help offset the cost of this new investment). So Hasty will use the double-declining-balance method, with a rate based on 200 percent of the straight-line rate. The first step is to find out what the straight-line rate is.

Since the truck has a useful life of five years, the annual straight-line rate is ⅕, or 20 percent. That means that the double-declining-balance rate will be twice this amount, or 2 × 20 percent, or 40 percent. This rate, however, will always be applied to the *book value*; it will be applied to the $20,000 original cost only in the first year (since the only time that cost equals book value is at the time of purchase). Let's see how this works.

The cost of the truck is $20,000. So the amount of depreciation for the first year will be .40 × $20,000, or $8,000. This is the amount that Hasty can write off its taxable income the year it purchases the truck. Now the book value of the truck is $20,000 − $8,000, or $12,000. This is the figure on which we base depreciation for the *second* year. In other words, the amount of depreciation in the second year will be the same 40 percent, but this time it is applied to the lower book value of $12,000; this results in depreciation of $4,800. Subtracting that from the previous book value of $12,000 leaves $7,200 for the third year.

By the end of the fifth year, the book value on the truck will have dropped to $2,592. This is still almost $600 over the $2,000 salvage value, so there's no problem. But let's suppose that the salvage value on the truck were $4,000, rather than $2,000. In that case, Hasty could not take the full amount of depreciation in the fifth year because *the book value can*

Declining-Balance Method

never drop below the salvage value. In other words, if the salvage value were $4,000, then $20,000 − $4,000, or $16,000, would be the *maximum* total depreciation that Hasty could take over the five years of the truck's useful life. If the amount of available depreciation is less than what the mathematics call for, then the company simply takes whatever's available.

The Sum-of-the-Years'-Digits Method	Sometimes a business may wish to depreciate an asset more at the beginning of its useful life, but not so much as to overly limit its depreciation toward the end of the depreciation period. What's needed in this situation is a kind of compromise between the strictly uniform straight-line method and the intentionally unbalanced declining-balance method. That compromise is found in the *sum-of-the-years'-digits method*, which produces more depreciation than the straight-line method early on but more than the declining-balance method later in the depreciation period.

This method tends to look more complicated than it is, simply because it involves use of a *depreciation fraction* rather than the sort of constant rates we've talked about so far (e.g., 20 percent, 40 percent). This depreciation fraction, which is different for each year, is multiplied by the depreciable amount to determine the *annual* depreciation. Let's look at an example to help clarify how this works.

Fernwood Dairy has recently installed five miles of fencing, at a cost of $24,000. The estimated useful life of the fencing is 10 years, and let's suppose that it has no salvage value at all; perhaps the scrap metal is worth something but it would cost more money than that to disassemble the fence and gather it all up. The first step in determining the amount of depreciation is to find the depreciation fraction.

While the fraction will differ every year, the denominator will always be the same: It's the sum of the digits for all the years of the asset's total useful life. Hence the name of this approach. Since the fence has a useful life of 10 years, the denominator is $10 + 9 + 8 + 7 + 6 + 5 + 4 + 3 + 2 + 1 = 55$. If you're thinking that adding up all these numbers could get tedious, you're quite right—especially for assets with an estimated useful life of 20 years or more! Fortunately, there's a shortcut.

The sum of the years' digits is equal to $n(n + 1) \div 2$. In this formula, n equals the useful life of the asset. In the case of the fence, it's 10 years. Thus, the denominator $= 10 (10 + 1) \div 2$, or $10 (11) \div 2$, or $110 \div 2 = 55$. Now we have the denominator, but what about the numerators? In each case, the numerator is equal to the *remaining years of useful life*. Thus, the numerator for the first year is the same as the number of years in the useful life of the asset, or in this case, 10. That makes the depreciation fraction for the first year $10/55$. Each year, the numerator goes down by one (since there is one less year of useful life remaining), so in year 2, it's $9/55$, then $8/55$ in year 3, $7/55$ in year 4, and so on, down to $1/55$ in year 10.

Here's an important point to remember in computing the amount of depreciation with the sum-of-the-years'-digits method: *Always* go back to the original cost in computing the amount, just as in straight-line depreciation. In other words, since the original cost of the fence is $24,000, the depreciation for each year will be based on this amount. In the first year, it will be $10/55 \times \$24,000$; in the second year, $9/55 \times \$24,000$, and so on. (By the way, notice that these fractions are not reduced to lowest terms. The fraction $10/55$ could be reduced to $2/11$, but that would give us a very misleading impression about the number of years remaining in the life of the asset. The numerator 10 helps indicate that we're in the first year of a 10-year depreciation schedule.)

Let's see what the depreciation amount for the first year will be using this method. Since the fraction is 10/55, we multiply 10/55 × $24,000, and the result is 240,000 ÷ 55 = $4,364 (rounded). It is, incidentally, customary in working with depreciation figures to round numbers to the nearest dollar. The amount of depreciation in the second year will be 9/55 × $24,000 = 216,000 ÷ 55 = $3,909. By the tenth year, depreciation will have dropped to $436.

The sum-of-the-years'-digits method looks as if it ought to have some complex mathematical logic behind it. But, disappointingly perhaps, it's really more like one of those mathematical tricks that just happens to work. The important thing to keep in mind with this method is that it allows relatively substantial depreciation early in the life of an asset, while still allowing relatively more depreciation than the declining-balance method toward the end of the asset's life.

So far, all the methods we've talked about base the useful life of an asset on years of ownership. This approach makes perfectly good sense for an asset that receives normal use at a normal rate. But sometimes that rate of use varies substantially from what we might expect, or it is heavier during some periods than during others. In that case, it may make better sense to figure the useful life in terms of *units of production*.

The Units-of-Production Method

For example, say that Tilly's Togs buys a press that prints designs on the front of tee-shirts. The cost of the press is $10,000, the salvage value is zero, and the estimated useful life is — well, it's hard to say in years because that would depend on how much use the machine gets. It might be more accurate to say that the machine will handle 100,000 shirts before it needs to be replaced. This is another way of saying that the press has an estimated useful life of 100,000 units. The depreciation per unit, then, is $10,000 (the depreciable amount) ÷ 100,000 (the total units in the press's useful life), or $0.10 per unit. In other words, Tilly can theoretically depreciate the press by 10¢ every time she produces another patterned shirt.

Notice that this approach provides a very realistic way of estimating depreciation, since it is based on actual use rather than the number of weeks or months that have elapsed since purchase. For this reason, the rate of depreciation will depend on how good business is right now. Let's suppose that Tilly's is a thriving business and the press handles 50,000 shirts in the first year. At 10¢ per shirt, Tilly's is entitled to $5,000 of depreciation in this first year.

Well, you might say, that looks like a very healthy annual depreciation, given that the total cost of the press was only $10,000. Quite right. But we must also consider the relatively heavy rate of use. Remember that the press has a useful life of only 100,000 units, and it's already printed 50,000 shirts. If things stay exactly as busy next year, Tilly will get another $5,000 of depreciation but will also have a worn-out machine on her hands. (And even if the machine is sturdier than expected and struggles on into a third productive year, no more depreciation is available.)

Notice, by the way, how different the scenario would have been if Tilly's were struggling. In that case, their total use for the year might be, say, 10,000 units. At that rate, the press would last for 10 years instead of two. And what if Tilly's stopped using the machine even temporarily? Then it would appear as if the machine had stopped depreciating, which is not really the case.

<table>
<tr><td>Accounting for
Partial Years</td><td>You might have noticed that up to this point we've been talking as if businesses bought all their computers, presses, trucks, or whatever on January 1 of each year. But of course, this is absurd. A company will buy what it needs when the need arises, and that's rarely on the first day of the year.</td></tr>
</table>

Accounting for
Partial Years

You might have noticed that up to this point we've been talking as if businesses bought all their computers, presses, trucks, or whatever on January 1 of each year. But of course, this is absurd. A company will buy what it needs when the need arises, and that's rarely on the first day of the year.

That's fine, the law says, but it's important to note the date and to calculate depreciation *only* from that date until the end of the year, not for the full year. For instance, to keep our illustration simple, let's suppose that Big City Research buys a paper shredder on October 1. The shredder costs $5,500 and has a salvage value of $500, and an estimated useful life of five years. We'll suppose for now that Big City is going to depreciate the shredder using the straight-line method. Thus, the depreciable amount is $5,500 − $500, or $5,000, and the rate is $\frac{1}{5}$ or 20 percent per year, or $1,000 per year for five years. So the depreciable amount for the first year *would* be $1,000, except that Big City didn't buy the shredder until October 1, when there were only three months left in the year. That means that under traditional methods Big City can take only $\frac{3}{12}$ (or $\frac{1}{4}$) of the depreciable amount: $1,000 × $\frac{1}{4}$ = $250.

In short, Big City Research can depreciate the shredder by only $250 the year they buy it. They are still allowed a full five years' worth of depreciation, though. They've used up only three months. So for the next four years, they'll depreciate the shredder at the normal annual rate of $1,000 a year. Four years and three months later, when nine months still remain in the depreciation schedule, they can claim the remaining nine months' worth of depreciation: $750.

What if Big City Research used the double-declining-balance method? In that case, their rate would be 2 × 20 percent, or 40 percent, applied to the book value. For the three months of the purchase year, that would mean a depreciation amount of $5,000 × .40 (the double declining rate) × $\frac{1}{4}$ (or three months) = $500. Remember, though, in the second year they can base the depreciation on the full 12 months. But it will be calculated on the book value, which becomes $5,000 − $500, or $4,500.

Of course, Big City might also choose to calculate depreciation according to the sum-of-the-years'-digits method. The trick here is that each year of depreciation is based on a fraction of the preceding year plus a fraction of the current year. In this case, because the purchase date is October 1, the depreciation for year 1 will be based on the remaining three months of the year, October 1 to December 31. But the depreciation for year 2 will be based on the last three months of year 1, plus the first nine months of year 2. It gets a bit more complicated than is worth explaining here, but the key point is that these traditional depreciation methods require that some adjustment be made to account for partial years of ownership.

Federal Reform:
ACRS and MACRS

The federal tax reforms of the 1980s brought many changes, including (some would say) a simplification of depreciation *for tax purposes*. The original *accelerated cost recovery system* (ACRS) was initiated as part of the Economic Recovery Tax Act of 1981; it applies to all property put into service between 1981 and 1986.

ACRS made some very significant changes to the concept of depreciation for tax purposes. First, salvage value was ignored; the depreciation was taken on the full cost, not cost minus salvage value. And the concept of "useful life" was replaced by the idea of a *cost-recovery class*. All property was placed into a class of 3, 5, 10, or 15 years, and which class an asset went into wasn't (and wasn't meant to be) directly related to its true useful life. And all property of the same class purchased in the same year was grouped together and depreciated as a group. In fact, under ACRS, calculating depreciation meant simply looking up the age and class of the asset in a table; the table gave a percentage that was then multiplied by the total cost of the assets of that class and age. Pretty easy, right? Don't forget, though, that since ACRS had little to do with the way the assets were really losing value, most companies were still depreciating assets on the company books using one of the more traditional methods.

Remember how we said that the purpose of the cost recovery methods of depreciation was to stimulate the economy, and that cost recovery depreciation didn't really have to make sense in terms of business accounting? One example of how much ACRS was more an economic tool than an accounting procedure is that the original ACRS regulations were adjusted by Congress shortly after they became law and, in 1986, were simply replaced by the *modified accelerated cost recovery system* (MACRS).

MACRS, which applies to assets placed in service in 1987 or later, added a 7-year class, as well as 20-, 27.5- and 31.5-year classes for real estate and utilities. What's more, most assets were moved from their ACRS class to the next longer class. If you're thinking that this made MACRS a worse deal for businesses than ACRS, you're right. Congress decided that the tax breaks provided by ACRS no longer needed to be so generous, so it changed the rules. And while most accounting procedures couldn't be changed so arbitrarily, Congress figured it was perfectly acceptable to change the cost recovery system it had invented in the first place.

Since 1987, business accountants have faced the interesting situation of having three different ways that assets are depreciated for tax purposes. Assets placed in service since 1987 are handled with MACRS. Yet ACRS applies to assets placed in service between 1981 and 1986. And for any assets still being depreciated that were in service prior to 1981, one of the traditional methods has to be used.

Your textbook has a list of the items that fit into the different MACRS recovery periods—and if you own a tugboat, wastewater plant, or race horse, you'll be interested to see that Congress specifically mentioned your asset. Many of the assets businesses deal with (cars, most trucks, computers, furniture, and so on) fall into the 5- or 7-year class. The 7-year class is particularly important because any asset that doesn't specifically belong to another recovery period is assigned to this class.

While the primary purpose of MACRS and ACRS was to give businesses the tax breaks that Congress wanted them to have, there's little doubt that it did simplify depreciation calculations for most businesses. That's because much of the computing has already been done for the user and incorporated into tables. There are really only two steps involved in using MACRS. First, the user must look up the recovery period for the asset, something that's easy to do with guidance from IRS publications.

Calculations with MACRS

The second step involves finding the depreciation rate in a table that lists the year of depreciation (or recovery) down the lefthand side and the total recovery period (e.g., three years, 10 years) across the top. For instance, the rate on an automobile (part of the 5-year class) for the second year is 32.00, meaning 32 percent, or .32. It's important to remember that the numbers in the table are percents; before using them to calculate the amount of depreciation, move the decimal two places to the left. Thus, the depreciation on a $20,000 car in year 2 would be $20,000 × .32, or $6,400. The depreciation on an $800 desk (part of the 7-year class) in year 4 is $800 × .1249, or about $100.

If this seems simple compared to, say, the sum-of-the-years'-digits method, it is. Your textbook contains the MACRS depreciation rate table; if you look at it, you'll see that you can calculate the deduction for any asset just by knowing its cost, class, and recovery year. MACRS even pretends that every asset is purchased halfway through the year and takes that into account in the rate table; notice that the table shows one more year than the class recovery period to account for half-years of depreciation in the first and last year. And, remember, you can depreciate all of the assets of the same class and year by adding together the total costs and doing one calculation. Just don't make the mistake of thinking that subtracting the cost recovery amount from the original cost will give you book value in the traditional sense.

SOME WORDS OF ADVICE

Tax laws are always changing and vary from state to state. It is wise, therefore, to address depreciation matters before making a major purchase, particularly if the investment represents a substantial portion of a company's income. An accountant may be needed to determine the most appropriate depreciation method, and if the business has more than a handful of assets, a computer will be handy in tracking depreciation.

Keep in mind, as a potential buyer, that tax deductions for depreciation often make a purchase more affordable than it might originally seem. Again, however, it is important to know the extent of such deductions before making a purchase. Further, not all assets are depreciable. Remember, there are two criteria: The asset's useful life must be more than one year, and land and personal property cannot be depreciated.

As a business manager, you will have little choice about how to calculate depreciation for federal tax purposes; the MACRS method will apply to all assets purchased after 1986. But, depending on state law, you may need to use a traditional method of depreciation for state tax purposes. (Which may not cause any added work, since your company may want traditional depreciation schedules to figure out just what the asset contributes to the company's net worth.)

Throughout our discussion, we've stressed how ACRS and MACRS don't try to make sense like the traditional depreciation methods. That is, in fact, not entirely true. Assets in the 3-, 5-, 7-, and 10-year classes are depreciated using the 200 percent double-declining-balance method at first and switching to the straight-line depreciation about halfway through the recovery period. Assets in the 15- and 20-year classes start with a 150 percent declining-balance method, then switch to straight-line, while assets in the 27.5- and 31.5-year classes are entirely straight-line depreciated. However, while there is a traditional method (or two) behind MACRS, the logic isn't all that obvious. When you also consider the somewhat arbitrary recovery periods, it's perhaps safer for nonaccounting types to simply view MACRS as being whatever Congress wanted it to be without worrying about the underlying logic.

Finally, don't under- or overestimate the value of the tax deduction for depreciation. Assets end up costing considerably less than the purchase price due to the tax deduction, but it doesn't make them free. A dollar spent for a depreciable asset is a dollar not available for another use, nor for profit to the owners. Also, it takes a while to recognize the tax savings — five or seven years for most common business assets.

KEY TERMS

Before you read through the text assignment and watch the video program, take a minute to look at the key terms associated with this lesson. When you encounter them in the text and video program, pay careful attention to their meaning.

Accelerated cost recovery system (ACRS): The method of depreciation required on all federal income tax returns for property acquired after January 1, 1981, but before January 1, 1987.

Accelerated depreciation: Depreciation that is greater than a straight-line rate in the early years of an asset's useful life. The declining-balance and sum-of-the-years'-digits methods are forms of accelerated depreciation.

Accumulated depreciation: A running balance or total of the depreciation on an asset to date.

Book value: The cost of an asset minus any depreciation to date.

Cost: The amount paid for a depreciable asset; this figure provides the basis for calculating depreciation.

Declining-balance depreciation: An accelerated method of depreciation that is based on a rate that is 200 percent, 150 percent, or 125 percent of the straight-line rate and uses book value as the base for computing depreciation from year 2 on.

Depreciable amount: The total amount that can be depreciated over the life of an asset.

Depreciation: The decrease in value of an asset caused by normal use, aging, or obsolescence.

Depreciation schedule: A schedule or table showing the depreciation rate, amount of depreciation, book value, and accumulated depreciation for each year of an asset's useful life.

Modified accelerated cost recovery system (MACRS): The method of depreciation required on all federal income tax returns for property acquired after 1986. This method, part of the Tax Reform Act of 1986, replaces the ACRS.

Salvage value: The value of an asset at the end of its useful life. In some cases, where an asset is not salable even as scrap, that value may be zero. Salvage value is not considered to calculate depreciation using the ACRS or MACRS.

Straight-line depreciation: A depreciation method in which depreciation is spread evenly over the life of an asset.

Sum-of-the-years'-digits method: An accelerated depreciation method that involves higher depreciation in the early years of an asset's life.

Units-of-production method: A depreciation method based on units produced or on some other precise measure of actual use (e.g., miles traveled, hours of operation), rather than on months or years of ownership.

PART II: WATCHING THE VIDEO PROGRAM

VIDEO VIEWING GUIDE

Before watching the video program, review the following questions. As you watch, be sure to collect the information necessary to answer them:

1. How does a business person know which assets can be depreciated for tax purposes and which cannot?

2. What is the difference between a tangible and an intangible asset, and how (if at all) does this distinction relate to depreciation?

3. From the business person's point of view, what are the major advantages in depreciating assets?

4. What motivation does the government have for allowing or encouraging depreciation on business assets?

5. How do the MACRS and ACRS cost recovery systems differ from traditional depreciation methods? In what ways are they similar?

6. For what assets would the straight-line depreciation method be most appropriate?

7. For what assets would an accelerated depreciation method be most appropriate? What is the most common accelerated depreciation approach?

8. When does it make sense for a business to use the units-of-production method of depreciation?

9. What factors should a business consider in determining the most appropriate depreciation approach? If you ran a business, would you use a traditional depreciation method in addition to MACRS, or would you just use MACRS?

VIDEO PROGRAM

The lesson's video program is Program 19 – Depreciating Business Assets. Remember, if you are watching this program on videotape, take time to replay sections of the tape any time you need to review a concept.

VIDEO VIEWING QUESTIONS

Immediately after viewing the video program for Lesson 19, take time to respond to the following questions. Give your answers some careful thought; they may provide the basis for additional discussion or a longer written response.

1. In a sentence or two, explain the difference between a depreciable asset and an expense. What are the financial implications of buying one or the other in terms of tax deductions?

   _____

   _____

   _____

2. List five depreciable assets a business might buy, and then list five assets that would be expensed.

   Depreciable: _____

   _____

   Expensed: _____

   _____

3. Name at least one asset that would logically be appropriately depreciated by each of the following traditional methods.

   Straight line: _____

   Declining balance: _____

   Sum of the years' digits: _____

   Units of production: _____

4. Which of the following factors is likely to be important in determining the traditional depreciation method a company uses with a given asset? (Check as many as apply. Be prepared to give reasons for your answers.)

   _____ Useful life of the asset

   _____ Intended use of the asset

   _____ Estimated rate of use

   _____ Cost of the asset

   _____ Current state and federal law

   _____ Current company profits or cash flow

   _____ Projected company profits

   _____ Estimated repair or maintenance costs for the asset

   _____ Company taxes

   _____ Current methods used by other companies with similar assets

   _____ Relative simplicity or difficulty of calculating depreciation using a given method

   _____ Current insurance rates related to an asset

   _____ Estimated salvage value of the asset

5. Decide whether each of the following statements is true or false. Then, in a sentence or two, give a reason for your answer.

   a. The only way to tell which depreciation method is best for a given asset in a given situation is to calculate the depreciation rates and schedules mathematically according to different methods.

   _____

   _____

   _____

   b. An asset can have great value to a company even if it cannot be depreciated at all.

   _____

   _____

   _____

6. Suppose that depreciation for tax purposes were no longer permitted. Which of the following do you think would likely occur? (Check as many as apply. Be prepared to give reasons for your answers.)

   _____ Businesses would invest more time and money in maintaining current assets

   _____ The cost of goods and services to the public would tend to go down

   _____ Businesses would invest more in land

   _____ Small businesses would have an easier time competing with big businesses

   _____ General economic expansion would increase nationwide

   _____ The cost of used equipment would decline

   _____ Businesses would pay more income tax

   _____ Business profits in general would fall

   _____ The quality of goods and services produced would rise

7. Describe the circumstances under which a company might choose to replace a depreciable asset before its useful life was over. Be specific in your answer, giving an example of an actual asset that might be replaced early in its useful life and the reasons a company might give for replacing it.

   _____

   _____

   _____

   _____

   _____

PART III: FOCUSING ON THE MATHEMATICS

READING ASSIGNMENT

After watching the video program, you should read one of the following Text Assignments, depending on the textbook you're using:

SOFTCOVER: Chapter 12 of the Miller, Salzman, and Hoelzle softcover text, *Business Mathematics*, pages 491-532.

HARDCOVER: Chapter 16, pages 554-590, and Appendix E, "Accelerated Cost Recovery System (ACRS)" of the Salzman, Miller, and Hoelzle hardcover text, *Mathematics for Business*.

As you read through the text, pay careful attention to the examples the book gives of the mathematics associated with the concepts you're learning about.

Then, after you've completed the text assignment, read through the Key Formulas below. This section provides a handy review of what you've learned. By the time you get to this point in the lesson, all of the formulas and calculations should be familiar to you. If they're not, go back and read the appropriate parts of the text and the Overview section of this lesson. You won't have much success completing the rest of your assignments if you are still confused about the information in the Key Formulas section.

KEY FORMULAS

The following key formulas are important to your understanding of this lesson. Be sure that you know each one and how to use it in solving problems related to asset depreciation.

KEY FORMULA:	Amount to be depreciated = Cost − Salvage value
Formula used for:	Determining the total amount that can be depreciated across the useful life of an asset.
Alternate forms:	Salvage value = Cost − Amount to be depreciated or Cost = Amount to be depreciated + Salvage value

Example:

Honey Hill Farms buys a hay baler for $50,000. It has a useful life of seven years and a salvage value of $5,000. What is the total amount to be depreciated? We begin with the total cost, then subtract the salvage value: $50,000 − $5,000 = $45,000. This is the maximum amount that Honey Hill can depreciate over the seven-year life of the baler.

Remember that in this formula:

1. Cost is what the individual or company pays for the asset.

2. Salvage value is the value of the asset at the end of its useful life; assets that cannot even be sold for scrap may have a salvage value of zero.

KEY FORMULA:	Straight-line depreciation = Amount to be depreciated ÷ Years of useful life
Formula used for:	Determining the annual amount of depreciation using the straight-line method.

Example:

In the example with Honey Hill Farms, since the total amount to be depreciated is $45,000 and the useful life of the baler is seven years, the annual depreciation according to the *straight-line* method would be $45,000 ÷ 7; about $6,428 per year.

Remember that in this formula:

1. The annual depreciation amount for the *straight-line* method is provided. Other forms of depreciation require a different method of computation.

2. In our example, the amount to be depreciated ($45,000) isn't evenly divisible by the number of years of useful life (7). Since the result is not an even number, it should be rounded to the nearest dollar.

KEY FORMULA:	Book value = Cost − Depreciation
Formula used for:	Determining the book value of an asset in any given year.

Example:

The annual depreciation on the Honey Hill Farms baler is $6,428. This means that the book value for the second year will be $50,000 (the cost) − $6,428 (the annual depreciation), or $43,572. The book value for year 3 will be $43,572 − $6,428 = $37,144.

Remember that in this formula:

1. The book value is the estimated dollar (or resale) value of an asset in any given year.

2. The formula can be used in two ways. Either subtract depreciation *for the year* from the current book value, *or* subtract *total depreciation to date* from the original cost of the asset. Both approaches yield the same answer.

3. Book value can never be less than salvage value.

KEY FORMULA:	Denominator for the sum-of-the-years'-digits method = $n(n + 1) \div 2$
Formula used for:	A shortcut to finding the denominator of the depreciation fraction used in computing depreciation by the sum-of-the-years'-digits method.

Example:

A pump costs $2,000, has no salvage value, and has an estimated useful life of five years. What is the denominator of the depreciation fraction that would be used to compute depreciation by the sum-of-the-years'-digits method? In this example, $n = 5$ because the useful life of the pump is five years. Thus, the denominator is $5 (5 + 1) \div 2 = 5 (6) \div 2 = 30 \div 2 = 15$.

Remember that in this formula:

1. The variable is n is the years of useful life.

2. The formula is only a shortcut to save time. If you like, you can check the answer by simply adding the digits for each year. In this case, since there are five years, we add $5 + 4 + 3 + 2 + 1 = 15$. The answer is the same either way, but the shortcut is very helpful in problems where the useful life is much longer (say, 30 years).

3. The answer derived from this formula is only the *denominator* of the fraction (the number on the bottom). To get the numerator, begin with the total number of years in the useful life of the asset for year 1 (5⁄15), then subtract one from this total for year 2 (4⁄15), and so on. For the last year of life (year 5), the depreciation fraction will be 1⁄15. Notice that while the numerator changes every year, the denominator is always the same.

4. Do not reduce the fraction to its lowest terms. For instance, in our example, the depreciation fraction for year 1 would be 5⁄15. This could be reduced to 1⁄3, but it is customary not to do this because the numerator indicates how many years of useful life remain for the particular asset in question.

KEY FORMULA: Depreciation = Depreciation fraction ×
Amount to be depreciated

Formula used for: Determining the annual amount of depreciation on an asset using the sum-of-the-years'-digits method.

Example:

As indicated with the preceding formula, the first-year depreciation fraction for the pump is 5⁄15. This fraction tells us that the pump has five years of useful life remaining and that the sum-of-the-years'-digits is 15. Since there is no salvage value, the depreciation is computed on the total cost: $2,000. Thus, the depreciation for year 1 is 5⁄15 × $2,000 = $667. In year 2, the depreciation fraction is 4⁄15. Thus, the amount of depreciation for that year is 4⁄15 × $2,000 = $533.

Remember that in this formula:

1. You subtract the salvage value from the cost to determine the total depreciable amount *before* applying the formula. (In our example, the pump had no salvage value, so the total cost could be depreciated.)

2. Be sure that the numerator of the fraction indicates the *remaining years of useful life*. Thus, in year 1, the numerator is *5* (five years of useful life remaining), *not* 1 (the number of the year).

3. In computing depreciation after the first year, go back to the *original cost*, not to the book value of the asset. In this example, depreciation for every year will be based on the original cost of the pump ($2,000), not on its book value for the year in question.

KEY FORMULA: Depreciation per unit = Depreciable amount ÷ Units of production

Formula used for: Determining the depreciation per unit in computing depreciation by the units-of-production method.

Example:

A delivery truck costs $22,000 and has a salvage value of $2,000 and a useful life of 100,000 miles. Find the depreciation per unit. We begin by determining the depreciable amount, which is cost minus salvage value: $22,000 − $2,000 = $20,000. In this example, units of production are given as miles. Thus, the depreciation per unit = $20,000 ÷ 100,000 = .20, or 20¢ per mile.

Remember that in this formula:

1. You determine the depreciable amount by subtracting salvage value from cost before applying the formula.

2. Units of production can take many forms. For instance, for a canning machine, the units of life might be the number of cans processed. For a videotape recorder, they might be hours of actual use.

3. The answer derived using this formula is always given in dollars and cents. Thus, .20 translates to *20¢* per unit. An answer of 1.50 would translate to $1.50 per unit.

4. The depreciation is limited to the depreciable amount. For instance, suppose the truck is driven 10,000 miles during its first year. The depreciable amount for that year is 10,000 × .20 = $2,000. Notice that the total depreciable amount on the truck is $20,000 (or the equivalent of 100,000 miles). This means that if the truck is driven 50,000 miles the first year and 50,000 more the second, there will be nothing left to depreciate in year 3 since 100,000 × .20 = $20,000, the full depreciable amount.

KEY FORMULA: MACRS depreciation = Cost of asset × Rate from MACRS table.

Formula used for: Determining the deduction from taxable income allowed for an asset placed in service after 1986.

Example:

A computer printer that costs $3,500 is in the MACRS 5-year class. In the first recovery year, the MACRS rate is 20.00, which means 20 percent. Since .20 times $3,500 is $700, that's the "depreciation" for the year. For the second year, the number is 32.00, so the depreciation is 32 percent of $3,500, which is $1,120.

Remember that in this formula:

1. The number from the table is multiplied by the cost, not by the book value. It's the number from the table that goes down, not the number it's multiplied by.

2. The depreciation in the first year is lower than in the second year because MACRS allows a half-year's depreciation for the first year regardless of when the asset was purchased. (As a result, an asset in the five-year recovery class is depreciated on into the sixth year, because that's where the missing half-year's depreciation comes from.)

DON'T FORGET

1. The total depreciable amount on a given asset is always the same, regardless of the method used to determine annual depreciation. But the schedules of depreciation, reflecting annual depreciation rates and totals, vary from method to method.

2. Only straight-line depreciation provides totally uniform annual depreciation across the life of an asset. Other methods tend to accelerate depreciation early in the life of an asset, allowing less depreciation toward the end of the useful life.

3. The units-of-production method is the only method based on actual use of the asset. Other traditional methods estimate the life in years. MACRS and ACRS use the concept of a *recovery period*, which is not at all the same as "useful life."

4. With methods other than MACRS or ACRS, it is important to deduct the salvage value from original cost to determine the depreciable amount before doing any other calculations.

5. Book value can never fall below salvage value. For this reason, the depreciation in the last year of an asset's useful life may be lower than would otherwise be permitted.

6. The rate for the declining-balance method is based on the straight-line rate. For the double-declining-balance method, use double the straight-line rate.

7. With the declining-balance method, use book value in computing depreciation. In year 1, book value is equal to cost.

PART IV: SOLVING BUSINESS PROBLEMS

PROBLEM SETS

Work the following problems in your textbook. Your instructor will tell you which problems, if any, are to be turned in. Some of the problems have answers provided in the back of the book; refer to these answers to make sure you are working the problems correctly.

SOFTCOVER: If you are using the Miller, Salzman, and Hoelzle softcover text, *Business Mathematics*, do the following problem sets:

12.1: Problems #22-32 (even numbers only) on pages 496-498.

12.2: Problems #22-32 (even numbers only) on pages 504-505.

12.3: Problems #18-28 (even numbers only) on pages 512-514.

12.4: Problems #8-18 (even numbers only) on pages 523-524.

12.5: Problems #24-34 (even numbers only) on pages 530-532.

HARDCOVER: If you are using the Salzman, Miller, and Hoelzle hardcover text, *Mathematics for Business*, do the following problem sets:

16.1: Problems #14-34 (even numbers only) on pages 559-561.

16.2: Problems #14-36 (even numbers only) on pages 566-568.

16.3: Problems #20-32 (even numbers only) on pages 574-576.

16.4: Problems #8-30 (even numbers only) on pages 581-583.

16.5: Problems #8-36 (even numbers only) on pages 588-589.

BUSINESS APPLICATIONS

Read each of the following scenarios and answer the questions about the decisions you would make in each situation. Give these questions some serious thought; they may be used as the basis for discussion or the development of a more complex essay. You should base your decisions on what you've learned from this lesson, applying both math skills and good business judgment to solve the problem at hand.

SCENARIO 1   Fairview Clinic plans to install a new therapy unit at a cost of $50,000. The unit has an estimated useful life of 10 years or 10,000 hours and no salvage value. Because of the newness of the unit (which was just developed within the past two years), it is very difficult to estimate repairs, but the unit is under warranty for the first two years following purchase. The clinic will amortize the cost of the unit and pay for it over a period of five years, rather than all in one lump sum. This is necessary since their current cash flow is fairly low.

Right now, the clinic serves an average of 200 patients daily, of whom perhaps 10 percent could take advantage of the therapy unit. The total number of patients and the number on therapy are both expected to double over the next 10 years. During that time, the clinic's property taxes will rise, but profits will go up, too. Not many other clinics will offer the range of services Fairview can offer, and their new therapy unit will help make the clinic more competitive.

The bookkeeper plans to use a straight-line depreciation approach for the therapy unit, but the accountant suggests that another approach might give a better representation of the unit's true worth to the company at any point in time. Besides, she tells the bookkeeper, the choice has only limited financial implications, since the federal tax deduction won't change.

What do you think? Given Fairview's current circumstances, is the straight-line approach as good as any? Or should the clinic consider other methods? Which method would you recommend? Why?

☐ Which depreciation method should Fairview use? Why is this a better choice than other options?

☐ Compare depreciation schedules across at least three different traditional methods for the first five years of the unit's useful life.

☐ Is the accountant right that the federal tax deduction won't change? Do any tax-related matters need to be considered?

☐ Suppose the bookkeeper points out that other equipment at the clinic is being depreciated using the straight-line method. Is that a good argument for using that same method with the therapy unit? Why or why not?

☐ What would be the advantages of leasing the unit (which would be an expense) versus buying the unit and depreciating it? What are the disadvantages?

Happy Times Amusement Park has recently installed a new roller coaster ride that cost $1.2 million. The roller coaster has an estimated useful life of 10 years or 600,000 rides. The roller coaster has been very popular and averages 100 trips per day; it could make as many as 150 trips if the park were open longer. Tickets are $2, and the coaster can carry 50 passengers per trip. It's usually full.

Right now, Happy Times is open eight months per year, five days per week (Wednesday through Sunday). The manager is considering expanding the schedule to seven days per week for the eight-month season. Because of weather, though, the park will probably continue to close for four months out of the year.

Currently, expenditures are running ahead of income for the park as a whole. That's one reason the manager is considering expanding the schedule to more hours per day and more days per week. Other plans include higher rates on popular rides and a general admission fee (which the park does not now charge). The total number of visitors is expected to go up about 10 percent per year for the next five to 10 years.

Depreciation on all the rides is computed by the units-of-production method. But the manager, who'd be the first to admit that he doesn't know a lot about accounting, is questioning this approach, feeling that the park might be cheating itself out of a better tax break right now when times are

SCENARIO 2

not too good and it could use a way of cutting costs. "There must be a better way to depreciate this thing so we can get a bigger break on our taxes," he thinks, "and I'm going to go talk to the accountant about it."

What do you think? Is the units-of-production method as good as any for Happy Times right now? Or would the park really receive a better tax break over the next few years with some other method?

- [ ] What depreciation method would you recommend for Happy Times right now? Why? (Justify your answer with actual dollar figures showing which approach puts Happy Times in the best financial position.)

- [ ] What are some advantages and disadvantages to Happy Times in using the units-of-production method?

- [ ] In general, under what circumstances does the units-of-production method make most sense for a business? Does Happy Times fit those circumstances? In what way?

- [ ] Suppose that Happy Times has 25 rides altogether, including the roller coaster. Should they use the same method to determine depreciation on all the rides? Why or why not? What factors would make the difference?

- [ ] Is the manager's effort to seek a better tax break on depreciating the roller coaster reasonable? Why or why not? What is the accountant likely to tell him about depreciating the ride for tax purposes?

- [ ] What other assets might Happy Times have that should be depreciated using the units-of-production method? Straight-line method? Sum-of-the-years'-digits method? Declining-balance method?

Allocating Costs and Profits 20

THE WALL STREET JOURNAL

"Old MacDonald's Farm will hereafter be known as MacDonald Enterprises Inc. . . . However, I expect to continue to have a close relationship with each of you."

From The Wall Street Journal.
Permission, Cartoon Features Syndicate.

Relatively few businesses these days are owned lock, stock, and barrel by just one person. The idea might sound appealing, for after all, if a *sole proprietorship* does well, then the owner gets all the profits. But in fact there are major disadvantages, too. Responsibility, for one thing. Unless the business is very small indeed, providing all the time, expertise, and money necessary to support it — especially in the beginning — may be more than one person can reasonably handle, however ambitious or committed he or she might be. Further, it's only sensible to point out that not all businesses *do* succeed, by any means. If a business suffers a loss and there is only one owner, there is no one with whom to share that loss.

Small wonder then that for a wide range of reasons, many persons find it advantageous to operate a business as a *partnership*. This means, of course, that profits (as well as losses) must be shared. But does it mean that if there are two partners, they'll split profits and losses fifty/fifty? No, not necessarily. There are countless ways to divide the proceeds and no general rules to dictate what percentage each partner should receive. With one exception, that is: State law usually stipulates that in the absence of any other agreement, profits (or losses) will be divided evenly among the partners. Otherwise, though, it's up to the partners themselves to decide what's fair. As we shall see, there are numerous alternatives.

We'll also address another important issue that business owners face: namely, determining how to allocate costs. Just as profits must be distributed equitably among those who helped generate them, so business expenses need to be allocated to the division, personnel, or product that caused them. Allocating costs provides a realistic basis for budgeting, for distributing resources within the company, and for managerial decisions involving expansions or cutbacks. As you might guess, a manager who couldn't allocate costs correctly and make use of the results would have a tough time running a business.

PART I: INTRODUCING THE MATERIAL

LEARNING OBJECTIVES

Upon completing your study of this lesson, you should be able to:

1. Describe the reasons that a business would want to allocate overhead rather than use a single overhead rate.

2. Given total overhead and floor space requirements, allocate overhead among departments or products based on floor space.

3. Given total overhead, units produced, and the value of each unit, allocate overhead among products based on sales value.

4. Given total overhead and number of employees, allocate overhead among departments or products based on number of employees.

5. Calculate the profits to be distributed to each of the partners in a business when the profits are to be distributed equally.

6. Calculate the profits to be distributed to each of the partners in a business when the profits are to be divided in an agreed ratio.

7. Calculate the profits to be distributed to each of the partners in a business when the profits are to be divided based on original investment.

If you're using the hardcover textbook, *Mathematics for Business*, there are some additional objectives for this lesson. Upon completing your study of the lesson, you should also be able to:

8. Describe the principle of dividing profits or losses by salary and agreed ratio and calculate the division of profits or losses, given total profit or loss, agreed ratio, and salary of each operating partner.

9. Describe the principle of dividing profits or losses by interest on investment and agreed ratio and calculate the division of profits or losses, given profit or loss, agreed ratio, and salary of each operating partner.

LESSON OVERVIEW

The majority of businesses today are owned by more than one person. A business owned by two or more persons is termed a *partnership*, in contrast to a *sole proprietorship*, a business with a single owner.

There are any number of reasons that people choose to go into business with a partner, not the least of which is the psychological comfort of having someone to help with the planning and management and to deal with the hundreds of everyday decisions that go with running a business. But in the real business world, partnerships must be based on something more substantive than companionship. Usually, people go into business together because each perceives that the other has something important to contribute to the business; something like money, time, or expertise.

For instance, say that Rockwell wants to start an import business. He's a world traveler with extensive knowledge of art and antiques but not much capital. Enter Calvin, an investor looking for a promising investment opportunity. Calvin agrees to capitalize Rockwell's effort in exchange for a good return on her investment. Calvin may or may not have anything to do with the actual running of the business; her primary contribution is money. Rockwell, in turn, contributes his expertise and the time he puts into traveling around the world, shopping for antiques, and marketing them through the new company's various outlets. It's a good combination, with each partner providing something the other needs.

No business can succeed without money, of course. Virtually every business requires supplies or equipment of some sort; retail businesses require inventory as well. So you may be thinking that funding is the single most important contribution a partner can make. But often specialized expertise is just as critical and just as hard to come by. Take Murphy, a would-be restaurant owner with some money to invest. He needs a partner to put up some of the initial capital required to rent a building, outfit a kitchen, buy furniture and supplies, and hire a good crew. But not just any partner will do. Murphy needs someone with knowledge of the restaurant business, preferably someone who can also be head chef. Of course, he can *start* a restaurant without that expertise; but keeping it going and making a success of it are something else altogether. What's more, if Murphy plans to apply for a loan, the bank (or other lending institution) is likely to ask whether Murphy has any experience in the restaurant business or is planning to form a partnership with someone who does. His odds of getting the loan are understandably less if the answer is no.

Splitting the Profits: What's Fair?

It might seem logical to assume that if there are two partners in a business, they might divide the profits evenly: 50 percent to one partner and 50 percent to the other. Sometimes that's how it works, but not always. Often, partners agree that the contribution one makes to the business is greater than the contribution made by the other, and they divide the profits accordingly.

For instance, consider our importers, Rockwell and Calvin. In their excitement over starting a new business, they might initially agree to divide everything equally, even though the bulk of the money for the startup came from Calvin. Thus, if the business makes a modest $1,000 profit the first year, each will receive $1,000 ÷ 2, or $500. On the other hand, Calvin might think that Rockwell has a pretty good deal. Here he is, touring the world at her expense, shopping for antiques, while she is risking her money. For that kind of investment and the risk that goes with it, she tells Rockwell, she wants 60 percent of the profits. That leaves Rockwell with 40 percent. Now if the business makes a $1,000 profit, $600 goes to Calvin and the remaining $400 to Rockwell.

Of course, this doesn't have to be a permanent arrangement, and most shrewd business people won't make it one. Calvin and Rockwell, for instance, might have a two-year contract covering the distribution of profits, during which time they'll see how the business goes. At the end of the two years, they can reconsider. This may be especially important to Rockwell, who finds himself doing *more* traveling than he would like and putting in 80-hour weeks marketing merchandise to a growing number of retailers across the country. It may occur to Rockwell as he's racing for a plane for the fourth time in a week that his investment of time and labor has become more valuable than Calvin's original financial investment, and they need to renegotiate their profit distribution agreement accordingly. The point is, the partners are under no legal obligation to split the profits in any way other than what they themselves have agreed to. What's important is how they mutually value the contribution of each partner at any given time. And if they can't agree, the partnership may have to be dissolved.

Dividing Profits by an Agreed Ratio

When Calvin and Rockwell agree to split their profits 50:50 or 60:40, they are using an *agreed ratio*—in effect, a formula for dividing the profits. This ratio might be mathematically determined, or it might just be the result of their mutual agreement. For instance, let's say that the marketing effort gets too big for Rockwell to handle alone, so he sells half of his interest to a new partner, Lucci. Calvin continues to get her 60 percent and Rockwell and Lucci split the remaining 40 percent, giving them each 20 percent of the profits. In other words, their agreed profit ratio is now 60:20:20, or 6:2:2, to reduce it to simpler terms. This is the same as saying that profits will be divided into 10 equal shares (6 + 2 + 2 = 10), and that of those shares, Calvin will get six, Rockwell will get two, and Lucci will get two.

To illustrate how this works, let's suppose that things are booming now for our once-tiny import business, and profits for the year are up to $40,000. Of this amount, Calvin gets six out of 10 shares, or $6/10 \times $40,000 = $24,000. Rockwell and Lucci each get two out of 10 shares, or $2/10 \times $40,000 = $8,000. And we can see from the totals that this accounts for all the profits: $24,000 + $8,000 + $8,000 = $40,000.

Dividing Profits Based on Original Investment

In our preceding example with Calvin and Rockwell, only one partner contributed money to the enterprise; the others contributed their time and talent. But often each partner makes a financial investment in the business and profits are divided accordingly.

For instance, let's say that Perkins, Skully, and Graves start their own traveling theater company, Roadside Productions, Inc. Perkins contributes $10,000, Skully $20,000, and Graves $30,000. Thus, their total investment in Roadside is $10,000 + $20,000 + 30,000 = $60,000. Of this amount, Perkins contributes $10,000 ÷ $60,000, or $1/6$. That will be her share of the profits. Skully's contribution, $20/000 ÷ $60/000, entitles him to $2/6$ of the profits. And Graves will receive $3/6$ of the profits for his contribution of $30,000 ÷ $60,000. Let's say that in its first year of production, the company clears $12,000 in profits. Perkins will receive $1/6 \times $12,000 = $2,000; Skully $2/6 \times $12,000 = $4,000; and Graves $3/6 \times $12,000 = $6,000.

A partner who makes a financial contribution to the business but takes no actual part in running the business is sometimes referred to as a *silent partner*. His or her contribution to the company begins and ends with that financial investment. Meanwhile, though, someone must run the business. And that person must be compensated for the effort.

Say, for instance, that Heath and Johnson own Land and Sea Tours, a service that provides guided fishing trips. Heath invests $100,000 to help Land and Sea buy equipment and set up shop. Johnson contributes no money, but since he's the experienced guide and fisherman, he devotes 50 hours a week to running the business. Heath, who has no interest in fishing, doesn't even stop by to visit; he just reads the monthly financial summary that Johnson mails to his condo in the city.

Because of his initial investment, though, Heath feels he's entitled to the lion's share of the profits, and Johnson readily agrees. Yet Johnson needs to earn a living, too. What motivation will he have for making Land and Sea successful if he's entitled to only a tiny portion of the profits? So they hit on a compromise: Johnson will receive $12,000 to be paid out of the profits, and any remaining profits will be divided according to an agreed ratio of 5:1. Now it may seem to you that Johnson is receiving a salary for his effort, but that's not actually correct. As an owner rather than an employee, Johnson really gets a premature withdrawal of owner's equity. But the effect on the amount of money left for further distribution to the partners is the same, and "salary" is a little easier to talk about than "premature withdrawal of owner's equity."

Let's say that profits for Land and Sea in a given year are $20,000. Out of this we first subtract Johnson's compensation of $12,000: $20,000 − $12,000 = $8,000. This remaining $8,000 is then divided according to the agreed ratio of 5:1. Heath receives ⅚ × $8,000 = $6,667. And Johnson receives ⅙ × $8,000 = $1,333.

Notice that in our scenario, Johnson made no financial contribution to the startup of the business. If he had, the profits might have been divided differently. For instance, let's say that out of that $100,000 Johnson contributed $25,000 and Heath $75,000. In that case, they might have agreed to split the remaining profits (after deducting Johnson's salary) in accordance with that original contribution, Johnson receiving one-quarter and Heath three-quarters. That would have given Johnson a total of $14,000: his $12,000, plus ¼ of the remaining $8,000 (or $2,000). And it would have left Heath with ¾ of the $8,000, or $6,000.

As we indicated earlier, sometimes all the silent partner is looking for is simple return on investment. Take Heath in our preceding scenario. In the final analysis, it is probably much the same to him whether Johnson opens a fishing tour business or candy store or used tire center. Therefore, his decision to go into business with Johnson is based not on a mutual passion for fishing, but on Heath's assessment of the profitability of the business.

In order to get the money needed to start a business, a person like Johnson, equipped with little more than a winning idea and some managerial know-how, may try to lure one or more investors with the promise of a definite return on investment. For instance, Johnson may tell Heath that he's likely to earn a 9 percent return on his $100,000 investment for the first year or two. From Heath's perspective, such an investment isn't too different from putting money into the bank or investing in stocks — except, of course, that the risk is likely higher. Maybe the bank is paying 8½

A Combination Approach: Salary Plus Agreed Ratio

Wanting a Return on the Investment

percent on certificates of deposit. Is Heath wise to invest in Johnson's business? Perhaps not.

Bring on the Cloudy Skies

Of course, despite our profitable scenarios, not all businesses succeed. Further, even those that are ultimately successful may have years when they suffer a loss. Not only is there no profit during these times, but the business without reserves to draw upon may actually wind up in debt. This is not an unusual situation for a new business that may have a large initial investment in buildings, equipment, and supplies, combined with limited income because it hasn't yet had time to establish a large clientele.

In a partnership, the partners commonly share in losses just as they share in profits, and the proportions and ratios are the same. That is, if three partners have an agreed ratio of 5:3:1 for dividing profits, they will apply that same ratio in splitting losses. Let's see how this works.

Keefer, Marx, and Horowitz are partners in Irma's Exotic Pets, which specializes in snakes and other reptiles. Their agreed profit ratio is 5:3:1. Import duties are running high this year, the cost of boa constrictors is up, and a virus wipes out half their aardvarks. All in all, Irma's has income of $100,000 and expenses of $118,000, resulting in a loss of $18,000.

Since $5 + 3 + 1 = 9$, Keefer's share of this loss is $5/9$, Marx's share is $3/9$ or $1/3$, and Horowitz's share is $1/9$. Thus, Keefer owes the business $5/9 \times \$18,000 = \$10,000$; Marx owes $1/3 \times \$18,000 = \$6,000$; and Horowitz owes $1/9 \times \$18,000 = \$2,000$. In other words, each of the owners must pay his or her share of the loss *to the business*. This is a little different from simply not earning any money for the year, and it's part of the risk in owning a business. In the beginning, when these three first bought the pet shop from Irma, Keefer might have been feeling quite pleased to have negotiated more than half the profits for himself. And indeed, his position would be a good one if the business did well.

Keep in mind that where a partner is being compensated with a "salary" or is promised a guaranteed return on investment, those amounts must be deducted from total profits *before* profits are distributed. For instance, say that Bailey, part owner of a catering service, is to receive a guaranteed 10 percent return on her original $50,000 investment. That's $.10 \times \$50,000 = \$5,000$ per year. She splits the remaining profits with her partner, Schultz, in an agreed ratio of 1:2. But what if the business earns only $3,200 in a given year? That's not enough to cover the money promised to Bailey, though it will cover a portion of it. Bailey and Schultz split the remaining loss. It works like this.

On the books, Bailey gets $5,000. But since profits are only $3,200, paying Bailey leaves a loss of $5,000 - \$3,200 = \$1,800$. The partners split the loss (just as they would have split the profits). Their 1:2 ratio tells us that profits or losses are split into three shares, with Bailey assuming $1/3 \times \$1,800 = \$600$, and Schultz assuming $2/3 \times \$1,800 = \$1,200$. Since the company already owes Bailey $5,000, she can simply deduct her $600 loss from this amount: thus, she actually receives $5,000 - \$600 = \$4,400$. But the company only has $3,200 left over. Where's the missing $1,200 going to come from? In theory, from Schultz, who receives no return on investment and must come up with the full $1,200 she owes out of her own pocket.

In practice, partners in a business with losses don't always just sit down and periodically write checks to bring everything back into balance. It's possible for companies to continue for some time with a "paper loss," which means that the partners have incurred a debt but they're not going to settle it up just yet. At some point, though, all this has to be straightened out and the partners will indeed be required to come up with additional funds to cover any losses.

Direct and
Indirect Costs

Obviously, not all the money that a business takes in represents profit. Would that it were so, but to paraphrase the old adage, it costs money to make money.

Take World of Sports, for instance, manufacturer of sporting goods. They have gross sales of more than $200,000 per month. But out of that income, they must pay rent on the factory, employee salaries and benefits, utilities, and advertising costs. In addition, they must buy and maintain manufacturing equipment and purchase the supplies with which to produce their goods. And they also have to pay taxes. What's left over after all this is the *net profit*, what many people think of as the true profit of the business.

Net profit is like the discretionary income of the individual consumer. A person who takes home, say, $1,200 per month can't just spend that money any way he or she likes. Portions of it must go for rent, clothing, food, utilities, and other ongoing expenses. Let's say those expenses add up to $1,000. That leaves $1,200 − $1,000 = $200 for the wage earner to spend or invest. That discretionary income is the consumer equivalent of a business's net profit.

And like a consumer, a business needs to keep track of its expenses. All business expenses can be classified as one of two types: a direct cost or an indirect cost. Direct costs are those directly associated with the production of goods. At World of Sports, for instance, direct costs would cover the cost of raw materials (e.g., the leather in a baseball glove) plus the labor required to produce the final product. Generally speaking, direct costs are those that go up when production goes up. The leather for 2,000 baseball gloves will cost more than the leather for 1,000, and the leather for zero baseball gloves doesn't cost anything at all.

Indirect costs, also called *overhead*, are ongoing expenses that do not directly contribute to the production of goods. For instance, overhead costs at World of Sports would include rent, utilities, salaries for the administrative staff, insurance, advertising fees, the cost of computerizing the accounting system, and so forth. Each of these things contributes in an indirect way to the success of the company and to the marketing and sale of the company's products. So it's not correct to look at the overhead costs as somehow "less important" or "less justifiable" than direct costs. But computerizing the accounting system will cost the same whether the company produces a record number of baseball gloves or none at all, so it's an indirect cost.

Distribution
of Overhead

Suppose that it actually costs World of Sports $12 to manufacture one Model A-34 baseball glove; that cost covers the materials used in production, plus the labor required to turn those materials into a salable product. Then if World can sell the glove to a distributor for $15, it will make a profit, right? Probably not. The only fair way to answer that question is to determine what portion of *overhead* goes into the manufacture and distribution of the Model A-34 glove.

After all, the workers who put the glove together are using company equipment during the process. They're housed in a building on which World is paying rent, and as they work, the company is paying for lights, heat, telephones, and so forth. The glove will be advertised in various catalogues and brochures, and that advertising must be paid for. And there's a company president overseeing the whole thing, and his or her salary needs to be paid. All in all, let's say that the overhead required to support production of the baseball glove is $8. If we add this to the direct costs of $12, we see that the company must price the glove at $20 just to break even and must charge more than $20 to realize any profit.

Realistically, World of Sports might decide to sell the gloves for $32. Now they're making a $12 gross profit ($32 − $20 = $12). But there's more to be analyzed here. Recall that overhead on the gloves is $8. In other words, it's 25 percent of the selling price of the glove: $8 ÷ $32 = $1/4 = 25%. Is that good or bad? Well, it depends. If the company discovers, in reviewing comparable overhead figures for other products, that its overhead generally runs about *15 percent* of sales, it might be time to consider whether the A-34 baseball glove is being manufactured and marketed efficiently. Maybe more money is spent on A-34 advertising, or maybe the assembly line takes up too much factory floor space.

Inequities in overhead don't necessarily mean something is wrong, of course. Often one department truly needs more space or a bigger staff than another. And some products simply cost more to produce than others. But let's say that World of Sports is devoting 15 percent of its total overhead to making baseball gloves, but those gloves represent only 5 percent of the company's profits. If water skis represent 25 percent of the company's profits and only 5 percent of its overhead, then it's possible that the company can be more profitable producing skis than it can producing gloves, and it could be time to think about reconfiguring the production space.

At the same time, let's not be hasty. Naturally, profit margin is important, too; it would be a dreadful error to stop making baseball gloves just because the overhead is higher than average. World of Sports can sell A-34 baseball gloves that cost $20 to make for $32, a healthy 60 percent markup. If it costs $95 to produce a pair of water skis that a distributor will pay only $100 for, the fact that the skis had a lower overhead allocation doesn't make them the preferred product.

Allocating Overhead: Why Bother?

It may occur to you that computing total overhead costs for a company is not so tricky. You just add together the costs for rent, lights, heat, executive salaries, and so forth, and come up with a grand total. So why not just stop there? Well, you could if your business were very small. Take Joe's Hot Dog Stand, for instance. Joe owns his own stand and it occupies only 16 square feet, so he isn't too concerned with what he's spending per square foot on overhead. He has no employees; he's sole proprietor and manager. He deals in one basic product — hot dogs — and has no thoughts of expanding. Thus, there are no departments or divisions; Joe's business isn't that complex. The big question is, can he afford to stay in business, given what it costs him to make and sell his hot dogs? One overhead figure will answer that question nicely. So that's all Joe needs to compute.

Many businesses, though, are considerably more complicated than Joe's. These business owners want to know how one department compares to another in terms of efficient use of resources, whether certain types of products may be produced more cheaply than others, or whether resources should be allocated differently among departments or production units. To answer these sorts of questions, the business owner must compare the overhead ratios for various products or departments to one another and to the ratio for the business as a whole. That's one way a company like World of Sports can decide whether to produce more base-ball gloves and fewer water skis, or whether to put more money into advertising and less into staff training.

One word of caution here, though: An unusually low overhead rate for one product or division can reflect a very efficient use of resources, or it *can* result from computing overhead in a way that ignores important cost factors. To understand this better, let's take a closer look at how overhead ratios are calculated. As with profit allocation, there are several choices.

Perhaps the most common way to allocate overhead is by the amount of *floor space* occupied by each department or production line within a company. This method works particularly well any time that physical space is a good indicator of what it costs the company to run a department or division. Consider an imaginary newspaper office, for instance. It produces essentially one thing; the newspaper. But different divisions contribute to that production, including, let's say, Reporting and Editing, Circulation, Production, and Advertising. These different divisions all occupy differing amounts of floor space, so their share of the overhead will also differ.

Computing Overhead by Floor Space

Suppose the paper occupies 50,000 square feet of floor space. Of this total, Reporting and Editing takes up 25,000 square feet, Circulation 5,000, Production another 10,000, and Advertising the final 10,000. If overhead is $200,000, let's see how it would be allocated among these four divisions.

Reporting and Editing takes up $25,000 \div 50,000$, or $\frac{1}{2}$ of the total floor space. So its share of overhead is also half: $\frac{1}{2} \times \$200,000 = \$100,000$. Circulation is squeezed into just 5,000 square feet, so its share is $5,000 \div 50,000 = \frac{1}{10} \times \$200,000 = \$20,000$. Production occupies 10,000 square feet, so its share will be $10,000 \div 50,000 = \frac{1}{5} \times \$200,000 = \$40,000$. Advertising is the same. Is this a good distribution of costs? That depends.

Reporting and Editing may not like the way things have come out. Why should it pay more overhead than anyone else when it has no more employees than the other divisions and requires less specialized equipment? The reason: They're taking up more floor space. Meanwhile, notice that Circulation is responsible for a fairly small share of the total, just $20,000. Is this a sensible allocation?

The whole issue turns on whether the square footage is proportional to the accumulated overhead costs. Often it is. Certainly things like heat, lights, and insurance on the building can defensibly be allocated on this basis. More importantly, though, square footage is often a reflection of the number of employees; it is, for example, likely that the Reporting and Editing Group has considerably more employees than, say, Circulation. And when that's the case, all the overhead costs related to employees (everything from the personnel department to the company picnic) can also be sensibly allocated by square footage.

When a business specializes in either selling or manufacturing a wide range of products, it often makes sense to allocate overhead on the basis of the sales value of those products. This is particularly true if the divisions are roughly equivalent in size. In that case, allocation by square footage would make each division responsible for roughly the same overhead. But if the value of what they produce is very different, that kind of equal distribution of costs might not seem fair.

Allocating Overhead by Sales Value

For instance, to keep our illustration simple, imagine a manufacturer, Rugby Coats, that produces just four products: ski jackets, rain slickers, sports coats, and silk jackets. Again, for the sake of simplicity, we'll suppose that during a given period the production totals are just 100 of each but the sales values differ. The sales value for ski jackets is $50, or a total of $100 \times \$50 = \$5,000$. The sales value for slickers is $40, or a total of $100 \times \$40 = \$4,000$. The sales value for sports coats is $60, for a total of $100 \times \$60 = \$6,000$. And the sales value for silk jackets (a hot fashion item this year) is $90, for a total of $100 \times \$90 = \$9,000$. That makes the total value of all jackets $\$5,000 + \$4,000 + \$6,000 + \$9,000 = \$24,000$.

Now let's allocate an overhead of $10,000. Again, it's just a matter of proportion, or setting up a series of ratios. The total value on the ski jackets is $5,000. That means this department's share of overhead is $\$5,000 \div \$24,000 = \frac{5}{24}$. Thus, $\frac{5}{24} \times \$10,000 = \$2,083.33$. The total value on the slickers is $4,000, so this department's share of overhead is $\$4,000 \div \$24,000 = \frac{1}{6} \times \$10,000 = \$1,666.67$.

The total sales value of the sports coats is $6,000, so their share of overhead is $\$6,000 \div \$24,000 = \frac{1}{4} \times \$10,000 = \$2,500$. And the share for the silk jacket division is $\$9,000 \div \$24,000 = \frac{9}{24} \times \$10,000 = \$3,750$.

Notice that the silk jacket division is paying the highest overhead, more than a third of the total. In some ways this seems very fair, since its product has the highest sales value and presumably the highest potential for profit. On the other hand, the manager must ask whether it really costs the company more to run this department. It may or it may not. Perhaps this division is actually a little smaller than the others. Perhaps its production takes less equipment, or has a smaller staff or use fewer supplies. The point is, it is important for the business manager to ensure that the way overhead is allocated reflects as closely as possible the way resources are really being used by the company.

In actual practice, though, figuring overhead based on sales value is not as useful (or as widely used) as you might think. The problem is that few companies have just a handful of products. In real life, a clothing manufacturer like Rugby Coats would likely have dozens of products, not just the four we used in our example. Besides, it's pretty unlikely that it'd be possible to track the overhead associated with sports coats versus silk jackets, since the odds are that the same employees and the same machines make both. All in all, the complexity of tracking costs considerably limits the use of allocation by sales value.

Still Another Method: Numbers of Employees

Overhead can also be computed according to the number of employees associated with a department or product. This approach may make good sense in a company where each employee takes up about the same floor space, uses similar equipment, and does similar work. In an accounting firm, for instance, or a group of technical writers, one employee likely costs the company the same overhead as another. If Project A requires twice the staff time as Project B, an overhead allocation method that charges twice as much to Project A makes a great deal of sense.

Like the other methods we've looked at, allocation by number of employees requires forming a ratio between each department, division, or project and the company as a whole. For instance, let's say that Arnold Consulting has 10 employees assigned to the Williams project, five on the Dewey Street renovation, and the remaining five on the Baldwin planning study. Their overhead for the period is $5,000. Since there are 20 employees in all, the Williams team will have an overhead of $\frac{10}{20} \times \$5,000$, or $2,500. The Baldwin and Dewey Street projects, with five employees each, will have identical overheads: $\frac{5}{20} \times \$5,000 = \$1,250$.

As you might guess, there's no simple answer to the question of which allocation approach is the right one. It depends on the nature of the business and the way in which overhead expenses are generated. Recall that earlier we noted the importance of distributing profits equitably, according to the relative contributions each partner provides to a business. The allocation of overhead is not too different, really. The desirable approach is the one that will match responsibility for overhead with the actual overhead costs each department or product creates. In other words, if the production line for the fiberglass multiwidget uses the most equipment, employs the most staff, and takes up the most space, we would logically assume that the product will carry the highest overhead. And if we later learn that the multiwidget is contributing relatively little to the company's profits, it might be time to do a little investigating.

Sometimes it is helpful for an owner or manager to compute overhead using more than one method, then compare the results in light of those factors that are contributing most to overhead costs. But the likelihood is that one way is simply going to make more sense than the others, and if the best method isn't obvious, it's easy enough to look at how overhead allocation is handled by others in the same business. If every competitor you have allocates overhead by number of employees, it might pay to consider the matter a bit further before deciding that sales value is the best approach for you.

Allocating overhead sometimes looks a little like smoke and mirrors: just a way of moving costs around on paper. But analyzed carefully, overhead allocations can provide the business owner or manager with some important insights on the relative costs of operating various departments or divisions within a company, and that's a vital clue to assessing overall efficiency.

SOME WORDS OF ADVICE

With respect to profit distribution, it's advisable for partners to formulate an agreement in advance of finalizing the partnership and to take their time in negotiating the particulars of that agreement, with an eye on each partner's anticipated contribution to the effort. A partner who contributes 50 percent of the initial funding and winds up with 90 percent of the management responsibilities may be less than delighted with a fourth of the profits.

As a prospective business partner, don't forget that as important as the investment of dollars is to a business, the value of expertise or commitment of time and effort must not be underestimated. All the funding in the world will not drive a business to success if it is poorly managed or run by persons with virtually no experience or skill in the field.

Remember that if the business partners together have agreed to fund either a salary or a guaranteed return on investment out of profits, this must be deducted *before* remaining profits can be distributed. Therefore, it is wise to make some realistic projections about the probable success of the business before becoming overcommitted. A partner who is also an experienced business manager may command a high salary, and rightfully so. But often the meager profits of a struggling young business will simply not support this kind of expense. Better to be realistic than to drive the business into debt. Similarly, resist the temptation to guarantee a silent partner an unrealistic return on investment just to get the startup funding in hand. Unrealistic expectations lead to profound disappointments, and occasionally to lawsuits. Remember that your promised return on an investment may be a legally binding agreement. More than one zealous entrepreneur has found his or her company being liquidated when the investors demanded their promised payoff.

Which brings us to another critical point: Keep in mind that partners share in losses as well as profits. So before becoming involved in any business, it's wise to ask yourself whether you could afford potential setbacks and whether you're willing and able to keep funding a business that may not stand on its own for the first few years. The promise of profits is tempting, but those profits are not assured, and every partner should have a contingency plan for how to cope with the bad times that may come.

Every company that's alive and well has overhead expenses of some kind. So it's important for the business manager to be familiar with methods for computing and allocating overhead and to know how to select the allocation approach that most closely approximates the way in which the company actually consumes resources. While there is no single correct answer, determining which method of allocation will provide the best indicator of relative costs from product to product or department to department is critical, so the issue can't simply be ignored.

It almost always makes sense to ask what others in the same industry are doing. For instance, if most clothing retailers are allocating overhead by sales value, then a company needs a good reason to use some other approach. That's not to say that it's always wrong to be different. But it's also only sensible to realize that such industry traditions are usually established on the basis of experience. Thus, if most retailers think that sales value is a logical approach to overhead allocation for their kind of business, they're probably right. Furthermore, a retailer who instead chooses to allocate overhead on the basis of square footage won't be able to compare overhead costs accurately with those of other comparable businesses, and that means giving up an important piece of information.

The careful manager will take time to analyze the results of overhead allocation in light of current production. It's important to ask which departments or divisions are showing the highest (or lowest) profitability, where resources could be used more efficiently, where expansion is called for, or where cuts are indicated. For instance, if a company is spending a disproportionate share of its overhead on the production of felt hats and no one is buying them, it's time to rethink the company's product line. On the other hand, if toy trains are selling at a great rate, the toy company has every right to be proud of its low overhead on this item, *if* it's computed appropriately.

Maybe it's low because the company really is devoting few resources to the production of the item. That's great. But maybe it's low because, despite the fact that the train department takes up a full fourth of the company's production area, the rate of production is so slow that overhead based on *sales value* is very low. If overhead were based on square footage, the train division would be charged with one-fourth of the company's total overhead expenses; and that, combined with slow sales, might make it look markedly inefficient. In short, choosing the "right" allocation method is important. It takes a combination of math skills, common sense, and thorough knowledge of how the company spends its money to come up with the best answer for any given company.

KEY TERMS

Before you read through the text assignment and watch the video program, take a minute to look at the key terms associated with this lesson. When you encounter them in the text and video program, pay careful attention to their meaning.

Agreed ratio: An agreed-upon ratio by which partners of a business divide the profits and losses of that business.

Allocation of overhead: Dividing the overhead among the various products or divisions within a company.

Capital: Money invested in a business.

Floor space: One basis for the allocation of overhead. The actual amount of physical space occupied by a department, office, or other division within a company.

Overhead: Any expenses involved in running a firm that are not directly connected with the production of goods. For instance, the cost of the wool fabric used in the production of a coat *is not* part of overhead; rent paid on the factory space where production occurs *is* overhead.

Partnership: A business owned by two or more people.

Salary plus agreed ratio: An arrangement by which one or more partners in a business are granted a salary out of profits, with remaining profits divided according to agreement. See *agreed ratio*.

Sales value: The value of sales for each department within a company. This is one basis for allocation of overhead.

Sole proprietorship: A business owned by just one person.

PART II: WATCHING THE VIDEO PROGRAM

VIDEO VIEWING GUIDE

Before watching the video program, review the following questions. As you watch, be sure to collect the information necessary to answer them:

1. What are some advantages in setting a business up as a partnership? What are some disadvantages?

2. Are there businesses that almost have to be run as partnerships rather than sole proprietorships? If so, what are some examples?

3. How do business partners determine an appropriate *agreed ratio* for dividing profits? What might be a reason to change that ratio over time?

4. What is a silent partner? What motivates someone to wish to be a silent partner in a business? What are some advantages/disadvantages to this arrangement?

5. Sometimes partners agree to pay a salary or return on investment out of profits before any further division is made. Is this a good idea or a risky one for a new business? Explain.

6. What exactly is overhead? Does the definition vary from business to business?

7. Why do owners or managers allocate overhead rather than simply using a single overhead rate for the business as a whole? Are there *any* businesses for which a single rate would work just as well? If so, give one or two examples.

8. Describe several ways in which overhead can be allocated. Then explain in general terms how an owner or manager knows which approach to use in allocating overhead.

9. Describe one or more business decisions that you, as a business manager, would make based on information on overhead allocation.

VIDEO PROGRAM

The lesson's video program is Program 20 — Allocating Costs and Profits. Remember, if you are watching this program on videotape, take time to replay sections of the tape any time you need to review a concept.

VIDEO VIEWING QUESTIONS

Immediately after viewing the video program for Lesson 20, take time to respond to the following questions. Give your answers some careful thought; they may provide the basis for additional discussions or a longer written response.

1. Name three advantages in setting a business up as a partnership.

   a. _____

   b. _____

   c. _____

2. Name two disadvantages in forming a business partnership.

   a. _____

   b. _____

3. Imagine that you are going to be partners with Chris Raymond in running a videotape rental store. Chris is putting up $40,000 cash but will be a silent partner. You are putting up $10,000 cash and will manage

the business, making whatever commitment of time and effort that takes. Explain exactly the arrangements you think would be appropriate and fair for dividing the profits of this business. Include the agreed ratio you think fits this situation. Explain the reasons behind your answer.

_____

_____

_____

4. Name two situations that might develop that would make you and Chris Raymond (Question 3) modify your partnership agreement. Be specific.

   a. _____

   b. _____

5. Which of the following businesses, if any, could be run more effectively as partnerships than as sole proprietorships? (Check as many as apply. Be prepared to give reasons for your answers.)

   _____ Gas station

   _____ Grocery

   _____ Department store

   _____ Pet shop

   _____ Candy store

   _____ Restaurant

   _____ Shoe repair store

   _____ Resort

   _____ Boat manufacturing company

   _____ Food processing company

   _____ Jewelry store

6. An investor, Woodrow Pierce, offers you $100,000 to help you start a new business. Pierce will be a silent partner. He wants a 12 percent (simple interest) guaranteed return on his investment and you would keep any remaining profits. Alternately, though, he'll accept an agreed ratio of 3:1 (three parts to him, one to you). Which offer is more appealing? Explain why. Can you think of a better offer that Pierce might accept? If so, describe it and explain your reasons.

_____

_____

_____

7. In your own words, describe the difference between direct costs and overhead.

_____

_____

8. Suppose you are owner of Smoof, Inc., which manufacturers only one product, the amazing SmoofBall, a plastic ball that returns to the thrower like a boomerang. Which of the following would normally be classified as overhead at your business? (Check all that apply, and be prepared to explain your answers.)

_____ Rent

_____ Utilities

_____ Taxes

_____ Costs of buying equipment

_____ Costs of maintaining equipment

_____ Costs of buying raw materials used in production

_____ Employee hourly wages

_____ Employee benefits

_____ Executive salaries

_____ Advertising

9. Imagine that you run a business that has two main parts: a bakery and an attached restaurant. Would you allocate overhead or use a single rate for the business as a whole? Explain. If you would allocate, describe the circumstances under which you might use each of the methods described in the video.

_____

_____

10. Name some decisions that a business owner/manager is in a better position to make *following* allocation of overhead.

_____

_____

11. Of the three approaches to allocating overhead that you've looked at (square footage, sales value, and number of employees), which approach would you recommend for each of the following types of businesses? Be prepared to give a reason for your answer.

_____ Cattle ranch

_____ Dentist's office

_____ Hospital

_____ Private school

_____ Grocery

_____ Dry cleaner

_____ Furniture manufacturer

_____ Auto manufacturer

_____ Hardware store

_____ Restaurant

PART III: FOCUSING ON THE MATHEMATICS

After watching the video program, you should read one of the following Text Assignments, depending on the textbook you're using:

SOFTCOVER: Appendix A at the end of this study guide, pages 541-552.

HARDCOVER: Pages 653-667 from Chapter 18 of the Salzman, Miller, and Hoelzle hardcover text, *Mathematics for Business*.

As you read through the text, pay careful attention to the examples the book gives of the mathematics associated with the concepts you're learning about.

Then, after you've completed the text assignment, read through the Key Formula below. This section provides a handy review of what you've learned. By the time you get to this point in the lesson, all of the formulas and calculations should be familiar to you. If they're not, go back and read the appropriate parts of the text and the Overview section of this lesson. You won't have much success completing the rest of your assignments if you are still confused about the information in the Key Formula section.

KEY FORMULA

The following key formula is important to your understanding of this lesson. Be sure that you know it and how to use it in solving problems related to profit distribution.

KEY FORMULA:	Profit distribution = Profits × (Partner's number of shares ÷ Total number of shares)
Formula used for:	Determining the amount of the profit to be given to a partner when profits are divided by an agreed ratio.

Example:

Meekler is a silent partner in an ice cream store that has two other partners. The store's profits for the year were $12,000. These profits are to be divided using an agreed ratio of 6:5:1, with Meekler's share being the smallest. Therefore, his share is $12,000 × ($1/12$) = $1,000.

Remember that in this formula:

1. This formula will work for any number of partners, but it can be applied only to the amount of profit left to be distributed. Don't use the gross (pretax) profit or profits figured before mandatory payments to managing partners or partners with guaranteed returns are made.

DON'T FORGET

1. If partners in a business make no other formal arrangements, most states require that profits will be divided equally. Otherwise, however, the law allows partners to make any arrangement that is mutually acceptable to them.

2. The profits that each partner will receive can be expressed as either a percentage or a ratio. For instance, if Partner A receives 60 percent and Partner B 40 percent, then the agreed ratio is 60:40, or 6:4, or 3:2. Obviously, the percentages received by the partners will always total 100 percent.

3. One common way of dividing profits is on the basis of original investment. When this method is used, each partner's proportionate contribution to the original investment forms the basis for the agreed ratio. For instance, if Partner A contributes $50,000 out of a total of $100,000, then her portion of profits will be $50,000 ÷ $100,000 = 50 percent. This portion will hold true regardless of how many other partners banded together to provide the remaining $50,000.

4. Profits may be affected by payments to managing partners or guaranteed returns to investors. In either case, the salary or interest on investment is deducted from total profits before any further division is computed. For instance, suppose Partner A contributes $100,000 with a guaranteed 10 percent annual return *plus* a 1:1 agreed ratio. If the annual profit is $12,000, it will be divided this way: First, A will receive $100,000 × .10 = $10,000 in interest on her investment. The remaining $2,000 will be split 50:50, so A will get an additional $1,000 and her partner the other $1,000.

PART IV: SOLVING BUSINESS PROBLEMS

PROBLEM SETS

Work the following problems in your textbook. Your instructor will tell you which problems, if any, are to be turned in. Some of the problems have answers provided in the back of the book; refer to these answers to make sure you are working the problems correctly.

SOFTCOVER: If you are using the Miller, Salzman, and Hoelzle softcover text, *Business Mathematics*, do the following problem sets from Appendix A at the end of this study guide:

A.1: Problems #1-22 on pages 545-547.

A.2: Problems #1-18 on pages 550-552.

HARDCOVER: If you are using the Salzman, Miller, and Hoelzle hard-cover text, *Mathematics for Business*, do the following problem sets:

18.4: Problems #1-22 on pages 658-660.

18.5: Problems #1-18 on pages 663-667.

BUSINESS APPLICATIONS

Read each of the following scenarios and answer the questions about the decisions you would make in each situation. Give these questions some serious thought; they may be used as the basis for discussion or the development of a more complex essay. You should base your decisions on what you've learned from this lesson, applying both math skills and good business judgment to solve the problem at hand.

Arnie Windsor and Kevin Kall decide to form a small publishing company where aspiring writers can pay to have their books published. Windsor, who knows next to nothing about the publishing business, puts up $80,000 in cash to help the company, Western Self-Publishing, get off the ground. Kall contributes just $10,000 (the maximum he can afford) but agrees to run the company. This turns out to be a major undertaking, demanding 20 to 30 hours per week of Kall's time.

According to their arrangement, Windsor will receive a 15 percent simple interest return on his investment annually, and remaining profits will be split 1:4, one part to Windsor, four to Kall. Unfortunately for Kall, the first five years are not good ones, and Western barely clears $8,000 per year in profits—far below his original optimistic projections. In its sixth year, however, the business begins to take off as its client base grows. The projected profit for the year is $15,000, which is well over anything Western has done to date.

What's more, the company could do even better if it could expand to include more space and a new computerized typesetting system. Windsor doesn't want to put up the money for the system, however, and Kall is reluctant to take it out of his share of the profits; this will be the first year he's realized much income at all from this venture. Several contracts hang in the balance. With the new typesetting capabilities, Kall might conceivably realize a profit as high as $25,000 for next year, with modest increases in the years to come.

An outside investor, Brady, has shown some interest in putting money into the business. Brady, who has some experience in the publishing industry, thinks she might like to be involved in running the business but is open to negotiating whatever arrangements would be comfortable for the current owners. She can afford to invest up to $60,000. That will cover the cost of the typesetting system in full, with about $10,000 left over.

Kall thinks it is definitely time to work out a new agreed ratio, together with other specifications for dividing profits, though he is uncertain as to what those new arrangements should be. But he isn't sure whether this is the right time to take on another partner. Windsor, for his part, is not in favor of taking on a new partner, but since he won't put up the money for expansion, Kall points out that there are not many options. Windsor

SCENARIO 1

counters that it is too early for expansion; the business is growing enough as is, and besides, it cannot support another partner just now.

What do you think? Are there relative advantages to be gained by taking Brady on as a third partner, or is Windsor right in pointing out that the business cannot really support another person right now? If you were in Kall's place, what new agreed ratio or other arrangements would you hope to negotiate in working out an equitable means of dividing profits?

□ Is this a good time for Western to expand and take on a new partner? Why or why not?

□ Suppose that Western *does* expand and that Brady becomes a partner in the firm. What agreed ratio or other arrangements would you recommend to ensure the fairest possible distribution of profits among the three owners? Be specific and explain the reasons behind your answer.

□ Suppose that Western *does not* take Brady on as a new partner right now. Is there still reason to renegotiate the agreement Kall and Windsor have for profit distribution? Why or why not? What agreed ratio and other arrangements would you recommend in that case? Be specific and explain the reasons behind your answer.

□ What are the specific major factors that Kall, Windsor, and (possibly) Brady need to consider in working out their agreed ratio or other arrangements for profit distribution? Which of the three do you think is making the greatest contribution to the company? Why?

□ Five years from now, it's possible that Windsor, Kall, and Brady (if she is part of the business) will need to review their agreed ratio for profit distribution. Why? Name two specific changes in their working relationship or in the business itself that would warrant totally new arrangements.

□ Suppose that Western Self-Publishing has a very bad year and loses $10,000. What are the mathematical implications of this turn of events under Windsor and Kall's *current* arrangement? In other words, how much would each receive or owe the business? Would this be fair to Windsor? To Kall? Why or why not?

SCENARIO 2 Garden Fresh Grocery is currently basing its overhead allocation on square footage. Up until now, rent and utilities have been the two major factors contributing to total overhead costs. The grocery has done major remodeling and expansion during the past five years, both of which have added to overhead, though the costs have been more than offset by rising profits.

This year, however, there are other changes. Garden Fresh has hired more than 20 additional employees, plus three additional department managers and a general manager; all four of them command salaries of $40,000 or more. In addition, they've installed a computerized checkout and inventory system and a state-of-the-art video system to prevent shoplifting and to help make managers immediately aware of accidents, spillage, blocked aisles, or other problems as they arise throughout the store. All of this makes the new general manager, Ted Ames, wonder whether it is still a good idea to base overhead allocation on square footage or whether they ought to consider some other approach.

The grocery is divided into four major divisions: Bakery and Deli, Meat Market, Produce, and Grocery. At a general meeting, the managers of the Produce and Grocery departments complain that they are paying an unfair share of overhead costs. They occupy twice the floor space of either the Bakery or Meat section but have no more employees. Further, each of their departments has one division manager, whereas the Bakery and Meat sections each have two. Worse yet, they argue, is the fact that both the Bakery and Meat departments require large investments in the purchase and maintenance of special equipment. It doesn't seem fair, they say, that they must pay a larger portion of overhead costs out of their budgets when it is the other departments that are incurring those costs. The Bakery and Meat managers counter that they take up less floor space and therefore cost the business less in rent and utilities. Further, they contend, their presence in the store brings in customers who would otherwise shop somewhere else. So in this way, they do carry their own weight.

Store manager Ames agrees that there are some inequities in the current computations and suggests allocating overhead by sales value for a year. The store's accountant, however, objects, maintaining that square footage is still the fairest method under the circumstances, despite differences in staff, sales value, and equipment use.

What do you think? Do you agree with the accountant that square footage provides the best basis for allocating overhead at Garden Fresh, or is Ames right to consider a new approach?

☐ Should Garden Fresh continue to use floor space as the basis for allocating overhead? Why or why not? Be specific in your answer.

☐ What other approach, if any, would you recommend? Give a reason for your answer.

☐ Right now, Grocery and Produce are carrying more of the overhead costs than the Meat or Bakery divisions. How, if at all, would this change if the allocation were based on sales value? Will each department look more or less profitable following the change?

☐ Suppose Ted Ames knows that overhead for the store as a whole represents 20 percent of gross profit. How might he use this information in analyzing overhead rates for each department?

☐ Suppose that rent is tending not to go up but other overhead costs are on the rise. How important is this information to Ames's decision about allocating overhead? Should it make a real difference, or should he just ignore it? Explain.

☐ Under what circumstances, if any, would it make sense for Garden Fresh to allocate overhead based on the number of employees in each department? Explain.

Financial Statements 21

UGH! I HATE DOING THESE ANNUAL PERFORMANCE WRAP-UP REPORTS!

SALES FIGURES, PROFIT & LOSS STATEMENTS...

IT'S A PAIN IN THE YEAR-END.

Perhaps no two business people would agree totally on what it takes to run a successful business, but one thing is critical to everyone: keeping track of the business's finances. The business that knows precisely what it's bringing in, and what it's spending, is in a much better position to make decisions and to spend money more wisely in the future. Of course, no amount of good bookkeeping will take the place of sound management. But if a business is losing money, then the sooner the business manager uncovers this unhappy fact and the reasons behind it, the greater the likelihood of turning the situation around.

Two important tools provide the business person with the information he or she needs for good financial decision making. These are, first, the *income statement*, which is essentially a record of business income and expenses over a specified period of time, and second, the *balance sheet*, a summary of the business's assets and liabilities (or debts) at a given point in time. Together, as we'll see in this lesson, these two kinds of records provide a financial profile of the business.

Like any statistical summary, the information provided by the income statement and balance sheet is necessarily limited. It obviously won't indicate whether staff are helpful and friendly to customers, or whether the products and services provided by the business are consistently those that customers want most. But it will provide a wealth of critical information that, if analyzed correctly, can help to show whether the current financial position of the business is a strong one; whether it can afford to expand or needs to clear away some of its debt load first, for example. It can also show whether the business is spending more on employee wages and benefits than in previous years, whether taxes are taking a bigger bite out of gross profit, or whether overhead expenditures are higher or lower than for similar companies in the industry. Such information is of considerable interest to the business manager, who needs to know how successful his or her business is in competing for its share of the market.

By the way, though income statements and balance sheets have no blank spaces for recording notes on friendly employees or successful products, the impact of such factors is sure to be reflected in these financial statements. Whether the business is successful or unsuccessful, one of the most important questions for the owner or manager to ask is why. As we'll see in this lesson, accurate financial statements help provide the answer.

PART I: INTRODUCING THE MATERIAL

LEARNING OBJECTIVES

Upon completing your study of this lesson, you should be able to:

1. Explain the purpose of an income statement and define the key terms used in income statements, including gross margin, net sales, cost of goods sold, net income, and operating expenses.

2. Know the formulas for determining gross margin and net income and calculate both, given the net sales, cost of goods sold, and operating expenses.

3. Calculate the cost of goods sold from initial and final inventory values, cost of goods purchased during the period, and freight.

4. Given a blank income statement and the required basic information, accurately complete the income statement.

5. Know the formula for conducting vertical analysis of an income statement and, given an income statement, find the percent gross margin, percent expenses, and percent net income.

6. Given a comparative income statement, identify by estimation the major areas of change across the period covered.

7. Explain the purpose of a balance sheet and define the key terms used in balance sheets, including assets, liabilities, and owner's equity, and know the mathematical relationship among these three quantities.

8. Given a list of business assets, correctly categorize each as a long- or short-term asset.

9. Given a list of business assets, correctly categorize each as a current asset, a fixed asset, a current liability, or a long-term liability.

10. Given a blank balance sheet and the required basic information, accurately complete the balance sheet.

11. Apply the formula for conducting vertical analysis to a given balance sheet to find the percents for each category.

12. Given a comparative balance sheet, identify by estimation the major areas of change across the period covered.

If you're using the hardcover textbook, *Mathematics for Business*, there are some additional objectives for the lesson. Upon completing your study of the lesson, you should also be able to:

13. Given the income statement of a hypothetical business and the published average category percents for similar businesses, identify areas of similarity and difference.

14. Given two year-end income statements from a hypothetical business, conduct a horizontal analysis to determine the percent of change.

15. Given two year-end balance sheets from a hypothetical business, conduct a horizontal analysis to determine the percent of change.

16. Given several year-end balance sheets and income statements from each of two hypothetical businesses, determine the strengths and weaknesses of each business and determine which business appears to be in the better economic position.

LESSON OVERVIEW

In addition to the business owner or manager, there are two people who typically share responsibility for helping to manage business finances. One is the bookkeeper, the person who is responsible for recording all the data that have to do with income, expenditures, purchases, and payments—in short, data that will ultimately be summarized on the income statement and balance sheet. This person is responsible primarily for seeing that such information is up to date and complete, but rarely if ever does the bookkeeper worry about such issues as why overhead keeps increasing faster than net profit, or the fact that liabilities grew twice as fast as assets in the preceding year.

Such worries tend to be the province of the accountant, whose job is usually not to enter data, but to interpret and analyze what's already there, and to offer explanations and recommendations. The accountant might point out, for instance, that the business was spending more on rent than most competitors, or that investment in new equipment was lagging well behind the industry average. Based on his or her interpretations of the company's finances, an accountant will sometimes recommend new staffing patterns, increased investment, relocation to help reduce property taxes, or other solutions.

In a very small firm, the business manager might wear one or both of these financial hats, but that would be fairly rare for a number of reasons. For one thing, recording all the important financial data, even for a very small business, is time-consuming; few business managers can afford to add this job to their already long list of tasks. Then, too, as you might guess, accounting has become a true specialty, with many complicated procedures, rules, and regulations to deal with. Like being your own lawyer, being your own accountant can lead to problems. And perhaps equally important, the insightful accountant can often see within the data forecasts and trends that would escape the eye of the less experienced observer.

All this is not to suggest, by the way, that the business person who can afford the luxury of hiring both a bookkeeper and an accountant can then afford to sit back while others handle the financial affairs of the business. As valuable as this specialized assistance can be, the business manager is, or should be, in the best position to ensure that financial records are as accurate and complete as possible and that the interpretations placed upon the financial profile of the business are consistent with the way the business is being run.

Beginning the Business Profile: The Income Statement

An *income statement*, as we indicated earlier, is a record of all business income and expenses for a given period. Normally, a business might have monthly or quarterly income statements, which would then be summarized in a longer annual income statement at the end of the year.

An income statement is somewhat like a budget in format, but it is very different in concept, since an income statement is a record of what *has already* occurred, not a plan of action. However, in picturing all the things that would go into an income statement, it may help to think of what information an individual would gather in preparing a budget. First, it would be important to note every source of income. For instance, a person who held more than one job or who wrote magazine articles on the side would need to record *all* those sources, not just the primary source of income. Next, it would be important to keep track of all expenditures—not just the big things like the mortgage payment, but everything, right on down to theater tickets and lunches in the company cafeteria.

Many bits and pieces of information contribute to a business's income statement. As you can see from the sample income statement below, there are several different categories.

INCOME STATEMENT

Gross sales	____
Returns	____
Net sales	____
Inventory, January 1	____
Cost of goods purchased	____
Freight	____
Total cost of goods purchased	____
Total of goods available for sale	____
Inventory, December 31	____
Cost of goods sold	____
Gross profit	____
Expenses	
Salaries	____
Wages	____
Rent	____
Advertising	____
Utilities	____
Taxes on inventory, payroll	____
Miscellaneous expenses	____
Total expenses	____
NET INCOME	____

Let's summarize these briefly. The first important entry is often *gross sales*, or the sum total of all the money the company has brought in as a result of selling its goods or services. The next entry, *returns*, shows the total dollar value of goods that were returned to the company and therefore not paid for. The difference between these two figures then is *net sales*, or the value of all goods and services for which the company was paid during the period: Net sales = Gross sales − Returns. Imagine, for instance, that Import Rug Company makes gross sales of $200,000 during the period, but several customers return their merchandise; one rug is too big for the space, another causes the buyer to sneeze, and so forth. If returns for the period total $40,000, then the net sales will be $200,000 − $40,000, or $160,000.

The next important item to compute is *cost of goods sold*, or what the business spends to make the merchandise available to the consumer. Remember that Import Rug Company has net sales of $160,000. But, of course, they had to pay something for the rugs, too. Let's say that they paid $100,000. Their *gross profit*, or profit before expenses, is the difference between this figure and the total value of net sales. Or, to summarize, Gross profit = Net sales − Cost of goods sold. Thus, the gross profit for Import Rug during this period is $160,000 − $100,000 = $60,000.

Unfortunately for Import Rugs, though, we haven't yet hit the proverbial bottom line in computing profit. Gross profit, remember, is what the company makes prior to paying its expenses. It costs Import Rugs something to do business (aside from what it spends on merchandise per se) and these *operating expenses* must also be deducted before the true profit can be known. For instance, let's say that Import Rugs spends $18,000 on employee salaries and wages, another $6,000 on rent, $2,000 to advertise its rugs, $1,000 on utilities, $3,000 on taxes, and another $1,000 on miscellaneous expenses such as the company retreat and a party to celebrate its tenth anniversary. That's a total of $31,000 in various expenses. Since Net income = Gross profit − Operating expenses, Import Rug's net profit (or net income) for the period is $60,000 − $31,000 = $29,000. Each of these numbers would be noted on (or at least contribute to numbers on) the income statement.

Computing cost would be fairly simple if a company like Import Rugs ordered one shipment of merchandise, put the rugs on the floor on display, then ordered nothing more until the last of those rugs sold. But, of course, that isn't how it works. For one thing, Import Rugs doesn't want to take the chance that a sudden flurry of consumer interest will leave it stripped of inventory. What's more, rug producers are constantly marketing their wares, tempting retail outlets like Import with new designs and discount prices. What this means, of course, is that retailers are continuously restocking their inventory well before they've exhausted the previous supply.

Add to this the fact that consumers keep buying merchandise, but not at a consistent rate, nor in a way that matches the dealer's inventory shipments. In other words, one buyer may purchase a rug that just came in two days ago, while another prefers one that's been in inventory for two years. Naturally, the business cannot very well refuse to sell the new rug until all the old ones are out of stock; few customers are likely to be patient with that kind of regimentation. So, all in all, the computation of cost can get a little tricky.

We might note that this computation is a lot less challenging for the business whose inventory system is fully computerized. The computer, after all, can keep track of merchandise cost sale by sale no matter how

Computing Cost from Inventory

fast goods come into or go out of the store. But even in the absence of that computational wizardry, there's a formula that simplifies the calculations for the merchant who knows the total value of inventory at the beginning and end of the period: Cost = Initial inventory + Cost of goods purchased during the period + Freight − Inventory at the end of the period.

Let's see how this formula works with our friends at Import Rugs. Their inventory at the beginning of the period is valued at $50,000. During the period, they purchase an additional $250,000 worth of rugs, with freight charges of $5,000. (Notice, by the way, that *freight* is considered a part of cost, not a part of overhead.) At the end of the period, their inventory is valued at $205,000. Thus, their *cost* = $50,000 (initial inventory) + $250,000 (purchases) + $5,000 (freight) − $205,000 (value at the end of the period) = $100,000.

Be careful not to confuse *cost of goods sold* with *operating expenses*. In our scenario, for instance, cost is what Import Rugs pays to buy and ship the rugs it sells. Expenses include wages, rent, heat, lights, advertising, or whatever it takes to run the business *over and above* stocking it with goods.

Turning Data into Information

The dollar figures entered on the income statement provide an important foundation for creating the total financial profile to which we referred earlier. They're not enough, though. Data of any kind require some basis for interpretation before they become useful information. For instance, if a doctor measures a patient's temperature and it is 101°F, we really have no way of knowing whether that's good or bad unless we also know that normal is 98.6°F. Knowing what's "normal" gives us a kind of benchmark for interpreting other measurements and giving them meaning that the numbers alone would not have.

One way to add meaning to the numbers on an income statement is through *vertical analysis*, a mathematical computation that represents every important item on the statement as a percent of net sales. Why net sales? Because that figure represents the total income of the business *before that business has spent any money*. Relating all other entries on the income statement to net sales provides a way of asking how the business used the income it collected. In other words, did most of it go for rent, or to cover the cost of buying new merchandise, or for staff salaries? If the company spent a large portion of its income on rent, was that due to increased rates? Or to the fact that the company opened a new branch office? Or to some other factor? And finally, what portion of those net sales dollars trickled down to net profit?

Depending on how the income statement is set up, a company might determine what portion of each sales dollar goes not only to major categories like rent or advertising but also to subcategories such as radio advertising, telephone solicitations, or mass mailings. As you might imagine, knowing what percent of the sales dollar went to these various categories helps the company decide how it ought to do business in the future. If mass mailings are twice as expensive as radio advertising and they're not bringing the company any real business, then perhaps they should be discontinued, and that portion of overhead can then go into buying more radio time or can be used in some other way. (Of course, the cost information has to be combined with information about how effective the different advertising was, information that no financial statement can provide.)

The formula for computing percent of net sales is the familiar $R = P \div B$ formula. In this formula, R equals rate, P is part, and B is base. As we're using the formula in this situation, R is the percent of net sales and

P is the dollar value of the particular item we're considering at the moment: gross profit, perhaps, or total overhead, or employee wages. And *R* is the total value of net sales.

Let's say that the manager of Chatham Computers wants to know how total overhead relates to net sales and how one portion of overhead (salaries and wages) relates to net sales for the period. Let's start with total overhead, which happens to be $31,000. This is the *part* in the formula. Net sales total $278,000; this is the *base*. Thus, $R = \$31,000 \div \$278,000 = .1115$, or 11.15 percent. (As always, we move the decimal two places to the right in converting a decimal figure to a percent.) In other words, the amount that the company spends on total overhead is roughly 11 percent of the amount of its total net sales.

Now let's look at salaries and wages specifically. This total is, say, $15,000 for the period. Thus, $R = \$15,000 \div \$278,000 = .0539$, or 5.4 percent. In other words, what the company spends on wages is roughly 5 percent of the amount of its net sales, which means it accounts for a bit less than half the overhead.

You may be wondering at this point what use the computer store manager will make of this information. That's a good question. If she has just this one isolated document to work with, then her ability to use the information effectively will necessarily be a little limited. But let's stop and think for a moment what it is that the manager is trying to find out.

Using the Information

The first question involves relative expenditures. Recall that overhead is about 11 percent of net sales. Compare this to the percent for total cost of goods sold: over 80 percent of net sales. Though these figures don't give us a complete picture of business operations at Chatham Computer, they do suggest that the relatively high cost of goods has a bigger effect on the bottom line than overhead. In other words, while it wouldn't be a waste of time for Chatham staff to be conscientious about turning off lights, that kind of conservation isn't likely to boost their profits as much as finding a distributor who will given them an extra 10 percent discount on their best-selling products. Still, as we noted a moment ago, there's a limit to what Chatham can learn by studying this one document.

Among the most important questions for any business to ask is how income and spending have changed over time. In order to get some sense of this, of course, Chatham will need to look at not just one income statement but two or three, or a whole series. Comparing the current income statement with the preceding one will suggest areas of increased or decreased spending. But this kind of comparison isn't sufficient for projecting trends. For instance, say that expenditures on wages and salaries are proportionately lower for the current period than for the preceding period. There could be many reasons for this. Perhaps Chatham is making more efficient use of its employees. If so, great. But it's equally possible that the expenditure is lower because some workers have been laid off temporarily or because a decrease in business has reduced the need for overtime. The owner or manager who has firsthand knowledge of the business is likely the only person who can place the proper interpretation on this kind of change.

On the other hand, consistent changes over time might well indicate a trend, perhaps one that calls for some managerial attention. For instance, suppose that total overhead, as a percent of net sales, is going up a few percent each period. That could simply be a reflection of business expansion. But if there is no such expansion occurring, then that kind of data suggests that overhead is threatening to get out of hand. An item-by-item analysis may help determine whether it's the rent increases, the big advertising budget, or some other factor that's causing the problem.

One of the best ways to look at change over time is through *horizontal analysis,* a measure of the percent of change from one year to the next. Recall, for instance, that the current percent of net sales for wages at Chatham is about 11 percent. Let's suppose that the percent of net sales for wages during the last period was 9 percent. What is the *percent of change*? To compute this, we first determine the *amount* of change: 11% − 9% = 2%. Then we enter our data into a formula: Percent of change = Amount of change ÷ Last year's amount. Be sure, when using this formula, to use *last* year's amount, not the current amount, as the denominator. In this case, the percent of change is two over nine, about 22 percent. By the way, things might have gone the other way. That is, last year's figure might have been higher; say, 14 percent. In that case, the percent of change would be (14%−11%) ÷ 14% = 3 ÷ 14 = 21%. But notice that the "3" in the formula is a three percent drop. In other words, the percent of net sales going to wages *dropped* by 21 percent. It is customary for accountants to use parentheses rather than a minus sign to indicate a decrease, so the item would probably show up on the horizontal analysis as (21 percent).

How Are Others Doing?

It's obviously useful for a firm to see how its own relative expenditures have changed over time. That kind of information helps the business person to see which areas of management have been most effective and to make some predictions about the future of the business.

But equally important, not to mention interesting, is a comparison with others in the same industry. Published data are available on the percent of net sales for each item on the income statement across a range of businesses, from supermarkets and pet stores to restaurants and retail clothing shops. These data help the business to see how its relative expenditures compare to those of businesses that provide similar products or services under similar conditions. This kind of comparison is one of the best measures of relative business efficiency.

Take Chatham Computer, for instance. Perhaps among computer equipment retailers, it isn't unusual for the ratio of cost to net sales to run about 80 percent. But suppose a comparison shows that the industry average for this ratio is 65 percent. That suggests that Chatham may be spending more than it should to get the merchandise into the store, which suggests some smarter buying might be in order. It might also show that Chatham's 5 percent ratio on wages is markedly low; perhaps the industry average runs around 10 percent. If Chatham is able to provide quality service without raising its overhead in this area, that's fine. But it's also possible that the ratio is low because they're understaffed or they're using less skilled salespeople, thus leading customers to go elsewhere. The point is, while the data do not provide all the necessary answers, they should prompt the business person to raise the right sort of questions.

Incidentally, you may be wondering whether comparisons with businesses in other industries are useful as well. The answer here is probably no. Where products and services differ markedly, it's illogical to expect similarities in the costs of providing those products and services. To put it another way, it simply makes no sense to compare the costs of running an ice cream parlor with those of running a used car dealership. True, a grocery store and a restaurant might have some things in common. Both sell highly perishable goods; both market their products directly to the public. But the differences are probably greater than the similarities, suggesting that any attempts to compare data would lead to more confusion than answers.

While the income statement summarizes the financial activities of a business across a given period of time, say a month or year, the balance sheet provides a summary of the financial condition of that firm *at a given point in time*. It shows what the business is worth by summarizing its *assets*, everything it owns, as well as its *liabilities*, everything it owes.

Filling Out the Profile: The Balance Sheet

Both assets and liabilities can be characterized as *long-term* or *short-term*, depending on whether the period of time involved is more or less than one year. There are some special rules for this; inventory, for example, is always a short-term asset because it *could* be (and usually is) converted into cash within a year or less. But a building is a long-term asset because although it could be sold, under most conditions a company will use a building for more than a year. Similarly, a bill from the electric company is a short-term liability, usually payable within 30 days or so. But a mortgage is a long-term liability, often running 15 years or longer, even though it could, theoretically, be paid off tomorrow.

Short-term assets are often called *current assets*. They include all the cash that the business has access to through checking and savings accounts, all the inventory that the firm has for sale at the time the balance sheet is prepared, and notes or accounts receivable. *Notes receivable* are short-term notes payable to the firm within the year. *Accounts receivable* consist of money owed by customers who have bought goods or services on credit.

Long-term assets are sometimes called *fixed assets* or *plant assets*. They include land, buildings, equipment, machinery, and furniture—in short, anything that is used by the firm over a long period of time.

Liabilities are also classified as short- or long-term. *Current liabilities*, or those that must be paid off within a year, include accounts payable (money owed to other firms) and short-term notes payable. *Long-term liabilities* include mortgages and long-term notes payable.

The difference between assets and liabilities is the *owner's equity*, also called the *proprietorship* or *net worth* of the business. If the assets and liabilities are equal, then the equity is zero. If assets outweigh liabilities, then the business has some net worth.

Owner's Equity

Imagine, for instance, Cooper's Corner Store, with assets of $150,000 and liabilities of $50,000. The net worth of this store is $150,000 − $50,000 = $100,000. This is another way of saying that if Cooper's were somehow put in the position of *having* to erase its $50,000 worth of liabilities, it could do so, given its current assets, and still retain a net worth of $100,000, which would be owner Cooper's equity. This relationship is summarized in the formula Assets = Liabilities + Owner's equity. The formula can also be expressed as Owner's equity = Assets − Liabilities.

Ideally, over time, the intention is that assets will grow faster than liabilities, resulting in increased owner's equity. Certain assets, like land and buildings, gain value over time because they appreciate; that is, their market value goes up. Other assets, like equipment, tend to depreciate (decline in market value); but since such items are replaced periodically, the total value of what the company owns tends to go up.

On the other hand, certain liabilities, such as the mortgage, might be expected to decline regularly. But others, such as money owed on new equipment, would be recurring. So while it may be desirable for assets to grow in *proportion* to liabilities, it's not a goal for the company to reduce liabilities to nothing. Large corporations often have hundreds of millions of dollars in liabilities but can still be in good financial shape because assets are even larger, leaving substantial owner's equity.

There's one other important point to make about the owner's equity figure. Many people get the idea that the company's owner's equity, the net worth, is what the company would be worth if it were sold. But that's not usually true. As an example, consider the Stayfast Suspender Company, a thriving company several decades back when suspenders were more common, but not too successful in recent years. Would you pay, say, $20 million for a suspender company just because that was the difference between assets and liabilities? Probably not. Instead, you'd look at the income statement and see that Stayfast has had nothing but lean times in recent years, and then you might ask yourself whether a suspender company is a good deal at *any* price. Stayfast does, of course, have some market value as a result of its salable assets. On the other hand, though, the bulk of those assets may be suspender-making machinery that would be hard to sell at anywhere near its book value. In summary, the net worth of a company is related to, but rarely the same as, its potential selling price.

Format of a Balance Sheet

Following is a simplified balance sheet of the type used in your text. Notice that it's divided into two main parts: assets on the top and liabilities and owner's equity on the bottom. The totals of the two halves will always be equal, *in balance*.

BALANCE SHEET	
Assets	
Current assets	
Cash	____
Notes receivable	____
Accounts receivable	____
Inventory	____
Total current assets	____
Plant assets	
Land	____
Buildings	____
Fixtures	____
Total plant assets	____
TOTAL ASSETS	════
Liabilities and Owner's Equity	
Current Liabilities	
Notes layable	____
Accounts receivable	____
Total current liabilities	____
Long-term liabilities	
Mortgages payable	____
Long-term notes payable	____
Total long-term notes payable	____
TOTAL LIABILITIES	════
Owner's equity	____
TOTAL LIABILITIES AND OWNER'S EQUITY	════

Notice, too, that assets are divided into current assets and plant (or fixed) assets, and that there is a subtotal for each. This allows the business person to see whether most of a firm's assets are represented by land, buildings, equipment, or accounts payable. This in itself could indicate something about the speed and extent to which assets gain value. For instance, a company that owns large tracts of land in an area where land is appreciating at a great rate can expect some significant increases in company assets without doing anything at all.

Liabilities are also divided into long- and short-term categories, again, to help draw a clearer picture of the company's current situation. Notice that ideally current assets should outweigh current liabilities. If they don't, the company may be headed for some cash flow problems. A printing company may have a press worth many thousands of dollars, but selling the press (a fixed asset) is no solution to a shortage of current assets, since once the press is sold, even if it's sold quickly for a good price, it's not available to produce any more revenue.

Analysis of a Balance Sheet

It is possible to do a *vertical analysis* of a balance sheet, just as with an income statement. Only this time, each item on the document is expressed as a *percent of total assets*. The formula is a simple one: Percent of total assets = Amount of the particular item ÷ Value of total assets.

For instance, let's find the percent of total assets for accounts receivable at Nelson Dairy. If the balance sheet shows accounts receivable of $37,280 and total assets of $152,400, the percent equals $37,820 divided by $152,400, which is about 25 percent. By comparison, if accounts payable are $49,230, the percent for accounts payable is $49,230 divided by $152,400, which is about 32 percent. The fact that payables are higher than receivables may be a problem or it may not. Some horizontal analysis can help answer the question.

The computation for horizontal analysis of a balance sheet is essentially no different from that for the income statement. Again, the question is one of change over time, a way of measuring increases or decreases. To determine the percent of change, begin by finding the *amount* of change and make that the numerator of the fraction. Use *last year's figure* as the denominator, and divide to find the percent of change.

For instance, suppose the Nelson Dairy balance sheet shows owner's equity of $54,320. Now, suppose that the previous equity totaled $50,200. In that case, the amount of change is $54,320 − $50,200 = $4,120. That makes the percent of change $4,120 ÷ $50,200 = .082, or 8.2 percent. Notice, by the way, that it's a change in the right direction: equity is on the rise. So while there are no guarantees that growth will continue, that's good news for the firm.

Getting the Overall Picture

How does the business person put all these bits and pieces together? It's tempting to say, "Get a good accountant." That response is only partly facetious. As you can guess from this discussion, when the numbers in a financial profile indicate trouble, there is often no clear-cut indication of the reason behind that problem. The accountant's experienced eye may spot patterns that others wouldn't notice, though as we've indicated already, only the business manager knows what goes on in the day-to-day running of the business or what plans the company holds for the future. Is the company, for instance, planning to relocate? Take on new staff? Sell off a portion of its inventory? Build a new plant? Answers to these and similar questions can greatly influence an accountant's interpretation of data.

In addition, it's important to look at the income statement and balance sheet together, since neither provides a complete picture of the financial position of the business. For instance, if assets are relatively low, a look at the income statement might suggest that high overhead could be one reason for that situation. On the other hand, high overhead might translate into *increased* assets, if a large portion of that spending is directed into newer, more efficient equipment. In short, it is virtually impossible to reduce all the potential patterns of spending and investment to a series of quick formulas. Business operations are too complex, and every business is a little different. But familiarity with these two important tools — the income statement and the balance sheet — is essential for any business manager evaluating the financial health of his or her own business.

Remember that the balance sheet is only a snapshot of where the business stands on a certain day of the year. It doesn't say anything about whether things are getting better or worse, or are basically unchanged. An accountant, in fact, is likely to label the balance sheet a "Statement of Financial Position as of December 31" to emphasize the single-point-in-time nature of the report.

SOME WORDS OF ADVICE

Business people almost always need to rely on the skills of trained bookkeepers and accountants to help keep the financial affairs of the business in order. But that dependence should not be so great that the manager or owner of the business no longer feels confident analyzing and drawing conclusions from both the income statement and the balance sheet. These reports provide important data, and the business owner/manager needs to work with the accountant in drawing meaning out of the numbers.

Both horizontal and vertical analysis should be conducted routinely. No single document in isolation can provide the wealth of information you can gain by looking at that document in relation to others. And often the current state of the business is less significant in and of itself than trends suggested by past performance — or projections based on those trends.

Perhaps it goes without saying that all data used in this important analysis must be both accurate and complete. Imagine, for instance, the implications if an estimate of current assets were to omit the purchase of an expensive new machine. Not only would the unrecorded cash expenditure make the current asset figure be off, but total assets would be incorrectly reported as well — and every other computation based on that figure, including owner's equity, would then be incorrect. (Admittedly, though, the biggest problem is that the IRS and state tax collection agencies quite reasonably expect your financial accounting to be accurate and complete, and there are severe penalties for negligent recordkeeping.)

These days, many firms have computerized their accounting systems. There are many advantages, not the least of which is a built-in system for data entry that takes some of the tedium out of bookkeeping. Such systems are much simpler to use than they were even a few years ago and do not demand great expertise in accounting, since many of the instructions are built right into the program. They're capable of generating speedy reports in a variety of formats, including horizontal and vertical analyses, though such reports are considerably more meaningful to persons who know how the figures were derived. All in all, the computer may do some of the work of a bookkeeper, but it replaces neither the business manager nor the accountant when it comes time to analyze the raw numbers.

KEY TERMS

Before you read through the text assignment and watch the video program, take a minute to look at the key terms associated with this lesson. When you encounter them in the text and video program, pay careful attention to their meaning.

Assets: Items of value owned by a firm.

Balance sheet: A summary of the financial condition of a firm at one point in time.

Comparative income statement: A summary of vertical analyses for two or more years that permits comparison of income or balance sheet items from one year to another.

Cost of goods sold: The amount paid by a firm for the goods it sold during the time period covered by an income statement.

Current assets: Cash, or items that could be readily converted into cash within a short period of time, usually a year.

Current liabilities: Debts a firm is obligated to pay within a year.

Fixed assets: Another term for long-term or permanent assets; those items a firm owns and plans to use for more than one year.

Gross margin: See *gross profit*.

Gross profit: The difference between the amount received from customers for goods (net sales) and what the firm paid for the goods (cost).

Gross sales: The total amount of money a firm takes in for the goods or services it sells; this figure is computed *before* returns are subtracted.

Horizontal analysis: A procedure for computing the amount (in dollars) and the percent of change from year to year across items on an income statement or balance sheet.

Income statement: A record of all income and expenses for a firm across a given period of time (usually a month, quarter, or year).

Inventory: The value of all goods on hand for sale.

Liabilities: The debts or expenses that must be paid by a firm.

Long-term liabilities: Those debts that a firm expects to continue for more than one year.

Net worth: The value of the business once all debts (liabilities) have been subtracted from the value of assets; also known as owner's equity.

Operating expenses: The everyday expenses, other than the cost of goods, involved in operating a firm; also known as overhead.

Owner's equity: See *net worth*.

Short-term liabilities: See *current liabilities*.

Vertical analysis of a balance sheet: A procedure by which every important item on the balance sheet is expressed as a percent of total assets.

Vertical analysis of an income statement: A procedure in which every important item on an income statement is expressed as a percent of net sales.

PART II: WATCHING THE VIDEO PROGRAM

VIDEO VIEWING GUIDE

Before watching the video program, review the following questions. As you watch, be sure to collect the information necessary to answer them.

1. Explain how an income statement and balance sheet complement each other and why it is important for a firm to use both in analyzing its current financial position.

2. What sorts of questions could an accountant expect to answer in looking at an income statement? At a balance sheet?

3. What are some similarities between these two documents? What are some differences?

4. What is the primary purpose of vertical analysis? What additional information does it provide from the income statement? From the balance sheet?

5. What is the primary purpose of horizontal analysis? What does it tell the business manager?

6. Many business owners/managers compare data from their own balance sheets and income statements to figures published for their industry as a whole. What is the purpose of such comparisons? How can the business person use the information provided by such comparisons?

7. Given the ready availability of computerized accounting programs, how important is it these days for a firm that uses accounting software to also employ an accountant?

VIDEO PROGRAM

This lesson's video program is Program 21—Financial Statements. Remember, if you are watching this program on videotape, take time to replay sections of the tape any time you need to review a concept.

VIDEO VIEWING QUESTIONS

Immediately after viewing the video program for Lesson 21, take time to respond to the following questions. Give your answers some careful thought; they may provide the basis for additional discussion or a longer written response.

1. In your own words, briefly describe how an income statement and balance sheet work together to create a financial profile of a business.

   _____

   _____

   _____

2. List two questions that an accountant might be expected to answer by reviewing the income statement of a firm.

   a. _____

   b. _____

3. List two questions that an accountant might be expected to answer by reviewing a firm's balance sheet.

   a. _____

   b. _____

4. A certain firm has never conducted a vertical analysis of its income statement or balance sheet. What important information, if any, is this firm ignoring by not performing this analysis?

   _____

   _____

   _____

5. A firm is conducting a horizontal analysis of its income statements and balance sheets. Would it be better to use the income statements and balance sheets for the past two, three, or five years? Explain your answer, relating your reasons to the purpose of horizontal analysis.

   _____

   _____

   _____

   _____

6. A glance at the balance sheet of a certain firm shows that liabilities outweigh assets. The firm is in its first year of operation. Is it likely to be in serious financial trouble? Why or why not? Where will the firm get the money to make up the difference between assets and liabilities?

   _____

   _____

   _____

7. A comparison with industry averages shows that the percent of net sales for a certain furniture store is quite a bit higher than the average for furniture stores in general. The figure for cost of goods sold is slightly higher than average; the figure for total operating expenses is quite a bit lower. What specific conclusions can you draw from this information?

_____

_____

_____

_____

8. Name three important decisions a manager would have difficulty making if he or she had no knowledge of the information contained on the firm's income statement and balance sheet.

a. _____

b. _____

c. _____

9. Name two tasks an accountant might perform that a computerized accounting program probably cannot handle as well.

a. _____

b. _____

10. A certain firm uses a computerized accounting program, and all data are entered by the bookkeeper. During the period, gross sales are $102,000 and returns are $15,000. The bookkeeper accidentally enters the returns as $1,500. In your own words, describe the relative significance (or insignificance) of this error and its probable impact on other data.

_____

_____

_____

_____

11. What is the probability that an error of the type described in Question 10 would be detected and/or corrected by the computer? Explain.

_____

_____

_____

_____

PART III: FOCUSING ON THE MATHEMATICS

READING ASSIGNMENT

After watching the video program, you should read one of the following Text Assignments, depending on the textbook you're using:

SOFTCOVER: Pages 537-554 from Chapter 13 of the Miller, Salzman, and Hoelzle softcover text, *Business Mathematics*.

HARDCOVER: Pages 596-614 from Chapter 17 of the Salzman, Miller, and Hoelzle hardcover text, *Mathematics for Business*.

As you read through the text, pay careful attention to the examples the book gives of the mathematics associated with the concepts you're learning about.

Then, after you've completed the text assignment, read through the Key Formulas below. This section provides a handy review of what you've learned. By the time you get to this point in the lesson, all of the formulas and calculations should be familiar to you. If they're not, go back and read the appropriate parts of the text and the Overview section of this lesson. You won't have much success completing the rest of your assignments if you are still confused about the information in the Key Formulas section.

KEY FORMULAS

The following key formulas are important to your understanding of this lesson. Be sure that you know each one and how to use it in solving problems related to financial statements.

KEY FORMULA: Net sales = Gross sales − Returns

Formula used for: Determining the amount of net sales when the value of gross sales and the value of returns are known.

Example:

Tiny Town Toys has gross sales of $82,000 during December and returns of $12,000. Therefore, its net sales for the month are $82,000 − $12,000 = $70,000.

Remember that in this formula:

1. Gross sales are equal to all the goods and services that customers buy, including those that they later return.

2. Returns are equal to the total value of those goods that customers initially buy but later return, and therefore (ultimately) do not pay for. Some return items are bought with cash, so that the firm temporarily has use of the buyer's money; other return items are bought with credit, so the firm never receives any actual money for them.

KEY FORMULA: Gross profit = Net Sales − Cost of goods sold

Formula used for: Determining gross profit when the figures for cost and net sales are known.

Example:

McCoy Grocery has net sales of $50,000 for the month of June. McCoy paid $30,000 for these goods. Thus, the gross profit for the period is $50,000 − $30,000 = $20,000.

Remember that in this formula:

1. Gross profit is the profit *before* expenses are paid, so it is not the bottom line, or net profit, for the firm.

2. The *cost* is what the merchant pays for the goods. Be careful not to confuse *cost* with *overhead*, which is sometimes referred to as "the cost of doing business." What a grocer pays for a can of soup comes under the heading of *cost*. What he or she pays for rent, light, heat, and the like, comes under the heading of *overhead* (also known as operating expenses).

KEY FORMULA: Net income = Gross profit − Operating expenses

Formula used for: Determining the firm's net income or net profit when gross profit and operating expenses are known.

Example:

Let's say that operating expenses for McCoy Grocery are $15,000 for the month of June. We already know from our previous computation that the gross profit for the period is $20,000. Thus, the net income (or net profit) is $20,000 − $15,000 = $5,000.

Remember that in this formula:

1. Net income is the same as *net profit*, or what some people think of as the true profit of the business.

2. Operating expenses are the same as overhead. They include all indirect cost items such as employee salaries, rent, utilities, and taxes. But they do *not* include *cost*, or what the firm pays to buy the goods it turns around and sells.

KEY FORMULA: Net sales = Cost of goods + Expenses + Net income

Formula used for: Determining the value of net sales when cost, overhead, and net profit (or net income) are all known.

Example:

We can use the figures from McCoy Grocery to recheck our earlier computation. We know from the previous examples that net profit is $5,000, expenses are $15,000, and cost is $30,000. Thus, net sales should total $5,000 + $15,000 + $30,000 = $50,000. Checking back to the formula for gross profit, we see that this is in fact the case.

Remember that in this formula:

1. Cost is what the firm pays for the goods it sells.

2. Expenses are the same as operating costs or overhead; these terms are interchangeable.

3. Net income is the same as the final profit; it is *not* the same as *gross profit*, which includes overhead.

KEY FORMULA: Cost of goods sold = Initial inventory + (Cost of goods purchased during the period + Freight) − Inventory at the end of the period

Formula used for: Finding the value of cost based on inventory values.

Example:

Claire's Gifts has an inventory valued at $40,000 at the beginning of the period. During the period, Claire purchases another $55,000 worth of goods, with shipping costs of $5,000. The value of Claire's inventory at the end of the period is $50,000. Thus, cost = $40,000 + ($55,000 + $5,000) − $50,000 = $50,000. In other words, the store paid $50,000 for the merchandise it sold during this period.

Remember that in this formula:

1. You must know inventory values at the beginning and the end of the period.

2. The value of the inventory at the end of the period is subtracted because those goods have not been sold yet.

3. Freight, or the cost of shipping, is considered a part of cost, not a part of overhead.

KEY FORMULA: R = P ÷ B

Formula used for: Finding the percent of net sales in a vertical analysis of an income statement *or* finding the percent of total assets in a vertical analysis of a balance sheet.

Examples:

Net sales for Mel's Hats are $10,000 for the month. Cost is $4,000. Thus, *cost as a percent of net sales* = $4,000 ÷ $10,000 = .40, or 40 percent. Similarly, total assets for Mel's Hats are $100,000. Current assets are $30,000. Thus, *current assets as a percent of total assets* = $30,000 ÷ $100,000 = .30, or 30 percent.

Remember that in this formula:

1. R or rate is a percent. When doing a vertical analysis of an income statement, you're looking for a percent of *net sales*. If doing a vertical analysis of a balance sheet, you're looking for a percent of *total assets*.

2. Your initial answer will always be represented as a decimal, e.g., .40 or .30. Move the decimal point *two places to the right* to convert a decimal figure to a percent: .30 = 30 percent, and .40 = 40 percent.

3. The B stands for base. In this context, the *base* is the basis for comparison: the net sales or the total assets. Be sure that this figure forms the *denominator* in the fraction.

4. The P stands for part. In this context, the *part* is any item from the income statement that is being expressed as a percent of net sales *or* any item from the balance sheet that is being expressed as a percent of total assets. Be sure this figure forms the numerator in the fraction.

KEY FORMULA:	Percent of change = Change ÷ Last period's amount
Formula used for:	Performing a horizontal analysis of the income statement or balance sheet when figures for two or more years are available.

Example:

Net sales at Shopper's City Shoes were $25,000 this month and $20,000 last month. Therefore, the percent of change = ($25,000 − $20,000) ÷ $20,000 = $5,000 ÷ $20,000 = .25, or 25 percent. Similarly, suppose that current liabilities for Shopper's City last month were $6,000, but this month they're $4,000. Therefore, the percent of change = ($6,000 − $4,000) ÷ $6,000 = $2,000 ÷ $6,000 = .333, or about (33 percent).

Remember that in this formula:

1. This formula can be used in the horizontal analysis of figures from *either* the income statement or balance sheet.

2. The *change* in the numerator of the fraction is equal to the *amount* of change that has occurred during the period. Shopper's City's current liabilities are down by $2,000, for instance; in other words, this is the *amount* by which current liabilities have decreased.

3. The denominator of the fraction is *always* the figure for the preceding period, *not* the current figure. Notice that we used $20,000 as the denominator for determining the change in net sales; we used $6,000 as the denominator for determining the percent of change in current liabilities. Be careful not to use the current figure, or your computations are likely to be very inaccurate.

4. The result will be expressed as a decimal, e.g., .25 or .333. To change to a percent, move the decimal point two places to the right.

5. Sometimes, as in our second example, the percent of change reflects a decrease. Accounting conventions call for putting negative results in parentheses, (33 percent), rather than using a minus sign.

KEY FORMULA:	Assets = Liabilities + Owner's Equity
Formula used for:	Ensuring that the two sides of the balance sheet do in fact balance, and determining the value of assets, liabilities, or owner's equity when the two other values are known.
Alternate form:	Owner's equity = Assets − Liabilities

Example:

Davis Hardware has assets of $230,000 and liabilities of $190,000. Therefore, the owner's equity is $230,000 − $190,000 = $40,000.

Remember that in this formula:

1. The owner's equity is the same as the net worth of the firm. This is the value of the firm *after* all its debts are paid.

2. In this formula, assets = *total* assets of the firm, both short- and long-term. Similarly, liabilities = *total* liabilities, both short- and long-term.

DON'T FORGET

1. When computing cost on the basis of inventory value, deduct the value of the inventory at the end of the period from the final figure. Be careful not to *add* this value to the total.

2. In a vertical analysis of an income statement, each item on the statement is represented as a percent of *net sales*. Thus, the value of net sales forms the denominator of the fraction. In a vertical analysis of a balance sheet, each item is represented as a percent of *total assets*. Thus, the value of total assets forms the denominator of the fraction.

3. Horizontal analysis looks at change from year to year (or period to period). To find the percent of change, make the *amount* of change the numerator and the figure for the *last period* the denominator. Remember that the change may reflect a decrease from period to period; show this by putting the results in parentheses, like this: (40 percent).

4. Total assets include both short- and long-term assets. Total liabilities include both short- and long-term liabilities.

5. When converting a decimal to a percent, move the decimal point two places to the right. Thus, .25 = 25 percent; .0004 = .04 percent; 1.25 = 125 percent.

PART IV: SOLVING BUSINESS PROBLEMS

PROBLEM SETS

Work the following problems in your textbook. Your instructor will tell you which problems, if any, are to be turned in. Some of the problems have answers provided in the back of the book; refer to these answers to make sure you are working the problems correctly.

SOFTCOVER: If you are using the Miller, Salzman, and Hoelzle softcover text, *Business Mathematics*, do the following problem sets:

13.1: Problems #1-4 on pages 541-542.

13.2: Problems #1-8 on pages 547-548.

13.3: Problems #1 and 2 on pages 553-554.

HARDCOVER: If you are using the Salzman, Miller, and Hoelzle hardcover text, *Mathematics for Business*, do the following problem sets:

17.1: Problems #1-7 on pages 600-603.

17.2: Problems #1-10 on pages 608-610.

17.3: Problems #1 and 2 on pages 614-615.

BUSINESS APPLICATIONS

Read each of the following scenarios and answer the questions about the decisions you would make in each situation. Give these questions some serious thought; they may be used as the basis for discussion or the development of a more complex essay. You should base your decisions on what you've learned from this lesson, applying both math skills and good business judgment to solve the problem at hand.

SCENARIO 1

Creative Costumes, Inc., is a small company in its second year of operation. The business is located in a busy, relatively low-rent downtown section of a mid-sized city. The area is undergoing major renovation, and Creative Costumes is a little anxious about the potential impact on its rent and property taxes. But at the same time, the renovation could bring more foot traffic (and thus more business) its way.

Right now, they have three major business problems: First, they're understaffed. They need at least one more part-time person, but even if they could get someone at the minimum wage level, this would add about $8,000 to the total they're spending on wages. Second, they're too crowded. Costumes and other supplies and equipment are jammed so tightly into the current space that owner/manager Ruby Simms doesn't think they're being displayed to advantage, and this may be costing them business. There is a new, bigger space opening up across the street within the month, but the rent is at least 30 percent higher than what they're paying now. Third, the business is low on inventory—particularly for certain types of costumes. Simms would like to double the inventory during the next year, but that would mean two things: moving to a bigger facility to house that inventory and borrowing some money to purchase what the company needs.

Simms's bookkeeper has just completed the balance sheet and comparative income statement shown on the next page. Simms hasn't had time to do more than glance at them, but a colleague recommends that she hire an accountant to help her review both documents, draw some conclusions, and make some plans for the future of the business. Simms is reluctant to spend money on an accountant, though, feeling that a stranger will not understand enough about her business to provide good advice.

What do you think? Is Simms right to be skeptical about the amount of help an accountant could provide, especially one who has not been involved with the business from the first? Or is she being impractical from a sound business perspective? Suppose Simms did hire an accountant. What advice do you think this person might offer? How might the accountant characterize the current financial health of Creative Costumes?

CREATIVE COSTUMES, INC.
Balance Sheet for December 31, 1990

Assets

Current assets		
Cash	$ 1,000	
Notes receivable	12,000	
Accounts receivable	15,000	
Inventory	5,000	
Total current assets		$33,000
Plant assets		
Store furnishings	$ 8,000	
Delivery van	12,000	
Computer and other equipment	6,000	
Total plant assets		$26,000
TOTAL ASSETS		$59,000

Liabilities and Owner's Equity

Current liabilities		
Notes payable	$10,000	
Accounts payable	12,000	
Total current liabilities		$22,000
Long-term liabilities		
Long-term notes payable	$24,000	
Owed on delivery van	11,000	
Total long-term liabilities		$35,000
TOTAL LIABILITIES		$57,000
Owner's equity		$ 2,000
TOTAL LIABILITIES AND OWNER'S EQUITY		$59,000

CREATIVE COSTUMES, INC.
Comparative Income Statement

	This Year		Last Year	
	Amount	Percent	Amount	Percent
Gross sales	$48,000	120.00%	$46,000	109.52%
Returns	8,000	20.00	4,000	9.52
Net sales	40,000	100.00	42,000	100.00
Cost of goods sold	$10,000	25.00%	$10,000	23.80%
Gross profit	30,000	75.00	32,000	76.20
Wages	$16,000	40.00%	$14,000	33.30%
Rent	6,000	15.00	5,500	13.10
Advertising	500	1.25	200	0.48
Utilities	1,200	3.00	1,000	2.38
Taxes	1,500	3.75	1,200	2.86
Miscellaneous	300	0.75	100	0.24
Total expenses	$25,500	63.75%	$22,000	52.38%
NET INCOME	$4,500	11.25%	$10,000	23.80%

□ Should Simms hire the accountant? Why or why not? (Be specific in describing the kinds of help this person could offer and the limitations to that assistance, keeping in mind what the firm is likely to be able to afford.)

□ Look carefully at the balance sheet and comparative income statement for Creative Costumes, Inc. What *specific* conclusions can you draw from these two documents about the relative financial health of this business?

□ What additional pieces of information do you think an accountant would be likely to request in assessing the financial status of Simms's company? What specific questions (if any) remain unanswered even with these two documents to work from?

□ Consider the three business decisions Simms is facing, one by one. What would you advise about adding staff, relocating, and increasing inventory? For each decision, state what you would advise if *you* were her accountant. Justify your advice with specific reasons based on what you know of the business from the financial documents and the scenario.

□ Name two changes in spending or money management that you feel could increase the likelihood of this firm's success.

SCENARIO 2   Designers' Original Furniture is a two-person company in its first year of operation. The owners, Dan Scoggins and Dave Todd, are both overjoyed at what they feel is an "overwhelmingly successful first year." They really did not expect the company to make much money for its first few years, so winding up with any net profit is something they view as a major victory.

They make all the furniture they sell by hand. Much of it is made out of scrap lumber, which they buy at low cost from various sources. They also finish and paint the furniture themselves, which means that every piece has a lot of hours in it. Right now, each is pulling in a salary of $10,000 per year, an amount that does not begin to cover their time. Each is spending, on average, 60 hours per week building and designing furniture, not to mention the many hours involved in scouting out suppliers and driving long distances to haul their own supplies. They occasionally hire someone to answer the phone, run errands, or pick up materials; hence the additional $4,000 spent on wages.

They're working out of a large warehouse, which doubles as their showroom. It's more space than two people need, even with the supplies and equipment required for the business, but they like the location. Also, they're reluctant to give up the space, for as Scoggins says, "At the rate we're going, we'll need to take on new staff before you know it."

They hired an accountant at an hourly rate to complete the income statement on the next page. The accountant also provided some data showing how furniture stores in general spend their money. Scoggins and Todd feel, after glancing at this table, that they are doing very well compared to others in their industry, but the accountant is urging a more cautious view. She would like to do a more thorough analysis of their financial profile, but they're not especially interested right now; neither feels they would learn enough to justify the accountant's $50 per hour fee.

What do you think? Do Scoggins and Todd know enough right now to make the business decisions they'll need to make over the next few years?

Or would they be wise to seek some further help? Are they justified in feeling that they're doing well by industry standards, or is the accountant right to be a bit skeptical?

DESIGNERS' ORIGINAL FURNITURE Current Income Statement		
	Totals for the Year	
	Amount	Percent
Gross sales	$72,000	102.90%
Returns	2,000	2.90
Net sales	70,000	100.00
Cost of goods sold	$25,000	35.70%
Gross profit	45,000	64.29
Wages	$24,000	34.29%
Rent	8,000	11.43
Advertising	500	0.71
Utilities	2,000	2.86
Taxes	4,000	5.70
Miscellaneous	2,500	3.57
Total expenses	$41,000	58.57%
NET INCOME	$4,000	5.70%

TYPICAL PERCENTS TABLE: FURNITURE STORES						
Cost of Goods	Gross Profit	Total Operating Expenses	Net Income	Wages	Rent	Advertising
68.9%	31.2%	21.7%	9.6%	9.5%	1.8%	2.5%

☐ Should Todd and Scoggins seek further help from the accountant at this point? If you say no, state why. If your answer is yes, specify at least two questions to which they might seek answers.

☐ Based on information from the scenario and the financial documents, how would you characterize the current financial health of Designers' Original Furniture?

☐ What specific additional information do you think an accountant would want to have before drawing final conclusions about this business?

☐ Do you think the owners' conclusion about the relative success of their business (in comparison to other furniture stores) is justified? Why or why not?

☐ Is there anything about Designers' Furniture or the way in which it is run that would make a comparison with industry averages difficult? If so, what? (If you identified a problem here, how would you recommend solving it?)

☐ Do you think Scoggins and Todd should remain in their current facility? Why or why not? If they move, what are the implications for next year's income statement?

☐ Name two specific changes in spending or money management that you think could increase this firm's chances for future success.

Cash Flow and Financial Ratios 22

There's a story that the famous American humorist James Thurber had overdrawn his bank account—and not for the first time. As a result, Thurber was "invited" to come in and see the bank manager to discuss the problem. In the course of the interview, the bank manager was horrified to find that Thurber had no inkling of the state of his finances and, in fact, didn't even bother to keep track of the checks he wrote.

"But then how do you know how much money you have in your account?" asked the dismayed banker.

"Goodness," replied Thurber, "I'd have thought that was your business."

Fortunately, most companies do a pretty good job of keeping track of the money flowing in and out. It may, however, take the help of a trained accountant to make sense of the raw numbers. Accountants are specialists at data interpretation. But that doesn't mean that they need only look at columns of figures to analyze a firm's financial health. Even experienced accountants generally use special techniques when it comes to finding meaning in the numbers.

Two techniques are particularly useful in getting the most out of the information presented on a firm's balance sheet. The first is to calculate a series of *financial ratios*, each of which provides an important piece of information on how well the business is doing. The second is to compare the results of those calculations to the financial ratios for other businesses. While it's true that every business is unique, dramatic variations from what's happening industry-wide sometimes signal potential problems.

Of course, before making specific recommendations about a business's future, an accountant will want the broadest, most comprehensive picture possible of the firm's financial activities. Often, that means examining another important indicator of financial health: the statement of cash flows. The statement of cash flows summarizes cash *inflow* and *outflow* across a given period. In general, it's intended to answer two important questions: (1) Where is the firm getting its money? and (2) How is it spending that money?

As we've often stressed, no one indicator can tell all there is to know about a firm's financial health. The skillful business person must put many pieces of the financial puzzle together to get a clear picture of how the firm is doing. In this lesson, we'll look at financial ratios and the statement of cash flows, two of the puzzle's most important pieces.

PART I: INTRODUCING THE MATERIAL

LEARNING OBJECTIVES

Upon completing your study of this lesson, you should be able to:

1. Explain why it is frequently worthwhile to calculate financial ratios and give examples of business decisions that might be based on such calculations.

2. Know the formulas for and, given the balance sheet of a hypothetical company, calculate the current ratio, acid test ratio, and ratio of net income to average owner's equity.

3. Explain the importance of adequate cash flow to a business and discuss the relationship among cash flow, liquidity, and investment and expansion opportunities.

4. Given cash flow projections for a hypothetical business, identify potential cash flow problems if they exist.

If you're using the hardcover textbook, *Mathematics for Business*, there are some additional objectives for the lesson. Upon completing your study of the lesson, you should be able to do the following:

5. Given the balance sheets of two hypothetical businesses, determine which indicates the more liquid business.

6. Know the formulas for and, given the balance sheet of a hypothetical company, calculate the accounts receivable turnover, average age of accounts receivable, and debt-to-equity ratio.

7. Distinguish among cash flow, operating cash flow, and free cash flow and discuss the advantages for companies that operate with free cash flow.

LESSON OVERVIEW

In assessing a firm's financial health, accountants generally look at three main documents: the income statement, balance sheet, and statement of cash flows. In the previous lesson, we talked about income statements and balance sheets and showed how to conduct horizontal and vertical analyses on them. But we didn't talk about how to use them as the basis for *financial ratios*, a special set of values derived from the information on the balance sheet.

Since financial ratios are calculated directly from the balance sheet, a brief reminder of what the balance sheet does is in order. The *balance sheet* sums up *assets*, what the firm owns, and *liabilities*, its debts. The summary includes current and long-term assets, current and long-term liabilities, *total* assets and liabilities, and owner's equity, which is the difference between total assets and total liabilities. An accountant looking at this summary statement can tell several things at a glance — for instance, whether the *owner's equity* is substantial, meaning that the business has a significant net worth. Or whether most of the firm's debts are short-term liabilities, like accounts payable, that could cause the firm cash flow problems in the near future.

An accountant can also tell what portion of assets exists in the form of cash or items that could quickly be converted to cash should the company need money in a hurry. This kind of information is invaluable in helping a company assess the strength of its own financial position and make plans for the coming months and years. But the accountant isn't likely to stop with a cursory review of the balance sheet. Creating certain financial ratios makes additional information about the company's financial health readily available.

Balance Sheet: A Summary of Debts and Assets

The first of these financial ratios is the *current ratio*, which is designed to measure a firm's *liquidity* — its ability to raise cash quickly without having to sell long-term assets. A total summary of assets won't provide this information because some assets, though extremely valuable, aren't particularly useful when it comes to paying off immediate debt.

Take Donaldson's Dairy, for instance. Its assets total over $2 million. But much of that total consists of long-term assets: land, farm buildings, cattle, and machinery. Donaldson certainly could sell these things, if necessary, to get the company out of debt. There are two problems with this, however. First, selling land, buildings, and equipment isn't like selling a delivery truck or a microcomputer. Finding a buyer can be a slow process; it may take months or even years. Unless, of course, Donaldson were to sell them well below their true value. Then he'd probably have a buyer but only a percentage of the cash he expected.

Second, if the business begins to sell the very things on which it depends to make its living, then bringing in future income will be much tougher. After all, what's a dairy without dairy cattle, pastureland on which to graze them, and milking machines to milk them? No business wants to find itself in the position of literally selling itself off to stay alive. So the key question underlying current ratio is this: Can this business raise enough money from *current* assets to cover its *current* liabilities?

Suppose that Donaldson's current assets are $400,000. Current liabilities are $150,000. That means the current ratio is $400,000 divided by $150,000, which is about 2.7. This figure is also expressed as 2.7:1, which is read "two point seven to one."

A current rule of thumb, based simply on experience, suggests that in order to be pronounced financially "healthy," a business ought to have a current ratio of at least 2:1. In other words, current assets ought to be at least double current liabilities. When this is true, the theory goes, a firm can meet its current obligations and might even be a safe bet to take on a little debt. Because banks tend to take a close look at the current ratio in deciding whether to grant a loan, it is sometimes referred to as the *banker's ratio*.

The Current Ratio: Comparing Current Assets to Current Liabilities

What About Inventory? Current ratio is affected by all the current assets, including cash on hand, accounts receivable, notes receivable, and inventory. But there's one problem with judging a company's financial health by the current ratio: It could prove very difficult for a firm in financial trouble to dispose of its inventory at a reasonable price.

Suppose that a retail furniture company has borrowed money to cover the cost of a recent expansion. If sales are slow and profits are down, the company may not be bringing in enough to cover its debts. Of course, it can raise more money by disposing of more inventory, but with sales already down, how will it do this? One answer is to reduce prices, but, of course, this cuts profits further. If this pattern continues too long, the firm may wind up selling all or most of its furniture at a loss and then have no capital with which to put itself back into business. In short, many accountants feel that relying on the sale of inventory to erase debt tends to put a company in a very precarious position.

These accountants tend to favor use of the *quick ratio*, also known as the *acid test ratio*, which compares only liquid assets to current liabilities. *Liquid assets* include only cash, cash equivalents (like stocks and certificates of deposit), and those things that could be converted to cash very quickly: namely, accounts receivable and notes receivable. Depending on its billing cycle, a company can normally expect to turn its accounts receivable into cash every 30 or 60 days, and don't forget that receivables can be sold to banks and others for cash. Notes receivable are normally a fairly reliable source of income, too, so they can be treated like cash for purposes of this ratio.

Recall that bankers like to see a *current* ratio of at least 2:1, so our dairy farm with its current ratio of 2.7:1 is in a good position to apply for a loan, should it care to do so. How will it look given the acid test ratio, though? Let's see.

Of their $400,000 in current assets, suppose that $200,000 is tied up in inventory. That leaves $200,000 in cash and other liquid assets — *liquid* meaning readily convertible to cash. Again, recall that their current liabilities are $150,000. That makes their acid test ratio $200,000 divided by $150,000, which is about 1.33, or 1.33:1. Most accountants say that the acid test ratio should be at least 1:1. In other words, cash or cash-convertible assets should be at least sufficient to cover *immediate* debts. That doesn't say anything about paying off the long-term loans, but it does mean that the firm can handle all of its accounts payable and notes payable without having to borrow money to do it. This is just one more indicator of financial health. Notice, by the way, that our hypothetical dairy farm came through very well, its acid test ratio of 1.33:1 indicating that it is well prepared to handle its current debt load.

How Well Are Investments Paying Off? The *ratio of net income after taxes to average owner's equity* is, to a large extent, a measure of how well business investments are paying off for the company. This ratio is one indicator of whether it's financially wise for the business to continue on its present course, or even to continue at all. Keep in mind that not all businesses are profitable for their owners. When a business earns *no* profit, and continues to earn no profit, then the owners are faced with a critical decision: whether to continue on the same course in hopes of a brighter future, even though this means financially supporting the business, or to dissolve the firm and invest any capital remaining (once debts are paid) in some other way. This ratio suggests to business owners whether they are, in fact, getting a good return on the money that's being put into the business, or whether they could earn just as much with less trouble through a conventional investment.

Let's say that the owners of a large manufacturing firm have invested a large amount of money in buildings, equipment, land, and inventory for a new subsidiary. They want to know whether this was a wise move. By comparing their net income *after taxes* to the average owner's equity, or net worth of the business, they can find out what kind of return they're getting on their investment. Let's say that their net income after taxes is $15,000. The owner's equity at the beginning of the year is $100,000; by the end of the year, it has grown to $200,000. This makes the average owner's equity $100,000 + $200,000 ÷ 2 = $150,000. So their ratio of net income to average owner's equity is $15,000 ÷ $150,000 = .10, or 10 percent. But is 10 percent good or bad?

There are two ways to answer this question. One is to look at this particular financial ratio for other firms in the same industry. If similar firms are averaging returns of 7 to 8 percent, then this company is doing well. But if averages are running say, 15 percent, then the picture is not so bright. Equally important, though, is a comparison between this return and the interest banks are currently paying on guaranteed savings. Let's say that Treasury bills, certificates of deposit, money market funds, and so on are giving returns of around 7.5 percent. That makes the 10 percent return look pretty good. But remember, it *should* be higher.

After all, putting money into these conservative investments isn't very risky. Investing in a business is. To compensate for that extra element of risk, business people like to see a fairly good return on what they're putting in. Our manufacturing company boasts a current ratio of 10 percent. So the question for the business owner(s) is, are those extra two and a half points (over the bank's 7.5 percent) enough? There's no simple answer to that; it depends almost totally on the investor's philosophy, other available options, and outlook on the future.

Few firms sell everything for cash, if for no other reason than that a "cash only" policy would probably lose the firm some customers who didn't want to pay cash and some who simply couldn't. It would also tend to cut down on sales of expensive items, since even cash-up-front types run out of money occasionally and must depend on credit to finance major purchases.

Of course, as we pointed out a bit earlier, extending credit doesn't change a company's current or acid test ratios. That's because accounts receivable, all those accounts on which credit customers have rung up purchases, are classified as both current and liquid assets. In other words, from the accountant's perspective, a credit purchase is pretty much the same thing as cash. Pretty much, but not quite. With cash, there's no risk. The money is paid and available to the firm for immediate use. But with credit, there's always the chance that some customers will not pay on time, or at all.

Millions of companies experience problems with customers or clients who cannot (or will not) pay all debts in full. Usually the impact on the firm's overall health is minor. But if the problem is widespread, it can threaten the firm's cash flow, and that in turn limits the firm's buying power and its ability to react to changing business conditions.

To determine how well a firm is doing in collecting the money owed to it, an accountant or business manager can compute the *accounts receivable turnover* and the *average age of accounts receivable*.

Collecting Money

The *accounts receivable turnover* is a measure of how fast the firm is collecting its bills. The result indicates, on average, how many times the firm collected payments from debtors during the accounting period (usually a year). Let's say that at Sam's Exotic Hardwoods, net sales for the year have been $200,000. Accounts receivable totalled $10,000 at the beginning of the year and $30,000 at the end of the year, making the average $10,000 + $30,000 ÷ 2 = $20,000. Thus, the accounts receivable turnover is $200,000 divided by $20,000, which is 10. In other words, Sam's collected money from its credit customers 10 times over the course of the year. Of course, this information in and of itself doesn't tell us very much because we don't know what Sam's billing cycle is.

To find the *average age of accounts receivable* (in days), we divide the number of days in a year (365) by the number of total turnovers: 10. Thus, the average age of accounts receivable at Sam's is 365 ÷ 10 = 36.5 days. If Sam's billing cycle is 60 days, Sam's average customer is paying on time. If payments are net 30 days, though, then these results indicate that at least some accounts are delinquent, and Sam's may need to get a little more aggressive about collecting its money—and perhaps a little pickier about extending credit to customers in the first place.

Notice, though, that what we've calculated is an average, and like all averages, it's prone to being misinterpreted. It may be that the vast majority of the customers pay more promptly than the average but a few accounts have balances long overdue. This is necessary information; it suggests that the problem isn't with Sam's bill-collecting policies in general but just with a very limited number of customers who may be taking advantage of their valued customer status to put more "flexibility" into the payment schedule than Sam's would like.

To Borrow or Not to Borrow

Most firms borrow money at one time or another—to take advantage of special pricing on merchandise, to buy equipment, to expand, to put on new staff, or for a host of other reasons. Two questions are paramount in any decision to borrow: First, can the firm qualify for the loan in the first place. Second, is borrowing a financially responsible idea, even if the firm can qualify for the loan?

A firm can go a long way toward answering both questions by examining its *debt-to-equity ratio*. Say, for instance, that Al's Repair Shop has current liabilities of $20,000 and long-term liabilities of $80,000. That makes total liabilities $20,000 + $80,000 = $100,000. Let's further suppose that total owner's equity at Al's is $40,000. In that case, the debt-to-equity ratio is $100,000 ÷ $40,000 = 2.5.

Notice that for Al's, liabilities far outweigh equity. The ratio of 2.5 tells us that for every dollar of equity that Al's owner has realized, creditors have invested $2.50 in the firm. That kind of return doesn't bode well for future investments at Al's. Of course, we don't have all the information a banker would have before making a decision to grant the loan. Perhaps Al's is a new operation, not really on its feet yet. Or perhaps the long-term liabilities reflect a recent investment in new equipment that will result in some healthy profits at Al's. What's more, perhaps the owners have collateral to secure the loan: land or other assets not directly connected to the business. Let's suppose, therefore, that all things considered, the banker decides Al's is a good risk for a short-term loan of $20,000. Does that mean Al's should take out the loan?

Not necessarily. If they *have* invested in new plant or equipment, perhaps their profits will rise. But what if they don't? Then Al's is saddled with more new debt. Keep in mind that if Al's owners consult with an accountant before taking out this loan, that accountant may look at several financial ratios before making a recommendation. Let's say Al's current ratio is 2.1:1 and its acid test ratio is 1.2:1. These figures suggest that Al's is within the recognized margin of safety for being able to cover short-term debt. The turnover on accounts receivable is 12.6; they're collecting their money, on average, every 28.9 days. That's not too bad, and most of the business is cash anyway.

Notice how this changes the picture just a bit. If we looked just at the debt-to-equity ratio, we might well advise Al's owners to close up shop and try a different line of work. But perhaps Al's is actually in a reasonably strong position to wipe out current debt, has a good cash flow now, and expects things to get even better once the new equipment starts paying off. All in all, the $20,000 loan may not be as risky from the lender's perspective as the debt-to-equity ratio would suggest.

The possibility of borrowing money notwithstanding, the ability of a company to meet its short- and long-term obligations, take on new inventory, employ new staff, or make any moves toward expansion depends more on readily available cash. After all, while borrowing is a reasonable option sometimes, no firm can afford to borrow *all* the money it needs. For one thing, borrowing costs money; interest rates charged on loans are often higher than the profit margins of the business. The more often a business can afford to finance its own growth, the more rapid that growth will be.

The term *cash flow*, though widely used in the business world, is somewhat imprecise. That's because there's no way to know whether the flow is *in* or *out*, whether it refers to income or expense. For purposes of this discussion, therefore, think of *cash inflow* as income, money coming into the firm. Think of *cash outflow* as money going out, money that the firm spends in one way or another.

A *statement of cash flows* provides important information on income *and* expenses. Some of this information can be gleaned from the income statement and balance sheet, but the statement of cash flows provides a more concise and more comprehensive picture of income and outgo without extraneous information. It shows where a firm is getting its income and how it's spending the dollars it makes.

To help conceptualize this summary, picture a firm at the beginning of its operating cycle. It must pour money into operations in order to make any money. For instance, the firm spends a certain amount on overhead, on inventory, and on employee salaries, just to name a few major expenses. The goal of the firm is to generate enough income so that it has more money at the end of the operating cycle than it had at the beginning. The firm that reaches its goal can take out some of the extra money in the form of profits; but it can also afford to finance the new operating cycle on a bigger, grander scale. And that, if all goes well, means higher profits next time around.

The format of the statement of cash flows is consistent and fairly simple. It's organized into three sections: operating activities, investing activities, and financing activities. *Operating activities* include anything connected with producing goods and services for customers — in other words, the on-going daily operations of the business. *Investing activities* include such things as the making or collecting of loans, the buying and selling of stocks

The Statement of Cash Flows

A Comprehensive, Systematic Picture

in other companies, and the purchase and sale of property. *Financing activities* include the sale and purchase of the firm's own capital stock, the borrowing of money, or the payment of dividends to the firm's stockholders.

Notice that each area is both a potential source of income for the firm and a target for spending or investment. For instance, the company earns income on the sale of its goods or services; that income is part of the cash flow under operating activities. But in addition, the company spends money—on materials and salaries. That expense is also part of the cash outflow under operating activities. Similarly, investing activities include both making and collecting loans. When the firm is making a loan, that's part of cash outflow; but the repayment and the interest collected on the loan are part of cash inflow.

Remember, the distinction depends on whether the firm is taking money in or sending money out. Keep in mind too that cash outflow can, and often does, strengthen the whole financial position of the firm. For instance, the firm may spend money to buy stocks that offer an excellent return, or it may buy more up-to-date equipment that doubles its productivity. These activities cost the firm money in the short run, money that's reflected as cash outflow for the period. But in the long run, they're intended to produce higher profits. The firm's goal is to keep inflow running ahead of outflow across the long term.

That's not the only objective, though. There's much to be said just for keeping the money in motion. In other words, when the company generates income, it endeavors to *use* that income in some productive way. The company that spends extra income in staff training, new equipment, or market research is likely to be miles ahead financially of the firm that spends all its extra income on office redecoration.

Mechanics of the Statement of Cash Flows

It's time to look at a statement of cash flows. Shown on the next page is one for a hypothetical company that did about $20 million worth of business in the last accounting period.

As we noted earlier, both inflow and outflow are represented on the same statement. Expenditures are enclosed in parentheses to indicate cash outflow; income figures, being cash inflow, aren't enclosed in parentheses. For instance, cash received from customers represents inflow, while such items as taxes and interest paid on loans are listed as outflow.

Notice that the purchase of assets is listed as a cash outflow, which makes sense since buying assets costs the company money. But remember, purchasing fixed assets has no immediate effect on the total assets shown on the balance sheet, since it's just converting one asset to another. Similarly, purchasing new inventory increases the value of current assets. It's still a cash outflow, though; it costs the company money to stock its shelves, money that could otherwise be spent on investments or something else. If you're getting the idea that the statement of cash flows shows something different from the balance sheet, you're quite right.

In our particular illustration, the net cash decreased. The company had a cash inflow of over $1 million from operating activities but an outflow of over $2 million in investing activities. This is *not* a loss of $2 million; far from it. It's $2 million of cash that went out of the company, but the money was exchanged for things of value, including almost $2 million of fixed assets. This is no different from a family deciding they need a new refrigerator; the purchase might result in a $1,000 cash outflow, but there's a valuable asset left over. While it makes sense to say, "I lost $1,000 in the

---

SPENCER HYDRAULICS
Statement of Cash Flows—Direct Method
For the Year Ended December 31, 1990
($s in thousands)

Cash flows from operating activities:		
Cash received from customers	$19,860	
Cash paid to suppliers and employees	(17,764)	
Interest paid	(50)	
Income taxes paid	(900)	
Investment income	50	
Net cash provided by operating activities		$ 1,196
Cash flows from investing activities:		
Purchase of fixed assets	(1,974)	
Purchase of intangibles	(60)	
Sale of property, plant, and equipment	18	
Acquisition of marketable securities	(50)	
Net cash used by investing activities		(2,066)
Cash flows from financing activities:		
Net proceeds from sale of bonds	500	
Sale of capital stock	1,000	
Payment of dividends	(750)	
Net cash provided by financing activities		750
Net decrease in cash		$ (120)
Schedule of noncash investing and financing activities:		
Stock issued in conversion of bonds		$ 200
Bonds issued to acquire fixed assets		$ 100
Reconciliation of net income to net cash provided by operating activities:		
Net income	$ 950	
Add (deduct) adjustments to cash basis:		
Depreciation	360	
Amortization of intangibles	30	
Deferred income taxes	20	
Gain on sale of equipment	(2)	
Increase in receivables	(90)	
Increase in inventories	(303)	
Increase in accounts payable	230	
NET CASH FLOW FROM OPERATING ACTIVITIES		$ 1,196

---

stock market," no one says, "I lost $1,000 because I bought a new refrigerator." The point is that there is nothing inherently bad about cash outflow — and there's certainly no way to avoid it when running a business.

By the way, the statement of cash flows is designed to reflect changes in cash or *cash equivalents* across the period. Thus, the statement won't reflect long-term investments because there's no cash flow associated with them. Short-term, highly liquid investments that will be reconverted to cash within three months or less will be reflected, however. Thus, a one-month certificate of deposit would be accounted for, but a 30-year bond would not.

In addition, it may have occurred to you that not every transaction a firm makes involves cash. Say, for instance, that a firm purchases a building by issuing the owner of the building stock in the firm. Such a *noncash exchange transaction* is not reflected directly in the statement of cash flows, but it is usually summarized in narrative form and attached to that statement.

**The Function of
the Statement
of Cash Flows**

The statement of cash flows is a useful summary of how money is moving into and out of the company, but it would be wrong to overestimate what it can do. It will not, for instance, indicate the net worth of a company, nor will it show how well that company is managing its income in comparison to similar firms. The owner of a sporting goods store can see from the statement of cash flows that he's earning more from sales than from investments, or that he's spending more on equipment than he's investing in stocks. He may also see that in a year of record profits, his cash position was actually down due to spending in various areas.

On the other hand, the statement of cash flows provides only broad summary data about where money is coming from and how it's being spent. The statement will have a line for "cash received from customers" but that's as detailed as it gets. There's no indication of what percentage of overhead is going toward employee benefits, or how profits on wet suits compare to profits on baseball uniforms. In general, the statement of cash flows is designed to answer broad questions like these:

☐ What amount of cash was generated by operations (or investments or financing)?

☐ What use was made of the cash the firm took in?

☐ How did the company finance its expansion or investments?

☐ How did the company use the money it took in on a new bond issue or sale of stock?

☐ What is the company's general cash position (that is, is inflow greater than outflow, and if not, why not)?

The statement of cash flows is a relative newcomer in the world of accounting. It has been a required component of formal business accounting for less than a decade. But most business persons agree that its concise summary of how a business is earning and using its immediate cash is among the best available indicators of total business health.

SOME WORDS OF ADVICE

If you're in the position of owning or managing a business, take time to become comfortable with the procedures involved in preparing or reading a statement of cash flows. This document, together with the income statement and balance sheet, provides a complete financial profile of a business. But all three are necessary (and, in fact, mandated by financial accounting standards) to provide a full picture of a company's financial health; if any one of these three key documents is missing, that picture is likely to be slightly distorted.

It's usually necessary to work with an accountant in order to derive the greatest possible meaning from both the balance sheet and statement of cash flows and to get them prepared in the first place. While all of the financial statements are relatively easy to understand conceptually, there are a lot of details to deal with that require a trained professional. As a business manager, would you know how to handle the remodeling you had done on the office by the carpenter who took the company's old delivery van as payment instead of cash? Probably not, and you wouldn't be expected to. But you would be expected to know that you have to reflect such transactions in your company's books and financial statements.

The financial ratios that can be derived from the statements are valuable, too. It's important to recognize that financial ratios are more than just an interesting assessment of how a firm is doing right now. Those ratios open windows that give the business owner or manager a peek at the future: Will the business need to borrow money? Is it in a good position to do so? Could the business cover all its short-term debt tomorrow if need be? Is the business collecting money in a timely and efficient fashion? Financial ratios can help answer these and a raft of related questions.

If you are gauging a firm's borrowing power through the use of financial ratios, it may be prudent to use the acid test ratio rather than just the current ratio. Many accountants (and bankers, too) consider it a better measure of a firm's liquidity since it is not dependent on the firm's sale of inventory as a means of reducing debt. Inventory is obviously an excellent potential source of income, but disposing of it quickly at a fair market price can be difficult.

As a business owner or manager, keep an eye on changes in financial ratios over time. For instance, an acid test ratio of 1.5:1 may be less significant than the fact that ratio is down from a former 1.9:1. Similarly, if the ratio of net income after taxes to average owner's equity is up from 10 to 15 percent, it might be important to see whether that trend continues for the future and to see how the figure compares to averages for the industry as a whole.

Finally, when monitoring cash flows, it's important to look at inflow versus outflow, of course; but keeping inflow high is not the only worthy goal. The shrewd business manager considers not only the bottom line but also how dollars from various income sources are spent. Using the inflow well is the secret to keeping it high for the future.

KEY TERMS

Before you read through the text assignment and watch the video program, take a minute to look at the key terms associated with this lesson. When you encounter them in the text and video program, pay careful attention to their meaning.

Accounts receivable turnover: Net sales divided by average accounts receivable.

Acid test ratio: The ratio of current assets to current liabilities.

Assets: Items of value owned by a firm.

Average age of accounts receivable: One year (365 days) divided by the accounts receivable turnover rate.

Balance sheet: A summary of the financial condition of a firm at one point in time.

Cash equivalents: Demand deposits and short-term, highly liquid investments that are readily convertible to cash and so near maturity that there is no significant risk of any change in face value due to fluctuating market conditions.

Current assets: Cash or items that can be converted into cash within a very short time, usually a year or less.

Current ratio: The ratio of current assets to current liabilities. Also called *banker's ratio*.

Debt-to-equity ratio: All liabilities divided by owner's equity.

Financing activities: Activities of a firm that include the sale and purchase of a firm's *own* capital stock, the borrowing of cash, and the payment of dividends to the firm's stockholders.

Inventory: The value of all goods on hand for sale.

Investing activities: Activities of a firm that include the making and collecting of loans, the purchase and sale of other firms' stocks, and the purchase and sale of property, plant, and equipment.

Liabilities: Expenses that must be paid by a firm.

Liquid assets: Cash or items that can be converted to cash quickly.

Liquidity: A measure of a firm's ability to raise cash quickly or to cover short-term debt.

Long-term liabilities: Debts that will be paid *after* one year.

Noncash exchange transaction: Financing or investing transactions that do not involve cash, such as the purchase of a building through a mortgage or through the issuing of stock.

Operating activities: The earnings-related activities involved in producing goods and services for customers.

Owner's equity: The net worth of a firm; the difference between total assets and total liabilities.

Quick ratio: See *acid test ratio*.

Ratio of net income after taxes to average owner's equity: Net income divided by average owner's equity; a measure of the average return a business is providing on the dollars invested to keep that business operational.

Short-term liabilities: Debts owed within the relatively immediate future, usually within one year.

Statement of cash flows: A required financial statement, classified into operating activities, financing activities, and investing activities, that provides information about the sources and uses of a firm's cash over time.

Stockholders' equity: Another term for owner's equity (depending on who owns the company); the difference between total assets and total liabilities.

PART II: WATCHING THE VIDEO PROGRAM

VIDEO VIEWING GUIDE

Before watching the video program, review the following questions. As you watch, be sure to collect the information necessary to answer them:

1. Suppose that an accountant has already reviewed this year's and last year's balance sheets for a firm. What additional information is provided through computation of financial ratios?

2. What is the main difference between the *current ratio* and the *acid test ratio*? Is this difference significant? If so, why?

3. How do various financial ratios relate to a firm's relative solvency? Ability to qualify for a loan? Ability to invest at a future date?

4. How important is it to work with an accountant in interpreting a balance sheet or a statement of cash flows?

5. What is meant by *cash flow* and why is it important to a firm's financial health? What is the difference between *cash inflow* and *cash outflow*?

6. What information, if any, does the statement of cash flows provide that could not be provided by the income statement and balance sheet?

VIDEO PROGRAM

This lesson's video program is Program 22—Cash Flow and Financial Ratios. Remember, if you are watching this program on videotape, take time to replay sections of the tape any time you need to review a concept.

VIDEO VIEWING QUESTIONS

Immediately after viewing the video program for Lesson 22, take time to respond to the following questions. Give your answers some careful thought; they may provide the basis for additional discussion or a longer written response.

1. Name three financial ratios that can be computed from a balance sheet, and describe in a sentence or two the kind of information each provides about the business.

   Ratio 1:_____

   _____

   Ratio 2:_____

   _____

Ratio 3: _____

_____

2. An accountant advises a firm to use the acid test ratio rather than the current ratio to measure its liquidity. Briefly, explain whether you think this is good advice and why.

_____

_____

_____

3. Is it important for a business person to work with an accountant in interpreting a balance sheet or statement of cash flows? Why?

_____

_____

_____

4. Name two pieces of information an accountant can provide about the financial health of a business that may not be readily accessible to the typical business person.

a. _____

_____

b. _____

_____

5. Imagine that you are a banker. A firm, Acme Minerals, has a quick test ratio of 1:1 and a current ratio of 1.8:1. Their ratio of net income after taxes to average owner's equity is 8.5 percent. They wish to borrow money on a short-term note with 11.5 percent simple interest. Based just on what you know, explain as specifically as you can why you probably would or would not grant this loan to Acme Minerals.

_____

_____

_____

6. A mail order firm, Holiday Candy, has an accounts receivable turnover rate of 10. Its billing cycle is 30 days. In a sentence or two, sum up your perceptions of how well this firm is doing in collecting the money its customers owe and suggest what, if anything, it might do differently. Use your math computations to justify your answer.

_____

_____

_____

7. Your firm has a five-year history of carefully prepared income statements and balance sheets. Now your accountant is recommending
that you also include the statement of cash flows. Name two reasons
why this might be a good recommendation.

a. _____

_____

b. _____

_____

8. Which of the following questions would the statement of cash flows
be most likely to answer for the accountant or business manager?
Check all that apply. Be prepared to provide specific reasons for your
responses.

_____ How much cash is generated by daily business operations?

_____ How much has the firm earned on investments during the
period?

_____ What portion of overhead was spent on rent?

_____ Has the firm increased or decreased its spending on
supplies?

_____ How much have taxes increased (or decreased) since the
last period?

_____ How much cash has the firm invested in new equipment?

_____ What is the rate of depreciation on the firm's new
equipment?

_____ Where did the firm get the dollars it spent on new
investments?

_____ What rate of interest will investments in stocks yield over
the coming year?

_____ How much interest did the firm earn (in dollars) over the
past year?

_____ Is the firm eligible for a bank loan?

_____ Is the firm solvent?

_____ Does the firm have a strong cash position?

9. Review the questions you checked in Question 8. Are there some that
could not be answered just as well through examination of the income
statement and balance sheet? If so, which ones? Briefly, explain why
this is so.

_____

_____

_____

PART III: FOCUSING ON THE MATHEMATICS

READING ASSIGNMENT _____

After watching the video program, you should read one of the following Text Assignments, depending on the textbook you're using:

SOFTCOVER: Pages 555-562 from Chapter 13 of the Miller, Salzman, and Hoelzle softcover text, *Business Mathematics.*

HARDCOVER: Pages 616-625 from Chapter 17 of the Salzman, Miller, and Hoelzle hardcover text, *Mathematics for Business.*

As you read through the text, pay careful attention to the examples the book gives of the mathematics associated with the concepts you're learning about.

Then, after you've completed the text assignment, read through the Key Formulas below. This section provides a handy review of what you've learned. By the time you get to this point in the lesson, all of the formulas and calculations should be familiar to you. If they're not, go back and read the appropriate parts of the text and the Overview section of this lesson. You won't have much success completing the rest of your assignments if you are still confused about the information in the Key Formulas section.

KEY FORMULAS _____

The following key formulas are important to your understanding of this lesson. Be sure that you know each one and how to use it in solving problems related to financial ratios.

KEY FORMULA:	Current Ratio = Current assets ÷ Current liabilities
Formula used for:	Measuring the relative liquidity of a firm when current assets and current liabilities are known.

Example:

Ford's Dry Cleaning has current assets of $50,000. It has current liabilities of $20,000. Its current ratio is $50,000 ÷ $20,000 = 2.5, or 2.5 to 1.

Remember that in this formula:

1. Current assets include cash, accounts receivable, notes receivable, and inventory. Current liabilities include accounts payable and notes payable.

2. The result of the computation is either a whole number or a decimal. In this case, the result can be expressed as either 2.5, 2.5:1 or 2.5 to 1.

3. A rule of thumb, based on experience, suggests that firms with a current ratio lower than 2:1 are likely to have financial difficulty. For this

reason, a firm with a current ratio of, say, 1.5:1 might have difficulty borrowing money from a bank. The current ratio is sometimes called the *banker's ratio*.

KEY FORMULA: Acid test ratio = Liquid assets ÷ Current liabilities

Formula used for: Determining whether a firm has enough liquid assets to cover all its short-term debts without depending on the sale of inventory.

Example:

Sally's House of Crafts has liquid assets of $30,000. It has current liabilities of $35,000. Its acid test ratio is $30,000 ÷ $35,000 = .86, or .86:1.

Remember that in this formula:

1. Liquid assets include cash, accounts receivable, and notes receivable. They do *not*, however, include inventory.

2. Current liabilities include notes payable and accounts payable.

3. A rule of thumb, suggests that a firm needs an acid test ratio of 1:1 *or higher* to be financially healthy. Such a ratio implies that the firm could erase all its short-term debt if it needed to without depending on the sale of inventory to do so. Notice that in our example, Sally's House of Crafts does not meet this criterion. The store does not have sufficient liquid assets to cover its short-term debt. This means they may have difficulty borrowing money and, further, if they encounter financial difficulties they may need to reduce selling price on their inventory in order to decrease their debt load. This result tells us that Sally's is not very "liquid" and that its overall financial position is, in at least this respect, fairly weak.

KEY FORMULA: Ratio of net income after taxes to average owner's equity = Net income after taxes ÷ Average owner's equity

Formula used for: Determining whether money invested in a business is providing a return that is higher, lower, or about on a par with what the owners could receive by depositing their money in the bank (or investing it in some other way).

Example:

Eastside Theater Company had a net income after taxes of $20,000 last year. Owner's equity at the beginning of the year was $80,000, and at the end of the year it was $120,000. That means that the *average* owner's equity for the period was $80,000 + $120,000 ÷ 2 = $200,000 ÷ 2 = $100,000. Thus, the ratio of net income after taxes to average owner's equity is $20,000 ÷ $100,000 = .20 = 20 percent.

Remember that in this formula:

1. Use the figure for net income after taxes, not before.

2. Find the average owner's equity first. Assuming you have figures for the beginning and end of one year, as in the example with Eastside Theater, simply add these together and divide by two.

3. Your result will be a decimal figure. As always, to convert this decimal to a percent, move the decimal point two places to the right. Thus, .20 = 20 percent.

4. The result is usually used in two ways. First, an accountant or business owner may wish to compare the ratio to that for other businesses. If similar theater chains are showing a return of 15 percent, then the 20 percent looks pretty good. Second, the accountant or business owner may wish to compare the ratio to current interest provided on more conventional investments, such as CDs and money market funds. The increased risk of being in business should have some rewards, among them a higher rate of return on business dollars than one would expect to get from just depositing the same amount of money in the bank. But given that most liquid, risk-free investments pay single-digit returns, Eastside is in good shape with its 20 percent return.

KEY FORMULA: Accounts receivable turnover =
Net sales ÷ Average accounts receivable

Formula used for: Determining how fast a firm is collecting its bills.

Example:

Shute Vacuum Company has accounts receivable of $78,000 at the beginning of the year and $82,000 at the end of the year. If their net sales for the year are $900,000, what is their accounts receivable turnover? First, their average accounts receivable is $78,000 + $82,000 ÷ 2 = $160,000 ÷ 2 = $80,000. Thus, their accounts receivable turnover = $900,000 ÷ $80,000 = 11.25. In other words, Shute collected money that was owed on accounts receivable 11.25 times during the year, or just under once per month.

Remember that in this formula:

1. Begin by determining the average accounts receivable. Assuming you have figures for the beginning and end of the year, as in the example, simply add these and divide by two.

2. Your result will be a whole number or decimal. This figure represents the number of times per year (if one year is the base period you're working with) the firm collected money on its accounts receivable.

KEY FORMULA: Average age of accounts receivable =
365 ÷ Accounts receivable turnover

Formula used for: Determining whether a firm is collecting its accounts receivable in a timely fashion, given its current billing cycle.

Example:

Let's continue with Shute Vacuum. Recall that their accounts receivable turnover, from the preceding example, is 11.25. Thus, the average age of their accounts receivable turnover is 365 ÷ 11.25 = 32.44. This may be good news or somewhat bad news, depending on the length of Shute's billing cycle. Let's say that accounts are due within 30 days; in that case, at least some accounts are delinquent since the average age is about two and a half days over this 30-day limit.

Remember that in this formula:

1. The 365 figure that forms the numerator of this fraction is derived from the fact that there are 365 days in a year. So the question is, how old is the average account *in days*?

2. The result is a whole number or decimal. It shows the *average* age of the firm's accounts. In our example, the average (32.44) is longer than the 30-day billing cycle. But this does not mean that *all* accounts are running late. Some customers could be paying early.

3. The result from this computation means little in isolation. The real question is, how fast does the company expect to have its money? If Shute is happy whenever customers pay within 60 days, then the news is good. But if Shute makes spending plans based on receivables that are paid in less than a month, there could be a problem.

KEY FORMULA:	Debt-to-equity ratio = Current assets + Long-term assets ÷ Owner's equity
Formula used for:	Determining whether the current debt load of a company is reasonable in light of industry averages.

Example:

McBean Canning Company has current assets of $50,000 and long-term assets of $150,000. Their current owner's equity is $100,000. Therefore, their debt-to-equity ratio is $50,000 + $150,000 ÷ $100,000 = $200,000 ÷ $100,000 = 2.0, or 200 percent. In other words, total liabilities are double the amount of owner's equity.

Remember that in this formula:

1. To form the numerator, add total current liabilities to total long-term liabilities.

2. The denominator, owner's equity, is based on the current figure, *not* on an average for the year.

3. The result is either a whole number or a decimal. To convert it to a percent, move the decimal point two places to the right. Thus, 2.0 becomes 200 percent.

4. Interpreting the results may require the assistance of an accountant and some figures on current industry averages. We really cannot say whether McBean should be concerned about its 200 percent debt-to-equity ratio without knowing the average for other canning companies. At the same time, though, a ratio indicating that liabilities are *double* current equity seems dramatic enough to make most business owners at least slightly uncomfortable. McBean would do well to see whether such a disparity is common in the canning industry and, if it's not, to figure out whether changes need to be made.

DON'T FORGET

1. Liquid assets include all current assets *except* inventory.

2. The current ratio, according to conventional wisdom within the business community, should be at least 2:1. In other words, total current assets should be at least double current liabilities.

3. According to the same experience-based rule of thumb, an acid test ratio of 1:1 or more is one good indicator of financial health. Such a ratio indicates that the firm could wipe out its short-term debt using only current assets (those readily convertible to cash), without relying on the sale of inventory.

4. The ratio of net income after taxes to average owner's equity should generally *exceed* the current rate of interest being paid on conventional investments. Otherwise, the business person is not receiving any increased return for the risk involved in owning and operating a business.

5. The average age of accounts receivable should be less than the length of the firm's billing period; if it is not, bills are probably not being collected in a timely manner.

6. The "ideal" figure for the debt-to-equity ratio varies widely from industry to industry. Thus, in interpreting this result, a business person should work closely with an accountant and should compare results for the firm with the average for the industry as a whole.

PART IV: SOLVING BUSINESS PROBLEMS

PROBLEM SETS

Work the following problems in your textbook. Your instructor will tell you which problems, if any, are to be turned in. Some of the problems have answers provided in the back of the book; refer to these answers to make sure you are working the problems correctly.

SOFTCOVER: If you are using the Miller, Salzman, and Hoelzle softcover text, *Business Mathematics*, do the following problem sets:

13.4: Problems #1-10 from pages 559-562.

HARDCOVER: If you are using the Salzman, Miller, and Hoelzle hardcover text, *Mathematics for Business*, do the following problem sets:

17.4: Problems #1-16 from pages 622-625.

_____ **BUSINESS APPLICATIONS**

Read each of the following scenarios and answer the questions about the decisions you would make in each situation. Give these questions some serious thought; they may be used as the basis for discussion or the development of a more complex essay. You should base your decisions on what you've learned from this lesson, applying both math skills and good business judgment to solve the problem at hand.

Reichert's Camera Company is in its fifth year of operation. Business has been good; net income is up more than 10 percent over last year, with a net income after taxes of $20,000. However, the business is outgrowing its current location and is also in need of new equipment.

  Business owner and manager Ray Reichert does not feel the firm can take enough money out of current cash flow to finance expansion, purchase of equipment, and possible relocation. He plans to apply for a 12-month simple interest note at First City Bank. He would like to borrow up to $60,000, if First City will approve the loan. The current simple interest rate on short-term notes is 14 percent.

  Reichert believes that the move and purchase of new equipment will boost net income another 10 to 20 percent. He feels that alone justifies borrowing the money. "Debts have a way of taking care of themselves," Ray maintains, "provided a manager knows how to spend the money well." Ray's accountant urges a more cautious view and suggests that Ray spend some time going over the balance sheet for the firm, shown here. Ray does so and concludes that the firm is in a very strong financial position.

SCENARIO 1

REICHERT'S CAMERA COMPANY		
Balance Sheet		
Assets		
Current assets		
Cash	$10,000	
Notes receivable	20,000	
Accounts receivable	42,000	
Inventory	80,000	
Total current assets		$152,000
Plant assets		
Land	$30,000	
Buildings	45,000	
Fixtures	10,000	
Total plant assets		$ 85,000
TOTAL ASSETS		$237,000
Liabilities and Owner's Equity		
Current liabilities		
Notes payable	$60,000	
Accounts payable	52,000	
Total current liabilities		$112,000
Long-term liabilities		
Mortgages payable	$60,000	
Long-term notes payable	32,000	
Total long-term liabilities		$ 92,000
TOTAL LIABILITIES		$204,000
Owner's equity		$ 33,000
TOTAL LIABILITIES AND OWNER'S EQUITY		$237,000

The accountant, meanwhile, is not convinced that Reichert's could repay the loan without difficulty, even though she concedes the bank may grant it. First City has indicated a willingness to *consider* granting the loan, if Reichert's will put up both its land and buildings as collateral to secure the loan in the event it cannot repay it. The accountant feels that losing the property through a loan default would absolutely devastate the firm, but Ray Reichert is persuaded that the risk is exaggerated. "No risk, no gain," he tells his accountant.

What do you think? Based on what you know of Reichert's situation from their balance sheet and the scenario, do you think they're in a good position to borrow money? Why or why not? Is the accountant right in being so cautious—or is she likely to talk Ray out of a good move that could only improve his position?

☐ Based on a review of the balance sheet, combined with information from the scenario, do you agree with Ray Reichert's assessment that his company is in a strong financial position? Why or why not? (Use specific math computations to justify your answer.)

☐ If you were in Reichert's position, would you apply for the loan? Explain why or why not.

☐ If you were in the bank's position, would you likely grant the loan, based on the information presented? Why or why not? (Use specific data to justify your answer.)

☐ As a loan officer for First City, do you think the information provided here would be sufficient in helping you decide whether or not to grant this loan? If you said yes, explain why. If you said no, explain what other information you might need and how you would use it.

☐ Why do you think Ray and his accountant have such different views regarding the financial position of the business? Isn't Ray likely to be taking a major risk if he acts contrary to his accountant's advice? Explain.

☐ Ray Reichert makes the comment that without risk there can be no gain. How do you feel about this remark in light of the company's current situation?

SCENARIO 2 The Jubilee Toy Company has a current ratio of 2.4:1 and an acid test ratio of .9:1. Their ratio of net income after taxes to average owner's equity is 10 percent (a little better than more conventional investments), compared to an industry average of a bit over 12 percent. The average age of their accounts receivable is 24.9 days on a 30-day billing cycle. Their debt-to-equity ratio is 90 percent.

Jubilee wants to purchase stock in a small video game company that is expected to have a bright future. Jubilee owner Bea Kendall has been contemplating this investment for some time and had expected to have plenty of cash on hand to finance it. But for some reason, despite record sales for the year, she finds that Jubilee is rather low on cash right now. This is puzzling to her, but she feels there are still two alternatives open.

Jubilee could take out a six-month simple interest note for $40,000 at 13 percent to finance the stock purchase. Kendall thinks this would be a good move since she expects the video game company's stock to increase its value at an annual rate of 15 percent or better. Or, Jubilee could trade a portion of its own stock for the game company's stock; the owners of the game company have indicated that they're more than open to this sort of agreement.

Kendall isn't sure which option makes more sense. As she ponders this decision, she can't help wondering what happened to all that money the firm took in on its record sales. Kendall's accountant suggests that a look at the statement of cash flows might provide some answers.

THE JUBILEE TOY COMPANY		
Statement of Cash Flows		
($s in thousands)		
Cash flows from operating activities:		
Cash received from customers	$54	
Cash paid to suppliers/employees	(46)	
Interest paid	(16)	
Income taxes paid	(36)	
Investment income	55	
Net cash provided by operating activities		$ 11
Cash flows from investing activities:		
Purchase of fixed assets	$(60)	
Purchase of intangibles	(12)	
Sale of property, plant, equipment	15	
Net cash used by investing activities		$ (57)
Cash flows from financing activities:		
Net proceeds from sale of bonds	$25	
Sale of capital stock	40	
Payment of dividends	(30)	
Net cash provided by financing activities		$ 35
NET DECREASE IN TOTAL CASH		$ (11)

What do you think? Is purchasing the video game company a good move for Jubilee right now? If so, how should it finance the purchase? Looking at the statement of cash flows, are you surprised that the firm is unable to come up with the money? How would you explain this?

☐ Is it a good idea for Jubilee to invest in more stock right now? Why or why not?

☐ If the firm *does* decide to invest, how should it finance the purchase of the stock? Why would you recommend that course of action?

☐ Based on what you know, rate the strength of this firm's financial position on an ascending scale of 1 to 10. Provide at least three specific reasons to justify your response.

☐ Given the record sales, it would seem that Jubilee ought to be able to come up with the cash to finance the purchase of the $40,000 worth of stock. How would *you* explain the fact that it cannot seem to do so? Do you think the problem is related to poor money management? Explain.

☐ If you could make one recommendation to Bea Kendall regarding the financial management of Jubilee Toy Company, what would it be?

☐ Suppose that Jubilee buys the stock with money borrowed from the bank. Name one specific financial consequence of this decision for the firm. Suppose they wind up trading stock. Name one specific financial consequence of *this* decision.

☐ Imagine that you are on the board of directors at the video game company and you have an opportunity to approve or disapprove the stock transaction. Which decision would you make, and why?

   a. Prevent Jubilee from buying any stock,
   b. Require cash for the stock, or
   c. Trade shares of your stock for shares of Jubilee.

Funding the Business with Stocks and Bonds 23

"You taught me how to sit, fetch, and roll over,
Roger, and I'll always be grateful for that. In
appreciation, I'd like to share with you some things
I've learned lately about junk bonds and leveraged
buy-outs!"

Have you wondered where large companies get the money they need to grow? Very often, a portion of it comes from the personal savings of the business partners. But rarely does that source provide sufficient income to launch any but the most modest of businesses. Nor is it practical to borrow all the needed capital from the bank. Banks are not big risk takers and generally are dead set against putting any more money into a new business venture than they feel very sure of recovering.

But while banks shy away from risk, individual or corporate investors sometimes welcome it, particularly when it carries with it the potential for high investment returns. That's often the case with stocks and bonds, two types of investments that provide working capital for corporations and, sometimes, the potential of high return for the individuals or corporations that buy them.

Stocks and bonds have some important elements in common. Both are investments. Both offer variable risk, depending heavily on the current state of the economy and on the financial soundness of the business or other entity in which the buyer is investing. But there are big differences, too, including one very basic distinction: A stockholder owns a portion of the business in which he or she invests, while a bondholder is not an owner at all, but a lender.

In this lesson, we'll define these two types of investments, talk about how the investor goes about selecting and obtaining stocks and bonds, and explore the relative risks and benefits of each investment.

PART I: INTRODUCING THE MATERIAL

LEARNING OBJECTIVES

Upon completing your study of this lesson, you should be able to:

1. Contrast proprietorships, partnerships, and corporations in terms of distribution of profits and responsibility for the business's liabilities.

2. Explain how a corporation raises capital through the sale of stock and define the key terms related to corporations, including stockholders, board of directors, executive officers, and dividends.

3. Describe the difference between common stock and preferred stock, know which is more prevalent, and describe the features of cumulative preferred, convertible preferred, participating, and nonparticipating stock.

4. Given a reproduction of a stock table from a financial newspaper, determine the prices (high, low, close, and year-to-date high and low), dividend, price-earnings ratio, and current yield for a specified stock.

5. Calculate the current yield of a stock, given its annual dividend and current price.

6. Calculate the price-earnings ratio of a stock, given its current price.

7. Explain how capital is raised by a corporation through the sale of bonds and contrast the effect on the ownership of the company of issuing stock versus issuing bonds.

8. Given a reproduction of a bond table from a financial newspaper, determine the rate and maturity, prices (high, low, and close), and current yield for a specified bond.

9. Given the appropriate commission schedule, calculate the commission charged to buy or sell a specified number of bonds or shares of stock.

If you're using the hardcover textbook, *Mathematics for Business*, there are some additional objectives for this lesson. Upon completing your study of the lesson, you should also be able to:

10. Given the appropriate commission schedule, determine how many bonds or shares of stock having a specified price can be purchased with a given amount of money.

11. Discuss the role that stocks and bonds (including so-called junk bonds) play in financing the takeovers and mergers of corporations.

LESSON OVERVIEW

Imagine two business partners in the late 1800s opening a lumber business in a small town somewhere in the Northwest. These two entrepreneurs, Fogel and Kline, have only a little money to put into the business, but for now a little is enough.

Business is slow at first, so they can take their time building up inventory, much of which comes right from Fogel's own land, where the two of them do most of the timber harvesting themselves. Their startup needs are minimal: a shed for storing their supplies and tools, some saws and axes, a wagon and team of horses for hauling the product. All of these things they own themselves, so there's no cash outlay. And if they do need something they can't immediately afford—down the road, say, when business picks up a bit—their credit is excellent at the local bank. The banker, Quigley, has known them both for most of their lives and, more importantly, knows that the town will need a constant supply of lumber as it expands, so a loan will be no problem.

For Kline and Fogel, starting a business has been a relatively simple matter. They already own much of what they need and have ready resources for obtaining the rest. Another factor is important in this scenario, too. Their lumber business is small, designed to serve the local community. Fogel and Kline aren't engaged in international trade or even distributing their goods nationwide. They don't have to worry about catalogs, or television advertising, or the problems of trucking goods across the country. If they did, perhaps their financial needs would be a lot different.

Today, most companies serve a wider community by far than that served by Fogel and Kline's 19th-century lumber business. And because this is so, their needs are greater right from the beginning. So are their risks.

Partnerships: A Partial Solution

In our scenario, Fogel and Kline had what is called a *partnership*, a business started by two or more persons. Since Kline and Fogel share equally in the running of the business, they probably divide the profits equally as well. That isn't always the case, though. As we discussed in the lesson on profit distribution, sometimes one partner is a *silent partner*, who puts up some money or other resources to get the business going but then leaves the day-to-day management to someone else.

Partners normally split the profits according to how much each contributes to the business. For instance, in our scenario, Fogel provides the land from which the business takes the timber. but let's say that Kline provides the team and wagon, together with most of the tools and the shed in which they store their goods. They may decide that their contributions are about equal, and so they will also split the profits equally. If the business *loses* money, they'll share equally in the losses, too. And because they are the only partners, they'll bear the full responsibility for any losses the business might suffer. Say, for instance, that they purchase additional land, thinking to provide resources for the years to come; unfortunately, business profits aren't sufficient to cover their payments. In that case, Kline and Fogel will have to make up the money out of their own pockets or lose the land.

As the example with the land illustrates, partnerships involve a considerable risk; each partner is both morally and legally liable for any debt the business incurs, in proportion to his or her share of the business. On the other hand, though, the risk is less than with a *sole proprietorship*, a business owned and run by just one person. Say, for instance, that Fogel sells out to Kline and goes off to start a general store in Nevada by himself. In that case, Kline bears full responsibility for all business debts. But, of course, that's the gloomy side of the scenario; it's also true that Kline, as the sole owner, will now receive all the profits of the business. That's his reward for bearing all the risk himself.

Limiting Liability Further

As mentioned, forming a partnership minimizes individual liability somewhat. After all, losses are less threatening when shared by two—or three, or more. But while that arrangement might have provided more than enough security for an 1880s lumber business, it would not satisfy the needs of most businesses today, many of which are in debt for millions of dollars—far more than two or three partners could likely bear alone if the business failed. There are, of course, exceptions to every rule; even today, some of the world's largest companies are partnerships or even sole proprietorships. But the risk of running a national business, combined with the need for more money than the partners can come up with, often speaks for having a different business structure.

A practical way of minimizing business risk is by forming a *corporation*, a business structure in which each investor stands to lose only what he or she has actually invested in the business and no more. Incorporation protects business owners against heavy loss and also gives them the right to issue stock, a practice that has benefits for those who issue the stock as well as those who buy it. Let's see why this is so.

Types of Stock

These days, few people can run a business out of a garage using "just a few things everyone has around the house." It happens, but it's rare. Most businesses need large sums of money to rent facilities, buy equipment, and purchase initial inventory. A common way of coming up with more capital is through the sale of *stock*. Each share of stock represents partial ownership in the company. Thus, if a company issues 1,000 shares of stock, a person who buys a single share owns $\frac{1}{1,000}$th of that company.

There are essentially two types of stock: common stock and preferred stock. Most of the stock sold is *common stock*. Those who purchase it have the right to attend annual corporate meetings, decide who sits on the company's board of directors, and vote on some matters of importance to the company. They often receive *dividends*, a portion of the profits paid to shareholders, though this is not guaranteed.

Holders of *preferred stock* have less uncertainty in their lives. Their stock has a *par value*, or face value, printed right on the front and an established *dividend*, based on a percent of par value. For instance, a stock with a par value of $100 and a dividend rate of 10 percent would pay a $10 annual dividend—provided the company earned enough to pay its shareholders a dividend at all, and provided that a dividend was declared by the board of directors. Keep in mind that the par value of the stock is not necessarily the same as its current market value, which may be above or below par, depending on investors' opinion of the company's projected future performance.

One critical difference between common and preferred stock is that preferred stockholders receive dividends *before* any dividend is paid to common stockholders. If there's not enough money to pay both, the common stockholders go without dividends. In the event that the company goes bankrupt, preferred stockholders are paid off before common stockholders but *not* before bondholders (more on this later).

Holders of *cumulative preferred stock* are also entitled to receive unpaid past dividends before common stockholders receive anything. For instance, suppose that West Hills Electric has a bad year and declares no dividend. Johnson, who holds ten $100 shares with a 10 percent dividend, would normally have received $100 ($10 per share). But since the company isn't doing well, Johnson receives nothing—for now. Next year, however, when profits are up, West Hills will pay Johnson not only the dividend for that year but the $100 they owe him from this year. All before common stockholders receive a cent.

Convertible preferred stock, as its name implies, may be exchanged in the future for a certain number of shares of common stock. You may be wondering why anyone would go for such a trade, since it means giving up a guaranteed dividend. Remember, however, that common stockholders often *do* receive dividends, too, sometimes big dividends. Most preferred stock is *nonparticipating*, which means that the shareholders usually get the dividend they've been promised even when times are bad, but they don't get a penny more when times are good. In other words, preferred stock isn't always preferable; sometimes it earns the shareholders considerably less than common stock.

Many business people would argue against spending much time discussing any kind of preferred stock. They correctly point out that only a small fraction of the stock in this country is preferred and that some very large corporations don't have any preferred stock at all. Others, though, suggest that even though "stock" almost always means "common stock," preferred stock is important to study if for no other reason than as a contrast to common stock when discussing the matter of guaranteed returns on the stockholders' investments.

Distributing Profits

Corporations are required by law to hold shareholder meetings at least once per year. These *annual meetings* must be open to all stockholders—who, after all, have a vested interest in how the company is run. Annual meetings are run by the firm's *board of directors*, a group elected by stockholders to represent their interests. The board of directors is responsible for responding to stockholders' questions and concerns, for hiring the firm's principal officers (president, vice president, etc.), and for distributing some portion of the firm's profits as dividends. They may decide to distribute most of the company's profits in this way, or very little, depending on the circumstances.

Say, for instance, that a small regional airline, South Central Air, makes a net profit of $500,000. They could distribute that entire amount in the form of dividends to stockholders. But the board may decide that the company needs to expand in order to remain competitive. So they will pour $400,000 of that net profit back into the expansion effort and distribute only the remaining $100,000 in the form of dividends.

Suppose that the company has issued 5,000 shares of preferred stock, each with a par value of $100 and a dividend rate of 8 percent. That makes the dividend per share $8 ($100 × .08). So the total dividends paid to preferred stockholders will be 5,000 × $8, or $40,000. That leaves $100,000 − $40,000 = $60,000 for distribution to common stockholders. Let's suppose there are 30,000 shares of common stock outstanding. In that case, the dividend per share will be $60,000 ÷ 30,000 = $2 per share.

The shareholders might like to see this dividend just a little bigger, but on the other hand, they likely understand why all the firm's profits can't be paid out in dividends. It's usually important for any firm to reinvest in its own growth so that next year's profits can be even bigger.

Evaluating Stock Performance

One way to measure a firm's financial success (and indeed, one way for potential investors to choose stock) is by looking at the *earnings per share*, which is found through this ratio: (Net income − Dividends on preferred stock) ÷ Numbers of shares of common stock outstanding.

In our example with South Central Air, the earnings per share would be ($500,000 − $40,000) ÷ 30,000 = $15.33. This is almost eight times the dividend paid to common shareholders (who receive just $2 per share). The difference reflects a combination of what the firm is paying its preferred stockholders plus what it is putting into investment. If this figure is higher than for other regional airlines, we might reasonably conclude that South Central is either investing more than other airlines or paying a higher dividend to preferred stockholders or both. This information is very useful to potential investors who are wondering what sort of return they're likely to get on their investment in South Central's common stock.

Two More Important Ratios

Two other ratios are important in assessing the current value of stock. One is the *current yield*, a ratio of annual dividend per share to current price per share. Let's say that a stock is currently selling for $50, and pays an annual dividend of $5. In that case, its current yield is $5 ÷ $50 = .10, or 10 percent. This is another way of saying that the investor can expect to recover annually about 10 percent on his or her investment, provided the company remains in a position to pay a dividend like this. How good that 10 percent looks depends on what other stocks (or other investments, for that matter) that the investor is considering are paying. If the average current yield for the market as a whole is 15 percent, then the investor may wish to hold out for something more promising. Investors in the stock market often feel, justifiably, that they're entitled to a better return than they can get simply putting the money into a certificate of deposit or Treasury bill, so the current yield is a pretty important number.

One other ratio often helps would-be investors with their stock-picking decisions. This is the so-called *price to earnings (P/E) ratio*: Price per share ÷ Annual earnings per share. Say, for instance, that the price per share is $20 and the annual net income per share is $5. In that case, the P/E ratio is $20 ÷ $5 = 4. Again, an investor will want to look at P/E ratios for similar firms and for the market as a whole in order to put this number into perspective. Let's say that the *average* P/E ratio for the market is around 13. That makes the 4 look pretty small, and small is good when it comes to P/Es because it means that the stock's price is low relative to the money it earns. But why is it so low?

There could be a couple of reasons. Perhaps this stock is what investment counselors call a "sleeper," a stock with high promise for the future, issued by a company that hasn't yet attracted the attention of investors. In other words, it's undervalued, with a relatively low price given the company's high net earnings. On the other hand, maybe the ratio is low not because the stock is underpriced but because observers don't really expect this company to do well in the future. Investors who take the time and trouble to research the company itself (not just look at stock prices) invest partly on the basis of a firm's long-term goals and how it manages its cash flow. Thus, a low P/E ratio may simply mean that the firm is out of favor with those who've done their investment homework.

Similarly, a P/E ratio may be high because a stock is overpriced in relation to net earnings for the company, in which case both the price and the P/E ratio are likely to fall sometime in the future. Or, it may be high because those investors who've researched the company predict it will do better in the future, so they're willing to pay more for it.

It's not unusual to hear a person say, "Boy, I wish *I'd* bought stock in that company when it was just starting out!" There was a time when the companies that make Polaroid cameras and Xerox photocopiers and IBM office machines were relatively small and had quite modest stock prices. But while these companies and others like them have routinely paid dividends over the years, the comments about getting in "on the ground floor" have more to do with the increase in the share price of the stock.

The value of stock, like that of almost every freely traded commodity, is set by supply and demand. When a company's future appears bright relative to the price of its common stock shares, more people want to own a piece of it and the share price goes up. But when a stock appears overpriced compared to the return it will provide, fewer are willing to invest, and even current shareholders may want to sell what shares they have. They do this through stockbrokers who work at *stock exchanges*, forums for buying and selling shares. The New York Stock Exchange (NYSE), located on Wall Street in New York City, is the most well known in the U.S., but there are others, including the large American (Amex) and NASDAQ exchanges and several smaller regional exchanges, most of which list many regional companies. There's nothing uniquely American about trading stocks; the large stock exchanges in London and Tokyo exert an influence on the world's economy similar to that of the major U.S. exchanges.

The current New York Stock Exchange really had its beginnings as a central auction, where auctioneers received a commission for each stock or bond sold. Then in May of 1792, a group of 24 concerned businessmen, in an effort to make the whole thing more organized and systematic, signed a document in which they agreed to trade securities only among themselves, to maintain fixed commission rates, and to avoid other auctions. Their agreement marked the beginnings of the modern stock exchange.

At that time, it cost $400 to be a member, and only members were allowed to trade. The cost of a "seat" on the stock exchange has gone up dramatically since then, but membership is still required of those who buy and sell directly. Being a member is still referred to as "having a seat" on the stock exchange (something of a misnomer since, as anyone who has visited the floor of a major stock exchange can testify, virtually no one ever sits down). The exchange is a veritable cauldron of activity, with members negotiating trades constantly and the latest stock values flashing by on an electronic board known as a "ticker."

The Stock Exchange: Classic Supply and Demand

Not all companies are traded at the NYSE. Some are partnerships or proprietorships, which means that they don't have any stock to trade. But not all large corporations are listed on the New York exchange; many are traded instead on the American or NASDAQ exchanges. And for every company traded on one of the major exchanges, there are dozens that aren't traded at all. Remember, all corporations have stock, but that stock is not usually not publicly traded. Willie's Fish and Chowder may well be a corporation, and hundreds of shares of stock may have been issued. But the odds are that most of the stock is held by Willie, his family, his friends, and perhaps a few outside investors. And if you decided you wanted to invest in Willie's stock, you'd likely talk to Willie to see what price he'd sell at rather than turning to the business section of the daily paper.

Members of the general public do not buy seats on the stock exchange so they can trade their stock; that would be far too expensive to make most investments at all profitable. More to the point, though, there are thousands and thousands of investors for each seat on the stock exchange. Seats are normally held by brokerage companies that specialize in stock market trading. In fact, people who want to buy or sell stock don't go to the stock exchange to trade as they did in the early days of the NYSE. They do most of their trading by telephone, through a licensed broker whose job it is to buy and sell securities on someone else's behalf.

Brokers: Licensed Stock Traders

Stock brokers are licensed by the Securities and Exchange Commission (SEC), which is the regulating body of the stock exchanges. The SEC sets strict standards of performance to which all brokers must adhere and strict financial requirements for brokerage companies, requirements designed to ensure the safety of stocks and money held by or passing through the brokerage company on behalf of a customer.

Brokers work for a *commission*, a percentage of sales. This rate was once set by the SEC, but now brokers are free to set their own rates, so they're more competitive. Some brokers charge a lower commission rate than others, but they provide no investment advice. They simply act as facilitators to put through trades according to clients' instructions.

Some brokers charge an additional fee for an *odd-lot differential*; that is, the purchase or sale of stocks in lots of fewer than 100. Let's say that Betty Schwartz buys $5,000 worth of stocks. Her broker charges a 3 percent commission, so his initial fee is $5,000 × .03 = $150. But Betty's purchase represents 250 shares: two *round lots* of 100 shares each, plus an additional 50 shares. The broker charges an additional fee of $1/8 for *every share* over and above the round lots of 100; in this case, there are 50 such shares. In the world of stocks and bonds, prices are expressed in dollars, so 1/8 is equal to 12.5 cents (an eighth of a dollar), or .125 in decimal terms. Thus, in addition to the $150, the broker will charge another .125 × 50 = $6.25 for the extra 50 shares.

The Language of Wall Street

Most of the language of Wall Street consists of numbers, the idea being to pack a lot of information into a concise code. After all, there are thousands of stocks traded on the major exchanges, so trying to summarize everything that happened during a trading day in a couple of pages of a newspaper is a formidable challenge calling for some clever shorthand. Thus, an excerpt from a stock table might look like this:

56 42 3/8 AmChm AMC 1.20 2.5 14 2007 48 5/8 48 48 3/8 + 1/8

The numbers to the far left (56 and 42⅜) show the high and low prices on this stock for the preceding 52 weeks. The abbreviation AmChm stands for American Chemical (a hypothetical company); AMC is the company's symbol on the exchange. The 1.20 shows that American Chemical is currently paying a dividend of $1.20. The 2.5 is the current yield, and 14 is the P/E ratio. The number 2007 shows the number of shares sold on this particular trading day *in lots of 100*; in other words, the total number of shares sold is 2007 × 100 = 200,700. The next three numbers provide a summary of prices on this stock throughout the day. It opened at 48⅝ ($48.625), then fell to a low of 48 ($48), but rallied a bit to close at 48⅜ ($48.375). The +⅛ on the far right shows that today's closing price was up ⅛ (or 12.5¢) over yesterday's close, which must therefore have been 48²⁄₈, or $48.25.

Volatility — or Plain Old Excitement

As this example shows, prices on Wall Street are rarely stable. The value of stocks changes not just yearly or monthly, but literally minute by minute. Of course, the typical trader isn't tuned in to these blow-by-blow shifts in the market. Some depend on the nightly business news or on the business page of the daily newspaper for a summary of the day's trading results. Others rely on a broker or other investment counselor to watch these ups and downs for them. All the same, anyone who's put a substantial amount of money into Wall Street can testify that the instability of the market is not well suited to all investors. Some find the risk stimulating, for along with it goes the potential for high profit. Others find it simply unnerving.

Over the long run, values on the stock market have tended to rise fairly steadily, paralleling a general growth in the economy as a whole. In the short term, however, individual stocks have often not fared well, and even the market as a whole has taken deep and serious dives. Most economists don't view these "corrections" as posing a threat to the long-term gains of the market as a whole; in fact, many stock prices hit new highs shortly after the drops. That was, however, small comfort for individual investors who faced substantial losses, particularly for those who were heavily invested in a limited number of stocks that did not rebound to previous levels

It's commonly said that the ups and downs of the stock market tend to reflect the prevailing faith of the public and the business community in the future of the country's business economy. The theory is that when the trade balance is fairly even, when the dollar is fairly strong (but not so strong that other countries will not buy our exports), and when the gross national product (the total of all the goods and services produced in the U.S.) is up, these factors tend to bode well for Wall Street. Similarly, when interest rates are down, money is "cheaper" and more readily available; thus, investment tends to increase and the value of stocks rises at a faster rate.

Investors are also theoretically more willing to take risks with their money if returns elsewhere (e.g., on savings bonds or certificates of deposit) are relatively poor. When general interest rates rise, many investors reason that it's foolish to take chances when they can get a good return just by putting their money in the bank. So trading volume on stocks declines and the value of stocks tends to fall off. Unfortunately, the market doesn't always react as the theories would have you believe, and there is no such thing as a perfectly safe stock market investment.

There are alternatives, though, and investors who are concerned about safety generally give at least some thought to investing in *bonds*. But just how safe are bonds, really? As we'll see, that depends a lot on who issues them, and under what circumstances.

Bonds: An Alternative Money Raiser

A company can go just so far in raising money through the sale of stock. Keep in mind that the number of shares issued is determined by the company itself. So it might issue 100 shares, or 10,000 or 1 million. But if the corporation is divided up into too many pieces, the value of owning any one piece is diluted. An investor might well consider owning one share in a corporation that has only 1,000 shares outstanding. But no one wants to own one four-billionth of a company. Likewise, what company wants to have 4 billion owners? In other words, there's a limit to how much capital a company can raise by selling bits of ownership through stock. There's another alternative, though: bonds.

A *bond* is a little like a long-term promissory note signed by a borrower who receives money from a bank. Like a note, it represents a promise to pay a debt in the future and to pay interest on that debt. With a note, however, the individual consumer or corporation is normally the *borrower*; with a bond, the consumer or investing corporation is the *lender*, and the issuer of the bond is the borrower.

The method of repayment is also a little different from that on a note. A person who borrows money usually pays off both interest and principal through a series of periodic payments. With a bond, the borrower pays a fixed amount of annual interest but does not pay anything on the principal until the bond comes due, at which time the principal is paid off all at once. This final payment is sometimes referred to as *retiring* the bond. Some bonds come due in a few years; others may have a maturity period of 20 or 30 years.

Corporate bonds are those issued by corporations who wish to borrow money for any of a number of reasons; perhaps to build new facilities, or to buy equipment, or to pay off other debts. *Municipal* bonds are issued by states, cities, or other governmental and quasi-governmental agencies to help finance projects that tax revenue alone won't cover. Municipal bonds may help build new schools, libraries, or hospitals; build or repair roads and bridges; establish parks or other recreational facilities; or otherwise contribute to the general welfare of the community. And there are other bonds (including the well-known *U.S. savings bonds*) that are issued by the federal government and used to finance federal programs or to help pay off other government obligations.

Cashing in Early

Persons who buy bonds are usually interested in long-term returns and often have no intention of converting the bonds to cash prior to maturity. Circumstances change, though. An individual investor may need money for a down payment on a house or to meet unforeseen medical expenses; a corporate investor may have an opportunity to transfer the money to another investment that promises a higher yield. It's possible to cash a bond in early, but it's not always possible to get back the full par, or face, value. That depends on the current market. Just as common stock values change based on how attractive an investment the stock is, bond prices also change depending on whether the return is a good value or not.

Most corporate bonds have a face value of $1,000. The interest rate, which is variable, is based on this par value. Thus, a $1,000 bond with an interest rate of 10 percent will pay $100 in interest each year. The value of the bond may fall below par or rise above par. But either way, the *amount of* annual interest will continue to be $100 (based on the par value); consequently, the *rate* of interest changes as the market value of the bond goes up or down. To illustrate (based on our $1,000 bond):

☐ When the bond price is at par, the yield is $100 ÷ $1,000 = 10 percent. (Note that the yield is the amount of annual interest divided by the par value of the bond.)

☐ When the bond price rises, the yield declines: $100 ÷ $1,100 = 9.09 percent.

☐ When the bond price falls, the yield goes up: $100 ÷ $900 = 11.11 percent.

In short, the interest *rate*, or yield, rises and falls in opposition to what happens to the market price of the bond, but the *amount* of interest paid remains constant. Further, the bond is redeemed at maturity *by the issuer* for par value, regardless of its market value at the time. However, in the interim, it may be sold to a number of buyers at prices above or below par.

That a long-term investment like a bond has a rather changeable market price might surprise you, but this makes sense if you think about it for a moment. The value of the bond on the open market depends on current interest rates in general. As interest rates rise, the interest on bonds must rise too; otherwise they wouldn't remain attractive investments to investors. But since the *amount* of interest paid on the bond is fixed at the time it's issued, the only way to push the rate up is by lowering the market price of the bond. To put it another way, it's more appealing to a potential investor to get a $100 return on a $900 investment than it is to get the same $100 on a $1,000 investment. Thus, when interest rates in general rise, bond prices tend to fall; when interest rates fall, bond prices tend to rise. (Note that this is just the reverse of how theory says that common stocks would react.)

Now let's look at things from the issuer's point of view. Remember that a bond is essentially a promise to pay; in other words, it represents a debt. So rising or falling interest rates have really nothing to do with the amount of money originally borrowed, nor with the promise to repay that money or interest on that money. Say, for instance, that Keystone Manufacturing sells 5,000 bonds with face values of $1,000 each to raise money for its new regional plant. Whether the market price of the bond has gone up or down has nothing to do with the amount Keystone needs to repay. From its point of view, everything about the bond is fixed: when it will be retired, what interest will be paid across the years, and the amount paid to the bondholder at maturity. The fact that the price of the bond on the open market may change dozens of times before it's retired doesn't affect Keystone at all.

The only exception to this "everything remains the same" rule is if the bonds are *callable*. If an issuer wishes to reserve the right to *call* the bonds (retire them before the maturity period is up), that right must be stated on the face of the bond at the time it is issued. The right to call protects the issuer from having to pay higher interest than can reasonably be covered through other investments.

Callable Bonds

Say that a company issues bonds at 10 percent. Then general interest rates fall to 8 percent, with no likelihood of an increase in sight. The issuer is now paying much more out in interest than can be recovered through other investments. It might now be a good idea to borrow the money instead, or even to retire the old bonds and reissue a new set at a lower rate. You may, of course, be thinking that the whole process of calling bonds and issuing new ones sounds like a lot of trouble to go to just for a couple of points in interest. True enough, the difference in interest on an 8 percent bond versus a 10 percent bond may not seem significant — until you remember that a company may have sold tens of thousands of bonds, making those two interest points worth millions of dollars. In fact, the difference may be so significant that a company is willing to call a bond *at a premium*; a $1,000 bond, for instance, might be redeemed at $1,100.

Reading the Bond Tables

Information on bonds, like that on stocks, is printed in tables often found in financial newspapers. Here's an example for a hypothetical company, Wolfley Research:

Wolfley   9½   05   8.8   50   98⅜   −¼

This table tells us that Wolfley bonds pay interest of 9½ percent, based on their par value of $1,000. The number 05 tells us that the bond will come due in the year 2005. The next number, 8.8, is the current yield (amount of interest divided by market price). The 50 is the number of bonds that sold today. Notice that bond tables give the exact number; recall that stock tables list the number of 100-stock lots sold. The 98⅜ tells us that the current market value of this bond is 98.375 percent of its face value, or $1,000 × .98375 = $983.75. This price is down ¼, or 25¢, from yesterday's closing market price.

Although most metropolitan daily papers carry the stock market reports, extensive bond trading information is harder to find. Part of it has to do with the amount of trading taking place; there are many more shares of stock traded each day (often over 100 million) than bonds. And bonds do not, under normal circumstances, change market price as much as stocks. Both of these characteristics come from one basic difference: Bonds *can* be bought and sold but are largely designed to be held; common stocks are designed to be publicly, and frequently, traded.

The Safe Investment — Usually

Bonds are often regarded as among the safest of all investments. In the case of U.S. savings bonds and many municipal bonds, this reputation is well earned. Such bonds are backed by the governments that issue them. In the case of federal bonds, keep in mind that the same government issuing the bonds also prints the money; thus, these bonds can lose their total value only if the entire economy falls apart.

All publicly held corporate and municipal bonds are rated by agencies, such as Standard and Poor's or Moody's, whose job it is to evaluate the relative safety of such investments. Ratings range from AAA (triple A), the highest rating, down through C, or sometimes D, the lowest. Bonds with a triple A down through triple B rating are generally considered secure investments. Those with a rating of double B on down are considered increasingly less secure and are sometimes referred to as "high yield" bonds or, less tactfully, as *junk bonds*. Those with a D rating are in default; interest that was owed to bond holders has not been paid.

High yield bonds are issued by corporations that may not be financially stable enough to cover the loan under current circumstances but that often plan to obtain the money through investments of their own. These bonds are quite risky compared to other bonds, but for this reason, they offer a higher yield; 12 percent or more is not unusual. This, of course, is the source of their appeal. Remember, the issuing company doesn't want to pay any more interest than is necessary, but it needs to attract investors, whose first rule is "If you want me to take more risk, you need to reward me with the promise of a better return."

High yield bonds are sometimes used to finance "buyouts," the takeover of one company by another. In simple terms, it works something like this. Suppose that one company, Green Industries, wishes to buy out another, White Manufacturing. Green doesn't have the money to finance the takeover, though; and even if it turned right around and resold White, it still couldn't pay off the loan with enough money left over to make all the hassle worthwhile. As it turns out, though, White Manufacturing isn't just one big company; it's a conglomerate, made up of several smaller operations—some of which *could* be sold separately, at a much higher profit margin than could be realized by selling the company as a whole.

If Green can get enough investors to buy its 12 percent bonds, it can come up with the money it needs to buy out White. Then it can turn around, sell the individual operations within the larger conglomerate, pay off the bonds, and still come out ahead. Of course, if any portion of this transaction fails to go as planned, Green may find itself in a difficult position: deeply indebted to its bond holders and unable to pay the ongoing interest owed to them. Unfortunately, once it becomes clear that Green is having trouble keeping up with its obligations, the market price of the bonds will fall through the floor, meaning that investors will take a big loss to get rid of them. In fact, the financial picture may become so bleak that the bonds become virtually worthless. Still, if things go well with the White Manufacturing takeover, bond holders who took the big risk could make windfall profits. All in all, there's considerable disagreement about the role of junk bonds as a corporate financing tool and about the wisdom of investing in them for anything except pure speculation.

SOME WORDS OF ADVICE

As an investor, take time *before* investing to find out just how stocks and bonds work. They have similarities (both are marketable investments) but there are also big differences. A stock represents an actual share in the company, while a bond is simply a promise to pay a debt. Therefore, as a stockholder, you are an *owner*; as a bond holder, you're a *lender*. Keep in mind, too, that while bonds can usually be sold, they are not as liquid as stocks. That is, they're not quite so readily convertible to cash. Therefore, it's usually best to view a bond as a long-term investment with a guaranteed return rather than something to be traded to make money.

Whether buying stocks or bonds, don't depend on just one source of information regarding the wisdom of various investments. In the final analysis, no one knows which companies will reap tomorrow's high profits, nor what the stock market will do, though some financial advisors or investment counselors are all too eager to give you the impression that they *do* know. Beware of such ambitious claims. This doesn't mean you shouldn't work with a consultant or broker, but select such an advisor carefully, and whenever possible, combine even the best professional advice with some research of your own. Keep in mind, too, that although a broker may *recommend* an investment, his or her advice is just that—a recommendation. It is not a promise of performance, nor is it legally binding in any way.

Most investment counselors advise against looking on the stock market as a good means of financing something as essential as an education or new home. In other words, where the financial need is fixed and certain, security is a vital consideration. Long-term returns on stock market investments have historically been quite good, especially for investors who *diversify* — invest in a variety of companies, that is, rather than in just one or two. But short-term stock investments often lose money for the investor, even when they look promising originally. It used to be that there were a number of "blue chip" stocks whose size and stability and ongoing dividends made them a rather safe investment. But now that the stock markets in general are more volatile than they used to be, it's easy to lose a substantial part of your investment even on these stocks if the timing of your buying and selling is bad.

The bond market tends to be somewhat less volatile and more stable over time than the stock market. That's as expected since bonds, unlike common stocks, pay a guaranteed annual return. What's more, many bonds, including all federal and most municipal bonds, are considered extremely safe investments. In exchange, of course, they pay a relatively low rate of interest, although that is partially offset by the fact that the income from federal and municipal bonds may not be taxed.

Corporate bonds are not tax-exempt, and they rarely offer the same security as government bonds. In exchange, their yield is higher. How much higher depends on the perceived risk involved, so be sure to check the ratings provided through Standard and Poor's or a similar agency before investing. You should also understand just what the money raised by the bonds is going for and how the ongoing interest payments will be covered. After all, the company is asking you to lend it money and you need to have some faith that it's going to spend it wisely. Your investment can only be as secure as the company's plans for repaying its debts.

Finally, it doesn't hurt to know your math. The ability to read stock and bond tables with ease and to calculate important ratios can put you well on your way to making sound investment decisions even in the absence of professional advice. At the very least, it will help you ask the right questions and make sense of the answers. You'll also need to estimate the commissions involved every time a broker buys and sells stocks or bonds for you. Commissions that seem small at the time can still knock a few percent off the return on your investment, and that might spell the difference between a good investment and money that would earn more for you sitting in the bank.

KEY TERMS

Before you read through the text assignment and watch the video program, take a minute to look at the key terms associated with this lesson. When you encounter them in the text and video program, pay careful attention to their meaning.

Annual meeting: A meeting open to all owners of stock where the management of the firm is open to questions from stockholders and where the board of directors is elected.

Bond: A promise by a corporation, government, or governmental unit to repay a sum of money at some stated time.

Capital: The amount of money originally invested in a firm.

Commission: A charge based on percentage of sales for buying or selling stock.

Common stock: Ordinary capital stock that does not share the privileges of preferred stock.

Convertible preferred stock: Preferred stock that is convertible into a specified number of shares of common stock at some future date.

Corporation: A form of business offering limited liability so that no owner may lose more than that owner has invested.

Cumulative preferred stock: Stock requiring that any dividends not paid in the past must be paid before common stockholders receive any money.

Current yield: The annual dividend per share of stock divided by the current price per share of stock. In the case of bonds, the current amount of interest paid per year divided by the market price of the bond.

Dividends: Money paid by a company to the holders of stock.

Earnings per share: The difference between the net income of a corporation and any dividends paid on preferred shares divided by the number of common shares outstanding.

Face value: See *par value*.

Nonparticipating stock: A form of stock that will never pay dividends above the stated rate.

Odd lot: Fewer than 100 shares of stock.

Odd-lot differential: An additional charge for buying or selling stocks when the number of shares is not an even multiple of 100.

Participating stock: Stock that could be affected by an increase in dividends.

Partnership: A business formed by two or more people.

Par value: The amount printed on a bond or stock certificate, usually the price at which the stock or bond is originally offered to the public.

Preferred stock: Stock that pays dividends before common stockholders receive any dividends.

Price-earnings (P/E) ratio: The ratio found when the price per share of stock is divided by the annual earnings per share.

Round lot: Any number of shares of stock that is a multiple of 100.

Stock: A certificate representing partial ownership of a corporation.

Stockbroker (or broker): A person who buys and sells shares of stock for the public.

Stockholders: The owners of a corporation.

PART II: WATCHING THE VIDEO PROGRAM

VIDEO VIEWING GUIDE

Before watching the video program, review the following questions. As you watch, be sure to collect the information necessary to answer them:

1. In what ways are stocks and bonds similar? In what ways are they different?

2. What factors go into determining the current value of stocks?

3. What factors go into determining the current value of bonds?

4. Do you think that a person who knew little or nothing of Wall Street operations could still invest profitably in the stock market? Explain.

5. How important are stocks as a means for most corporations to raise money? How important are bonds? If corporations did not have these alternatives, where would they get their money?

6. How do rising or falling interest rates affect the value of stocks or bonds on the open market?

7. Why would a company choose to sell bonds rather than simply borrow the money it needed from the bank?

8. For what sort of person are stocks a good investment? Corporate bonds? Government bonds? Junk bonds?

9. Do you believe the Dow Jones Industrial Average is a good, fair, or poor indicator of the country's general economic health? Why?

VIDEO PROGRAM

This lesson's video program is Program 23 — Funding the Business with Stocks and Bonds. Remember, if you are watching this program on video-tape, take time to replay sections of the tape any time you need to review a concept.

VIDEO VIEWING QUESTIONS

Immediately after viewing the video program for Lesson 23, take time to respond to the following questions. Give your answers some careful thought; they may provide the basis for additional discussion or a longer written response.

1. Briefly, in your own words, define *stock*.

_____

_____

2. Define *bond*.

   _____

   _____

3. Name two similarities between stocks and bonds.

   a. _____

   b. _____

4. Name two important differences between stocks and bonds.

   a. _____

   b. _____

5. You have a friend who has $2,000 to invest toward his four-year-old child's college education. He is considering buying stocks with an 8.5 percent dividend, a 15-year corporate bond with a triple B rating and 10 percent interest rate, or a 15-year U.S. savings bond with a 6 percent interest rate. Name one potential advantage of each choice.

   The 8.5 percent stocks: _____

   The triple B 10 percent bond: _____

   The 6 percent savings bond: _____

6. Briefly, in your own words, explain why many investment counselors recommend diversifying when you invest in the stock market.

   _____

   _____

   _____

7. Name two factors that you think might affect the rating of a corporate bond given by an agency such as Standard and Poor's or Moody's.

   a. _____

   b. _____

8. Imagine that you recently bought 100 shares of stock in Interstate Chemical. You paid $80 per share. Today, you see in the paper that the value per share has dropped to $70, and the dividend is down. Which of the following are you *most likely* to do: buy more, sell what you have, or do nothing and see what happens? Explain your answer.

   _____

   _____

   _____

9. How do you respond to the following comment: "The stock market is strictly for big-time investors. There's no room there for the small investor who doesn't want to trade on a daily basis."

   _____

   _____

   _____

10. You have a friend who predicts that eventually stock market volatility will be a thing of the past. "Stocks will then gain or lose a few cents a day," he claims, "but rarely more than that. Brokers will be able to make long-term predictions with extraordinary accuracy." Briefly, state why you would agree or disagree with this statement.

_____

_____

_____

PART III: FOCUSING ON THE MATHEMATICS

READING ASSIGNMENT

After watching the video program, you should read one of the following Text Assignments, depending on the textbook you're using:

SOFTCOVER: Pages 423-438 from Chapter 10 of the Miller, Salzman, and Hoelzle softcover text, *Business Mathematics.*

HARDCOVER: Pages 634-653 from Chapter 18 of the Salzman, Miller, and Hoelzle hardcover text, *Mathematics for Business.*

As you read through the text, pay careful attention to the examples the book gives of the mathematics associated with the concepts you're learning about.

Then, after you've completed the text assignment, read through the Key Formulas below. This section provides a handy review of what you've learned. By the time you get to this point in the lesson, all of the formulas and calculations should be familiar to you. If they're not, go back and read the appropriate parts of the text and the Overview section of this lesson. You won't have much success completing the rest of your assignments if you are still confused about the information in the Key Formulas section.

KEY FORMULAS

The following key formulas are important to your understanding of this lesson. Be sure that you know each one and how to use it in solving problems related to stocks and bonds.

KEY FORMULA: Current yield = Annual dividend per share ÷ Current price per share

Formula used for: Determining the current yield on a share of stock when the dividend and price are known.

Example:

Suppose that the current price for a given stock is $40 per share. The current annual dividend is $4. In that case, the current yield is $4 ÷ $40 =.10, or 10 percent.

Remember that in this formula:

1. The annual dividend and current price per share are both available from a stock table.

2. The answer may be a whole number or decimal; if it's a decimal, round it off to the nearest tenth. To convert a decimal to a percent, move the decimal point two places to the right; thus, .10 = 10 percent.

3. To determine whether the current yield is good news or bad, you must compare it with yields for similar stocks, for the market as a whole, and for alternative investments.

KEY FORMULA: P/E ratio = Price per share ÷
                        Annual income per share

Formula used for: Determining the price-earnings ratio.

Example:

Suppose the current price per share for a given stock is $81. The annual net income per share is $9. The P/E ratio is therefore $81 ÷ $9 = 9.

Remember that in this formula:

1. The result will be a whole number or decimal, *not* a dollar figure.

2. The result is often rounded to the nearest whole number. Thus, a result of 9.89 would be rounded up to 10. A result of 6.23 would be rounded down to 6.

3. As with the current yield, the P/E ratio must be interpreted in comparison to ratios for similar firms and for the market as a whole.

4. A low P/E ratio may indicate that a stock, though valuable, has yet to be discovered by investors, or it may mean that investors foresee a dim future for the company. Similarly, a high P/E ratio may indicate that the stock is overpriced given its low earnings, or forecasters may be predicting a growth spurt in the near future. A P/E ratio by itself can't actually show whether a stock is a good or a bad investment.

KEY FORMULA: Earnings per share = (Net income − Dividends
                        on preferred stock) ÷ Number of shares of common stock outstanding

Formula used for: Assessing corporate earnings on the basis of stock.

Example:

The Grover Company has a net income of $50,000. It paid $20,000 in dividends on preferred stock and has 10,000 shares of common stock outstanding. Thus, the earnings per share are $50,000 − $20,000 ÷ 10,000 = $30,000 ÷ 10,000 = $3 per share.

Remember that in this formula:

1. The result is always a dollar figure and should not be rounded.

2. The denominator is the *number* of common shares outstanding, not the dollar value of those shares.

DON'T FORGET

1. A stock represents a portion of ownership in a company; a bond, on the other hand, is a debt, a promise to repay a certain amount on a certain date.

2. Preferred stocks have a par value, and the dividend is based on a percent of that par value. Common stocks may or may not have a par value. But it doesn't make any difference to the dividend because the dividend, if any is paid at all, is simply the total amount allocated for dividends on common stocks divided by the number of shares outstanding.

3. The commission on sale or purchase of stock is based on a percent of the total sale, but there may also be an additional fee for odd-lot (fewer than 100 shares) sales.

4. In the world of stocks and bonds, the fraction $\frac{1}{8}$ represents $\frac{1}{8}$ of a dollar, or 12.5¢, which may also be expressed as the decimal .125. Similarly, $\frac{3}{8}$ = .375, or 37.5¢, and $\frac{5}{8}$ = .625, or 62.5¢, and so on.

5. The par value of a bond and the *amount* of annual interest that will be paid on that bond are fixed at the time of the sale. These do not change. However, the *market value* of the bond, and hence the *interest rate* or *yield*, shift with market conditions. This means that subsequent buyers of the bond probably paid a different purchase price and are receiving a different return from the return of the person who bought the bond in the first place.

PART IV: SOLVING BUSINESS PROBLEMS

PROBLEM SETS

Work the following problems in your textbook. Your instructor will tell you which problems, if any, are to be turned in. Some of the problems have answers provided in the back of the book; refer to these answers to make sure you are working the problems correctly.

SOFTCOVER: If you are using the Miller, Salzman, and Hoelzle softcover text, *Business Mathematics*, do the following problem sets:

10.6: Problems #6-42 (even numbers only) on pages 429-432.

10.7: Problems #2-24 (even numbers only) on pages 437-438.

HARDCOVER: If you are using the Salzman, Miller, and Hoelzle hardcover text, *Mathematics for Business*, do the following problem sets:

18.1: Problems #2-20 (even numbers only) on pages 638-639.

18.2: Problems #2-50 (even numbers only), 51, and 52 on pages 646-648.

18.3: Problems #2-24 (even numbers only) on pages 652-653.

BUSINESS APPLICATIONS

Read each of the following scenarios and answer the questions about the decisions you would make in each situation. Give these questions some serious thought; they may be used as the basis for discussion or the development of a more complex essay. You should base your decisions on what you've learned from this lesson, applying both math skills and good business judgment to solve the problem at hand.

SCENARIO 1

The Wells Appliance Company is in its fifth year of operation. Profits were very high during the first two years, then fell somewhat in the third year, when the company had some problems with two of its leading products and bad attendant publicity. Wells is struggling hard to improve its image by providing better service and by putting more money into research and development to improve the performance of its products. The effort seems to be paying off; profits are climbing again, although at a slower rate than before.

Since the company began, Wells has issued 5,000 shares of preferred stock, about half of them being cumulative preferred stock. There are about 40,000 shares of common stock outstanding. The par value of preferred stock is $40, with a dividend of 10 percent. Last year, Wells realized a net income of $220,000 but paid no dividend to stockholders, electing instead to put the entire amount into research on new products. This year, the net income is up to $380,000, and the company's board of directors is trying to decide what to do with this money. So far, the most popular options seem to be to:

a. Put all the net income into dividends and issue an additional 40,000 shares of common stock to raise more capital, or

b. Use half the money to pay dividends to stockholders and put half into further research and product development, or

c. Use a portion of the money to pay dividends and put the remainder into the purchase of grade B bonds with a yield of 15 percent.

The callable grade B bonds are being offered by a 10-year-old electronics firm with a reputation for innovative ideas but a history of difficulty in securing funding to carry out those ideas. The electronics firm needs the additional funding to complete development of a revolutionary product that will be very profitable if they can bring it to market. Wells chairman of the board Fred Miller thinks there's a good chance these bonds would be called early—well before their 10-year maturity date—because the new product will produce such impressive revenue. If he's right, Wells will forgo some interest but will have earned a very nice return in the interim.

Several board members think this a reasonable plan, but director Chambers suggests that it would be better to simply buy the common stock of the electronics company. "After all," she says, "why settle for 15 percent?; If the product is successful, the share price will go through the roof and we could triple our investment."

What do you think? Does Wells have an obligation to pay dividends to its stockholders, or could it use more profitably net income in some other way? Do you think the bonds would be a good investment for Wells just now, or should the company concentrate on improving its products through more research?

☐ Which of the three options—a, b, or c—do you feel holds the most promise? Explain your reasons for choosing the option you selected, and point out at least one problem with each of the other two options.

☐ Suppose *you* were on Wells's board of directors and had a chance to present an option of your own. Based on what you know, how do *you* think the company should spend this year's $380,000 net income? Remember that your answer does *not* have to agree with a, b, or c. And you can divide the money, spending a portion of the $380,000 one way and another portion another way.

☐ Is Chambers's assessment correct that if the electronics company is worth investing in at all, Wells would be better off buying common stock instead of the bonds because it would be more profitable? Is there any difference in the risk of the two approaches?

☐ Notice that about half of the current preferred stockholders have cumulative preferred stock. How much influence should this have over the board's decision? Explain.

☐ Do you agree or disagree with the notion of issuing more stock? Explain. What are the financial implications of issuing more shares of stock at this point?

☐ Suppose that Wells decided to raise some money by selling bonds of its own. Do you think this would be a good option right now? Why or why not? If you were responsible for grading its bonds, what rating (triple A down to D) do you think Wells's bonds would *most likely* receive, based on the limited information you have on this company? What additional information would you want to have in assigning this rating?

☐ Suppose Wells decides to follow the advice you gave in the second question. What do you think its financial position is likely to be next year as a result of taking this advice? In presenting your answer, compare and contrast the results of *your* advice with the results of following one of the other options.

SCENARIO 2   Henry Scoggins, president of Swiftside Construction, is seeking a good long-term investment to strengthen his company's financial future. Henry's broker, Alice Risby, recommends Midas Manufacturing, one of "Wall Street's new high fliers." This company's stock values have soared over the past year, and for whom many observers predict a continued bright future for it. "This," Risby assures Scoggins, "is as close as Wall Street ever comes to a sure thing."

A glance at the stock table in the newspaper reveals this information about Midas Manufacturing:

57⅛ 22⅛ MidMan MDM 2.5 4.4 9 3700 56⅜ 54¼ 57⅛ +⅜

In addition, Alice informs Henry that Midas's net income was up 50 percent this year, to well over $40 million. The annual net income per share is $6.52, and the average P/E ratio for Wall Street stocks as a whole has been running between 13 and 14.

Swiftside's investment portfolio consists of about 70 percent stocks, with the remainder primarily in municipal bonds, an investment Henry Scoggins tends to favor. So far, the company has realized a good overall return, with the majority of stocks performing well and only a few "losers."

Scoggins is intrigued with the idea of Midas Manufacturing; it sure looks like a winner. On the other hand, there are several opportunities to invest in municipal bonds, with 15- to 20-year issues available at 7 percent. Risby isn't impressed with this idea. She tells Scoggins he's put enough into these "super safe" investments. "If you want to put more into bonds," she tells him, "why not consider corporate bonds? The yield is much better, and the maturity period is sometimes shorter." She suggests a double B bond with a return of 11 percent, or grade B bonds with a return of 12 percent.

Scoggins is tempted but very afraid of the risk. Risby insists that the higher return makes up for the risk; besides, the majority of these bonds get retired without a hitch. But Scoggins feels he needs to be more prudent in investing money for the company. "After all," he tells her, "it isn't all *my* money. It belongs to stockholders, too. I just don't feel I ought to take chances with it."

What do you think? Is Scoggins right to be so cautious about his investments, or is his prudent attitude likely to cost the stockholders better profits in the long run? What about Midas? Is it as good an investment as Risby is making it out to be? And shouldn't Scoggins trust his broker's advice rather than relying so much on his own intuition?

☐ Should Scoggins invest in Midas Manufacturing? Why or why not? Use the specific data in the scenario to support your answer.

☐ Suppose that Scoggins has $50,000 of his own to invest, over and above what he invests for the company. What portion of this amount, if any, should he put into Midas? What portion, if any, should he put into corporate bonds? Municipal bonds? Do you have other suggestions? Regardless of your answer, explain your response.

☐ Scoggins seems a bit reluctant to take his broker's advice without a great deal of thought and reflection. Is this a wise position for a business person to take, or is he being overly cautious? Explain your answer and state what, if anything, you would do differently.

☐ Risby seems to be of the opinion that corporate bonds, on the whole, make a better business investment than municipal bonds. Do you agree or disagree with her position on this?

☐ Suppose that Scoggins puts $100,000 of the company's money into Midas and that stock values go up at the same rate they went up this past year. If Scoggins *sells* the Midas stock a year from now, how much will he make in profit? How does this profit compare to what he would make by investing the whole $100,000 in either of the corporate bonds Risby mentioned? The municipal bonds?

Statistics for the Business World 24

The Government are very keen on amassing statistics. They collect them, add them, raise them to the nth power, take the cube root and prepare wonderful diagrams. But you must never forget that every one of these figures comes in the first instance from the village watchman, who just puts down what he damn pleases.

Sir Josiah Stamp

Numerical facts make up a big portion of our world, so much so that it's almost impossible to get through the day without being bombarded by facts and figures about the weather, Wall Street, the economy, sports, health and medicine, population growth, prices, and a dozen other topics. For the business person, making sense of business-related data is vital; the information can (and often should) influence decisions about an individual company's growth, marketing practices, advertising, pricing—virtually every decision that affects how that business is run.

Some people maintain that numbers are a language unto themselves, and perhaps there's something to that. But unlike words, numbers have very little meaning in and of themselves. They need to be interpreted. Often, that means comparing them to other numbers or putting them into some new kind of framework that reveals the patterns so often inherent in business data. *Statistics*—the branch of mathematics concerned with the collection, analysis, interpretation, and presentation of numbers— helps business people and others find the hidden patterns and organize numbers in ways that help make their meaning clear.

In this lesson, we'll take a look at statistics, focusing on just a few of the terms and concepts that this science of numbers uses to make predictions and draw conclusions based on sets of data. Numbers may well have a language of their own, but as we'll see in this lesson, decoding the message properly often takes some statistical know-how.

PART I: INTRODUCING THE MATERIAL

LEARNING OBJECTIVES

Upon completing your study of this lesson, you should be able to:

1. Locate examples of how statistics are routinely used to communicate business-related information.

2. Determine the mean, median, and mode of a list of numbers and accurately explain when each is the most appropriate measure of central tendency.

3. Calculate the weighted mean from a list of values and weightings.

4. Explain a normal distribution and give some examples of qualities that are normally distributed.

5. Use the concept of dispersion to demonstrate how two distributions can be widely different in spite of having similar means and medians.

6. Calculate the range of a given frequency distribution.

7. Explain the concept of percentiles and give examples of the use of percentiles in describing data points.

8. Use Consumer Price Index information in calculations of the cost of items at different times and in different parts of the country.

If you're using the hardcover textbook, *Mathematics for Business*, there are some additional objectives for this lesson. Upon completing your study of the lesson, you should also be able to:

9. Find the mean for a frequency distribution for grouped data.

10. Describe the usefulness of standard deviation and the relationship it has to normal distributions and the normal curve.

11. Calculate the standard deviation for a limited set of data.

12. Use information about the mean and standard deviation of a data set to estimate the approximate percentile rank of a given data point.

13. Explain what a price relative is and calculate any price relative, given the appropriate price information.

LESSON OVERVIEW

The science of statistics is concerned with collecting data, finding ways to display them, and making predictions or drawing conclusions based on those data. Because there's something about numbers that inspires belief and trust in many people, the way in which data are collected, presented, or displayed and the way in which they're interpreted are very important. Those who analyze the data must take care to draw their information from the right sources, to ensure that it's as accurate and complete as the time for collecting and processing will allow, and to present it in a way that clarifies meaning without distorting the truth. Those who use or rely on data, in turn, must take time to question the source, to find out how the data were collected, and to use their sound judgment in determining whether the conclusions or predictions are likely to be accurate, given how the information was put together.

Suppose a new data collection company, Numbers, Inc., decides to conduct a survey to determine the current rate of unemployment in a given city. At the end of two weeks' work, they report that unemployment in the city has fallen 6 percent. Should we believe them? Well, that depends.

Suppose it came out that Numbers, Inc., got its information through a sidewalk survey. They simply stopped people on the corner, at random, to ask whether they were currently employed or not. After they'd talked to 100 people, they tallied the results, compared them with previous unemployment figures, and drew their conclusions. Most of us wouldn't have much faith in the results of such an informal survey, and with good reason.

All Statistics Are Not Created Equal

First of all, the number of people questioned is quite small. Unless Numbers, Inc., is working in a *very* small town with a population of only a few hundred working people, its survey isn't likely to be *representative* of the population as a whole. Further, we might like to know when and where the street corner survey was conducted. If it was at 8:15 a.m. on a busy downtown corner right in the heart of the business district, then chances are that many of the people surveyed were on their way to work; most of the unemployed people were elsewhere, so they simply didn't get included in the survey.

Further, what assurance do we have that the responses were accurate? Perhaps the information that some people would provide to an official government census taker is a little different from what they'll provide to someone who's stopping people on the street corner; not everyone feels comfortable with that kind of public confrontation. And isn't it reasonable to think that people who were unemployed might not want to share that fact with a total stranger and therefore might be less inclined to participate in the survey in the first place? In short, there's plenty here to make us skeptical about these unemployment figures.

On the other hand, though we're often right to question the accuracy or the source of specific information, numbers tend to give us confidence; and when data are well used, that confidence is justified. For instance, suppose the sales manager in a large metropolitan real estate office tells her workers that from now on she expects them to make a minimum of 50 phone calls per day, since the most successful sales people are those who make at least that many calls. If she can then whip out a graph illustrating her point and showing that persons who make 50 or more calls a day are also likely to earn $50,000 or more per year, her argument will be pretty compelling. But if she's making this claim just based on general observation and her own instincts, her new rule will seem very arbitrary. Most people like to see some proof or evidence to back up what they regard as a hunch or statement of opinion. And when they ask for proof, what they often want are numbers.

Confidence in Numbers

But even so, it's important to keep in mind that some numbers have a way of looking more *precise* than they actually are. This doesn't mean they're inaccurate; it means they're accurate within a given *range* and so must be interpreted with care. Not all data are subject to a big margin of variability, but some are.

For instance, when an inventory clerk says that the store sold 37 Model R171 dishwashers last month, he doesn't mean "37 more or less"; he means 37 right on the button. This makes sense, because dishwashers come in whole units; you can't sell half a dishwasher. But when a weather forecaster tells his audience that the current temperature is 90°F, he really means "roughly 90°F, give or take half a degree." Temperatures of 89.8°F and 90.3°F would still be reported as 90°F. What the forecaster is really saying is that the temperature is really 90°F *plus or minus* half a degree.

And when the nightly newscaster says that "42 percent of registered voters support the President's new policy," there is some imprecision associated with that figure, perhaps plus or minus 2 or 3 percent. That's because there is a limit to how many people can be asked the question. Obviously, if it were somehow possible to ask every registered voter his or her opinion about the new policy, the answer could be exact. But since it is not usually possible to question *every* member of the group under consideration (the *population*, statisticians call it), data gatherers must base their information on a *sample*—a smaller and, one hopes, representative group.

Great care is taken, usually, in selecting such a sample to make sure that they're indeed representative of the population as a whole. But since the sample isn't as large as the population, there's the chance of some error. As you might imagine, the size of this *margin of error* depends a lot on the relative size of the population and the sample. Presenting national unemployment rates deduced from a sample of 100 people would have a large margin of error, while asking a *random sample* of half the students at a large college what they thought of the parking situation would certainly be almost as good as asking every student. The goal of a statistician is to choose a sample size that provides the amount of precision necessary. If the information has to be very precise (have a small margin of error, that is) the sample will have to be much bigger than if the goal is "a rough idea."

In any event, the most important concept here is to realize that many of the numbers you encounter are not precise. Relatively few basketball players are exactly 6'9" tall, and it's unlikely that it's rained exactly half an inch. A 12-inch wide shelf isn't exactly a foot wide; it's just that given how closely we choose to measure it, we say it's 12 inches. And, most importantly, if a newscaster says that an election poll shows someone is "favored by a margin of 53 to 47 percent in a poll with a margin of error of 4 percent," realize that you shouldn't view this saying that "the favorite" will get 6 percent more of the vote. While this is the most likely of all of the results possible, what the poll really said is that the results would fall somewhere in the range of 57 to 43 percent (53+4 to 47−4) at one end to 49 to 51 percent (53−4 to 47+4) at the other, meaning that the apparent favorite might not even win.

Unfortunately, reporters and their audiences both tend to prefer the nutshell version of the statistical news, and there are relatively few people who could accurately interpret the results given in most television and newspaper news stories. Whether that's a serious problem or not can be debated, but you'd certainly agree that a business manager who doesn't understand precision and margin of error could make some pretty bad decisions based on statistical data. (And notice that while the manager might well claim the data were inaccurate, it was in fact the manager's ability to use the data that was a problem.)

So far, we've talked about statistics only in broad, general terms. Let's look now at some of the specific ways business people and others group or manipulate numbers to help make sense of them.

Imagine that an exercise enthusiast, Helen Roberts, runs a diet center in which she promotes constant, vigorous exercise as the key to weight loss. To keep track of how her clients are doing, Helen decides to make a chart based on how many miles each client walks each day. She has 20 clients, each of whom walks somewhere between one and 10 miles. So Helen's data set looks like this:

Miles walked daily:

| 1 | 3 | 10 | 2 | 4 | 6 | 9 | 3 | 2 | 10 |
| 9 | 8 | 7 | 7 | 3 | 5 | 4 | 8 | 8 | 1 |

In this form, however, Helen's diet center data are a little difficult to digest (no pun intended). Helen still doesn't have much sense of how many people are walking various distances. To get a clearer picture, she makes a *frequency distribution table*, based on the number of miles walked and the number of clients who walk each distance. Here are the results:

Miles Walked	Number of Clients
1	2
2	2
3	3
4	2
5	1
6	1
7	2
8	3
9	2
10	2

This helps a little. Now Helen can see that two of her clients are walking only a mile a day, while two walk 10 miles. But she thinks it would be more helpful yet if she combined some of her data to form fewer categories. She decides to form three groups: Group A, three miles or less; Group B, four to six miles; and Group C, seven miles or more. Now her frequency table looks like this:

	Miles Walked	Number of Clients
A:	3 or less	7
B:	4-6	4
C:	7 or more	9

Grouped data are obviously easier to display, and often easier to graph too. They do lose a little precision, though. Sometimes that's important, sometimes not. For instance, Helen can no longer tell how many people in her group walk four miles as opposed to five or six, but for her immediate purpose, that kind of detail is not particularly important.

Notice how much easier it is to draw some conclusions based on this re-organized data. For instance, it's now easy to see that nine of Helen's clients (almost half the group) are doing a good bit of walking. If these are also the people who are losing the most weight, Helen might want to expand her study to a larger, better controlled sample in hopes of showing that there's a relationship between distance walked and weight loss. But if it's those four in the middle group who are losing the most weight, Helen will need to do some more investigating to see what other factors are influencing their weight loss.

But suppose that the avid walkers *are* the ones losing the weight. Can't Helen feel comfortable in making the connection between distance walked and weight loss? Absolutely not. For one thing, her small sample certainly isn't representative of all the people who walk and lose weight. For another, it's a small sample, so that even if it were somehow representative, there'd be a huge margin of error in the results.

But the third problem is the most critical; Helen has no *control group* for her sample. There's no way she can say that the people who lost the most weight were the same as the others except that they walked more. In fact, the obvious question is whether the people who lost the weight might not have simply eaten less; certainly, there's nothing in Helen's data to prove they didn't. They might all have taken up soccer in their spare time, or they might all have come down with the flu. Perhaps surprisingly, Helen's modest set of data couldn't even disprove a statement that people who walk more lose *less* weight. Admittedly, that doesn't seem right, but the point is that nothing Helen has done is sufficient to disprove this hypothesis.

What can Helen do to prove the connection between walking and weight loss? She would need to get a large sample of people—thousands—from all over the country (or the world, if she wanted to have her results apply worldwide). The people would have to be of all ages, live in all different types of places, have all different kinds of jobs; they would, in other words, have to be representative of the population Helen wants to apply her results to. Then they would have to be divided randomly into at least two groups. One group—the control group—would be told not to walk; the other would have to walk a lot.

Throughout the study, Helen would have to monitor that the "walkers" were walking and the "nonwalkers" weren't. She'd also have to verify that the groups remained the same in all other aspects except how much they walked. For example, perhaps the walkers were spending so much time walking that they didn't have time to do their work, which made them worry, which made them lose their appetite, which made them eat less, which made them lose weight. Helen would have to be confident that this wasn't the reason for any differences she found. And the study would have to continue for quite some time to ensure that the weight loss was permanent. Only then could Helen analyze the data and perhaps be able to say with some confidence that those who walk more lose more weight.

Of course, the problem with all this is that to do the job right would take more time and much more money than Helen wants to devote to the job. How much easier it is just to say "Well, walking burns calories and burning off calories causes weight loss, so walking is good for people trying to lose weight." Under this approach, Helen can assign people to walk with some certainty that it will do some good.

Unfortunately, Helen probably doesn't know enough statistics to keep her from saying "In a study I did, walking more caused people to lose more weight." But that conclusion is wrong, and Helen is wrong to say it. Not "stretching the truth" and not "a little inaccurate," but just plain wrong. When statistics are criticized as being used to mislead people, the finger is pointed at the wrong place. The statistics themselves aren't misleading, any more than the statement "The capital of Texas is Austin" is misleading. It's the misinterpretation of the statistics that's the problem. Just as you'd think Helen foolish if she said Austin is the biggest city in Texas just because it's the capital, you should think her foolish to conclude that "people who walk more lose more weight" based on the information she gathered.

The dangers of using statistics inappropriately are very real; many a costly mistake in marketing or production has come about because someone misinterpreted a set of numerical data. Fortunately, there are several statistical concepts that are easy to understand and can be used effectively by anyone exercising just a little bit of care.

The Mean — The All-American Average

Quote statistics on height, weight, test scores, or any of a hundred other factors, and the first thing many people want to know is where they fit in. One way of measuring this is through the *average* for any given set of data. For instance, suppose that a 38-year-old woman weighs 125 pounds. She may think that's too much until she finds out that the *average* for women her age and height is 140. That news could make her feel thin enough to celebrate with a hot fudge sundae. But what does that word *average* mean exactly?

In statistics, it can mean any of several things. Take our 125-pound woman. When her physician tells her that 140 pounds is average for her height, he might mean that if you added up the weights of all women in the same age and height and divided that total by the number of women in the group, 140 would be the result. Or he might mean that about half the women of her age and height weigh less than 140 and about half weigh more. Or he might mean that 140 is the most common weight among women in this group. These three *measures of central tendency* — the *mean*, *median*, and *mode*, respectively — are all kinds of *averages*. Though the meaning of the term is a little different in each case, they're all ways of describing the *middle* of the data set. Each one represents a single number that can be used to describe a larger set of numbers in some meaningful way.

These different averages can all be useful, and most statisticians would argue that it is helpful to have all three in interpreting the true central tendency of any data set. Still, what most people refer to when they say *average* is the mean, not the mode or the median.

The mean is simple enough to compute. Just total the numbers in the data set and divide by the number of *numbers* in the set. For instance, suppose these are the assessed values (in thousands) of the 10 homes in the 1600 block of Dupont Avenue:

$125 $140 $152 $155 $170 $171 $172 $179 $181 $185

If we add these values together, the total is $1,630,000. To find the mean, we divide this total by the number of houses: $1,630,000 ÷ 10 = $163,000. We can, therefore, say that the mean assessed value of the homes in the 1600 block of Dupont Avenue is $163,000.

The Weighted Mean

In the example, every home on Dupont Avenue had a different assessed value. But often that isn't the way of things. A given number may occur more than once in a data set, and when this happens it's convenient, although not necessary, to compute a *weighted mean* that takes this recurrence into account.

For instance, suppose that Henry Beasley sells handcrafted diamond rings. To keep things simple for Henry (and for us) we'll imagine that there are only four possible prices that he sells his rings for. Here's a frequency distribution listing the number of rings Henry sold last year at each price:

Number Sold	Price
20	$ 4,000
5	$10,000
5	$15,000
2	$20,000

So what is the *average* price of a ring sold at Henry's? He can't just add up the four selling prices and divide by four, since different numbers of rings were sold at each price. Henry could, of course, add up all 32 selling prices and then divide by 32. But there is a considerably easier way to figure this *weighted mean*. Henry has only to multiply each number (in this case the selling price) by the number of times it occurs, like this:

$$20 \times \$ 4,000 = \$80,000$$
$$5 \times \$10,000 = \$50,000$$
$$5 \times \$15,000 = \$75,000$$
$$2 \times \$20,000 = \$40,000$$

Then Henry adds the results of the multiplications for a total of $245,000 in all. He then divides this figure by the total number of rings (20 + 5 + 5 + 2 = 32) to get the weighted mean of $245,000 ÷ 32 = $7,656.25. This is considerably less than the $12,250 that he would have gotten had he incorrectly found the average of the four selling prices. (Actually, one *could* argue that the "average selling price" really is $12,250, the average of the selling prices. But $12,250 is definitely not the average sale, which is a much more useful number — and undoubtedly what Henry really wanted to know.)

Unfortunately, even this weighted mean is still a bit misleading. A buyer talking with Henry for the first time might be surprised to discover that in a business where the "average ring sells for $7,656" there are no rings at all at that price. Remember, though, that the purpose of an average is to describe something about the data's tendency to cluster around a central point. Averages don't even try to tell anything about the individual pieces of data.

GPA:
Student Favorite
Weighted Mean

One of the most common applications of the weighted mean computation is the grade point average (GPA). As you are likely aware, the grade point averages of most high school and college students are typically reported numerically. But how it is possible to average As, Bs, and Cs and then come up with a numerical result that reflects the importance of each course?

The trick is to assign a number value to each letter grade, then multiply this value by the number of credit hours allotted to the course. For instance, let's say that college freshman Alvin Karp takes a modest three courses. Here's his grade report for the term:

Course	Credit Hours	Grade
Physics	5	A
Calculus	5	A
Drama	2	F

To determine Alvin's GPA, we must first know that As are assigned a value of 4 points, B = 3, C = 2, D = 1 and F = 0. We multiply these values by the "frequency" (in this case, credit hours for each course), then divide by the total number of credit hours Alvin is carrying. Thus, physics = 5 × 4 = 20; calculus = 5 × 4 = 20; and drama = 2 × 0 = 0. The total is 20 + 20 + 0 = 40. And the GPA is 40 ÷ 12 = about 3.33. Since 3 = B, Alvin has a little better than a B average, despite the fact that he didn't receive a single B.

Now imagine that Alvin has a friend, Rose, who takes the same classes. Rose receives As in drama and calculus but fails physics. That's two As and an F, just like Alvin. Unfortunately for Rose, an A in drama isn't as valuable to a grade point average as one in physics. A little arithmetic shows us that Rose's GPA is only 2.33, a full point lower than Alvin's.

The *median* is the midpoint in a set of numbers. It's the point at which we can say, "Half the numbers in the data set lie above this point; half lie below." To help visualize this, consider this very simple data set: 1, 2, 3, 4, 5. The middle number here is 3; it's the *median*, or the number that falls halfway between 1 and 5. It also happens to be the *mean*: 1 + 2 + 3 + 4 + 5 = 15, and 15 ÷ 5 = 3. Usually, however, it doesn't work out this way. Consider this data set, for instance: 1, 2, 3, 99, 100. Here, the median is again *3*. But the mean is (1 + 2 + 3 + 99 + 100) ÷ 5 = 41.

The concept of *median* as the midpoint can be very useful, especially if it's presented in combination with other data that help the user visualize the whole data set. For instance, suppose that the five motels in Ocean View City charge the following rates for a one-night stay:

$$\$40 \quad \$40 \quad \$50 \quad \$70 \quad \$160$$

What's the *average* cost of overnight lodging in Ocean View City? Well, that depends on how you look at it. The *mean* is ($40 + $40 + $50 + $70 + $160) ÷ 5 = $72. But that's surely a misleading figure, given that rates at all but one motel are lower than $72. The median figure, however, is $50; that's the number in the middle of the data set. And in this case, it's perhaps a better measure of how prices run at Ocean View City.

Notice that the prices for motels at Ocean View City are arranged from lowest (far left) to highest (far right). This is critical to finding a median, since if the numbers were in random order (say $40, $50, $160, $40, $70) picking the number in the middle wouldn't work. When you arrange the numbers in order so you can find the median, you're creating an *ordered array*, a somewhat fancier name for a list of numbers written in order (ascending or descending; it doesn't matter). Of course, the data sets in the preceding examples are very small, so picking out the middle number is no real challenge; it's just a matter of taking a look. But suppose the data set is much bigger: dozens of numbers, hundreds, or even thousands.

Median:
The Number
in the Middle

What then? String them all out and try to spot the middle? That wouldn't be very practical, or probably very accurate.

Fortunately, there's a mathematical solution. Divide the *number of numbers* by 2. If the result is a decimal fraction (say, 21.5), then the next whole number up (e.g., the twenty-second number) gives the location of the median. If the result is a whole number (like 26), then the median is halfway between the number in that position and the number in the next position; that is, it's the mean of the twenty-sixth and twenty-seventh numbers. Notice that this technique provides only the *position* of the median; it does *not* tell you anything about the value of the median.

For instance, let's say that there are 153 numbers in a data set. Where is the median? To find out, we divide by 2, and the result is a fraction: $153 \div 2 = 76.5$. Thus, the median is the number in the seventy-seventh position of the ordered array. Suppose, though, that there are only 152 numbers. Then the *median* is the *mean* of the numbers in the seventy-sixth and seventy-seventh positions. We don't know what those numbers are without looking at the data set, but let's suppose that the seventy-sixth number is 204 and the seventy-seventh number is 230. In that case, the median would be $204 + 230 = 434 \div 2 = 217$.

Mode: The Trendy Number

The word *mode* is sometimes used in everyday conversation as a synonym for *vogue*, *trend*, *style*, or *current fashion*. Those connotations are somewhat useful in helping remember the meaning of *mode* in the mathematical sense, too, since the *mode* is the most commonly recurring number in a data set. Remember the motels at Ocean View City? Two charged $40 for their overnight accommodations (and no other room price occurred more than once), so $40 is the *mode* in that data set.

Consider this data set: 17, 17, 17, 12, 13, 14, 18, 18, 18. Here two numbers (17 and 18) each occur three times. This set is said to be *bimodal*, meaning that it has two modes. While a data set can have only one mean and one median, it can have many modes.

Now consider this set: 4, 6, 73, 12, 42, 97. Here no number occurs more than once. This data set has no mode.

Dispersion: The Spread of Data

Measures of central tendency, as their label suggests, all focus on the center of the data set. The assumption is that the number that best describes that data set will be somewhere in the middle; the meaning of *middle* depends on which measure of central tendency you choose. What about the end points, though—the extremes that define the range of the data? Aren't they important too? Yes, indeed.

Imagine, for instance, that you hear that the mean score on a recent math test was 73. That figure becomes much more interesting, and much more meaningful, if you also find out that the *range* of the scores was from 13 to 104. Now think how different your impression might be if you learned that the scores ranged from 71 to 75. Those very different ranges give us an entirely different picture of the data and may tell us some useful things about the students who took the test, or about the test itself.

A narrow range, for instance, might mean that students in the group were very similar in ability, or it could be that while some items on the test were simple for nearly everyone, others were difficult for nearly everyone, so scores didn't really discriminate among students. Similarly, a broad range might indicate a wide range of abilities among students or a test that discriminated very well among students who really knew the material and those who did not. None of these conclusions is supportable based only on the range, but notice that these possibilities wouldn't have even come to mind if you had just looked at the averages.

Consider, for instance, the average cost of homes in two different areas. In Area A, homes range in price from $50,000 to $150,000, with many homes in the $100,000 bracket. Here the median is around $100,000 and the mean is also around $100,000. Now compare Area B. Here the homes range in price from $98,000 to $102,000. Again, the median and mean are around $100,000, but the range is very different. If we visited Area A, we might expect to see quite a variety of home styles, but we'd expect much less variety in Area B. Clearly, averages alone cannot tell the whole story.

The *standard deviation* is a way to measure the distances (the deviations) from the mean of each data point in a given set of data. Numbers that cluster together around the mean have small standard deviation, while those that are a long way from the mean have bigger standard deviations.

The Standard Deviation

The hardest thing about computing the standard deviation for any data set is remembering all the steps. None of them are difficult, but they must all be done, and they must be done in order. Let's begin with a small data set (10, 20, 25, 40, 100) and compute the standard deviation step by step.

Step 1: Find the mean for the set. The mean for this data set is 10 + 20 + 25 + 40 + 100 ÷ 5 = 195 ÷ 5 = 39. This number provides the base for determining individual deviations from the mean in Step 2.

Step 2: Find deviations from the mean for each number in the set. To find the deviation for any number, subtract the value of the mean from the value of the number. Thus, the deviation for the first number in our set is 10 − 39, or −29. Keep in mind that when you subtract a larger number from a smaller one, the result is always a negative number, indicated with a minus sign. Now, let's put the values into a table:

Data value:	10	20	25	40	100
Deviation:	−29	−19	−14	1	61

Step 3: Find the square of each deviation from the mean. A negative number *squared* always produces a positive number. Thus, −2 squared (or -2^2) is −2 × −2 = 4. This means that *every* square will be a positive number, regardless of whether the deviation is positive or negative. If we add these results to the table, it will look like this:

Data value:	10	20	25	40	100
Deviation:	−29	−19	−14	1	61
Square of Deviation:	841	361	196	1	13,721

Step 4: Find the mean of the sum of the squares of all individual deviations. First, total the squares: 841 + 361 + 196 + 1 + 3,721 = 5,120. The *mean* of this total is 5,120 ÷ 5 (the number of numbers in the data set) = 1,024.

Step 5: Find the square root of this mean. The mean of the sum of the squares for all deviations is called the *variance*. And the square root of the variance is the standard deviation. The square root is simple to compute with a calculator, so if you have one handy, you can easily figure out that the standard deviation of this data set is 32 (32 × 32 = 1,024).

Using Standard Deviations

If you're like most people, the fact that a data set has a standard deviation of 32 is not too meaningful. Why do we care? Actually, as we'll see, there's quite a bit a standard deviation can show you under certain circumstances. But for the moment, it's enough to realize that a data set with a mean of 39 and a standard deviation of 32 isn't clustered very tightly around that mean. There is, in other words, a considerable amount of *dispersion*.

Can we use this standard deviation to make predictions about where future data will fall? No, not really. You see, this is a very small data set. We kept it small deliberately so that the illustration of how to compute standard deviation would be fairly simple; if we had 100 numbers in the set, the illustration would be very long and complex, even though all the steps would be just the same. But this mini-data set with only five figures may not be at all typical of how the data would look if we collected 100 times this much information.

For example, let's say these are test scores on a 150-item test. Right now, the score of 100 is well beyond one standard deviation. In fact, it's almost beyond two standard deviations, since 39 (the mean) plus 64 (two standard deviations of 32) is 103. But this isn't likely to hold true anymore if we collect dozens, or hundreds, of test scores. In our limited sample, the median score is 25, and the score of 100 looks unusually high. But that may just be a fluke; certainly most people get scores higher than 10 or 20 on tests with 150 items. The point is that when you start with very few data points, the statistics are likely to change dramatically with just a couple of additional pieces of data.

But suppose we test 5,000 people. We might well find that the mean is up to 101, and perhaps scores of 110 or 120 wouldn't be at all unusual. The scores of 10, 20, and 25 are likely to be exceptionally low when we look at a larger sample, with perhaps two-thirds of people scoring in, say, the 85 to 115 range. The standard deviation, which was 32 in our small sample, might drop to 15 or less.

Incidentally, you could justifiably be worried about how many days it might take to calculate the standard deviation of something with 5,000 data points using the five-step process described earlier. Fortunately, all the tedious arithmetic is no problem for even the smallest computer or even for some advanced calculators. Generally, finding the mean and standard deviation is just a matter of pressing the right button after entering all of the data points, so it's not nearly the problem our explanation might lead you to believe.

Also, we should mention that there is a formula that sums up the process for finding standard deviations. Unfortunately, it uses some symbols that make it look a little forbidding, so it's sometimes easier to go through the steps first (as we just did). The formula looks like this:

$$s = \sqrt{\frac{\Sigma d^2}{n}}$$

In this formula, *s* is the standard deviation, Σ is the Greek letter sigma, which in mathematics stands for *the sum of*, *d* is the deviation from the mean of each individual number in the data set, the small number *2* at the upper right of the *d* is an indication that this value is to be *squared* (multiplied times itself), and the *n* stands for the *number of numbers* in the data set. If you check, you'll see that the formula simply tells you in symbols to do the same math as the process we described earlier in words.

The concept of standard deviation is particularly useful in working with something called the *normal curve*, a graphic representation of a large data set that looks a little like a hill with even sloping sides left and right. The right and left slopes are mirror images of each other, and the peak of the hill itself comes right in the middle. This is important. In a so-called *skewed* data set, the hill might emerge a little to the left or to the right of the midpoint, giving the curve a pronounced slant to one side.

We talk about a normal curve, but what we're really discussing are data sets that when plotted produce such a curve. Normal curves themselves wouldn't be important except that many sets of data in the real world approximate a *normal distribution*, and when they're graphed, the results do create a normal curve.

Which still isn't all that exciting, but thanks to the work of some clever mathematicians, we know there's more to a normal distribution than meets the eye. For one thing, the mean, median, and mode of a normally distributed data set are identical. And, if the distribution is normal, just over two-thirds of the data values (about 68 percent, actually) will fall within one standard deviation of the mean. What's more, about 95 percent will fall within two standard deviations of the mean, and about 99 percent will fall within three standard deviations of the mean. Here's an illustration of how this might look:

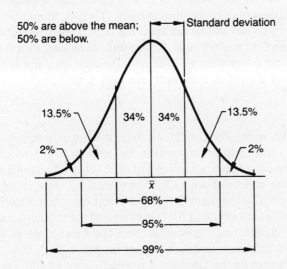

The interesting thing is that these percentages hold true for every normally distributed data set. Don't get the idea, though, that there's only one shape of normal curve; that's not correct. Normally distributed data sets can have big ranges (which makes the normal curve wide) or small ranges. They can have values widely distributed throughout the range (which makes the middle of the curve more of a hump than a peak) or the vast majority of the data can be clustered near the center. But all of these variations are reflected in the value of the standard deviation, so the percent of the data points falling within a certain number of standard deviations from the mean remains the same for any normally distributed data set.

As we just pointed out, when data are normally distributed, about two-thirds (actually, closer to 68 percent) of the data points in that set will fall within one standard deviation of the mean (one-third above, one-third

What Data
are Normally
Distributed?

below), and about 95 percent will fall within two standard deviations of the mean. So can we use this information to estimate performance on our sample 150-item test?

Maybe, maybe not. There are some things we have to know first. Remember our five-person test score data set, the one we used in computing standard deviation? That set would not create a normal curve because, among other things, it isn't big enough. Mathematically, a perfect normal curve represents an infinite number of data values. While it isn't necessary (or possible) to have an infinite number of data values to plot, it is necessary to have a sample large enough to approximate an infinite data set.

In other words, if we give the same test to 5,000 people, we have a much better chance of having a normal distribution. Certain test scores, by the way, often *do* end up more or less normally distributed, with most scores falling in the middle of the range and a few people scoring very high or very low. As you'd suspect, however, this will be true only when the test does a good job of discriminating between those students who know the material on which the test is based and those who do not. If we made the test ridiculously simple so that virtually every respondent would get most every question right, or so difficult that very few people could answer the questions, the chances of a normal distribution would be almost nil.

Other sorts of data are normally distributed. Take the height of the average adult male in the United States, for instance, which is about 5'10", or 70 inches. Most adult males, then, will tend to be close to this height. If the standard deviation (measured in inches) is two, then more than two-thirds of all adult men will be between 5'8" and 6' tall. About 95 percent will be between 5'6" and 6'2" tall. There will, of course, be a few who are 5' or shorter and a few who are 6'8" or taller, but they are five standard deviations from the mean and represent only a tiny fraction of the total population.

More About Normal Curves   Recall that with normally distributed data, the mean, median, and mode all fall at the same data point, right in the middle. As a result, the two halves of the normal curve are mirrors of each other. And the dividing line falls right in the middle of where the curve peaks. Thus, in our example with heights, 5'10" is the mean height for adult men, but also the median (with half of all men taller and half shorter) and the mode (the most common height). And for any deviation from the mean, just as many data points fall that far above the mean as that far below it.

Some data sets do *not* produce a normal curve at all. For instance, suppose we plotted the costs of new houses in the current year. Would they form a normal curve? Well, they might, but it's very unlikely. One reason for this is that the mean cost of a new house is not likely to come right in the middle of the range of costs. It's likely to be toward the low end of the range. That's because, typically, there are more houses for sale at or below the mean price than there are at or above the mean price.

This stands to reason if you think about it, since the cost of one extravagant new home balances out the cost of several very modest homes. That's precisely why the mean winds up a little above the midpoint of the range as a whole. Let's say that the mean price for new houses turns out to be $130,000. Maybe the median price is only $115,000, with half of the houses costing more than $115,000 and half less. Perhaps the single most common price (the mode) is only $99,000. And given that the mean, median, and mode aren't the same, this data set isn't normally distributed, which means that all the guidelines about how much of the data is within a certain number of standard deviations won't work.

Remember our example about the test scores? It ties in with the idea that some instructors "grade on a curve." What's meant by this is that the instructors treat the assignment of grades as if the grades should be normally distributed. The mean, median, and modal grade is a C, with equal numbers of Bs and Ds and equal numbers of As and Fs. Notice that for every above-average grade, there has to be a below-average grade to balance it, regardless of whether the scores themselves were high or low. (Grading on a curve is apparently a bit out of fashion, however, since the median grade point average is now above 3 in many colleges and school districts.)

Finally, students may sometimes hear themselves referred to as being at a certain *percentile*; for example, "Mary scored at the 67th percentile in comprehension." A percentile is simply a way of measuring position on the curve. The 10th percentile, for instance, is the point at which 10 percent of all data in the set have values lower than the value in question, while 90 percent have values that are higher. Mary, who's at the 67th percentile on a test, has outperformed 67 percent of those students tested, which means that 33 percent received the same or higher scores. (Percentiles are often used with normal distributions, but notice that the concept is meaningful even for data that aren't normally distributed.)

Standard deviations and normal curves are very useful for looking at data that were all collected at about the same time. Sometimes, though, it's handy to look at changes in statistics from one period of time to another.

Statistics and (Mostly) Rising Prices

Take prices. As any consumer can testify, most prices *tend* to go up. Pocket calculators and computers don't cost as much as they used to, but they're an exception to the rule of inflation. Nearly everything else costs more. The question is, how much more? It's simple, statistically, to answer this question, using something called the *price index*.

Let's say that Harry Dalton lives in Waterville, where he's a teacher. His salary has gone from $25,000 ten years ago to $32,000 today. Harry thinks this is a pretty modest increase compared to increases in the cost of living, but right now he's basing this judgment on his own general impression of how tough it is to pay the bills. Would some math computation bear out Harry's impression? Let's try to decide using just one indicator, food costs. Suppose that a cart full of groceries that cost $50 at the Waterville Food Mart 10 years ago costs $85 for the same products today.

First, let's see how much Harry's income has gone up. The formula for a *price relative* is 100 times the price or amount for the current year divided by the price or amount in the base year. The *base year* is whatever the year is that we're comparing the current situation to, so in this case, it's 10 years ago. The price relative for Harry's income is 100 times the result of dividing his current salary by the base year salary. Thus, the price relative is $100 \times (\$32,000 \div \$24,000) = 100 \times 1.33 = 133$ percent. The result is always a percent, in this case a percent of increase. This is another way of saying that Harry's income is 133 percent of what it was 10 years ago, or that it's gone up 33 percent.

Now, how about those grocery prices? In this case, the base is again the 10-year-old figure: $50. Thus, the price index is $100 \times (\$85 \div \$50) = 100 \times 1.7 = 170$ percent. In other words, groceries in Waterville cost 170 percent of what they cost 10 years ago. If the increase in groceries is typical of other costs in Waterville, then our friend Harry is quite right in thinking that his paycheck hasn't kept pace with inflation. Obviously, though, there's no reason to expect that price increases for rent, car insurance, long-distance telephone calls, and other items just happened to match the increase in groceries. Some broader measure is required.

The Big Picture

The Bureau of Labor Statistics publishes a monthly *Consumer Price Index*, which indicates changes (sometimes they *do* go down) in prices for the nation as a whole and for various major cities across the country. Here is one part of such a report:

	Chicago	Detroit	Los Angeles-Long Beach	New York New Jersey	Philadelphia
All items	187.3	190.2	189.6	193.5	190.8

The figures in this table are expressed as a percentage of a 1967 base of 100. In other words, what you could have bought for $100 in Chicago in 1967 would cost $187.30 at the time of this report. Notice that among those cities listed, prices have risen more in New York than anywhere else. But that does *not* mean that prices are necessarily higher in New York than in the other cities listed. They *could* have been much higher in Chicago to begin with, so even though they've increased more in New York, they may still be higher in Chicago. In other words, this table does not provide information on dollar amounts, but only on the extent of the changes.

Suppose that an automobile cost $10,000 in Los Angeles in 1967. How much would it cost at the time of this report? Well, we should point out that the listings for "all items" that appear in this report represent an average; they do not reflect increases in specific items like automobiles. But for the sake of our illustration, let's suppose that this average increase is the same as the increase for automobiles: 189.6. This number is a percentage, and we'll use it that way in answering our question. The car cost $10,000 in 1967, so it costs $10,000 × 189.6% = 10,000 × 1.896 = $18,960. (Remember, to change a percent to a decimal, move the decimal point two places to the left.)

Notice that in this example, as in the others we've presented, the numbers by themselves mean little. But we can use the tools of statistics to look at those numbers in a new way and to give them a meaning that makes them more useful in analyzing today's world or predicting tomorrow's.

SOME WORDS OF ADVICE

Statistical data are all around us. We're barraged with statistics daily, many of them aimed at persuading us to adopt some new point of view, to change our behavior, or to buy something. But some data are more useful than others. When we hear that the current temperature at the airport is 86°F, we have considerable confidence that this information is right because we know something about how it's gathered, and there's little or no guesswork involved. Other data, however, deserve to be questioned. If we hear, for instance, that "Crime is down 40 percent," it's worthwhile to ask:

☐ What sort of crime? Is this an average of *all* crimes or just certain crimes? Does a shoplifting incident have the same impact as a murder?

□ How were the data to back this claim gathered? Where does this information come from?

□ How recent is this information? When were the data assembled?

□ Precisely what previous information is this 40 percent decrease based on? Were the former figures obtained in the same way?

□ Is there evidence that nothing that would affect this figure changed except the number of crimes? (In practice, for example, the figures might be based on the number of *reported* crimes. But what if people simply don't think it's worth their time to report minor crimes any more? This might have produced a 40 percent drop without any real drop — and maybe even an increase — in the actual number of crimes.)

Until these and related questions are answered satisfactorily, there's good reason to be a little skeptical about such information.

Of course, most of us place a certain amount of trust in reports given in the press or on the nightly news. We feel confident that persons who report on crime rates or unemployment rates do not (as in our early example) simply stand on the street corner for half an hour prior to the broadcast interviewing passersby at random, then rush in to face the camera, equipped with these highly questionable data. Indeed, most of them rely upon well-trained, qualified data analysts whose job it is to gather and report statistics accurately.

Nevertheless, there's a limit to how accurate any data can be, given the practical constraints on sample size and representativeness, so even when statistics are not reported as having a specified margin of error, we'd be wise to think of them this way. Statistics have a way of looking more precise than they have a right to look, given the difficulties inherent in gathering them.

If you find yourself in the position of gathering or reporting statistical information, you may wish to keep this question of overstated precision in mind. Can you support your interpretation of the data? If your sample is small, if it's not representative, or if you should have had a control group and you didn't, the answer is probably no. Remember, it's not the statistics that lead people astray; short of miscalculations or just plain fudging of the data, the statistics are what they are. It's the misinterpretation and overinterpretation of the statistics that cause the trouble.

Finally, expand your own knowledge of basic statistics to help you make good use of data in your business life. Statistics provide strategies for organizing data effectively and for analyzing it to mark changes or predict trends. Anyone can gather sets of numbers. But collections of numbers are rarely useful unless we can see the patterns that tell us what the numbers mean. Statistics offer an important tool for decoding numbers: for making the patterns visible and the implications clear.

KEY TERMS

Before you read through the text assignment and watch the video program, take a minute to look at the key terms associated with this lesson. When you encounter them in the text and video program, pay careful attention to their meaning.

Average: Usually used to refer to the *mean*; in the broader sense, though, an *average* may be any measure of central tendency.

Base year: Some past year with which something today is being compared.

Bimodal: Having two modes. Usually refers to a set of numbers in which two numbers occur equally often (and more than once each).

Consumer Price Index: A monthly publication of the Bureau of Labor Statistics (an agency of the federal government) showing changes in the cost of living by city and for the nation as a whole.

Dispersion: The spread of data.

Frequency distribution table: A table showing the number of times one or more events occur.

Grouped data: Data (taken from a table) combined into groups to simplify analysis and graphic representation.

Mean: One type of average; one measure of central tendency. The mean is the *sum* of all numbers divided by the *number* of numbers.

Measure of central tendency: A number that tries to estimate the middle of a list of numbers. Measures of central tendency include the mean, median, and mode.

Median: The middle number in an ordered array; half the numbers in the array will fall above the median and half below.

Mode: The most common number in a list of numbers. If each number occurs only once, then the list has no mode.

Normal curve: The bell-shaped curve resulting when data are plotted with a normal distribution.

Ordered array: An arrangement of numbers from lowest to highest, designed to facilitate computation of the median (the middle number in an ordered array).

Price Relative: The quotient of the current price to some price in a past base year multiplied by 100.

Range: The difference between the largest value in a data set and the smallest value in that set.

Raw data: A list of numbers that have not been subjected to any kind of analysis.

Standard deviation: A statistic that measures the distances (deviations) of various values from the mean of the data set. It can be defined as the *square root of the mean of the squares of the deviations*.

Weighted mean: A mean calculated by use of weights, so that each recurring number in the set is multiplied by its frequency. It can be thought of as a shortcut to computing the mean for data sets in which many numbers occur more than once.

PART II: WATCHING THE VIDEO PROGRAM

VIDEO VIEWING GUIDE

Before watching the video program, review the following questions. As you watch, be sure to collect the information necessary to answer them:

1. Do you agree or disagree with the statement "Statistics are only for professional accountants and mathematicians; the average business person doesn't really need them."?

2. Name several business contexts in which statistics are likely to be used.

3. What specific factors could add to the credibility of statistics? What specific factors would detract from their credibility?

4. What is the purpose of sampling? How does it work?

5. When would the mean be an especially important measure of central tendency? How about the median? The mode? Is it always important to use all three measures together?

6. Why is the idea of dispersion so important? Does dispersion relate to central tendency? If so, how?

7. What sorts of data sets would likely be represented by a normal curve? What sorts would not?

VIDEO PROGRAM

The lesson's video program is Program 24 — Statistics for the Business World. Remember, if you are watching this program on videotape, take time to replay sections of the tape any time you need to review a concept.

VIDEO VIEWING QUESTIONS

Immediately after viewing the video program for Lesson 24, take time to respond to the following questions. Give your answers some careful thought; they may provide the basis for additional discussions or a longer written response.

1. Give two recent situations in which you have had to deal with some statistical information.

   a. _____

   b. _____

2. Name three situations in which an understanding of statistics *could* be helpful to a business person. Be specific.

a. _____

b. _____

c. _____

3. Suppose you hear on the nightly news that "U.S. productivity went up 5 percent in the past year." In your own words, describe your response to this statement: whether you believe it, how you would interpret it, and what questions (if any) you would still want to have answered.

_____

_____

_____

4. Describe the role that sampling plays in gathering and interpreting data.

_____

_____

_____

5. Suppose you were going to gather data on the following topics. Which do you think would lend themselves well to sampling? (Check as many as apply. Be prepared to give a reason for your response.)

_____ National unemployment

_____ Unemployment within your community

_____ Citywide crime rates

_____ National opinions on who should be the next president of the United States

_____ Students' opinions on who should be president of a class of 150 students

_____ The current percent of students who drop out of high school

_____ The average GPA for the 10,000 students at a given university

_____ Student attitudes on grading practices at the same university

_____ Cost of living increases over the past ten years

_____ American attitudes on crime

_____ The percent of fourth-grade students at a given school who passed the geography test

6. Sometimes statistics can be very misleading. Provide one example (real or invented) that helps illustrate how statistical data are sometimes presented in a misleading way.

   _____

   _____

   _____

7. Your friend recently read a report claiming that "people who eat more carrots live up to 10 percent longer." Should she believe the report? Why or why not? How would you encourage her to interpret this sort of information? What, if anything, would make such a report *more* believable?

   _____

   _____

   _____

8. Name one data set for which the *mean* would be an especially important indicator of central tendency.

   _____

   Name one for which the *median* would be especially important.

   _____

   Name one for which the *mode* would be especially important.

   _____

9. Describe any two data sets that could likely be graphed as normal curves.

   a: _____

   b: _____

   Now name any two that could not.

   a: _____

   b: _____

10. Chris Walker just learned that her score on the math midterm was two standard deviations above the mean. How many people in a class of 40 *probably* scored higher than Chris? (Hint: While there is no single right answer, some suggestions will be more logical and more defensible than others.) What letter grade do you think Chris is *most likely* to receive? What grade do you think you would give her? If you knew that there were 100 items on the test, could you determine Chris's score based on what else you know now? If you say yes, show how. If you say no, explain why not and describe what specific additional information you would need.

    _____ _____

    _____

    _____

PART III: FOCUSING ON THE MATHEMATICS

READING ASSIGNMENT

After watching the video program, you should read one of the following Text Assignments, depending on the textbook you're using:

SOFTCOVER: Pages 583-588 from Chapter 14 of the Miller, Salzman, and Hoelzle softcover text, *Business Mathematics*.

HARDCOVER: Pages 687-707 from Chapter 19 of the Salzman, Miller, and Hoelzle hardcover text, *Mathematics for Business*.

As you read through the text, pay careful attention to the examples the book gives of the mathematics associated with the concepts you're learning about.

Then, after you've completed the text assignment, read through the Key Formulas below. This section provides a handy review of what you've learned. By the time you get to this point in the lesson, all of the formulas and calculations should be familiar to you. If they're not, go back and read the appropriate parts of the text and the Overview section of this lesson. You won't have much success completing the rest of your assignments if you are still confused about the information in the Key Formulas section.

KEY FORMULAS

The following key formulas are important to your understanding of this lesson. Be sure that you know each one and how to use it in solving problems related to business statistics.

KEY FORMULA: Mean = Sum of all values ÷
Number of values in the set

Formula used for: Finding the mean for a given data set.

Example:

John Davis has five thoroughbreds in his stable. They have won 3, 4, 7, 12, and 2 races, respectively. The *mean* number of races won by John's horses is $(3 + 4 + 7 + 12 + 2) \div 5 = 28 \div 5 = 5.6$.

Remember that in this formula:

1. It is not necessary to put the numbers in any sort of order before adding them to find the mean. They can be in random order.

2. The numerator in the fraction is the *sum* of all the values.

3. The denominator in the fraction is the *number* of values. In this example, John Davis has five horses, so the denominator is 5.

4. The answer can be rounded, depending on the nature of the answer and the amount of precision required. For instance, if you are solving

a money problem (average price of new televisions, let's say), you might want to round to the nearest cent or even the nearest dollar. In our example, saying that a horse has won 5.6 races may seem a bit silly (since it's hard to win six-tenths of a race), so the number would likely be rounded up to six.

KEY FORMULA: $s = \sqrt{\dfrac{\Sigma d^2}{n}}$

Formula used for: Computing the standard deviation for a data set.

Example:

Irma Bell recorded the 8:00 a.m. temperatures at the lighthouse where she works for five mornings in early December. Here they are: 10°F, 12°F, 16°F, 10°F, and 20°F. What is the standard deviation of this data set?

As we mentioned, there is a five-step process to let you compute the standard deviation. The math is not difficult, but it is tedious. With real-world data sets, you would likely find the standard deviation by using a business or scientific calculator or a computer. But no matter how we find the result, the standard deviation of Irma's temperatures will be 3.63.

Remember that in this formula:

1. There are several steps involved in computing the standard deviation by hand, and it is important not to leave any of them out.

2. The *mean of the sum of the squares of the deviation* is the *variance*. This is *not* the same as the standard deviation. In the example, the variance is 13.2. To find the standard deviation, you must find the *square root* of the variance.

KEY FORMULA: Price relative = 100 × (Price in specified year ÷ Price in base year)

Formula used for: Determining the percent of change in a price (or other figure) from the base year to another year.

Example:

Homes in Betty Rogers's neighborhood averaged $50,000 in 1960. This year, the average cost is $100,000. What is the price relative? Keep in mind that 1960 is the *base year*, so the average price in that year will be the denominator in the formula: $100,000 ÷ $50,000 × 100 = 2 × 100 = 200 percent. In other words, the price of a new home in Betty's neighborhood, on average, is 200 percent of the 1960 cost.

Remember that in this formula:

1. The price in the base year (the year against which the comparison is being made) always forms the denominator.

2. The price for the specified year is the numerator.

3. The result is always a percent. In the example with Betty Rogers, it's 200 percent, which is the same as the decimal figure 2.00. Remember, to convert a decimal to a percent, move the decimal point two places to the right. To convert a percent to a decimal, move the decimal point two places to the left.

4. This formula is widely used with prices, but it works equally well with other things; taxes, for instance, or salaries. In fact, the formula can be used to compute any sort of numerical change, so long as the figures for specified year and base year are known.

DON'T FORGET

1. The mean, median, and mode are all measures of central tendency. All are types of averages.

2. To find the median, it is necessary first to arrange numbers in an *ordered array* from low to high (or high to low; it doesn't matter). Thus, the data set 10, 8, 2, 6, 4 could be arranged as follows: 2, 4, 6, 8, 10. And the median, the middle number, is 6.

3. The *mode* is the most frequently occurring number in any data set. There is no mathematical formula for computing this number. It must be identified through observation or computer analysis. There can be more than one mode in a data set or no mode at all.

4. The range and standard deviation are helpful in interpreting data sets where the mean and median are the same but the dispersion, or spread, of data, is very different for each set.

5. The square of a negative number is a positive number. Thus, $-7 \times -7 = 49$.

6. The standard deviation is a measure of the extent to which numbers in a data set differ from the mean for that data set. It's defined as the square root of the *mean of the square of all individual deviations from the mean of the data set*. This sounds more complex than it is, and it's undoubtedly more useful to recognize what a standard deviation is and why it's important than to memorize the formula.

PART IV: SOLVING BUSINESS PROBLEMS

PROBLEM SETS

Work the following problems in your textbook. Your instructor will tell you which problems, if any, are to be turned in. Some of the problems have answers provided in the back of the book; refer to these answers to make sure you are working the problems correctly.

SOFTCOVER: If you are using the Miller, Salzman, and Hoelzle softcover text, *Business Mathematics*, do the following problem sets:

14.2: Problems #7-36 on pages 585-588.

HARDCOVER: If you are using the Salzman, Miller, and Hoelzle hardcover text, *Mathematics for Business*, do the following problem sets:

19.2: Problems #6-30 (even numbers only) on pages 692-694.

19.3: Problems #2-26 (even numbers only) on pages 697-698.

19.4: Problems #8-40 (even numbers only) on pages 703-704.

19.5: Problems #2-16 (even numbers only) on pages 706-707.

BUSINESS APPLICATIONS

Read each of the following scenarios and answer the questions about the decisions you would make in each situation. Give these questions some serious thought; they may be used as the basis for discussion or the development of a more complex essay. You should base your decisions on what you've learned from this lesson, applying both math skills and good business judgment to solve the problem at hand.

Al's Electronics is having a close-out sale on video camcorders. There are five models and they vary widely in price. The following chart shows the model listings, the number of each Al's has on hand, and the list price of each model.

SCENARIO 1

Model A	20 units	$ 650
Model B	10 units	$ 800
Model C	10 units	$ 950
Model D	5 units	$1,000
Model E	5 units	$1,600

Marketing manager Sheila Grady is planning to advertise the close-out sale in the newspaper and wants to include information on the average cost of video cameras at Al's. Owner Al Pierce tells Grady to list the $650 price as the "average," since they have more cameras at that price than any other. "That's the truest representation of our average price," he tells her, "not to mention the fact that it will be good for business. The average all over town is running $800 or more. Here's our chance to beat the competition cold." Grady isn't so sure, though, that this figure is an accurate representation of the average price. She is concerned about misleading customers. Al tells her not to worry: "As long as you're telling the truth (and we are, technically) you can't be doing anything wrong."

What do you think? Based on what you know of averages, do you think the $650 figure is a good representation of the average price on the cameras? Or should Al's present this information some other way? Is Grady right to be so concerned about the ethics of presenting data in a certain way, or is she creating an issue that really doesn't exist here?

- ☐ Is $650 the "average" price of cameras at Al's? Explain.

- ☐ Do you think Grady should or should not use this figure in her advertisement? If she *does* use it, how should she present it?

Be specific. If you say she should *not* use it, give a reason for your response.

☐ Suppose that you were writing the ad for Al's close-out sale and you wanted to include the concept of "average price." How would you word the ad?

☐ Imagine that you are a customer who comes to buy a camera at Al's based on an advertisement that claims the "average price of video camcorders at Al's is $650." Are you likely to agree with Al's statistics?

☐ Compare the mean, median, and mode prices of camcorders at Al's. Of the three, which *best* represents the average price? Why? Now consider the *range* of prices. How important should this figure be in putting together the advertisement?

☐ In advertising products, do you think business people are justified in using statistics to make their prices or other terms look better than they might otherwise look? Why or why not? What responsibility does the public bear for *interpreting* statistical data correctly and cautiously?

SCENARIO 2

Biology teacher Bill Bradmore has just administered a midterm test to his Biology 101 class. The 100-item test produced a wide range of results among Bradmore's 20 students. Here are their scores in terms of number of items correct:

| 88 | 78 | 15 | 48 | 50 | 75 | 80 | 95 | 20 | 72 |
| 56 | 60 | 85 | 49 | 52 | 36 | 98 | 68 | 74 | 76 |

Normally, Bradmore gives everyone with a score of 90 and up an A, 80 to 89 a B, 70 to 79 a C, and 60 to 69 a D. Those with scores below 60 fail. In looking over the data, however, Bradmore is afraid this usual method will produce too many failing scores. He feels uncomfortable about that. He is vaguely aware, however, that there are ways to involve the standard deviation and similar statistics in the calculations, and he's thinking about learning how to do that. But he isn't certain if this would be more fair or not, or even if what he's remembering is appropriate at all.

What do you think? Should Bradmore just keep things simple and stick to his usual grading method? Or is he right in thinking that there might be a better way? Will computing the standard deviation help him to come up with a better grading approach?

☐ What is the *range* of scores on this test? What *might* that range suggest about the test or about the students taking the test?

☐ What is the mean score? What is the median score? What further information do these two scores offer about the test or the students? What do the mean and median suggest about the appropriateness of Bradmore's usual grading method?

☐ Is Bradmore correct in thinking that some method involving the standard deviation might be useful in assigning grades to his students? If so, what would be the advantages and disadvantages of such a method?

□ Assuming that you were teaching the class and had to make this decision, how would you assign grades? What method would you use? What approximate scores would get an A, a B, and so on?

□ If these biology test scores were graphed, would they form a normal curve? Why might Bill Bradmore care whether they do or not?

□ Suppose that Bradmore continues to administer this same test in future years, always with similar results. Would that argue for or against considering the standard deviation in assigning grades? Explain.

Communicating with Graphs and Charts 25

*Developing an effective chart is a bit like having a baby —
easy to conceive, much harder to deliver.*

Today, we seem to be inundated with numbers. They come at us from the
government, from business and industry, in newspapers, on television —
everywhere we look. And often they are thrown together in such bunches
that it's hard to understand what they all mean. Translating the numbers
into pictures helps us make sense of them and often allows us to see things
in the data that we would never be able to pick out if we had just numbers
to stare at.

In this lesson, we'll discuss the advantages of representing business-
related information with charts and graphs. We'll consider several different forms of graphic presentation — bar charts, line graphs, pie charts, and
several varieties of each — and learn when each can be used most effectively. We'll also stress the educational and persuasive power of an effective visual display of data, showing how this effectiveness can work to a
business's advantage in such contexts as reporting and marketing.

And because graphs *are* so persuasive, we'll also talk in some detail
about how they can be misleading. In most cases, such confusion is unintentional. But every business person should recognize that graphs can
be purposely distorted in order to mislead the user. By pointing out things
business people and others should keep in mind when they view graphics,
we hope to make you a better interpreter of numerical information.

PART I: INTRODUCING THE MATERIAL

LEARNING OBJECTIVES

Upon completing your study of this lesson, you should be able to:

1. Given sample sets of business data, identify which data sets could be communicated better through graphs.

2. Given graphs that are misleading or inappropriate representations of the underlying data, identify the problem.

3. Construct bar and line graphs illustrating a given set of business data provided in tabular form.

4. Construct a bar graph illustrating a given set of business data provided in tabular form as grouped data.

5. Construct a comparative line graph illustrating two or more given sets of business data provided in tabular form.

If you're using the hardcover textbook, *Mathematics for Business*, there are some additional objectives for the lesson. Upon completing your study of the lesson, you should also be able to:

6. Construct a circle graph illustrating a given set of business data provided in tabular form.

7. Plot a set of business data as a scatter plot and use the graph to estimate a best fit curve and to identify outlying data points.

8. Given one or more sets of business data in tabular form and an indication of the audience for the information, determine which type of graph would best illustrate the information.

9. Given business-related graphs that communicate poorly due to design and format problems, identify the problem with each and suggest how to redraw the graph.

LESSON OVERVIEW

Perhaps the most important part of coming to grips with graphing business information is simply understanding why it's worth the effort. After all, good charts can take quite a while to turn out, so why bother?

In her classic book, *Charting Statistics*, author Mary E. Spear presented an observation about the function of graphs that bears repeating. Spear wrote:

> In the present day, when visual education in all aspects
> has become not only an aid to, but a vital part, of learn-
> ing, our attention is called more than ever to the almost
> limitless possibilities in the field. The eye absorbs written
> statistics, but only slowly does the brain receive the mes-
> sage hidden behind written words and numbers. The cor-

rect graph, however, reveals that message briefly and simply.

You may find this commentary even more insightful if you consider that it was written *four decades* ago. As you might guess, the visual orientation of today's business audience is greater than ever before.

By the way, before proceeding further, it might be good to address a potentially confusing issue. Do you think there is a difference between a chart and a graph? That's actually a pretty tough question. At one time, the word "chart" was used primarily for information in tabular form (what we would probably call a table), while a graph was the diagram that showed the variation in a quantity compared to other quantities. For better or worse, that distinction has blurred, so while mathematicians and statisticians would correctly argue that the correct use is "bar graph," "line graph," and the like, the average person, along with many dictionaries, views the terms "chart" and "graph" as synonymous.

Graphs, if well done—and you cannot place too much emphasis on this important *if*—can make even very complex data almost immediately understandable as well as appealing to the eye. This point is important, for if people feel comfortable with the data, they're more likely to understand and remember it. Further, graphs don't take as long to scan or to interpret as numerical tables or written copy. The paragraph and the chart below present the same information. Which do you find easier to use?

Some Graphic Examples

> The company's history shows continuous growth over the past five years; this growth has consistently been in the range of 4 to 6 percent, with the exception of 1984, when the actual growth was closer to 2 percent. Unfortunately, this growth rate has never approached the projected growth rate, which had been set at the 7 to 10 percent level. The discrepancy was reduced in 1987, when the projected increase was dropped to the 6 percent range.

Percentage of Increase in Sales

- - - - Projected Revenue from Sales   ——— Actual Revenue from Sales

And which do you prefer, the table below or its equivalent graph?

Sales of Product 1 in 1984 —	$12 million
Sales of Product 1 in 1985 —	4 million
Sales of Product 1 in 1986 —	4 million
Sales of Product 2 in 1984 —	$ 2 million
Sales of Product 2 in 1985 —	16 million
Sales of Product 2 in 1986 —	8 million
Sales of Product 3 in 1984 —	$ 9 million
Sales of Product 3 in 1985 —	12 million
Sales of Product 3 in 1986 —	9 million

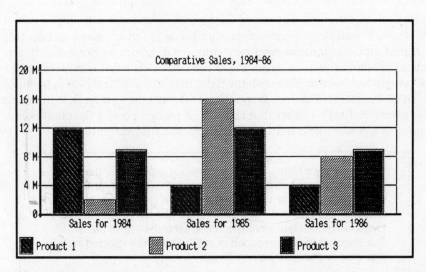

Well, they say that one picture is worth a thousand words, and maybe that's true. But the more important question is whether the verbal information can get through at all. As you can see from these examples, putting the information in graphic form often does wonders for turning a tangle of data into a clear message.

Graphing to Save Time

Perhaps the examples we've just shown convince you that information is often easier to understand when it's presented graphically. But a good business manager will also demand to know just how the investment of effort in making the graph will be repaid.

If you doubt the effectiveness of good graphs, consider some information from a survey performed a few years ago by the American Management Association (AMA). The graph on page 507 shows how top executives spent their working hours. Notice the large amount of time devoted to meetings.

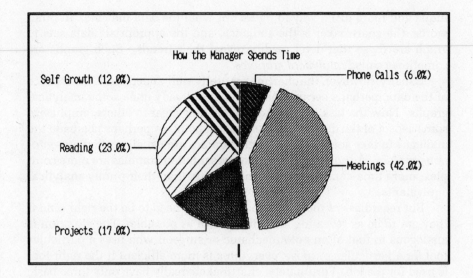

Now consider that another study, this one performed by the Wharton School of Business, found that reaching a consensus in management meetings happened 28 percent faster when information was presented using color charts and graphs. And because managers reached consensus 28 percent faster, they reduced the amount of time needed in the meetings by 15 percent.

Given that the AMA study suggests that almost half of the executives' time was spent in meetings, a 15 percent time savings is about 16 working days a year, or almost a day and a half a month. What could hard-working business people do with one or two extra days a month? Quite a bit, no doubt. And their companies would profit as well; for a $30-per-hour manager, the savings in salary alone would be about $4,000 a year.

The preceding calculation presents a rosier picture than it should. For one thing, it's likely that the presenters using the high-quality visuals were better presenters overall than those who worked without graphic backup. And who knows whether the time saved in meetings would be put to some productive use. Still, there's sufficient evidence to support the claim that the appropriate use of high-quality graphics can increase efficiency and save money.

Remember, a good chart or graph can have many purposes, but its primary goal is to turn *raw data* into useful information. That is, a graph can be used to translate a confusing or apparently unrelated list of numbers into a picture that makes immediate sense. Such lists, or *data sets* as they are called, exist in enormous variety in all human endeavors that use statistics or numerical values: science, mathematics, engineering, the social sciences, economics, and business.

What Data Should Be Graphed?

Charts and graphs express sets of numbers visually, but they also give insight into the past and sometimes into the future. Good charts help interpret the numbers and often reveal new information. Therefore, the kinds of data to be graphed should be those that have meanings or implications not already clear to the intended audience. In other words, the choice of what to graph, and in how much complexity, depends on who the graph is for.

Sometimes the implications of the data set may not even be clear to the immediate user. In such situations, a graph is less a presentation technique and more just a way to figure out what the data indicate. In other words, the chartmaker is the audience, and the appropriate data sets to graph are those that don't readily reveal their trends. Such graphs are sometimes called *analytical graphics*.

Usually, however, the chartmaker pretty well understands the essence of the data, perhaps because he or she has already done some analytical graphs. Now the task is to make the meaning clear to others, emphasize some aspect of the data in order to make a point, or perhaps persuade the audience to take some action. Such graphics are usually called *presentation graphics*. As you might imagine, presentation graphics are more complex, more time-consuming, and more costly than their purely analytical equivalents.

But regardless of the audience, the graphs need to be the right kind if they are to be as revealing and informative as possible. The situation is analogous to that of an auto mechanic or surgeon who uses a particular tool for a particular purpose; everything is more efficient if the right tool is used for the job. Fortunately, chartmakers really have only three basic types of charts to deal with, bar charts, line graphs, and pie charts.

Bar Charts   A *bar chart* is one of the most common ways used to display numerical information. In a vertical bar chart, the height of a bar corresponds to the magnitude of a particular value in a data set.

For example, let's say you want to show the differences in sales among the six major divisions within a company. Your graph might look like this:

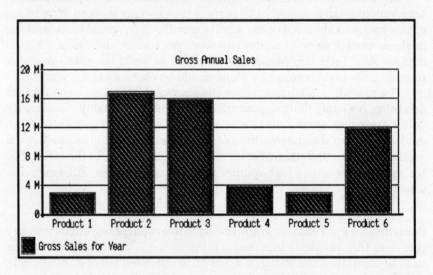

This graph, though plain, carries a lot of information. And there's room for some more. Suppose you want to show those same differences and simultaneously compare projected sales against actual sales. There's nothing to stop you from plotting two data sets on the same set of *axes*. (Axes, pronounced ak-seez', is the plural of axis; it's easier to say than axises.) Then the bar chart would look like the one on page 509.

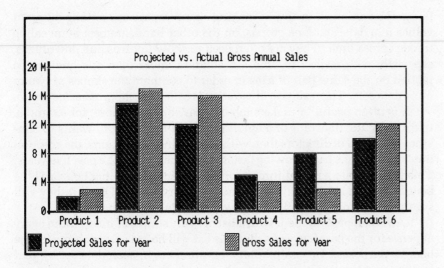

Notice how much information we have in this graph, and how difficult it would be to write a succinct paragraph that contains all this information.

Choosing Appropriate Groups of Data

Drawing an effective bar chart is largely a matter of having an appropriate data set to graph. Bar charts are not as good at showing trends as they are at comparing different pieces of data. As a result, they are more often used when all the data are from a single point in time but for different groups.

The other critical factor is the grouping of the data for graphing. Imagine that Holichek, the personnel officer of a large company, wants to know the ages of all the firm's employees in preparation for reviewing the company's package of insurance benefits. To prepare the bar chart, Holichek first needs to determine the number of employees at each age; that is, the frequency of occurrence of each value in the data set. How many are 18, how many are 19, how many are 20, and so on? Then she can prepare a graph in which the vertical axis represents the number of employees of each age and the horizontal axis represents ages ranging from youngest to oldest. She'll draw the bars for each age, each bar corresponding to the number of employees of that particular age.

See any problem here? The way Holichek is going about this, she'll likely have over 50 bars, far too many to look at effectively. What's more, she's made comparisons more difficult by trying to compare individual years. Since she is probably really trying to find out how various age groups compare, her next move should be to reduce the number of bars by grouping several ages in one category.

For example, imagine that Holichek's company has employees of every age from 18 to 72; her bar graph would contain 55 bars if each bar were to represent a single age. A graph that grouped the ages into categories such as under 20, 21-25, 26-30, 31-35, and so on would be much more helpful. This second graph, with perhaps 10 bars representing all the data, would be much easier to read and would also be more useful, allowing easy comparisons among the different groups.

One final note: Be aware that some people make a distinction between bar charts and *column* charts. Conceptually, they're identical; it's just a matter of whether the bars go from left to right or from bottom to top as values increase.

Line Graphs

Bar graphs are most useful in making size comparisons among different values in a data set. *Line graphs*, on the other hand, are best at revealing trends across time. They are often used to show upturns and downturns, especially with respect to time. In addition, more than one line can be plotted on the same pair of axes in order to compare the shapes of two or more data sets. The resulting illustration is called a *comparative line graph*.

It is often useful to make such comparisons. Suppose, for example, that Lewis, the treasurer of a small nonprofit corporation, wants to convince the board of directors that, with a few minor exceptions, the corporation's income has been growing faster than expenses for the past five years. This is so despite a recent three-month drop in income that concerns the board. He can simply tell the board that everything is OK, but they will surely press him for details. They will want to see for themselves.

Lewis can present them with a list of every source of income and every expense for the past five years, but this list will be too cumbersome for the board's purposes. He can tabulate the numbers in each data set by year and present the resulting table to the board. This is better, but why not take the process one step further? What Lewis really needs is a clear, concise illustration of the relative amounts and trends of the two data sets, expenses and income, with respect to time. A comparative line graph will provide just that.

What such graphs are not so good at is showing comparative information about individual data points at a single point in time. That's not to say that you can't tell the value of any individual data point from a line graph. You can, but the format of the line graph is less suitable for this than the format of a bar chart. What it really boils down to is whether you're trying to show the change in the data for the same thing across time; if so, you need a line chart.

Scatter Plots

Another name for the line in a line graph is the *curve*. Sometimes the number of items in a data set suitable for a line graph will be really big. Plotting the individual points on the graph will be possible, but connecting each dot to the next with a separate line segment will be impossible or counterproductive. This is because there will be too many points bunched too closely together to draw clean lines between each of them. In addition, if some of the points of the graph lie far away from the majority of points, drawing zigzag lines to them will create a comical distortion of the main trends of the graph.

The solution, in this case, is not to try. The main trends of such a graph, called a *scatter plot*, will be visually apparent once all the points are plotted. Points that are far away from the major group of points are no less valid, but they represent relatively unusual happenings. The majority of points, like the Milky Way's points of light in the night sky, will suggest a band rather than a clean line. No lines are drawn connecting any of the points.

To make the scatter plot more useful, it's often valuable to draw a line that represents a sort of average of this band of points. The line is called the *best fit curve*. Unfortunately, where this curve should fall isn't always (or even usually) obvious. Determining just where the best fit curve should go is usually left to computers.

As an example of a scatter plot to analyze business data, consider the situation of Thomsen, the manager of an outdoor municipal swimming pool. The city's governing body wants to know how pool use is related to air temperature and other factors. The commissioners disagree about the relative importance of the temperature, the school calendar, the flow of tourists to and from the region, and so on. They are trying to decide when it makes economic sense to operate the pool.

To begin to answer the commissioners' questions, Thomsen checks the pool records and discovers that the noontime air temperature varied from about 60°F to about 110°F during the previous swimming season and that daily attendance varied from a low of 12 to a high of 193. He decides to graph his data as a scatter plot to present at the next commission meeting. He puts attendance along the y-axis and uses the x-axis for temperatures. In both cases, he chooses subdivisions that will allow all the data to be plotted on one sheet of graph paper and that will not squash the plotted points into such a small space that the graph loses clarity. He then plots each day's data as a separate point.

What Thomsen ends up with is a graphic depiction of the rise and fall of pool use with temperature, not too surprising. The majority of the points on his graph fall in a band that shows the expected: that pool use goes up when the temperature goes up. But the graph shows clearly that there are some exceptions. Thomsen finds that changes in temperature don't produce much of an increase in attendance until the temperature hits 80°F. And pool use actually falls off once the temperature hits 100°F.

By the way, if you're wondering why scatter plots weren't listed as one of the three major chart types when we began this overview, it's because they are often considered just a variation on the line chart. After all, the best fit curve is very similar to what would result from an ordinary line chart.

Pie Charts

Pie charts, also known as circle graphs, are good for showing the relationship of the parts of anything to the whole. For example, you could show what portions of a corporate budget went for various expenses with this pie chart:

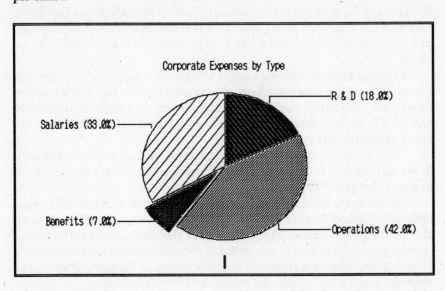

Notice that one "slice" of the pie has been pulled out in order to add emphasis. You might think this an odd thing to do, but suppose that this chart is being presented in a workshop on employee benefits. Then the idea of "exploding" the employee benefits wedge makes a lot of sense.

Pie charts require a bit more mathematics than line or bar graphs. There are two reasons for this. First, the values plotted are parts of a whole rather than just the raw values. This means that each number has to be converted to a percentage of the total. And second you need some math to know how to draw that portion of a circle.

Let's use the example of Rameriz, whose board wants to see where the income for their nonprofit corporation came from in the previous month. To do this, Rameriz would first need to assemble the raw data. The corporation received income from the following sources in the following amounts: donations, $35,339; grants, $17,000; subscriptions and dues, $6,395; educational video rentals, $2,327; and miscellaneous, $1,134.

Next Rameriz would add the separate incomes to get the total income, which turns out to be $61,516. Rameriz then divides each of the individual incomes by this total to get the portion of the total income that came from each source. For example, in the case of donations, Rameriz would divide $35,339 by $61,516 to get approximately .57.

Unfortunately, it's not immediately clear how to draw the wedge representing 57 percent of a circle. So the second step — converting the percentage into the number of degrees of a circle that percentage represents — is necessary. Since a circle has 360 degrees, the part of the circle allocated to donations would be .57 multiplied by 360 degrees, which is about 205 degrees. Thus, Rameriz would use a protractor to create a wedge occupying 205 degrees of the circle and would label it "donations." He'd then proceed to perform the same steps for the other categories.

While these calculations would be a bit cumbersome, the end result would be a simple and easy-to-use illustration of relationships that the board would be able to grasp instantly. Furthermore, each person would not have to do all these tiresome calculations for himself or herself. Rameriz would have done it for them; that is part of his job.

Common Errors in Graphing Data

Good charts should be clear, just like good writing. If the chartmaker puts in too many lines or too many labels, the result is confusion. Too many bars on a bar chart, too many lines on a line graph, and too many wedges in a pie chart all have the same effect — a reduction in the readability of the chart.

A similar kind of confusion arises when a chartmaker tries to include too small a wedge in a pie chart. If Rameriz had, in our last example, broken his "miscellaneous" category into five or 10 smaller components and tried to include them as separate wedges, most would have been too small to label neatly or even notice.

These kinds of errors make the graph look odd and are therefore easy to see and correct. More serious kinds of error occur when a chart distorts in a way that is not apparent.

For example, imagine that Preston, a newspaper reporter who regularly covers school board meetings for *The Daily News*, writes a news story about student test scores. The grouped data that she collects at the school board meeting show the average national percentile ranking of the students at each grade who took standardized tests earlier in the year. If she turns these data into a line graph, the results will be misleading.

The data used by Preston are separate data for each grade. There is no continuity across the test scores, no change over time. But that is exactly what a line graph suggests. If each grade's percentile score is plotted on the graph and then the dots are connected, it will appear that the scores reveal trends as a single group passes from grade to grade. That is, it may appear to the newspaper's readers that a group of students are "smart" in third grade and get "dumber" around ninth grade, but by 11th grade get almost as smart as they were in third grade.

But this is wrong. The students in the various grades are separate groups and took separate tests *in the same year*. And since the data are for one year only, no one can predict future trends. The results for next year's groups may be quite different.

A better choice of graph for this data would be a bar chart, with each bar representing the average percentile score obtained by a particular grade. Bar charts are good at comparing different groups, and it is perfectly accurate to say that this year's third grade had a higher average score than this year's ninth grade. It would also be perfectly sensible to make a graph of how, say, the class of 1999 scored when they were third-graders, then fourth-graders, then fifth-graders, and so on. Now we have a single group being measured over time—the perfect setup for a line chart.

A different sort of distortion can occur when the chartmaker accidentally or deliberately chooses improper scaling that makes minor fluctuations look very big or that make big fluctuations look very small. All of us have seen examples of line graphs meant to persuade us that something is "going off the top of the chart," whether it is automobile sales, world population, or the cost of health insurance. It's easy to make the stock market look like it's crashing, for example, by using what might be called the zoom-lens technique. The chartmaker zooms in on a minor downturn in the market and graphs only that segment, using a vertical scale that doesn't show the full range of possible values. This kind of distortion is not always easy to spot in a fast-paced medium like television, where the graphic images may create a particular impression and then vanish before complete analysis is possible.

A Word about Computer Graphics

Not long ago, the best graphs you could hope to get from your microcomputer were simple (and rather unattractive) bar, line, or pie charts, usually with very plain headings and labels. If you wanted something really slick, a visit to your friendly professional graphic designer was probably in order. There, someone with good artistic skills and visual sense would listen to your ideas and translate your concepts into pictures. The results were often good—even striking.

But there were some disadvantages. One was the time it took. Even a skilled graphic artist can work just so fast; it might be two or three weeks between your visit and the time you received the graphics. Then there was the problem of changing the graphic. Many people have gotten their graphs back from the graphic artist only to discover that a slight mistake or misconception by the artist produced a chart that was unusable or usable only with an embarrassing preface: "Uh, there's been a slight change in this figure . . . ." And then there was the cost; $100 a chart isn't an unreasonable figure for handcrafted graphics of moderate complexity.

These problems can be reduced if you use a microcomputer and appropriate software to produce your own graphs. Obviously, you can expect rapid results. A simple bar graph (assuming you have your data together) may be turned out in as little as five minutes; something more complex— let's say a line graph for one data set superimposed on a stacked bar graph for three additional data sets, with everything elaborately labeled—could be produced in less than an hour.

Further, you are in control of what gets produced. If you don't like where the title is, you can move it. If district sales figures take a sudden leap, you can produce a new graph with little effort; you don't have to use the old one and ask your listeners to visualize the new figures. And mistakes aren't disastrous; you can correct them yourself, on the spot. In fact, you can use data from a spreadsheet or database program as the basis for your chart. In many cases, changes in the graphs will be made automatically for you when data within the spreadsheet or database are changed.

And best of all (for most people, anyway), you don't need to be an artist to get decent results. You don't have to draw the graphs yourself. You simply select a design (e.g., bar graph, pie graph), and the computer uses the data you provide to produce the graph for you. But how good are the results?

Unfortunately, they are rarely the equal of those produced by an experienced, and expensive, graphic artist. But they are better than virtually any business person could create on his or her own. They're more visually attractive and better designed than most hand-drawn graphs. Equally important, the software offers the perfect deal: precision without tedium. The computer determines (with unerring accuracy) the size of the components, for example, in a pie graph, how big each slice of the pie will be, based on the numerical values you feed in. So there's no guesswork. Face it—how easy would it be to slice off just 17.35 percent of a pie? Just don't believe that the right computer software will somehow give you some special artistic sense that you never had before. Sad to say, it won't.

SOME WORDS OF ADVICE

Charts and graphs are with us every day. Whether we actually produce any charts ourselves or not, they appear in the newspapers we read and in the television programs we watch, in advertisements, documentaries, arguments, and explanations. Because charts may be used to deceive as well as inform, it's critical to understand how they work.

Most business people will, and certainly should, be chartmakers at one time or another. Remember, even if no one else needs to see it, sketching a rough graph can often bring order to a data set that, at first glance, appears to have no order. Graphing becomes second nature to most scientists and engineers—and to most good business managers, who often make critical decisions based on the comparisons and trends revealed by the charts.

Just a few decades ago, it might have been a plausible excuse to say "Well, I just don't know what a good graph looks like." These days, however, effective graphs are everywhere. The nightly news broadcast, the newspaper, magazines, annual reports; all these communicate often and well using graphs. And if a Wall Street analyst asked a corporation president for information about trends in the company's quarterly sales figures over the last five years, which would most likely be used: a written paragraph, a table of numbers, or a chart? If the company wants to show the trends clearly and efficiently, it's likely to be the chart.

Nothing is likely to turn a novice chartmaker into an overnight artist. There are, though, a couple of tips that will help keep your graphs useful, if not stunning. For one thing, don't try to fit too much on a single graph. If you do, you defeat the purpose of good graphics. Here's a simple test: You should be able to sum up the main point of every graphic in one statement. If you can't, maybe your concept is complex enough to require two or three graphs, or more.

Similarly, you need to have a clear idea of what you want your graph to show before you try making it. This may seem obvious, but it pays to stop for a second before you start plotting things to visualize whether the finished graph is likely to tell you what you want to know. If you're using a computer, don't expect your software to make these decisions for you. Even if you tell it to graph something that doesn't make sense, or you tell it to use a pie graph to depict something that would be clearer using a line graph, it will go right ahead and follow your orders. But who do you suppose will get the blame for a graph nobody can decipher?

Finally, remember to keep it simple. The raw data should always be available to answer the need for more details, but don't treat a graph as just a long table of numbers in a slightly different form. In business presentations, it's much more common to try to show too much with a graph than too little, an error that undermines the whole purpose of the graph. Look at the effective graphs used in newspapers and on television. Almost without fail, they deal with just one data set and they deal with it so straightforwardly that you can't possibly be confused. In short, when in doubt, simplify.

KEY TERMS

Before you read through the text assignment and watch the video program, take a minute to look at the key terms associated with this lesson. When you encounter them in the text and video program, pay careful attention to their meaning.

Axis: One of the perpendicular reference lines from which numerical values are measured on a graph. By convention, the x-axis is horizontal; the y-axis is vertical. Three-dimensional graphs also have a z-axis.

Bar chart: A graph in which the height or length of a bar represents the magnitude of the variable being graphed.

Best fit curve: The center line of the main swath of points in a scatter plot.

Comparative line graph: One graph with multiple lines showing how two or more data sets relate.

Curve: Another name for the line of a line graph.

Line graph: A graph that shows how some variable changes with respect to another variable, most often time.

Pie chart: A graph that shows the whole of a data set as a complete circle and the parts that make up the whole as pie-shaped wedges. (Also called a circle graph.)

Raw data: A list of numbers before analysis.

Scatter plot: A line graph in which the curve is determined by the most dense clusters of a large number of plotted points. Sometimes also called a scatter diagram or a dot plot.

Stacked bar chart: A bar chart in which each bar is subdivided into segments. Conceptually, each individual bar is like a pie chart, making a stacked bar chart a very effective way to present a lot of information.

Variable: Numerical value that changes with respect to something else, often time. Examples are stock prices, rents, taxes, and income.

PART II: WATCHING THE VIDEO PROGRAM

VIDEO VIEWING GUIDE

Before watching the video program, review the following questions. As you watch, be sure to collect the information necessary to answer them:

1. What is the purpose of a good chart? Is it enough simply to make a set of numbers visible, or must the chartmaker have a purpose in mind before starting?

2. What are the three main types of graphs or charts? Cite examples of data sets that would be best represented by each of the three types.

3. What effect has the spread of computer graphics had on chartmaking? What are some of the advantages and disadvantages of using a computer to produce charts?

4. How did the use of charts for business purposes get started? Is the use of charts in business growing or slowing?

5. What are some of the common *unintentional* mistakes that people make in producing charts? What, if any, are some *intentional* errors?

6. What are some of the important concerns in producing charts for sharing with an audience? Be able to answer the question for a variety of different audiences.

7. How might the sales manager for a small steel producer use charts for business? Be able to list three specific applications.

VIDEO PROGRAM

The lesson's video program is Program 25 — Communicating with Graphs and Charts. Remember, if you are watching this program on videotape, take time to replay sections of the tape any time you need to review a concept.

VIDEO VIEWING QUESTIONS

Immediately after viewing the video program for Lesson 25, take time to respond to the following questions. Give your answers some careful thought; they may provide the basis for additional discussion or a longer written response.

1. A family keeps track of its expenses for a year. Here are the results, in percentages: housing, 30; food, 21; automobile, 14; clothing, 10; medical, 5; savings, 8; miscellaneous, 12. What is the best type of chart to use for this information, and why?

    Pie –

    Shows parts of a whole

2. List three common errors people make when plotting line charts. Then put a checkmark next to the error you think is the most serious.

    a. *Too many items or lines*

    b. *Too many points*

    c. _____

3. Discuss the importance of the audience to charting. In other words, how might your approach to charting differ from audience to audience?

    _____

    _____

    _____

4. Suppose a hotel wants to chart its occupancy rate, month by month, over the last five years. What is the best choice of chart type for this information? Why?

    line Chart

    _____

    _____

5. Imagine that you produce a lot of business graphs and would like to have a microcomputer and appropriate software to help in the process. Sensibly enough, though, you have to demonstrate to your supervisor that this would be cost effective. List some of the major points you'd use to persuade her to approve the purchase.

    _____

    _____

    _____

6. The local power company includes a bar chart with each month's electric bill to consumers. The chart shows the customer's average daily electricity use for the preceding 12 months. Would a line chart be just as effective? How about a pie chart?

    Line Chart: _____

    Pie Chart: _____

7. Speculate a bit on the future of chartmaking. Do you think it is likely to continue increasing in popularity as it has in the past decade or two? Or do you think that it's a passing fad that will die down in the coming years?

PART III: FOCUSING ON THE MATHEMATICS

READING ASSIGNMENT

After watching the video program, you should read one of the following Text Assignments, depending on the textbook you're using:

SOFTCOVER: Pages 569-582 from Chapter 14 of the Miller, Salzman, and Hoelzle softcover text, *Business Mathematics.*

HARDCOVER: Pages 676-687 from Chapter 19 of the Salzman, Miller, and Hoelzle hardcover text, *Mathematics for Business.*

As you read through the text, pay careful attention to the examples the book gives of the mathematics associated with the concepts you're learning about.

Then, after you've completed the text assignment, read through the Key Formula below. This section provides a handy review of what you've learned. By the time you get to this point in the lesson, all of the formulas and calculations should be familiar to you. If they're not, go back and read the appropriate parts of the text and the Overview section of this lesson. You won't have much success completing the rest of your assignments if you are still confused about the information in the Key Formula section.

KEY FORMULA

The following key formula is important to your understanding of this lesson. Be sure that you know how to use it in solving problems related to pie charts.

KEY FORMULA: (Individual value ÷ Total of all values) × 360 degrees = Degrees in wedge

Formula used for: Determining the size of a "slice" in a pie chart by indicating the arc of its outside edge.

Example:

Duckworth, who manages the warehouse of a small wholesale company, decides to illustrate her division's expenditures by making a pie chart. She has grouped the expenses, which total $200,000 by category as follows: labor — $80,000, facilities — $60,000, maintenance and repairs — $30,000, taxes — $20,000, and "other" — $10,000.

To find out how big the pie slice for labor should be, she calculates ($80,000 ÷ $200,000) × 360 degrees. The answer, 144 degrees, is how big an arc of the circle is taken up by the outer edge of the labor wedge of the pie. Duckworth will then go through the process for the remaining five categories.

Remember that in this formula:

1. One major reason why this step is necessary is so that you can use a protractor to draw the pie wedge. If a computer were plotting the chart, the calculation would be done automatically.

2. Duckworth has the option of "exploding" one of the pie slices to call attention to it. In the scenario, this probably wouldn't be done, because all of the wedges are of equal importance. But if she were talking to management about the cost of labor, exploding the labor wedge might have made sense.

DON'T FORGET

1. Finding the best fit curve on a scatter plot also takes some calculation, but because the number of data points is apt to be large, most best fit curves are calculated using computers.

2. Calculating where to draw the different parts of each bar on a stacked bar chart is similar to finding the size of a pie chart wedge. The difference is that instead of being multiplied by 360 degrees, the ratio of the individual value to the total is multiplied by the length of the total bar. For example, if a bar representing the 21 to 30 age group were two inches long and 150 out of 200 in that age group were male, then the portion of the bar for males would be (150 ÷ 200) × 2, or 1.5 inches.

PART IV: SOLVING BUSINESS PROBLEMS

PROBLEM SETS

Work the following problems in your textbook. Your instructor will tell you which problems, if any, are to be turned in. Some of the problems have answers provided in the back of the book; refer to these answers to make sure you are working the problems correctly.

SOFTCOVER: If you are using the Miller, Salzman, and Hoelzle softcover text, *Business Mathematics*, do the following problem sets:

14.1: Problems #1-43 on pages 575-580.

HARDCOVER: If you are using the Salzman, Miller, and Hoelzle hardcover text, *Mathematics for Business*, do the following problem sets:

19.1: Problems #1-14 on pages 681-687.

BUSINESS APPLICATIONS

Read each of the following scenarios and answer the questions about the decisions you would make in each situation. Give these questions some serious thought; they may be used as the basis for discussion or the development of a more complex essay. You should base your decisions on what you've learned from this lesson, applying both math skills and good business judgment to solve the problem at hand.

SCENARIO 1   Van Gundy, director of the Big Valley Public Library, is required to prepare an annual report each year for the library's board of directors. The final version of the report will bear the signature of the board president, but the bulk of the work is always delegated to Van Gundy.

The report is used for internal planning but also to generate income. That is, the annual report will be included with documents that go to the city, county, and state governments and are linked to the annual subsidies the library gets from each of those sources. The annual report may also be used in grant applications to foundations, the Friends of the Library and other civic groups interested in the library, and possibly individual donors. It is, therefore, a very important document with a wide variety of potential audiences.

Van Gundy loves the library and wants it to flourish. He believes strongly in what he sees as the mission of the library: to make as much information as possible available to everyone in Big Valley. He believes that libraries are an important feature of democracy and that societies with good libraries are better than societies with bad libraries or no libraries. Therefore, he wants the library to have lots of money so that it can buy more books, subscribe to more periodicals, add to its on-line search capabilities via computer, expand summer hours of operation, and so on.

Beyond that, he believes the library staff salaries, including his own, are much too low. He makes $20,000 annually, though the average for similar libraries in the region is $25,000. His chief assistants make $15,000; the average is $18,000. This year, he would like to persuade the board and the governing bodies that jointly fund the library to approve substantial salary hikes.

The annual report will present the highlights of the year's accomplishments at the library. It will discuss trends, goals, and budgets and will contain a lot of numerical data. Financial data from the treasurer, staff productivity data from Van Gundy's records, written explanations, and an overview will be included, and the report may contain illustrations such as charts and graphs if Van Gundy decides to include them. Van Gundy's report must be believable but also persuasive if he is to achieve his ends. He decides to persuade through the extensive use of charts, but he isn't quite sure how best to present the information or, for that matter, what information to present.

What do you think? What parts of Van Gundy's information could be effectively presented with charts? What parts couldn't? How can he most effectively use his time in preparing the report and its graphics?

☐ What general type of graph — pie, bar, or line — would be most appropriate for showing the relationship of staff salaries to total library expenses during the past year? If staff salaries appear to be a relatively large part of total library expenditures, is Van Gundy obligated to use that chart, or should he try an alternate approach?

☐ What type of graph would be best suited for showing the relationship between staff salaries at Big Valley Library and those at five other libraries in the region? What steps, if any, does Van Gundy need to take to make sure the data are truly comparable?

☐ Suppose there are 15 comparable libraries in the region. Given that Van Gundy wants to show that salaries at his library are too low, what type of graph would show this most dramatically?

☐ Van Gundy gives some thought to plotting his library along with only the five other libraries that have the largest salaries. Does this seem appropriate to you? Why or why not?

☐ If Van Gundy wants to show the change in staff salaries with respect to time, what graph type would be the best? How about if he wants to compare the change in Big Valley staff salaries with the change in staff salaries at other regional libraries over the past five years? If it makes his graph more persuasive, is he justified in using only four years of data rather than five?

☐ Because of his position, Van Gundy has many ways to manipulate the data to make the case he wants. What are the most important factors for Van Gundy, or anyone in a similar position, to consider when deciding how to use graphic information designed to persuade?

Blackman, the owner of a small furnace-making company, is giving some thought to buying a graphics package for the company microcomputer. His thought is that the computer, currently used primarily for a limited amount of word processing, could draw up various charts that would help clarify the advantages of the company's furnaces compared to those of their competitors.

SCENARIO 2

His staff members, however, don't see the merit in this purchase. One remarks that the software will undoubtedly be hard to learn, while another comments that the graphs produced by the computer won't look good enough to give to clients. Another points out a more basic problem: there doesn't seem to be all that much worth graphing. It's true that they have some heat retention tables that might be easier to understand in graphic form, but this hardly seems a reason to buy a whole new software package.

Blackman counters that the reason they've never done much graphing is that they haven't had an easy way to do it. "Once the software is here," he ventures, "I'll bet we find hundreds of useful things to do with it."

What do you think? Will Blackman be wasting his money buying graphing software? Or is he right that there are probably many sets of data that could be better handled in graphic form?

☐ Should Blackman buy the software? What is the single most important reason for your answer?

☐ Blackman mentions developing graphs to share with clients, but a staff member questions whether such graphs would be "good enough." What do you think?

☐ What are three improvements that Blackman and his staff might see immediately if they buy and use the microcomputer software? Then cite one improvement that is likely to develop over time.

☐ A week later, Blackman brings in an elaborate brochure put out by the computer company that shows some stunning graphs produced on the very model of computer his company uses. Some members of the staff are swayed by the prospect of doing graphs of such high quality, but some others comment, "All that stuff was done by professional artists who had nothing but time and talent. We could never do anything like that." Which perspective is likely closer to the truth?

☐ One problem Blackman admits to is a lack of experience in graphing on the part of his staff. Is this a major problem, or is the staff likely to catch on without any real training?

The Future of Business Mathematics 26

Reprinted by permission: Tribune Media Services.

This is an interesting time in business mathematics. At this very moment, there are roughly as many people working in business who have always had computers as an integral part of daily operations as there are who remember the days before computers. This means that half the business population is still in awe of the changes the computer has made in business, while the other half views the computer as a routine tool.

Not that this phenomenon is new. Most of us, for example, would admit that the airplane was a great invention, but few of us are dazzled by the fact that you can now get from New York to Los Angeles in six hours. But there are still many older people for whom this is an amazing situation; the technology they grew up with didn't allow coast-to-coast travel in six *days*. A similar situation developed with radios after World War I, the telephone and electricity around the close of the 19th century and railroads around the Civil War. In each case, for the people who grew up with the invention it was an integral part of life, while those who could remember what life was like without it never ceased to be amazed by the change.

Suffice it to say that business mathematics, and business in general, would be nothing like it is today without computers. In this concluding lesson of *By the Numbers*, we'll examine the role computers (and their smaller counterparts, hand-held calculators) play in business. We'll give particular emphasis to a few of the techniques businesses use to create and analyze data that didn't even exist before the use of computers became widespread.

PART I: INTRODUCING THE MATERIAL

LEARNING OBJECTIVES

Upon completing your study of this lesson, you should be able to:

1. List a number of business mathematics calculations that can be done much more rapidly with a special-purpose business calculator than by hand or with tables.

2. Give examples of application programs for small computers that can be of substantial help in business mathematics calculations and analysis.

3. Discuss some of the dangers inherent in using calculators and computers to solve business mathematics problems.

4. Given a list of sample business mathematics problems, identify which could be efficiently handled by a computer-based spreadsheet, by a graphics program, or by a database management program.

5. Explain the importance of yield management in many modern businesses and discuss the role that computers play in making effective yield management possible.

6. Explain the role that computerized forecasting plays in many modern businesses and discuss the potential advantages and disadvantages of relying on such forecasts.

7. Discuss the magnitude of current and predicted computer use and describe major trends occurring in business computer use.

If you're using the hardcover textbook, *Mathematics for Business*, there is an additional objective for this lesson. Upon completing your study of the lesson, you should also be able to:

8. Given a hypothetical business problem requiring calculations most easily done with a computer-based spreadsheet, determine the most appropriate rows, columns, and relationships for the spreadsheet.

LESSON OVERVIEW

As we implied at the outset, it wasn't so very long ago that computers were viewed as truly high tech, the wave of the future, something comprehensible only to a remote and esoteric band of intrepid scientists. At the start of the 20th century, people regarded the automobile with something of the same combination of amazement and distrust.

As time went on, the initial fear of the automobile gave way to acceptance, then demand, and finally to consumer pressure for more power, more features, more luxury. Something like that has happened with computers. Millions of business people are using computers daily, with millions more becoming computer literate every year. And those of us already adept at using computers want them to do more, to do it better, and to do it faster. But, ironically, because most of our demands were answered in the past, we've grown exceedingly hard to impress.

Computer manufacturers are justifiably quick to point out that if air travel had made the same advances as computer technology, a coast-to-cost trip would take less than a minute and cost less than a dollar. In fact, most analysts rank computers with inventions like the steam engine and electric light in terms of immediate, widespread, and continuous impact on business. And, to hear computer scientists talk, the developments of the next decade will be even more impressive. All of which suggests that every prospective business manager should know something of how these impressive tools can be applied effectively.

Do Computers Think?

Even for a person who works with computers regularly, it's easy to give the computer credit for more than its fair share of intelligence. After all, computers do many of the same tasks that used to be done by armies of clerical workers. But it's important to remember that these capabilities have been painstakingly "taught" to the computer by a human programmer.

To get some idea of the still-gigantic difference between human intelligence and what the computer can do, take just one second to look about you. In that single second, just over the time it takes to blink your eyes, your brain has taken in enough visual information to fill hundreds of computer disks. And what you absorb visually is just a small portion of what your brain is actually taking in, assimilating, and integrating with previous experience.

Furthermore, computers (at this point at least) are capable of replicating only a very limited kind of human thinking. They can, for example, match words, numbers, and shapes. They can sort things from big to small or A to Z or 1 to 100 in some other logical, orderly, easily programmable fashion. They cannot, however, distinguish ugly from beautiful or clever from ordinary. They cannot, in other words, make judgments. Their "thought" processes are notably lacking in flexibility, creativity, and spontaneity. They can make only the choices they've been taught to make, using precisely the rules they've been programmed to use.

Fortunately, some tasks can be performed very well through the application of consistent, clear-cut rules, and therein lies the key to knowing when to rely on computers for help with business tasks. For example, suppose you are the loan manager for a bank. When an applicant comes in for a loan to purchase a new automobile, a computer can use her current salary, length of employment, outstanding debts, and other important criteria to decide whether she'll likely be a good risk. Now, if the computer approves her loan but she later defaults, has the computer made a mistake? Not really. The true responsibility rests with the people who made up the guidelines that the computer used, guidelines that will have to be revised if there are too many problems. But to the extent that the guidelines are effective, the computer can apply them consistently and fairly to everyone. Whether you get a car loan will depend not on your race, sex, hair color, or an uncle who works at the bank, but on the appropriate predetermined criteria.

Business Forecasting

If computers can't really think, you would hardly think they could predict the future. But they can—in a way. The concept is called *business forecasting*, and it can be a very helpful tool if used with caution and perhaps a little skepticism.

Business forecasting is a process that takes advantage of the computer's power to identify patterns and analyze sets of variables too complex to convey meaning to even the most logical and inquiring human mind. Suppose that Marichal is director of marketing and sales for a large national advertising company with clients in every major industry. Marichal has helped make his agency successful largely because he has an excellent track record at predicting which sorts of products will sell and to which groups. He has, in fact, developed a reputation throughout the industry for anticipating consumer needs as well as for forecasting the demise of products whose popularity is on the wane.

Perhaps it isn't all instinct, however. Nor is it luck. Marichal's professional secret may be the astute use of computerized business forecasting. Instead of sitting down with other staff to list out all the factors that could determine the fate of this year's hot products, Marichal and his colleagues do the work with computers. They don't have to rely on their own capacity to sort things out. They think of all of the factors that might influence marketing success and sales growth—things like the state of the economy in general, regional economic health, shifts in employment, identified needs within the target population, price fluctuations, shifts in the size of the market—and feed that information into a computer.

The program takes that information and looks for trends and *correlations*—mathematical connections between different variables. Perhaps car sales go up and down in relation to employment rates, or perhaps the price of bonds drops when interest rates climb. The computer can often find correlations in data sets too big or too complicated for humans to sort through. But simply finding the correlations is not enough to qualify as forecasting.

Forecasting is essentially a process of using history to predict the probability of certain business trends or events. How well this works with a computer depends on several factors, not the least of which is the user's thoroughness in entering all relevant data. This implies first that a user like Marichal must be well versed in all the relevant statistical information, and second that he or she must use considerable expertise in determining which information is most important. The computer's software may provide some guidance here, but final decisions still rest with the user.

The programs used for forecasting vary enormously in complexity. Some are simple, menu-driven packages that even beginning computer users may find relatively easy to work with, provided they have access to the business information required. Others are sophisticated enough for use by professional forecasters, but even these are not so esoteric as to rule out use by the business person. And there is a whole layer of complexity above this; professional economists, actuaries, demographers, and statisticians often use extremely complex software running on mainframe computers to make their predications. But even their programs differ more in sophistication than in concept.

But regardless of the details, every business person should know that computers can play an important part in helping to make sense of, and generate accurate predictions from, available business data. The use and sophistication of forecasting programs is likely to continue to grow, and shrewd business managers may want to have this tool available.

Yield Management— Another Computerized Forecasting Technique

Another way computers are changing the face of business is by making *yield management* possible. Yield management is a concept used most frequently—and successfully—in airline bookings and hotel and motel reservations. In simplest terms, its goal is to assure that profits are maximized by balancing the percent of rooms or seats filled against the amount of profit made on each one.

Let's look at a simple example. If an airline sold coast-to-coast plane tickets for $1, it's likely that every seat on every flight would be filled. On the other hand, if every seat were offered only at full fare, many times — the majority of times, in fact — planes would leave with a lot of empty seats. Some travelers would, of course, be in a situation where they had to pay whatever the airline charged because they *had* to make the trip. But for most others, the need to travel is at least somewhat price-sensitive.

A yield management system uses past information to determine the prices for tickets and rooms on a given day or flight. That historical information will show that factors such as day of the week, season of the year, holidays, conventions, and so on influence just how much demand can be expected. If demand at the full price is expected to be low — as it would be, for instance, at a business hotel on Friday and Saturday nights — rates will be dropped. But if a special event is in town and every room will likely be sold out, demand will be high, which means prices will be kept high.

In much the same way as business forecasting tries to use correlations to predict what might happen in the future, yield management tries to identify the factors that will help set the optimal price. All this might theoretically be done manually, but in practice, the amount of data to be recorded and examined is too large to handle without a computer. Consider that an airline with a modest 100 flights per day has to decide on pricing on each of those flights; that could result in as many as *36,000* sets of prices in a year.

What's more, a good yield management system is continually monitoring itself. The computer doesn't say, "Well, I don't think there will be much demand for rooms on this night a year from now, so let's drop the rate and keep it there." Instead, the computer has a record of when reservations are typically received and from what types of clients. If, for whatever reason, there's an above-average number of early reservations for business travelers willing to pay the higher rates, the computer will adjust and say, "Let's hold up on those deep-discount rooms; it looks like there are more people than expected ready to pay the higher price."

The widespread use of yield management has produced some interesting situations. At any given time, there are thousands of different fares for trips on U.S. airlines, and fare information now has to be updated daily. Six people sitting in the same row of an airline may have paid six different prices for their tickets. Similarly, you might call a hotel twice to ask the rate for a room and get two different answers. Usually, it's not because the reservation clerks are confused; it's because the room rates have actually changed between calls. As you can see, none of this complexity could be dealt with without a computer.

But while the sophistication of yield management techniques is new, the underlying concept isn't as innovative as it might sound at first. For example, a department store's after-Christmas sale could be viewed as a type of yield management activity. The store says, "Let's lower the price of tinsel; we'll take less on each box, but we'll sell a lot more of them." Business in general doesn't just set one price and wait for the business to flow in. Rather, each business tries to price its products or services at a level that keeps total and per-item profitability in balance. Yield management, though, is a particularly systematic and refined approach to pricing — and it's all made possible by the power of the computer.

Deciding What to Computerize

Forecasting is one of the more intriguing uses of computers in business, but it's only one possibility among hundreds. Reasonably priced computer programs are available to manage the customer lists, keep the company books, track the inventory, and even answer the telephone. But there are millions of businesses in the United States and no two are exactly alike. Given that the implementation of a computerized system — whether it be for word processing, database management, accounting, electronic publishing, or whatever — is a fairly major expense in terms of dollars, time, and effort, how should a wise business person approach computerization?

Certainly not by automatically computerizing everything. Capability must be balanced against need. Such common-sense advice seems hardly to bear repeating, but computerization seems to offer its own seductive allure. After all, what business wouldn't want to present itself as modern, efficient, up-to-date, and progressive? A computer on every desk may seem to offer the desired amount of window dressing to turn potential clients' heads. Technology for its own sake has rarely proved worthwhile, however, especially in business.

A skillful business manager can tell whether declining sales are more likely due to reduction in product quality, lack of staff motivation, or inability to keep track of customers' orders efficiently. Two of these three probably can't be fixed by computerization, but a jumbled-up order system probably could. Obviously, knowing what computers can and cannot do is a critical part of judging what role they might play in your business.

That's not to say that computers aren't sometimes bought impulsively or with only a vague idea of how they might help the business. They often are. But not by good managers, who instead make decisions about using computers for a given task by asking questions like these:

- ☐ Will computerizing the task enhance our profitability?

- ☐ Will we enjoy our work more?

- ☐ Do we have the expertise (or potential for expertise) to make good use of what computers can do?

- ☐ How will our work be different?

- ☐ What work will we be able to give up?

- ☐ What new responsibilities can we take on with the additional time available?

- ☐ What costs will we incur?

- ☐ From the day we plug in the computers, how long will we need to wait before we see a real improvement in efficiency?

- ☐ What can we do — and what will we need to do — to get staff ready for this change?

- ☐ Will computerizing the task put us in a more competitive position? How about five years from now? Ten years from now?

Computerization clearly has much to offer the business person whose optimism is well grounded in reality. Our advice is that you try to develop a good feel for what computers can and cannot do in a business setting and then examine each major business task to truly determine where involving a computer can be cost-effective.

You can walk into almost any stationery store and pick up a columnar pad that lets you construct a lined grid with horizontal rows and vertical columns. You might, for instance, use such a pad to keep a record of your personal business expenses from month to month. Across the top, at the head of each column, you'd list the names of the months: January, February, and so on. Down the side you'd list kinds of expenses: mileage, business lunches, books, seminars, supplies, gifts, etc. Your columnar pad is a modest, noncomputerized version of a *spreadsheet*.

In both printed and computerized versions, a spreadsheet consists of rows and columns containing interrelated information. The columns are often lettered and the rows numbered (or vice versa). The points at which rows and columns intersect are called *cells*, and you can reference the cells by using the column letter and row number — Cell F13, for example. Each cell has a unique definition; that is, it contains information contained nowhere else within the spreadsheet. For example, to continue with our personal business expenses illustration, one cell within your columnar pad might contain mileage for January, another business lunch totals for April, and another the money spent on gifts during December.

A spreadsheet is much more than a collection of raw numbers, though. The columns, rows, and cells provide a handy way to refer to groups of information. This structure can be very useful for discussing the information, but it's even more helpful when it comes time to relate one group of data to another. Suppose, for example, that the business mileage figures on your handwritten spreadsheet are in Row P and you've figured out that the actual cost of driving your car is 21.4 cents per mile. Simply place the 21.4 figure in a cell (let's say Cell D4), and then you can say that you'll find the mileage costs for each month by multiplying the figures in Row P by those in Cell D4.

A spreadsheet on a computer is not much different from its paper and pencil version. Picture a grid comprising numerous columns and rows of numbers, all somehow interrelated. Just like its paper counterpart, a computer spreadsheet grid can represent a budget, or employee data, or student records, or basketball statistics, or any of a thousand other things that can be concisely and logically expressed using numbers.

A computerized spreadsheet is more than a place to store numerical data, however. It offers a special feature, a capability that immediately appeals to anyone who has ever spent long, tedious hours hunched over a calculator. It can perform mathematical calculations automatically and not on just one number at a time but on whole sets of numbers, in seconds. How important is that capability?

Well, if you were told to calculate your company's income for the coming year and you knew it was projected to increase by 10 percent, you could easily perform the calculation on scratch paper, or even in your head. But suppose your company sells lead weights and you have to find the volumes of over 100 different spherical weights. How many times will you multiply 1.333 times 3.14159 times the cube of the radius (the formula for the volume of a sphere) before you wish you sold something else instead? You could give that formula once to the spreadsheet program and it would perform all 100 calculations in seconds. Not only would it ease the pain in your neck, but you'd have the data you needed much faster and without the inevitable errors. More data, better organization, simpler calculations, no waiting. No wonder the business community stood up and cheered when computerized spreadsheets made their debut.

Spreadsheets: What Are They?

Computerizing the Spreadsheet

An Example of Spreadsheet Use

Picture yourself in charge of putting together a budget for a large construction project on which your company wants to submit a bid. Let's say the project involves designing a new sports stadium for the community. The budget is complex. You'll need to account for the time of more than 500 workers, including architects, drafters, engineers, construction supervisors, subcontractors, and a host of others. Suppose you spend three weeks putting the budget together, only to find that your supervisor isn't happy with the final figure. Unless you lower it, he protests, your company will not stand a chance of landing the contract.

"It's very simple," he tells you. "We'll just cut the square footage in the bleacher seating area by 10 percent. Just redo the budget with that one small change, and let me know when you've got the new figures." But is that a small change? Not at all.

Consider what's involved: First, there are the building materials — not just the seats themselves, but concrete, steel supports and reinforcements, nuts and bolts, paint and sealers, and so forth. Then there are reduced labor costs; the salaries and benefits of the workers constructing the bleachers will be less. But the drafters putting together the final drawings will have to rework the design, and an engineer will have to approve the revision; all this will cost, not save, money. And perhaps other portions of the total design will be affected, too, making it necessary to have other parts of the plans reviewed to ensure that changes do not violate local building codes. One change leads to another, and any budget figure is often dependent on one or more others.

Now let's say you have to redo the stadium budget by hand (knowing all the while that your boss is impatiently awaiting the results of your computations). It is likely to take you many hours, even if you have the help of a powerful calculator. Will everything be accurate? Perhaps — if you're very good at math, if you recheck all your figures, and if you don't forget anything (such as the fact that you'll now have room for one less concession stand under the smaller bleachers).

But there's another problem, one that can seriously affect your ability to render a competitive bid. Your extensive time investment in revising the budget may lock you into a decision you won't be happy with later. Suppose that just as you're reaching the end of your calculations, the boss has a brainstorm: "I've got it," he tells you exultantly. "Instead of cutting down on the bleacher area, we'll cut back on the grandstand roof, so we only put half of those seats under cover."

You like the idea at once. Unfortunately, you no longer have three days in which to make calculations. You have to have your bid in final form within 24 hours or you won't get your submission in on time. So you go with the smaller-bleachers budget because that's already completed. All too often, real-world decisions are influenced heavily by cost and time constraints. If the data were already in a computerized spreadsheet, however, you could come up with several new alternatives each day, and you could figure out the implications of each in a timely manner and with no undue stress.

Answering "What If" Questions

This ability to change some of the figures and have the computer automatically recalculate all the related figures is extremely useful. If you systematically change one set of numbers and then observe the effect of the change on other numbers, you can quickly examine a wide variety of alternate situations.

This approach is sometimes called "what if." For example, a spread-sheet can quickly tell you what the implications are if:

- [ ] all employees receive a 5 percent pay raise,

- [ ] each mid-level manager devotes one less staff day to a project,

- [ ] sales of a product drop 10 percent, as projected,

- [ ] property taxes rise by 3 percent,

- [ ] base prices of all new cars already in inventory are dropped 7 percent, or

- [ ] working hours are decreased from 40 to 37.5 per week.

In other words, you can change any figure within the data set and see how that change affects all other figures. In real life, numbers aren't static. They change continually. Spreadsheets allow you to deal with actual changes for the present and projected changes for the future. And the number of different things that can be profitably analyzed with a spread-sheet is very impressive.

For better or worse, though, a computer-based spreadsheet program doesn't provide any real guidance about which of the myriad things that *can* be analyzed *should* be analyzed. What you see on the screen are empty rows and columns. In the realm of computer software, a spreadsheet program is probably as close to a blank slate as you can come. That is to say, the program consists primarily of the *capability* to manipulate and change data. But you must put the data in yourself, and you must teach the program how one entry relates to another.

For example, let's say that you are using spreadsheets to keep track of sales. You have a 40 percent markup over wholesale price on certain items and a 30 percent markup on others. You can give the program these relationships and feed in the wholesales prices, and it will automatically calculate the retail price of each item for you. As we mentioned, you do not have to specify the relationship of every item. You tell the program the formula once and tell it which figures are affected (e.g., everything in cells B1 through B148 has a 40 percent markup), and all prices in those 148 cells will be figured at once.

We've talked about budgets and cost calculations, but the business applications of computer spreadsheets are virtually limitless. This may sound like hyperbole, but it's not really. The variety of tasks commonly conducted with spreadsheets is very broad and includes:

Potential Applications of Spreadsheets

- [ ] inventory management,

- [ ] cash flow analysis,

- [ ] sales records and projections,

- [ ] profit analysis,

- [ ] investment projections,

- [ ] financial planning,

- [ ] amortizations of mortgage payments or insurance benefit payments,

- [ ] tax preparation,

    □ scheduling of workers and equipment,

    □ quality control analysis,

    □ performance records (for everything from regional sales offices to the company bowling league),

    □ engineering design, and

    □ scientific recordkeeping.

In fact, virtually anyone who deals with numbers on a daily basis has potential use for spreadsheets. Countless businesses routinely make use of spreadsheets to manage employee records, track expenses, project sales, or otherwise manage data effectively. A good business manager will consistently consider the advantages of computerized spreadsheets and the ways in which they can provide the information to make sound decisions.

A calculator can do many of the same mathematical calculations that a spreadsheet program excels at. But spreadsheets work particularly well in two kinds of situations. First, a spreadsheet is helpful if you have a lot of calculations to do, even though each calculation may be quite simple.

Then again, suppose your calculations are complex, perhaps involving several steps. For example, let's suppose you have to figure sales tax on the items in your retail store. Sales tax is 6 percent. OK, you say, that doesn't sound too difficult. But what if not everything is subject to sales tax? If you do the calculations by hand, you'll need to screen every item individually. If you use a spreadsheet program, you can tell the program what characteristics to look for (e.g., a specific letter in the stock number or what department the product is sold by) and it can screen the items, figure out what markup applies, determine retail price, and calculate the 6 percent sales tax—all within a few seconds. Now suppose your inventory consists of 243 different items (a very small inventory by retail business standards). How long will it take you to do the same task using your calculator? Perhaps long enough to pay for a spreadsheet program the first time it's used.

Using a Business Calculator

There's a tendency among some people to consider calculators as a sort of poor relation to the computer. This is unfortunate, although perhaps understandable, and every business person should have a good idea of just what a business calculator can do.

We say that a negative view of calculators might be understandable for a couple of reasons. First, there are a lot of people whose only contact is with the basic calculators that do the basic arithmetic operations but nothing more. These calculators, which usually cost $20 or less, are incredibly useful, but they don't help much in some of the more complex business math problems. Someone who knows only about these calculators might be tempted to think that's all a calculator can do.

Then there are people who know how useful a small computer can be and can't imagine that a calculator could do anything nearly as useful. There's a conceptual difference, however, that needs to be considered. A computer can do hundreds of different things; the same computer used for word processing in the morning can be doing a spreadsheet in the afternoon. That's because the computer can run different programs. Most calculators, on the other hand, have exactly the same capabilities when you turn them on. The question, though, is whether those built-in capabilities are the ones you need.

Often, they will be. The average hand-held business calculator costing perhaps $50 can figure out present and future values, calculate payments and interest rates on loans and annuities, amortize loans, and compare the results of different investment opportunities. Remember all of the tables that you had to use when working compound interest, annuity, and sinking fund problems? The equivalent information is available from a business calculator with just a couple of keystrokes. All in all, if the problem you have to solve is covered by the calculator's built-in functions, a solution is near at hand.

Of course, you might say that all of these things can easily be done by a computer running the correct software. That's entirely correct. But there are no $50 computers, let alone $50 computers that come complete with keyboards, display screens, and software. And while it's no longer true that you can't fit a computer into a briefcase, it's still hard to imagine a banker or broker pulling out a computer at lunch to analyze quickly how a deal is shaping up.

The easiest way to investigate whether a business calculator can make a substantial improvement in your efficiency is to look over the operations manual for one you might consider buying. The manual will discuss the different types of problems that can be solved; if the problems are ones that you face regularly, the calculator might be a good investment.

Other Computerization Possibilities

While a spreadsheet is perhaps the computer application most closely related to business mathematics, it's certainly not the only one. For example, we mentioned in the last lesson how helpful computers can be in making up charts and graphs of business data. And computerized business accounting programs are widely used to track accounts payable and receivables and to prepare invoices. Most of this software can even be used to prepare income statements and balance sheets.

When it's time to pay employees for their work, payroll management software can greatly speed up the process. And when it's time to pay governments their taxes, computer tax calculation programs are used. Indeed, the use of computers for payroll recordkeeping is so advantageous and so widespread that the Internal Revenue Service now requires that large businesses deliver their tax accounting records in computer-readable form.

And while many people don't rely on their database management programs for performing math calculations, many database managers have a set of math functions built in that can perform some rudimentary computations. Even more important, however, is the ability of most database management programs to select a subset of the database using some specific criteria and then transfer those data to a spreadsheet for further analysis. For example, the database could be used to identify the payroll records for all employees at salary levels 12, 13, and 14, then a spreadsheet could be used to determine the net effect on salaries, benefits, taxes, and cash flows of giving each of these employees a raise of a specified amount.

In summary, it's perhaps best just to point out that the computer has gone from being a rarity to being an essential tool for business people at all levels and in all industries, which means that every business manager needs to know something of what computers can do. In the same way that you'd certainly expect a manager know that there were trucking companies available to ship the business's goods to market, modern business people can legitimately be expected to know just what computers and calculators can add to a business's efficiency.

SOME WORDS OF ADVICE

It's difficult to hit a happy balance when discussing computers in business. Thousands of managers have become overly enamored with computers, applying them to tasks that were more effectively handled by hand or with calculators. On the other hand, thousands more have resisted computerization, dooming their businesses to unnecessary inefficiency and expense.

Fortunately, the majority of businesses have hit the nail pretty close to the head. Those who suffered through the early days of small computers may, in fact, marvel at how straightforward things have gotten in recent years. The computers generally work as expected, the software is considerably more powerful and less quirky, and almost everything costs less than it did. All things considered, there's good reason for business people to be bullish about the possibilities of computerization.

When thinking about modern-day business mathematics, it's virtually impossible to ignore spreadsheets as a potential tool. A properly set up spreadsheet can provide literally a hundredfold increase in productivity on certain types of tasks, an increase that is too big to overlook. But potentially even more profitable is the ability to look at different alternative solutions to any business problem. This "what if" feature makes it truly possible to select from the best of many alternatives instead of settling for the one that happens to get the big investment of time early on.

Finally, keep in mind that for numerous types of business computations, especially those involving compound interest, a hand-held business calculator is often less expensive, and sometimes even preferable to a computer. Given the relatively low cost, there's likely no reason to rely on compound interest tables and hand computations when there are more than a handful of problems to solve.

KEY TERMS

Before you read through the text assignment and watch the video program, take a minute to look at the key terms associated with this lesson. When you encounter them in the text and video program, pay careful attention to their meaning.

Cell: The small portion of a spreadsheet formed by the intersection of a row and a column. A cell contains one single piece of data and is often referenced by a letter and a number (e.g., B3).

Correlation: A relationship between two quantities where a change in one is mathematically related to the change in the other. Finding correlations is a critical part of business forecasting.

Forecasting: When related to computers, an application where large amounts of historical data are analyzed to find trends and correlations, which are then used to predict what might happen in the future.

Spreadsheet: On a computer, an application where data entered into columns and rows can be interrelated so that changes in one piece of data are reflected in the interconnected data. (The term also refers to the paper and pencil version.)

PART II: WATCHING THE VIDEO PROGRAM

_____ **VIDEO VIEWING GUIDE**

Before watching the video program, review the following questions. As you watch, be sure to collect the information necessary to answer them:

1. Do you agree or disagree with the assertion "Computers are overrated as a factor in increased business productivity. Most of the time they don't make any useful contribution."?

2. Name several business contexts in which spreadsheets are likely to be used.

3. What specific advantages can come from using a computerized spreadsheet? How, if at all, do these advantages show up in a business's bottom line?

4. What does it mean to ask "what if" questions of a spreadsheet? Do you see this as a major or a minor feature of a spreadsheet?

5. Besides spreadsheets, what are some of the math-related computer applications that are commonly used in business?

6. When might a hand-held calculator be almost as valuable as a computer for solving business problems? Are there times when it might be more valuable?

7. What additional advances in computer technology might be expected during the next few years? Will these likely produce much change in the way business mathematics is done? Why or why not?

_____ **VIDEO PROGRAM**

The lesson's video program is Program 26 — The Future of Business Mathematics. Remember, if you are watching this program on videotape, take time to replay sections of the tape any time you need to review a concept.

_____ **VIDEO VIEWING QUESTIONS**

Immediately after viewing the video program for Lesson 26, take time to respond to the following questions. Give your answers some careful thought; they may provide the basis for additional discussions or a longer written response.

1. Give two examples you know of where use of a computer has significantly improved productivity.

   a. _____

   b. _____

2. Now give two examples you know of where using computers did not improve, and may even have hurt, the business.

   a. _____

   b. _____

3. Suppose a friend told you that her boss had decided her colleagues were all getting their own microcomputers and a spreadsheet program. However, she is skeptical that much of an improvement will come from this purchase. What kinds of questions would you ask to decide whether she is right to be concerned or whether the computers are likely to bring a considerable improvement?

   _____

   _____

   _____

4. Imagine that your household is a business and that it has a microcomputer with a spreadsheet. Think of three tasks that could be efficiently performed with a spreadsheet.

   a. _____

   b. _____

   c. _____

5. Suppose you encountered someone who simply didn't believe that there was any way to predict what might happen in the future, no matter how much information you collected. Using the idea of a correlation, give an example that might help convince this person that some predictions are indeed warranted.

   _____

   _____

   _____

6. For each of the three types of programs listed below, think of one practical application for which you might put that program to good use in a business you know. Be specific. If, for example, you think you might use a program in generating a report, state what kind of report, name the general audience for it, and describe, in broad terms, what some of the content might be.

   Accounting: _____

   _____

   Database management: _____

   _____

   Forecasting: _____

   _____

7. Your cousin recently got a hand-held business calculator as a present and is wondering whether to take the time to learn how to use it. List two questions that you might ask to determine what advice you should give.

   a. _____

   b. _____

PART III: FOCUSING ON THE MATHEMATICS

_____READING ASSIGNMENT AND KEY FORMULAS

This lesson on the future of business math does not have either a reading assignment or any key formulas. However, given that this is the end of the course and you likely have an examination coming up, it might be wise to use the time to review the Key Formulas sections of the previous lessons in order to see how well you remember these critical concepts.

PART IV: SOLVING BUSINESS PROBLEMS

_____PROBLEM SETS

Since there is no reading assignment associated with this lesson, there are also no problems to be worked. However, your instructor may choose to assign a set of review exercises that will help you review what you do and don't remember from the previous lessons.

_____ BUSINESS APPLICATIONS

Read each of the following scenarios and answer the questions about the decisions you would make in each situation. Give these questions some serious thought; they may be used as the basis for discussion or the development of a more complex essay. You should base your decisions on what you've learned from this lesson, applying both math skills and good business judgment to solve the problem at hand.

SCENARIO 1

Davis is a building contractor whose firm specializes in home construction and remodeling. Davis is familiar with computer-based spreadsheets and has even worked with them from time to time, though he has not purchased one for his own business. He feels now, however, that a spreadsheet could be of great benefit in the firm's everyday calculations, and he is interested in a program that will help him and his staff assemble the best possible bids for housing or remodeling projects. If it works well, Davis thinks, it might be one step that would take the firm closer to expanding. After all, efficiency is the key to success.

"The thing is," Davis explains, "our calculations are particularly complex because the data are so elusive—it's like you just can't quite get hold of them. Almost every day, some cost shifts. Or some material becomes unavailable and we have to substitute something else. Here we are trying to come up with an estimate that makes sense, and before we can even get to the bottom line, some of our information has become outdated. We've got to get faster, and we need the flexibility of making projections based on different scenarios—what if the cost of roofing tile goes up 12 percent, for example? It would also be handy to know how we need to budget costs to come out with a 15 percent profit margin; we've had trouble narrowing those figures down as well."

Davis is also interested in graphics. "Just something practical," he explains. "We're not making fancy presentations, so we don't need anything dazzling. But I figure that sometimes—even with your own staff—if you want to get a point across, it's a lot easier to do if you've got a graphic summary than if you're looking at a whole page full of figures. Know what I mean?"

But Davis's enthusiasm is tempered by two concerns. The first is the bad experience that some of his competitors have had. "Those guys over at Judson Construction lost their shirts on a bid when the spreadsheet made a mistake and they put in way too little for concrete. I wouldn't want anything that I couldn't trust to give us the right answer." The second is the amount of time learning the software would take. "I'd really like something that's relatively easy to use. We haven't got weeks that we can stop everything else and sit down and learn this program. I want something we can learn without investing weeks of time and energy."

What do you think? Based on the information contained in the scenario, do you think Davis should proceed with getting a computer-based spreadsheet and a graphics program in his work? Is he right to think that these programs will make a significant difference in his business?

- Should Davis buy the computer-based spreadsheet program? Why or why not? If you recommend he buy it, what are the major features he should look for?

- To what extent, if at all, might Davis be disappointed with what a spreadsheet program can do? What advice might you give him about "reasonable expectations?"

- Davis mentions getting a graphics program, but he treats it almost as an afterthought. Should he buy the graphics program at all? If you recommend he buy it, should he wait until he sees how the spreadsheet works?

- Davis mentions that at Judson Construction "the spreadsheet made a mistake." Comment on the accuracy of this perception.

- Suppose for the moment that Davis proceeds with purchasing the spreadsheet program. How do you recommend he decide if it was, in fact, a sensible purchase?

Myrtle's Freshest Flowers, a small flower shop in the old area of downtown, has always been run just exactly as Myrtle Nevis wanted it run. Sole proprietor and the only staff of the shop, she ran the business rather flexibly, to put it mildly. If Myrtle wanted a day off, the shop was closed; if she wanted to hang around the shop a little longer, hours were extended. (This somewhat quaint approach appeals to a certain segment of the town, which patronizes Myrtle's in spite of the inconvenience.)

Myrtle's methods for keeping track of inventory and shipments are equally relaxed. When she runs out of a certain flower, she just doesn't make any arrangements that use that flower. Myrtle couldn't tell you anything about how many flowers she used in a given period or what they cost. Nor could she even tell you what she sold during the period.

One of the few things keeping Myrtle in business is that her son Jim takes care of what passes for the company books, making sure that tax returns are filed and keeping track of the checking account. It also helps that Myrtle does all of her sales on a cash basis. Nevertheless, her son is concerned.

"One small computer with an easy-to-use spreadsheet would do wonders," he claims. "A computer's no big deal these days, Mom, and getting one doesn't mean you have to change the way you do business. You can still stay open late sometimes and close sometimes, and you can still do all the business by cash. But with a minimal investment of money, time, and energy, we can get a much better understanding of where the business money comes from and goes."

But Myrtle's daughter disagrees with her brother's advice. "Leave her alone, Jim. Everything is going along fine with nothing but a $10 calculator. Just what big advantage do you think a new computer would bring? My guess is that a computer would just goof things up!"

What do you think? Is Myrtle's Freshest Flowers in need of computerization? Or is Myrtle's daughter right in thinking that in spite of its idiosyncrasies, the flower shop is doing just fine and a computer would have a negative effect?

□ Whose advice should Myrtle take? What is the single biggest reason for your answer?

□ Jim may have a point about the advantages of having a computer, but most computer experts would say that his analysis was pretty sketchy. What are some of the major factors Jim didn't consider?

□ Jim talked about getting a spreadsheet, but is this the best type of application for Myrtle to start with? Why or why not?

□ What about her daughter's comment that everything is going fine "with a $10 calculator"? Is that statement true? If not, is it a matter of more technology or is there another solution?

□ Name five pieces of new information Myrtle might get using a computerized spreadsheet. Which, if any, of that information is available without a computer?

□ There's one factor that many people—including, perhaps, Jim—often forget when considering a computerized record-keeping or analysis system of any kind: the amount of effort it takes to keep the information up to date. How might this potential problem affect the advice you gave in Question 1?

SCENARIO 2

APPENDIX A

A.1 Distribution of Profits and Losses in a Partnership

1. Divide profits (in a partnership) by equal shares.
2. Divide profits (in a partnership) by agreed ratio.
3. Divide profits (in a partnership) by original investment.
4. Divide profits (in a partnership) by salary and agreed ratio.
5. Divide profits (in a partnership) by interest on investment and agreed ratio.

In a partnership, a business is owned by two or more people. These partners may have invested equal amounts of money to start the business, or one may have invested money while the other invested specialized knowledge. The partners must agree on the relative amounts of money and time that will be invested in the business. They must also agree on the method by which any profits will be distributed. This section considers the various methods by which partnership profits may be distributed.

The partners may simply agree to share all profits equally. (In fact, if there is no formal agreement stating the terms under which profits are to be divided, most states require that profits be divided equally.)

1. Divide profits by equal shares

Three partners opened a music store, and agreed to divide the profits equally. If the store produced profits of $57,000 in one year, each partner would get

Example 1

$$\frac{1}{3} \times \$57,000 = \$19,000$$

as the annual share of the profits. • •

Partners may agree to divide the profits using some given rule. For example, two partners might agree that profits will be divided so that 60% goes to one partner and 40% to the other. Profit divisions are sometimes given as a ratio; this division could be written 60:40, or in a reduced form, 3:2, with profits said to be divided in an **agreed ratio**.

2. Divide profits by agreed ratio

Three partners divide the profits from a business in the ratio 2:3:5. How would profits of $47,500 be divided?

Example 2

Solution   The ratio 2:3:5 says that the profit should be divided into 2 + 3 + 5 = 10 equal shares. The first partner gets 2 of these 10 shares, or

$$\frac{2}{10} \times \$47,500 = \$9.500.$$

The second partner gets 3 of the 10 equal shares, or

$$\frac{3}{10} \times \$47,500 = \$14,250.$$

Finally, the third partner gets 5 shares, or

$$\frac{5}{10} \times \$47,500 = \$23,750.$$

To check, the sum of the three shares, \$9,500 + \$14,250 + \$23,750, is the total profit, or \$47,500.   • •

3. Divide profits by original investment

A common way of dividing the profits is on the basis of the **original investments** made by each partner. The fraction of the total original investment supplied by each partner is used to find the fraction of the profit that each partner receives.

Example 3   Ed Porter, Fran Jones, and Wes Wilson formed a partnership. Porter contributed \$15,000, Jones \$20,000, and Wilson \$25,000. The three signed an agreement that profits would be distributed based on the original investment. If the firm made a profit of \$75,000, find the share received by each.

Solution   The total amount contributed to start the company was

$$\$15,000 + \$20,000 + \$25,000 = \$60,000.$$

Of this total, Porter gave

$$\frac{\$15,000}{\$60,000} = \frac{1}{4}.$$

Therefore, Porter is entitled to ¼ of the profits, or

$$\frac{1}{4} \times \$75,000 = \$18,750.$$

Jones gave

$$\frac{\$20,000}{\$60,000} = \frac{1}{3}$$

of the total, and gets ⅓ of the profits, or \$75,000 × ⅓ = \$25,000. Finally, Wilson gave

$$\frac{\$25,000}{\$60,000} = \frac{5}{12}$$

of the total, and gets 5⁄12 of the profits or

$$\frac{5}{12} \times \$75,000 = \$31,250.   • •$$

Suppose the firm in Example 3 had a loss of $36,000 in one year. Find the share of the loss that each partner must pay.

Example 4

Solution   Just as partners share profits, they may be called on to share losses. Here Porter must pay ¼ of the loss (see Example 3), or

$$\frac{1}{4} \times \$36,000 = \$9,000.$$

Jones must pay ⅓ of the loss, or $12,000, while Wilson must pay 5/12 of the loss, or $15,000.   • •

Sometimes one partner contributes money to get a business started, while a second partner contributes money and also operates the business on a daily basis. In such a case, the partner operating the business may be paid a salary out of profits, with any additional profits divided in some agreed-upon ratio, called dividing profits by **salary and agreed ratio**. As mentioned in the introduction to this chapter, a partner who makes only a financial investment, but takes no part in running the business, is a **silent partner**.

4. Divide profits by salary and agreed ratio

Lin Chao and Joan Frisk start a new dry-cleaning business. Frish contributed $50,000, while Chao contributed $25,000. The business will be run by Chao. The partners have agreed to pay Chao a salary of $14,000 per year, and then divide the remaining profits according to the original investment. Find the amount each partner would get from a profit of $26,000.

Example 5

Solution   The profit is first used to pay Chao's salary. Of the $26,000, Chao gets $14,000, leaving

$$
\begin{array}{ll}
\$26,000 & \text{total profit} \\
-\ 14,000 & \text{Chao's salary} \\
\hline
\$12,000 & \text{profit to be divided,}
\end{array}
$$

The balance of the profits will be divided in the ratio of the original investments, which total $50,000 + $25,000 = $75,000. Of this total, Chao contributed

$$\frac{\$25,000}{\$75,000} = \frac{1}{3},$$

and thus receives

$$\frac{1}{3} \times \$12,000 = \$4000.$$

Frisk receives the balance of the $12,000, or $8,000.
   In summary,

$$
\begin{array}{ll}
\$14,000 & \text{salary} \\
+\ 4,000 & \text{share of profits after salary} \\
\hline
\$18,000 & \text{total received by Chao.}
\end{array}
$$

Frisk receives only the $8,000.   • •

5. Divide profits by interest on investment and agreed ratio

Sometimes one partner will put up a large sum of the money necessary to start a firm, while other partners may actually operate the firm. In such a case, an agreement to divide profits by **interest on investment and agreed ratio** may be reached by which the partner putting up the money gets interest on the investment before any further division of profits.

Example 6   Laura Cameron, Jay Davis, and Donna Friedman opened a restaurant. Cameron contributes $125,000 to the opening of the restaurant, which will be operated by Davis and Friedman. The partners agree that Cameron will first receive a 10% return on her investment before any further division of profits. Additional profits will be divided in the ratio 1:2:2. Find the amount that each partner will receive from a profit of $50,000.

Solution   Cameron is first paid a 10% return on her investment of $125,000. This amounts to

$$\$125,000 \times 10\% = \$125,000 \times 0.10 = \$12,500.$$

This leaves an additional

$$
\begin{array}{ll}
\$50,000 & \text{total profit} \\
-\ 12,500 & \text{amount to Cameron} \\
\hline
\$37,500 & \text{to be divided.}
\end{array}
$$

The additional profit of $37,500 is to be divided in the ratio 1:2:2. First divide this amount into $1 + 2 + 2 = 5$ equal shares. Cameron gets 1 of these 5 shares, or

$$\frac{1}{5} \times \$37,500 = \$7,500.$$

Davis and Friedman each get 2 of the 5 shares, or

$$\frac{2}{5} \times \$37,500 = \$15,000.$$

In summary, Cameron gets

$$
\begin{array}{ll}
\$12,500 & \text{return on investment} \\
+\ 7,500 & \text{share of profit} \\
\hline
\$20,000 & \text{total to Cameron.}
\end{array}
$$

Both Davis and Friedman get $15,000.   ● ●

Example 7   Suppose the restaurant in Example 6 had a profit of only $8,500. What would be the distribution of this amount?

Solution   The partners agreed to give Cameron a 10% return, or $12,500. The profits were only $8,500, leaving a loss of

$$
\begin{array}{l}
\$12,500 \\
-\ 8,500 \\
\hline
\$\ 4,000.
\end{array}
$$

This loss of $4,000 will be shared in the ratio 1:2:2, just as were the profits. Cameron's share of the loss is

$$\frac{1}{5} \times \$4{,}000 = \$800,$$

while the share of both Davis and Friedman is

$$\frac{2}{5} \times \$4{,}000 = \$1{,}600.$$

Cameron gets $12,500, minus her share of the loss, or

$12,500	due to Cameron
− 800	her share of loss
$11,700	actually received by Cameron.

Davis and Friedman must each contribute $1,600 toward the loss. The $11,700 that Cameron actually receives is made up as follows.

$8,500	profit
1,600	from Davis
+ 1,600	from Friedman
$11,700	Total to Cameron • •

Divide the following profits. Round all answers to the nearest dollar.

A.1 EXERCISES

	Partners	Investment	Method	Profits
1.	1	$12,500	Equal shares	$72,000
	2	$15,000		
	3	$18,200		
2.	1	$16,000	Ratio 3:5	$120,000
	2	$20,000		
3.	1	$25,000	Ratio of investment	$90,000
	2	$75,000		
4.	1	$125,000	$25,000 salary to	$250,000
	2	$100,000	partner 2; balance	
	3	$80,000	divided 4:2:4	
5.	1	$70,000	10% return to	$60,000
	2	$20,000	partner 1; balance	
	3	$10,000	in ratio 1:4:5	
6.	1	$30,000	12% return to	$132,000
	2	$100,000	partner 2; balance	
	3	$20,000	in ratio of investment	
7.	1	$40,000	$8,000 salary to	$80,000
	2	$50,000	partner 1; $15,000	
	3	$60,000	salary to partner 2;	
			balance divided equally	

	Partners	Investment	Method	Profits
8.	1	$75,000	$20,000 salary to	$140,000
	2	$25,000	partner 2; 10% return	
	3	$50,000	to partner 3; balance	
			divided 3:1:1	
9.	1	$80,000	15% return to	$10,000
	2	$10,000	partner 1; balance	
	3	$40,000	divided in ratio 1:4:5	
10.	1	$200,000	12% return to	$20,000
	2	$50,000	partner 1; balance	
	3	$50,000	divided in ratio 2:4:4	

Work the following word problems.

11. Two partners make a profit of $32,000. If they have no agreement on dividing profits, find the share of the profits that each will get.

12. If five lawyers agree to divide their profits equally, find the share that each gets if the firm makes a profit of $144,000.

13. Three partners contribute $15,000, $40,000, and $65,000, respectively, to start a new company. Find the share that each gets if the profit is $80,000 and profits are divided in the ratio of the original investments.

14. Powell, Reedy, and Adams have started a new office supply firm. Powell contributed $120,000 to the firm, Reedy $80,000, and Adams $100,000. Find the division of a profit of $72,000 if profits are divided in the ratio of the original investment.

15. Four partners have agreed to divide profits in the ratio of 2:5:6:7. Find the division of a profit of $120,000.

16. Suppose the partners in Exercise 15 have a loss of $80,000. How much of the loss would be paid by each partner?

17. Mary Finch and Pete Renz have started a new travel agency. Finch will run the agency. She gets a $25,000 salary, with any additional profits distributed in the ratio 1:4. Find the distribution of a profit of $45,000.

18. Tom Pollack, Fred Scott, and Alice Neinken have started a new bookstore, to be run by Scott. He will get a salary of $17,000, with any additional profits divided in the ratio 3:1:2. Find the division of a profit of $53,000.

19. Bob Coker has invested $80,000 in a new hardware store. His partner, Will Toms, will actually run the store. The partners agree that Coker will get a 10% return on his investment, with any additional profits divided in the ratio 1:3. Find the division of profit of (a) $60,000 and (b) $6,000.

20. Wilma Dickson has invested $250,000 in a small electronics plant, to be run by her partner, John Ardery. They agree that she will receive a 15% return on her investment, and that any additional profits will be divided in the ratio 2:3. Divide a profit of (a) $90,000 and (b) $30,000.

21. Three partners invest $15,000, $25,000, and $30,000 in a business. The partners agree that partner 1 will receive a 10% return on investment, with partner 2 receiving a salary of $12,000. Any additional profits will be divided in the ratio of the original investments. Divide a profit of $110,000.

22. A plumbing wholesale business has three partners. Partner 1 invested $50,000 in the business, and is given a 10% return on investment. Partner 2 invested $75,000, and earns a 6% return on investment, plus a salary of $21,000. Partner 3 invested $100,000 and earns a 12% return on investment. Any additional profits are divided in the ratio 2:1:2. Divide a profit of $180,000.

A.2   Distribution of Overhead

1. Allocate overhead by floor space.
2. Allocate overhead by sales value.
3. Allocate overhead by number of employees.

Businesses have many expenses in addition to the cost of the materials and labor that are actually used to make a product. Rent on the factory building must be paid, insurance premiums and executive salaries must be paid, office supplies must be ordered, and so on. These general expenses, which cannot be avoided but which do not go directly for the production of goods and services, are called **overhead**. The cost of an office typewriter would come under overhead, while the cost of sheet metal used to actually make a product would not.

A company can usually decide on the total overhead expenses fairly quickly; however, a problem often comes up in dividing the overhead among the various products or lines of business of a company. Various methods are used by different firms to divide overhead. The choice of a method often depends on industry practice. In any case, the **allocation of overhead** is usually done by forming a ratio of each product or department to the total firm. There are several ways of forming this ratio.

Overhead can be allocated by department according to the **floor space** used by each department of the company.

1. Allocate overhead by floor space

Lindquist Press has three departments, with floor space as shown.

Example 1

Department	Floor Space
Magazine printing	50,000 square feet
Book printing	30,000 square feet
Catalog printing	20,000 square feet
Total	100,000 square feet

Allocate an overhead of $275,000.

Solution   The magazine printing department has a floor space of 50,000 square feet out of a total of 100,000 square feet. Therefore, this department is allocated

$$\frac{50,000}{100,000} = \frac{1}{2}$$

of the overhead, or

$$\frac{1}{2} \times \$275,000 = \$137,500.$$

When finding the expenses of this department, the company accountants would assign an overhead expense of $137,500 for the department.

The book printing department uses

$$\frac{30,000}{100,000} = \frac{3}{10}$$

of the floor space, and so would be allocated 3/10 of the overhead, or

$$\frac{3}{10} \times \$275,000 = \$82,500.$$

Finally, catalog printing would be allocated

$$\frac{20,000}{100,000} = \frac{1}{5}$$

of the overhead, or

$$\frac{1}{5} \times \$275,000 = \$55,000. \quad \bullet \ \bullet$$

2. Allocate overhead by sales value

It is common to allocate overhead according to the **sales value** of each department or product, as shown in the next example.

Example 2   Acco Hardware Manufacturing produces four products, with monthly production and value as shown.

Product	Production	Value of Each
Wheelbarrows	2,500	$40
Ladders	5,000	$25
Shovels	6,000	$10
Hammers	25,000	$3

Allocate an overhead of $50,000.

Solution   First find the total value of each item.

Product	Production	Value of Each	Total Value
Wheelbarrows	2,500	$40	2,500 × $40 = $100,000
Ladders	5,000	$25	5,000 × $25 = $125,000
Shovels	6,000	$10	6,000 × $10 = $60,000
Hammers	25,000	$3	25,000 × $3 = $75,000
		Total	$360,000

Of the total value of $360,000, wheelbarrows produced $100,000. Therefore, the fraction

$$\frac{\$100,000}{\$360,000} = \frac{5}{18}$$

of the total overhead must be applied to wheelbarrows. The total overhead
is $50,000 so

$$\frac{5}{18} \times \$50,000 = \$13,888.89$$

must be applied to wheelbarrows. Also,

$$\frac{\$125,000}{\$360,000} \times \$50,000 = \frac{25}{72} \times \$50,000 = \$17,361.11$$

of overhead will be applied to ladders, and

$$\frac{\$60,000}{\$360,000} \times \$50,000 = \frac{1}{6} \times \$50,000 = \$8,333.33$$

to shovels. Finally,

$$\frac{\$75,000}{\$360,000} \times \$50,000 = \$10,416.67$$

is applied to hammers. Check that the sum of the various allocated over-
heads is the total overhead of $50,000.   • •

*3. Allocate overhead by
number of employees*

Overhead can also be allocated by the number of employees associated
with a department or product.

Example 3

Allocate an overhead of $12,000 to each department according to the num-
ber of employees in the department.

Solution Form a ratio of the number of employees in the department to
the total number of employees.

Department	Number of Employees	Ratio of Employees	Overhead of Department
1	7	$\frac{7}{20}$	$\frac{7}{20} \times \$12,000 = \$4,200$
2	2	$\frac{2}{20}$	$\frac{2}{20} \times \$12,000 = \$1,200$
3	5	$\frac{5}{20}$	$\frac{5}{20} \times \$12,000 = \$3,000$
4	6	$\frac{6}{20}$	$\frac{6}{20} \times \$12,000 = \$3,600$
	Total 20		Total $12,000

• •

A.2 EXERCISES

Allocate overhead as indicated. Round to the nearest dollar.

1.

Department	Floor Space
A	2,000 square feet
B	3,000 square feet
C	10,000 square feet

Overhead: $12,000

2.

Department	Floor Space
A	32,000 square feet
B	57,000 square feet
C	11,000 square feet

Overhead: $280,000

3.

Department	Floor Space
1	6,200 square feet
2	7,200 square feet
3	6,800 square feet
4	9,800 square feet

Overhead: $76,000

4.

Department	Floor Space
1	6,200 square feet
2	14,200 square feet
3	31,900 square feet
4	4,100 square feet

Overhead: $360,000

5.

Product	Number Produced	Value of Each
M	10,000	$15.00
N	20,000	$5.00
P	40,000	$2.50

Overhead: $21,875

6.

Product	Number Produced	Value of Each
X	5,000	$20
Y	8,000	$25
Z	4,000	$50

Overhead: $62,500

7.

Product	Number Produced	Value of Each
1	60	$7
2	250	$12
3	80	$20
4	120	$10

Overhead: $8,000

8.

Product	Number Produced	Value of Each
1	150	$6
2	200	$12
3	75	$3
4	125	$8

Overhead: $10,000

9.

Department	Number of Employees
A	200
B	500
C	300

Overhead: $80,000

10.

Department	Number of Employees
J	1,000
K	7,000
L	2,000

Overhead: $900,000

11.

Department	Number of Employees
1	70
2	90
3	15
4	25

Overhead: $90,000

12.

Department	Number of Employees
1	80
2	10
3	60
4	50

Overhead: $70,000

13. Dayton Auto Parts allocates its $360,000 overhead by the floor space used by each department. Allocate the overhead for the following departments.

Department	Floor space
Hoses	2,000 square feet
Carburetors	8,000 square feet
Water pumps	6,000 square feet
Fuel Pumps	9,000 square feet
Gaskets	1,000 square feet
Filters	4,000 square feet

14. City Office Supply wishes to allocate its $75,000 overhead among its various departments by floor space. Allocate the overhead for the following departments.

Department	Floor Space
Typing paper	750 square feet
Copy machine paper	600 square feet
Copy machines	1,000 square feet
Office furniture	1,500 square feet
Filing cabinets	500 square feet
Calculators	650 square feet

15. A wholesale lumber mill wishes to allocate its overhead of $15,150 by the sales value of each product. Allocate overhead for the following products.

Product	Number Produced	Value Per Unit
Construction 2 × 4's	15	$200
Plywood	20	$400
Veneers	10	$600
Wood chips	50	$75
Furniture wood	30	$150

16. Allocate the $8,732 overhead of Victor Meats by sales value of products, using the information in this chart.

Product	Number Produced	Value Per Unit
Beef	10	$800
Lamb	7	$300
Pork	5	$750
Chicken	14	$120
Sausage	12	$150
Luncheon meats	15	$300

17. Allocate an overhead of $4,500 for Chalet Manufacturing according to the number of employees per department. Use the information in the following chart.

Department	Number of Employees
Office	20
Sales	35
Manufacturing	75
Finishing	12
Shipping	8

18. The Beaver Drug Company wishes to allocate an overhead of $11,400 among its departments according to the number of employees per department. Use the following chart.

Department	Number of Employees
Headache remedies	25
Pain killer	30
Cold remedies	40
Foot powder	15
Eye wash	20
Skin lotion	25